THE
STRUCTURE
OF
PROCEDURE

By

ROBERT M. COVER

and

OWEN M. FISS

Professors of Law, Yale University

Mineola, New York

THE FOUNDATION PRESS, INC.

1979

Cover & Fiss—Struct. of Proc.
3rd Reprint–1997

FOREWORD

We invite you to rethink procedure.

In 1974 we began to experiment with the traditional first-year civil procedure course. We were led by two impulses. The first was to make the course less an exercise in professional training, in the narrowest sense of that term, and more an exploration of theoretical and abstract issues. The second was to drop the limitation, "civil," and to consider procedure as a unified attribute of law that transcends the traditional professional categories—those implied by the terms "civil," "criminal," or "administrative."

We were expressing our own intellectual tastes. We were also responding to our environment. The decade of the 1960s was one of the most innovative periods in American law. Procedure—now taken in its broadest sense—was a focus of much of that innovation. Some of the reform occurred on a constitutional level, as evidenced by Supreme Court decisions on the right to confrontation, the exclusionary rules, the jury, federal habeas corpus, and restrictions on state power to control solicitation by attorneys. Other developments occurred on the level of rule, statute, and practice: the class action changed dramatically in 1966; new federal civil discovery rules emerged in 1970; federal rules of evidence finally became effective in 1975. Institutional changes proliferated: a national legal services program emerged; the federal injunction became a tool for reorganizing ongoing social institutions such as schools and prisons, and as part of that effort a new procedural institution, the special master, evolved. Viewed cumulatively, these innovations have been rightly termed by others as a Due Process Revolution. It was only natural that, after a while, the revolution would reach the classroom.

Rapid and wide-spread change in legal doctrine and institutions, in our conceptions of due process, made the intensive training in rulesmanship—long a primary goal of the first-year civil procedure course—somewhat beside the point. The basic propositions, ones that had long lain dormant and unexamined, now demanded attention. Their axiomatic status had been called into question. We also realized that such a re-examination should not be confined by the traditional labels of the law school curriculum, those that made a sharp distinction between civil and criminal procedure. Procedure should no more be a course in the chronology of specific kinds of law suits than torts should be a course in claims adjustment.

The right-to-counsel cases, such as *Gideon*, *Gault*, and *Argersinger*, to pick but one line of decisions that tested the traditional categories, formally involved non-civil proceedings. Two of them involved criminal proceedings; the third, a juvenile one. Yet they were bound to have analytical implications for all types of adjudication. That was quickly realized by commentators and advocates; and we have found it illuminating, indeed necessary, to introduce these cases into the first-year "civil" procedure course.

The relationship was a reciprocal one, the structure in one system illuminating others. A simple study of the rules of either civil or criminal discovery is illuminated by the more general inquiry into information acquisition and exchange in civil, criminal, and administrative proceedings. In all this, our attention was not to obscure the differences among the various types of proceedings, such as differences in the stakes and in party structure, but only to ask whether the differences truly mattered, or mattered in the way that we had been taught.

The shape that our innovations assumed was also strongly influenced by two contemporaneous developments that occurred in the academy: one was the rise of clinical education; and the other, the proliferation of inter-disciplinary work. Starting in the late 1960s clinical education became a larger part of the law school curriculum. Some teachers believed that intense professional activity, whether it be real or simulated, was the most effective way of training lawyers. They were supported in their beliefs by increasing student demands for "relevance" and by pangs of social conscience, calling for public service even during the educational period; they were also supported—indeed encouraged—by a major funding program launched in the late 1960s by the Ford Foundation. Clinical education grew, and it had important implications for procedure courses; in the past the procedure courses had been seen as the principal vehicle for transmitting the very skills or insights that supposedly were best taught by the clinical method.

The traditional first-year civil procedure course—as best exemplified by the well-known opening one hundred pages or so of the original Field and Kaplan casebook—operated at the middle level, that is, some analytic reflection, some skill training. In the face of the clinical possibility it was hard to maintain the middle level. It seemed almost absurd to teach plead-ing, for example, through a discussion of Rule 8 and a few scattered appellate opinions, if students could actually draft complaints. And when the aim of professional training was abstracted from the traditional first-year course, much of it seemed insufficiently analytic to sustain itself.

Some instructors responded by transforming the first-year civil pro-cedure course entirely into a clinical one (usually of the simulated variety). We have taken the other road. We tried to make the course more analytic, more theoretical. We have viewed clinical education not as a model to be followed, but rather as a source of new opportunities. It freed the first-year academic procedure course from an overriding obligation to teach "how to" skills. Such skills are important, but they are, in our judgment, most effectively taught in a clinical program or supervised work experience: through summer employment or the early years of actual practice, through work in a legal aid office, through clinical courses or seminars in trial practice. We have also tried to teach such skills through a "side course"—written assignments supervised by teaching assistants (second-year and third-year students who have had some experience in practice, either through summer employment or working in the Law School's clinical program). This enabled us to devote the major portion of our class discussion and our pedagogic energy to an exploration of the more theoretical issues. Those did not respect the traditional professional categories.

Interdisciplinary work has pushed us in the same direction. The need for interdisciplinary studies in law, for increasing the role of social scientists and humanists, could be traced back to Roscoe Pound's plea for a sociological jurisprudence, or to the Legal Realism of the 1920s or 1930s; but it was not until the 1960s—oddly enough while the Warren Court was working its revolution in professional domains and clinical education was becoming more important—that interdisciplinary work became a fully legitimate part of the standard law school curriculum. At first the substantive courses felt the impact; economics, philosophy, and history became integral parts of scholarship and teaching in torts; then property; then contracts. In time, procedure was included.

Interdisciplinary work inevitably lessens the focus on professional training, and raises more general theoretical questions. The purpose of much of the research is not to improve professional technique, although that is often a useful by-product, but rather is to understand why people behave the way they do and to guide power wielders in designing institutions or formulating rules. Interdisciplinary work also tends to obliterate the traditional curricula categories, such as "civil," "criminal," and "administrative" procedure. While those categories may have a great deal of meaning for the practicing lawyer, they have less significance for the academic inquirer approaching his task from an analytic, rather than a professional lawyer's, perspective. Harry Kalven and Hans Ziesel were aware that their book, The American Jury, pertained only to the criminal jury. For one instant they considered calling the book The American Criminal Jury. We suspect they chose their title largely because their findings on judge/jury divergence transcended the professionally rooted categories—they spoke to the jury as a unified institution.

We began this collaboration in 1974, and at that time the three forces —the Due Process Revolution of the Warren Court era, the advent of clinical education, and the increasing role for interdisciplinary work—led us in the same pedagogic directions: toward a more theoretical course, and toward one not confined to procedure denominated "civil." Two of those developments, those occurring in the academy, also required us to develop new *kinds* of teaching material—both for the so-called "side course" and, even more importantly, for exposure to the interdisciplinary scholarship.

The "side course" largely consists of pleading exercises, memoranda, briefs, and a set of problems on discovery. The material for the "side course" has changed from year to year, and is largely developed by our teaching assistants. It consists of imaginative but plausible factual situations that will instill skills and test generalities; the material is quite similar to that employed in the familiar law school examination. The greater challenge consisted of developing the material that would provide the basis for the discussions in the main course, the exploration of the more theoretical issues.

We started with the case method. Our first efforts were devoted to putting together a new collection of cases, ones that would raise the theoretical issues and that would lead the student to think of procedure as a unified attribute of law. We began with Goldberg v. Kelly, and in the years following we have revised the selection and arrangement of cases many times (though we have never considered abandoning Goldberg v. Kelly as the introductory case, even after the Supreme Court decision in Mathews v. Eldridge). In the course of these revisions we introduced more and more secondary material, both to give the student a basis for considering the theoretical issues and to integrate the interdisciplinary scholarship into our teaching. As it turned out, as the 1970s wore on, the volume of interdisciplinary scholarship on procedure increased enormously (as witnessed by the fact that most of the essays in this volume were written during that period). We then realized that we had two books, not one: a collection of readings and a casebook.

These readings have been assembled with an eye towards our casebook. But we believe that they may be useful to others and should not await the completion of our work on the casebook. The readings may be used in the traditional first-year civil procedure course (an afterword suggests in detail how that might be done). They may also play a role in the familiar advanced courses in criminal and administrative procedure. Most importantly, however, we believe the readings will be of value to other procedure teachers who, responding to the forces that impelled this collaboration, are also experimenting with their courses. In that instance, the readings, and even more, the categories we have chosen to organize and present the readings, might be seen as giving preliminary shape to a field of inquiry very much in flux. They might be seen as a first step in reforming the curriculum and revising the research agenda.

ROBERT M. COVER
OWEN M. FISS

Yale University
July, 1979

TABLE OF CONTENTS

Page

FOREWORD iii

PART I. GENERAL PERSPECTIVE

CHAPTER 1. VALUING PROCESS 2

  A. A General Enumeration of the Values of Process 3

      Frank I. Michelman, The Supreme Court and Litigation
      Access Fees 3

  B. Efficiency 6

      Richard A. Posner, An Economic Approach to Legal Pro-
      cedure and Judicial Administration 7

  C. The "Fraternal" Values 17

      Jerry L. Mashaw, The Supreme Court's Due Process
      Calculus 18

  D. The Limits of Instrumental Explanations 27

      Arthur A. Leff, Law and 27

      William L. F. Felstiner, Influences of Social Organiza-
      tion on Dispute Processing 38

CHAPTER 2. THE INDEPENDENCE OF PROCEDURE? .. 47

  A. The Place of Procedure in a General Theory of Law ... 48

      William H. Simon, The Ideology of Advocacy 48

  B. The Interdependence of Substance and Procedure 75

    1. The Impact of Substance on Procedure 75

      Robert M. Cover, Reading the Rules: Procedural
      Neutrality and Substantive Efficacy 75

    2. The Impact of Procedure on Substance 86

      Hal S. Scott, The Impact of Class Actions on Rule
      10b–5 86

  C. Separating Substance and Procedure as a Strategy for
      Reform 95

      Thomas C. Grey, Procedural Fairness and Substan-
      tive Rights 96

CHAPTER 3. THE CONCEPT OF A FORMAL PROCEDUR-
      AL SYSTEM 105

  A. The Boundaries Within a Procedural System 105

    1. The Line Between Negotiation and Adjudication .. 105

      Martin P. Golding, Dispute Settling and Justice ... 106

      Melvin A. Eisenberg, Private Ordering Through Ne-
      gotiation 115

CHAPTER 3.   THE CONCEPT OF A FORMAL PROCEDUR-
AL SYSTEM—Continued   Page
  2.   The Line Between Legislation and Adjudication ____ 133
       David L. Shapiro, The Choice of Rulemaking or
       Adjudication in the Development of Administra-
       tive Policy _____ 134
  3.   The Line Between Public and Private Adjudicatory
       Institutions _____ 144
       Bernard D. Meltzer, Labor Arbitration and Discrim-
       ination _____ 145
B.   Formal Roles and Procedural Systems _____ 151
  1.   Ambiguity in Role _____ 151
       Mortimer R. Kadish & Sanford H. Kadish, Discre-
       tion to Disobey _____ 152
  2.   Person and Office _____ 168
       John T. Noonan Jr., The Passengers of *Palsgraf* ___ 168
       Jerome N. Frank, The Judging Process and the
       Judge's Personality _____ 183

PART II.   THE ELEMENTS OF ADJUDICATION

CHAPTER 4.   ADVERSARIES _____ 190
A.   The Dynamics of the Conflict Relationships: Strategic
       Behavior _____ 191
       Arthur A. Leff, Injury, Ignorance and Spite—The
       Dynamics of Coercive Collection _____ 191
       Marc Galanter, Why the "Haves" Come Out Ahead 199
B.   The Party as a Functional Construct: The Justifications
       for the Creation and Limitation of Party Status 212
       Christopher D. Stone, Should Trees Have Standing? 212
       Kenneth E. Scott, Standing in the Supreme Court—
       A Functional Analysis _____ 222
       William M. Landes and Richard A. Posner, The Pri-
       vate Enforcement of Law _____ 235
C.   Group Litigation: Functional and Natural Bases for
       Party Status _____ 242
  1.   The Functions of a Class Action _____ 242
       Harry Kalven, Jr. and Maurice Rosenfield, The Con-
       temporary Function of the Class Suit _____ 243
       Gerald A. Wright, The Cost-Internalization Case for
       Class Actions _____ 252
  2.   The Natural Basis for Group Litigation: Limits Up-
       on a Legal Construct _____ 255
       Stephen C. Yeazell, Group Litigation and Social Con-
       text _____ 255
       Derrick A. Bell, Jr., Serving Two Masters: Inte-
       gration Ideals and Client Interests in School De-
       segregation Litigation _____ 271

Page

CHAPTER 5. DECISION CENTERS _____ 283

  A. The Ideal of Independence _____ 284

      Martin Shapiro, The Logic of the Triad _____ 284

  B. Internal Organization of Decision Centers _____ 292

    1. Patterns of Authority _____ 292

      Mirjan Damaška, Structures of Authority and Comparative Criminal Procedure _____ 292

    2. Choice Among Decision Centers: Structures of Coordination _____ 306

      Arthur T. von Mehren and Donald T. Trautman, Jurisdiction to Adjudicate: A Suggested Analysis 307

      Burt Neuborne, The Myth of Parity _____ 324

  C. Knowledge and Experience of Decisional Personnel ___ 332

    1. Professional v. Lay _____ 332

      Harry Kalven, Jr. and Hans Zeisel, Reasons for Judge-Jury Disagreement _____ 333

      Richard O. Lempert, Jury Size and the Peremptory Challenge _____ 349

    2. Experts _____ 356

      Donald L. Horowitz, The Personnel of the Adjudicative Process _____ 357

      Joel B. Harris, The Title VII Administrator: A Case Study in Judicial Flexibility _____ 361

      Stephen Wexler, Expert and Lay Participation in Decision Making _____ 370

CHAPTER 6. INFORMATION AND KNOWLEDGE _____ 376

  A. Knowledge and Belief as Social Constructs _____ 377

    Robert K. Merton, The Sociology of Knowledge _____ 377

  B. Legal Discourse as a Communication System _____ 380

    Martin Shapiro, Toward a Theory of Stare Decisis ____ 380

  C. From Information to Decision _____ 387

    Laurence H. Tribe, Trial by Mathematics _____ 388

  D. Measuring the Importance of Structural Variables in the Informational Processes _____ 405

    Mirjan Damaška, Presentation of Evidence and Factfinding Precision _____ 405

CHAPTER 7. ADJUDICATORY ACTION: ITS FORMS AND MEANING _____ 420

  A. The Forms of Action: Their Variety and Interrelationships _____ 420

    Owen M. Fiss, The Civil Rights Injunction—The Sources of Uniqueness _____ 421

    Robert M. Cover & T. Alexander Aleinikoff, Dialectical Federalism: Habeas Corpus and the Court __ 437

CHAPTER 7.   ADJUDICATARY ACTION: ITS FORMS AND
                 MEANING—Continued   Page
    B.   The Latent Function of Judicial Action _____ 446
         Martha L. Minow, The Judgment of Solomon and the
             Experience of Justice _____ 447
         Douglas Hay, Property, Authority and the Criminal
             Law _____ 451
    C.   Efficacy _____ 465
         1.   The Conditions of Efficacy _____ 465
              Robert L. Crain, The Politics of School Desegrega-
              tion _____ 466
              William K. Muir Jr., Prayer in the Public Schools __ 474
         2.   The Desire for Efficacy and its Influence _____ 484
              Alexander M. Bickel, The Supreme Court at the Bar
              of Politics _____ 484

CHAPTER 8.   THE INTERRELATIONSHIP OF STRUCTUR-
                 AL   ELEMENTS—ALTERNATIVE   CON-
                 CEPTIONS OF ADJUDICATION _____ 492
    Abram Chayes, The Role of the Judge in Public Law Litiga-
    tion _____ 492
    Lon L. Fuller, The Forms and Limits of Adjudication _____ 508

Afterword: A Map for Misreading _____ 522

Acknowledgments _____ 526

A Selected Bibliography _____ 531

Index _____ 541

Part I

GENERAL PERSPECTIVE

Chapter 1

VALUING PROCESS

This first chapter is designed to raise questions about the values and objectives of procedural systems. We want to raise questions both about the objectives that various procedure systems ought to serve and the objectives that they, in fact, do serve. We have found, however, that simply enumerating abstractly formulated "values" or "ends" of procedure is an unsatisfying exercise. You will want to consider precisely what implications flow from taking a particular value seriously or pursuing a certain end. Moreover, you will want to understand what we give up in terms of one value when we pursue other values in too single-minded a fashion.

You may notice that "procedural due process" cases play an important role in the discussions in some of the articles in this chapter. It is a strange characteristic of the traditional law school curriculum that those cases are more often treated in constitutional law courses (where they occupy a most marginal position) than in procedure courses. Actually, it is in such cases as Goldberg v. Kelly, Mathews v. Eldridge, and Arnett v. Kennedy that we find the most extended and serious judicial discussions about the nature and purposes of procedure. It is only when the nature or adequacy of a particular procedural structure is itself brought into issue that one finds a court addressing questions normally taken for granted: What do we wish procedure to do in this kind of case? What sort of procedural system will accomplish that set of aims? What will it cost in money, and in values not readily monetized? How would such a system feed back upon norms and institutions already functioning in this and related areas?

The Michelman, Posner, and Mashaw essays which follow address these questions from different postures. It should be noted, however, that all three presuppose an instrumental focus on procedure. We *use* procedures to accomplish certain ends, whether the end be efficient implementation of substantive norms or recognition of the essential humanity of people affected by decisions. The Felstiner and Leff articles at the end of this chapter suggest a very different way of looking at procedure. Procedures—like other social and cultural institutions—are not susceptible of taking just *any* shape in *any* social or cultural context. Although they are formed with their uses in mind, they also *exhibit* the larger society and culture within which they operate. The Felstiner and Leff essays are designed to remind us of the explanatory power of the focus on such extra-legal considerations. Felstiner provides a typology of dispute-processing devices and considers the implications of their use within the context of divergent ideal-types of social and economic organization. His conclusions are intended to have, and do have, implications for attempts to "borrow" or "adapt" dispute-processing devices from one society to another or from one sphere of activity (e. g., labor relations) to another (e. g., torts). Leff's work raises questions about the force of a human tendency to impose consistency and coherence—meaning—upon large areas of thought and action even at substantial "cost" in other terms. Such "meaning," of course, must derive from a cultural context considerably broader than the universe of formal dispute-processing devices. What a given society does with its disputes will be influenced by this broader system of meaning.

All of the questions in this section are introductory in the sense that they present a series of problems which should be with us as we address, in detail, a particular procedural system. None of these questions can be set aside, at least until after we complete such a study.

SECTION A. A GENERAL ENUMERATION OF THE VALUES OF PROCESS

What are the values served by process? This question arises in many different contexts. In the excerpt that follows, Professor Michelman is responding in part to the Supreme Court cases, including United States v. Kras, 409 U.S. 434 (1973), and Ortwein v. Schwab, 410 U.S. 656 (1973), that sustained filing fees which had the effect of limiting court access for indigents. *Kras* involved an individual seeking discharge of his debts in a voluntary bankruptcy proceeding, while *Ortwein* involved judicial review of a reduction in welfare allowances for the aged. Michelman asks whether there can be a defensible rule with the following characteristic: "The rule defines a subgroup (call it X) of all persons, such that whenever a person is within X, that person is denied due process if he is refused access to court because of inability to pay a state-imposed fee." Michelman attempts to formulate and test principles and litigation contexts to explain this rule. In this testing he first looks for the reasons underlying the societal provisions for litigation.

As you read this excerpt consider whether Professor Michelman's typology of process values is exhaustive. Next consider whether procedure necessarily furthers all of the four types of values enumerated. If you can conceive of procedure which may further some but not all of the values, consider whether furtherance of any particular one of the values may be a necessary condition for an event to be called "procedure" or a necessary condition for the procedure to be called "fair" or "just."

Frank I. Michelman, **The Supreme Court and Litigation Access Fees: The Right to Protect One's Rights***

   . . . [T]here are generally accepted *reasons* for making litigation possible. I think we take little risk of serious distortion if we try to frame those reasons in terms of the values (ends, interests, purposes) that are supposed to be furthered by allowing persons to litigate.

I have been able to identify four discrete, though interrelated, types of such values, which may be called dignity values, participation values, deterrence values, and (to choose a clumsily neutral term) effectuation values.

* *Source:* 1973 Duke L.J. 1153, 1172–77 (1973). Professor of Law, Harvard University.

Dignity values reflect concern for the humiliation or loss of self-respect which a person might suffer if denied an opportunity to litigate. *Participation values* reflect an appreciation of litigation as one of the modes in which persons exert influence, or have their wills "counted," in societal decisions they care about. *Deterrence values* recognize the instrumentality of litigation as a mechanism for influencing or constraining individual behavior in ways thought socially desirable.[73] *Effectuation values* see litigation as an important means through which persons are enabled to get, or are given assurance of having, whatever we are pleased to regard as rightfully theirs.

. . .

Dignity values. These seem most clearly offended when a person confronts a formal, state-sponsored, public proceeding charging wrongdoing, failure, or defect, and the person is either prevented from responding or forced to respond without the assistance and resources that a self-respecting response necessitates.

The damage to self-respect from the inability to defend oneself properly seems likely to be most severe in the case of criminal prosecution, where representatives of civil society attempt in a public forum to brand one a violator of important societal norms. . . .

Of course, one immediately sees that there are some nominally "civil" contexts where the would-be litigant is trying to fend off accusatory action by the government threatening rather dire and stigmatizing results (for example, a proceeding to divest a parent of custody of a child on grounds of unfitness), which are exceedingly difficult to distinguish from standard criminal contexts in dignity value terms. Still these cases do not by themselves show that the dignity notion is uncontainable. Challenging though it may be in a few cases to draw the line between the quasi-criminal and the noncriminal context, the determination usually will not be insuperably difficult.

But this is hardly to say that dignity considerations are entirely absent from civil contexts. Perhaps there is something generally demeaning, humiliating, and infuriating about finding oneself in a dispute over legal rights and wrongs and being unable to uphold one's own side of the case. How serious these effects are seems to depend on various factors including, possibly, the identity of the adversary (is it the government?), the origin of the argument (did the person willingly start it himself?), the possible outcomes (will the person, or others, feel that he has been determined to be a wrongdoer?), and how public the struggle has become (has it reached the courts yet?).

That listing of factors might seem to lend a degree of plausibility to a general right of court access for civil defendants though not for civil plain-

---

73. A possibly more accurate (but less distinct) label would have been "social welfare values." The category is intended to stand for all interpretations of litigation as a means for maximizing value across society, as distinguished from securing to the victorious party his due. In a given case, value maximization might be effectuated through an act of redistribution of wealth (the immediate impact of the judgment or decree itself), rather than through an act of (negative or affirmative) deterrence strictly speaking (the impact on future behavior of knowledge of the decision and its grounds). . . .

tiffs. But the idea is really not very persuasive on close inspection. Consider Ortwein's situation. He was not accused of any crime. Indeed, the government was able to work its will against him without starting any public proceeding; the choice to take the dispute to a public forum was Ortwein's own. On the other hand, Ortwein's adversary was the government; and the government's actions did imply that he was demanding more than his lawful entitlement.[76] That a person's self-respect might be seriously injured by inability to have that charge tested in a credibly impartial tribunal seems entirely likely.

Nor does it seem that such a likelihood can readily be ruled out in various other plaintiff contexts that easily come to mind: a citizen wishes to sue a governmental body for breach of contract or for tax refund; a customer wishes to sue an automobile mechanic for breach of warranty; a member wishes to challenge his expulsion from a private association (or a worker, his dismissal from private employment); a tenant wishes to sue his landlord for having evicted him for a malicious or erroneous (and allegedly unlawful) reason; an aggrieved party wishes to sue another for defamation, or for assault, or for malpractice, or for breach of trust. It seems that denial of access would noticeably arouse dignity concerns in all these cases. No doubt, there are variations in the degree of injury, depending on permutations of relevant factors; but dignity concerns seem widespread through the juridical sector.

Participation values. The illumination that may sometimes flow from viewing litigation as a mode of politics has escaped neither courts nor legal theorists. But I can see no way of trenchantly deploying that insight so as to rank litigation contexts for purposes of a selective access-fee relief rule. (Certainly the Supreme Court's emergent rule cannot be construed to reflect any such ranking.)

But if participation values cannot help us differentiate among litigation contexts, they can contribute significantly to the argument for a broad constitutional right of court access. Participation values are at the root of the claim that such a right can be derived from the first amendment, a claim that I shall not pursue. And they also help inspire the analogy between general litigation rights and general voting rights . . . .

Deterrence values. Litigation is often, and enlighteningly, viewed as a process, or part of a process, for constraining all agents in society to the performance of duties and obligations imposed with a view to social welfare. A possible link between deterrence values and access fees is, of course, supplied by the obvious frustration of those values which results if the person in the best position, or most naturally motivated, to pursue judicial enforcement of such constraints is prevented by access fees from doing so. The pervasiveness of deterrence factors throughout the juridical sector, like that of dignity and participation factors, adds force to the argument for breadth or generality in any right of court access. In order to establish beyond serious debate that society's interest in constraining agents to the performance

---

76. The situation illustrates a more general point . . . : there is no particular reason to assume that the party to a controversy who becomes plaintiff in a lawsuit is "the aggressor" in the controversy viewed in its entirety.

of legal duties has a nigh universal relevance, one need only refer to the lively contemporary interest in a "cost-internalization" rationale for tort law, to the related literature that would connect the very definition of legal rights to a goal of economic optimizing, and to the utilitarian considerations commonly thought to support the imperative of *pacta sunt servanda.*

Effectuation values. In the effectuation perspective we view the world from the standpoint of the prospective litigant as distinguished from that of society as a whole or as a collectivity. Value is ascribed to the actual protection and realization of those interests of the litigant which the law purports to protect and effectuate (in this perspective one would shamelessly refer to those interests as the litigant's "rights") and more generally to a prevailing assurance that those interests will be protected; and litigation is regarded as a process, or as a part of a process, for providing such protection and assurance. Notions of necessary legal protection for rights may be intuitive or philosophically elaborated. Elaborations may range from the extremely abstract and deontological (inferring legal rights, say, from a transcendental Idea of Freedom) to the borderline utilitarian (viewing rights as necessary to the preservation of a satisfying social order). They may vary in tone and emphasis from the legalistic (strict social contract theories, or looser contractarian theories which entail legal protection for rights as a necessary part of the ethical justification for civil society's coercive aspects) to the humanitarian and psychologically oriented (rights regarded as one of the lenses through which we view and find meaning in, or media through which we express and give meaning to, our notions of self, personality, social relationship). However articulated, defended, or accounted for, the sense of legal rights as claims whose realization has intrinsic value can fairly be called rampant in our culture and traditions. Of course, this sense is aroused more naturally and appropriately by some claims and predicaments than by others; and that phenomenon suggests the possibility of accounting for a selective rule of access-fee relief by reflection on effectuation values. . . .

———

Professor Michelman has written a richly textured analysis of what he labels "formal" and "associational" aims of procedure in "Formal and Associational Aims in Procedural Due Process," 18 Nomos, Due Process 126 (1977). In that article he develops the theory of "values" in process considerably further than in the excerpt provided here.

SECTION B.　EFFICIENCY

Perhaps the most familiar justification for procedure is that it contributes to the maximization of value—value as defined by the individual and collective preferences expressed in part through the substantive norms of the law. Procedure, by this view, ought to be the means by which correct decisions—according to such norms—are rendered more probable and more public.

Frequently, however, one objection to a procedural component is that it costs too much. When such an observation is made in the course of judicial opinions, and in much of the literature on procedure, it is usually made with reference to direct costs as they appear in the budgets or balance sheets of courts and agencies. Such costs, however, are only one component of an analysis which considers the *social* costs of a procedure or set of procedures. Procedural components may impose costs on others. And if such costs are not observable on the dockets and in the budgets of courts, they are often ignored. Systematic social cost-benefit analyses may be most important, therefore, for their power to transcend accounting and include consideration of factors not apparent on balance sheets. In the essay that follows, Professor Posner introduces the concept of "error costs." Consider to what extent the concept is necessary and useful in analyzing the justifications for procedure and its components in any particular case or class of cases.

Ask yourself, as you read, whether any convincing method is presented for placing a value on the costs of error where non-economic injury is at stake. If not, how far has Posner's method advanced us in analyzing such cases? What sort of claim is made for the method by Posner himself? Even if Posner's method can be applied, does it leave anything out? What would Posner say of Michelman's four categories of process values?

Richard A. Posner, **An Economic Approach to Legal Procedure and Judicial Administration***

A Framework of Analysis

An important purpose of substantive legal rules (such as the rules of tort and criminal law) is to increase economic efficiency [in the sense of maximizing value]. It follows . . . that mistaken imposition of legal liability, or mistaken failure to impose liability, will reduce efficiency. Judicial error is therefore a source of social costs and the reduction of error is a goal of the procedural system. The reader may challenge the last proposition by citing, for example, the rule excluding from criminal trials evidence obtained by an illegal search. Such evidence is highly probative; its exclusion reduces the accuracy of the fact-finding process in criminal trials. But this type of exclusionary rule is exceptional, and is recognized—and often bitterly criticized—as such.

Even when the legal process works flawlessly, it involves costs—the time of lawyers, litigants, witnesses, jurors, judges, and other people, plus paper and ink, law office and court house maintenance, telephone service, etc. These costs are just as real as the costs resulting from error: in general we would not want to increase the direct costs of the legal process by one dollar in order to reduce error costs by 50 (or 99) cents. The economic goal is thus to minimize the sum of error and direct costs.

Despite its generality, this formulation provides a useful framework in which to analyze the problems and objectives of legal procedure. It is usable

* *Source:* 2 J. Legal Studies 399, 400–08, 417–20, 441–48 (1973). Professor of Law, University of Chicago.

even when the purpose of the substantive law is to transfer wealth or to bring about some other noneconomic goal, rather than to improve efficiency. All that is necessary is that it be possible, in principle, to place a price tag on the consequences of failing to apply the substantive law in all cases in which it was intended to apply, so that our two variables, error cost and direct cost, remain commensurable.

To illustrate the utility of the economic approach, consider the question whether the defendant in an administrative action (such as deportation, license revocation, or the withdrawal of a security clearance) should be entitled to a trial-type hearing. The tendency in the legal discussion of this question has been to invoke either a purely visceral sense of fairness or a purely formal distinction between penal and nonpenal sanctions. The economic approach enables the question to be framed in rational and functional terms. We ask first whether error costs would be substantially increased by denial of a trial-type hearing. Error costs (discussed in detail in the next part) may here be regarded as the product of two factors, the probability of error and the cost if an error occurs. If the facts on which the outcome of the administrative proceeding turns are the kind most accurately determined in a trial-type hearing, the probability of error if such a hearing is denied is apt to be great. If, in addition, the cost of an error if one occurs would be substantial because the sanction applied by the agency, whether in formal legal terms penal or not, imposes heavy costs on a defendant, total error costs are likely to be significantly increased by the denial of a trial-type hearing. The increment in error costs must be compared with the direct costs of a hearing; but these will often be low. The cost inquiries required by the economic approach are not simple and will rarely yield better than crude approximations, but at the very least they serve to place questions of legal policy in a framework of rational inquiry.

The Costs of Error in Civil Actions

A.   An Analysis of Error Costs in Accident Cases

Suppose a company inflicts occasional injuries on people with whom it cannot contract due to very high transaction costs. Victims of these injuries could prevent them only at prohibitive cost (we will initially assume), but the company can purchase various relatively inexpensive safety devices that would reduce the accident rate significantly. In the absence of legal sanctions it has no incentive to purchase such devices since, due to the costs of transacting, it cannot sell anyone the benefits of the devices in increasing safety. If the tort law makes it liable for the costs of these accidents,[5] and is enforced flawlessly, the company will purchase the optimum quantity of safety devices. If the law is not enforced flawlessly, a suboptimum quantity of safety equipment will be procured.

The goal of a system of accident liability is to minimize the total costs of accidents and of accident avoidance. If we assume that the only feasible method of accident avoidance is the purchase of a particular type of safety equipment, then those total costs are minimized by purchasing the quantity

5.   Under either a strict-liability or a negligence standard. . . .

of that equipment at which the marginal product of safety equipment in reducing accident costs is equal to the marginal cost of the equipment. This marginal product is the rate at which the number of accidents inflicted by the company declines as the quantity of safety equipment purchased increases, mutiplied by the cost per accident. The marginal cost of safety equipment is simply the unit price of such equipment if, as we shall assume, that price does not vary with the amount of equipment that the company purchases. These relationships are depicted in Figure 1. The intersection of the marginal product and marginal cost curves determines the socially optimum quantity of safety equipment for the company to buy and install (q_s).

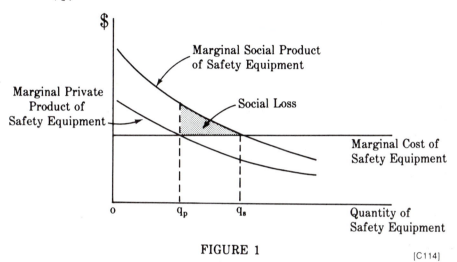

FIGURE 1

[C114]

The company, however, is not interested in minimizing the social costs of accidents and accident avoidance; it is interested only in minimizing its private accident and accident-avoidance costs. The former are the social costs of the firm's accidents multiplied by the probability that the firm will actually be held liable—forced to pay—for those costs. Since legal error presumably causes erroneous impositions as well as erroneous denials of liability, we must add a third term to the firm's cost function: the amount of money that it is forced to pay out in groundless claims. That amount is a function of the legal-error rate and disappears when that rate is zero. We ignore it for the moment.

The company minimizes its private accident and accident-avoidance costs by equating the marginal product of safety equipment in reducing its accident liability to the marginal private cost of that equipment (which we assume is the same as the marginal social cost). This marginal private product is simply the marginal social product weighted by the probability of the firm's being held liable. If that probability is one, the marginal social and private products are the same. But when the probability is less than one—that is, when the legal-error rate is positive—they diverge, leading to a social loss as shown in Figure 1. The higher the error rate, the greater the reduction in the purchase of safety equipment and the greater the social loss.

The analysis is incomplete because we have ignored the possible effect of a positive error rate, operating through the third term in the company's cost function (liability resulting from groundless claims), on the firm's purchase of safety equipment. Suppose that the errors against the company took the form exclusively of accident victims' exaggerating the extent of their injuries. By increasing the company's private accident costs, these errors would increase the marginal private product of safety equipment. Thus, while errors in favor of the company would lower the company's marginal private product curve in Figure 1, errors against the company would shift it back upward. In fact, however, although all errors in favor of the company operate to lower its marginal-product curve, only some errors against the company operate to raise it. The purchase of additional safety equipment will not prevent the erroneous imposition of liability in a case in which no accident would have occurred in any event—the victim fabricated it—or in which the accident was inflicted by someone else and could not have been prevented by the defendant. Such errors do not increase the value of safety equipment to the firm and hence the marginal private product of that equipment. But even here a qualification is necessary. Additional safety equipment might strengthen the company's defense against a suit arising out of an accident actually caused by someone else. The company might be able to argue that, in view of all of the safety precautions it had taken, it could not have caused the accident.[9] Still, it seems a reasonable conclusion that a positive error rate will result in a net reduction in the company's marginal private product of safety, and hence in a net social loss.

A glance . . . at Figure 1 will confirm that this social loss will be greater, the more serious the accident. . . .[10] To be sure, the stakes have another effect that is not captured in Figure 1, which treats the error rate as completely exogenous . . . . [A]n increase in the stakes in a case will usually induce the parties to spend more money on the litigation. This in turn will reduce the probability of an erroneous result, and so, by our previous analysis, the social loss from error. Aggregate error costs might actually be smaller in a class of big cases than in a class of small ones.

. . .

Thus far we have assumed that legal error will have no effect on the behavior of accident victims. In fact, by increasing expected accident costs net of compensation, error encourages prospective victims to engage in self-protection. If adequate compensation were paid in every accident case, the net cost of accidents to the victims would be zero and their incentive to take precautions also zero. But if by reason of error the expected compensation is only (say) 80 percent of the expected accident cost, the net cost of accidents to victims becomes positive and they have an incentive to adopt precautions that cost less than the uncompensated accident costs that they prevent.

9. Groundless claims might impose costs in another form: the company might spend heavily on lawyers, etc., to resist them. However, it might economize on these costs in the cases where, due to legal error in its favor, it was not sued at all, or where the claimant was unable to make a strong case.

10. A higher accident cost per case raises both marginal-product curves by the same proportion. . . .

The effect of error is thus to shift safety incentives from injurers to victims. If the victims can prevent the same accidents at lower cost than the injurers, such a shift will produce a net social gain rather than a social loss, but where this is possible the injurers should not be liable in the first place. If, as we assume, the substantive law places liability where it will encourage the most efficient methods of loss avoidance, the shift in safety incentives brought about by error in the legal process will produce a net social loss. But the loss may be slight.   .   .   .

The analysis of legal-error costs would be very different if the purpose of the underlying substantive law were not to improve the allocation of resources but were instead to compensate victims of certain accidents. The amount of undercompensation due to legal error would be equal to the product of the error rate, the cost per accident, and the number of accidents that occur for which the injurer should be held liable. That number will be greater the higher the error rate, for we know from the previous discussion that the number of accidents rises with the error rate, and therefore undercompensation must rise with the error rate. Besides the error rate, the principal factors determining the total amount of undercompensation are the effectiveness of the law (albeit imperfectly enforced) in deterring accidents, and the scope of the law. For identical error rates, the number of accidents occurring for which the injurer should be held liable will be greater if the legal standard is strict liability than if it is negligence. The costs of error are therefore likely to be higher under a strict-liability than under a negligence standard if failure to compensate where compensation is due is reckoned as a cost, and not merely as a transfer of wealth. Finally, to make undercompensation commensurable with the social loss of Figure 1, we need to know the rate at which a dollar in undercompensation is equated to a dollar in scarce resources consumed; it need not be one to one. In short the cost of legal error may differ dramatically depending on whether the purpose of the underlying substantive law is viewed as allocative or distributive.

B.   Biased and Unbiased Error

It is useful to distinguish between "biased" and "unbiased" error. Unbiased error in our usage is any error that is as likely to operate against one party to the dispute as it is to operate against the other. Such an error gives judgment to undeserving plaintiffs in about half of the erroneously decided cases and to undeserving defendants in the other half; accepting perjured testimony is an example. A biased error is one more likely to defeat plaintiffs than defendants or vice versa. The previous analysis assumed unbiased error.

Two types of biased error may, in turn, be distinguished. The first arises from a deliberate decision to bias a source of error (as in the rule that the guilt of a criminal defendant must be proved beyond a reasonable doubt). Consider a social-loss function that consists of two terms: the social loss of Figure 1, due to failure to impose liability on injurers in all cases in which they should be held liable, and the social loss that results when the judicial system awards compensation to a victim who could have averted an accident by appropriate safety precautions at lower cost than the injurer.[11] Assume that if the parties have the same burden of proof,[12] the probability of an accurate determination of liability in both situations will be 90 per cent, meaning that in 10 per cent of the cases in which injurers should be held liable they are not held liable, while in 10 per cent of the cases in which victims should be held liable (denied compensation) for failure to take cost-justified safety precautions they receive compensation. Now let the standard of proof be changed to require that the defendant prove nonliability to a certainty. Victims will win every case. The probability of injurers' being held liable when they should be held liable will rise to one, causing the social loss from legal errors favoring injurers to fall to zero. But the probability of victims' being held liable when they fail to take proper safety precautions will fall to zero, which will cause the social loss from such failures to rise. We cannot be certain whether our total loss function will be higher or lower without knowing the specific values of the relevant parameters, but probably it will be higher. What we have done, in effect, is to impose a standard either of strict injurer liability (with no contributory negligence) or strict victim liability, depending on which probability has gone to zero. Both standards are less efficient than the alternatives. The effects of moderate bias, however, cannot be appraised a priori.

A second type of biased error occurs when a source of error affects the parties' chances unequally. Consider the rule—still followed in some states— that the victim of an accident must prove his freedom from contributory negligence. In a fatal accident to which there were no witnesses, the effect of the rule, if followed to the letter, would often be to prevent recovery even though the victim was in fact free from contributory negligence: the rule would never operate in favor of victims. But courts do not apply the rule in such cases. Instead they presume in the absence of contrary evidence that the victim was exercising due care. The effect is to increase the injurer's incentive to take precautions and reduce the victim's. This is an improvement if we assume that the injurer is more likely to be negligent than the victim; the modified rule is better if the reverse is more likely .   .   .   .

Settlement Out of Court

The .   .   .   preceding [section] considered the costs of erroneous judicial determinations. Now we turn to the direct costs of legal dispute resolution. These include the costs of trials .   .   .   and the costs of settling cases without, or before completion of, litigation.   .   .   .

---

11. There is no presumption that an injurer can avoid a costly accident more cheaply than a victim; in general an efficient allocation of responsibilities for accident prevention will require that prospective victims take some safety precautions. These optimal precautions are to be distinguished from the second-best precautions . . . that prospective victims take only because of errors in the legal process that permit injurers to escape full liability.

12. The burdens of proof (in technical legal language, "risk of nonpersuasion") would be approximately equal if plaintiff, to prevail, had only to establish that his version of the facts was more probably true than the defendant's. . . .

Since settlement costs are normally much lower than litigation costs, the fraction of cases settled is an important determinant of the total direct cost of legal dispute resolution. The necessary condition for settlement is that the plaintiff's minimum offer—the least amount he will take in settlement of his claim—be smaller than the defendant's maximum offer. This is not a sufficient condition: the parties may find it impossible to agree upon a mutually satisfactory settlement price. But we shall assume that settlement negotiations are rarely unsuccessful for this reason [27] and therefore that litigation occurs only when the plaintiff's minimum offer is greater than the defendant's maximum offer. The plaintiff's minimum offer is the expected value of the litigation to him plus his settlement costs, the expected value of the litigation being the present value of the judgment if he wins, multiplied by the probability (as he estimates it) of his winning, minus the present value of his litigation expenses. The defendant's maximum offer is the expected costs of the litigation to him and consists of his litigation expenses, plus the cost of an adverse judgment multiplied by the probability as he estimates it of the plaintiff's winning (which is equal to one minus the probability of *his* winning), minus his settlement costs.[28] Anything that reduces the plaintiff's minimum offer or increases the defendant's maximum offer, such as an increase in the parties' litigation expenditures relative to their settlement costs, will reduce the likelihood of litigation. Hence measures to reduce litigation costs might actually increase the total costs of legal dispute resolution, by making trials, which are usually costlier than settlements, more attractive than before the measures were introduced.

27. Typically there are only two parties to a legal dispute. Presumably the problem is acute only when there are many parties; then each has a strong incentive to hold out for a large part of the expected value of the transaction. This may be a problem in some multiparty litigation.

28. If a party is either risk averse or risk preferring rather than risk neutral the expected utility of litigation may be smaller or larger than its expected value. We assume risk neutrality except where otherwise indicated, but the analysis could easily be modified to take account of the existence of nonneutral attitudes toward risk.

We shall also ignore John P. Gould's interesting point, in The Economics of Legal Conflicts, 2 J.Leg.Studies 279, 290 (1973), that when both parties expect to lose the case if it is litigated, each can increase his expected wealth by litigating and at the same time betting with the other party against himself. To illustrate, suppose the stakes in the case are $1000 to each side and each side thinks it has only a 10 per cent chance of winning. Then (if we ignore the costs of settlement and of litigation) plaintiff will accept any offer from the defendant of more than $100 to settle the case. Defendant has an expected loss of $900 so he will settle for anything less than that amount. Assume that the parties decide to litigate and bet each other on the outcome. Plaintiff bets $10,000 that he will lose; defendant bets $10,000 that *he* will lose. The expected value of litigation to the plaintiff is now $9000 plus $100, or $9100, which exceeds any settlement offer the defendant would make, while the expected value of litigation to the defendant is $9000 − $900, or $8100, which exceeds the maximum expected value of a settlement to the defendant (zero). However, Gould's point is probably not empirically important. Such a betting contract could not lawfully be enforced; nor could it be enforced practically: each party would have an incentive to improve the odds by failing to litigate vigorously and by deliberately committing mistakes that made it more likely that he would lose.

Anything that increases the plaintiff's minimum settlement offer or reduces the defendant's maximum offer will increase the likelihood of litigation. An increase in the plaintiff's subjective probability of prevailing or in his stakes will do this, but so will an increase in the defendant's subjective probability of prevailing since it will induce him to reduce his maximum settlement offer. An increase in the defendant's stakes in the case will reduce the likelihood of litigation by leading him to increase his maximum settlement offer. In the important special case where the stakes to the parties are the same, it can be shown that an increase in those stakes will increase the likelihood of litigation. In that case, litigation cannot possibly occur unless the plaintiff's subjective probability of prevailing is greater than one minus the defendant's subjective probability, for otherwise the plaintiff's minimum settlement offer will be equal to or smaller than the defendant's maximum offer. Assuming that this minimum condition for litigation is satisfied, any increase in the stakes must increase the likelihood of litigation by making the plaintiff's minimum settlement offer grow faster than the defendant's maximum settlement offer.

The approach suggested here assumes that the subjective probabilities, the stakes, and the costs of litigation and of settlement are mutually independent, but they are not. A change in the stakes will affect the amount of money that the parties spend on litigation and this in turn will alter the probabilities of a particular outcome. Settlement costs are probably a function of both litigation costs and stakes. A change in one party's expenditures on litigation, triggered by a change in the stakes or subjective probability of winning of that party, may lead the other party to alter his expenditures on the case, which may induce a further change in the first party's expenditures. . . . [T]he interdependence of the parties' expenditures makes it impossible to predict the level of those expenditures unless special, and somewhat arbitrary, assumptions about the parties' reaction patterns are adopted. This indeterminacy makes the conditions for settlement indeterminate, since not only the plaintiff's and defendant's litigation costs but also their subjective probabilities of prevailing if the case is litigated are functions of their expenditure decisions. . . .

The Interaction Between Error Costs and Direct Costs

The relationship between error costs and direct costs can be summarized in a loss function having three terms. The first term is error cost. This is a function of the probability of error, which in turn is a function of the fraction of cases litigated, the amount of private expenditures on litigation, and the amount of public expenditures.[52] The second term is the sum of the private and public expenditures in cases that are litigated, and is equal to the total of those expenditures in all cases multiplied by the fraction of cases litigated. The third term is the total expenditures (all private) on cases that are settled,

---

52. On judges' and clerks' salaries, court house buildings, juries, etc. Although normally assumed to be a small part of the overall costs of the legal dispute resolution system, they are by no means trivial. In fiscal year 1971, the budget of the federal court system alone was $174 million. . . .

and is equal to the total private expenditures in all cases multiplied by the fraction of cases settled multiplied by the fractional cost of settling rather than litigating. An increase in the fraction of cases litigated, or in the public or private expenditures on litigation, will reduce the probability and hence cost of an erroneous judicial determination. An increase in public expenditures on litigation will reduce the relative cost advantage of settling rather than litigating (the government's subsidy of litigation has increased), and an increase in the relative cost advantages of settling will reduce the fraction of cases tried.

These relationships make clear why it is difficult to predict a priori the effect on overall efficiency of changes in the relevant variables. For example, an increase in the fraction of cases litigated will increase the social costs of legal dispute resolution only if the difference between the total costs of litigating cases and the total costs of settling them is greater than the reduction in error costs brought about by increasing the fraction of litigated cases. Otherwise it will reduce the total costs of legal dispute resolution. An increase in public expenditures will reduce error costs both directly and by inducing a larger fraction of cases to be tried, but it will increase the total direct costs of legal dispute resolution both directly and by making litigation relatively more attractive than settlement. Thus there can be no presumption that increasing the public expenditures on the court system will increase social welfare. An expenditure of another $1 million on the court system might cost society several millions—or benefit society by several millions. Finally, an increase in the fractional cost of settlement versus litigation, by lowering the cost of settlement relative to that of litigation, will reduce the direct costs of legal dispute resolution but indirectly increase the error costs. Thus, as argued earlier, measures that increase the attractiveness of settlement in comparison to litigation cannot be regarded as unequivocally desirable.

[Professor Posner then examines several examples of the "complex interplay between error and direct costs," including discovery, substantive law reform, the jury, and res judicata. Also examined is delay in court.]

.   .   .   To most experts in judicial administration, delay between the filing and final disposition of a legal claim is an unmitigated evil and the proper focus of judicial reform. This is an odd way to look at the matter. Delay is an omnipresent feature of social and economic life. It is only excessive delay that is undesirable, and what is excessive can be determined only by comparing the costs and benefits of different amounts of delay.

A major cost associated with queuing as a method of rationing goods is the opportunity cost of the time people spend in the queue. Where the parties' time is their own while they wait (as when a theatergoer is forced to "wait" for six months to see a popular musical), the queue is merely a "figurative" queue. The court queue is a literal queue for defendants incarcerated awaiting trial and for some owners of property "tied up" in litigation. Otherwise it is a figurative queue, but this does not mean that it is costless. Court delay increases error costs because the adaptation of legal rules to altered circumstances is retarded and because evidence decays over time, increasing the probability of an erroneous decision. Clearly, at some level of delay error costs would become prohibitive. Delay also increases error costs by widening the gap between damages and judgments that is created by the fact that the legal interest rate is lower than the market rate and interest is usually allowed not from the date of the event giving rise to the suit but only from the date of judgment. This particular source of error cost from delay could be eliminated simply by increasing the interest rate and computing interest from the date of violation.

Delay is also a source of benefits. Presumably it enables a reduction in the number of judges and other court personnel, court houses, etc. It may increase the settlement rate. A hidden benefit of delay in administrative proceedings is the additional incentive it gives regulated firms to increase technical efficiency between rate proceedings. The analysis of the costs and benefits of delay is especially complicated in criminal cases. One effect of delay is to increase both the punishment costs and litigation costs of defendants not admitted to bail; another effect is to reduce the punishment costs of those defendants who are admitted to bail.

Whether existing levels of delay are optimum is very difficult to judge, in part because the usual statistics of delay do not measure the court queue— the waiting period—accurately. Delay is generally measured from the filing of the defendant's answer to the complaint to the final disposition of the case. This interval is too long because it includes time during which the parties are not waiting at all, but litigating or preparing to litigate or attempting to negotiate a settlement. It is too short because it excludes the period between the event giving rise to the legal dispute (or the earliest time when a settlement might have been made) and the filing of the answer.

In 1972, the average interval between answer and final disposition, in personal-injury cases tried before juries in state courts, was 21.7 months, an increase of only three months since 1963. Delays in other kinds of cases, and in the federal courts, appear to be substantially shorter. The situation in a few major cities, however, is a good deal worse. Statistics that actually measure either the court queue or the costs and benefits of court queues of different length are unavailable.

The marked difference in waiting times between jury and nonjury trials is interesting because it suggests that courts are encouraging the choice of the cheaper method of trial by subjecting the more expensive to a much longer queue. A more straightforward method of accomplishing this end would be to charge a substantial fee for plaintiffs demanding a jury trial. The use of price as a method of rationing access to the courts would have the additional advantage, compared to queuing, of providing the court system with information on whether there is in fact a strong demand for prompt trials. But the use of the price system is not among the commonly proposed methods of reducing court delay, and the methods commonly proposed—such as procedural reform to simplify the trial of cases and thereby increase the effective litigation capacity of the courts, and the appointment of additional judges— have, in comparison to the use of price, some serious drawbacks.

The effect of the usual procedural reforms that are suggested (greater use of summary judgment, admissions, judicial notice, and the like) is to increase the productivity of litigation expenditures. The relationship to delay is obscure. An increase in the productivity of evidence will, as we have seen, induce litigants to purchase more of it. Thus, while it is repeatedly suggested that delay in Interstate Commerce Commission proceedings (for example) could be reduced if only the ICC would permit evidence without the cumbersome procedures, such as the best-evidence rule and the right of cross-examination, of common law proceedings, such simplification would induce the parties to increase the quantity of their litigation inputs—expert witnesses and the like—and this might result in even more protracted proceedings, albeit ones of higher quality.

The proposal to reduce delay by adding judges—usually considered the sovereign remedy—ignores several realistic possibilities that might undermine the effectiveness of the measure. The reduction in delay brought about by the addition of judges might be offset by the lower settlement rate in the personal-injury area, and perhaps in other areas, that can be foreseen if delay is reduced; the additional litigation would create a new source of delay. Moreover, with litigation a speedier method of dispute resolution, disputants who under existing conditions of delay substitute other methods of dispute resolution (such as arbitration) because they value prompt resolution would be attracted back to the courts, and again a new source of delay would be created. An analogy may be drawn to building a new freeway: by improving road transportation the freeway induces some people who previously used other modes of transportation to switch to driving, and this leads to new congestion.

The essential point is that minimization of delay is not an appropriate formulation of the goal of judicial reform. The goal, it has been argued in this article, is to minimize the sum of the error costs and of the direct costs of legal dispute resolution. The problem of delay must be placed within that larger framework of inquiry. Indeed, unless that is done, delay cannot even be defined in a meaningful fashion. . . .

There is now a substantial literature of economic analysis of procedure and administration of justice. See, for example, G. Becker and W. Landes, Essays in the Economics of Crime and Punishment (1974). Posner's general work, Economic Analysis of Law (2d ed. 1977), provides an overview of the general analytic framework within which the above-excerpted essay fits. For a criticism of that framework, see Leff, Economic Analysis of Law: Some Realism about Nominalism, 60 Va.L.Rev. 451 (1974).

SECTION C. THE "FRATERNAL" VALUES

The Supreme Court has recently introduced explicit cost-benefit analysis into its jurisprudence in determining what sort of hearing due process requires for protection of various interests. In the article which follows, Professor Mashaw considers the leading case applying such a method—Mathews v. Eldridge—and criticizes both its application of the cost-benefit analysis and the method itself. As you read, ask yourself what the process values are which Mashaw believes are slighted through this method. Are they necessarily incapable of being considered in a sufficiently sensitive approach to cost-benefit analysis?

Jerry L. Mashaw, **The Supreme Court's Due Process Calculus—Three Factors in Search of a Theory of Value***

During the 1970s the Supreme Court has undertaken an intensive review of administrative hearing procedures for conformity with constitutional requirements of due process of law. The landmark case of Goldberg v. Kelly[2] in 1970 confirmed the Court's unwillingness to limit its review by traditional notions of property interests and also suggested, in its specification of the constitutionally requisite elements of adjudicatory procedure, that the Court was prepared to assume a highly interventionist posture. What followed was a "due process revolution"—a flood of cases seeking to extend, or simply to apply, *Goldberg*'s precepts.

The basic task that this burgeoning due process case load has presented to the courts has been to give content to the requirements of due process while maintaining an appropriate judicial role in the design of administrative procedures. Although *Goldberg* may have indicated the Court's willingness to impose a detailed model of requisite adjudicatory procedure upon a particular administrative function, no recent Supreme Court has believed that a single model is readily and consistently applicable to all administrative functions. What is required, therefore, are general criteria for review that will lend consistency and principle to the Court's decisions while permitting different administrative functions to be reviewed on their own terms. At the same time, those general criteria should be sufficiently concrete to structure administrative behavior without resort to a judicial test of every procedure that lacks some element of the paradigm process advanced in *Goldberg*.

In the Court's latest attempt to formulate this due process calculus, Mathews v. Eldridge,[4] Justice Powell's majority opinion articulates a set of criteria with a comprehensiveness that suggests a preliminary integration of the Court's recent efforts.[5] In the majority's words, from which there is no dissent,[6] the Court must consider:

> first, the private interest that will be affected by the official action; second, the risk of an erroneous deprivation of such interest

---

* *Source*: The Supreme Court's Due Process Calculus for Administrative Adjudication in Mathews v. Eldridge: Three Factors in Search of a Theory of Value, 44 U.Chi.L.Rev. 28, 28–30, 46–59 (1976). Professor of Law, Yale University.

2. 397 U.S. 254 (1970).

4. 424 U.S. 319 (1976). [In upholding the Social Security Administration's termination procedures which had been challenged by plaintiff Eldridge in connection with the termination of his disability insurance benefits, the Court in

Eldridge decided that a full evidentiary hearing was not required prior to the divestiture of a substantial interest when some opportunity to contest had been provided and no overriding governmental interest in summary process was apparent. Ed. Note.]

5. *Eldridge* may also represent a turning point in the Court's resolution of procedural due process issues. Since *Eldridge*, plaintiffs in due process cases have been uniformly unsuccessful,

---

6. See note 6 on page 19.

through the procedures used, and the probable value, if any, of additional or substitute procedural safeguards; and finally, the Government's interest, including the function involved and the fiscal and administrative burdens that the additional or substitute procedural requisites would entail.[7]

Although this functional formulation impliedly invites an intrusive, particularistic review and specification of procedures, it is tempered by judicial restraint. "In assessing what process is due in this case, substantial weight must be given to the good-faith judgment of the individuals charged by Congress with the administration of the social welfare system that the procedure they have provided assure fair consideration of the entitlement claims of individuals." [8]

The thesis of this article is that the *Eldridge* approach is unsatisfactory both as employed in that case and as a general formulation of due process review of administrative procedures. The failing of *Eldridge* is its focus on questions of technique rather than on questions of value. That focus, it is argued, generates an inquiry that is incomplete because unresponsive to the full range of concerns embodied in the due process clause .   .   .   .

The Supreme Court's analysis in *Eldridge* is not informed by systematic attention to any theory of the values underlying due process review. The approach is implicitly utilitarian but incomplete, and the Court overlooks alternative theories that might have yielded fruitful inquiry. My purpose is, first, to articulate the limits of the Court's utilitrian approach, both in *Eldridge* and as a general schema for evaluating administrative procedures, and second, to indicate the strengths and weaknesses of three alterntive theories—individual dignity, equality, and tradition. These theories, at the level of abstraction here presented, require little critical justification: they are widely held, respond to strong currents in the philosophic literature concerning law, politics, and ethics, and are supported either implicitly or explicitly by the Supreme Court's due process jurisprudence.[61]

---

and a marked tendency has emerged to avoid "balancing" analysis by finding the due process clause inapplicable. Montamye v. Haymes, 427 U.S. 236 (1976) (lack of hearing prior to transfer of prison inmates); Meachum v. Fano, 427 U.S. 215 (1976) (lack of hearing prior to transfer of prison inmates); Bishop v. Wood, 426 U.S. 341 (1976) (lack of hearing prior to employment termination of city policemen); Paul v. Davis, 424 U.S. 693 (1976) (lack of hearing prior to distribution of list of names of people charged but not convicted of shoplifting).

6. Although Justice Brennan questioned the application of these criteria to the facts, he refrained from questioning the criteria themselves. 424 U.S. 319, 349–50 (Brennan, J., dissenting); see

Richardson v. Wright, 405 U.S. 208, 212 (1972) (Brennan, J., dissenting).

7.   424 U.S. at 335.

8.   Id. at 349.

61.   In early due process cases the Supreme Court concentrated on tradition. The oft-cited statement in Davidson v. New Orleans, 96 U.S. 97, 104 (1877), that the Court's approach to due process problems should be "by the gradual process of judicial inclusion and exclusion," epitomizes the conservative, precedent-oriented, historical approach. As governmental functions increased, however, the Court was faced with due process problems that had no compelling historical analogies. If the Court was not to be a continual stumbling block to "prog-

A. Utilitarianism

Utility theory suggests that the purpose of decisional procedures—like that of social action generally—is to maximize social welfare. Indeed, the three-factor analysis enunciated in *Eldridge* appears to be a type of utilitarian, social welfare function. That function first takes into account the social value at stake in a legitimate private claim; it discounts that value by the probability that it will be preserved through the available administrative procedures, and it then subtracts from that discounted value the social cost of introducing additional procedures. When combined with the institutional posture of judicial self-restraint, utility theory can be said to yield the following plausible decision-rule: "Void procedures for lack of due process only when alternative procedures would so substantially increase social welfare that their rejection seems irrational."

The utilitarian calculus is not, however, without difficulties. The *Eldridge* Court conceives of the values of procedure too narrowly: it views the sole purpose of procedural protections as enhancing accuracy, and thus limits its calculus to the benefits or costs that flow from correct or incorrect decisions. No attention is paid to "process values" that might inhere in oral proceedings or to the demoralization costs that may result from the grant-withdrawal-grant-withdrawal sequence to which claimants like Eldridge are subjected. Perhaps more important, as the Court seeks to make sense of a calculus in which accuracy is the sole goal of procedure, it tends erroneous-

ress," a more flexible approach was needed. Indeed, the history of due process in the Supreme Court might be characterized as a continuous search for a theory of due process review that combines the legitimacy of the evolutionary theory with a flexibility that permits adaptation to contemporary circumstances. Dignitary or natural right, utilitarian, and egalitarian theories have all been incorporated to this end.

Dignitary ideas, although used occasionally in a supportive role both before 1900 and in some contemporary cases, were employed most frequently as the primary mode of analysis from about 1933 through the early 1950s. The proliferation of new government functions associated with the New Deal legislation and, later, with emergency war measures, stimulated a judicial reaction that was captured in the Court's emphasis on individual rights and dignitary values. The reactive natural rights style, predicated upon the Justices' perception of the "fair" solution in each case, had an ad hoc quality that soon became disturbing. The apparent inconsistency of the Supreme Court's due process jurisprudence led Sanford Kadish in a seminal article to describe the Supreme Court's decisions as in "chaotic array." Ka-

dish, Methodology and Criteria in Due Process Adjudication—A Survey and Criticism, 66 Yale L.J. 319 (1957).

In the late 1950s and early 1960s various utilitarian formulations began to supply a structure for analysis. In Cafeteria & Restaurant Workers Local 473 v. McElroy, 367 U.S. 886, 895 (1961), for example, the Court, per Mr. Justice Stewart, stated that two factors must be considered in due process cases: "the precise nature of the government function involved . . . [and] of the private interest that has been affected by government action." The statement of the utilitarian approach culminates in the *Eldridge* opinion's three-factor calculus.

Equality as a due process value has received considerable attention in criminal (or quasi-criminal) cases, but little outside that area. Perhaps the best example of the explicit use of equality concerns with respect to an administrative function is found in Ashbacker Radio Corp. v. FCC, 326 U.S. 327, 330 (1945). There the Court, per Mr. Justice Douglas, stated that the right to a hearing "becomes an empty thing" unless all parties affected by the process have an equal opportunity to be heard.

ly to characterize disability hearings as concerned almost exclusively with medical impairment and thus concludes that such hearings involve only medical evidence, whose reliability would be little enhanced by oral procedure. As applied by the *Eldridge* Court the utilitarian calculus tends, as cost-benefit analyses typically do, to "dwarf soft variables" and to ignore complexities and ambiguities.

The problem with a utilitarian calculus is not merely that the Court may define the relevant costs and benefits too narrowly. However broadly conceived, the calculus asks unanswerable questions. For example, what is the social value, and the social cost, of continuing disability payments until after an oral hearing for persons initially determined to be ineligible? Answers to those questions require a technique for measuring the social value and social cost of government income transfers, but no such technique exists. Even if such formidable tasks of social accounting could be accomplished, the effectiveness of oral hearings in forestalling the losses that result from erroneous terminations would remain uncertain. In the face of these pervasive indeterminacies the *Eldridge* Court was forced to retreat to a presumption of constitutionality.

Finally, it is not clear that the utilitarian balancing analysis asks the constitutionally relevant questions. The due process clause is one of those Bill of Rights protections meant to insure individual liberty in the face of contrary collective action. Therefore, a collective legislative or administrative decision about procedure, one arguably reflecting the intensity of the contending social values and representing an optimum position from the contemporary social perspective, cannot answer the constitutional question of whether due process has been accorded. A balancing analysis that would have the Court merely redetermine the question of social utility is similarly inadequate. There is no reason to believe that the Court has superior competence or legitimacy as a utilitarian balancer except as it performs its peculiar institutional role of insuring that libertarian values are considered in the calculus of decision.

Several alternative perspectives on the values served by due process pervade the Court's jurisprudence, and may provide a principled basis for due process analysis. These perspectives can usually be incorporated into a broadly defined utilitarian formula and are therefore not necessarily antiutilitarian. But they are best treated separately because they tend to generate inquiries that are different from a strictly utilitarian approach.

B. Individual Dignity

The increasingly secular, scientific, and collectivist character of the modern American state reinforces our propensity to define fairness in the formal, and apparently neutral language of social utility. Assertions of "natural" or "inalienable" rights seem, by contrast, somewhat embarrassing. Their ancestry, and therefore their moral force, are increasingly uncertain. Moreover, their role in the history of the due process clause makes us apprehensive about their eventual reach. It takes no peculiar acuity to see that the tension in procedural due process cases is the same as that in the now discredited substantive due process jurisprudence—a tension between the efficacy of the state and the individual's right to freedom from coercion or socially imposed disadvantage.

Yet the popular moral presupposition of individual dignity, and its political counterpart, self-determination, persist. State coercion must be legitimized, not only by acceptable substantive policies, but also by political processes that respond to a democratic morality's demand for participation in decisions affecting individual and group interests. At the level of individual administrative decisions this demand appears in both the layman's and the lawyer's language as the right to a "hearing" or "to be heard," normally meaning orally and in person. To accord an individual less when his property or status is at stake requires justification, not only because he might contribute to accurate determinations, but also because a lack of personal participation causes alienation and a loss of that dignity and self-respect that society properly deems independently valuable.

The obvious difficulty with a dignitary theory of procedural due process lies in defining operational limits on the procedural claims it fosters. In its purest form the theory would suggest that decisions affecting individual interests should be made only through procedures acceptable to the person affected. This purely subjective standard of procedural due process cannot be adopted: an individual's claim to a "nonalienating" procedure is not ranked ahead of all other social values.

The available techniques for limiting the procedural claims elicited by the dignitary theory, however, either appear arbitrary or render the theory wholly inoperative. One technique is to curtail the class of substantive claims in which individuals can be said to have a right to what they consider an acceptable procedure. The "life, liberty, or property" language of the due process clause suggests such a limitation, but experience with this classification of interests has been disappointing. Any standard premised simply on preexisting legal rights renders a claimant's quest for due process, as such, either unnecessary or hopeless. Another technique for confining the dignitary theory is to define "nonalienating" procedure as any procedure that is formulated democratically. The troublesome effect of this limitation is that no procedures that are legislatively authorized can be said to encroach on individual dignity.

Notwithstanding its difficulties, the dignitary theory of due process might have contributed significantly to the *Eldridge* analysis. The questions of procedural "acceptability" which the theory poses may initially seem vacuous or at best intuitive, but they suggest a broader sensitivity than the utilitarian factor analysis to the nature of governmental decisions. Whereas the utilitarian approach seems to require an estimate of the quantitative value of the claim, the dignitary approach suggests that the Court develop a qualitative appraisal of the type of administrative decision involved. While the disability decision in *Eldridge* may be narrowly characterized as a decision about the receipt of money payments, it may also be considered from various qualitative perspectives which seem pertinent in view of the general structure of the American income-support system.

That system suggests that a disability decision is a judgment of considerable social significance, and one that the claimant should rightly perceive as having a substantial moral content. The major cash income-support programs determine eligibility, not only on the basis of simple insufficiency of income, but also, or exclusively, on the basis of a series of excuses for partial or total nonparticipation in the work force: agedness, childhood, family responsibility, injury, disability. A grant under any of these programs is an official, if sometimes grudging, stamp of approval of the claimant's status as a partially disabled worker or nonworker. It proclaims, in effect, that those who obtain it have encountered one of the politically legitimate hazards to self-sufficiency in a market economy. The recipients, therefore, are entitled to society's support. Conversely, the denial of an income-maintenance claim implies that the claim is socially illegitimate, and the claimant, however impecunious, is not excused from normal work force status.

These moral and status dimensions of the disability decision indicate that there is more at stake in disability claims than temporary loss of income.[73] They also tend to put the disability decision in a framework that leads away from the superficial conclusion that disability decisions are a routine matter of evaluating medical evidence. Decisions with substantial "moral worth" connotations are generally expected to be highly individualized and attentive to subjective evidence. The adjudication of such issues on the basis of documents submitted largely by third parties and by adjudicators who have never confronted the claimant seems inappropriate. Instead, a court approaching an analysis of the disability claims process from the dignitary perspective might emphasize those aspects of disability decisions that focus on a particular claimant's vocational characteristics, his unique response to his medical condition, and the ultimate predictive judgment of whether the claimant should be able to work. . . .

C. Equality

. . . Notions of equality can . . . significantly inform the evaluation of any administrative process. One question we might ask is whether an investigative procedure is designed in a fashion that systematically excludes or undervalues evidence that would tend to support the position of a particular class of parties. If so, those parties might have a plausible claim that the procedure treated them unequally. Similarly, in a large-scale inquisitorial process involving many adjudicators, the question that should be posed is whether like cases receive like attention and like evidentiary development so that the influence of such arbitrary factors as location are minimized. In order to take such equality issues into account, we need only to broaden our due process horizons to include elements of procedural fairness beyond those traditionally associated with adversary proceedings. These two inquiries might have been pursued fruitfully in *Eldridge*. First, is the state agency system of decision making, which is based on documents, particularly disadvantageous for certain classes of claimants? There is some tentative

---

73. The *Eldridge* Court, in distinguishing *Goldberg* largely on the ground that terminated welfare recipients were more desperate financially than terminated disability recipients, thus ignored a very substantial similarity . . . . The potential for feelings of demoralization, rejection, or simple righteous indignation seems essentially the same in both types of cases.

evidence that it is. Cases such as *Eldridge* involving muscular or skeletal disorders, neurological problems, and multiple impairments, including psychological overlays, are widely believed to be both particularly difficult, due to the subjectivity of the evidence, and particularly prone to be reversed after oral hearing.

Second, does the inquisitorial process at the state agency level tend to treat like cases alike? If the GAO's study [a] is indicative, the answer is decidedly no. According to that study, many, perhaps half, of the decisions are made on the basis of records that other adjudicators consider so inadequate that a decision could not be rendered. The relevance of such state agency variance to Eldridge's claim is twofold: first, it suggests that state agency determinations are unreliable and that further development at the hearing stage might substantially enhance their reliability; alternatively, it may suggest that the hierarchical or bureaucratic model of decision making, with overhead control for consistency, does not accurately describe the Social Security disability system. And if consistency is not feasible under this system, perhaps the more compelling standard for evaluating the system is the dignitary value of individualized judgment, which . . . implies claimant participation.

D.   Tradition or Evolution

Judicial reasoning, including reasoning about procedural due process, is frequently and self-consciously based on custom or precedent. In part, reliance on tradition or "authority" is a court's institutional defense against illegitimacy in a political democracy. But tradition serves other values, not the least of which are predictability and economy of effort. More importantly, the inherently conservative technique of analogy to custom and precedent seems essential to the evolutionary development and the preservation of the legal system. Traditional procedures are legitimate not only because they represent a set of continuous expectations, but because the body politic has survived their use.

The use of tradition as a guide to fundamental fairness is vulnerable, of course, to objection. Since social and economic forces are dynamic, the processes and structures that proved functional in one period will not necessarily serve effectively in the next. Indeed, evolutionary development may as often end in the extinction of a species as in adaptation and survival. For this reason alone tradition can serve only as a partial guide to judgment.

Furthermore, it may be argued that reasoning by analogy from traditional procedures does not actually provide a perspective on the values served by due process. Rather, it is a decisional technique that requires a specification of the purposes of procedural rules merely in order that the decision maker may choose from among a range of authorities or customs the particular authority or custom most analogous to the procedures being evaluated.

This objection to tradition as a theory of justification is weighty, but not devastating. What is asserted by an organic or evolutionary theory is that

---

a. A General Accounting Office consistency survey of state disability determinations. The study found a definite lack of consistency among state agencies and between state agencies and the federal adjudicators. Ed. note.

the purposes of legal rules cannot be fully known.   Put more cogently, while procedural rules, like other legal rules, should presumably contribute to the maintenance of an effective social order, we cannot expect to know precisely how they do so and what the long-term effects of changes or revisions might be.   Our constitutional stance should therefore be preservative and incremental, building carefully, by analogy, upon traditional modes of operation. So viewed, the justification "we have always done it that way" is not so much a retreat from reasoned and purposive decision making as a profound acknowledgment of the limits of instrumental rationality.

Viewed from a traditionalist's perspective, the Supreme Court's opinion in *Eldridge* may be said to rely on the traditional proposition that property interests may be divested temporarily without hearing, provided a subsequent opportunity for contest is afforded.   Goldberg v. Kelly is deemed an exceptional case, from which *Eldridge* is distinguished.   .   .   .

Conclusion

The preceding discussion has emphasized the way that explicit attention to a range of values underlying due process of law might have led the *Eldridge* Court down analytic paths different from those that appear in Justice Powell's opinion.   The discussion has largely ignored, however, arguments that would justify the result that the Court reached in terms of the alternative value theories here advanced.   Those arguments are now set forth.

First, focus on the dignitary aspects of the disability decision can hardly compel the conclusion that an oral hearing is a constitutional necessity prior to the termination of benefits when a full hearing is available later.   Knowledge that an oral hearing will be available at some point should certainly lessen disaffection and alienation.   Indeed, Eldridge seemed secure in the knowledge that a just procedure was available.   His desire to avoid taking a corrective appeal should not blind us to the support of dignitary values that the de novo appeal provides.

Second, arguments premised on equality do not necessarily carry the day for the proponent of prior hearings.   The Social Security Administration's attempt to routinize and make consistent hundreds of thousands of decisions in a nationwide income-maintenance program can be criticized both for its failures in its own terms and for its tendency to ignore the way that disability decisions impinge upon perceptions of individual moral worth. On balance, however, the program that Congress enacted contains criteria that suggest a desire for both consistency and individualization.   No adjudicatory process can avoid tradeoffs between the pursuit of one or the other of these goals.   Thus a procedural structure incorporating (1) decisions by a single state agency based on a documentary record and subject to hierarchical quality review, followed by (2) appeal to de novo oral proceedings before independent administrative law judges, is hardly an irrational approach to the necessary compromise between consistency and individualization.

Explicit and systematic attention to the values served by a demand for due process nevertheless remains highly informative in *Eldridge* and in general.   The use of analogy to traditional procedures might have helped rationalize and systematize a concern for the "desperation" of claimants that seems as impoverished in *Eldridge* as it seems profligate in *Goldberg;* and the absence in *Eldridge* of traditionalist, dignitary, or egalitarian considerations regarding the disability adjudication process permitted the Court to overlook questions of both fact and value—questions that, on reflection, seem important. The structure provided by the Court's three factors is an inadequate guide for analysis because its neutrality leaves it empty of suggestive value perspectives.

Furthermore, an attempt by the Court to articulate a set of values that informs due process decision making might provide it with an acceptable judicial posture from which to review administrative procedures. The *Goldberg* decision's approach to prescribing due process—specification of the attributes of adjudicatory hearings by analogy to judicial trial—makes the Court resemble an administrative engineer with an outdated professional education. It is at once intrusive and ineffectual. Retreating from this stance, the *Eldridge* Court relies on the administrator's good faith—an equally troublesome posture in a political system that depends heavily on judicial review for the protection of countermajoritarian values.

The path to a more appropriate and successful judicial role may lie in giving greater attention to the elaboration of the due process implications of the values that have been discussed. If the Court provided a structure of values within which procedures would be reviewed, it could then demand that administrators justify their processes in terms of the degree to which they support the elaborated value structure. The Court would have to be satisfied that the administrator had carefully considered the effects of his chosen procedures on the relevant constitutional values and had made reasonable judgments concerning those effects.

A decision that an administrator had not met that standard would not result in the prescription of a particular adjudicatory technique as a constitutional, and thereafter virtually immutable, necessity; but rather in a remand to the administrator. In meeting the Court's objections, the administrator (or legislature) might properly choose between specific amendment and a complete overhaul of the administrative process. Perhaps more importantly, under a due process approach that emphasized value rather than technique, neither the administrator in constructing and justifying his processes, nor the Court in reviewing them, would be limited to the increasingly sterile discussion of whether this or that particular aspect of trial-type procedure is absolutely essential to due process of law.

————

1. Are the questions put by the dignitary and egalitarian approaches any more "answerable" than those put by the utilitarian calculus? Or is it simply that Professor Mashaw is reacting to the utilitarian pretense of answerability?

2. Is the egalitarian approach analytically distinct from the others, as Professor Mashaw suggests, or can it be viewed merely as a particularization of the dignitary approach? What are the differences?

SECTION D. THE LIMITS OF INSTRUMENTAL EXPLANATIONS

Human decisional processes, whatever their commonalities, vary from society to society, from culture to culture. Far more even than the physical tools of agriculture, war, or industry, they exhibit the living arrangements and symbol systems of their users. This phenomenon is hardly surprising. The very definitions of "dispute," "decision," "resolution," "peace," to say nothing of evaluative terms—"wise," "good," "fair"—depend primarily upon the particular institutions, expectations, and systems of meaning in which they occur. Professor Leff considers the impact on legal institutions and processes which follows from the fact that people strive to place their legal institutions—with their functional characteristics—within more or less coherent systems of meaning. Professor Felstiner considers the operation of three different forms of dispute processing—adjudication, mediation, and avoidance—in the context of opposing ideal types of social organization.

Arthur A. Leff, **Law and***

.   .   .

The First Tribe

Let us suppose there exists somewhere a primitively-organized people, call them the "Jondo."[2] This tribe is so primitive that it has divided itself into only two moieties, or subgroups, totemically specified as the Fish-Jondo and the Maize-Jondo. Each moiety is eponymously charged with the production of one of the two Jondo food staples.

The Jondo also possess an elaborate cosmology that includes a complex classification of the heavenly bodies, which are believed to give direction to the sublunary activities of the tribe and its members. In the tribe's world vision, most of the visible stars are organized into vegetable-like constellations; other heavenly bodies, like the moon, sun, planets, meteors, and comets, being more "active," are associated with various animals. This play of the sky sends to every Jondo messages about how his tribe is ordered to be "in tune" with the universe.

Ordinarily, each of the two Jondo moieties stays on its own clearly demarcated side of the village. On two occasions, however, all the Jondo come together. One jointure occurs "when the Great Cod enters the Maize Ear," that is, when the moon rises full in a particular constellation of stars that the Jondo call the "Maize Ear." This celestial event normally occurs in early

* *Source:* 87 Yale L.J. 989, 989–1005 (1978). Professor of Law, Yale University.

2. My treatment of the Jondo is most certainly not to be taken as "doing anthropology." One does not practice that discipline on imaginary data, and even if I were working with information about a real tribe, I am not equipped to do a real job of anthropological interpretation. The Jondo are not a tribe but a metaphor; I am attempting to illustrate some of the difficulties of "legal science" in terms of this imaginary society, but I am not trying to say anything at all about the Jondo as a unit of human organization.

autumn, and when the sky so arranges itself, all the Fish-Jondo cross to the Maize-Jondo side of the village, help with the maize harvest, and celebrate with a big post-gleaning party.

The other major all-tribe event takes place in early spring, when "the Maize Ear is eaten by the Great Cod," that is, when the maize constellation disappears below the horizon under the setting new moon. At that point all the Maize-Jondo go to the Fish-Jondo (river) side of the village, help cope with the annual run of the river cod, and have another party when it is over.

Now by and large these heavenly arrangements coincide with the two "harvests." But only by and large. Because of yearly variations in the ripening time of maize and the spawning lust of codfish, moon, stars, and organic nature almost never perfectly coincide. Thus, not infrequently part of the spawning run and/or part of the maize harvest is lost. Indeed, sometimes, when heaven and earth are too much out of phase, it begins to look as if *all* of a particular harvest might be lost. When that happens, the "Astronomer Royal" of the Jondo must declare the moon "bewitched," and order the temporary merger of all the Jondo on the basis of where an unbewitched moon *would* be, or, as he puts it, where it "really" is.

After the maize is harvested, it is placed in a number of "grain elevators" shaped like gigantic fish located on the Fish-Jondo side of the village. When the codfish catch is completed, it is salted and cured and then stored in a series of deep burial chambers in the Maize-Jondo territory. Throughout the year, the Fish-Jondo "swim" (very stealthily, at night) over to the Maize-Jondo's burial chambers and, until interrupted by the Maize-Jondo watchmen, "go fishing" for the preserved cod. The Fish-Jondo take as "bait" sacks of maize, which they leave behind them when, discovered, they flee with their "catch."

This, as one might imagine, leads to disputes. Under such a distribution system the fish-grain exchange ratio is determined almost unilaterally by the Fish-Jondo. So the Jondo also have a legal system, albeit one that recognizes only one cause of action, which may fairly be translated as "tortiously fishing with insufficient bait." When such a complaint is filed, the matter is taken for solution to the Jondo's chief judicial officer, the "Sacred Hermaphrodite."

Among the Jondo, be it said, "hermaphrodite" does not mean half-male, half-female; it means half-fish and half-grain. The Jondo Sacred Hermaphrodite is always the eldest male member of the same family. This family belongs to the Maize-Jondo moiety and resides on that side of the village. But the males in the family suffer from a nasty hereditary skin disease that makes them appear almost "scaly." This dematological misfortune is hardly mitigated by the family's position as maritally "unclean" to both totems, which leads to a shocking amount of inbreeding.

In any event, the alleged tortious fishing is tried before the Sacred Hermaphrodite. He listens to both sides, then tears open a codfish, wraps it around a maize ear, buries it in a warmed pit, and a day or two later "reads" the decayed result. Generally he awards some compensatory grain to the Maize-Jondo, but since this Jondo skin disease is genetically linked to adult imbecility, the award occasionally goes the other way. When it does, the

Maize-Jondo have for a while a very hungry time of it indeed. But then again, Sacred Hermaphrodites who botch the decision two years in a row are always found, before the third year's "trial," floating face down in the river, having sought, perhaps successfully, to join the Great Cod himself in an epiphanic embrace.[3]

What then is one to make of the Jondo? One approach might be to ignore the Jondo cosmology and just describe what they do. The first thing to be noted would be the existence of the tribe, which proves that they have ordered their society so that it is viable at the crude biological level. But more than that, the Jondo can be seen to make a series of moves clearly conducive to material prosperity. They are committed to the specialization of labor in the acquisition of their two staples, and that leads, one might surmise, to productive efficiencies. But when either production group must temporarily be augmented by a pool of less-skilled labor in order to bring in the "harvest," the needed workers are regularly available. And the produce, once acquired, is stored and cared for in what again looks to be a technologically efficient manner, again involving labor specialization.

Moreover, a balanced diet is achieved as protein and fat are exchanged for carbohydrate, and vice-versa. When this primary system of exchange generates temporary misallocations, an adequate legal system is in place to cope with the problem. Since that legal system uses a judge recognized as independent of either major grouping within the society, his judgments are accorded tribal respect. And that legitimacy seems not to be misplaced; an objective study of the final exchange ratio between moieties for any extended period would show that all of the Jondo are more or less equally well nourished.

In brief, it would appear thoroughly plausible to describe the Jondo as organized to achieve economic goals in their tribal and individual endeavors. One could, without blushing, speak of the economic efficiency of the Jondo.

But the same activities among the Jondo could be described in a different vocabulary, tied to a differently perceived pattern. One could see the Jondo, in all things, merely acting out the implications of their cosmology. Fish-Jondo fish and Maize-Jondo cultivate, each apart from the other, in mere imitation of similar empyreal divisions; the distinctions between animal and plant, moving body and fixed body, active and passive, all occur on earth, as they do in heaven. The Jondo come together when the sky does, and depart again on the same sort of cue. Fish-Jondo can move, but Maize-Jondo are more rooted. So the Fish-Jondo swim, bearing grain as bait, to catch their penned totemic brothers. When the Fish-Jondo have greedily fished unfairly, neither Fish nor Maize can be trusted to decide: the arbiter must be a totemic Maize Ear who nonetheless bears the scales of the Great Cod.

---

3. The elders among the Fish-Jondo visit the Hermaphrodite to tell him that the Great Cod has appeared and asked for him "to come home." The Maize-Jondo elders then come and publicly rejoice in their totemic brother's honor. The Hermaphrodite joyously makes for the river closely accompanied by the ecstatic elders of both totems, and throws himself face down in the water, with the eldest Fish and eldest Maize helping him to maintain his embrace.

Here, then, it would not be absurd to suggest that the "explanation" of Jondo society lies in its symbolic intellectual structure. One *can* see all Jondo activities as but metaphoric dramatizations of the all-inclusive coherence of heaven, earth, and Jondo.

But it cannot be overlooked for long that both analyses would finally end up with a "not quite." Surely the "economic" analyst would puzzle over the Jondo's repeated failure to hit the optimal labor allocation for harvest maximization. And for all its apparent workability, a more accurate adjudication device could be designed than one that relies almost totally upon the decisions of a congenitally imbecilic trier of fact.

From the other side, an observer attuned to the structure of Jondo cosmology would have to be troubled by the phenomenon of the bewitchable moon. After all, if the Jondo just waited they would have no need for an Astronomer Royal charged with the task of creating imaginary lunar positioning. Eventually the moon would get where it was going, and the Jondo could then mingle in perfect accord with heavenly behavior, and while anthropological cosmologists would admire the Jondo solution to a possible bias problem in a culture of two equal moieties—by linking the Sacred Hermaphrodite geographically to Maize, and metonymically to Fish—they would have a very difficult time with the Sacred Hermaphrodite's mortality patterns: some embrace the Great Cod early, some much later, and some die without any transcendence ceremony at all. What is the pattern *there*?

If, however, one were to stand far enough back from the data of Jondo life to encompass both material and metaphorical frameworks, the anomalies would quickly dissipate. One would just say of the Jondo that at least two different things are important to them: biological survival, which depends on some degree of whole-tribe labor and a fair intratribal allocation of staples; and living with a system of meanings such that heaven and earth are joined in an all-inclusive, internally coherent pattern. Neither pattern can be said to be prior or primary, either logically or socially. Only by what might be called a general equilibrium solution of *everything* could the Jondo have a system of being and meaning that would "work out" correctly and elegantly in each sphere of desire. Lacking that, there must be some "loss," either in the generality and power of their meaning system, or in the yield from their economic system. Thus in order to preserve the elegance of their cosmic vision, the Jondo will give up some food; to keep from starving, they will suffer some degree of aesthetic decay. But what they will do only in extremity, if then, is accept the total destruction of either their material or their metaphoric universe.

The Usa

The Jondo do not really exist. They were invented solely to illustrate a way of talking about social phenomena that might aid in understanding the workings of a real society. Let me, therefore, try to use a similar method to talk about the Usa.[8] The Usa control a vast and rich domain. Politically

---

8. I have decided to refer to our own society as that of "the Usa" to make it easier to use the metaphorical paraphernalia developed by my trope of the Jondo. This time, however, the society involved is not imaginary. It exists,

and economically they are organized so complexly that any Jondo coming among them would likely expire from mere bewilderment. Instead of having two moieties, two staples, two totems, the Usa are divided into literally countless classes—territorial, familial, occupational, political, ideological. A seeming infinity of resources is divided, subdivided, traded, combined, produced, and reproduced. Where the Jondo had only the problem of allocating their produce between Fish-Jondo and Maize-Jondo, among the Usa there is a vast network of distribution, allocation, production, and exchange serving to satisfy as fully as possible each and every Usa's needs and wants.

Since the Usa form so large and various a society, one cannot in any reasonable space describe anything approaching the fullness of Usa life. Indeed, almost any single element or institution of Usa society is too complex to describe totally.

There appear to be, however, aspects of Usa society that might be illuminated, if only dimly, by casting on them the same kind of light played over Jondo society. Consider . . . the Usa "Trial."

A. The Trial

Among the Usa, as among most other peoples, every so often there are disputes. The other techniques and institutions available to the Usa to deal with such mutual unhappiness—screaming at each other, refusing to do business with each other, refusing to go to dinner together, reciprocal libel and slander, and so on—for some reason do not work. When that happens, one of the annoyed Usa will take the initiating steps toward bringing into play the Usa Trial.

First, he will seek out a Trial Champion, one of an expensively trained caste of Usa who, for a price, will press the disputant's claim. The Champion will begin this new phase of the interaction between the parties by serving, on behalf of his employer, a Challenge. This document, ordinarily couched in a special, archaic vocabulary, will accuse the other of some behavior understood among the Usa to be rotten. The Challenge will demand that the other disputant appear, at a particular time, in a special place, before a caste of quasi-sacred functionaries, the "Judges," to give the lie to the charge. This usually forces the recipient to hire a Trial Champion of his own to file, on *his* behalf, the Answer. In equally ritualized language, the Answer may deny the calumny, deny that it *is* a calumny, and/or assert a counter-calumny of its own.[12]

---

and therefore can be misdescribed, and to the extent I do so, my commentary will also be off the mark. Thus if I fail to draw a picture of these particular elements of our society that the reader feels is adequate, he should feel free to disregard whatever else I say.

Moreover, to some extent my description will certainly be inaccurate. It will, for one thing, be necessarily incomplete. For another, the use of "tribal" language will, to some extent, if only connotatively, falsify perceived reality. And finally, my observations are empirical, but only in a sense of that term that most sociologists, for instance, would consider a mere mockery.

12. There are other possible responses to a Challenge, for instance, that the dispute is not the sort that can be settled in the Usa Trial, or at least not before this particular Judge.

Once the Challenge is given and accepted, there usually ensues a substantial and costly period of preliminary sparring between Champions. During this time, the Champions engage in divers reciprocal harassment and data-gathering activities controlled, but only to some extent, by the Judges. Many disputes leave the Trial system during these early formal interactions as the parties exchange things of value (money, submission ceremonies) to signal their formal accommodation to each other.[13] But sometimes, after substantial delay (for this is one of the few places in Usa society where one cannot exchange something of value for a better place in line), the parties and their Champions will actually find themselves together at the "special place," ready to confront and terminate their dispute.

These "special places" are almost unique in architecture and interior decoration among the Usa. The rooms are large and imposing, nothing like "home" or most "work" rooms among the Usa, and have lavished upon them a large number of Usa awe symbols—very high ceilings, carved plaques, banners. An area in the Trial room is set aside for each of the combatant teams. These areas are of equal size, have equal accouterments, and are symmetrically placed equidistant from a raised, central platform where the Judge sits. The Judge is "really" just another Usa, but he is always dressed up in a peculiar costume signaling his temporarily supraordinary status. He is addressed with archaic honorifics, and he is understood to be omnipotent *within that room.* That is, during the proceedings no licit power on earth exists superior to his, and the parties and the Champions from time to time practice elaborate deference ceremonies to signal their subservience to that power.

Frequently, the Judge is assisted in some of his functions by a group of helpers, typically twelve in number. They too are ordinary Usa, but they too are visually distinguished at the Trial: they sit together in a sharply differentiated space, which is also sometimes raised (though never as high as the seat of the judge). This separated helpers' space is usually perpendicular to the spaces of Judge and parties, connecting them, but only peripherally.

Unlike the Judge, the helpers wear no odd costumes and are not trained for their roles at all. In theory, they are initially chosen by a random selection device, supplemented by another winnowing process designed to remove potential helpers with too close an affinity to one of the contestants or his Champion. But in practice, this second procedure removes from the final panel of twelve anyone who might have particular expertise, or even knowledge, of anything relevant to the dispute.

Once the proceedings are under way, almost a weird symmetry obtains. The contestants alternate moves according to strict rules of precedence and subsequence, and the temporal symmetry applies even to sub-moves. No party has an opportunity not shared by the other, and when simultaneity is impossible, corrective reversals are the rule; he who starts the initiating dyad of moves, for instance, finishes the concluding dyad.

13. As a general rule, the parties can,
by mutual agreement, withdraw from
the Trial even into its latest stages.

Moreover, the ordinary rules of Usa discourse are superseded at the Trial in favor of a new set of rules about who may talk when and about what. Disputes about this special Usa Trial etiquette frequently must be posed to the Judge for authoritative determination, for the rules governing this etiquette represent arcane knowledge, and possession of it is one of the most valuable assets of both Champions and Judges. Trial etiquette bears only the slightest relationship to ordinary Usa modes of investigation and description. To pick just one instance, in most situations the Usa rely extensively, even in important matters, upon reports by other Usa of what still other Usa claim to have observed. But during the Trial (subject to some peculiar exceptions) such method of discovering what happened is formally "unclean" and excluded.

At the close of the Trial, the dais-raised, oddly dressed Judge, sometimes aided by his group of helpers, will declare the "winner" of the confrontation. Much of the time this will entail giving an answer to complicated questions of fact as if only two quantities—all and none—exist. For instance, if the dispute involves the proper understanding of complex communications between two parties over time, the Judge and his helpers will likely behave as if the only interpretations available are (a) contract or (b) no contract.

In any event, the Judge will at last tell one of the parties to do something with respect to the other (or tell him that he doesn't have to), and this decision (subject to the severely limited "appellate" power of other oddly dressed people in other symmetrical rooms whose discourse rules are even more straitened) may be aggressively enforced by the Usa society; behind every Usa Judge stands ultimately the naked power of the 101st Airborne Division of the Usa army.

It should be recalled, however, that the initiating Challenge demands that the challenged party "give the lie" at the Trial to the nastiness therein asserted. Although a great deal else goes on before, during, and sometimes after the Trial, the purpose of the Trial itself, at least in form, is primarily to ascertain the truth about an event, to determine whether particular states of fact did or did not obtain some time in the past.

This is significant for an understanding of the place of the Trial in Usa society. A large and growing number of serious, intelligent, and reasonably persuasive studies of the Usa Trial and associated institutions have pointed out the extent to which they are integrated into the Usa production, distribution, and consumption systems. The substantive legal rules applied at the Usa Trial seem largely designed to further the "efficiency" of the Usa system. Obviously, if the rules are so designed, the facts to which those rules are applied must also be accurate, for surely an efficiency-oriented "law" applied to a false view of the world can have none but inefficient effects. If efficiency demands, for instance, that promisors keep their promises, it would hardly be efficient to enforce promises never made, or to fail to enforce ones that were. And if liability is imposed after accidents to deter negligent behavior, how silly it would be to deter the careful and reward the reckless.

B. The Ludic Metaphor

All this is but to say—what is obvious—that the Usa Trial is part of the total Usa society, and serves some of the same economic purposes served by other institutions in that society. . . .

The Usa do, of course, farm, work, and trade. But even the most casual observer of Usa society cannot help but note that its members take part, either as participants or spectators, in a vast array of activities that they call "sports" and "games." . . . Indeed, although no careful empirical analysis has been made, it would not appear laughable to suggest that the Usa expend more time, energy, and interest on their sports and games than on any other kind of activity, notably more than they spend in their more directly "economic" activities, like "working" or "trading."

. . . Indeed, when one looks at those activities considered "games" or "sports" among the Usa, some striking generalizations come immediately to hand. One notes first of all that games or sports in Usa society [18] are ordinarily played in clearly demarcated spaces set off from the background of other activities. There are boards, fields, arenas, stadiums, and so on. These spatial arrangements, indeed, are frequently integral to the play, as when particular significance is given to transgressing a boundary.[19]

Moreover, this boundedness is not limited to space. Games are notably subject to rules designed to signal formal beginnings and ends, either in terms of elapsed time [20] or a stated number of iterations of moves within the game,[21] or in terms of the exhaustion of a given and unreplenishable supply of consumable resources.[22]

Second, the players in any game are treated for purposes of the game as formally identical.[23] They each have the same access to the field and the mechanisms of play, and the same formal entitlements (if not simultaneously, then at least in equal succession).

Third, the rules that govern the game are absolutely binding during any play thereof. They are not open to question in any nongame terms— justness, for instance, or legitimacy or efficiency—for they do not so much regulate the activity as constitute it.[24]

---

18. I shall hereafter frequently use "game" to cover both those activities so denominated among the Usa, and those usually called "sports" by them. For present purposes whatever distinguishes "game" from "sport" in our culture's ordinary language seems of little significance.

19. Consider, for example, the foul line and "the stands" of baseball, the sideline of football, the gutter of bowling.

20. E. g., football, soccer, basketball.

21. E. g., baseball, bowling, horseshoes.

22. E. g., checkers, bridge, Monopoly.

23. This generalization must be tempered by reference to the use of "handicaps" in some agonistic games when the probable outcome is so clear, given what is known about the actual contestants, that all suspense would be removed were structural inequalities not built into the particular contest. Also, the identity referred to in text means the formal equality of each player on a team, not vis-à-vis the members of his own team, but in relation to his "opposite number" on another team.

24. That is not to say that the rules of games cannot be changed, but only that they are immovable during any

Last, and most important, the aim of the game activity is "in" the game, that is, the aim is defined as part of the game, or better, as part of that which defines the game. The most significant thing about games, therefore, is that they have a resolution, a definition of the *meaning* of every act within the game, including, ordinarily, a definition of what it means to say that one has "won" or "lost." A game is an activity in terms of which you can know with some precision what you did and how you came out. Although no human activity can be totally free of ambiguity, a "game" is so set up as to reduce ambiguity to a minimum. "Can he do that?", "Is that permitted?", "What does that mean?" are questions designed to be, most of the time, easily answerable in terms of the game itself.

In Usa games, therefore, if one achieves the defined "end" of the game but in so doing ignores any of the defined constraints, *one has not won.* This is true even if there is no enforcement power in all of Usa society able to do anything about it, for all definitional systems are self-enforcing

.   .   .   .

.   .   .   .   Although as a psychological matter, it is perhaps perceived by most Usa as better to win than to lose, it seems that, given how hard it is in the ordinary "playing" of "real life," including economic activity, to determine how one came out, it is a joy independent of victory to be engaged in an activity that allows for a determinate result. Even clearly losing may, at least some of the time, be a pleasant alternative to a lifetime of never knowing.[28] If utility is tied to knowing the result, then the result must be easy to determine. It is therefore not enough that "win" be the product of clear definition, but it is also important that the objective embodiment of that defined state be easily perceived. There must be some reasonably precise "scoring" system, a significance system in terms of which one can determine the "result" of every "move," and of the aggregate of all moves, which together constitute a play of the game.

One of the most common devices to achieve that clarity in Usa games is the definition of results in ordinal rather than cardinal terms. That is, the central vocabulary of most Usa games is that of comparatives—faster, heavier, longer, more—and those particular comparatives called superlatives —fastest, heaviest, longest, most—which remain merely ordinal, differing only in that they are comparative to all prior plays of the same game. Since these comparative terms use "natural" standards of the natural world, they have the added advantage of well-known, simple, and precise calibration. But other games and sports have other ways of defining the achievement of the "significant" or "meaningful" act. Certainly (to pick just one instance of many) the positional victory of "chess" is not a simple matter of achieving some physically palpable ordinality.

---

particular play. If any normative element justifies this rigidity, it is that the players have freely chosen to play the game by those known rules.

28. One chess grandmaster observed:
      If a combination forcing a win has been found, nothing avails the opponent, for the demonstration of the win can be grasped. In Life it is different. There the struggles are not so indubitably terminated as in a game. The game gives us a satisfaction that Life denies us.
      E. Lasker, Lasker's Manual of Chess 114 (1947).

In all of the ludic activity of the Usa, however, the rules are formulated such that a certain amount of something is defined within the game as the "right" amount. More is not better, nor (most of the time) is it worse; it is, strictly speaking, in terms of the game, *irrelevant*.

This aspect of Usa ludic rules is perhaps, clearest when one considers games that define achievement against spatial constraints. For example, the home run in baseball is a ball hit into the stands, on the fly, in fair territory (all as defined). For purposes of the game it makes not a whit of difference how close to the stands a fly ball is hit so long as it falls short, nor how far a home run is hit so long as it clears the fence. In football, there are no additional points for a football kicked far over the crossbar, nor is there more of a victory in chess for blocking a King's move with two threatening pieces for each possible square. In Usa games, enough is enough.

Moreover, this same "more is not better" rule applies to the ultimate result of most games, the "final-win" rule. Baseball, for instance, is won by the team that gets *more* runs. *One* more run will do it and more than that will not do it any more. A team that wins 1–0 wins; a team that wins 2–0 or 12–2 or 27–4 still just wins. In terms of such a game, enough is all.[29]

Or, to put the matter in other terms, in all games there is a defined point past which the return to increased production does not merely diminish but vanishes. Because of the definitional structure of the game, optimal production is not "as much as possible," but "just enough."

To summarize, the Usa play and watch a huge number of games, with a range and intensity of interest that identifies the activity as highly significant in their culture. Moreover, every game is freely chosen, in the sense that playing and watching are not, like labor, tied to biological necessity, or even (except for Usa gamblers and professionals, who are not playing at all, but working) to material wants. Once in the game a player cannot question the rules; they *define* the game, and although the penalty for violating them may be expulsion in some organized Usa games, in all games rule violation brings aesthetic defeat; the penalty for winning by cheating is winning by cheating.

Moreover, games are so designed that whatever the rules define as "score" or "win," the players all have *formal* equality of opportunity to achieve them. No player or "side" may properly do anything that the other may not do, simultaneously or in equal turn. Whatever the actual powers of the players, as far as the game is concerned the players are indistinguishable.

In addition, games *define* playing, winning, and losing; they give palpable *significance* to physical and mental activity. More particularly, it is the nature of the game solution that it be, so to speak, an aesthetic solution to a practical problem: one does something and can be seen to do something that "fits" the rule that gives it significance. One is not attempt-

---

29. Asserting that clarity of result, or significance, is a source of human pleasure does not imply, of course, that it is the only source. Winning (or losing) 27–2 is a different experience for most people from getting the "same" result 1–0, and it may have significantly different effects on the lives of the players *outside* the context of the particular play . . . .

ing to amass or consume; once the point in the pattern is found and fitted, the returns to increased production are zero.

C. The Game of the Trial

Returning from the playing fields of the Usa to the Usa Trial itself, what appears is a process for investigating empirical evidence that looks very much like an agonistic game.[33] The Trial does seem more or less well adapted to providing the more or less accurate data needed for the rational operation of the Usa "economic" system. It appears, that is, largely capable of answering the question "what happened" at the legally relevant time.

But the connections between the appearance of the Trial and the vast corpus of games in the enveloping society indicate that the Trial is not *only* a vehicle for determining fact. It is, after all, inherently implausible that an epistemological inquiry in the form of an agonistic game maximizes thoroughness and accuracy of factual determination.

What one observes, rather, is an artifact like the Jondo trial, the embodiment of two separate social impulses. Jondo society balances the requirement that the protein-carbohydrate exchange ratio not flout the demands of biology too grossly and the equally exigent need to maintain the central place of cosmological metaphors in Jondo life. In this Usa instance, the nonmaterial realm is not cosmological but, in the broadest sense, ludic.

Nor can this ludic element in Usa society easily be dismissed as peripheral or trivial. The values of the game—formal equality of opportunity, freely assumed behavioral constraints presented as unassailable rules, the perfect clarity of the meaning of mere activity—are manifest as values in other nongame activities. Rule-bound "artistic" activities—metrical poetry, for instance, and almost all music—seem to be affected by some of the same ludic impulses .   .   .   .   Indeed, the Usa concept of justice, which sometimes seems to describe little more than bilateral symmetry and reciprocity, can itself be seen as deeply ludic.

But this does not mean that the Trial among the Usa is just a game. Indeed, that it is not just a game is the most significant thing about it. For one thing, it is *not* for all the players freely chosen.[36] But much more important, the very fact that the Trial actually allocates things of material and emotional value means that it is *not* clearly demarcated as a game, either pictorially or causally. The outcome of a trial has an *effect*, hence another meaning in the world outside the sacred time and place. It is like a game of chess in which, when the King is mated, a real king dies. The meaning of each move is thus not defined wholly in terms of any game, but simultaneously in terms of that real world the complexity and uncertainty of which may be the source of the Usa game impulse in the first place.

If, however, the Usa Trial is not a game, it is not not a game either. It is, like the Jondo Sacred Hermaphrodite, an amphibian cultural artifact

33. That is, a contest, a game played against an opponent.

36. The ability to buy one's way out of most Trials does not affect this contention. "Freely chosen" means that the only cost of not playing is not playing.

that embodies, simultaneously, at least two different social mechanisms. Like the Sacred Hermaphrodite, who is connected causally to food allocation and metaphorically to the universe, the Usa Trial reflects simultaneously the causal and metaphoric universes, both integral parts of Usa life but neither dominant over the other .   .   .   .

————

Compare Professor Leff's analysis with Simon's critique of "ritualist advocacy" in chapter 2, p. 63, infra.

————

William L. F. Felstiner, **Influences of Social Organization on Dispute Processing***

Man is an ingenious social animal. Institutionalized responses to interpersonal conflict, for instance, stretch from song duels and witchcraft to moots and mediation to self-conscious therapy and hierarchical, professionalized courts. The dispute processing practices prevailing in any particular society are a product of its values, its psychological imperatives, its history and its economic, political and social organization. It is unlikely that any general theory encompassing all of these factors will be developed until there have been many piecemeal attempts to understand something of the influence of each.

This paper first outlines several types of social organization and analyzes certain forms of dispute processing. It then suggests that these forms of dispute processing either depend on an availability of resources (such as coercive power or pre-dispute information) which varies with social organization or have different negative consequences in different social contexts. Finally, the paper explores the implications of this linkage between social organization and dispute processing for certain reforms currently advocated in the U. S.   .   .   .

I.   Ideal Types of Social Organization

.   .   .   Two ideal types of social organization will be contrasted: a technologically complex rich society (TCRS) and a technologically simple poor society (TSPS). In a TCRS the family unit is nuclear (conjugal) and biological. Marriage and its functional equivalents are unstable, are not arranged, and constitute a liaison between individuals rather than between family groups. Relationships between extra-nuclear family members are either unimportant—in that they are not a source of companionship, therapy, economic or political support, education, ceremony or self-definition—or they tend to be grounded not upon kinship but upon the same factors which give rise to relationships outside the family. Adults infrequently live in the same neighborhood as their parents, siblings or adult children. Financial assistance in old age is the responsibility not of the family but of the state. Working members of a family do not share work sites or occupations.
.   .   .

* *Source*: 9 L. & Soc'y Rev. 63, 63–89 (1974). Senior Research Associate, Social Science Research Institute, University of Southern California.

[In a TCRS friendships are unstable since long-term interpersonal relationships are difficult to maintain. Vocational mobility is high, although more from job to job than from occupation to occupation. Residential mobility is also high.]

In a TSPS the family unit is generally extended and frequently includes significant fictive elements. Marriage is either a relationship of restricted contact reflecting purdah considerations or else tends to be unstable. . . . In a TSPS . . . people tend to be aggregated with their parents, children and other kin in residence, in work and in responsibility.

In a TSPS the geographical range of non-family liaisons is restricted. Friends tend to be neighbors, neighbors tend to rely on each other for economic cooperation and significant public works projects require community cooperation as much as government assistance. . . . The full picture of interpersonal relations is a complicated, highly articulated cross-cutting network in which individuals are involved on their own account and as representatives of kin-based groups. It is conventionally contrasted to the nuclear family centered, unconnected, single-stranded organization of societies resembling a [TCRS].

The contrast in residential mobility between a [TCRS] and a TSPS is not as stark as the difference in type of family relationship. . . . [M]oves in a TSPS are much more dependent upon tying into an existing social network at the destination and involve more economic hardship, social and cultural alienation and emotional trauma than do moves in a TCRS.

Vocational mobility is also lower in a TSPS. . . . Ascriptive preferences and nepotism are commonplace. A significant proportion of the labor force is self or family employed and thus involved in work which is restricted in locale. Social contacts tend to precede rather than follow vocational opportunities.

The crucial role of large-scale organizations in a TCRS is not duplicated in a TSPS. Employment may be with major enterprises, but is generally not; credit is extended by individual money lenders and merchants rather than by commercial banks and large stores; consumer purchasing is carried on in small shops; primary education is provided in small local schools; and health services are indigenous and individualized rather than imported and bureaucratic. Only in the administration of welfare (i. e., public works projects, famine relief) and other government activities does the citizenry of a TSPS confront bureaucracies comparable to those which dominate social life in a TCRS.

II. Components of Forms of Dispute Processing

The basic question underlying this paper is whether the consequences of, and the availability of resources required by, *any* form of dispute processing vary with social organization. This proposition will be explored through analysis of adjudication, mediation and avoidance as they are applicable to disputes in which individuals or small groups are involved.

Adjudication and mediation are distinguishable from negotiation and self-help by the necessary presence of a third party, someone who is neither

asserting nor resisting the assertion of a claim in his own behalf nor is acting as the agent of such a party.   Conventionally we label as adjudication
that process in which the third party is acknowledged to have the power to
stipulate an outcome of the dispute, although in many instances such power
will be exercised only when the adjudicator is unable to persuade the disputants to agree to an outcome.   In mediation, on the other hand, outcomes [7]
are produced by the third party only when he can secure disputant consent to
proposals of accommodation.   By avoidance I mean limiting the relationship with the other disputant sufficiently so that the dispute no longer remains salient.   Avoidance resembles [the] notion of exit.   But avoidance,
unlike exit behavior, does not necessarily imply a *switch* of relations to a new
object, but may simply involve *withdrawal* from or contraction of the dispute-
producing relationship.

In adjudication, outcomes may be sensitive to a wide range of extrinsic
factors including class membership, political alliances, economic consequences and corruption, but in the main the behavior of the disputants is
evaluated by reference to generalized rules of conduct.   Most such rules are
not immutable, but they are stable.   Adjudication as a consequence tends to
focus on "what facts" and "which norms" rather than on any need for
normative shifts.[9]   This concentration on the behavior of the disputants,
rather than on the merits of abstract rules, creates a significant potential for
psychological trauma.   The effect of losing a dispute is to be told that what
you consider as history was either an illusion or a lie, that what you considered normatively appropriate behavior is characterized as anti-social, and
that what you consider your property or your prerogative will now, because
of your failings, by fiat become your enemy's.

The psychological consequence is frequently to alienate the loser from
the adjudicative process.   The process is generally endowed with a high
degree of legitimacy derived from its ritual and trappings as well as from the
participants' prior socialization.   The loss of the case puts the loser in an unstable psychological condition.   He must change either his attitude toward
the process or toward his past behavior.   Although some losers may be convinced of their errors by the adjudication, that many will change their attitude toward the process rather than toward their past behavior is suggested
by the least effort principle.   This "psycho-logical" rule indicates that
change will be made in the direction which involves the actor in making
the least significant other changes in his cognitive structure.   Change in
attitude toward past behavior may also involve changes in attitude toward
the role and behavior of close associates, toward related behavior, and
toward important values and elements of self-definition.   It is thus likely
to require more effort than a change in attitude toward a rarely encountered
and generally alien institution.   One would, therefore, expect that loser
compliance with adjudicative decisions is produced not by their merits, but

7. Disputes have outcomes rather than
resolutions for the same reason that
they are processed rather than settled.

9. If most adjudication were concerned
with the wisdom of rules it would
not be nearly as psychologically
threatening.   A loss then could be
rationalized as a difference of opinion
about future utilities rather than understood as negative labeling of past
behavior. . . .

by the coercive power which they command. Unconvinced of their original error, losers respond to an adverse decision only because the consequences of not responding would be worse.

The predicted association of adjudication and coercive power appears to be borne out empirically. . . .

The relationship between social organization and adjudication appears to depend not only on the availability of coercive power, but also on the presence or absence of social groups.[13] Most adjudication systems operate as an aspect of specific groups. Adjudicative entrepreneurs who sell their services to an unassociated set of disputants seeking third party assistance (the American Arbitration Association, for example) are uncommon. Exactly why this is so is not entirely clear. To the extent that dispute processing is politics by another name, it is obvious that political struggles can only have meaning if they take place within the political unit which will feel their consequences. To the extent that adjudication is a process of evaluating behavior in the light of a particular normative system, the norms must originate with and be used by some specific group. To the extent that adverse adjudicated decisions will be ignored unless compliance can be coerced, compliance will depend on the threat of some sanction acceptable to, and generally administered by, a group. To the extent that judicial specialization reflects general social role differentiation, many societies are simply not sufficiently differentiated to produce wandering adjudicators. . . .

Adjudication requires expertise in the social rules governing behavior and, frequently, in the secondary rules governing the conduct of disputes. This expertise is relatively easy to create on a mass basis. The expertise required of a mediator is different. Since successful mediation requires an outcome acceptable to the parties, the mediator cannot rely primarily on rules but must construct an outcome in the light of the social and cultural context of the dispute, the full scope of the relations between the disputants and the perspectives from which they view the dispute. Mediation, then, flourishes where mediators share the social and cultural experience of the disputants they serve, and where they bring to the processing of disputes an intimate and detailed knowledge of the perspectives of the disputants. . . . [16] [S]ince the outcomes it produces are consensual and are generally compromises, mediation need not be backed by coercive power.

Why is it important for a mediator who does not know the disputants to acquire insight into their priorities and feelings as a part of the mediation

13. . . . [G]roups are collections of individuals in long-term relationships whose actions toward each other and toward outsiders are importantly influenced by the existence and standards of the group.

16. That mediation depends upon understanding the particular perspectives of particular disputants as well as on understanding the context in which they act is an example of the importance of the influence of symbolic interactionism on role theory. Rather than emphasizing the deterministic effect of role expectations, symbolic interactionists stress the importance of the interpretation process used by individuals in human encounters. To them a dispute cannot be analyzed as a set confrontation between conflicting role expectations but rather involves individuals who continually redefine themselves and their situations and realign their behavior accordingly. Thus an understanding of the disputants' perspectives as well as the biography of a dispute is crucial in mediation. . . .

process? Let us assume that mediated outcomes are of two kinds. They may be personality independent in the sense that the mediator is able to suggest a result which adequately meets the interests of each disputant as those interests would be identified by any persons in their positions. In such situations the mediator's ingenuity is affected only by his understanding of the disputants' manifest interests. It may well be feasible to acquire such information adequately during the mediation.

On the other hand, an outcome may be personality dependent in the sense that an acceptable scheme which sufficiently meets the demands of both disputants must reflect these demands as they idiosyncratically view them. In this case the feelings of the disputants are crucial and the possibility that a mediator will acquire sufficient insight during mediation is more doubtful. . . . [T]he information presented to the mediator is probably not as rich as the more general information available to a mediator who has widely-shared experience with the disputants. It would be imprudent to set theoretical limits to the successes of mediative geniuses, but for the run-of-the-mill mediators upon whom institutionalized mediation must be based long-term and relatively intimate prior association with the disputants may be highly functional in all settings and necessary for reaching personality dependent outcomes.[18]

Adjudication and mediation are relatively visible processes. They tend to be public to the group in which they take place, notorious within the group and didactic for the group. Avoidance, on the other hand, is more difficult for an outsider to identify and is less frequently reported. Even a recital of a few characteristic avoidance techniques will, however, demonstrate how common it is. Note, for instance, the unexceptional nature in the U. S. of adolescent children limiting contacts with their parents to perfunctory matters because matters of importance have proved to be too contentious, of friends curtailing their relations because of past quarrels, of consumers switching their trade from one retail merchant to another after a dispute, of casual workers (gas station attendants, waitresses, dishwashers, gardeners, housekeepers) quitting jobs because of problems with employers, of children moving out of their parents' houses because of unreconcilable values and of neighbors who visit less because of offensive pets, obstreperous children, loud parties and unseemly yards.

The most important social characteristic of avoidance for dispute processing theory is its variable costs. To understand that variation one has only to focus on Gluckman's [a] classic distinction between single-interest linkages and multiplex relationships, those which serve many interests. The cost of avoidance is always a reduction in the content of the relationship which has been truncated or terminated. If the relationship was geared to a single interest, only that interest is affected. If the relationship was multiplex, all the interests are affected, even though the cause of the avoidance grew out of only

18. Labor mediation is probably a special case. It tends to involve a limited set of issues most of which have been confronted in principle before. Most of the participants are professionals, and the outcomes are more affected by economic and political considerations than by personalities . . . .

a. Max Gluckman, The Judicial Process Among the Barotse of Northern Rhodesia 19 (1955). Ed. note.

one. The difference, for example, is between losing a sibling only and losing a sibling who is also a neighbor, a companion, a therapist, a political ally, an economic co-adventurer and a ceremonial confederate.

III.   The Effect of Social Organization on Institutionalizing Different Forms of Dispute Processing

For our purposes, then, the key to adjudication is groups and coercion, to mediation is shared experience, and to avoidance is its variable costs. Within any society on an institutional basis, we should expect to find less adjudication where groups are infrequent and the coercive power which can be marshalled is weak, less mediation where shared experience is rare and less avoidance where avoidance costs are high. What insights concerning the distribution of forms of dispute processing might these propositions produce in the ideal type societies described earlier? In a TSPS either adjudication or mediation will occur at the level of face-to-face groups such as kin units, factions and villages. The coercion necessary for adjudication rests ultimately on the group's power to expel contumacious disputants. Since the group's functions are central to the members' well-being, participation in group adjudication and adherence to adjudicated outcomes are self-generating. The size of such groups and the intensity of relations within them make mediation a realistic alternative to adjudication: the requisite knowledge of dispute context and participant perspective are available without inordinate mediator efforts. Whether groups in any particular society will use both institutionalized adjudication and mediation, or one more than the other, may then be a function of considerations other than social organization. Values and their psychological derivatives may in some contexts be crucial ingredients. . . . [D]espite the conventional notion that mediated compromises better preserve the continuing relationships characteristic of small communities or multiplex groups, adjudication is quite common in such situations.
.   .   .

As the size of the groups on which one focuses in a TSPS grows, from village to tribe or from extended family to sub-caste, adjudication will become the dominant form of dispute processing. Mediation is no longer feasible because, whatever the shared general social and cultural experience, no specific mediators nor occupants of specific social positions will possess as a matter of existing experience sufficient information about the particular perspectives and histories of the particular disputants to be able efficiently to suggest acceptable outcomes. Adjudicative expertise in rules, on the other hand, is either widely possessed where the rules are not specialized (in the sense that they are readily available only to professionals) or can be generated on a mass basis where specialization is important.

The frequency of avoidance as a form of dispute processing in a TSPS should be affected by its high costs. These costs would be incurred whether avoidance takes place within the kin group, within a non-family multiplex relationship, or in economic activities. Within the family if disputants terminate or decrease their contacts, relations between groups, which may have political and economic as well as social connotations, are jeopardized as well. Where marriages are arranged, decisions about who marries whom are generally made on prudential grounds, in a corporate process and under the influence of past social relations. As a result, disputes which are processed by avoidance will cast a long shadow, interfering with the future marriage prospects of many group members. Use of avoidance as a technique where the disputants, such as parent and grown child or siblings or affines, live and work and conduct other important activities together, is logistically difficult and psychologically dangerous—the repressed hostility felt toward the other disputant is likely to be shifted to someone or something else. Even worse, the failure to express or act upon predictable hostility will in many societies lead to accusations of witchcraft against the person who hides his antagonisms. Yet physical separation, by moving residence or work, may be socially infeasible, economically disastrous and emotionally traumatic. Since many relationships beyond the family are multiplex, avoidance as a reaction to dispute impairs not only the interest out of which the dispute arose, but all other interests shared by the disputants. As Moore points out for the Chagga, "the continuing control exercised by the lineage neighborhood nexus over its members is illustrated by every dispute it settles. No man can hope to keep his head above water if he does not have the approval and support of his neighbors and kinsmen." [b] This analysis should not be construed to imply that avoidance would never or rarely occur in small communities in technologically simple societies. In fact, in nomadic tribes, where avoidance by physical separation is easy, dispute processing by such tactics is commonplace. The point is rather that avoidance has high costs in a TSPS and one would as a result expect significant use of other forms of dispute processing which are more likely to aid the maintenance of threatened, but important, social relationships.

In both a TCRS and a TSPS adjudication is predictable at the level of the state which is a group with an important normative system and substantial coercive power .   .   .   .

In both types of societies adjudication may also be an important form of dispute processing within large-scale organizations. Such organizations must establish a normative system to govern their operations: coercive power is located both in their power to expel constituents and in their power to vary tasks and rewards. Rules and compulsive power may explain why adjudication can work if it is established. But they do not entirely explain why it is established   .   .   .   .   Mediation within organizations may be equally feasible since in the operations of an organization extensive shared social, cultural and personal experience is generated. And adjudicative and mediative institutions may co-exist within an organization. .   .   .

Between outsiders who have some contact with a large organization and the organization, a significant amount of dispute processing may be a special form of avoidance termed "lumping it." .   .   .   It would be uncommon for such grievances to be mediated since there is little incentive for the organization to change its posture. Because of the discrepancy in size and power even the threat of withdrawal by the individual is futile to coerce compromise by the organization. And no adjudication short of the government courts

b. Sally Falk Moore, Law and Social   Study, 7 L. & Soc'y Rev. 719, 738
   Change: The Semi-Autonomous Social   (1973). Ed. note.
   Field as an Appropriate Subject of

may be possible because no other power exists to coerce decisions against the organization.

The clearest difference between dispute processing in a TSPS and a TCRS should be located in disputes between individuals or family and social groups. The availability of adjudication and mediation and the high costs of avoidance in a TSPS have been examined. The opposite conditions are predictable for a TCRS: adjudication and mediation of such disputes will be hard to institutionalize and avoidance will carry significantly lower costs. The obstacle to adjudication of interpersonal disputes in a TCRS is the limited coercion available to agencies other than government courts. The forms of coercion available in nongovernment adjudication in a TSPS depend either on membership in groups, especially kin-related groups, or on participation in multiple interest relationships. In a TCRS such groups and associations are either non-existent or weak. One cannot be influenced by public opinion if there is no relevant public, nor exiled from a group to which one does not belong. What sanction in a neighborhood of single interest relationships might a neighborhood adjudicator employ? With what, after childhood, can most parents threaten a child or an uncle a niece?

At the same time structural factors exist in a TCRS which reduce the utility of adjudicating interpersonal disputes in government courts. To the extent that such courts are staffed by specialists, as one would expect them to be in such a society unless it is organized according to a revolutionary socialist ideology, the rules they apply will tend to become specialized, importantly procedural and alien from everyday norms. Specialized rules will require litigants to hire professional counsel. Professional counsel means added expense, inconvenience and mystification. . . . If court litigation may be fairly characterized as costly, slow and alienating, we can expect relatively little use to be made of it in situations in which, as in most interpersonal disputing, the economic stakes are low, unless, as in divorce and custody cases, a government imprimatur is an absolute necessity. . . .

Institutionalized mediation of interpersonal disputes will also be infrequent in a TCRS. Because of the crucial importance of shared experience in mediation, the less role differentiated a social unit, the more mediators will be available for disputes of varying origin. In the technologically simplest societies all adult members, having generally the same experience, are equipped on that dimension to mediate all disputes. But in a TCRS, where role differentiation is intense, few persons are qualified by experience to mediate any disputes: almost everybody's role set is too specialized to be common to a significant number of potential disputants. . . .

The relatively weaker bonds of family, of friendship, of job and of place in a TCRS make institutionalizing adjudication and mediation difficult, but they also reduce the negative consequences of avoidance. Avoidance behavior between generations within a family, for instance, generally will not seriously threaten either disputants' economic security, political position or ceremonial or therapeutic opportunities. Reducing as well as eliminating contact within a continuing social framework is relatively easy where relations are more formal than functional. Difficult vocational relationships may be terminated with better alternatives than unemployment. New friendships may be struck and old contacts turned sour may be easily avoided . . . .

Where there are pockets within a TCRS where social organization is more like that postulated for a TSPS, then one would expect that avoidance, having higher costs, would be less important and that adjudication and mediation, being more feasible, would be more frequently institution-alized.[25] Such pockets are likely to arise where there are unassimilated ethnic minorities with a strong tradition of internal government or where a pattern of social discrimination severely limits the economic, residential and social mobility of distinctive minority groups. . . .

To summarize . . ., adjudication and mediation, on the one hand, and avoidance, on the other, are complementary. Where adjudication and mediation are feasible, avoidance is costly: where avoidance has tolerable costs, adjudication and mediation are difficult to institutionalize. This com-plementarity has a logical base. The same set of social circumstances which makes one set of processes available frustrates the other and vice-versa.[26] The predicament of unorganized individuals who have a dispute with large organizations of which they are not members may be an exception: adjudica-tion and mediation are generally unavailable and avoidance costly to the in-dividual. It is this social pathology which has probably led to recent calls for ombudsmen in government, in universities and for public utilities. . . .

25. The opposite should, of course, be equally true. Estimates of the utility of the ideal types described in this paper made by testing any of their constituents against the attributes of real societies, if indeed such a test is a fair measure of the use of ideal types, must be careful to insure that reference is made to the modal con-dition of the real society, and not to minority instances which are organized on contrasting lines. . . .

26. Reduced to its simplest form, this paper argues that mediation and ad-judication will not be institutionalized where they will not work. But what is "work"? The manifest function of these institutions is to bring disputes to an end. But many social institu-tions, courts among them, may thrive although they do not fulfill their os-tensible purpose. The actual function of dispute processing institutions may not be what they do for disputants, but what they do for the third par-ties by way, for instance, of reinforcing their prestige or political authority. Whether a dispute processing institu-tion will flourish when nurtured pri-marily by such a latent function should depend on whether disputants themselves seek to end disputes. Where they do, it is difficult to un-derstand why they would activate a process which rarely produced that re-sult. . . .

Chapter 2

THE INDEPENDENCE OF PROCEDURE?

Anyone who has taught procedure for a while will recognize the problem. Should one attempt to take the categories "substance" and "procedure" seriously? Or should one rather destroy the distinction as metaphysical nonsense? The practitioner usually comes across the distinction between "substance" and "procedure" in answering *Erie*-type questions, in choosing the law to be applied in a conflicts situation, in determining whether a rule may be retroactively applied. In all such cases, trenchant criticism has been leveled at the process of pigeon-holing a rule—e. g., the statute of limitations is "substantive"—without a consideration of the values or policies served by the conclusory characterization. And, if one is to consider values and policies to be the basis for decision, why does one need the procedure/substance characterization at all? One ought only need state why it is good or sensible to apply the statute of limitations of the forum (or of the lex loci, as the case may be).

When the substance/procedure distinction arises in such a concrete form —where rules and outcomes may turn on it and where it is so often thoughtlessly employed—it is indeed difficult not to agree with some Realists, such as Walter Wheeler Cook (see, e. g., W. W. Cook, The Logical and Legal Bases of the Conflict of Laws 154–93 (1942)), that there may be something to these generalizations, but oh, . . . are they impediments to good sense whenever someone uses them!

In the essays in this chapter we have attempted to avoid rehashing the old substance-versus-procedure practical questions. Despite the excellence of some of the recent literature dealing with both *Erie*-type questions and choice of law issues, we assume the contours of those debates are already familiar or are, at least, easily accessible. See, e. g., John Hart Ely, The Irrepressible Myth of *Erie*, 87 Harv.L.Rev. 693 (1974). Intead, we have here chosen articles that explore the relationship of substance to procedure in the contexts of a critique of institutions, of legal theory, or of the general structure of legal doctrine. In none of these articles is the issue a mere issue of characterization of rules.

William Simon's article considers the justifications for the institution of adversarial representation. He finds that the "ideology of advocacy" has its roots in the purported problematic relation between substance and procedure. The reprinted portions of this extensive article consider the problematic relationship of procedure and substance in three theories of law. In his analysis, Simon criticizes the ways in which each theory is used to justify the institutions of professional domination.

Professor Cover's essay is an attempt to explore the extant structure of trans-substantive procedural rules and to suggest reasons for the aspiration to enunciate values and to enforce policies which are equally sound regardless of the particular substantive policies to which they are applied. Cover also

47

suggests areas in which the trans-substantive aspiration ought to be qualified by criteria of sensible enforcement of particular substantive objectives.

Hal Scott's article provides an almost unique case study demonstrating in detail the operation of an "old saw." Maine's fine old phrase, later repeated by Maitland, that "substantive law has at first the look of being gradually secreted in the interstices of procedure" was intended to apply to more "primitive" stages of legal development. H. Maine, Early Law and Custom 389 (1891); F. Maitland, The Forms of Action at Common Law, in Equity and the Forms of Action at Common Law 295 (1932). Many have commented, however, that procedure remains "somehow" a breeding ground for substantive change. Scott goes beyond such generalizations and convincingly demonstrates the precise relation between procedural change—the class action rule—and substantive innovation in federal securities law.

Thomas Grey, in the final essay in this chapter, explores the justifications behind giving procedural protections more extensive and firm constitutional support than that afforded most substantive interests. His analysis penetrates one of the few areas of law in which many scholars, and all but a few judges, have been content to have a dichotomous substance/procedure characterization be the determinant of legal rights and obligations. We refer, of course, to the "distinction" between "procedural" and "substantive" due process.

SECTION A. THE PLACE OF PROCEDURE IN A GENERAL THEORY OF LAW

As you read the following essay, consider why Simon's critique of the "ideology of advocacy" must be tied to a general exploration of the place of *procedure* in legal theory. What other "ideologies" are entailed in the general perspective that Simon sketches—"Legal personality"? "Strategic behavior"? In this same vein, see J. Vining, Legal Identity: The Coming of Age of Public Law (1978).

William H. Simon, **The Ideology of Advocacy***

Conventional morality frowns at the ethics of advocacy. Public opinion disapproves of what it considers the lawyer's most characteristic activities. Popular culture can reconcile itself to him only by pretending that all his clients are virtuous. The lawyer's response takes the form of a dialectic of cynicism and naiveté. On one hand, he sees his more degrading activities as licensed by a fundamental amorality lying beneath conventional morality. On the other hand, he sees his more heartening ones as serving an institutional justice higher than conventional morality . . . .

The formal, articulate expression of the lawyer's response is the "Ideology of Advocacy." The purpose of the Ideology of Advocacy is to rationalize the most salient aspect of the lawyer's peculiar ethical orientation: his explicit

* *Source*: The Ideology of Advocacy: Procedural Justice and Professional Ethics, 1978 Wis.L.Rev. 29, 30–64, 91– 113 (1978). Staff Attorney, Legal Services Institute; Boston, Massachusetts.

refusal to be bound by personal and social norms which he considers binding on others. The most elaborate expressions of the Ideology of Advocacy occur in officially promulgated rules of ethics, in doctrinal writings on legal ethics, the attorney-client evidentiary privilege, and the constitutional right to counsel, and in writings on the legal profession .   .   .   .

Of course, there is a growing body of writing addressed to the profession which is critical of the conduct of lawyers and professional organizations. Yet, most of these discussions take place within the framework of the Ideology of Advocacy and do not involve criticism of its premises. The more prominent of these discussions have been of two types. First, doctrinal writings on legal ethics and judicial procedure often take the form of a debate between the partisans of a "battle" model and the partisans of a "truth" model of adjudication .   .   .   . Yet, almost all of the distinctive ethical views of lawyers can be rationalized in terms of one or the other of the models, and the differences between them are greatly exaggerated in the debate. Both models accept the basic principles of the Ideology of Advocacy and are primarily concerned with defending those principles.

Second, there is a substantial body of sociology and social criticism which focuses on the legal profession. Some of this literature argues that lawyers compromise their clients' interests in order to advance their own interests. Other studies focus on an elite within the profession and argue that the elite has used professional ethics and organization to achieve prestige and economic privilege at the expense of the less powerful members of the profession and of the lower classes generally. Studies which emphasize the exploitation of clients explicitly accept the Ideology of Advocacy and criticize lawyers for failing to live up to it. Although studies which emphasize elite domination purport to criticize legal ethics and professionalism, they do not deal with the basic principles expressed by the Ideology of Advocacy. Instead, they focus on principles such as restrictions on membership in the profession and prohibitions on advertising and solicitation. Such studies are concerned less with the nature of legal services than with their distribution. In suggesting that the increased availability of legal services allegedly inhibited by professional ethics and organization would be desirable, these writings often rely on the Ideology of Advocacy .   .   .   .

I.   The Principles of the Ideology

   .   .   . The first principle [of the Ideology of Advocacy] is the principle of neutrality. This .   .   . principle prescribes that the lawyer remain detached from his client's ends. The lawyer is expected to represent people who seek his help regardless of his opinion of the justice of their ends. In some cases, he may have a duty to do so; in others, he may have the personal privilege to refuse. But whenever he takes a case, he is not considered responsible for his client's purposes. Even if the lawyer happens to share these purposes, he must maintain his distance. In a judicial proceeding, for instance, he may not express his personal belief in the justice of his client's cause.

The second principle of conduct is partisanship. This principle prescribes that the lawyer work aggressively to advance his client's ends. The lawyer will employ means on behalf of his client which he would not consider proper in a non-professional context even to advance his own ends. These means may involve deception, obfuscation, or delay. Unlike the principle of neutrality, the principle of partisanship is qualified. A line separates the methods which a lawyer should be willing to use on behalf of a client from those he should not use. Before the lawyer crosses the line, he calls himself a representative; after he crosses it, he calls himself an officer of the Court. Most debates within the Ideology of Advocacy concern the location of his line . . . .

The principles of neutrality and partisanship describe the basic conduct and attitudes of professional advocacy . . . . [I]t should be noted that the two principles are distinct in important respects. Many occupational roles, for instance the bureaucrat and the doctor, are expected to serve the general public without regard to the ends of those who seek their help. Yet, they are not expected to engage in the partisan pursuit of individual ends. On the other hand, political representatives are expected to be partisan, but they are not expected to serve all comers without regard to their ends. Only the lawyer seems to insist on making a virtue of both neutrality and partisanship.

Two further principles, though less obvious, are also assumed . . . . The first is the principle of procedural justice. In its most general usage, procedural justice holds that the legitimacy of a situation may reside in the way it was produced rather than its intrinsic properties. Another aspect of the principle is that, given adequate procedures, one can act justly by conforming to them regardless of the consequences to which one's conduct contributes. In this essay, the term "procedural justice" is used more specifically to refer to the notion that there is an inherent value or legitimacy to the judicial proceeding (and to a more qualified extent, the entire legal system) which makes it possible for a lawyer to justify specific actions without reference to the consequences they are likely to promote . . . .

The second foundation principle of the Ideology of Advocacy is professionalism. In its most general usage, the term professionalism refers to the notion that social responsibility for the development and application of certain apolitical and specialized disciplines should be delegated to the practitioners of these disciplines. In this paper, the term is used more specifically to describe the notion that the law is an apolitical and specialized discipline and that its proper development and application require that legal ethics be elaborated collectively by lawyers in accordance with criteria derived from their discipline . . . .

II. The Lawyer as Champion (The War of All Against All)

The fullest justification of the Ideology of Advocacy rests on Positivist legal theory. The term Positivist is used here to refer to the kind of theory which emphasizes the separation of law from personal and social norms, the connection of law with the authoritative application of force, and the systematic, objective character of law. Positivism was the basis of the profession's conception of advocacy in the late 19th and early 20th centuries, and it is still an important component of the professional self-image of some lawyers, despite its repudiation in most areas by the intellectual leaders of the bar. Even lawyers who reject Positivism as a general jurisprudential theory are sometimes prone to fall back on it when justifying their professional roles.

A.   Positivist Advocacy

.   .   .   In the Positivist view, society is an aggregate of egoistic individuals each pursuing his own ends.   .   .   .

Ends are natural, individual, subjective, and arbitrary. Social norms result from the random convergence of individual ends. By contrast, it is possible to construct a system of rules which is artificial, impersonal, objective, and rational. The best way to provide order is to create a sovereign (e. g., monarch, legislature, party) which is neutral toward the various ends of the citizens and which acts through rules. Rules will give a regularity to social life and thus eliminate uncertainty. Oppression will be eliminated once power is concentrated in the hands of a neutral ruler. An obstacle remains. The legitimacy of the sovereign rests solely on the unique end of order which all share. Yet, from the point of view of each citizen, this end extends only to the orderly behavior of the others. People will constantly be tempted to violate the rules in order to pursue their own individual ends. No one will be willing to pay the price of resisting such temptation without some assurance that the others will also obey. The solution is to have the rules provide for the administration of rewards and punishments in a manner calculated to insure general obedience.

The rules will define for each citizen a private sphere of autonomy. Within this sphere, he need not account to anyone for his actions. So long as he remains within his sphere, he need not fear coercion by the sovereign. The sovereign's enforcement of the rules against the other citizens will insure that they do not trespass within his sphere. Where disputes arise, they must be resolved in accordance with the rules. Since the sovereign cannot itself apply the rules to every particular dispute, it must appoint judges to act on its behalf. It is important that the judges apply the rules with impersonal regularity. They must not refer to their own personal ends. Otherwise, they would create uncertainty, and their decisions would be oppressive. The rules cannot specify a specific result for each situation to which they apply, but the judge will be able to determine the proper result in any given situation because the rules have a systematic quality. The system may involve formal logic, linguistic analysis, empirical observation, or some combination of these methods. The system enables the judge to reason from the general prescriptions of the rules to particular results. The judge applies the rules to the factual premises of the given situation. The disposition of the case is dictated by the system. The judge has no discretion; he is bound by the system.

The need for lawyers in the Positivist theory arises from the strangeness of the law. Since the legal system is independent of personal ends and social norms, its prescriptions often appear alien. They may be very complicated, and the sovereign may find it convenient to express them in an esoteric language. Thus, the rules are not easily apprehensible. But the individual needs to know how he can further his ends without causing the sovereign to intervene with sanctions. Otherwise, he will be in the very state of uncertainty that government was supposed to remedy. Moreover, if other citizens can gain a superior understanding of the rules, they can use this knowledge to oppress him by maneuvering him into situations where sovereign power will operate to his disadvantage. The solution is to create a class of legal specialists and to require its members to serve every citizen regardless of his ends.

The function of the lawyer is to explain how, and under what circumstances, the sovereign will intervene in his client's life. The lawyer enables his client to pursue his ends effectively by predicting the likelihood of assistance or sanction which attaches to alternative courses of action. He does so by the same type of systematic reasoning which the judge uses to decide cases. From another perspective, this function can be described as informing the client of his rights. A right is an opportunity to invoke or resist the force of the sovereign in a certain way. Rights are defined by the rules of the legal system.

The lawyer's various other services as advocate are all ancillary to this basic task of prediction. In litigation, he simply sets in motion the system which vindicates (or refutes) his prior predictions. The lawyer presents the court with the factual premises to which the rules are to be applied. The outcome of the case is determined by the autonomous operation of the system of rules on these premises. At best, the lawyer anticipates the outcome; he does not determine it.

The lawyer's neutrality is essential to the proper performance of his basic task of prediction. Since the legal system is independent of personal ends and social norms, the lawyer's ends and his notions of social norms have no relevance to the prediction of the sovereign's actions. Because ends are individual, subjective, and arbitrary, if the lawyer attempted to take his ends into account in advising his client, he would reduce the accuracy of his predictions and the effectiveness of his services. If the attempt caused him to take an unrealistically liberal view of the scope of permissible conduct, the client would suffer unexpected state interference and would thus be deprived of a measure of the certainty which he was promised. If it caused him to take an unrealistically restricted view of the scope of permissible conduct, then the lawyer would be abusing his position to oppress his client.

The lawyer's partisanship arises from his duty to assist the client in the pursuit of his ends. The lawyer cannot legitimately recognize any limitation on this pursuit aside from the rules of the legal system.

The rule that the lawyer cannot reveal a confidence of the client without the client's consent is designed in part to enhance access to legal advice by insuring that the client will not be prejudiced by seeking such advice. It is also, more fundamentally, a reflection of the fact that the lawyer is, in effect, an extension of the client's will. Since he cannot consult his own ends or his own notions of social norms, the lawyer has no basis other than the interests of his client for deciding whether or not to reveal confidences. [The] criticism that the lawyer acts as a "tool" of his client is entirely correct but beside the point. A tool is precisely what the client needs in order to invoke his rights and maximize his autonomy .   .   .   .

B.   The Critique of Positivist Advocacy

.   .   .   The Positivist version of the Ideology of Advocacy fails in two broad respects. First, Positivism's failure to take account of the problematical relation between substance and procedure undermines its promise to eliminate uncertainty and oppression. Second, Positivist notions about the relation between law and personal ends are inconsistent with the Positivist notion of the advocate's role. The Positivist version of the Ideology of Advocacy purports to show that the advocate enhances his client's autonomy. Yet, given Positivism's psychological assumptions, the advocacy it prescribes can only subvert this autonomy.

1.   *The Procedural Problems*

Procedure comes as something of an afterthought in Positivism, and the problems it creates are never fully acknowledged. Two procedural problems in particular—the problems of enforcement and access—represent serious dangers of uncertainty and oppression for which Positivism makes no adequate provision.

Positivist discussions of procedure begin with a belated recognition of a basic contradiction: in the Positivist system, the sovereign is both the only guarantee of order and the greatest threat to it. Since obedience to the rules does not come naturally, the sovereign must be charged with the power and duty to enforce them. But this task poses a terrifying prospect. The only effective means of enforcement involve torture, deprivation of liberty, invasion of privacy, or confiscation of property. These means are necessary both to get the information needed to determine that the rules have been violated and to deter future violations. Fact-finding holds the further danger that the sovereign will constantly be finding new evidence or revising his reasoning so as to upset previous determinations on which people have relied. Moreover, once the facts have been determined, there remains the further problem that the sovereign and its agents are likely to act inconsistently in applying the rules to different situations. No matter how elaborately the legal system is constructed, ambiguities will remain, and in choosing among alternative interpretations, the judges will act inconsistently, and will thus produce unpredictable results. Thus, within his own system, the Positivist finds the very danger of disorder which he had set out to remedy.

To meet this problem, Positivism proposes a second body of rules which limit the enforcement powers of the sovereign. As the purpose of the first set of rules is to impose regularity on conduct in the social world, the purpose of the second is to impose regularity on the actions of the sovereign. The first kind of rule is called substantive, and the second kind procedural. The procedural rules require that certain evidence be produced before the sovereign may act on the premise that a substantive rule has been violated. They limit the ways in which the sovereign can procure evidence and prescribe the manner in which it can be presented. They limit the authority of the sovereign to make and revise findings of fact and interpretations of rules. And they specify the sanctions which the sovereign may apply upon finding that the rules have been broken.

The establishment of this second body of rules has a curious consequence. The substantive rules reflect the basic purpose of the system, the securing of order in the social world. The procedural rules are designed to deal with a technical problem. Once the system is set into motion, however, the procedural rules play the more fundamental role. Order depends on the citizens' compliance with the substantive rules, and compliance depends on the application of sanctions by the sovereign. The application of sanctions is governed by the procedural rules. The key to the system is the operation of the sovereign, and the ultimate test of the legitimacy of any of the sovereign's acts is procedural. For the citizen, this means that compliance with the substantive law does not guarantee immunity from state sanctions. Nor does liability necessarily follow from violations of the substantive rules. The procedural rules legitimate results which may be substantively wrong. Having repudiated personal notions of justice at the outset of its system, Positivism ends by refusing to guarantee the citizen even the legal justice defined by the substantive law. All the citizen can count on is a day in court.

The citizen's bewilderment may be a matter of indifference to the Positivist, but it is not so easy for him to shrug off another difficulty. The second body of rules has not solved the problem of disorder. The risk of disorder from the sovereign has been diminished only by impairing the efficiency of the sovereign's enforcement powers and hence by increasing the risk of disorder from the citizens. The procedural rules give the citizens a broad range of discretion. The existence of this discretion undermines the Positivist claim to secure order through the delegation of power to a neutral sovereign who exercises it through a system of rules. The citizens can use their procedural discretion to thwart the enforcement of the substantive rules and to affect the exercise of state power in accordance with their individual ends. Once the existence of this discretion is recognized, the actions of the sovereign appear to result, not from the neutral, systematic application of rules to given factual premises, but from the strategic exercise of procedural discretion by private parties.

For instance, the procedural rules which require that evidence be produced before sanctions can be applied and which limit the ways in which evidence can be obtained enable people to conceal violations of the substantive rules by not leaving evidence or by withholding or destroying it. The rules which govern evidence at trial enable people to thwart the enforcement of the substantive law by excluding or discrediting probative evidence or by introducing misleading evidence. Procedural rules permit people whose claims have no substantive validity to put others to the risk of proof. They enable people to frustrate enforcement by delaying and by imposing expenses on their adversaries. They permit people to influence enforcement by strategic choices as to whether to initiate proceedings, when to do so, and before which tribunal to do so. They make it possible for some to influence rule interpretation by framing legal issues for decision in factual contexts favorable to the interpretation which suits their ends. . . .

. . .   [L]itigation has been used in this manner on behalf of lower- and middle-income individuals against dominant economic interests. The claim of spokesmen for large corporations that many recent class actions represent "legalized blackmail" reflects an accurate perception that the procedure is not being used merely as a more efficient way of enforcing a substantive claim, but also as an instrument of private policy for the vindication of expectations which are not justified by the substantive law. The availability of the class action device may have a critical impact on the result independently of the substantive merit of the claim. Analogously, the threat of mass assertions of due process rights by criminal defendants or welfare recipients is a potential instrument by which substantive concessions could be exacted from enforcement officials. . . .

In creating a critical role for private discretion, procedure undermines the basic Positivist guarantee of order. Uncertainty becomes inevitable because the actions of the sovereign cannot be reliably predicted. The sovereign's actions are determined by procedural discretion. This discretion is not exercised by the citizens in any systematic fashion, but rather it is exercised instrumentally in the pursuit of their individual, subjective, and arbitrary ends. The problem is not just that procedure complicates the analysis. More importantly, the procedural rules create a situation in which outcomes depend on contingencies which are not susceptible to legal analysis. They depend on private decisions which are not controlled by the rules. Moreover, oppression still threatens. Positivism's claim to eliminate oppression is plausible only to the extent that people see state intervention as governed by a neutral system of rules. The system as a whole can be shown to be just vis-à-vis all the citizens, but no particular outcome can be shown to be just except by tracing it to the system. However, once the role of procedural discretion is recognized, the actions of the sovereign appear to be determined by private power. As such, they constitute oppression.

Thus, to the extent that procedure checks public anarchy, it unleashes private anarchy. The debate within Positivism between authoritarians and libertarians is concerned with striking the balance between public and private disorder. Yet, by this point, Positivism has conceded its failure to secure the basic goal of order .   .   .   .

.   .   . [The Legal Realists] suggest two strategies for dealing with the tension between substance and procedure without abandoning the basic Positivist premises. Neither is successful.

One strategy is to eliminate the distinction between substance and procedure by collapsing the two sets of rules into a single set. This can be done by reading the procedural rules as qualifications to the substantive rules. In this way, law can still be viewed as the prediction of the application of force from a unitary body of rules. The predictions simply become more complicated. This strategy seems to underlie some of the more familiar rhetoric of discussions of legal ethics. For instance, lawyers argue that a person has a "right" to plead the Statutes of Frauds or Limitations to defeat an otherwise valid claim or to object to probative hearsay because the rules authorize such actions. And they insist that a person has a "right" to breach contracts because the law does not specifically enforce prohibitions of breach but merely imposes damages. Significantly, however, such rhetoric rarely embraces the more extreme consequences of this line of thought. Lawyers never argue that a person has a right to commit murder so long as he does not leave behind proof beyond a reasonable doubt of his act. Nor do they assert that a person may lawfully swindle others if he flees to Brazil before the sovereign brings him to trial. Their reluctance to go this far has not been due to mere timidity. The distinction between substance and procedure reflects a real conflict within the Positivist system between the total dependence on the sovereign's power and the extreme danger from it. The procedural rules which are needed to limit the sovereign's power give discretion to citizens which undermines order. The experience of this discretion and of the disorder which it creates cannot be eliminated by a merely rhetorical or conceptual change.

Another strategy which Realism suggests is to make the sovereign's enforcement power more effective and to limit the discretion of citizens to manipulate the system. But this approach merely turns the problem on its head. Limiting the discretion of the private parties only increases the discretion of the sovereign and thus enlarges the danger of disorder from that source. For example, if the rules were changed to abolish the discretion of criminal defendants to escape enforcement by excluding illegally seized evidence, the effective discretion of the sovereign to torture, wrongly imprison, and confiscate property in the quest for evidence would be enlarged greatly.

The second procedural dilemma of Positivism arises from the question of access to the legal system. Positivism recognizes that the strangeness and complexity of the law creates a new danger of oppression. The danger is that some will be able to anticipate state intervention better than others and that they will use their knowledge to the disadvantage of the less informed. Positivism's basic response to this danger is a promise to make counsel available to people regardless of their ends. Availability can mean either access for those who can pay, or some guaranteed level of access regardless of wealth. But neither approach is adequate.

Availability means merely formal access when Positivist legal theory is linked to the theory of the self-regulating market, as it commonly was in the late 19th and early 20th centuries . . . .

The profession's more recent response to the problem of access is to acknowledge some responsibility for making legal services available to those who cannot pay for them. Yet, in terms of Positivist theory, this solution is little more plausible than the formal one. There is no practical way of equalizing access to legal services sufficiently to preclude oppression. . . .

Thus, knowledge of the rules will necessarily be unequally distributed, and as a practical matter large numbers of people will be denied any substantial access to the legal system. Those who can afford a large amount of legal services will be able to use their superior knowledge to maneuver others into situations where the sovereign's interventions will benefit them at the expense of the others. It may turn out that the sovereign's interventions routinely serve the ends of those with superior knowledge of the rules.

The problem of access is aggravated by the problem of enforcement. The citizen needs legal services not only to learn his rights, but also to enforce them against the trespasses of others. The advantaged can make far better use of their procedural discretion than the disadvantaged. They can engage in far more elaborate and sophisticated procedural strategies. They can use the procedural rules to increase the expenses of the disadvantaged in asserting their claims so that the latter must give up or compromise before their claims have been determined.

At the same time, any attempt to alleviate the problem of access by increasing the availability of legal services will only aggravate the problem of enforcement. The expansion of legal services multiplies the number of people able to exploit their procedural rights so as to thwart the commands of the substantive law and escalates their ability to do so.

The problems of enforcement and access undermine the Positivist image of the lawyer. They make it implausible to portray the fundamental legal activity as the prediction of the actions of the sovereign. The lawyer does not merely anticipate outcomes, he makes them. This is so for two reasons. First, the notion of the lawyer as predicting events depends in large part on the notion of the law as a system with a momentum of its own, operating independently of the will and conduct of any particular actors. Yet, in fact, the outcomes of legal proceedings depend on strategic procedural choices in which the lawyer participates. In becoming the tool of the client, the lawyer does not merely enable his client to vindicate expectations based on a determinate set of rights. Rather, he becomes an agency for the exercise of discretionary power. Second, the notion that the lawyer predicts events also depends on the assumption that there is no scarcity of legal services so that a lawyer's decision to represent a particular client has no significant impact on the distribution of legal knowledge. Yet, the problem of access refutes this assumption .   .   .   .

2. *The Tyranny of Advocacy*

.   .   .   [E]ven after acknowledging the failure of the legal system to check uncertainty and oppression, the Positivist can still argue that the lawyer enables individual clients to pursue their ends more effectively within the limits imposed by both the legal system and social disorder. Yet this second perspective involves difficulties as serious as those of the first .   .   .   . [I]t appears from Positivism's own premises that the lawyer who adheres to the Positivist version of the Ideology of Advocacy must end by subverting his client's autonomy. The problem is that the lawyer's task of explaining the impact of the legal system on the client's personal ends cannot be accomplished without some direct understanding of these ends. Yet, Positivism forbids the lawyer to seek or rely on such an understanding .   .   .   .

The Positivist version of the Ideology of Advocacy focuses on the person for whom the law is a mystery. Such a person, even if conscious of and articulate about his ends, would not know which aspects of them the lawyer would need to understand in order to gauge the impact of the legal system on his life. In order to isolate these aspects, he would need the legal knowledge for which he relies on his lawyer. The lawyer, on the other hand, has no reliable way of learning the client's ends on his own. Because these ends are subjective, individual, and arbitrary, the lawyer has no access to them. Because the lawyer's only direct experience of ends is his experience of his own ends, he cannot speculate on what the client's ends might be without referring to his own ends and thus biasing the neutral predictive analysis he is supposed to perform. Any attempt to frame inquiries to the client concerning his ends or to interpret the client's ambiguous replies will necessarily involve the intrusion of the lawyer's own ends. Thus, consciously or not, the Positivist lawyer is faced with a dilemma: On the one hand, he cannot give intelligible advice to his client without referring to ends; on the other hand, he cannot refer to ends without endangering the client's autonomy, and thus, undermining the basic purpose of his role. . . .

The strategy [that Positivism has developed for dealing with the dilemma] is to impute certain basic ends to the client at the outset and to work to advance these imputed ends . . . . By imputing ends to the client at the outset, the lawyer obviates dangerous inquiries into the particular ends of the particular client. On the other hand, if most people actually do share the imputed ends to some degree, then the lawyer will usually advance the client's actual ends when he works to advance the imputed ends. The ends which Positivism imputes are derived from the basic Positivism premise of egoism, but they go beyond this initial premise to emphasize characteristics of extreme selfishness. The specific ends most often imputed are the maximization of freedom of movement and the accumulation of wealth.

The notion that the advocate should serve, not the individual ends of the client, but rather certain standard ends imputed to him is implicit in cases dealing with the effectiveness of advocacy. The law of procedure repeatedly recognizes that critical decisions are made by the lawyer without any participation by the client. Occasionally, such a decision results in disaster to the client, and the issue arises whether he has been represented effectively. This issue is often seen to depend on whether the lawyer's decision was strategically reasonable under the circumstances in which it was made. A strategically reasonable decision is one well calculated to advance certain ends. Yet, these discussions often proceed in total ignorance of the actual ends of the particular client. Rather, the strategic reasonableness is assessed with respect to the imputed ends of Positivism. The lawyer is not criticized for failing to ascertain his client's ends, but only for failing to advance the ends which have been imputed to him . . . .

This Positivist strategy is a complete failure. It can only precipitate, rather than mitigate, the lawyer's subversion of the client's autonomy. The Positivist's vague, crudely drawn psychological assumptions cannot begin to do justice to the specific complexity of his client's actual ends . . . .

. . . The client of whom Positivism is most solicitous is the naive person, face to face with the alien force of the state, threatened with a massive disruption of his life. Confronted with the need to act in this strange situation, the client must make sense of it as best he can. The lawyer puts himself forth quite plausibly as the client's best hope of mastering his predicament. If he is to avoid being overwhelmed by chaos, he must acquiesce in his lawyer's definition of the situation. He must think in a manner which gives coherence to the advice he is given. He may begin to do this quite unconsciously. If he is at all aware of the change, he is likely to see it as a defensive posture forced on him by the hostile intentions of opposing parties, of whom his perception is mediated by the categories of his lawyer's framework of analysis. His only strategy of survival requires that he see himself as the lawyers and the officials see him, as an abstraction, a hypothetical person with only a few crude, discrete ends. He must assume that his subtler ends, his long-range plans, and his social relationships are irrelevant to the situation at hand. This is the profound and unintended meaning of Holmes's remark:

> If you want to know the law and nothing else, you must look at it as a bad man, who cares only for the material consequences which such knowledge enables him to predict, not as a good one, who finds his reasons for conduct, whether inside the law or outside of it, in the vaguer sanctions of conscience.[62]

The role of the bad man, conceived as an analytical device for the lawyer, becomes, under pressure of circumstances, a psychological reality for the client .   .   .   .

Despite its complete irrationality, this Positivist strategy for dealing with the problem of the inaccessibility of personal ends has become so widely accepted that many lawyers have come to equate the manipulation of the client in terms of imputed ends with neutral advice to the client on his rights. For instance, lawyers constantly express astonishment at the willingness of intelligent laymen, aware of their rights, to make inculpatory statements to the authorities. They can think of no other explanation for this phenomenon besides confusion or pressure from the interrogators, and they thus conclude that no one can be expected to make an "informed decision" on such matters without the assistance of counsel.[65] But the lawyer's assistance does

62. Holmes, The Path of the Law, 10 Harv.L.Rev. 457, 459 (1897).   .   .   .

65. E. g., Griffiths & Ayres, A Postscript to the *Miranda* Project: Interrogation of Draft Protestors, 77 Yale L.J. 300 (1967). This article exemplifies the unconscious influence of ideological assumptions on empirical research. It is based on an actual, unstaged incident in which members of the Yale University community were interrogated individually on two occasions by agents of the FBI about their involvement in illegal draft protests. In the first series of interrogations, despite the fact that the agents gave *Miranda* warnings, all of those questioned discussed their involvement. After these sessions, those questioned attended a meeting at which they were then informed of their rights, this time in more detail and by a "friendly source," that is, three Yale law professors. At the subsequent interrogations, all refused to give any information to the agents. The authors attribute the change of mind to the "greater understanding" resulting from the meeting and suggest that the agents' *Miranda* warnings had been ineffective because they were mechanically and tersely given and because of psychological pressures inherent in the interrogation situation, stemming in part from middle-class habits of courtesy and cooperation and a natural fear of the alien, coercive force of the state. They conclude that mechanical recitals of the *Miranda* provisions by officials are not enough and that a person requires an "advocate" at interrogation proceedings.

The central thrust of the article is its portrayal of the psychological pressures involved in interrogation. It shows no awareness whatsoever of the possibility of pressure from a "friendly source" or an "advocate." Yet, from the authors' account of the incident, the following conclusions seem at least as plausible as theirs. First, the three friendly sources gave more than information; they also conveyed, tacitly or explicitly, the impression that cooperation with the FBI in an not take the form of neutral information or the alleviation of pressure. Along with his knowledge of the law, the lawyer brings his own prejudices and his own psychological pressures. These derive from the conception of the roles of lawyer and client which is implicit in Positivism generally and in the strategy of imputed ends. As Justice Jackson put it, "[A]ny lawyer worth his salt will tell the suspect in no uncertain terms to make no statement to the police under any circumstances." [66] The Positivist lawyer is not an advisor, but a lobbyist for a peculiar theory of human nature . . . .

The Positivist psychology either makes advocacy impossible or forces the lawyer into the strategy of imputed ends. Because the imputed ends ignore the most important dimensions of the client's personality, the strategy leads to the manipulation of the client by the lawyer in terms of the lawyer's own moral and psychological prejudices. In this manner, the lawyer becomes the agent of the result he was supposed to prevent. He subverts his client's autonomy.[70] . . .

investigation into the political expression of students was contrary to the expected standards of behavior of members of a liberal university community. Second, the fact that the second interrogation was conducted under the indirect scrutiny of third parties, while the first was not, was a factor encouraging the students to refuse cooperation the second time when they had cooperated the first time . . . . Third, put to the test, the students' middle-class instincts of cooperation proved stronger with respect to other students and faculty, members of the same upper-middle professional-class to which the student subjects belonged, than with respect to the police, members of a lower social class and an occupational group held in low esteem by the upper-middle professional class.

66. Watts v. Indiana, 338 U.S. 49, 59 (1949) . . . .

70. A Positivist might attempt to avoid the criticism made here by qualifying or retracting the principle of the subjectivity of ends. He might assert that ends are sufficiently shared, or at least understood, so that even strangers can achieve some understanding of each other's ends. This being so, the lawyer could respect his client's autonomy by making strong efforts to come to an understanding of his ends. The Positivist might assert that, although many lawyers do engage in the strategy of imputed ends, there is nothing in Positivism, so revised, which requires that they do so.

I doubt that Positivist Advocacy can be made more acceptable by such a re-

vision. In the first place, to the extent that the revision avoids the problem of the inaccessibility of ends, it becomes less plausible ethically than the version stated above. There are severe limitations on the extent to which a person, particularly a stranger, can understand with any depth the ends of another without actually sharing those ends. The language in which we describe ends is often vague and indeterminate. To understand its meaning in a specific context, one must often share the moral outlook of the person who uses it . . . . Thus, in order to suggest that the advocate can gain an understanding of his client's ends, the revision must assume a substantial degree of sharing of ends throughout the society. Yet, to the extent that such a sharing exists, the insistence that the advocate refrain from holding either himself or his client to personal or social norms becomes untenable. In the Positivist version, the ethical validity of adversary advocacy depends heavily on the premise that values are subjective, arbitrary, and individual. If there were a substantial sharing of values in society, then the reference to such values by judges and lawyers would not be likely to cause uncertainty. If lawyer and client did share values, then the lawyer's adherence to such values would not constitute oppression of the client.

In the second place, the notion that ends are inaccessible accurately describes the experience of lawyers in some areas of practice. This is particularly true in criminal law, where the client is likely to be from a different social background than the lawyer. Albert

III. The Lawyer as Para-Bureaucrat (The Half-Hearted Appeal to Truth)

[After analyzing the connection between the Ideology of Advocacy and the Positivist theory of law, Mr. Simon turns to a second theory of law as a foundation for the ideology, one called Purposivism. This Purposivist theory is said to have been derived from the writings of Pound, Brandeis, Fuller, Llewellyn, Freund, Hart and Sacks, and Hurst.]

.   .   .   In the Purposivist view, society is populated not by atomistic egoists but by people held together by shared experiences and norms. The purpose of law is not just to maintain order, but also to coordinate the actions of citizens so as to further their common purposes as effectively as possible.

Unlike the subjective and individual values of Positivism, the social norms of Purposivism are intuitively perceived and accepted throughout the society. To a large extent norms are self-enforcing because people are spontaneously disposed to conform to them. Nevertheless, spontaneous conformity to social norms is insufficient to secure their fullest implementation. The most effective implementation of social norms requires the application of technique. Unlike norms, technique cannot be intuitively apprehended. Technique involves abstract cognition and requires aptitude, study, and training. The law is a technical apparatus for the advancement of social norms.

The application of technique involves the exercise of power. In contrast to Positivism, Purposivism does not require that power be monopolized by the state. Purposivism recognizes that lawyers and private citizens exercise power. The exercise of power by private citizens is justified by the same principle which legitimates its exercise by the state: its tendency to further the shared norms of the society.

Moreover, the exercise of power is not entirely constrained by rules. Rules are only one among a variety of legal tools for the advancement of social norms. Judges reach behind rules directly to the social purposes the rules are intended to serve, and when they find the rules wanting in the light of the relevant purposes, they abandon or modify the rules. The predictability of judicial decisions remains a goal of the legal system, but it has a different significance than in Positivism. First, the mechanical application of rules is not viewed as the best way to achieve predictability. Predictability can often be better achieved by appealing directly to the intuitively perceived shared norms of the society. Second, predictability is not the pre-

Alschuler has written, "Most criminal defendants do not understand our [sic] system of criminal justice and cannot be made to understand." Alschuler, The Defense Attorney's Role in Plea Bargaining, 84 Yale L.J. 1179, 1310 (1975). In this situation, Alschuler suggests, no meaningful choice by the client as to the exercise of certain procedural rights is possible. If this is true, then it can only be because most defense lawyers do not understand their clients and cannot be made to understand. If the lawyer understood his client, he would be able to give him the information about the criminal justice system which the client would need in order to make an autonomous choice. The strategy of imputed end, is not merely a theoretical ploy. It is a response to the experience of the inaccessibility of client ends in actual practice. It seems unlikely that the problem can be solved merely by telling lawyers to try to learn their clients' ends.

eminent goal of the system. It must be weighed against competing purposes, and it may be occasionally sacrificed to them.

The lawyer's role is a social function designed to facilitate the advancement of norms through the application of legal technique. Legal technique involves the use of institutional forms to manipulate the social world productively. But the lawyer's role requires more than knowledge of legal technique. It also depends on his knowledge of the shared norms of the society. It is only through the intuitive normative understanding which the lawyer has by virtue of his membership and experience in the society that he can use legal technique productively.

In further contrast to Positivism, the role of the Purposivist lawyer is constructive, rather than predictive. He uses institutional forms to create generally rewarding patterns of interaction. He works in the interstices of the patterns created by legislators and judges. The individual's personal ends, though identical or compatible with those of others, are submerged in the minute practical considerations of his particular activity. The lawyer discerns these ends and houses them in an institutional form congruent with the larger patterns of the society. He thus links the concrete and particular with the abstract and general, but not through a system of rules held together by formal logic. He does so by bringing out the latent harmonies among different individual concerns and giving them a secure institutional foundation. His approach is technical and instrumental. He reasons not from rule to conclusion, but between ends (shared purposes) and means (institutional forms).

The implications of Purposivism for advocacy are not as immediately clear as are those of Positivism. Indeed, at first glance, Purposivism seems to present troubling difficulties for the Ideology of Advocacy. The most basic difficulty arises from the necessity of reconciling the Purposivist emphasis on shared values and social harmony with the large measure of social antagonism presupposed by the institutions of adversary advocacy. On the one hand, it is difficult to see how any substantial conflict could exist in a society founded on shared ends. On the other hand, given the existence of such conflict, it is difficult to see how it could be resolved in terms of shared ends, since conflict often arises from differing ends. It is particularly difficult to see how the institutions of adversary advocacy could resolve such conflict, since these institutions seem to preserve and engender social antagonism. In Positivism, where conflict is presumed to be natural and order depends on force, this fact is not an objection. But in Purposivism, where order depends on the tacit acceptance of social norms, the antagonistic nature of adversary advocacy seems a fatal defect .   .   .   .

IV.   The Lawyer as Acoylte (The Sanctification of Ceremony)

.   .   .   Ritualism [the third version of the Ideology of Advocacy] responds to the critique of Positivism and Purposivism by changing the terms of the debate. It acknowledges the irrationality and inefficiency of the legal system, and then embraces it anyway. In a sense, it represents a synthesis of the two other versions, though only one of several possible syntheses.

Ritualism refuses to follow Positivism in insisting that the legal system be viewed as independent of social ends; and it refuses to follow Purposivism in seeing the legal system as simply a means to such ends. The Ritualists suggest that judicial procedure be viewed as both means and end. Procedure can be seen as serving ends, but serving them less by producing them than by embodying them. This logical compromise is accompanied by similar compromises in politics and psychology. The Ritualists think the Positivists right in insisting on the presence of conflict in the social world. And they agree with the Purposivists that law is impossible without shared values. Thus, instead of strife on the one hand and harmony on the other, they propose to substitute the illusion of harmony. The Ritualists see with the Purposivists that men have other ends in common beside order, but they concede to the Positivists that it would be impractical to attempt to realize these ends. Thus, instead of retreat into private realms on the one hand and struggle for concrete social achievement on the other, they propose to substitute the performance of public ceremony.

A.   Ritualist Advocacy

Among the adherents of Ritualism there are both cynics and naifs

.   .   .   .

Cynical Ritualism emerged in the writings of a few of the legal Realists who were not inclined toward Purposivism, and who did not join in the call to reform judicial procedure along instrumental lines to make it a more effective mechanism for the attainment of truth. Rather, they adopted an attitude of bemused resignation toward the irrationalities of the system. The classical Positivists had taught that, though the legal system as a whole could be shown to be rational in terms of the overriding goal of order, particular results could not be evaluated by social criteria because the system was necessarily independent of society. Some Realists—most notably, Thurman Arnold [a]—later suggested that particular results could not be criticized for precisely the opposite reason. They suggested that the system was submerged in society, where it served subliminal cultural needs too subtle to be susceptible to critical analysis. They explained that judicial procedures, including the advocate's role, served a dramatic function by expressing values which were deeply rooted, though only partially articulated, in the culture. These values, such as liberty, equality, and above all, individual dignity, are metaphysical abstractions which only complicate the practical affairs of life, but whose magical power over the culture is such that men cannot bring themselves to let go of them. Judicial procedure is perfectly designed to assuage the fears and longings engendered by such irrational attachments. By allowing these values to be symbolically enacted in its public forums, the society reassures its members that the values have not been forgotten and are still part of their lives. But by confining them to the realm of drama, it guarantees that they do not get in the way of the efficient fulfillment of material needs.

The naive form of Ritualism has emerged more recently, sometimes in connection with discussions of the Warren Court's reforms in criminal pro-

a.   See T. Arnold, The Symbols of Government (1935).   Ed. note.

cedure.   The Warren Court and its supporters occasionally acknowledged that some of its holdings in this area could not be justified either as deductions from the language of the Constitution on the one hand, or as instrumental to the control of official discretion or the assurance of the accuracy of determinations of guilt or innocence on the other hand.   It was occasionally suggested that the procedures required by such decisions were justified by their service as expressions of fundamental moral value, such as individual dignity, trust, equality, and fraternity.   In [one view], the trial is an end in itself in the same way that religious rituals and artistic performances are not means to ulterior purposes but are intrinsically valuable.   The procedures enable the society to communicate to outsiders and to reaffirm to its members the kind of society it is and hopes to be.   The rituals and performances cannot be viewed as means to this expression because they constitute it.   The manner of expression and the content expressed are unintelligible apart from each other.   The role of counsel is thus viewed as an expressive element in the expressive system of the trial.   It is structured by the values the system embodies, and it contributes to the over-all expression as one of the musicians in an orchestra contributes to the performance of a symphony.   .   .   .

The principles of the Ideology of Advocacy occupy a prominent place in both versions of Ritualism.   The lawyer's neutrality makes it possible for everyone to have a lawyer and to participate in the legal system regardless of his ends.   Neutrality thus expresses and implements the value of equality.   Partisanship also expresses the value of equality.   The vigorous presentation of alternative views by each side gives the trial the form of a contest between equals.   Both principles are also closely linked to the value of individual dignity.   Neutrality embodies a recognition that all individuals have rights regardless of their ends.   Partisanship expresses the value of individual dignity by allowing the litigant wide latitude in the presentation of his case.   The discretion allowed the litigant emphasizes the respect with which society views his claims, and perhaps also (from the naive point of view) a sense of trust in him.   .   .   .

B.   The Critique of Ritualist Advocacy

Two kinds of objections can be raised to the Ritualist version of the Ideology of Advocacy.   First, it can be questioned whether the judicial proceeding is regarded, or should be regarded, as an embodiment of shared social values.   Second, the propriety of the analogy of the judicial proceeding to theatrical or ceremonial performances can be disputed.

1.   Ignoring Experience

The cynical version of Ritualism depends on the assumption that the judicial proceeding functions to gratify beliefs actually held by the general public.   Yet, it appears that this assumption is erroneous.   Although Legal Realism, from which cynical Ritualism grew, purported to place a high value on systematic empirical research, the cynical Ritualists were generally content to rely on their intuition in the matter of lay attitudes toward the legal profession and judicial procedure.   Had they been inclined to look seriously into the matter, they would have been surprised to find that the moral notions so readily attributed to the multitudes are in fact a matter of indifference to vast numbers, probably the great majority, of the American people.

In fact, the multitudes do not thrill to the ritual incantation and celebration of such values as equality and individual dignity. Indeed, of all the various manifestations of such values, none seems to have a more slender following than those which are specifically associated with the judicial proceeding. Moreover, not only does the judicial proceeding tend to be held in low esteem by the population as a whole, but it is even less well regarded by those who have actually had the experience of participating in it directly as litigants. The facts turn out to be not only a refutation of Arnold's theory, but something of a joke on him. Arnold seemed to assume that, while liberal professionals might be skeptical of adversary advocacy because of its shortcomings as a method of attaining the truth, the general public uncritically appreciated the judicial proceeding because it served popular political superstition. In fact, it appears that the attitudes which Arnold attributes to the nation as a whole are actually most typical of that minority to which the professionals themselves belong, the group which Herbert McClosky refers to as "the articulate classes." [140]

The naive version of Ritualism depends less on assumptions about the views actually held by the public. Naive Ritualism was first elaborated when the Warren Court's most notable procedural decisions were producing a storm of hostile criticism throughout the country. In this situation, those who sought to justify these decisions could not comfortably appeal to prevailing social beliefs. Thus, the naive Ritualists did not insist that people actually respected equality, trust, and individual dignity or that they actually viewed the judicial proceeding as an expression of these values. Rather, they suggested that these values *should* be respected and that the judicial proceeding *should* be viewed in this way, in the same manner that a beautiful work of art should be appreciated and understood.

But if the Ritualist emphasis on the importance of such values as trust, equality, and individual dignity can be accepted with some qualifications, the Ritualist interpretation of the judicial proceeding as a dramatic expression of these values cannot. The public disdain for adversary advocacy does not arise from philistinism or insensitivity. It is a natural and perceptive response to the operation and design of the institutions prescribed by the Ideology of Advocacy.

The source of the Ritualist error is evident. In a limited sense, the trial *is* a ritual in which ideals *are* affirmed and celebrated. But it is not the ordinary citizen who participates in the celebration or who experiences the affirmation of trust, equality, and individual dignity. The litigants are not the subject of the ceremony, but rather the pretext for it.

Most litigants find the trial a completely irrational and oppressive experience. Far from seeing his dignity affirmed, the litigant is more likely to feel it is being assaulted. Far from celebrating mutual trust, the average litigant feels that he is involved "either in achieving or in checkmating

---

140. McClosky, Consensus and Ideology
in American Politics, 58 Am.Pol.Sci.
Rev. 361, 362 (1964) . . . .

chicanery. . . ." Far from feeling engaged in a contest of equals, he is constantly reminded of his inferiority.

In fact, the celebration of trust, equality, and individual dignity in the judicial proceeding is done exclusively by, and for, the lawyers. The only manifestation of trust which occurs in the judicial proceeding is the willingness of the lawyers (and the judge) to rely on each other's professional honor. This willingness stands in sharp contrast to their attitude toward the litigants and the general public. The lawyer often unflinchingly mouths his client's lies, but he holds himself and his legal brethren to a higher moral standard than that which he expects and encourages in ordinary citizens. Thus, in litigation, a critical moral distinction is drawn between statements of the client or of witnesses repeated by the lawyer, which are regarded with extreme skepticism and statements backed by the lawyer's professional honor, on which other lawyers willingly rely.

The elaborate patterns of courtesy and respect of the trial are entirely for the lawyer's benefit. In the courtroom, a place of special prominence from which laymen are excluded is reserved for the lawyers. Though the lawyer openly heaps contempt on the opposing party, he calls the opposing counsel a brother, refers to him with elegant courtesy, and criticizes him only with gentle circumlocution. The judge refers to the lawyer by titles such as counselor or officer of the court. Even where the judge must reprimand the lawyer, he honors him by assuming him to be bound by a code which the client is assumed to be incapable of understanding.

It may seem peculiar that the lawyer should routinely yield to the judge obsequies which, in almost any other sphere of life, would seem intolerably degrading. Yet, this exaggerated deference is really part of the ceremonial patterns which confirm the lawyer's distinctive dignity. The formal courtesy which the judge returns to the lawyer is all the more satisfying as coming from so exalted a source. . . .

The ritual incarnation of social values is accomplished by the lawyers and by the judge without any help from the litigants. It is the lawyers who perform the ceremony. It is they who assert rights and see their assertions recognized by the judge. They set the rhythm of the proceeding. In alternating turns, each shapes the trial, partly in accordance with his own itinerary and partly in response to his adversary's. Out of this interplay of performances, a sense of resolution or wholeness may emerge and be crystallized and confirmed by the judge. To be sure, he gives judgment only to one side, but he expresses his conclusions in the terms established by both.

Throughout all this, the litigant, if he is well advised, will sit mutely and foolishly. If he should attempt to assert his individual dignity by speaking out, the judge will admonish him to let his lawyer do the talking. If he should persist, he may be bound and gagged, or excluded entirely from the ceremony which is purportedly honoring his individuality. Usually, the client will hesitate to do anything without furtive, whispering conferences with his lawyer. He will have to rise and sit awkwardly in accordance with the unfamiliar etiquette of the court. The physical design of the courtroom, and particularly the bench where the judge sits, will intimidate him. Unaccustomed to striking the proper balance between sycophancy and assertiveness, he will stammer when addressing the judge.

The client's only opportunity to tell his own story is to take the stand. Yet, if he does so, his testimony will be rigidly controlled by the lawyers and the judge in accordance with a complicated body of rules which make no sense to him. He will be repeatedly interrupted, and he will be prohibited from saying much of what he wishes to say. But even the opportunity to make this expurgated, truncated personal statement can be had only at great cost. The litigant must submit to a cross-examination in which he is forced to respond, in accordance with a highly restrictive and peculiar logic and an oppressive etiquette, to a series of questions designed to distort his position and perhaps also to abuse him personally. Testifying in an adversary proceeding is a humiliating experience. Witnesses are expected to tolerate abuse, condescension, and authoritarian discipline of a sort they would never willingly submit to in private life.

Except for such brief and unsatisfying participation, the litigant will be an alien spectator at his own trial. The language of the trial will be largely foreign to him. It is not himself whom he will see represented, but a puppet manipulated by his lawyer in the character of "plaintiff" or "defendant." His lawyer will have dressed and groomed him in a manner calculated to please the trier. He will have drilled him in detail on how to behave throughout the proceeding so as to present an image consistent with the legal position the lawyer has taken. . . .

2. Collapsing Result into Process

The Ritualist analogy of the judicial proceeding to drama and ritual is ingenious and in some respects enlighting, but it is also fundamentally misleading. These analogies eliminate the problems of instrumentalism and the long run, but they do so in a question-begging manner. Dramas and rituals do not involve issues of instrumentalism and the long run because dramas and rituals do not produce distinct consequences; their purpose is not to alter the landscape against which they are played. But a trial does have a consequence; it is a decisionmaking procedure. It is designed to alter the landscape in a very precise fashion.

The significance of the Ritualist analogies can be clarified by comparing them to another possible analogy for the trial: the game. The anthropologist Claude Levi-Strauss [, in The Savage Mind 32 (Chicago ed. 1966),] has contrasted the notions of ritual and game thus:

> Games . . . appear to have a disjunctive effect: they end in the establishment of a difference between individual players or teams where originally there was no indication of inequality. And at the end of the game they are distinguished into winners and losers. Ritual, on the other hand, is the exact inverse; it *conjoins*, for it brings about a union (one might say communion in this context). . . .

Of these two alternatives, it is clearly the game which is the proper analogy for the trial. For the trial works to distinguish winners and losers. The

Ritualist approach simply ignores that at the end of the trial one of the parties may imprison or coerce the other or deprive him of property. To ignore such facts is to commit the reverse of the mistake which the Ritualists attribute to instrumentalism. . . . [I]t is to collapse result into process.

The problem is not that procedures cannot be seen as expressive phenomena, but that the results which are produced by the procedures must also be seen as a part of what is expressed. The Ritualists cannot acknowledge this because, more often than not, the results of the judicial proceeding contradict the values which the procedures are supposed to express. It becomes more difficult to see the trial as a manifestation of social harmony when it is recalled that, at the end, one of the parties may inflict some sort of pain on the other. It becomes more difficult to see the trial as a "contest between equals" when it is recalled that its outcome will be determined in substantial part by the state of the substantive law and the nature of the available evidence. Where these factors put one party at a disadvantage, are they to be considered illegitimate handicaps? Suppose the result of the trial is that an ignorant person loses his savings through the enforcement of an unfair contract which he entered in reliance on the advice of the other party. What will have been said about trust? Suppose the result of the trial is that a person will be sent to a cesspool of a prison. What will have been said about the dignity of the individual?

The Ritualists can justify the trial only by detaching it from its social context and by closing their eyes to the practical consequences which the judicial system implements. This perspective is a real psychological possibility for the lawyer. For him, the trial does end when the procedures are exhausted. The rhythms of his life continue as before; he merely turns to another proceeding. But it is absurd to impute this perspective to the litigant. The litigant cannot ignore the outcome; he will suffer or benefit from it. After the trial, he turns not to another proceeding, but to the task of adjusting his life to the change which the trial has wrought. . . .

3. The Jurisprudence of Resignation

. . . Ritualism represents a policy of resignation. It is based on a strategy of avoiding disappointment by moderating expectations of success and putting the best possible face on failure. Ritualism acknowledges the irrationality of adversary advocacy just enough to establish credibility. It glamorizes adversary advocacy just enough to discourage criticism. As Alvin Gouldner [, in The Coming Crisis of Western Sociology 384 (1970),] writes of Erving Goffman's "dramaturgical" sociology, "[i]t is an invitation to the *enjoyment* of appearances.

C. A Revision: The Game Analogy

. . . Goffman [b] sees the world as drama or ritual, but the performance is to a large extent false. The individual does not take on a role in order to express his harmony with the others, but to escape his terror of

---

b. E. Goffman, The Moral Career of the Mental Patient, in Asylums: Essays on the Social Situation of Mental Patients and Other Inmates (1961); E. Goffman, Interaction Ritual: Essays on Face-to-Face Behavior (1967); E. Goffman, The Presentation of Self in Everyday Life (1959). Ed. note.

them. The mask which the individual puts on is not a message to his fellows, but a shield against them.

In Goffman's world of radical alienation, individual identity is so fragile and dessicated that every gaze from another person is perceived as a threat. Every social encounter is a crisis in which individuals struggle desperately to maintain their autonomy by erecting barriers to penetration by the others. In such situations, ritual and role provide breathing space. They shelter the individual from the siege of foreign gazes and temporarily relieve him from the constant pressure of having to improvise defenses.

This perspective can be readily applied to the judicial proceeding. By giving the proceeding a formal structure based on a moral rhetoric with which the participants have some familiarity, and by giving them fixed roles to play, the system offers the individual a little comfort and privacy in a situation of great stress. The litigant may welcome the identity which his lawyer fashions for him, for it frees him from the strain of adjusting his outward appearance to a new and frightening situation, and gives him a mask with which to shield his inner feelings from the intimidating presence of hostile strangers. He knows that he can satisfy everyone's expectations by adhering to the script. Similarly, by creating the formalized alliance of lawyer and client, the system enables the two actors not only to protect their separate identities from each other, but also to cooperate in the protection of their joint identity from the pressure of others.

The principle of neutrality relieves the client from the pressure of having to account for himself to the lawyer. The principle of partisanship encourages the lawyer to run interference for the client against the advances of others. The lawyer is similarly benefited. Because he portrays himself to his client as indifferent to all purposes, he does not have to defend his own. Because he is expected to be partisan toward the ends of his client, he need not fear public criticism for his activities.

This line of thought travels some distance from the purer forms of Ritualism. It is like Purposivism in that it sees the proceeding as in part instrumental to an ulterior purpose. . . . But this ulterior purpose is not the kind of purpose on which Purposivism usually focused, that is, concrete social achievements. The new version is like Positivism, in that it works to delineate pockets of autonomy within which the individual can exist without accounting to others. But the pockets are much smaller, and they depend on a delicate balance of social forces, not just on state power. And the new view also suggests a compromise between the Positivist and the Purposivist visions of the social world. On the one hand, individuals are seen as alien and hostile, desiring barriers behind which they can isolate themselves from the others. On the other hand, they do not need much coercion to cooperate with each other. There is a spontaneous reciprocity of assistance in the task of safe-guarding order, which is now known, in Goffman's phrase, as "impression management."

A second strength of Goffman's approach is that, though it often speaks in terms of drama or ritual, it is actually based on an analogy to game, as Levi-Strauss explains the term. Goffman does not overlook the fact that the patterns of interaction which he studies function to divide the society into winners and losers. Far from viewing such patterns independently of the results they produce, he insists on what he calls "consequentiality." He recognizes not only that patterns of interaction are refuges for the harried ego, but also that they produce concrete social changes.

The game analogy rationalizes the contradictions between substance and procedure. The game is a social phenomenon in which the satisfactory quality of the outcome depends almost entirely on the proper implementation of procedures. People usually feel that when the rules are followed the outcome of a game is just, precisely because the rules have been followed. They usually are not inclined to assess outcomes in terms of an independent set of criteria. This is particularly true of the game of chance, where the only substantive criterion is negative: that the results have no discernible significance. It should not therefore be surprising that some philosophers find the game the most satisfying example of procedural justice.

For many, the game analogy will appear dubious because the game appears to depend to such a large degree on chance and arbitrariness, and it appears remote from meaningful political activity. Yet, the game might be a useful metaphor for authoritative patterns of interaction, such as the judicial proceeding, to someone who believed that such patterns were arbitrary or had no substantial meaning. To see the central institutions of the society as constructed along the principle of the game of chance is to cease to hold the society to any substantive standards of meaning or consistency. To one willing to accept this conclusion, the game, particularly the game of chance, might be a satisfactory model for social institutions. If the central institutions of the society are viewed in terms of the game of chance, then the arbitrariness of the results they produce is a virtue which proves the integrity of the system. On this view, the threat of contradiction would arise only if the results should actually produce meaningful patterns.

Abraham Blumberg's article, The Practice of Law as a Confidence Game, [1 Law & Soc'y. Rev. 15 (1967),] suggests that many criminal defense lawyers view the legal process in Goffmanian terms. Charles P. Curtis has defended the view of law practice in terms of the game analogy as a special ethical prerogative of the lawyer. The lawyer, he suggests, is under much greater strain than the client because of his conflicting obligations to the public and to his client. The game analogy helps him to view his activities in a way which reduces the strain of his dual commitment. Thus, he writes, "Never blame the lawyer for treating litigation as a game. . . ." [164] On the other hand, Douglas Rosenthal's study of personal injury litigation suggests that lawyers lead clients to view the litigation in terms of the game analogy. Rosenthal emphasizes the passive nature of the client's role and his manipulation by the lawyer. He notes of one litigant: "The lawyer talked her into exaggerating her pain under oath by acknowledging that there were special 'rules' in the 'game' of trial tactics." [165] He quotes another as saying, "the lawyer is a reassuring presence who takes away your guilt feelings. He says, 'Hey, this is the way the game is played.' . . ."

---

164. C. Curtis, It's Your Law (1954); Curtis, The Ethics of Advocacy, 4 Stan.L.Rev. 4 (1951).

165. D. Rosenthal, Lawyer and Client: Who's in Charge? (1974).

The greatest strength of the game analogy is its realism. It is more consistent with the actual experience of large numbers of people than the ritual or theatrical analogies. Moreover, it is a view which can be shared by both winners and losers, both lawyers and litigants. The lawyer is far more likely to be successful in inducing the client to see the litigation as a game than as a ritual.

Yet, the realism of the game analogy is not really a virtue, for the experience to which it defers is itself false and unworthy of respect. To encourage the client to see the results produced by the legal system as arbitrary is to discourage him from considering that they might have a meaning other than the one the legal system attributes to them. A litigant disposed to reflect on the meaning of the consequences produced by the legal system might decide that, while the judicial proceeding does not express such values as harmony, equality, and dignity, neither is it arbitrary. For instance, he might decide that it expresses such phenomena as cruelty, injustice, and oppression. The game analogy abandons the claim that there is any principle by which the way the system works to distinguish winners from losers can be justified, but in doing so, it also rejects the claim that there is any principle by which it can be criticized. The game analogy subverts criticism of the legal system at the same time that it debunks the system.

Moreover, although the game analogy appeals to losers as well as winners, its appeal seems to be limited to the two extremes. As Alvin Gouldner writes of Goffman's sociology:

> A dramaturgical model . . . is for those who have already made it in the big game, or for those who have given up playing it. It has appeal to those members of the middle class who generally mask their alienation out of concern to maintain a respectable appearance and to those "dropouts" in the Psychedelic Culture who feel no need to conceal their alienation; both groups are alike in that they are not moved to protest against and actively oppose the system that has alienated them.

Even more serious is the failure of the game analogy to distinguish between winners and losers in the attitudes it encourages toward the legal system. It induces the same kind of complacent cynicism in both the powerful and the weak. The game analogy admits that the actions of the litigants influence concrete consequences, as the actions of players influence who wins a game. However, it ignores the wide variation among the players in the legal system in the capacity to influence consequences. The problem is not so much that differences in power give some an advantage over others, since such power differences can be seen as the result of previous games. Rather, the problem is that the analogy conceals the extent to which people with power could, if they wanted to, stop playing the game, or attempt without great risk to alter its rules in accordance with some substantive standard of meaning. The game analogy encourages the winners to think of themselves as lucky but helpless beneficiaries of a situation they have not made and can do nothing about.

D.   The Finale: The Friendship Analogy

In a recent article, Charles Fried has defended legal ethics in terms of yet another analogy: friendship.[169] Unlike drama, ritual, and game, friendship is an analogy, not for the legal system, but for the lawyer-client relation itself. It is interesting because it illustrates a tendency to think of the lawyer-client relation as having a value apart from and even antagonistic to the legal system as a whole. . . .

. . . Fried's principal purpose is to defend lawyer-client relations as "good in themselves." . . . Fried is concerned with the embodiment of ideals such as "the ideal of personal relations of trust and personal care." But now the relevant ideals are embodied, not in the legal system as a whole, but in the attorney-client relation itself. This relation is seen less as a component of a larger structure and more as an independent entity. . . .

. . . [Fried] attempts to rationalize legal ethics by emphasizing the personal worth of the relations defined by the professional norms of partisanship and neutrality. Fried suggests that partisanship is like friendship in that it involves "an authorization to take the interests of particular concrete persons more seriously and to give them priority over the interests of the wider collectivity." At the same time the lawyer's neutrality bespeaks a deference to the "concrete individuality" of the client which is similar to the deference one friend would show to another. The fact that the lawyer's concern is not reciprocated in kind by the client does not differentiate the relation from friendship. On the contrary, it exemplifies the lawyer's freedom to bestow and the client's "freedom to receive an extra measure of care" which also exists in friendship. Fried argues that, after one has recognized in the lawyer-client relation the qualities generally valued in friendship, one should accept the lawyer-client relation as good in itself. . . .

Fried writes: "[L]ike a friend [the lawyer] acts in your interests, not his own; or rather he adopts your interests as his own. I would call that the classical definition of friendship." Now this is clearly an error. The classical definition of friendship emphasizes, not the adoption by one person of another's ends, but rather the sharing by two people of common ends. Moreover, the classical notion of friendship includes a number of other qualities foreign to the relation Fried describes. These missing qualities include affection, admiration, intimacy, and vulnerability. On the other hand, if Fried's definition is amplified to reflect the qualification, which Fried repeatedly acknowledges, that the lawyer adopts the client's interests *for money,* it becomes apparent that Fried has described the classical notion, not of friendship, but of prostitution. . . .

Fried's lawyer is a friend in the same sense that your Sunoco dealer is "very friendly" or that Canada Dry Ginger Ale "tastes like love." The friendship analogy is one of those "self-validating, analytical propositions" which Marcuse describes as typical of "the closing of the universe of discourse":

> The unification of opposites which characterizes the commercial and political style is one of the many ways in which dis-

169.   Fried, The Lawyer as Friend: The Moral Foundations of the Lawyer-Client Relation, 85 Yale L.J. 1060 (1976) . . . .

course and communication make themselves immune against the expression of protest and refusal. How can such protest and refusal find the right word when the organs of the established order admit and advertise that peace is really the brink of war, that the ultimate weapons carry their profitable price tags, and that the bomb shelter may spell coziness? In exhibiting its contradictions as the token of its truth, this universe of discourse closes itself against any other discourse which is not on its own terms.[178]

. . . For Fried, the legal system is a condition of the value of the lawyer-client relation, but it is not the source of this value. Legal friendship arises from the fact that the client has a special need for help in order to exercise the autonomy which the legal system guarantees. The fact that this autonomy is a moral value legitimates certain of the lawyer's anti-social conduct, but it does not give it the special pathos and dignity celebrated by the friendship analogy. These qualities arise, not from the specifically legal character of the client's need, but from the fact that the need is integrally related to the integrity of the person, that it is "implicated in crises going to one's concreteness and individuality." Although Fried argues, somewhat halfheartedly, that the need is a special one which is different from needs for non-professional services, he expressly indicates that the need for legal help is similar to the need for other professional services, particularly, medical help.

Of course, the legal system defines the patterns and boundaries of the relation, but these patterns and boundaries seem to limit, more than to promote, the qualities emphasized by the friendship analogy. Fried does not contemplate that the lawyer do many things which friends might be expected to do for each other, such as to destroy evidence, lie to the court, or do anything else which would violate the law or the Code of Professional Responsibility. After first extolling friendship in glowing and unqualified terms, Fried breaks the bad news that the lawyer is only a "special-purpose friend." Although the lawyer-client relation has value apart from considerations of fairness and efficiency, that value must yield in some situations to the need to maintain the integrity of the legal system. The legal system thus appears as a threat to the lawyer-client friendship. . . .

Social norms no longer provide any kind of satisfaction. Rather they pose an intolerable burden, and even their ceremonial enactment is threatening. Fried argues against the Purposivist notion of responsibility—which he portrays in a Utilitarian caricature—as a "monstrous conception." Where the classical Purposivists saw social norms as energizing creative individual behavior, the friendship analogy sees them as frightening individuals into retreat. The autonomy Fried celebrates is much different from the aggressive egoism portrayed in the classic Positivist writings. It is defensive and passive.

If the Ideology of Advocacy is a rationalization of the ethical orientation of lawyers, then the friendship analogy seems both its culmination and its

178. H. Marcuse, One-Dimensional Man:
Studies in the Ideology of Advanced
Industrial Society 88, 90 (1964).

finish. The lawyer's distinctive identity has emerged from behind the facade of the legal system and is now openly celebrated as an end in itself. The irony of this development is that at the same time that it celebrates the legal profession more openly than previous defenses, the friendship analogy also comes closer than previous defenses to acknowledging the failure of the legal profession to accomplish the task for which the lawyer's role was created in the first place, the reconciliation of public and private ends. Previously, the lawyer justified his role in terms of the resolution of individual differences through order, justice, welfare, or ceremony. Yet, in fact, to the extent that he was sensitive to outcomes at all, he experienced them not as resolutions, but as arbitrary concessions to one of two opposing spheres. In emphasizing the remoteness and coolness of public ends, the friendship analogy admits that the magic with which the lawyer once claimed he could resolve the clash of individual wills is a fraud.

Yet, the admission is only implicit. The friendship analogy diverts attention from failure by conflating the lawyer with a less problematical social role. The same effect occurs in the familiar comparison of the legal role with that of doctors (also used by Fried) or clergymen. Such comparisons emphasize the commitment of all three professionals to individual clients, patients, or penitents against the claims of the collectivity, as illustrated particularly by the norms of confidentiality to which all three adhere. Yet, they gloss over a critical difference. The insistence of the doctor and the clergyman on maintaining the confidence of those they serve represents a commitment to the values with which their professional activities are concerned above competing social values. On the other hand, the lawyer's insistence on confidentiality represents a compromise *among* the values with which he is professionally concerned, or perhaps even a sacrifice of these values to extrinsic values. The doctor and the clergyman insist that for them health and salvation must take precedence over justice. The lawyer asserts that his relationship with his client must take precedence over justice, but in doing so he forgets that his relationship was originally defined and rationalized in terms of justice.

In the friendship analogy, the plaintive tone of Ritualism reaches its highest pitch. The lawyer tacitly concedes his failure, but rather than apologize for it, urges the society to lower its expectations. Unable to justify his role in terms of public means and ends, he urges that it be accepted as an end in itself. . . .

----

1. Simon claims that the ideology of advocacy permits the lawyer to work by imputing "certain basic ends to the client . . . and to work to advance these imputed ends." Assuming Simon is correct, how serious is the resulting loss of autonomy to the client? Might it be the case that the relatively simple set of "imputed ends" used by lawyers is not the result of the ideology of advocacy, but rather of the very limited set of solutions that legal institutions can effect in any given social and political environment? If the range of effective solutions is sufficiently small, does the problem of "imputed ends" disappear? For differing views on the extent of the range of potential legal "solutions," see chapter 7.

2.   Procedure may be an attribute of a fallen world—of the differentiation of egos.   To what extent does Simon's critique amount to a commentary on our fall from grace, and to what extent is it peculiar to the specific set of institutions supporting existing patterns of domination?

SECTION B.   THE INTERDEPENDENCE OF SUBSTANCE AND PROCEDURE

1.   THE IMPACT OF SUBSTANCE ON PROCEDURE

Discourse on procedure, and especially on legislation which purports to regulate procedure, presupposes that it is both possible and intelligent to consider process rules and principles apart from particular substantive objectives.   Such discourse, and such rules, are often intended to be "trans-substantive" in character and effect—that is, they are intended to be equally or similarly relevant to many different sorts of substantive disputes.   The idea of trans-substantive procedural values and rules is related to, but not identical to, the ideal of procedural autonomy and procedural "neutrality" (here speaking of the neutrality of the process rather than of the decisionmaker)—an ideal that lies at the heart of John Rawls' attempt to lay the philosophic foundation of the liberal-egalitarian institutions of contemporary American society.   J. Rawls, A Theory of Justice (1971).   In the essays which follow, two aspects of procedural neutrality are considered.   First, Professor Cover considers the circumstances in which the trans-substantive values of process ought to be resistant to the demands of instrumental manipulation in the service of substantive objectives, and also addresses the circumstances in which such manipulation constitutes the intelligent response to a process question.   Next, Professor Hal Scott considers the nature and extent of "unintended" changes in substantive law which may follow upon "procedural" innovation.

Robert M. Cover, **Reading the Rules: Procedural Neutrality and Substantive Efficacy***

We have become so transfixed by the achievement of James Wm. Moore and his colleagues in creating, nurturing, expounding and annotating a great trans-substantive code of procedure that we often miss the persistent and inevitable tension between procedure generalized across substantive lines and procedure applied to implement a particular substantive end.   There are, indeed, trans-substantive values which may be expressed, and to some extent served, by a code of procedure.   But there are also demands of particular substantive objectives which cannot be served except through the purposeful shaping, indeed, the manipulation, of process to a case or to an area of law.   What follows is by no means an attempt to denigrate or undermine the ongoing trans-substantive achievement of the Federal Rules of Civil Procedure.   Rather it is an exploration to rediscover the feel of a tension.   .   .   .

I.

.   .   .   It is useful to test our intuition about the substance-oriented manipulation of procedure in a remote context where, hopefully, we may

---

* *Source*: For James Wm. Moore: Some   84 Yale L.J. 718, 722–40 (1975).   Professor of Law, Yale University.
Reflections on a Reading of the Rules,

assume a degree of unanimity among readers about substance. The first rough sketch of my intuition thus emerges from .   .   .   cases involving the issue of whether particular persons were or were not slaves.

Robinson v. Smyth [16] was decided by the English Court of Common Pleas in 1799; it is short enough to reproduce in its entirety:

> .Shepherd Serjt moved to put off the trial in this case on ac-
> count of the absence of a material witness. He stated that the action
> was brought for wages supposed to be due to the Plaintiff as a sea-
> man, upon a voyage from the West Indies to London, and that
> the defence to be established by the evidence of the absent witness,
> was that the Plaintiff was slave to the Defendant who had paid a
> valuable consideration for him.

> Sed per Curiam. This is an odious defence, to which the Court
> will give no assistance. If the Defendant were to offer to put it on
> the record, we should not give him a day's time. It is as much a
> denial of justice as the plea of alien enemy, which is always dis-
> couraged by the Court.

> Shepherd took nothing by his motion.

This case seems a most troubling one despite (or, rather, because of) the admirable sentiment against slavery expressly stated as a ground for the exercise of discretion.   Yet it is not easy to articulate what it is that is trouble-some about the case.   It is certainly not the result.   Indeed, one can easily contemplate a perfectly acceptable decision reaching the same result:

> Sed per curiam: It is notorious that seamen, without wages
> from their voyage, are impoverished, incapable of awaiting the nor-
> mal measure of the pace of litigation. If that time is given the de-
> fendant in this action it is unlikely that the plaintiff, with no wages
> from his voyage, will be able to subsist without departing again,
> thereby losing his claim. Under such circumstances, there is less
> likelihood that injustice will be done by denying defendant's motion
> than by granting it.

> Shepherd took nothing by his motion.

This hypothetical version of *Robinson* answers a question about the ele-ment of timing in litigation with a justification that contains at least an im-plicit, generalizable principle about its uses.   It is responsive to the defend-ant's motion in precisely the terms in which the motion is made.   Thus it seems quite clear that the case is troublesome because of the nature of the justification, a manipulation of a procedural component to an admirable (from our moral perspective) substantive end.   Needless to say, we would be at least as troubled by a case in which the same procedural amenities were withheld from a black person petitioning for freedom because the jurisdiction held freedom suits in disfavor.

Having reached the conclusion that it is the (admirable) substantive justification for the procedural step in *Robinson* that is troublesome rather

16. Robinson v. Smyth, 1 Bos. & Pul.
454, 126 Eng.Rep. 1007 (C.P.1799) . . . .

than the procedural step itself, we must concede that there are many examples of substantive justification for procedural steps which do not trouble us in the same way . . . .

Within a month of *Robinson*, the Virginia Supreme Court of Appeals considered a question of standing in Pleasants v. Pleasants; [18] the issue was whether to permit a person who had already been discharged as executor of an estate to petition a court of equity in order to compel legatees to free slaves who had passed to them under a will. The will directed the beneficiaries to set the slaves free "when the laws should allow of it." The Virginia Act of 1782, permitting manumission, was passed after the executor had been discharged. The Virginia court allowed the petitioner to present the slaves' claims to freedom, despite its certainty that he did so neither in his capacity as executor nor as heir at law. The court permitted the discharged executor, son of one testator and brother of the other, to represent the claim for freedom [in these words]:

> On mature consideration, I am of opinion, that the suit in Chancery cannot be sustained upon the ground of the appellee's [Robert Pleasants'] claim as heir at law to take the slaves for the condition broken, it being the practice of that Court to relieve against forfeitures and not to aid or enforce them. Neither will his claim as executor, have that effect; because, having long since assented to the several legacies and bequests of these people, he had fully executed his power over the subject. At the same time, *those characters furnish a commendable reason for his stating the case of these paupers to the Court; and it ought to be heard and decided upon without a rigid attention to strict legal forms, since it can be done, without material injury to the other parties.*

. . . [T]he holding in *Pleasants* may be functionally equivalent to judicial ratification of a self-appointment as guardian ad litem. Unquestionably the power given him to bring the suit was extraordinary, and would not be generalized to parallel situations outside the area of slavery. My intuitive sense of approval for *Pleasants* is fully as strong as my sense of disapproval for *Robinson*. . . .

Robinson seems to me to sit outside the limits of [the] continuum of more to less acceptable manipulations of process. It is thus particularly important to understand what is disturbing in it. The difficulty seems to me fourfold. First, the case seems to further no consistent, coherent substantive policy, given what is presumed to be the operative rule of law to be applied. Since slavery is presumed to be an acceptable defense to the action for wages, we are confronted by the use of process as a means of undermining the formal rule of law. Now qualification or mitigation of substance through process is not unusual or necessarily problematic. But it usually takes the form of imposing presumptions or allocating burdens to structure the usual litigation risks of uncertainty in a fashion which recognizes a substantive preference. What is highly unusual about *Robinson* is that it ignores this route altogether

18. 6 Va. (2 Call) 319 (1799), 6 Va. (2 Call 2d ed.) 270 (1799). . . .

in undermining the rule of law; it purposefully refuses to permit uncertainty to be reduced.   And it does so without any reference to cost or efficiency criteria which may, in many situations, acceptably impose a limit on the amount of trouble or expense we are prepared to undertake to reduce uncertainty.

The only sense that can be made of the combination of the substantive rule of law in this case with the procedural ruling and its articulated justification is that slavery is to be formally recognized, but the holding of this form of interest is to be purposefully rendered insecure.   It might be noted that this kind of objective, if it can be justified at all, is usually justified as a "transition" stage in the development of substantive law.   It suggests a position of disequilibrium which, when resolved, will eventuate in a more stable substantive configuration that will presumably not need, and should not use, such manipulation of procedural components to achieve its ends.   In a sense this type of justification is itself a recognition of the character of the process as a departure from a norm, as problematic.

The second disturbing characteristic of *Robinson* inheres in its failure to achieve equality of treatment of litigants.   Recall that my suggested alternative to the court's opinion would have justified the decision by invoking the litigation plight of impoverished seamen.   It would have stressed that the extension of time sought would unfairly and disproportionately burden the other litigant, thus providing a generalizable, trans-substantive principle which would presumably benefit and burden parties regardless of their positions on the matter before the court.

The third problem in *Robinson* inheres in the unpredictable character of the justification when applied to process.   That a claim or defense is "disfavored" does not generate any plausible or predictable pattern of impact on process.   If the "disfavored" rubric will justify failure to extend time to secure an absent witness, it may, but need not, eventuate in a predilection to dismiss pleadings for trivial errors, a careful scrutiny of testimony for trivial inconsistencies, an enlargement of privileges to exclude testimony which would support the disfavored claim, a narrowing of privilege to permit testimony against the disfavored claim, etc.   Indeed, the sum effect of calling an action disfavored seems to be that lightning may strike at any time or in any way; we know only which party it will strike.

Finally, *Robinson* is troublesome because the court chooses to make a point of the lack of procedural justification for the decision.   There are a broad variety of procedural desiderata and a decision often involves a choice among them.   While a decision such as the one I suggest as an acceptable alternative implicitly sets off one procedural value against another, the Court of Common Pleas expressly failed to do so.   It may be justifiable, once a trade-off between process values is inevitable, to make the choice in one direction rather than another because of the substantive end that will thereby be served; in any event, such a form of decision appears less nakedly as a disregard for a process value.   But it seems intuitively troublesome to ignore these values altogether.

    .   .   .   In *Pleasants* [, on the other hand,] the court is confronted with a problem of remote participatory rights, the issue of access to litigation for those against or for whom a decree will not run.   Indeed, one may go further in terms of our present rules governing participation and stress that Pleasants himself would have neither been injured nor benefited as a practical matter if his participation had been denied.   The conferral of rights of participation upon those whose interest is remote or, in a sense, gratuitous, must represent in large part a judgment about the likelihood of a particular form of litigation taking place without such participation, and about the desirability of encouraging such litigation.   It is difficult to imagine how such judgments can be made in a trans-substantive fashion.   One might wish to encourage litigation in order to deter a certain kind of conduct (by structuring litigation risks and making adverse results more likely) or in order to protect a certain class of persons considered particularly vulnerable to some specified form of predatory conduct.   But those judgments must be made on an individual basis for each substantive question.

Apart from substantive preferences, it is difficult to decide what conditions will determine a decision to permit such remote participation.   But the concept of litigation plights and the likely consequences of permitting participation may furnish some of these.   Those conditions could indeed be embodied in a rule which might read:

> A person not seeking relief on behalf of himself or herself will be permitted to seek relief on behalf of others if:
>
> (a) There is reason to believe that those persons on behalf of whom relief is sought are unable or substantially less able to seek relief effectively on their own behalf.
>
> (b) The representative party will actively and adequately represent the interest of those on behalf of whom he sues.
>
> (c) Effective adjudication on the merits will not be impeded.

But such a rule would be inadequate if it did not also permit consideration of the effect of enhanced remote participation on the substantive objectives of whatever scheme is being enforced.

Thus in *Pleasants* one may discern two dimensions to the court's decision.   One dimension concerns itself with the procedural variables: the form of litigation determined by Pleasants' petition serves the end of effective litigation on the merits; the persons on behalf of whom relief is sought are indeed in a vulnerable litigation situation; the prior position of the petitioner as executor under the will is ground for expecting adequate representation.   But without the sense that there is public favor for encouraging and facilitating private manumission (a sense which pervades the opinions in *Pleasants*) there is no sufficient reason for not leaving the matter to action by those aggrieved.   In a precisely analogous case the Supreme Court of North Carolina refused to give leave to a discharged executor to sue.[31]   And that decision was quite proper given that court's express judgment that the substantive policy of the state was not hospitable to the creation of a class of free Negroes through private manumission.   Thus it seems to me that

---

31.   Pride v. Pulliam, 11 N.C. (4 Hawks)
49, 60 (1825).

questions of remote participatory rights and representation will always involve a series of trans-substantive values which create conditions for conferring such rights, but must also involve judgments that cannot be made without particularized attention to their effect upon substantive policy.

.   .   .

II.

The fine tuning of remedial and procedural instruments for implementing substantive preferences which I have suggested was at work in the slavery cases is severely retarded once procedural norms are codified in a trans-substantive structure . . . .   It is extraordinary that our legal system holds a divided view of procedure: Our norms for minimal process, expressed in the constitutional rubric of procedural due process, are generally conceded to constitute a substance-sensitive calibrated continuum in which the nature of the process due is connected to the nature of the substantive interest to be vindicated; yet our primary set of norms for optimal procedure, the procedure available in our courts of general jurisdiction, is assumed to be largely invariant with substance.   It is by no means intuitively apparent that the procedural needs of a complex antitrust action, a simple automobile negligence case, a hard-fought school integration suit, and an environmental class action to restrain the building of a pipeline are sufficiently identical to be usefully encompassed in a single set of rules which makes virtually no distinctions among such cases in terms of available process.[37]   My point is not that the Federal Rules are not workable over such a broad range.   But it may be worth asking in what sense that codification works well because of its trans-substantive aspiration, and in what sense it works in spite of it . . . .

.   .   .   The class action has constituted the most widely noted and most problematic case for construction of the Federal Rules.   Commentators could hardly fail to note the variety of contexts in which the remedial clout purchased by the class action has far-reaching effects on substantive law. Some . . . have argued for a cautious approach to the application of the [class action] Rule to antitrust laws because of the inhibiting effect on legitimate business activity of both the increased likelihood of private litigation and the possibility of enormous recoveries.   Others have argued that the private class action should be embraced precisely because it is a form of private enforcement, which may well be more efficient and cheaper in deterring unwanted and illegal activity than public enforcement.   But with the single significant exception of truth in lending cases,[43] courts have not analyzed class action cases as presenting problematic questions of substantive law: of antitrust, securities regulation or environmental policy.   Rather, they have treated the

---

37. It is clear that certain basic distinctions have already permeated the application of the Federal Rules, though ordinarily not found within the text of the Rules themselves. For example, the use of the pretrial conference is largely directed to encouragement of settlement in most routine actions. But in "big" or "complex" actions, the conference(s) is (are) directed to planning future stages, whether trial or discovery.

43. The truth in lending cases have been a partial exception largely because the $100 minimum recovery per violation can be and has been read as inconsistent with the multiplier effect of 23(b)(3) class actions. These cases began to take a strange turn with the significant opinions of Judge Marvin Frankel in Ratner v. Chemical Bank N. Y. Trust Co., 54 F.R.D. 412 (S.D. N.Y.1972). . . .

text of the trans-substantive rule as more or less controlling on the issue of its availability.

Some opponents of the class action have argued that it is precisely the characteristics noted above that make application of the rule problematic under the Rules Enabling Act, a statute which provides that the rules not "abridge, enlarge or modify" substantive rights of parties.[45] The first section of this article leads to the conclusion that the manipulation of procedural tools to effectuate substantive objectives is by no means undesirable and often seems necessary. Thus if the Enabling Act were read to forbid a Federal Rule to have substantive impact, it would create an anomaly. Federal Rules, intended to provide a flexible structure for achieving substantive ends, would remove from the courts a useful arsenal for remedial policy by freezing process in a single posture for all cases. But there is a way of reading the Enabling Act which neither renders it a dead letter, as courts have tended to do, nor construes it as a bulwark against change. Such a reading would start with the premise suggested above, that absent a trans-substantive structure of rules, courts must often justify decisions about procedure with a combination of substantive and procedural objectives and values. The Rules Enabling Act might then be read to mean that the courts, in applying the Federal Rules of Civil Procedure or any subsequently enacted similar body of rules, may not forsake their responsibility to justify substantive impact in terms of substantive values. It would not be enough to point to Rule 23; one would have to justify invoking it.

The Rules Enabling Act, then, would operate to render explicit the obligation of the courts to make the same sort of determination when applying Federal Rules or similar codifications as they would make when justifying a form of non-rule remedy such as equitable relief. Insofar as the application of the federal rule to the particular area were not well-established, it would require the degree of elaborate inquiry into substantive objectives which marked the Supreme Court's discussion of non-rule remedies in cases like J. I. Case Co. v. Borak,[47] Bivens v. Six Unknown Named Agents of the FBI,[48] Brown v. Board of Education (II) [49] and Hawaii v. Standard Oil.[50] Insofar as the general applicability of the federal rule to the substantive area were well-established, the inquiry would center on the utility of its specific incidence. Above all, the Rules Enabling Act would not be read to forbid the application of a federal rule because it altered substantive rights. However, it would forbid the *reasoning* by which a rule altered the right simply because it is a rule of procedure. As part of the repository of our collective procedural imagination the Federal Rules of Civil Procedure would be read to include remedial structures which could be applied where appropriate in light of substantive objectives.

At this point it is well to consider the argument that the Rules, as a quasi-legislative enactment, should restrict the courts in much the same way as statutes should. In this view, however desirable it is for courts to exercise

45. 28 U.S.C. § 2072.

47. 377 U.S. 426 (1964).

48. 403 U.S. 388 (1971).

49. 349 U.S. 294 (1955).

50. 405 U.S. 251 (1972).

a residual power to manipulate all process norms (including Rules) to achieve substantive objectives, they no longer have the power to make such decisions as to the Federal Rules of Civil Procedure. The answer to such an argument is twofold. First, remedial creativity is exercised apart from the Federal Rules, and the extension of that creativity to application of the Federal Rules is not inherently beyond the power of a court. In imposing a limitation on the power to alter substantive rights *through* the Federal Rules, Congress was not concerned with the danger of explicit remedial creativity accompanied by substance-oriented justifications. Rather it was concerned lest the power granted to regulate procedure enlarge the power of the courts to make substantive law. So long as courts make explicit their substance-oriented justifications for procedural steps, they will place themselves in precisely the same position they occupy with respect to (nonconstitutional) questions of standing, equitable relief, or any other remedial characteristic. Congress will know what choice was made and will be able to correct it or not as it chooses. Moreover, the problematic character of the Federal Rules under the Constitution must color our treatment of them as controlling. They are not passed by Congress, but are promulgated pursuant to the Rules Enabling Act. Justices Black and Douglas have long dissented from promulgation on the grounds of the unconstitutionality of that procedure. If the Federal Rules are to be read as removing the power of a court to treat substantive objectives as overriding where they otherwise would control, have they not "abridged, modified or enlarged" substantive law in a fashion more far-reaching than some outcome-determinative test would suggest?

The model of decisionmaking under the Federal Rules that I have suggested hardly constitutes a cure-all for our procedural ills. For in the past several years the application of the Federal Rules of Civil Procedure to federal habeas corpus actions has worked along just such a model with, at best, mixed results. Far from precluding use of tools such as interrogatories for purposes of discovery, the Supreme Court has simply turned the question into one of case-by-case determination of whether the needs of effective adjudication of the particular issue warrant the use of such a tool. In Harris v. Nelson,[51] the Court stated:

> We conclude that, in appropriate circumstances, a district court, confronted by a petition for habeas corpus which establishes a prima facie case for relief, may use or authorize the use of suitable discovery procedures, including interrogatories, reasonably fashioned to elicit facts necessary to help the court to "dispose of the matter as law and justice require."

Most important for our purposes is the Court's reasoning concerning the *source* of authority for discovery, such as it may be, in habeas corpus:

> Clearly, in these circumstances [the absence of specific congressional guidance on methods of "securing facts"], the habeas corpus jurisdiction and the duty to exercise it being present, the courts may fashion appropriate modes of procedure, by analogy to existing rules or otherwise in conformity with judicial usage. . . .

---

51. 394 U.S. 286 (1969).

Their authority is expressly confirmed in the All Writs Act, 28 U.S. C. § 1651. This statute has served since its inclusion, in substance, in the original Judiciary Act as a "legislatively approved source of procedural instruments designed to achieve 'the rational ends of law.'"

Justice Harlan's dissent in *Harris*, though prompted by his satisfaction on the record that the discovery sought in the instant case was not necessary to a fair hearing, also raised in stark form the difficulty inherent in a case-by-case approach to procedure.

> If discovery procedures are developed case by case, there will at least be a very long period during which procedures will differ from district to district. . . . It is unlikely that the rules thus generated will be the best that could have been devised.

As a result, Harlan concluded that the model of "rules" setting consistent and coherent standards ought to be invoked in the establishment of a code of habeas corpus rules of procedure. But Harlan's suggestion of referring the habeas procedure question to a Rules Advisory Committee was followed with ironic results: The proposed Habeas Rules [a] . . . refer the question of discovery to the discretion of the court for case-by-case treatment along the lines suggested by the Court in *Harris*.[56]

In some sense Harlan has certainly been proven correct. One cannot re-invent a procedural system for every case. And the question of what is to be presumptively or generally available may be best settled by rule. But where the only or primary issues at stake are substantive, justifications in substantive terms may be necessary.

Sero v. Preiser,[57] a recent application of the method of Harris v. Nelson, is an example. In that case the Second Circuit upheld a habeas corpus class action on behalf of "more than 500" New York state prisoners who had received special four year sentences as young adults for misdemeanors which would have entailed shorter sentences if treated as adult crimes. The places and conditions of confinement for those "young adult" (16 to 21 years old) offenders were the same as for adult offenders.

In upholding the class action the court grounded its authority in the All Writs Act and found the content of its procedural tool by analogy to Rule 23. But it went further:

> A number of other persuasive justifications enforce our conclusion that the class action was appropriately used in this case. Because many of those serving reformatory sentences are likely to be illiterate or poorly educated, and since most would not have the

---

a. The Habeas Rules referred to in the text became effective with changes not relevant to this discussion on February 1, 1977. Ed. note.

56. Habeas Corpus Rule 6, § 2255 Rule 6, in Comm. on Rules of Practice and Procedure, Amendments to the Federal Rules of Criminal Procedure, Proposed

Rules Governing Habeas Corpus Proceedings, Proposed Rules Governing § 2255 Proceedings for the United States District Courts and Proposed Amendment to the Federal Rules of Appellate Procedure 62,113 (1973).

57. United States ex rel. Sero v. Preiser, 506 F.2d 1115 (2d Cir. 1974).

benefit of counsel to prepare habeas corpus petitions, it is not improbable that more than a few would otherwise never receive the
relief here sought on their behalf.

This invocation of the litigation plight of young, poor prisoners is highly
reminiscent of the justification for the holding in *Pleasants* .   .   .   .

Why, indeed, may the All Writs Act (or alternatively, some notion of
a residual constitutional power of a court) not be read to provide the same
flexibility of process for ordinary civil actions to which the Federal Rules apply as that provided for habeas corpus? The significance of that question may
be demonstrated by contrasting *Sero* with the opinion of the Supreme Court
in Eisen v. Carlisle & Jacquelin.[59]   In *Eisen* the Court, eschewing constitutional grounds for its decision, ruled that actual notice must be sent to all
known or readily ascertainable class members in a 23(b)(3) action, even if
the cost of such notice would be so high as effectively to preclude the action
being brought.   The Court grounded its opinion in the language of Federal
Rule 23(c)(2):

> [T]he Court shall direct to the members of the class the best
> notice practicable under the circumstances, including individual no-
> tice to all members who can be identified through reasonable effort.

Eisen is remarkable for its absolute silence on the issue of the impact
that this ruling would have on substantive issues of antitrust and securities
law enforcement.   Instead of considering a vague term, "practicable," as an
invitation to inject substantive preferences, the Court treats the Rules notice
provision as a clear legislative command which is binding and susceptible to
only one resolution.   I must stress that my criticism of *Eisen* does not go to
the result.   It may be eminently reasonable (though I doubt it) to refrain
from the use of such a procedural device in terms of antitrust policy.   But it
seems absurd to refrain from a remedy which *may* make sense in substantive
terms because of lack of individualized notice to persons who cannot conceivably be harmed thereby as a practical matter.   In *Eisen* both economic
considerations and the statute of limitations made it a virtual certainty that
no individual actions would conceivably be brought if the class action failed.
Thus a class member would lose no viable litigation opportunity even if notice failed to reach him, while the defendants' securing of a res judicata bar
would constitute no better barrier to subsequent law suits than that afforded
by cost barriers to individual suits and the statute of limitations.

If the All Writs Act may serve as a repository of power to create the
process needed by a particular case or substantive interest, *absent* a rule or
body of rules, why could it not serve equally to provide a basis for modification of rules where they do exist?   Such a scheme would neither destroy the
Federal Rules of Civil Procedure nor violate some notion of separation of
powers.   Indeed, just as *Sero* and *Harris* have hardly shaken the normal presumption that habeas corpus petitioners' actions will have no recourse to
discovery or class actions, so an application of the All Writs creative power
to modify the Federal Rules in extraordinary circumstances such as *Eisen*

59. Eisen v. Carlisle & Jacquelin, 417
U.S. 156 (1974).

would not alter the presumptive applicability of the Rules as they stand. As to separation of powers, I have already argued that the most problematic character of the Federal Rules of Civil Procedure under the Rules Enabling Act emerges from letting the mere fact of a rule's existence control the promotion (or lack thereof) of substantive values. The use of the All Writs Act to implement substantive values is simply a device for avoiding such a bind.

. . . Professor Moore has persistently struggled against the elevation of form over substance. I think he will agree that the Federal Rules of Civil Procedure, themselves, ought never to become the categories to which substance must bend. Indeed, he might prefer to find his source for this perspective not in the All Writs Act, but in the text of the Federal Rules themselves, in the oft-quoted but little used authority of Rule 1: "They [the Rules] shall be construed to secure the just, speedy, and inexpensive determination of every action."

————

1. Might it be helpful to consider the Federal Rules of Civil Procedure not as a set of trans-substantive norms, but rather as a repertoire of possible moves available to participants so that each case works out a mosaic of predefined set pieces chosen by the individual participants? Would the "repertoire" metaphor undermine the argument in Cover's article?

2. Professor Cover's suggested methodology requires courts to think extensively about procedural possibilities. But perhaps the courts are better off simply acting in a common-sensical way without worrying about the structure of justifications. The reported comment (here paraphrased) of baseball's Yogi Berra might here be apposite: "I ask, how can yah think and hit at the same time? " See M. Mantle, The Education of a Baseball Player 188–89 (1967).

3. To what extent can the trans-substantive quality of the Federal Rules be understood as a function of the peculiar institutional arrangements used to discharge the obligations of the Rules Enabling Act (28 U.S.C. § 2072)? These institutional arrangements give a primary role to an Advisory Committee, consisting largely of academics, practitioners, and judges (acting in a non-judicial capacity). The work of that Committee is supposed to be reviewed by various government agencies, but the responsibility for review is not clearly defined in form or practice. The rules written by the Advisory Committee are passed on to the Judicial Conference; then to the Supreme Court; and then to Congress. Congress must act affirmatively to stop the rules from going into effect (a procedure that curtails the veto power of the President). The quality of the Supreme Court's review remains a mystery—some justices believe that anything more than a ceremonial transmittal would be inconsistent with Article III; the Court holds no hearing, proceeding, or argument prior to its transmittal. The Judicial Conference does not seem suited for a thorough review, and it is not clear that it engages in any such review under these circumstances. The Advisory Committee thus emerges as the central law-making agency, and one can well understand their reluctance to make substantive choices. See, generally, Clark, The Role of the Supreme

Court in Federal Rule-Making, 46 J.Am.Jud.Soc'y 250 (1963); Lesnick, The Federal Rule-Making Process: A Time for Re-examination, 61 A.B.A.J. 579 (1975); Hazard, Book Review, 87 Yale L.J. 1284 (1978).

2. THE IMPACT OF PROCEDURE ON SUBSTANCE

Hal S. Scott, **The Impact of Class Actions on Rule 10b–5***

Securities law literature largely ignores the role of the class action device in the recent expansion of liability under section 10(b) of the 1934 Securities Exchange Act and SEC rule 10b–5. Indeed, both courts and commentators maintain a dichotomy between the "substantive" considerations of 10b–5 and the "procedural" considerations of rule 23. Commentators, of course, argue that increased use of class actions in the 10b–5 setting is likely to enhance the effectiveness of the rule in forcing disclosure. But these observations do not depend on the possibility that the use of class actions will prompt changes in the substantive requirements of a 10b–5 cause of action. They assume instead that no change in substantive law will result from the introduction of the class action device. [This article challenges that assumption.] . . .

I. The Operational Effects of the Class Action Device

Hall v. Coburn Corp.,[6] a consumer class action in the New York Court of Appeals, illustrates the relationship between class actions and changes in substantive law. A large number of buyers entered into retail installment contracts for carpeting with different sellers. Suing as a class, the buyers alleged that material parts of the contracts were printed in smaller than eight-point type, the minimum size required by statute. The action was brought against a finance company, the assignee and printer of the contracts. Each plaintiff sought recovery of the credit service charge.

Plaintiffs' decision to base the claim on print size, a theory of statutory liability per se, probably was motivated by two considerations. First, if they had brought the action against all sellers on the terms of the contracts, on a theory of unconscionability or common law fraud, they would have been subject to the defense that the question presented was not "one of a common or general interest of many persons." Each contract had different terms and contractual parties. Second, the credit charge in the contracts was authorized by New York law.

Affirming the trial court dismissal of the case, the court of appeals interpreted prior class action case law as requiring "something more" than identical facts and found that class actions were permissible only in those cases involving "closely associated relationships growing out of trust, partnership or joint venture, and ownership of corporate stock." Moreover, the court rejected the theory based on the print size of the contract type, admittedly a technical statutory violation, finding that it did not strike at the "real evil" of retail credit buying—the amount of credit service charge. Finally, the

* *Source:* 38 U.Chi.L.Rev. 337, 337–71 (1971). Assistant Professor of Law, Harvard University.

6. 26 N.Y.2d 396 . . . (1970).

court felt there were other remedies available to the class, such as administrative action by the newly created State Consumer Protection Board.

The result in *Hall* does not seem compelled by prior class action case law. The court, instead of imposing an additional requirement that the case involve trust, partnership or joint venture, or ownership of stock, could easily have held that class actions were available where there were identical facts. Further, it is clear that individuals have successfully maintained actions under the same statutory liability theory advanced in *Hall*.[14] As for the alternate remedies, the statute expressly authorizes a private right of action, and one of the powers of the State Consumer Protection Board is to cooperate with and assist consumer class actions in proper cases. What then explains the result?

The court was evidently unwilling to allow a "technicality" to be used in a class action where it would produce large damages and have the effect of broadly undermining existing legislative policy regarding legitimate credit charges. Although identical facts had been pleaded—the print size was identical and common to all of the contracts—the court considered these facts, when alleged in a class action, an improper basis for liability.

The *Hall* analysis can be compared profitably with the approach of the Sixth Circuit in Mader v. Armel.[17] There, owners of stock in Certified Mortgage Corporation, the target of a successful merger, brought a 10b–5 class action against the officers and directors of Certified to recover the decrease in the value of their stock allegedly resulting from the merger. Plaintiffs claimed that the merger had been accomplished by misrepresentations and omissions of material facts in proxy statements.

The district judge originally ordered the case to proceed as a class suit as required by [Fed.R.Civ.P.] 23. Later, however, he found that the merger did not involve a sale within the meaning of rule 10b–5 and granted defendants' motions to dismiss and for summary judgment. In ordering dismissal, the court indicated that if the case had proceeded to trial the ruling maintaining the class action would have been vacated, in part, because each member of plaintiff class would have had to prove his reliance on the alleged misrepresentations.

The Court of Appeals for the Sixth Circuit reversed and remanded in a two-part opinion. First, the court held that a merger does constitute a sale within the meaning of rule 10b–5. Second, it held that the suit had properly been maintained as a class action.

Defendants' objection to the propriety of the class action was that questions of fact and law were not common to the class.[20] They contended that

---

14. Ben Constr. Corp. v. Rivers, 29 A. D.2d 1048, 289 N.Y.S.2d 866 (1961); Gramatan Co. v. Jones, 23 A.D.2d 940, 260 N.Y.S.2d 54 (1965) (by implication); Ben Constr. Corp. v. Snushall, 44 Misc.2d 878, 880–81, 254 N.Y.S.2d 948, 950 (Sup.Ct.1964).

17. 402 F.2d 158 (6th Cir. 1968), cert. denied 395 U.S. 977 (1968).

20. Fed.R.Civ.P. 23(b)(3) is the section of rule 23 under which 10b–5 actions are generally brought. . . . Before a suit can be maintained on a class basis, rule 23(b)(3) requires that the court find "that the questions of law or fact common to the members of the class predominate over any questions affecting only individual members . . . ."

not all of the shareholders might have relied on the misrepresentations, suggesting that some might have signed the proxies without reading the proxy statements, while others might not even have signed them.

The court of appeals responded to this argument by questioning the reliance requirement itself. It distinguished the case relied upon by the district court, List v. Fashion Park, Inc.,[21] stating that "*List* was not a class action suit. It involved only one plaintiff." It went on to decide that actual reliance on the misrepresentation was not required. It was sufficient that plaintiffs presumably had relied on the honesty and fair dealing of the company when they purchased their shares. Thus, the court dispensed with defendants' class action objections by presuming, as a matter of law, that the element of the claim that might give rise to uncommon questions was present.

In both *Hall* and *Mader* the focal point was the necessity for "common questions." In *Hall* the court was unwilling to allow a class action even though the strict liability theory presented only common questions. The court felt that such a theory would undercut legislative policy. In *Mader* the court found common questions by changing the *List* reliance requirement.

Both cases point out how courts can maintain different requirements for substantive causes of action in individual and class suits. *Hall* does not state that a strict liability theory would be unavailable in an individual action. It is the consequences of allowing the theory in a class action which bother the court. In *Mader* the court frankly states that the *List* requirement may be good law in individual actions but is not required in class actions.

However, the analytical approach in the two cases differs substantially. The *Hall* court's decision not to allow a class action is based on the court's judgment on the merits of plaintiffs' claim. The existence of a valid cause of action and a valid class action pose the same question for the court. In *Mader*, however, the issues are viewed separately. Since the court perceives itself as making a "procedural" ruling on the propriety of the class action, it seems not to appreciate fully the change it is making in the reliance requirement. Thus, it does not discuss the appropriateness of the change.

More fundamentally, these two cases reflect different responses to the pressures of class actions. Although the *Hall* court recognized that a wrong had been suffered by a large class of buyers, it considered the substantive effects of maintenance of a class action, identified its policy preference, and disposed of the class action accordingly. The *Mader* court, on the other hand, responded to the pressures of a large class of defrauded investors by asking the procedural question about common questions and eliminating an element of 10b–5 liability that threatened the class suit. It is the response of *Mader*, rather than that of *Hall*, that typifies the course of development in the securities law area.

21. 340 F.2d 457 (2d Cir.), cert. denied
382 U.S. 811 (1965).

II. The Class Action Catalyst in 10b–5 Expansion

. . . At least since the 1966 amendment of rule 23 of the Federal Rules of Civil Procedure, if a class action is to be maintained, [the] elements of substantive liability must be funneled through rule 23's requirement that "questions . . . common to the members of the class predominate . . . ." Given the considerable pressure in securities law to adopt and foster class actions, there is a tendency, after viewing the elements of a 10b–5 claim solely in terms of the common questions proscription, to restrict the operation of any element that would frustrate commonality and fragment or prevent recovery by the class . . . .

. . . The most common target of a non-common questions defense is reliance; defendant simply claims that some members of the class relied and some did not. Defendant will usually point out a particular non-relying member of the plaintiff class—often but not always the plaintiff-representative—to substantiate his point about reliance differences.

In the preponderance of cases this non-common questions defense has not been successful. The result of failure to sustain the defense has been the near elimination of reliance as an element in class actions. However, few courts explicitly reject the defense with a statement that reliance is not required. They follow more circuitous paths to this end.

A common device is to postpone the reliance inquiry and treat reliance as a problem of proof of damages. As the Second Circuit said in Green v. Wolf, ". . . separate trial can be had on that issue as on damages." [49] Thus, possible differences in reliance do not defeat the action. No case adopting this approach has yet completed trial on the merits and therefore reached the problem of making separate determinations of reliance for each member of the class. However, when a class numbers in the thousands it is somewhat unrealistic to expect that each class member will be called into court for the purpose of determining reliance.

Reliance presents a much more difficult factual inquiry than does the damage issue. The latter will typically require only some indication of a purchase or sale in the time period of liability—a matter which can be handled by a master without an adversary process. Reliance, on the other hand, involves intensive examination of the plaintiff's conduct, background and state of mind. It has been the central issue in many 10b–5 individual actions. These considerations make it likely that deferring the reliance inquiry effectively eliminates the dispositive effect of reliance . . . .

Another possible treatment of reliance in class actions is to change, rather than eliminate, the substantive requirement. Thus, a court could ask whether the "reasonable investor" would have relied. This standard eliminates the necessity for more than one factual inquiry, since all plaintiffs are, presumptively, reasonable investors. This formulation of the reliance element, may, however, be a mark of its demise, for the new definition is peril-

---

49. 406 F.2d 291, 301 (2d Cir.), cert. denied 395 U.S. 977 (1968).

ously close to the definition of materiality in SEC v. Texas Gulf Sulphur Co.[a] If the test of materiality is whether a reasonable man would attach importance to a fact, it is hard to conceive of a situation where importance would be attached by a reasonable man but where a reasonable man would not rely. Thus, in Gerstle v. Gamble Skogmo, Inc.,[54] an action under section 14(a) and SEC rule 14a–9, the court remarked that "if the 'reasonable man' test has been satisfied . . . personal reliance can be inferred and reliance by the individual shareholder may be inferred." There can be little doubt that this definition departs significantly from the *List* test of causation in fact.

Still other courts deal with reliance by finding that it exists a priori. Thus, in Weisman v. M. C. A., Inc.,[56] the court proposed that reliance exists whenever there is a purchase of stock—which is always. Even if the case involves a sale, there must necessarily have been a prior purchase. The court viewed reliance as characteristic of all holders of stock in that they rely on the good faith and fair dealing of corporate management.

A similar form of a priori reliance relates to market prices. In Herbst v. Able[57] the court found a material omission of fact and misrepresentations resulting in overstated earnings. Plaintiff class was comprised of holders of convertible debentures who exercised their conversion rights during the omission-misrepresentation period. The court reasoned that since the market price of the stock went up during the omission period, and since all purchasers (holders of convertible debentures) "presumably" react to increased market prices, there was a fraud on the market common to all members of the class. Thus, through the heroic assumption that market prices are the sole explanation for purchases, the court neutralized differences in reliance .   .   .   .

A few courts have yielded to the common question dilemma by stating that reliance is not a necessary element of a cause of action under 10b–5. Thus, in Kahan v. Rosenstiel,[59] a suit for attorney's fees, the Third Circuit had to decide whether a mooted class action in which Kahan had been counsel had stated a meritorious cause of action. The court stated that "proof of reliance is not an independent element which must be alleged to establish a cause of action," because it would make recovery for the class difficult and because any material defect in a statement carries with it the implication that a "reasonable shareholder" had relied.

The tide may be turning toward express elimination of reliance with the Supreme Court's decision in Mills v. Electric Auto-Lite Co.[62] In *Mills*

a. 401 F.2d 833 (2d Cir. 1968), cert. denied 394 U.S. 976 (1969), on remand, 312 F.Supp. 77 (S.D.N.Y.1970), aff'd in part, 446 F.2d 1301 (2d Cir. 1971), cert. denied 404 U.S. 1005 (1971). Ed. note.

54. 298 F.Supp. 66 (E.D.N.Y.1969) [, mod. on other grounds 478 F.2d 1281 (2d Cir. 1973)] . . . .

56. 45 F.R.D. 258, 269 (D.Del.1968) . . . .

57. 47 F.R.D. 11, 16 (S.D.N.Y.1969) [, order modified 49 F.R.D. 286 (S.D.N.Y. 1970)].

59. 424 F.2d 161, 173–74 (3d Cir. 1970) (Adams, J.), rev'g 300 F.Supp. 447 (D.Del.1969), cert. denied 398 U.S. 950 (1970).

62. 396 U.S. 375 (1970) (Harlan, J.), rev'g 403 F.2d 429 (7th Cir. 1968), rev'g 281 F.Supp. 826 (N.D.Ill.1967).

plaintiffs sued derivatively and as a class of minority shareholders to set aside a merger, alleging a failure by Auto-Lite's directors to disclose in a proxy statement recommending the merger that they were under the control and domination of the acquiring company. The suit was grounded on section 14(a) of the 1934 Act and SEC rule 14a–9. The district court, ruling on plaintiffs' motion for summary judgment, decided that there was a material omission, but that a hearing would have to be held to determine whether there was a causal connection between the omission and the injury. After the hearing, the court held that since the votes of minority shareholders were necessary to approve the merger, the requisite causal relationship had been shown. The court of appeals reversed on the causation point, explaining that the test of causation was the same as the test of reliance—whether the injured parties relied on the misrepresentation. However, "rightly" [66] concluding that it would be impossible to determine the reliance of thousands of individuals, the Seventh Circuit adopted another test: plaintiffs would prevail unless defendants could show that the merger was fair. Justice Harlan's opinion for the Supreme Court rejected this fairness approach, holding instead that where "the proxy solicitation itself, rather than the particular defect in the solicitation materials, was an essential link in the accomplishment of the transaction," reliance need not be established.

Mills clearly does not dispose of the reliance question in 10b–5 actions. . . . But, faced with "thousands of investors" who may or may not have relied, all three courts in *Mills* accommodated the class by restricting the reliance element. The same problem of determining reliance by each of the "thousands of investors" in a class suit must be resolved under 10b–5. Indeed, the reliance cases so far reviewed indicate that 10b–5 law is fast approaching the *Mills* result. . . .

. . . Unlike reliance . . ., the requirement that a misrepresentation or omission be material generally does not provide a basis for differentiating members of a plaintiff class. The cause of action arises out of some incident of alleged misconduct by defendant. If that incident is material for one member of the class, it is material for all members of the class. In these situations, the materiality notion remains strong.

However, in another setting—where several minor and usually different misrepresentations or omissions are alleged to constitute a "deceptive device" [107] or an "artifice to defraud" [108]—the class action device facilitates a finding of materiality and thus broadens the incidence of liability under 10b–5. Green v. Wolf Corp.,[109] a leading case, is illustrative. Plaintiff class alleged misrepresentations in three prospectuses issued over more than

---

66. This is Justice Harlan's characterization of the Seventh Circuit's conclusion . . . .

107. Section 10(b) . . . provides: "[It shall be unlawful] [t]o use or employ . . . any manipulative or deceptive device or contrivance in contravention of such rules and regulations as the Commission may prescribe as necessary or appropriate in the public interest or for the protection of investors."

108. Rule 10b–5 . . . provides: "[It shall be unlawful] [t]o employ any device, scheme or artifice to defraud . . . ."

109. 406 F.2d 291 (2d Cir. 1968) [, cert. denied 395 U.S. 977 (1969)].

a year. Each document overstated the amount of cash available for distribution to shareholders. Defendants argued that the proposed class—all those who bought stock during the year—could not be maintained because the content and the materiality of the various statements differed. The theory was that the first of the misrepresentations may not have been material and, therefore, a member of plaintiff class who bought before the second, perhaps material, misrepresentation could not recover. The court held, however, that all the statements were alike in material respects and that even if there were differences, the series of misstatements constituted a common course of conduct in a scheme to defraud. . . .

Under the "scheme" approach, a potential plaintiff who bought after a single misrepresentation that was not itself material can nevertheless recover by instituting a class action on behalf of those in his situation, plus others who purchased after subsequent or prior misrepresentations by defendants. The plaintiff relies on these other misrepresentations to establish a scheme to defraud a class of investors. Moreover, materiality is provided by later misrepresentations or the cumulative effect of several non-material misrepresentations. The common questions objection that the statements differ fails because all statements are pursuant to the scheme. Thus, the class action device operates in conjunction with the scheme rubric to impose liability in situations where an individual action could not be successful. . . .

One by-product of a broad use of the scheme theory in class actions may be the expansion of the number of defendants. This may be necessary when the misrepresentations have been made by different parties over a long period of time. Plaintiff must, in that case, show some connection between the defendants if a common course of conduct or scheme theory is to succeed. An allegation of conspiracy may provide the necessary connection.[121] The most striking use of a scheme-plus-conspiracy approach to ease materiality requirements occurred in Harris v. Palm Springs Alpine Estates, Inc.[122] A class of investors in a "secured 10% Earnings Program" of the Los Angeles Trust Deed and Mortgage Exchange sued the company, its officers and 40 groups of real estate subdividers. The court seems to have relied on a prior action by the Securities and Exchange Commission, SEC v. Los Angeles Trust Deed & Mortgage Exchange,[123] in holding that there was a proper allegation of both a conspiracy linking defendants and a scheme linking a number of misrepresentations for the purpose of withstanding a motion to dismiss. Given this holding, differences of materality of misrepresentations surrounding the sale of securities to the more than 8,000 investors were of no consequence; defendant's common question defense to the class action was dismissed.

Using the scheme strategy in class actions under 10b–5 helps avoid problems of matching plaintiffs, time periods, misrepresentations and defendants. If plaintiff establishes a scheme, all members of the plaintiff class will have a claim against all defendants, and the materiality of particular misstatements need not be shown. But the expansion of 10b–5 liability

121. The use of this theory is traceable to antitrust precedents . . . .

122. 329 F.2d 909 (9th Cir. 1964).

123. 186 F.Supp. 830 (S.D.Cal.1960).

through class actions based on a scheme to defraud is not without limitation. A scheme approach necessarily implies a larger class of plaintiffs, and there may be significant practical and procedural problems, relating to representation, conflicts among the members of the class and notice, which limit the effectiveness of this approach . . . .

III. Expanded Use of the Class Action Device: Explanations and Implications

. . . If substantive law is changing as a result of the pressures of conservation of judicial resources, compensation and deterrence, it is important to see how these pressures are being served by the expansion of 10b–5 liability.

The assertion that class actions conserve judicial resources is open to serious challenge. Class actions are instituted under 10b–5 in situations where no, or very few, individuals would bother to bring suit. The expectation that class actions would save time was premised on the assumption that many individuals would sue separately. This is somewhat unrealistic, insofar as apathetic individuals with small claims are likely to be unaware of their rights. Indeed, the unlikely incidence of individual actions is used as an argument to support the compensation objective. . . . [T]he management problems in class actions can consume a great deal of judicial time. Further, the complex nature of the procedural problems can trigger a series of motions and appeals on these issues long before a court reaches the merits.

That class actions will increase compensation is similarly problematic. . . . [A]pathy [appears] with regard to the collection of damages. In securities cases where a plaintiff class is easily identified and transfer records are kept, this problem may be circumvented by mailing a check directly to those who bought or sold between certain dates. However, where . . . a large percentage of stock is held in street name or in trust by a large institution, the problem of identifying persists. Further . . ., where a thousand investors were involved, individuals in a mobile society are difficult to trace, even if they can be identified.

Pomerantz [a prominent plaintiff class action attorney] suggests an alternative distribution system, based on the doctrine of *cy pres*, in which damages would be a form of automatic relief given to that class most similar to the one actually harmed. This form of relief already may occur in a derivative suit where the shareholders have changed by the time the corporation recovers damages. Conceivably it could be implemented in antitrust cases . . . by lowering the price-differential on odd-lot commissions for a time sufficient to cover the damages. The theory would be that a close identity exists over time between odd-lot purchasers. It is, however, difficult to imagine an equally satisfactory solution in a *Texas Gulf Sulphur* situation. The closest class to the actual sellers is probably the present shareholders who are, however, indirectly (that is, through the corporation) defendants. The next best class is probably the public at large, which might obtain uncollected damages through escheat. This alternative, however, is far from compensation of the injured class, and may be a better argument for deterrence than for compensation.

Another reason the class may not be well compensated is that attorney's fees often consume a major portion of any damage award. These fees are substantial whether the case is settled or is fully litigated. The possibility of large settlements and consequent large attorney's fees is the basis for the contention of corporate defendants and their attorneys, that "strike suits" are common; courts, too, have recognized the danger of strike suits. The incentive for strike suits under 10b–5 will no doubt increase with the relaxation of substantive requirements since plaintiff attorneys will have increased leverage in bargaining situations. Although rule 23(e) seeks to prevent such suits through judicial approval and notice to the class of any settlement, the practical problems of implementing these safeguards have not been resolved. It is unclear, for example, whether a court can compel a named party plaintiff and his attorney to continue an action once they reach an out-of-court settlement, or whether the class interests would be protected if they were so compelled.

Moreover, compensation for defrauded investors is often paid, indirectly, by innocent shareholders of the defendant corporation. If the corporation is a defendant, or if it indemnifies its executives, any recovery will decrease the equity of existing shareholders. If compensation is desirable, it is difficult to see why, especially in a large public corporation, it should be achieved at the shareholder's expense.

The limiting case of this anomaly arises when the corporation is liquidated because of a damage award. This may be not only unfair to the shareholders but also extremely uneconomical. Creditors and employees as well as shareholders would be directly affected. Some thought should be given to the "capitalization" of class action damages by a judicially created security interest for plaintiff class in the corporation. This would avoid the harshest feature of class action damages, the lump sum payment. Existing shareholders could reasonably be expected to favor dilution of their interests over bankruptcy.

The final benefit alleged to result from expanded liability under 10b–5 is deterrence of securities fraud. This is acknowledged to be the principal objective of the Act. But the crucial question—which has never been addressed empirically—is whether and how well the current state of 10b–5 law serves the deterrence goal.

Given the costs associated with changes in the substantive law evoked by the class action device and the questionable achievement of the other two pressures used to justify these changes, it is imperative that the question of deterrence be examined on a systematic basis. It could be evaluated from a number of perspectives: through the use of market data before and after disclosures, through an examination of the Securities and Exchange Commission's ability to detect violations, through interviews of corporate managers and their counsel to test their knowledge of the potential effects of 10b–5 violations, and through an analysis of market institutions which presently facilitate the use of inside information. Until comprehensive analysis of data along these lines is available, the evolving expansion of liability under 10b–5 class actions may be both undesirable and unwarranted.

———

1.   Professor Scott locates the impact of the class action in two different realms—on the reliance requirement and on the materiality requirement. With reliance, the requirement is relaxed or dropped in an effort to accommodate the class action; with materiality, the class action "facilitates" a finding that the requirement is satisfied.   Are these "effects" equivalent?   Are they both "substantive"?

2.   Are there *any* important procedural devices that do not have similar "unintended" substantive effects?   From that perspective you might speculate as to the substantive effects of our diffuse and redundant patterns of decisional authority (see Chapter 5), or as to the substantive effects of various modifications in discovery.

3.   The role of the class action in "reminding the judge that resolution of the dispute between the parties may affect, and correspondingly be affected by, the interests of individuals not before the court" has been described, in Developments in the Law—Class Actions, 89 Harv.L.Rev. 1318, 1366–67 (1976), as follows:

> The heuristic function of class actions is most apparent in cases where relief awarded to the immediate parties would obviously affect the interests of absentees or would be obviously affected by the actions of absentees.   For example, where a number of individuals claim rights to a share of a fund too small to satisfy in full every individual's claim, courts readily allow a class action to be brought to allocate the fund among the competitors.   A series of suits by individual competitors might result in a situation where each competitor possessed the right to claim in full against the fund, putting the holder of the fund in the quandary of having to decide which of a number of equally binding judgments to obey.   Moreover, since the fund is limited, each competitor would be affected by the outcome of every other competitor's lawsuit.   To whatever extent recovery rights are awarded one competitor, the difficulties other competitors would face in recovering would be increased.

4.   For other essays in this volume dealing with the topic of class actions, see the following essays: Cover (chapter 2), Yeazell (chapter 4), Kalven and Rosenfield (chapter 4), Wright (chapter 4), Bell (chapter 4).

SECTION C.   SEPARATING SUBSTANCE AND PROCEDURE AS A STRATEGY FOR REFORM

The preceding sections of this chapter have stressed the interdependence of procedure and substance in a variety of contexts.   Despite that interdependence, accepted constitutional doctrine conceives of procedural protections as being constitutional mandates even where substantive constitutional guarantees are difficult or impossible to find.   The distinction between substantive and procedural due process has remained important in constitutional law while the procedure/substance dichotomies in other areas have become objects of skepticism or even of scorn.   In the following article, Professor Grey considers whether the differential treatment afforded to questions of "process" creates a sufficiently intelligible or coherent line for constitutional lawyers.

Thomas C. Grey, **Procedural Fairness and Substantive Rights***

. . . In my view, there is a paradox here. The Constitution is indifferent to the very intense and yet fragile interests of applicants for government jobs or for clemency [even to the point of not insisting upon procedural protections] as long as the officials in charge of deciding on those applications are left unguided by substantive rules governing those decisions. The Constitution is indifferent to whether those decisions are subject to substantive rules. If such rules are adopted, the Constitution is almost entirely indifferent to their content. The Constitution is even indifferent to the question whether the benefits in question are available at all. But if the benefits are made available, and the conditions for bestowing them are defined by rules, the Constitution closely constrains the discretion of the rule-making authorities to design the procedures under which individual claims for the benefits in question are granted or rejected . . . .

In explaining this paradox, it does not suffice to make reference to the importance and fragility of the individual interests at stake. By hypothesis, those interests are not sufficient to require the benefits to be granted at all. Nor does it suffice to advert to the inclinations of officials to slight those interests in their decisions whether or not to grant the benefits, when those inclinations are as much present when bestowal of the benefits is not governed by rules. Indeed, the rule-making authorities are left with full discretion to slight those interests as much as they wish in establishing the substantive terms of the rules governing the bestowal of benefits.

It is tempting to resolve the paradox legalistically; to argue that the Constitution requires fair procedure, but not clemency or job security or welfare. . . .

The truth is that nothing in the language or historical background of the constitutional due process clauses requires or even strongly suggests such [a position]. The constitutional text forbids deprivation of "life, liberty or property without due process of law." Historically, the rights of life, liberty, and property were regarded as natural (and constitutional) rights which the legislatures could neither create nor destroy. The characterization of legislatively created benefits like job tenure or welfare payments as property—much less life or liberty—would not have occurred to the framers of our due process clause.

Traditionally, benefits such as these—benefits which governments can grant or withdraw in their discretion—have been described as "privileges" rather than rights, and as such outside the protection of the due process clauses. Where there was legislative discretion to create and define the substantive terms of a benefit program, there was equal legislative discretion to give structure to the procedures under which that program was administered. With respect to such discretionary programs, the process established

* *Source*: 18 Nomos, Due Process 182. 190–202 (1977). Professor of Law, Stanford University.

by the authority with the discretion to define the program was the only process which was "due."

Modern courts have rejected this traditional position and the "right-privilege distinction" that underlies it. But their rejection cannot be based on the language or the historical meaning of the due process clauses. It must be justified by arguments from contemporary moral ideals implicit in the general concept of procedural fairness. And those arguments must confront the paradox presented by constitutional indifference to the substantive content and indeed to the very existence of benefit programs, combined with deep constitutional concern for the procedures through which those programs are administered once established.

As a first approach to the paradox, one might argue that it is not the content but the source of the programs which gives special force to the requirement that they be accurately enforced. Statutes such as those creating job security or establishing a welfare program may not themselves be required by justice or morality, but they have been passed by a democratically elected legislature, and as such represent the popular will. On this view, which stems from notions of the separation of powers, due process constraints are designed to prevent the circumvention of the legislative will by bureaucrats or executive officials through the kind of careless or intentional misapplication of statutes which can be caused or permitted by excessively informal procedures.

This attempt to justify review for procedural fairness as a device to protect legislators from bureaucrats cannot withstand analysis. Any procedure invalidated on grounds of due process has itself been either mandated directly by the legislature itself, or created by executive officials under express or implied legislative authority. Procedures lacking such legislatively granted authority are unlawful without reference to constitutional due process; they are invalid because they violate statutory law. Due process—if it is to be the vital notion it has been in our constitutional law—must be a restraint on legislative as well as on executive procedural design.

Further, norms of due process are not applicable only to the enforcement of democratically promulgated substantive laws. Even a dictator may establish substantive laws the administration of which can be criticized as procedurally unfair. His substantive criminal code might not be very different from our own; but if in trials of alleged offenders, evidence was taken in secret, the judge was dependent on the executive, and the defendant was not allowed to be heard, the dictator would be subject to legitimate criticism for procedural injustice as well as for undemocratic rule. The same point can be made with respect to the application of norms of procedural fairness in the many situations where the applicable substantive norms are not legislated or promulgated at all; as, for example, when a parent decides a dispute between children or indeed whenever customary substantive norms are applied. It is, in short, simply not useful to regard procedural due process merely as an aspect of the theory of separation of powers, or as a protection of government by popular consent.

A second approach [to the paradox] would treat the special concern for procedural fairness as based on the morality of contractual obligation.

Where substantive norms—whatever their source or status—govern a dispute, they generate in the parties to the dispute the legitimate expectation that these norms will be accurately applied. Even if the substantive rules are themselves only the product of a legislative balancing of conflicting interests, or indeed even if their content is quite arbitrary and devoid of any intrinsic moral force, the frustration of the expectation that they will be followed is felt as injustice. Morality does not require me to help my neighbor move his furniture, even though he would be happier if I did; but if I *promise* to help him and then do not (without adequate excuse), I have wronged him. Similarly, the constitution may not require governments to grant job tenure to their employees or welfare payments to their needy citizens, but statutes establishing such programs create expectations which if frustrated trigger a universal sense of injustice. Due process norms then operate to enforce a kind of "truth-in-lawmaking," to prevent frustration, through unduly inaccurate procedures, of expectations generated by substantive norms which by their terms guarantee benefits . . . .

[But] the promissory theory does not adequately resolve the paradox of due process. If we think of a benefit program established by law as a promise or set of promises establishing rights in the beneficiaries, why should we look only to the substantive provisions of the law defining the program as terms of the promise? The program establishes not only substantive entitlements, but also procedures for determining in individual cases whether the substantive terms are met. Government employees may not be fired except for cause—as determined by the following procedure. People meeting certain conditions are entitled to welfare—as determined by the following procedure.

Now imagine a due process attack charging that the procedures are error-prone, so that the expectations generated by the program will be unfairly frustrated, the promise will be broken. What is the promise? Is it that *every* claimant who in fact meets the terms of the program will receive the benefit? No one could sensibly read it that way; a procedure could not possibly be devised which would be wholly error-free. On the other hand, the terms of the program itself "promise" only that persons will receive the substantive benefits, subject to the error rate one would expect to result from application of the procedures established by the statute. Yet this promise will invariably be kept if the statute is enforced according to its terms. And if the statutorily prescribed procedures are not complied with, we again need no concept of due process or fairness to find them illegal— they violate the terms of the statute itself.

It might be argued that I have posed a false dilemma in describing a statute as promising either an (impossible) foolproof set of procedures or simply the enforcement of its own procedural terms. Perhaps popular expectations do not form around the actual, highly technical, procedural terms of statutory programs, although they do around the basic substantive terms. A benefit program might be thought to generate the expectation that its substantive terms will be enforced with a "normal" or "reasonable" degree of accuracy in application. The standard of normality would be determined by reference to the sorts of procedural safeguards commonly provided for already existing programs of a similar type. The moral force of that standard is again promissory—when a new statutory right is established, its beneficiaries can fairly expect that it will be enforced with the degree of accuracy and formality of procedure with which they have been accustomed in their similar previous dealings with the state. They cannot fairly be expected to look to "the fine print"—that is, the statute's own specifications of procedure—and to modify their general procedural expectations accordingly.

The difficulty with this suggestion appears when one probes more deeply into the factors that must be considered in making the judgment what is a "normal" level of procedural formality for the administration of a given statutory benefit. When one tries to assess how much and what kind of procedure would "normally" be attached to the adjudication of claims to a statutory benefit, one searches for some other benefit like it in relevant ways in order to establish a standard. What are the proper criteria of similarity? What other benefits would one compare, for instance, to those created by a statutory welfare program? Some might find the most relevant comparison in private or institutional charity programs, which are generally regarded as providing benefits as a matter of grace with virtually complete freedom of choice in the donor—a comparison which would suggest that very few or no procedural protections are required in welfare programs. Others might argue that the relevant comparison is to other economic subsidies established by law, such as those for farmers or the maritime industry. Still others would argue that because errors against welfare claimants, as distinguished from other subsidy beneficiaries, will lead to real misery and degradation, the relevant comparison is to the criminal law, where the most rigorous procedural safeguards are erected against the undeserved misery which results when a defendant is falsely convicted. Against this, it can be urged that the welfare program implicates a far more significant public interest than does the criminal process in simple, inexpensive and informal procedures—perhaps because of the great number of very similar claims, perhaps also because in welfare programs money spent on cumbersome procedures means less money to be spent directly on the needy recipients.

My point in listing these arguments is neither to be exhaustive nor to endorse any or all of them; but rather to point out that the quest for a "normal" level of procedural formality is by no means a simple factual inquiry. It is rather an exercise in evaluation; a search for the reasonable or appropriate level of procedure, which must take account of the values tugging in favor of greater or lesser procedural formality. Other things being equal, the stronger the substantive case for the benefit being provided to those claiming it, the stronger the case for procedures designed to prevent erroneous denials of the benefit. In the limiting case of a benefit which has behind it no independent claim of right—so that apart from the statute guaranteeing it, no one had any case for having it provided—it seems that it would be impossible to determine a "normal" or "reasonable" level of procedure which its recipients could properly expect. In the case of such a benefit, the only procedure that could reasonably be expected would be that procedure actually specified in the statute . . . .

In general, the promissory theory of procedural fairness is, like the separation of powers theory, inadequate to resolve the paradox of due process. Upon analysis, it turns out that judgments of the appropriate level or procedure required in the administration of a benefit program must vary according to judicial evaluation of the force of the substantive case for providing the benefit in the first place. It thus remains a puzzle why special constitutional norms of justice should be applied to the procedures under which such benefits are provided, but the substance and even the existence of the benefit programs themselves are left to the discretion of the legislative authority.

In my view, the paradox of procedural fairness as I have stated it is not resolvable. A decision to treat a legislatively created benefit program as subject to the constitutional-moral constraints of due process, while regarding the substance or existence of the program as a matter of legislative grace, would be simply an unjustifiable anomaly . . . .

Using the example of welfare benefits, let me explain what I mean by this perhaps somewhat startling assertion. If I am correct in my thesis, the application of norms of procedural fairness to welfare decisions means that the courts regard claims to welfare benefits as claims of substantive right with a basis beyond the welfare statutes themselves. The overriding of legislative judgment as to the proper procedure for administering welfare programs means that the courts regard the *substance* of the welfare programs as no longer entirely a matter of legislative discretion, subject to legislative alteration at will and indeed to legislative withdrawal.

Surely this conclusion is contradicted by the emphatically proclaimed judicial position that the substance of welfare programs is not subject to probing judicial review, and by the general understanding that there is no judicially enforceable "constitutional right to welfare." [14] Surely if a legislature repealed its welfare program altogether, the courts would not require it to reenact the program and enjoin it to raise tax moneys to support it. Surely, the objection continues, when the courts speak of an "entitlement" to welfare as the ground for judicial scrutiny of the procedures used in the program, they refer only to the fact that the legislature has chosen to structure the substance of existing welfare programs through reasonably definite rules governing eligibility and benefits provided.

Let me take the last point first, to explain what I mean by the existence of a substantive right to welfare. A right—as I mean the concept—is more than a legislatively created entitlement. To illustrate the point, consider the following example. Suppose that a legislature, unhappy with the procedural restraints placed upon its welfare program by the courts, sought to escape from those restraints by removing the entitlement element from its program.

As a first effort in this direction, the legislature might simply designate the welfare program as one designed only to express public charity or generosity, and not to confer any entitlement to benefits on the eligible recipients. Rules governing eligibility and amount of payment could be redefined—

---

14. On the refusal to give substantive scrutiny to the provisions of welfare laws, the leading case is Dandridge v. Williams, 397 U.S. 471 (1970).

perhaps by way of a statutory preamble—as no more than internal directives from the legislature to the executive, designed to channel the public charity in the way most desired by its collective donors, the taxpayers.

I think most constitutional lawyers would agree that a legislature would not (and should not) be allowed to escape the constitutional requirements of due process in welfare administration by this kind of purely formal recasting of its welfare laws.   But to reach this conclusion, one must abandon the premise that the legislature has plenary control over the substance of the program.   There is nothing impossible in logic or unprecedented in practice about a legislatively created program, structured by internal directives to its administrators, which incidentally confers benefits on individuals who have no legally enforceable entitlement to those benefits.[15]   If a legislature would not be allowed to recharacterize its welfare program into this mold and thereby escape the imposition of the restraints of fair procedure by the judiciary, a first substantive check on legislative discretion in the name of a right to welfare has been imposed.

Now suppose that the legislature—frustrated in its first attempt to escape the judicial requirements of due process—takes the further step of repealing the substantive provisions governing eligibility and benefit levels. The legislature might, for example, repose in a commissioner of welfare authority to dispense "to persons whom he in his absolute discretion determines to be needy and worthy of public assistance, such sums as he in his absolute discretion determines to be appropriate."   Such legislation would remove any entitlement to welfare benefits by converting the state's welfare program into one ungoverned by substantive standards.   In my view, it would not and should not work, any more than did the purely verbal attempt to legislate away the entitlement status of welfare benefits.

The most likely outcome of this statute would be that the commissioner would enact, in the form of administrative guidelines or regulations, rules to determine who should be eligible for welfare and for how much.   These rules would perhaps closely resemble the preexisting statutory framework. But whether they did or not—and whatever efforts were made to label the rules "internal" or "administrative"—they would and should be treated as substantive standards defining the entitlement to welfare, and due process constraints would be imposed on their administration.   The courts would, I think, say that the replacement of statutory standards by "internal" regulations was no less futile in destroying the entitlement status of the benefits than had been the formal statutory preamble.

In the unlikely event that no such regulations or guidelines were adopted, another aspect of due process doctrine would, I believe, be brought into play.   If the decisions of the commissioner followed no standards, an applicant denied benefits could, I think, successfully challenge the denial on the basis that it was arbitrary.   Such a challenge—which in our constitutional tradition would fall under the rubric of due process—would not be based on a claim of procedural unfairness .   .   .   .   It would be a claim

15. Welfare programs themselves were until very recently regarded in this light. . . .

of substantive injustice—substantive due process—against the lawless administration of the welfare program. A court accepting the argument would order that the program be administered according to ascertainable standards —which then would themselves trigger the requirements of fair procedure in their application.

If I am right in my assessment of how courts would deal with these legislative attempts to remove the "entitlement" nature of welfare benefits, my argument reveals an important respect in which welfare benefits are a kind of constitutional "right" not entirely subject to the substantive control of the legislature. For it is by no means the case that every benefit—even every important benefit—bestowed by government would be treated in the same way. For instance, the power of executive clemency is almost invariably exercised without the guidance of substantive rules, under the virtually absolute discretion of the relevant authorities. Similarly, the hiring of public employees in the first instance need not as a matter of constitutional requirement be carried out according to rules and standards whose application is then subject to judicially imposed requirements of fair procedure. Conversely, even if public hiring *were* internally directed by guidelines stating criteria for personnel officials to use in hiring applicants, the courts would I think not treat these regulations as creating entitlements to be hired in those meeting the criteria set forth, entitlements enforceable in proceedings subject to the constraints of constitutional due process.

On the other hand, it must be conceded that welfare is not a full-fledged, judicially enforceable, constitutional right. A legislature balked in its attempt to get free of procedural restrictions imposed on its welfare program would retain the power to reduce the cost of that program by cutting benefits across the board, reducing the number of recipients, or even eliminating the welfare program altogether. The courts would not closely scrutinize the steps taken and the lines drawn in such a substantive cost-cutting program—at least such is present constitutional doctrine.

The reasons for the courts' reluctance to intervene with the substance of welfare programs in this way lie, I believe, in the courts' present judgment of the proper limitations on their institutional competence and authority. Even if they considered that some guarantee of minimum material support for those unable to support themselves was a fundamental individual right—a right properly deserving of constitutional status—they might quite properly think it was a right beyond their power to enforce against infringement by direct legislative withdrawal of funds. At least— in the extreme case of total legislative withdrawal from public assistance— enforcement of the right to welfare would require the judiciary to order the disbursement of large sums of public money, to draft a complex scheme of social legislation, and to force the collection or diversion of massive tax revenues. None of these tasks are within our traditional conception of the judicial role, and that institutional consideration would probably prevent straightforward judicial protection of the right to welfare.

On the other hand, judicial enforcement of the requirements of the rule of law and of procedural fairness in the structure and the administration of welfare programs are quite reasonably within traditional conceptions of the judicial role. The difference is one of degree rather than kind—enforcement of formal procedures does cost public money—and it would be, I think, a mistake either to predict or inflexibly to prescribe that the courts never move on to scrutinize the substance of welfare programs. In the meantime, however, the right to welfare remains—with its partial judicial enforcement, confined to the procedural realm—as an obligation of government more stringent than a mere privilege, and indeed as a kind of "shadow constitutional right."

Let me try to summarize the general conception of procedural fairness suggested and tentatively sketched in this essay. Procedural fairness involves a special moral concern for the correct and accurate decision of disputes which affect substantive rights. Its norms impinge from the outside on decision-making institutions, and require of those institutions more concern for the substantive rights which would be threatened or infringed by erroneous decisions than the institutions (or officials) would otherwise be inclined to show, given the natural balance those institutions are likely to strike between the competing claims of accurate decision, cost, and institutional self-interest.

It makes sense to impose special procedural controls from outside the authoritative decision-making institution—whether through the moral check of conscience, or the external institutional check of judicial review—only when the substantive right placed at hazard has its source outside the decision-making institution itself. Thus "entitlements" created only by the decision-making institution's own rules should not be protected by external restraints of procedural fairness. These, in the old terminology of the law, are "mere privileges." The kinds of substantive rights which properly trigger due process restraints are categorical moral rights or, in the legal context, rights with a hierarchical status above the rules of the decision-making institution. In the usual case—where the decision-making institution's authority derives from the legislature—the only substantive rights having this status are constitutional rights. Some constitutional substantive rights may be judicially enforced largely or only through procedural due process constraints, because institutional constraints on judicial power prevent their more direct enforcement . . . .

---

1. Professor Grey finds a "paradox" when government is left theoretically unfettered as to substantive choices, but is substantially constrained in the processes by which any of the ("free") choices made are to be subsequently implemented. But is it not, at one level, simply common sense to maintain that substantive choice must entail certain procedural consequences? For example, one may not ask in a substantive vacuum whether it is "just" to use a lottery procedure to determine "who will die." While it may be "just" to use such a procedure to choose who must go on a "necessary" suicide mission in war, it is most emphatically "unjust" to use the same lottery to determine who shall be hung as a murderer. See Greely, The Equality of Allocation by Lot, 12 Harv.C.R.–C.L.L.Rev. 113 (1977). See also D. Daube, Collaboration with Tyranny, in Rabbinic Law (1965). Shouldn't "due process" reflect such judgments?

2.   Grey further suggests that a quasi-substantive due process constraint is likely to operate whenever a program is administered in a fashion inconsistent with an institution's internal regulations, procedures, precedents, and the like.   Actually, in a case which was decided after Grey's article was published, Mr. Justice Rehnquist has cast doubt upon such a supposition when he commented as follows:

> Respondent also contends that petitioners [essentially the University of Missouri-Kansas City Medical School] failed to follow their own rules respecting evaluation of medical students and that this failure amounted to a constitutional violation under Service v. Dulles, 354 U.S. 363 (1957).   We disagree with both respondent's factual and legal contentions . . . .   As for the legal conclusion that respondent draws, both *Service* and Accardi v. Shaughnessy, 347 U.S. 260 (1954), upon which *Service* relied, enunciate principles of federal administrative law rather than of constitutional law binding upon the States.

Board of Curators of the University of Missouri v. Horowitz, 435 U.S. 78, 92 n. 8 (1978) (in which the procedures leading to respondent Horowitz' dismissal for academic deficiencies were held not to be violative of federal due process).   One wonders whether literally lawless incoherence in a government program violates the current Court's version of the Constitution.

3.   Is Professor Grey correct in maintaining that it is the Court's view on the substance of a program that determines both whether a given process is necessary in adjudication and whether a degree of internal order and consistency is required in administration?   While Grey suggests that welfare decisions must have consistent, articulated, specified standards for eligibility if the program is to exist at all, he would not maintain that similar characteristics must mark, say, administration of the projects of the National Endowment for the Arts.   Is he right?

4.   Does Grey's critique of the preferred place for "procedural due process" apply with equal validity to the constitutional strategy of regulating *process* but not *substance* in the criminal law?   For an analysis of that strategy the reader may wish to consult Underwood, The Thumb on the Scales of Justice: Burdens of Persuasion in Criminal Cases, 86 Yale L.J. 1299 (1977).

Chapter 3

THE CONCEPT OF A FORMAL PROCEDURAL SYSTEM

We began our inquiry in the domain of values. We asked how process might be valued; and then, in the chapter on the relationship between substance and procedure, we speculated on the relationship between two categories of values. We now turn to the institutions that embody and implement those values.

Central to any understanding of legal procedures are courts and adjudication—the process of invoking the power of a court or agency; the process of informing the judge, jury, or agency; the process of transforming that information into a decision, and then implementing the decision. The focus on adjudication is justly deserved; in Part II of this book we propose to examine the various elements of the adjudicatory process in some detail. But first, we wish to pause and consider adjudication as a part of a larger system that embodies and implements procedural values. That in turn introduces two ideas we believe central to this systemic perspective—"boundaries" and "roles." They are the subject of this chapter.

SECTION A. THE BOUNDARIES WITHIN A PROCEDURAL SYSTEM

The systemic perspective views adjudication as one among many devices for performing the same function, whether that function be settling disputes or generating norms. So placed, the question naturally arises as to how to differentiate adjudication from other types of processes. The task becomes one of identifying the boundaries of adjudication and also of testing the strength of those boundaries.

1. THE LINE BETWEEN NEGOTIATION AND ADJUDICATION

In these first essays we begin with a limited conception of adjudication as a means of settling disputes. As so conceived, the conventional wisdom is to distinguish adjudication from other processes of dispute settlement, more consensual ones, denoted by the term "negotiation" or "conciliation." Both Professors Golding and Eisenberg, in the selections that follow, provide material for questioning that understanding. (Professor Shapiro's essay on courts in chapter 4 also speaks to the issue, though more in terms of the ideal of impartiality.)

Professor Golding distinguishes adjudication from "bilateral bargaining" and "good offices," but sees adjudication as part of a larger category—called "jural-like forms of dispute settling." He includes within that category "adjudication," "conciliation" (or "mediation"), and "therapeutic integration" (in conjunction with this last category, you might look at Martha Minow's essay on the judgment of Solomon, in chapter 6, pointing to the many-layered quality of adjudication). Golding notes some differences among "adjudication," "conciliation," and "therapeutic integration," but on the whole he seems more intent on uncovering the similarities and continuities—the boundary crossings. He pursues this intention by trying to construct a unified set of procedural rules, ones that would govern all types of jural-like dispute-settling mechanisms. Professor Eisenberg continues this theme. He points to common bases of decision—principle—in both adjudication and conciliation, thereby contradicting the conventional understanding of these two forms of dispute settlement.

Martin P. Golding, Dispute Settling and Justice *

. . . Our first task is to examine the activity of dispute settling. In effect, we will attempt to supply a partial answer to a series of questions posed by the legal realist Karl N. Llewellyn. "What," he asked, "is a court? Why is a court? How much of what we know as 'court' is accidental, historically conditioned—how much is essential to the job? " [1] However, the institutions we formally know as courts are not the only ones that undertake the settling of disputes. There is, rather, a variety of dispute-settling processes engaged in by various kinds of bodies, public and private, formal and informal. These processes, which resemble each other in significant respects, might be called *jural-like* forms of dispute settling. . . .

Jural-like dispute settling involves (1) a dispute settler, a particular *third party* (who may be more than one individual) who "stands between" (2) *particular disputants* and settles, or attempts to settle, (3) *their particular dispute*. There must be (4) some kind of *hearing* of the dispute, the presentation to the third party of each disputant's side of the controversy. And (5) the materials so received must be *used* by the third party in arriving at the settlement. There is a sad tale of two farmers disputing the ownership of a bean patch. They appeared before the Emir, who summarily ordered that the farmers be decapitated and took the land for himself. Now the Emir brought the matter to an end, but he did not settle the *farmers'* dispute. He did not even hear it. Jural-like dispute settling requires a setting of "persuasive conflict," [2] as we may call it, and the use of its materials by the third party. . . .

From this we see that jural-like dispute settling, which always involves a third party, must be distinguished from the resolution of conflict through bilateral negotiation or bargaining. Of course, if the parties should agree to settle their dispute by tossing a coin, we would have an analogy to jural-like dispute settling. But it would be only an analogy, for although there is something like a third party, the element of persuasive conflict would be absent.

* Source: Philosophy of Law (ch. 6) 106–25 (1975). Reprinted by permission. Professor of Philosophy, Duke University.

1. Jurisprudence (Chicago: University of Chicago Press, 1962), p. 374

. . . .

2. The term comes from Thomas Nixon Carver, Essays on Social Justice (Cambridge: Harvard University Press, 1915), p. 85. Carver distinguishes five chief forms of conflict: militant, gambling, persuasive, economic, and recreational.

We also see that jural-like dispute settling should be distinguished from "good offices." In good offices, diplomacy may be used by a third party to bring warring nations to direct negotiations or to agree on a method for the pacific settlement of their conflict. Good offices are designed to enable the contending of the parties to be carried on through *verbal* means. Militant conflict is thus transformed into persuasive conflict. Whenever there is a tendency toward persuasive conflict and the emergence of a third party there will be an analogy to jural-like dispute settling. Nevertheless, good offices do not quite fill the bill, for the third party is not strictly a dispute settler. He provides an environment for negotiations, and he carries and interprets communications between the parties. He does not, as the dispute settler does, *use* the materials of the persuasive conflict in order to effect a settlement. The process of good offices can easily break down if one of the disputants perceives the third party as taking on a more mediational role, for this could be viewed as a violation of the kind of *neutrality* expected in good offices. Neutrality, of course, is also expected of a dispute settler. It is one of the main elements of fairness. But this poses one of the most difficult problems in the design of dispute-settling institutions—how to harmonize neutrality with the necessity of securing and using the materials that are the basis for settling a dispute. . . .

. . . The persuasive conflict which takes place in the presence of the dispute settler, the presentation of the sides of the dispute, is an offshoot of an antecedent conflict. But this can be a conflict of desires, of interests, of claims, of demands, of rights, or simply an inability to "get along." Conflict on the normative level may have an underlying basis in disagreement over questions of fact, and the third party, in certain kinds of dispute settling, will have to decide factual issues. . . . An important function of the institution of jural-like methods of dispute settling is the forestalling of militant conflict and "self-help." . . . It is possible to design jural-like methods that serve the wider interests of justice, but it is doubtful that militant conflict often serves this end.

Persuasive conflict and the use of its materials—two essentials of jural-like dispute settlement—are not uniform phenomena, however. Dispute settling varies in the kind of use to which the materials are put, which depends on the kind of dispute settling in which the third party is engaged. Though all forms of dispute settling are alike in that they involve a hearing and a use of its materials, these common characteristics are not manifested in the same way in all the forms. We shall return to this point shortly.

First, however, a few general remarks remain to be made about the *settlement* of disputes. . . . Sir William Markby, a nineteenth-century British jurist[, in Elements of Law § 201 (6th ed. 1905),] . . . writes:

> All that the judge absolutely requires is authority to settle all disputes which come before him. . . . A tribunal without law, though scarcely within our experience, is not a contradiction.

Now I am in perfect agreement with the view that a dispute might be resolved in the absence of any substantive law governing the issues between the parties. The availability to the third party, Markby's judge, of pre-existent laws typifies only a subclass of a particular variety of jural-like dispute settling. My objection to Markby concerns the first part of the quotation.

Markby apparently holds that it is a condition of jural-like dispute settling, and its only condition, that the third party should have authority to issue a *binding decision* in the case before him. (We may assume a setting of persuasive conflict.) And he seems to identify the *settlement* with the binding decision that is issued. But bringing a dispute to an end by a simple fiat, binding as it may be, is not a guarantee that it has been settled. The Emir, in our tale of the two farmers, did *not* settle the farmers' dispute. Whether or not a decision of this kind settles a dispute depends, first of all, on its logical relationship to the terms or subject of the dispute. I shall later try to show how adherence to standards of procedural fairness promotes genuine settlement.

Secondly, moreover, we should bear in mind that the persuasive conflict in the presence of the third party is an offshoot of an antecedent conflict. Whether a binding decision settles a dispute or not depends also on the relationship it is supposed to have to the original conflict. If, for example, the antecedent conflict is comprised in part of conflicting attitudes between the parties—hard feelings—it is not at all obvious that a binding decision will resolve them. It might even exacerbate them. Similarly, a binding decision might leave conflicting interests in their original state of opposition. When is a dispute to be considered settled? Is it at the point at which the decision is made? If the terms of a decision are not carried out, if the decision is not actually enforced, has the controversy been settled? The answers depend on what we mean by "settling a dispute." Markby's meaning is not the only one. Dispute-settling processes may have a variety of *aims* and, therefore, different forms of jural-like dispute settling are possible and various functions may be served by a third party in his capacity as a dispute settler.

Now it might be said that what Markby means by "settling a dispute" is an authoritative or binding decision as to which party is right and which is wrong, a decision as to whose contentions are in some sense justified and whose not. And it might further be argued that this is the only kind of jural-like dispute settling that ought to be regarded as "legal." . . .

We shall consider three chief forms of dispute settling: (1) *adjudication,* (2) *conciliation,* and (3) *therapeutic integration.* . . . Civil litigation, commercial arbitration, and (labor) grievance arbitration provide examples of the first. Mediation of industrial disputes provides examples of the second. And certain kinds of family counseling provide examples of the third. . . .

Adjudication

[Adjudication] is the only one of the three in which the third party "decides" the dispute before him—that is, makes a determination as to who is in the right and who is in the wrong. This determination can involve deciding questions of fact, if a disagreement over facts is at the basis of the dispute, and it can also involve deciding questions of law or other normative issues. The settlement itself consists in an *award* to the winning party, which is intended as a *final* resolution of the dispute. The award also has the character of a binding decision. It is, so to speak, the "content" of such a decision. The source of the adjudicator's authority to make an award of this kind may derive from the State, as in civil litigation, or from a private agreement of the parties, as is usual in commercial arbitration. Clearly, in this type of dispute settling—because a binding decision is involved—there is special need for *procedural safeguards* to insure the fairness of the process, although the parties naturally have a greater freedom to set the procedures when it is conducted under private auspices.

The aim of adjudication, then, is the final settlement of disputes by the kind of award just described, and this appears possible only when certain conditions are met. There must, first, be "joinder of issue." For the dispute between the parties to be decided, they must meet head on, with one side denying what the other claims. . . . [I]f Jones claims that I owe him $100 and I deny it, we have joined issue. We can then each present our arguments (the factual, legal, or other normative grounds of our contentions) to the third party, and he can decide, on the weight of the arguments, whose position is justified. The materials of the persuasive conflict function as premises for drawing such a conclusion, which in turn is the basis of the award.

A second condition for the occurrence of adjudicatory settlement is that the conflict must be of a kind that can be settled by making an award. Leaving aside the question as to the senses in which the adjudicator's act of "making an award" can be binding (legally, morally, or otherwise), the award that Jones, for example, is in effect claiming must be within the power of the third party to grant. The binding decision that expresses the making of the award is something like a *command,* a directive, and it seems that not everything can be commanded. I can be told to *do* something for, or *give* something to, Jones, but I cannot be flatly commanded to love him. (I can, however, be commanded to act in a loving manner and to try to develop loving dispositions.) Adjudication is possible only for conflicts that can be settled by feasible awards.

Last, let us consider the finality of the settlement. As mentioned earlier, the persuasive conflict that takes place in the presence of the third party is an offshoot of an antecedent conflict. There is no guarantee, however, that his binding decision, which is supposed to stamp "finis" to the controversy, will in fact settle the original conflict. The antecedent conflict of interest, for example, may partly remain in its original unresolved state after the binding decision is issued. (In cases of litigation between members of a family, it frequently happens that the original conflict is actually exacerbated.) We are guaranteed finality of settlement only for the dispute that is ultimately framed in the persuasive conflict. For the purpose of adjudicatory dispute settling, the persuasive conflict must be conceived as *superseding* the antecedent conflict. This does not hold for the other forms.

Conciliation

In the second kind of jural-like dispute settling, the aim is to achieve settlement of disputes by an *adjustment* or *compromise* between the claims, demands, or interests of the parties. It is not the job of the third party to decide the dispute and make an award—in effect, impose a settlement—but rather to bring the parties to an arrangement that both willingly, though perhaps grudgingly, *accept*. The terms of the settlement may be accepted by them as a final resolution or as a temporary stopgap. Given that the task is securing the agreement of the parties, it might be thought that how this is done is immaterial (e. g., by unfairly tricking one of the sides) and that it is therefore unnecessary for the dispute settler to maintain a stance of neutrality. But aside from the consideration that adherence to standards of procedural justice promotes genuine settlement, experience shows that conciliational processes break down if one party has reason to suspect the dispute settler of partiality. And even if acceptance of the terms is secured, the aggrieved party might well renege. Individuals in conflict submit their dispute to a third party because they are unable to resolve it through bilateral negotiation, and mutuality of confidence in his neutrality is generally a requisite of a successful outcome. This is especially true of conciliation, which usually is a voluntary affair from the start.

Because the third party is not called upon to decide the dispute that he hears, joinder of issue in a strict sense is not a condition of the conciliation process. Of course, there must be some kind of conflict between the parties: one wants to practice on his trumpet and the other wants to conduct a delicate experiment; labor demands a one-dollar increase in hourly wage and management offers only fifty cents. The positions here are in some way "incompatible"—otherwise there is no dispute to settle. . . .

Just as the conciliator does not decide the dispute, he also does not decide between the arguments (factual or normative) that the sides present to support their claims or demands. The conciliator's use of the materials of the persuasive conflict therefore differs in important respects from the adjudicator's. He does not weigh the arguments in order primarily to decide who is right or whose demands are justified. Rather, the arguments give him an understanding of the complexities of the conflict and a sense of the weight that the *sides* assign to their claims and counterclaims, of what interests are at stake and what significance is attached to them, of what is "negotiable" and what is not. He learns what common interests could supply a basis for a settlement, and thus can formulate and present *proposals* to this end.

When a dispute is settled by conciliation it often happens that the parties will have to compromise over what each feels he is legally or morally entitled to. Resolution is unlikely as long as a party "stands on his rights" or sticks to a demand "on principle." The conciliator has the job of "de-ideologizing" the conflict, and will try to get the parties to focus on the broader interests that are at stake. One of his functions is that of bringing rational considerations into the discussion, and he must tactfully use his own persuasive powers to overcome hostility and deep-seated needs to assert one's superiority. Plainly, conciliation requires special skills over and above the ability to "run a court." Although we expect adherence to standards of fairness, the conciliatory process is naturally also characterized by a greater flexibility and informality than we are accustomed to in civil litigation. . . .

Therapeutic Integration

.   .   .   This [third] form of dispute settling seems especially appropriate for conflicts arising out of personality differences and "psychic incompatibility," and particularly for individuals whose relationships are intimate and affective.   It is useful for us to think of it in terms of its best example, *intensive family therapy*.   .   .   .

Intensive family therapy should be distinguished from family therapies designed to enable the parties to "cope" with each other on a more or less temporary basis.   These are closer to conciliation, and for all we know may be more effective.   Family therapy of the intensive kind seeks to bring about deep *psychic change* through which the personalities are integrated and the inner *sources* of conflict removed.   Obviously anything like strict joinder of issue is out of place here.   Although the parties are, by hypothesis, in conflict, they may not be able to formulate what the conflict is or where it lies.   The therapist must get at the roots of their troubles, and this he does through the persuasive conflict that takes place in his presence.   Its materials are interpreted by him as *symptoms* of the underlying conflict.   As in conciliation, the third party does not have the job of deciding between the claims and arguments of the parties, but one of the serious problems in the therapeutic process is that parties do often seek to win over the therapist to their side.

Therapeutic integration stands at an extreme opposite to an adjudicatory award: plainly it cannot be couched in a command to do or to give. (In conciliation, at least the *terms* of the settlement can usually be put this way.)   The fact that a procedure for change (e. g., self-expression, correcting misunderstandings, or gaining insight into difficulties) is outlined to the parties does not mean that therapeutic change is necessarily brought about.   This depends on the skill of the therapist, a skill that is exercised in terms of his psychotherapeutic theory and, it seems, a substantive notion of "health" or ideal of family life.

Another point of contrast with adjudication is that it would be highly misleading to view the persuasive conflict of the therapeutic process as superseding the antecedent conflict.   Supersession, as a matter of plain fact, hardly occurs.   The two conflicts are almost indistinguishable aspects of the same conflict.   But there is, nevertheless, a significant difference between them—the persausive conflict occurs in *the presence of a third party*, and a *neutral* one at that.   It is very pertinent that the literature on family therapy should so much emphasize the therapist's "use of himself," his "empathetic neutrality," and his capacity to "relate to the parties in an impartial, unbiased manner."   Neutrality is as functionally vital here as in other kinds of jural-like dispute settling   .   .   .   .

Procedural Justice

The second subject we have set for exploration in this chapter is *procedural justice*.   .   .   .

Does the need for fairness in procedure follow in some way from the very nature of the activity of jural-like dispute settling?   This is our main question. If this is the case, a society that provided agencies for the settling of disputes between individuals would necessarily have to build procedural justice into the design of such institutions.

I think that this view has some initial plausibility when we consider that jural-like dispute settling involves the attempt to settle the *particular disputes of particular parties*. We would be hesitant to say that a system which provided "courts" in which the dispute settler was always fatally biased against one of the parties (e. g., if one of the disputants were always made the judge) had really provided jural procedures for settling disputes, let alone just procedures. Now, it seems clear that jural-like dispute settling will wither on the vine if parties in conflict have no confidence in the fairness of the proceedings. For if the contenders have any choice in the matter, they generally will not submit their dispute to a third party whose neutrality, for example, is suspect. But the view we are considering goes further than the question of confidence, important as that is. It suggests that the desire for institutions and methods in which we can have this kind of confidence is in part based upon something more fundamental—namely, a special kind of connection between jural-like dispute settling and procedural justice.

Unfortunately, there is no name for this connection. One might describe it by saying that the concept of "dispute settling" is parasitic on the concept of "fair dispute settling." Putting the connection in this way has the advantage of not making it self-contradictory to speak of corrupt dispute settlers or unfair trials. It does imply that we cannot understand what a trial or hearing is without the concept of a fair trial or hearing. It amuses us that the ancients determined guilt by examining the entrails of chickens. But, by analogy with the above, we can identify this as a "judicial," and not simply a magical, proceeding because the ancients believed that the relevant questions could be decided in this way *and* the determination of such questions is an element of a judicial proceeding.

Nevertheless, the above statement of the connection is somewhat obscure, and I prefer the formulation . . . that adherence to standards of fairness *promotes* the settlement of disputes. A few points should be noted about this. First, adherence to fairness does not guarantee that the outcome of a jural-like process will be fair by some substantive standard. It does not even guarantee that the outcome will in fact be a settlement of the parties' dispute. On the other hand, violation of fairness does not preclude the possibility of a genuine settlement, but such an eventuality would be more a matter of accident than design. Finally, adherence to fairness does increase the likelihood that the outcome is a genuine settlement, and *this* is not a matter of accident or of some purely contingent correlation between fairness and jural-like dispute settling, but rather a consequence of the nature of the activity. I shall try to show the plausibility of this thesis in the treatment of the standards of procedural justice . . . .

Standards of Procedural Justice

.   .   .   [L]et us now turn to the standards of procedural justice
.   .   .   .   For convenience, the list will be put under three headings:

Neutrality

1. "No man should be judge in his own cause."

2. The dispute settler should have no private interest in the outcome.

3. The dispute settler should not be biased in favor of or against a party.

Persuasive Conflict

4. Each party should be given fair notice of the proceedings.

5. The dispute settler should hear the argument and evidence of both sides.

6. The dispute settler should hear a party only in the presence of the other party.

7. Each party should be given a fair opportunity to respond to the arguments and evidence of the other party.

Settlement

8. The terms of the settlement should be supportable by reasons.

9. The reasons should refer to the arguments and evidence presented.

.   .   .   Numbers 1, 5 and 9 seem to have a special status, for they, in a sense, define jural-like dispute settling. The first has also been construed to demand of a society, if it is to be a just society, that it provide mechanisms or agencies for the settling of disputes .   .   .   .   And obviously, these institutions ought to operate in a fair manner, giving the parties a sense of fair treatment. One reason is that fairness, I think, *promotes settlement* and the other is simply the matter of *confidence*, without which the institutions will not survive. The dispute settler, therefore, should be neutral as between the parties; he should be impartial and unbiased. Standard 2 helps to insure neutrality and maximize confidence.

So do the standards governing the persuasive conflict. They comprise, in a sense, the *operational* definition of neutrality—neutrality in practice. Suspicion of bias, and perhaps bias itself, can be overcome or kept within bounds if the dispute settler must hear both sides, and that in the presence of both parties. But adherence to these standards does more than help insure neutrality and equalize the parties. It raises the "litigation quality" of the whole process: disputed issues are brought out into the open and the scope and terms of the conflict receive clarification. Not only is the sense of fair treatment maximized, because a party will have some assurance that the dispute settler's actions will be based on material that the party has heard and to which he has had a chance to respond, thus mitigating the effects of "surprise," but also a more adequate and objective basis for action is achieved . . . .

We can see, I think, how these standards bring together various components of the concept of justice and how they tie in with third-party neutrality. They are, however, in need of qualification for the other forms of dispute settling. Although it would be quite improper for a judge in an adjudication to invite one of the parties for lunch to tell his side of the dispute in private, this would not be out of place in most conciliations. It is, in fact, not an uncommon practice in labor mediation. The explanation of this is plain. In adjudication the dispute settler *decides* the dispute, and in effect imposes the settlement; in conciliation the parties *agree* to the settlement. If the excluded party is satisfied with the dispute settler's proposal, he will accept it despite the private lunch. And if he is bothered by the private lunch, he can simply refuse to accept the proposal. Of course, the agreement of both parties must be secured, and hence the need for objectivity, impartiality, etc. Neutrality, here, is first of all openness and receptivity in a fashion that maintains parity and, secondly, objectivity and impartiality in explaining the position of one party to the other, in showing the reasonableness or unreasonableness of a demand, and in pointing the path to an agreement. The conciliator, it should be remembered, enters the conflict because the parties are unable to resolve it though bilateral negotiation.

A further explanation of this variation between adjudication and conciliation is that only in the former is there "joinder of issue" in a strict sense, so that the process is dominated by narrower notions of what is *relevant* to deciding the dispute. Each party will, therefore, be quite concerned about what material is presented to the adjudicator and what might influence his decision. Finally, there is the matter of substantive justice, to which conciliation has a more complex and problematic relation than adjudication. Procedural justice should serve the interests of substantive justice, and we have already considered some of the difficulties that lie in the way. In conciliation, however, it is not simply substantive justice which is at stake, if it is at stake at all, but a workable arrangement that the parties can "live with" and for which each has to compromise what he feels he is entitled to. Conciliation, therefore, is characterized by a greater flexibility, and this reflects back on the standards of fair procedure.

Therapeutic integration is an even more complicated story, and we cannot go into details on how it affects the standards of fairness. Interestingly, most family therapists and marriage counselors are quite cautious about seeing a party in private. They will do so only if there is pressing need, and will inform the party that their conversation will not be held in confidence if it reveals an issue that should be brought out into the open. The dispute settler must keep neutral, and not appear to "take sides." (It is striking how the literature on all the forms of jural-like dispute settling emphasizes this.) One reason why the question of standards of fairness in therapeutic integration is so difficult and elusive is that the persuasive conflict does not supersede the original conflict, so that the therapist is a *participant* in the family conflict. He is a participant who is not deciding a dispute or seeking an agreement, but a participant who is affecting human relationships through the therapeutic technique. But he is a participant of an odd kind—a neutral participant. He must be receptive to both sides, give each an opportunity to respond to the other, be objective, receive adequate information, and so on.

After the persuasive conflict we come, finally, to the settlement. The eighth standard of procedural justice tells us that the terms of the settlement (the adjudicatory decision, the conciliatory proposal, the therapeutic measures) should be based upon reasons, for justice excludes arbitrariness. And, according to the ninth standard, these reasons should refer back to the materials presented in the persuasive conflict. *How* they should make reference to the materials of the persuasive conflict raises questions about deliberative reasoning and also policy questions. In adjudication conducted within the framework of a legal system, the dispute settler's use of these materials is determined by the relevant law; and in therapeutic integration it is determined by psychotherapeutic theories and a concept of "health." A conciliation might also have to take into account wider economic factors. This standard, like the others, is context-dependent and its details need to be worked out.

In coming to the last group of standards we see the plausibility of the thesis that adherence to procedural fairness *promotes* the settlement of disputes rather than merely bringing them to an end. Jural-like dispute settling aims at settling the particular disputes of particular parties. Standards 8 and 9 work in cooperation, so to speak, with the previous standards. Aside from the important issue of confidence—and we have seen how complex the matters are that go into making for confidence—adherence to the standards of fair procedure, taken together, focuses the terms of the settlement on the parties' dispute. If dispute-settling processes should serve the cause of justice, they should also settle disputes. Settling the parties' dispute takes us back to neutrality, objectivity, equality, and impartiality in the hearing stage of the process. But all these considerations also support the contention that the need for fairness in procedure follows from the very nature of jural-like dispute settling . . . .

————

Melvin A. Eisenberg, **Private Ordering Through Negotiation***

. . . Nowhere does the contrast between official processes and their private counterparts appear greater than between adjudication and negotiation. Adjudication is conventionally perceived as a norm-bound process centered on the establishment of facts and the determination and application of principles, rules, and precedents. Negotiation, on the other hand, is conventionally perceived as a relatively norm-free process centered on the transmutation of underlying bargaining strength into agreement by the exercise of power, horse-trading, threat, and bluff. But as applied to dispute-negotiation, at least, this perception of negotiation is by no means self-evident; on

* *Source*: Private Ordering Through Negotiation: Dispute-Settlement and Rulemaking, 89 Harv.L.Rev. 637, 638– 65 (1976). Professor of Law, University of California at Berkeley.

the contrary, observation suggests that such negotiation consists largely of the invocation, elaboration, and distinction of principles, rules, and precedents. . . . [T]his article proceeds on the theory that the verbal behavior of negotiating disputants can to a considerable extent be taken at face value and that in most cases of dispute-negotiation the outcome is heavily determined by the principles, rules, and precedents that the parties invoke. In the balance of this Article I shall refer to this theory as the norm-centered model of dispute-negotiation (using the term "norm" to mean a standard of conduct with ethical connotations, and the term "model" to mean an abstracted representation of a complex process).

Since the ultimate validity of this model turns on the actors' subjective intent, it cannot be demonstrated directly—any more than the ultimate validity of a theory of adjudication which posits that outcomes are heavily determined by the official norms of the legal system, rather than by the personal and political views of judges. No other theory of dispute-negotiation, however, has been demonstrated to be valid in this sense, and the norm-centered model has two advantages over its few competitors: It treats the verbal content of negotiation as meaningful, and it provides coherent organization to a wide range of empirical observations . . . .

A.   The Universe of Norms

. . . Because of the paucity of case histories of dispute-negotiation in our own culture, I shall draw a case from the book *Social Control in an African Society* [(1963)], by the anthropologist Philip Gulliver, which deals with dispute-settlement among the Arusha of northern Tanzania. Negotiation holds a central role as a dispute-settlement technique in Arusha society. Arusha social organization is based on age, kinship, and residence. Disputes are usually dealt with by negotiation, conducted under the leadership of notables, in age-group conclaves, kinship moots, or community assemblies. Although the assembly has power to levy fines in certain cases, neither the assembly nor the conclaves and moots are adjudicative bodies, and notables generally do not act as adjudicators or even mediators. . . .

The following is one of many Arusha case histories recorded by Gulliver . . . :[12]

> [*Kadume's Case*]   . . .   About ten years before [this dispute] arose, Kadume's mother had separated from his father, Makara; and taking Kadume and the other children with her, she went to live on her own brother's farm . . . . Makara remained on his farm alone . . . and he came to depend a good deal on his immediate neighbor and half-brother, Soine, and his wife. On Makara's death his land was occupied by Soine.
>
> Later Kadume . . . obtained the two cattle and three goats left by his father. Although these cattle were stalled . . .

---

12. . . . *Kadume's Case* involved members of an interdependent group. Cases set in such a context may involve elements not present in a nondependent context. . . . However, while these elements may have affected the outcome, the aspects of the case that are of concern at this point are susceptible to independent interpretation.

on the land of Lembutua, his mother's brother, an arrangement was made for them to graze in the daytime in the paddock of Soine. Kadume was accepted as a full member of the inner lineage founded by Mesuji [the father of Makara and Soine].

About a year after the establishment of the grazing arrangement, Kadume claimed possession of all of his father's land which Soine was then cultivating for the fourth or fifth season. Soine refused to give up the land and, after a quarrel, refused to allow Kadume to continue to graze his animals in the paddock.

Kadume went to the lineage counsellor who convened a conclave of the inner lineage. This ended in failure and further quarrelling. Soine held to the arguments that Kadume's mother had deserted Makara and left him wifeless and uncared for, except by Soine himself and his wife; that Kadume had never cultivated his father's land; that Soine himself had only a small farm, but that he had rightful claims in the estate of Mesuji (i. e., the land Makara had inherited from Mesuji); and finally, that Kadume already had a piece of land on his mother's brother's farm where he was living. . . .

Later, at Kadume's insistence, the counsellor convened an internal moot which was held at Soine's homestead. . . . Kadume . . . had persuaded a lineage notable, Kirevi, to speak for him. Kirevi began the moot, and he argued that Kadume, the only adult son of Makara, had the right to inherit his father's land now he was a [mature] man. . . . He pointed out that Kadume had already inherited Makara's animals, and by the same right he should now take the land.

Soine, in reply, relied on the same arguments he had used in the earlier conclave. . . .

[Kirevi then argued that Soine's failure to turn over the land to Kadume would cause dissension within the inner lineage, and Olamal, a relative of Kadume, suggested that if the senior generation (of which Soine was a member) did not help the junior generation now, the juniors when they became mature might refuse to help the seniors.]

The counsellor commended Olamal for his speech, but said that he must look after his fathers in their old age whatever they did now. Then, turning to Soine, the counsellor said that perhaps it would be a good thing to talk of giving Kadume his father's land. . . . [A half-brother of Soine then] . . . agreed aloud that they should consider giving Kadume the land. Silence followed this statement, signifying agreement on the point. In effect Soine had tacitly expressed his willingness to allow Kadume some of the land, for when he spoke he entered immediately into a consideration of what part of the land Kadume might occupy.

Kadume broke into Soine's speech to demand that he be given the whole of his father's land; but Soine replied that Kadume had land already at his mother's brother's farm, as much almost as Soine's own farm. 'Does Lembutua (the mother's brother) want to drive you away? Are you and he not friends?' Kadume was silent, but, stirred by the insistence of Soine and the counsellor, he admitted that Lembutua did not want to evict him from that land. 'And have you not planted coffee there? Ee, and bananas and trees also?' Kadume agreed that he had. 'Then you have a farm,' announced Soine; 'And you do not need all of Makara's land. Take that portion beyond the bananas—that is yours.' He indicated the area referred to.

There was some discussion, and then the members of the moot all walked over onto the land in question nearby. The establishment of the new boundary took some time—about half an hour—and a good deal of bargaining, but it was successfully concluded in the end. . . .

The whole moot concluded by retiring to Soine's house to drink beer in commensal cordiality. Agnates took the opportunity to congratulate both Soine and Kadume on the success of the agreement, and on the conclusion of the inheritance settlement.

Was negotiation of this dispute based on principles, rules, and precedents? Gulliver thought not. He believed that Soine retained approximately half the land "despite the enunciated norms of inheritance." This interpretation is certainly not compelled by the conduct of the negotiation, since the parties proceeded in large part through the invocation, elaboration, and distinction of various standards which they treated as norms. Rather, Gulliver's view, made explicit elsewhere in his book, appears to reflect the not-uncommon concept that adjudication is the model of principled dispute-settlement, and that variation from that model in itself implies a drift away from principle toward power.

To explore the limitations of this view it is necessary to compare the universe and operation of norms in dispute-negotiation, on the one hand, and adjudication, on the other. At this point, three differences may be identified, having to do with the problems presented by *conflicting, colliding,* and *person-oriented* norms.

First, norms may be said to *conflict* when they are mutually inconsistent across the entire spectrum of their applicability. For example, the doctrine of contributory negligence is inconsistent with the doctrine of comparative negligence. Typically, when two norms conflict one becomes dominant, in the sense that it is generally accepted as the "better" or "valid" norm. The other norm, while subordinate, may, however, be given some degree of continued recognition.

Second, norms may be said to *collide* where each has a sphere of action within which it is admittedly valid, but they point in opposing directions in cases in which their respective spheres of applicability intersect. For example, in a number of recent cases involving suits for damages against media of various sorts, the principle of right to privacy has pointed to a verdict for the plaintiff, while the principle of freedom of speech has pointed to a verdict for the defendant.

Third, norms may be said to be *person-* rather than *act-oriented* where their applicability depends on the personal characteristics of the disputants rather than on the nature of their acts.[18] For example, in a society that does not recognize testamentary disposition, the norm "sons inherit" is act-oriented; its applicability does not usually depend on the personal characteristics of a particular father and son. In contrast, a norm such as "brothers should help each other" might be described as person-oriented, because, despite its apparent generality, its application depends almost entirely on the personal characteristics of the individual parties—a wealthy brother should not seek economic help from a poor one; an unkind brother may not be entitled to any help at all.

In adjudication (or, at least, that style of adjudication prevalent in complex Western cultures) the universe and operation of norms is highly stylized and tightly controlled. Where norms conflict, a court will characteristically treat one norm as not only subordinate but totally invalid—so that a court which adopts the doctrine of contributory negligence will deny the validity of comparative negligence. Where norms collide, a court will characteristically select one as determinative of the outcome of the case and reject the other as inapplicable—so that in a case to which the norms of privacy and free speech might be applicable, a court will typically hold that the outcome is controlled by one or the other, but not both. Finally, courts tend to treat person-oriented norms as either invalid or irrelevant [20]—so that in the United States the socially recognized principle that brothers owe each other special obligations will typically give rise to neither a cause of action nor a defense.

In contrast, the universe and operation of norms in dispute-negotiation is typically open-ended. Thus it is characteristic of dispute-negotiation that when norms collide account is taken of both, although the eventual settlement may reflect an adjustment for relative applicability and weight. Similarly, the parties in dispute-negotiation may accord partial or even full recognition to a norm that is generally deemed subordinate or even legally invalid, so that a negligent plaintiff who has no "right" to prevail in a tort action because of the doctrine of contributory negligence may nevertheless make a

---

18.   .   .   .   Act- and person-oriented norms are, of course, polar analytical constructs rather than mutually exclusive categories. Thus in status-oriented societies these categories may intersect or even merge, since different kinds of acts are expected from different kinds of persons .   .   .   .

20. It should be noted, however, that despite this tendency, person-oriented norms can be and often are explicitly administered by courts. Prominent examples in our own culture include norms governing divorce that turn on the application of such standards as "irreconcilable differences,"   .   .   . and norms that make child custody turn on the child's best interests or welfare .   .   .   .

Systems employing the inquisitorial method seem to make somewhat greater use of such norms than those employing the adversary method .   .   .   . Furthermore, even where person-oriented norms are not officially relevant, they may be considered in a shadowed or covert way .   .   .   .

favorable settlement by reason of the legally invalid but socially real principle of comparative negligence.   Finally, parties to dispute-negotiation can and frequently do take person-oriented norms into account as freely as act-oriented norms.

Because adjudication is often regarded as the paradigm of principled decisionmaking, dispute-settlement processes in which the universe and operation of norms differ sharply from adjudication are often perceived as not turning heavily on principle for that reason alone.   But whether a process turns heavily on principle depends on the extent to which principles determine the outcome, not on the nature of the principles nor the precise manner in which they determine the outcome.   A process that accommodates colliding norms, and freely recognizes subordinate, legally invalid, and person-oriented norms, is not intrinsically less principled than a process that selects between colliding norms, treats subordinate norms as invalid, and focuses on acts rather than personal characteristics.

Viewed in this light, not only the outcome but also most of the conduct of *Kadume's Case* can be explained in terms of the norm-centered model of dispute-negotiation.   In drawing the conclusion that, "[t]he result [in *Kadume's Case*] was that, *despite the enunciated norms of inheritance*, Kadume obtained only about half of his father's land," Gulliver focused solely on the act-oriented and dominant norm, "sons inherit."   But the verbal behavior of the parties and other relevant Arusha material indicate that two subordinate and person-oriented norms were also applicable to the dispute: (1) A well-off relative should not begrudge means of sustenance to a needy relative (Kadume already had a farm almost as big as the land in dispute, Soine did not);   (2) One who voluntarily cares for an aging relative until the latter's death should share in his estate (Soine took care of Makara until his death, Kadume did not).   Out of the collision between the act-oriented dominant norm favoring Kadume, and the person-oriented subordinate norms favoring Soine, an outcome issued which accommodated all of the relevant norms by tacitly recognizing that *as a matter of principle* Kadume and Soine *each* had a right to the land.[25]

B.   The Element of Reconciliation

I turn now to the effect on dispute-negotiation of a drive on the part of the disputants to reconcile differences for the purpose of maintaining interpersonal harmony.   This element of reconciliation is most commonly associated with a context of interdependence—where it may grow naturally

25.   .   .   .   Considerations having to do with conflicting, colliding, and person-oriented norms are applicable in the analysis of many other legal institutions.   For example, one advantage of arbitration over official adjudication is that an arbitrator has power to take person-oriented and subordinate principles into account, and to adjust for colliding principles.   The American jury, involving as it does both laymen and secrecy, may be seen as a device for permitting the covert consideration of person-oriented norms in what is otherwise a highly act-oriented process.   Instances of justifiable rule-departures by officials   .   .   . frequently involve the substitution of a subordinate (and often person-oriented) rule or principle for the dominant act-oriented rule or principle that has been officially adopted by the legal system   .   .   .   .

out of a personal relationship between the disputants, or where it may be imposed upon them by a group of which they are members—but it is also found among non-interdependent disputants who share a cultural ideal of interpersonal harmony. On the surface, this element may seem to lead to outcomes based on compromise without regard to principle, merely for the sake of peace. It will be shown . . ., however, that the element of reconciliation does not necessarily preclude a powerful role for principles, rules, and precedents, although it may transmute the manner in which they operate. Again, such a showing can best be made by examination of a case history. The case I shall use is set in Java, and reported by the political scientist Daniel Lev [, in Judicial Institutions and Legal Culture in Indonesia, in Culture and Politics in Indonesia 246 (Holt ed. 1972)]:

> [*T's Case*] In late 1960 I [Lev] agreed to accompany an American visitor on a trip across Java. In Jogjakarta we registered at the city's largest hotel. . . .
>
> After registering, T and I went to our room. T went to the bathroom, where the toilet was an old-fashioned one with a wall tank and cord. When T pulled the cord the cover of the tank and the whole mechanism inside came down (though no water), near-ly hit him and crashed onto the toilet bowl, knocking a huge chunk out of it. . . . During the afternoon, while I sat on the ver-anda writing and T slept, a servant came to the room and handed me a note which informed us that the hotel expected Rp. 5,000 for replacement of the toilet. I was astonished at this and without thinking everything over went directly to the hotel office and asked to see the manager. . . . For half an hour or more he and I argued about the bill. I told him that it was not T's fault the tank's insides had come down and that had T been hit by the falling metal, clearly the hotel would have been been responsible for dam-ages. . . . The manager would not accept this reasoning and said that T had not been hit by the metal and, since such a thing had never happened before, T must be responsible for the damage . . . . Finally I told him that we would not pay the bill, that it was best to take the matter to court, and that I would ask Judge S [a friend] . . . to talk the problem over. . . .
>
> [In the course of the next several hours the manager and I met at various times to establish our relative power positions by in-dicating which influential officials we knew, a game often played in this kind of conflict and one that involves a good deal of bluffing. As it happened, a new element was introduced into the affair when a friend from Djakarta stopped at the hotel and mentioned that not long ago another toilet tank had fallen from the wall in the hotel. When the manager was reminded of this, the situation changed somewhat.]
>
> I finally called up Judge S, fully intending to take the case to court or at least to scare the manager into withdrawing his claim . . . . Judge S's reactions left me momentarily speechless. He agreed the civil code was on our side. Then he said, "Well, but

of course you are willing to pay part of the expenses for replacing the toilet, aren't you? Offer the manager some money in payment of the damages, to show good will, and then come to a settlement somewhere between his demand and your offer." When I recovered my composure I said that T was convinced he was not wrong, and why should he pay anything? Judge S replied, "Yes, of course, but that is beside the point. What is important is that you show good will and settle by damai (peace, compromise) if at all possible. Only if the manager demands full Rp. 5,000 and refuses the offer to damai should you take the case to court."

Later . . . accepting Judge S's advice . . . we offered the manager a thousand rupiah. He carried on a bit but finally accepted without demanding more, we had some tea and small talk together, and the issue was never raised again.

In response to an inquiry concerning this case, Professor Lev added that ". . . [I] certainly intended to return to that hotel, as it was the only one convenient enough to stay in [in Jogjakarta] at the time. When I did return later, the manager and I became friends, and the incident was never raised again between us."

Lev's analysis of *T's Case* is that it illustrates how the "penchant for compromise . . . contrasts with a legal culture that tends to be concerned with substance and 'right.'" There are, however, at least two other possible interpretations of *T's Case*, each of which is consistent with the norm-centered model of dispute-negotiation. First, the outcome may have simply reflected an accommodation of conflicting facts and norms. After all, it could not be unequivocally established that T was not at fault—perhaps he pulled too hard on the cord. Furthermore, even if T was not at fault, he was nevertheless a cause-in-fact of damage to hotel property. Although modern legal systems have adopted the principle that liability for property damage should normally be predicated on fault, the social sphere continues to recognize a subordinate principle that one is responsible for any property damage that one has caused in fact, regardless of fault. Thus the compromise settlement in *T's Case* may have reflected the likelihood that T was at fault and the strength, in this context, of the causation-in-fact principle.

Assume, however, that (as was probably the case) the settlement was not based on the accommodation of conflicting norms and facts to which both parties gave some degree of recognition. The case can still be interpreted as one in which the outcome turned heavily on principle. Even if it was clear to Lev that T was not liable on the basis of the relevant legal rules—that is, even if Lev gave no recognition to any counter-norm or alternative facts— the manager may nevertheless have *believed in good faith* that T was liable. On that assumption, if Lev, as *T's* stand-in, had refused to pay anything, he and the manager would have been left in a state of permanent opposition: The case would have been one in which a claimant had put forth a claim of right, founded, he believed, in justice, and the respondent had answered by denying that the claimant had any right whatsoever on his side—surely a slap in the face that would have made a continued relationship between the parties extremely difficult. On the other hand, if in such a case the respondent makes a payment in satisfaction of the claim, he tacitly admits that the claimant has some degree of right; while the claimant, by accepting, indicates that the books are now closed on the matter. In *T's Case* the hotel manager did not get the full amount he claimed. He was not, however, placed in a position where his claim of right was rejected out of hand. Instead his claim was accepted, but with the modification that a colliding defense was also accepted. The claim and defense were mutually accommodated, and an amicable relationship between the parties could and did continue.

In short, it is oversimplified to regard the element of reconciliation as necessarily standing in opposition to principle, rule, and precedent. Rather, these elements are likely to interact: In cases where the disputants place a premium on the continuance of an ongoing relationship, the element of reconciliation is likely to provide each disputant with an incentive to give some weight to his opponent's good faith claim or defense and the norms and factual propositions that underlie it, even if he regards the norms as invalid and the facts as wrong. Admittedly, a disputant may also surrender in such a case even though he does not regard the claim or defense as either reasonable or asserted in good faith. Perhaps, indeed, that is just what happened in *T's Case*. But in most such cases a perception of reasonableness or good faith will be critical: While interdependence or a shared ideal of interpersonal harmony may induce disputants to place a high premium on peace, the parties are unlikely to achieve peace through a settlement based on a norm or factual proposition that one regards as neither valid nor asserted in good faith.

C.   The Role of Precedent in Dispute-Negotiation

1.   *The Invocation of Precedent*

The normative model of dispute-negotiation posits that principles, rules, and precedents will heavily determine negotiated outcomes, even when they conflict with self-interest. Internalization of moral standards and the pressure of peer-group and public opinion contribute to the force of principles and rules in such negotiation. The source of the power of precedent requires exploration, however, because the mere performance of an action does not necessarily give rise to a moral obligation to perform the same action again. In some cases past actions may be transposed into principles or rules, as where the actions were taken by persons who are regarded as models to be emulated, or where widespread repetition gives rise to a perception that a course of conduct has become a rule of conduct. Equally important, where the precedent consists of an interaction between the respondent and a third party who was situated similarly to the claimant, the claimant may appeal, through invocation of the precedent, to an underlying (although often merely implicit) norm that one should deal evenhandedly with similarly situated others—the principle of equal treatment. This principle is potentially applicable whenever two or more persons stand in a similar relation to a third person. . . .   Failure to accord equal treatment . . . is likely to bring on very strong resentment, and few are willing to meet the invocation of precedent with the answer, "Too bad." Instead the party against whom the precedent is invoked is likely either to yield to the claim or to attempt to make a principled distinction of the precedent. Distinctions, in turn, will be met either with reasoned counter-argument or with the invocation of a counter-principle.[35]

Another explanation of the influence of precedent has been put forth by Thomas Schelling in his book The Strategy of Conflict [(1960)]. Schelling suggests that two parties who are unable to communicate can concert their actions by choosing a course of conduct that each believes the other will choose because that course is more conspicuous or prominent than any alternative. (For example, a husband and wife who lose each other in a department store might try to reunite by meeting at a location each believes to be prominent in the minds of both.) He then argues that comparable considerations apply even in cases where the parties can communicate, so that "a cynic" might often be able to predict the outcome of negotiation "on the basis of some 'obvious' focus for agreement, some strong suggestion contained in the situation itself, *without much regard to the merits of the case.* . . ." Observing that "[p]recedent seems to exercise an influence that greatly exceeds its logical importance or legal force," Schelling concludes that precedents—and even standards of fairness—derive a large part of their force from the fact that they provide solutions which are prominent.

This view has little operational significance as applied to principles and rules, because few principles are sufficiently specific to provide a prominent solution, and in any event explicit negotiation usually involves a number of principles and rules, no one of which is structurally more prominent than the others. It does seem likely that the force of precedent stems in part from the prominence effect; but by overlooking the powerful normative implications that precedent may acquire, Schelling gives that effect a wholly disproportionate weight. Furthermore, although Schelling treats the prominence effect as if it were an independent variable, in fact its force will depend largely on the opportunity of the parties to communicate and the type of negotiation involved. A prominent solution will exert its strongest pull where both parties will be better off if they concert their actions, and communication between them is blocked. In such a case each party will be motivated to concert, and can do so only by selecting a course of action he believes will be conspicuous to the other. Both parties, if they are economically rational, will therefore embrace that solution willy-nilly. The presence of an opportunity to communicate, however, will in itself diminish the significance of the prominence effect, because if the parties want to agree, they can do so by means other than the selection of a prominent solution.

Furthermore, when the purpose of negotiation is dispute-settlement, the process tends to be a zero-sum game (that is, a contest in which the winner's gains are exactly balanced by the loser's losses).[41] Characteristically, if the

---

35. When there has been prior interaction between the claimant and the respondent, precedent may derive its force from the claimant's perception of the prior interaction as a tacit agreement that the parties will conduct themselves in a certain way with regard to the subject matter of that interaction. . . . The later varying action may then be regarded by the claimant as a violation of the agreement.

41. . . . As in most cases where a process is labeled zero-sum, this characterization pertains only to outcomes,

respondent negotiates and settles he cannot be better off, and may very well be worse off, than if he does not. Under those circumstances it is highly unlikely that the respondent will make a settlement simply because there happens to be a prominent settlement-point on which his attention can be focused. Of course, a precedent may nonetheless have significant weight in dispute-negotiation because of its normative implications. But where those implications are weak, and the principle of equal treatment is inapplicable, a precedent will usually influence the outcome of dispute-negotiation through the prominence effect only if it happens to fall within the settlement zone established by norms or other strong forces at play in the particular case. An otherwise prominent solution—even the single prominent solution—that is not within that zone will have little or no effect.

2. *The Precedential Effect of a Settlement*

The force of precedent in dispute-negotiation is not confined to the effect of past precedents on present disputes. Rather, its force, as in adjudication, is double-edged: In resolving their dispute the parties are also likely to take into account the precedential effect of the contemplated settlement on future behavior. A characteristic response in dispute-negotiation is, "If I agree to do this for you, I will have to do it for everyone else." Why "have"? Partly because the respondent may no longer be able plausibly to argue infeasibility, but more importantly because "everyone else" will surely invoke the principle of equal treatment. Thus one dimension of this response is to spell out to the claimant the full implications of the parties' negotiation in light of the intense strength of the principle of equal treatment. A second and perhaps more fundamental dimension of this response is that it constitutes a shorthand way of turning an issue of expediency into one of principle. To the implied question, "Can't you do this for me?," this response impliedly answers, "The issue is not whether I can do this for you, but whether I should do this kind of thing for persons situated like you."

D. Dispute-Negotiation and Adjudication

The preceding sections have dealt primarily with continuities between the processes of dispute-negotiation and adjudication. This section will deal primarily with discontinuities between them. An exploration of these discontinuities is of interest both in itself—among other things, it helps explain why a disputant would prefer one process rather than the other—and because it illuminates the elements of each process. . . .

1. *The Binary Character of Adjudication*

The classical model of adjudication, at least in complex Western cultures, is characterized by the dominant role of an official, neutral third party who is vested with formal power to impose a settlement after affording the disputants an opportunity to make arguments and present proofs. For convenience, I shall refer to this model as traditional adjudication. It is sometimes suggested, directly or by inference, that this form of adjudication is

and excludes both transaction costs and indirect benefits derived either from engaging in the process or from conferring a benefit on the other party.

distinguishable from negotiation (and other forms of dispute-settlement) because it is a zero-sum game. But zero-sum outcomes are characteristic of all dispute-settlement processes, including dispute-negotiation. If *B* damages *A*'s car, and *A* claims the cost of repairs, *A*'s gain in dispute settlement can only come at the expense of *B*'s loss, whether the dispute is settled by traditional adjudication, dispute-negotiation, or other means.[47]

There is, however, a closely related factor, bearing both on outcomes and on the manner in which the outcomes are rationalized, that does tend to distinguish the two processes. Dispute-negotiation has a *graduated* and *accommodative* character: In reaching and rationalizing outcomes, any given norm or any given factual proposition can be taken into account according to the degree of its authoritativeness and applicability (in the case of a norm) or probability (in the case of a factual proposition). In contrast, traditional adjudication tends to have a *binary* character: In reaching, and even more clearly in rationalizing outcomes, any given proposition of fact is normally found to be either true or false, colliding norms are generally treated as if only the more compelling norm were applicable, conflicting norms are generally treated as if only the dominant norm were applicable, and each disputant is generally determined to be either "right" or "wrong." One cause of this binary character is that the very purpose of resorting to adjudication may be to achieve a clear-cut determination of which disputant is right. The binary character of traditional adjudication also reflects a second deep cleavage between that process and dispute-negotiation. While dispute-negotiation is usually controlled by the disputants themselves, and is therefore characterized by its *intimacy,* traditional adjudication is characterized by the central role given to a *stranger.*   .   .   .

2. *The Impact of the Stranger*

(a) The Selection and Application of Norms.—It has been shown that in social relations a broad spectrum of norms can be taken into account in a wide variety of ways, while in traditional adjudication the selection and application of governing norms is highly stylized. The insertion into the dispute of a stranger is a major cause of this stylization. Since the stranger typically draws his authority from the principle of objectivity, in reaching, and particularly in rationalizing, his decision he is likely to stress his compliance with that principle and to downplay the amount of his discretion. One way in which the stranger can achieve that end is by treating norms in a binary fashion, rather than attempting to assign appropriate degrees of weight. Furthermore, a decision that is rationalized on the basis of the norms advanced by one of the two disputants requires a smaller commitment of resources by the stranger than an accommodative solution, and involves less risk that the stranger will settle the dispute on the basis of norms that neither party deems relevant.

---

47. If transaction costs were taken into account, adjudication would not be a zero-sum game. Assume plaintiff is entitled to $40,000 if he prevails, and each party spends $10,000 in attorneys' fees. If plaintiff wins, he nets $30,-000 and defendant loses $50,000. If defendant wins, each loses $10,000. [This "minus sum" characteristic is explored at much greater length at p. 191, infra. Ed. note.]

The impact of a stranger is even more pervasive in the area of person-oriented norms. Since such norms tend to be intimate in nature, a stranger typically has little standing to dictate behavior on their basis. Furthermore, a stranger is typically not in position to determine the applicability of such norms, which usually depends upon intimate familiarity with the parties. To determine whether the norm "One who takes care of an aging relative should share in his estate" is applicable, an adjudicator would have to determine not only the texture of the relationship between the decedent and the claimant, but that between the decedent and other potential claimants to his estate—no easy task even for an intimate, but a herculean one for a stranger. For both these reasons, a stranger is usually much readier to invoke act-oriented than person-oriented norms.

All of this is pungently summed up in comments on *Kadume's Case* made to Gulliver by an Arusha magistrate: [54]

> . . . [The magistrate] was certain that, had the case come before him in court, he would have awarded all the disputed land to the son, Kadume. This decision would be based directly on the rule that a son has the right to inherit his deceased father's land in precedence to his father's brother. I pointed out that, in the moot in question, the father's brother, Soine, had been allowed to retain part of the land. The magistrate commented that it had been a good settlement in the circumstances. It had, he said, taken account both of Soine's special relationship with his brother before the latter's death, and of Soine's shortage of land in contrast with Kadume who had a farm on the land of his mother's brother. Additionally, the magistrate noted, the settlement had been such as to permit full lineage unity to continue without great strain. 'Those men (i. e., counsellor and notables) were right,' he declared. 'They know the custom of inheritance, but they also know the people of the lineage and their affairs. But I cannot judge like that for I am a magistrate of the court. I must follow the custom. The law is that a son inherits his father's property. If I fail to follow the law, people will say that I am wrong—and the chief and District Commissioner [will say so] too.'

---

54. . . . Another example of the way the stranger tends to apply act-oriented norms is given by Gulliver in his description of *Sendu's Case.*

Sendu had been allocated a piece of land by the chief in 1941, and in 1942 he allowed two younger brothers to have the use of part of it. In 1954 one of these brothers died, and the other, Leshiloi, claimed the field the decedent had cultivated. In the quarrel that followed Sendu sought to evict Leshiloi altogether. The case eventually went through a court of first instance and two appellate levels.

In each of the three successive courts the magistrate . . . de-clared that it was Sendu's duty to assist his younger brother . . . and to give him the use of some land. The magistrate of the Arusha Appeal Court actually advised Sendu to allow Leshiloi to remain on the land cultivated for twelve years by the two younger brothers; the magistrate of the local court and the District Commissioner in his Court merely counseled the general obligation to be generous and to observe fraternal responsibility. These were all merely *obiter dicta,* and the actual judgments awarded the whole area to Sendu . . . .

Thus, the stranger-adjudicator is likely to treat as irrelevant some principles the disputants themselves regard as relevant, and consequently to have at his command less than the sum total of principles potentially applicable to a dispute. In a real sense, therefore, traditional adjudication may actually be a less principled process than dispute-negotiation.[55]

(b) Fact-determination.—Just as the universe and operation of norms is more constricted in adjudication than in dispute-negotiation, so is the universe of techniques for fact-determination. In dispute-negotiation most factual issues can be determined by explicit or tacit agreement, since the participants in the process will have personal knowledge of most of the material facts. Where the disputants do not have personal knowledge, they can often agree on the truth of a proposition on the basis of their mutual acceptance of a relator's credibility. If agreement on a factual proposition cannot be reached, a further cluster of techniques is available. The disputants can assume the truth of the proposition provisionally, and proceed to develop and examine its implications; they can bypass the proposition provisionally, to determine whether a settlement can be reached if its truth is left open; or they can make a settlement whose terms accommodate, in an appropriate way, conflicting versions of the proposition or doubt as to its validity. Finally, if none of these techniques proves effective, the disputants can terminate negotiation entirely.

The insertion of a stranger into a dispute, coupled with the binary character of traditional adjudication, entails radical changes in the modes of fact-determination. Propositions of fact that could be quickly agreed to in dispute-negotiation must be laboriously reconstructed to the stranger's satisfaction. The linear nature of the process may make it difficult or impossible to develop and test hypotheses on a provisional basis or provisionally to bypass contested propositions. The compulsion to reach a decision may preclude the adjudicator from declining to render judgment when he is genuinely undecided. Exclusionary rules, necessitated by the role of the stranger, may prevent consideration of relevant evidence, and thereby the establishment of important facts. The binary character of the process may force the adjudicator to treat as unquestionably true propositions he regards as only probably true. In sum, the modes of fact-determination associated with traditional adjudication may be not only less efficient but actually less reliable than those associated with dispute-negotiation.

(c) Choice of remedy.—In choice of remedy, too, dispute-negotiation is considerably more flexible than adjudication, and for the same reasons. Just as the stranger is ill-equipped either to select or to apply person-oriented principles, so he is ill-equipped to determine whether a person-oriented reme-

---

55. It may be more difficult to enforce even act-oriented norms through adjudication than through negotiation, because of problems posed by the requirement that factual propositions be proved to the satisfaction of the stranger. For example, in a dispute involving a claim of employment discrimination, both disputants may know perfectly well that the respondent has wrongfully discriminated against the complainant in subtle but important ways, but it may be virtually impossible to prove discrimination to the satisfaction of the third-party adjudicator if the respondent acted within the form of all relevant rules . . . .

dy—an apology, a handshake, an invitation—would be either appropriate or effective; and just as a stranger typically lacks the moral authority to invoke person-oriented norms even when he believes himself capable of selecting and applying them, so he typically lacks the moral authority to order a person-oriented remedy even when he believes it would be efficacious. Similarly, a stranger-adjudicator cannot easily decree a remedy logically unrelated to the claim before him, such as topping off a tree to improve the claimant's view in lieu of paying damages for defamation.

(d) Emotional effect of participation.—The elements considered so far concern the manner in which outcomes are reached and rationalized in adjudication and dispute-negotiation. A second set of elements concerns the emotional effect of participation in each of these processes. The major discontinuities in this area relate to the disputant's sense of control, and of being judged.

In dispute-negotiation, the settlement is made by the parties themselves. Each party therefore controls the process, or at least shares jointly in its control. As a consequence, the disputant must be treated with dignity, at the risk of a breaking-off; may participate freely and directly, unless he voluntarily chooses to negotiate through affiliates; and may have his full say, although some of what he says may seem rambling or irrelevant. Correspondingly, dispute-negotiation does not entail a passing of judgment upon the disputant by a superordinate party. Indeed, it may not involve any definitive judgment at all. Since a negotiated settlement can take account of competing norms, the disputants can recognize the validity of the norms invoked by the claimant and still accord a degree of recognition to those relied on by the respondent to justify his actions. In some cases it may suffice that the respondent admits either that he *might* have been wrong, or that the claimant's belief that he was wrong is held in good faith. Thus, participation in the process need not be overly threatening, and a reasonable degree of harmony between the parties can be maintained both during and after resolution of the dispute, as in *T's Case.*

Where, on the other hand, the dispute is settled by a stranger-adjudicator, each disputant is by posture a supplicant and by role an inferior. He must tacitly admit that he cannot handle his own affairs. He must appear at times and places which may be decidedly and expensively inconvenient. He must bend his thought and expressions, perhaps his very body, in ways that will move the adjudicator. He must show various signs of obeisance—speak only when permitted, be orderly, and act respectfully if not deferentially. He not only has little or no control over the process, but may be sharply limited in both the content and form of his say and the extent of his participation. Indeed, because of the superstructure necessitated by the role of the stranger —particularly limitations on cognizable evidence and norms—the proceeding is likely to be conducted in a manner so technical that each disputant can participate only through an intermediary who himself assumes a large degree of control over the disputant by virtue of his technical mastery. Finally, the settlement is not fashioned by the disputants themselves, but comes down in the form of a judgment by a superordinate, while the binary nature of the process so structures the dispute that the judgment must recognize one party as "right" and brand the other as "wrong." The prospect of subjection to such a judgment, coupled with the lack of control over the process leading up to the judgment, tends both to generate a state of tension and to drive the disputants irreconcilably apart, whatever the outcome.[63]

E.   The Role of Affiliates in Dispute-Negotiation

In the dispute-negotiation cases considered in the previous sections, affiliates of the original actor-disputants participated in lieu of or in addition to the actors themselves. For example, both Soine and Kadume were joined in the moot by their allies, who often spoke for them, while *T* appeared only through his representative, Lev.   .   .   .

1.   *Accounting and Demanding*

Since dispute-negotiation usually turns in large part on whether the respondent has violated some norm, a settlement often cannot be achieved unless the respondent accounts for his past actions by explicitly or implicitly admitting that a norm-violation has occurred. The difficulties involved in admitting fault might therefore provide a substantial obstacle to settlement in many cases, if the account had to be rendered by the actor himself. One set of institutions whose purpose or effect is to overcome this obstacle are those involving the concept of *party*, in which the roles of *actor* and *accountant* are split between different persons, so that the negotiator can concede a norm-violation without admitting *his own* fault. The legal profession is an obvious example of such an institution.   .   .   .

A counterpart to the respondent's use of an affiliate to render his account is the claimant's use of an affiliate to present his demand. The claimant may employ an affiliate for this purpose because the affiliate is a better negotiator, or because the respondent does not want to negotiate and the affiliate has power to constrain negotiation, or simply because the claimant is averse to dealing personally on the subject matter of the claim. Whatever the reason, one effect of demanding through an affiliate is to relieve the respondent of the embarrassment of dealing directly with the very person he has wronged. A second effect—particularly where the respondent also

---

63.   .   .   .   These emotional ramifications tend to reinforce the impact of the stranger in narrowing the universe of available remedies: An apology that would once have sufficed may not bridge a gap made irreconcilable by the very act of resort to adjudication.

In addition to the discontinuities discussed in the text, there are also important economic differences between the two processes. Adjudication normally involves heavier transaction costs, in terms of both time and money, than dispute-negotiation. Moreover, because of the binary nature of traditional adjudication the most unfavorable outcome each disputant may incur is usually worse than the most unfavorable outcome he may incur in negotiation. All other things being equal, application of the minimax principle (that each party to a contest will choose a strategy minimizing the other party's maximum possible gain, and maximizing his own minimum possible gain) will give rise to a preference for a nonbinary process. Despite all this, there are cases where a disputant may prefer adjudication. For example, a claimant may seek an authoritative declaration that he was right, an institutional disputant may be more interested in making law than in recovering damages, and a disputant who represents others may want to shift responsibility for disposition of a dispute to a third party   .   .   .   .

negotiates through an affiliate—is to help set the stage for the assumption by the affiliates of an adjudicative function.

2. *The Element of Adjudication*

An adjudicative function of a sort is an implicit element of the norm-centered model of dispute-negotiation even in cases involving only the original actor-disputants, since resolution of a dispute will turn in large part on the judgment each party renders on the norms and facts adduced by the other. However, this element tends to be enhanced and made explicit when an affiliate enters the picture, because the affiliate normally brings to the dispute a degree of objectivity which the actor-disputant cannot attain. For example, in his study of the insurance-settlement process, H. Laurence Ross[a] found adjusters to be concerned not solely with minimizing claims costs, but also with making settlements that are fair—meaning, for this purpose, mutually satisfying to the parties and reflective of "what the claim is worth" in an objective sense. . . .

Similarly, negotiation conducted jointly by an actor and his allies on an institutionalized basis tends to slide imperceptibly into adjudication by the allies. Thus, in Arusha dispute-settlement mechanisms affiliates may put considerable pressure upon the disputant to go along with a settlement they judge appropriate.

> . . . dependence [on one's associates] means not only assistance —which is what the Arusha themselves always stress—but the liability of constraint. A man's associates, though certainly supporting him, may come to urge, even insist, on a settlement which he would prefer to reject. Not only can he not afford to do without their support in the particular instance, but he is bound up with them in the permanent relationships involved in the groups and categories to which he and they both belong. . . . It is possible to say that a disputant is judged privately by his associates, who will thus determine their support of him before a wider group. However close they are to him, and however strongly they may support him, they, or some of them, are likely to take a more dispassionate view than he himself does.

How can an affiliate, tied as he is to one party, achieve the objectivity required to fill an adjudicative function? To begin with, since he is not alleged to be personally at fault, the affiliate's emotions are usually not as highly engaged as those of the actor-disputant. If, as is frequently the case, the affiliate is a professional, objectivity may itself be a norm in which he is schooled. The lawyer is perhaps the most prominent affiliate of this type, but other professionals may also play such a role. An example is the architect, who represents the owner during the construction period. According to Johnstone and Hopson [, in Lawyers and Their Work 316–17 (1967)]:

> As part of their administration of the construction process, architects informally adjudicate many disagreements that develop.

a. H. L. Ross, Settled Out of Court (1970). Ed. note.

. . . The architect listens to both sides, personally examines the site if necessary, and then makes a ruling. Sometimes the owner is unaware of the controversies involving his interests. The architect assumes the dual role of agent for the owner and neutral adjudicator of conflicts involving the owner's interests as against the contractor. The amazing thing is that architects successfully perform these diverse roles without the interested parties objecting to the conflict of interest. This combining of agent and neutral adjudicator tasks, so foreign to the lawyer's way of working, is traditional for architects.

Structural factors may also promote objectivity.[77] Ties to one party may well be balanced by pulls in the other direction. The insurance adjuster may be under pressure to attain a high rate of file-clearance; the Dean may be interested in keeping the peace; the customer-relations service may be under a general directive to go along with the customer in doubtful cases; negotiating allies may be anxious to achieve reconciliation between the actor-disputants. Thus the affiliate may be oriented toward both disputants (although in different degree), so that he is institutionally as well as emotionally free to consider the claim on its merits.

Finally, in many cases objectivity is attained through placement of the adjudicative function not in one affiliate but in two—one representing the claimant, and one the respondent. Such paired affiliates are likely to find themselves allied with each other as well as with the disputants, because of their relative emotional detachment, their interest in resolving the dispute, and, in some cases, their shared professional values. Each affiliate therefore tends to take on a Janus-like role, facing the other as an advocate of his principal, and facing his principal as an advocate of that which is reasonable in the other's position.

This type of role is brought into its sharpest focus when the paired affiliates are lawyers. Because a lawyer is both a personal advisor and a technical expert, each actor-disputant is likely to accept a settlement his lawyer recommends. Because of their training, and the fact that typically they become involved only when formal litigation is contemplated, lawyers are likely to negotiate on the basis of *legal* principles, rules, and precedents. When these two elements are combined, the result is that paired legal affiliates typically function as a coupled unit which is strikingly similar to a formal adjudicative unit in terms of both input and output. Indeed, in terms of sheer number of dispute-settlements effected, the most significant legal dispute-settlement institution is typically not the bench, but the bar. . . .

---

1. In thinking about Schelling's theory of the role of precedent, and Eisenberg's discussion of it, you might look at Martin Shapiro's essay, A Theory of Stare Decisis, here in chapter 6.

77. It should be stressed that objectivity is neither predicated on nor equivalent to neutrality . . . .

2.   In the first part of his essay Professor Eisenberg stresses the continuities between adjudication and negotiation. He does this by pointing to the role of principle in each. He then turns away from that theme and stresses the discontinuities, building his case largely out of alleged institutional features of the two methods of dispute-settlement. Drawing on earlier work by Lon Fuller—The Forms and Limits of Adjudication, 92 Harv.L.Rev. 353 (1978) (here in chapter 8); Two Principles of Human Association, in 11 Nomos, Voluntary Associations 3 (1969); Human Interaction and the Law, 14 Am.J.Juris. 1 (1969); Mediation—Its Forms and Functions, 44 S.Cal.L.Rev. 305 (1971)—Eisenberg emphasizes both the "binary character" of adjudication and the status of the third party as a "stranger."

The excerpt from Gulliver's account of *Kadume's Case*, which Eisenberg quotes, seems to support that view; but one can only wonder whether Eisenberg takes sufficient account of some modern litigation, exemplified by the typical school desegregation case. Hart v. Community School Bd. of Brooklyn (383 F.Supp. 699 (E.D.N.Y.1974), 383 F.Supp. 769 (E.D.N.Y. 1974), aff'd 512 F.2d 37 (2d Cir. 1975)), involving an effort to desegregate the Mark Twain Junior High School in the Coney Island area of New York City, is as much an instance of adjudication as is *Kadume's Case*; and as a case such as *Hart* makes abundantly clear, there are myriad possible solutions to the problem. To use a phrase Fuller borrowed from Michael Polyani, it is polycentric. It is often impossible to tell which side won, and, of course, equally impossible to think of the judge who supervises the reorganization of the school system over a long period of time as a "stranger." See the Harris, Fiss, and Chayes essays in chapters 5, 7 and 8. Similarly, against Eisenberg's discussion of the choice of remedy, which suggests that the so-called "stranger" is "ill-equipped to apply person-oriented remedies," you should consider not just the modern equity experience, but more obvious counter-examples such as defamation litigation or even contemporary criminal litigation. See the Symposium on The Paper Label Sentences, 86 Yale L.J. 590 (1977). See also Eisenberg, Participation, Responsiveness, and the Consultative Process: An Essay for Lon Fuller, 92 Harv.L.Rev. 410 (1978). At various points in the above essay Eisenberg inserts the word "traditional" before "adjudication;" but is that qualification sufficient to rescue his claim?

2.   THE LINE BETWEEN LEGISLATION AND ADJUDICATION

Adjudication is not simply a method of solving a dispute, such as one over who owns a particular parcel of land. It also may be viewed as a process for establishing future standards of conduct for the participants and, even more, for the public. From that perspective adjudication bears a striking similarity to legislation or rulemaking. The task of setting boundaries, of locating adjudication within a procedural system, thus also requires that adjudication be distinguished from legislation.

Part of the distinction between adjudication and legislation derives from the political status of the agencies that typically engage in each activity—for example, the appointive status of courts and the elective status of legislatures. This is a theme explored more in chapter 5 under the "independence of decision makers." Here we are concerned not with such factors, but rather with the formal differences between the two processes. How are information and views about the proper rule presented in the two processes? Who can participate in the processes, and what does participation mean? Are there differences in the quality of the rules that emerge from the two types of proceedings, as to either their scope or their binding effect?

We believe that these formal questions might profitably be explored in the administrative law context, more specifically, in the context of deciding whether an administrative agency should proceed by adjudication or by rule-making (or, in our terms, "legislation"). Such a context minimizes the political-status question because administrative agencies have such a hybrid political status and because the two ways of proceeding—adjudication and rulemaking—could be employed by the very same agency. The formal questions are likely to be more prominent. At the same time, because administrative agencies are somewhat unique in having the power to choose how they shall proceed, a body of scholarship has emerged in administrative law on the issue. We include Professor Shapiro's well-known essay on the subject, but you may also want to read Professor Glen Robinson's more recent study, The Making of Administrative Policy: Another Look at Rulemaking and Adjudication and Administrative Procedure Reform, 118 U.Pa.L.Rev. 485 (1970).

David L. Shapiro, **The Choice of Rulemaking or Adjudication in the Development of Administrative Policy**[*]

One of the most distinctive aspects of the administrative process is the flexibility it affords in the selection of methods for policy formulation. While a legislature must normally confine itself to the declaration of generally applicable standards of conduct, and a court must deal with a problem as defined by the particular controversy before it, an administrative agency may often choose between these approaches or may even reject them both in favor of more informal means of regulation. . . .

[One hazard in considering the merits of the various approaches] is the difficulty and importance of drawing a workable distinction between rule-making and adjudication, for analysis cannot proceed very far if the point of departure itself lacks validity. The language of the Administrative Procedure Act is not much help; it first defines "rule" broadly enough to cover virtually all agency action having future effect and then defines "adjudication" as the process leading up to everything else, "but including licensing."[8] One possible approach is not to affix a label to a proceeding as a whole but to identify any aspect of it that declares generally applicable policy as "rulemaking" and any aspect applying that policy to identified persons as "adjudication." But this is to define away the problem, for then all declarations of policy in any form of proceeding become "rulemaking." For purposes of deciding on what occasions a particular method of policy formulation is suit-

---

[*] *Source*: 78 Harv.L.Rev. 921, 921–57 (1965). Professor of Law, Harvard University.

8. Administrative Procedure Act §§ 2 (c), (d), 60 Stat. 237 (1946), 5 U.S.C. §§ 1001(c), (d) . . . .

able it is helpful to rely primarily on the distinction that "rulemaking"—the process leading to the issuance of regulations—is typically a proceeding that is entirely open ended in form, specifying only the class of persons or practices that will come within its scope, while "adjudication" is a proceeding directed at least in part at determining the legal status of persons who are named as parties, or of the acts or practices of those persons. Such an approach may be unsatisfactory in many contexts, for by stressing one factor to the exclusion of others it leaves some of the hardest questions unresolved, may occasionally be inaccurate, and may permit some formal agency actions to escape identification entirely. But our interest is primarily with the typical case, and thus an illustration may well be as useful as an abstract definition. . . .

An especially apt and timely example of "hard-core" rulemaking is the [1964] trade regulation rule of the Federal Trade Commission entitled "Unfair or Deceptive Advertising and Labeling of Cigarettes in Relation to the Health Hazards of Smoking," in which the Commission declared: [13]

> [I]n connection with the sale, offering for sale, or distribution in commerce . . . of cigarettes it is an unfair or deceptive act or practice within the meaning of section 5 of the Federal Trade Commission Act . . . to fail to disclose, clearly and prominently, in all advertising and on every pack, box, carton or other container in which cigarettes are sold to the consuming public that cigarette smoking is dangerous to health and may cause death from cancer and other diseases.

Instead of promulgating such a regulation after notice and hearings, the Commission could have initiated adjudicatory proceedings against one, some, or all of the major cigarette manufacturers, looking to the issuance of orders to cease and desist from specified unfair practices. Indeed, this was the method principally relied upon by the Commission for most of the first half-century of its existence, and industry representatives argued that it was the only one available under the governing statute. But the Commission vigorously defended both its authority to act by rulemaking and the wisdom of its choice in an exhaustive supporting statement, listing ten reasons why a "regulation" was preferable to "adjudication" in this particular instance. The contrast between the method selected by the Commission and the one expressly rejected furnishes an appropriate framework for considering the problem of choice.

A. The Uses of Adjudication: The Articulation of Standards

. . . [T]he choice between rulemaking and adjudication is not necessarily the choice between the articulation of a rule and an ad hoc approach in which each case is governed only by a general statutory provision. Agencies, like courts, frequently evolve detailed and precise rules in the course of adjudication. . . . Rules declared in adjudication have varied in form from the imposition of minimum time limits for the observance of statutory obligations to the declaration of presumptions that are based on

13. Section 408.1, 29 Fed.Reg. at 8325
[1964] . . . .

prior experience and that shift to the respondent the burden of going forward. The soundness and lawfulness of any given rule may be subject to challenge, but the existence of general authority to act in this manner can hardly be questioned, and it is evident that the effect of such a rule is to narrow and simplify the issues requiring resolution in subsequent cases.

Nevertheless, the process of adjudication, including the decision whether or not to prosecute, is often used without any effort to clarify and elaborate general statutory standards, while the rulemaking process has no real function except elaboration. It is possible to have a regulation providing that each case will turn on its own facts, but the regulation would serve virtually no purpose unless perhaps it was designed to announce that more specific proposals had been considered and rejected. . . .

B. The Advantages of Rulemaking in Achieving Fair and Effective Administration

. . .

1. Notice and Opportunity for Comment

One of the substantial advantages claimed for rulemaking is that it requires the agency to allow general participation in the deliberative process by all those who may be affected by the rule, while no such opportunity is afforded in adjudication. As put by the FTC: [32]

> The Administrative Procedure Act, in its provisions governing formal rule-making proceedings, requires that all interested persons be given an opportunity to express their views on a proposed rule before it is finally adopted (sec. 4(b)). . . . [Q]uite apart from considerations of fairness, their participation in the rule-making process is likely to assist the agency in formulating a practical and sound rule. Where rules are made, not in formal rule-making proceedings, but in adjudicative proceedings, the requirement is ordinarily not met. Views of all interested persons are not solicited or received—only the views of particular litigants. Though a decision may have far-reaching significance by reason of the rule it lays down, and affect many persons besides the particular litigants, only the latter will have participated in the rule-making process; and, in many cases, even they will have had no opportunity to express their views on the rule declared by the court or tribunal.

This statement is a persuasive one, but several important qualifications, some of which may be implicit in the passage, should be noted. . . .

. . . [E]ven in the course of adjudicatory proceedings, agencies are not powerless to permit general comment on proposed rules if they wish to do so. The device of the brief amicus curiae, which has become increasingly common in Supreme Court proceedings, has also been used by administrative agencies. Thus, on several occasions the NLRB has invited or accepted comments on contemplated rule changes in the context of a pending case.

---

32. Statement of Basis [and Purpose of Trade Regulation Rule, 29 Fed.Reg. 8325,] 8366 [1964] . . . .

True, the use of such a device rests within the discretion if not the whim of the agency, but there is no reason why it cannot fulfill any perceived need for general reaction to a proposed policy. Especially since section 4 of the APA permits participation in rulemaking to be limited to written submissions and since an amicus may be allowed to make an oral presentation, the difference between the two approaches in terms of opportunity for comment does not seem substantial.[37]

. . . [T]he FTC's suggestion that even a party who participates in an administrative adjudication may not be afforded a chance to express his views may not be entirely accurate. In a . . . case involving a complaint of discriminatory discharge in violation of section 8(a)(3) of the NLRA, the Labor Board had, without warning, reversed its long-standing policy of tolling backpay during the period between an examiner's dismissal of a complaint and the Board's reversal. The reviewing court stated that under section 5 of the APA,[39] the Board should have notified the employer that it was considering a change in the rule.[40] This holding, not entirely without precedent, points up the close relationship between the notice provisions of section 5, the section governing adjudication, and those in section 4. . . .

2. *Advance Planning*

Courts do not select the issues to be litigated before them, except insofar as they have a discretionary power of review, and it has been suggested that when an agency acts like a court, it too must depend more on the accident of litigation than on conscious planning. This is admittedly so in those instances in which an agency cannot adjudicate except on the complaint of a private party, or in which the agency's prosecuting and judging functions have been divided.[43] Indeed, this division has been criticized precisely because it vests so much policymaking authority in one who is not responsible to the agency itself. But many agencies, like the FTC, have the power to initiate cases as well as to decide them, and these agencies can exercise virtually the same degree of planning in the commencement of adjudicatory proceedings as they can in rulemaking. . . .

3. *"Retroactivity" and Reliance*

"Rules made in adjudicative proceedings," the FTC has stated, "are ordinarily retroactive in application, while, under the Administrative Procedure Act, rules made in formal rule-making proceedings . . . are prospective only. . . . In a formal rule-making proceeding, the possibility of un-

37. Some questions may turn on the fact that an amicus is not a "party" to the administrative proceeding . . . . In addition some statutes provide for evidentiary hearings in rulemaking proceedings.

39. 60 Stat. 239 (1946), 5 U.S.C. § 1004 (a).

40. NLRB v. A. P. W. Prods. Co., 316 F.2d 899 (2d Cir. 1963). The court con-

cluded that remand to permit the employer to argue against the change would be an "exercise in futility" in view of the arguments already made by the dissenters on the Board. Id. at 906.

43. Both limitations exist in the case of the NLRB, the agency perhaps most adamant in the refusal to resort to rule-making.

doing consummated transactions is excluded." [47]   Once again, however, the distinction is subject to several qualifications that may leave substantial doubt as to its value.   .   .   .

When we turn to "rules made in formal rule-making proceedings," we find that retroactivity is by no means unknown.   Assuming that the FTC's description is intended to embrace if not be coextensive with "legislative regulations," there are instances in which such regulations have been sustained although plainly determining the legal consequences of events occurring before their issuance.[50]   And more importantly, regulations often affect substantial reliance interests even when their form is entirely prospective. .   .   .   Following "formal rule-making proceedings," the Commission declares that after a certain date, the use of a particular designation in a trademark or trade name will constitute a deceptive practice unless the designated product has certain characteristics.   The regulation plainly applies to existing products, in which a substantial investment in formulation and advertising may have been made, as well as to products not yet on the market; indeed, if it did not it might be vulnerable to a charge of arbitrariness.   Past conduct has not been branded as unlawful as a result of the new policy, but the difference to one deprived of his trademark is marginal at best.

On the adjudication side, the weight in the quoted passage is borne by the word "ordinarily."   Many orders issued in adjudicative proceedings, including most orders to cease and desist,   .   .   .   are addressed to future conduct and often do not upset existing reliance interests.   Furthermore, the concept of prospective overruling, recognized as valid and at times plainly desirable in judicial proceedings, has on occasion been applied by administrative agencies when reliance interests seemed to compel it.   Thus the SEC has in several instances refused to apply a change or clarification in its policy to a pending case when the applicant "may not inappropriately have relied"on a different policy announced in an earlier decision.   And even the NLRB, which in one decision declared that "to establish an *in futuro* rule for all pending cases would create an administrative monstrosity," [56] limited another policy change to cases filed in the future "in order to avoid undesirable confusion as to the impact of this new policy on cases currently pending before the Board   .   .   .   ." [57]   Moreover, courts have at times insisted on purging or mitigating the retrospective effects of an adjudicative order.

About the most that can be said is that a rule declared in a regulation is more likely than a rule declared in adjudication to be limited in application to determining the legal status of future conduct, although either may operate to defeat expectations justifiably based on prior policy   .   .   .   .

---

47. Statement of Basis [, supra note 32, at] 8367–68.   .   .   .

50.   .   .   .   [It has been suggested] that a rule setting forth the legal consequences of prior conduct is not retroactive if it simply prescribes action to be taken in the future.   .   .   .   It can be persuasively argued, however, that any rule is "retroactive" when it purports to ascribe certain consequences to conduct occurring before its issuance.   Even under this latter, more encompassing, definition, many rules will not be "retroactive" yet will upset substantial expectations   .   .   .   .

56. Deluxe Metal Furniture Co., 121 N.L.R.B. 995, 1006 (1958).

57. Ideal Elec. & Mfg. Co., 134 N.L.R.B. 1275, 1278 (1961)   .   .   .   .

4. *Uniformity of Application*

The FTC emphasized in its accompanying statement that when a practice is widespread in an industry, a rulemaking proceeding operates even-handedly to bar that practice on the part of all, while an order directed to only one permits his competitors to gain an unfair advantage. Again, however, the reference is to tendencies rather than to rigid distinctions. Adjudicatory proceedings may be and have been brought by the FTC against virtually all those in an industry employing a particular practice, and the Commission has exercised its discretion to delay the effectiveness of an order until similar orders have been issued against all offenders and their validity has been determined. Authority to obtain temporary injunctions pending the completion of adjudications exists in several areas and has been sought in others. Moreover, the issuance of a regulation does not guarantee its effectiveness; it may well be necessary to bring individual violators to book by commencing adjudicatory proceedings against them while others are complying with the law.

5. *Flexibility of Procedure*

Particular emphasis has been placed on the contention that the trial-type hearings required in adjudication are basically unsuited to the formulation of policy, as is the requirement of the separation of functions imposed by the APA. In rulemaking proceedings, the argument runs, agencies are relatively free to consult with their staffs, to receive far-ranging submissions of data, and to limit or eliminate the use of oral testimony and cross-examination unless the governing statute calls for a determination to be made on the record.

This is undoubtedly a telling point in favor of the rulemaking process, but it too can be overstated. . . . [T]here is nothing in the APA that compels all issues to be treated alike in the course of an adjudication, or which precludes the introduction in such a proceeding of data bearing on broad questions of policy. And as Professor Davis points out, the appropriate methods of presenting and refuting evidence concerning the parties and their activities may often be different from the methods suitable for considering facts bearing on essentially legislative matters, particularly those not in dispute.[64] Thus, if the trade regulation rule proceeding on the hazards of smoking had taken the form of a consolidated cease-and-desist proceeding against the major manufacturers, it is by no means clear that the evidence on smoking and health, on the nature of the industry, or on past and present advertising practices would have been subject to any objections that could not have made in the course of rulemaking. And, of course, in adjudication as well as in rulemaking, the agency itself may preside at the hearing, may receive presentations from its staff, and may draw on its general experience in formulating a rule.

A related question is whether the use of the adjudicatory route is more time consuming because of the many procedural safeguards that must be

---

64. See 1 Davis, Administrative Law §
7.20 (1958); 2 id. § 15.14.

observed.   It is certainly true that fifty separate proceedings against named individuals constitute a much heavier administrative burden than a single rulemaking proceeding and that considerable amounts of time have been wasted treating questions of policy like facts to be determined in an accusatory trial.   But proceedings can be consolidated, and it may well be possible further to streamline adjudicatory procedures without sacrificing important interests.   Moreover, the amount of time that elapses between institution and completion is often a function of the complexity of the issues, the soundness of the agency's legal position, and the opportunity to resort to judicial review.   .   .   .

[6.]   *Accessibility and Clarity of Formulation*

A further aspect deserving mention is that the enunciation of rules in adjudicatory proceedings frequently has the effect of "hiding the ball" from those who are not initiated into the mysteries of a particular agency and its works.   A good example is the NLRB's "contract-bar rule," the name for the aggregate of rules under which the Labor Board determines when a collective agreement will bar a petition for a certification election.   One exhaustive study of this rule as it has evolved over the years has praised it as the evident result of "careful study and weighty deliberation," based on principles that are "clear and intelligible." [79]   And so it is in large part, for anyone who has the time to put together all the cases in which different branches of the rule may be found and to check all the recent decisions to make sure that nothing has changed.   Failing this, the lawyer must rely on some commentator's summary, which may oversimplify, omit, or simply be out of date.   As a result, even experienced practitioners may be hard put to state the rule accurately.

The issuance of regulations, then, can serve the function of readily accessible codification, a function not to be denigrated at a time when rules seem to be multiplying faster than the population.   Other, less formal methods, like manuals and reports issued by the agency, are available too, but their very informality may tend to detract from their accessibility and reliability.   Moreover, an effort at formal statement in a regulation is likely to force the agency to focus on issues previously only dimly perceived and lead it to be more circumspect than it might be within the liberal confines of an opinion, informal summary, or annual report.

[7.]   *Judicial Review*

As a final note, the declaration of policy by means of regulations may make more available the process of judicial review.   There are many instances when the threat of administrative sanctions, such as nonrenewal of a license, may deter interested persons from testing the validity of an agency's position even though they believe that position to be invalid.   In such instances, a formal announcement of the agency's position in a regulation may permit an individual to obtain judicial review even before any action has been taken

79.   Feldesman, Contract Bar to Representation Elections, 29 Geo.Wash.L. Rev. 450, 463 (1961).

in a particular case, if he can show that his ordering of his affairs is plainly affected by the very existence of the regulation. At the same time, however, the threat of review may operate to discourage an agency from taking any steps that would expose a questionable stand to judicial scrutiny .   .   .   .

C. Reasons for Administrative Reluctance to Resort to Rule-making

.   .   .   [Professor Shapiro first lists a tactical reason for preferring adjudication—the greater vulnerability of rulemaking to judicial challenge. Then he turns to more general reasons.]

The Binding Effect of Regulations and Precedents

Administrative agencies appear to be freer to disregard their own prior decisions than they are to depart from their regulations. It has been observed that when agencies develop policy through adjudication they are generally as devoted to the doctrine of stare decisis as are courts of last resort. But how devoted is that? And to what extent do courts require agencies to adhere to their own precedents? These questions have at least two aspects. First, is an agency precluded from changing its policy for pending and future cases because of its own prior decisions, and second, may an agency depart from its existing rules of decision in a given case without adequate explanation, or even establish directly conflicting lines of authority from which to choose? On the first of these, it seems clear that the principles of stare decisis do not prevent an agency from making an announced and reasoned change in policy, although the agency's earlier decisions may affect the court's view of the controlling law. Just as an agency may amend its regulations, so it may alter the course of its decisions unless in either instance the court is convinced that the prior construction or application of the statute was the only permissible one. The principal difference between the amendment of a regulation and a reversal of a rule of decision may reside in the ability of the agency to apply its new policy to completed transactions or other prior conduct .   .   .   .   .

When we come to the second aspect, the difference between rulemaking and adjudication appears more pronounced. If there is to be any measure of predictability and consistency in the process of adjudication, and if the decision maker is not free to rely on unarticulated criteria, then a change in the rule of decision in a given case should apply not only to the case at hand but to similar cases arising in the future. In theory at least, an inadequately explained departure solely for purposes of a particular case, or the creation of conflicting lines of precedent governing the identical situation, is not to be tolerated. But the theory does not always prevail. A rule of decision may be distorted or ignored in one case only to be resurrected in full vigor in the next. Or two different rules may be formulated to govern wholly disparate fact situations and, by imperceptible degrees, move toward each other so that ultimately the cases decided under each are virtually indistinguishable and the results almost squarely in conflict. Often these developments are simply stages in the evolution or synthesis of new and more rational rules, but the process can be painfully slow and litigants may suffer in the meantime .   .   .   .   .

.   .   .   There are clear indications that when an administrative rule, either substantive or procedural, is embodied in a regulation, a court will be much less willing to sustain an agency's disregard of that rule, at least in the absence of a satisfactory explanation of why the regulation is not controlling. The concept that regulations "have the force of law"—the analogy to legislation and to the binding effect of the governing statute—appears to have played a significant role. This same analogy is not so apparent when the question is simply one of the application of a rule of decision in the course of adjudication.

It seems fair to conclude that by eschewing regulations in favor of the declaration of rules by adjudication, an agency is likely to regard itself as freer, and will in fact be given greater freedom by the courts, to ignore or depart from those rules in specific instances without giving sufficient reasons. Part of the blame for what seems an unreasonable distinction must be laid at the door of the courts for failure to develop a consistent approach in determining the effect to be given to regulations and to rules of decision. Both regulations and decisions can of course be inadequate or ambiguous, and can give rise to inconsistent interpretations, but the point suggested here is that the respect that an agency must accord a given rule, even one that is clear and precise, may depend on the form in which it appears. Freedom to disregard a rule or to choose from among inconsistent policies is not necessarily a blessing. Not only does it complicate the process of decision but it may make the agency more susceptible to pressures unrelated to the merits of a case.

Application to Prior Conduct

It has been suggested above that the distinction between a regulation and an adjudication with respect to "retroactivity" has on occasion been overstated; regulations that affect the legal status or consequences of past conduct or that defeat justified expectations are not unknown, and adjudication can have a purely prospective effect. But the question remains whether, by choosing one mode of proceeding rather than another, an agency retains greater freedom to apply a new policy to prior conduct if it wishes to do so   .   .   .   .

Courts have occasionally taken the position that even regulations that appear to do no more than interpret self-operative statutory provisions should be limited to prospective effect when reliance interests based on prior regulations are at stake. But the conceptual problem has focused on regulations regarded as "legislative," in that they impose requirements or create exemptions that plainly could not have existed in their absence. The leading case is Arizona Grocery Co. v. Atchison, T. & S.F. Ry.,[126] holding that once having prescribed a reasonable maximum rate, the ICC could not award reparations with respect to rates within the prescribed limit without first having lowered the maximum for the future. For present purposes the interesting aspect of the case is the Court's rationale, resting as it did on a highly theoretical approach to the nature of administrative action: "Where, as in this case, the Commission has made an order having a dual aspect, it may not in a subsequent proceeding, acting in its quasi-judicial capacity, ignore its own pro-

126. 284 U.S. 370 (1932) . . . .

nouncement promulgated in its quasi-legislative capacity and retroactively repeal its own enactment as to the reasonableness of the rate it has prescribed." The clear implication is that if the Commission's original action had been one regarded as "quasi-judicial," such as an order limited to the awarding of reparations, the result would have been different. It may well be that the extent of the railroad's justifiable reliance would not have been so great in the case of a prior award of reparations only, and that the administrative need to act retroactively would have been more evident if no power to prescribe for the future existed. The difficulty with the opinion, however, is that the Court's view of the ICC's act as "legislative" appeared to preclude it from a searching inquiry into these questions of need and reliance. . . .

When we turn to cases in which a rule declared in adjudication has subsequently been explicitly modified or abandoned, we find that the approach of the courts has been a good deal more pragmatic, and that the balance between administrative need and actual impact on legitimate reliance interests has been the principal criterion.[134] Indeed, there may have been some tendency to tolerate too much because of the resemblance between administrative adjudication and the process of judicial decision, where at least in theory law is still generally found and not made, and where prospective overruling is regarded as something of a novelty. In both areas, however, the law appears to be moving toward a resolution in which, as Judge Cardozo suggested, the guiding principle is not "metaphysical conceptions of the nature of judge-made law" but rather "considerations of convenience, of utility, and of the deepest sentiments of justice." [135] The distinction drawn between rulemaking and adjudication in this respect was well stated in the . . . decision in NLRB v. A. P. W. Prods. Co.: "[I]n addition to cases where the function of an administrative order as a future command precludes its retroactive overruling . . . [citing *Arizona Grocery*], there may be some instances where the adverse effects of retroactive overruling so far outweigh any possible benefits that administrative agencies may not properly exercise the power. . . ." [136]

This is not to suggest that the application of this principle, even by the courts that have embraced it, has been consistent, or that the relevant decisions can all be reconciled. To take judicial review of NLRB reversals of policy as an example, courts appear to have disagreed on whether and to what extent an employer can be held for unfair labor practices committed during

134. There are also a number of cases dealing with efforts by agencies to change policies announced in private rulings or advice or in a consistent course of administrative practice. Whether such changes can defeat reliance interests based on the prior policy is a question on which courts have differed, both in their results and their rationale. . . . Although differences among agency techniques of policy formulation may be matters only of degree, such practices can in general be distinguished from the more formal processes of rulemaking and adjudication dealt with here. It may be, of course, that reliance on a private ruling exceeds that resulting from a regulation of general applicability . . . .

135. Cardozo, The Nature of the Judicial Process 148–49 (1921). . . .

136. 316 F.2d 899, 906 (2d Cir. 1963). The word "command" in the quoted passage is somewhat ambiguous. The maximum rate order in *Arizona Grocery* did not, of course, prohibit the carrier from charging a lower rate.

a period when the Board would not have exercised jurisdiction over the controversy.[137]   Outside the area of jurisdiction, one court held that branding conduct as unlawful in a cease-and-desist proceeding was a sufficiently adverse consequence to invalidate a Board order based on a change in policy declared after the fact,[138] while other courts have rejected the argument that a change in policy should not be applied to increase the liability for backpay accruing before the change was announced.[139]   But whether or not these results are consistent, the opinions in these and other cases do largely reflect an attempt, in considering the impact of adjudication on reliance interests, to make a careful analysis of the need for and the burdens resulting from the action under review.   .   .   .

---

3. THE LINE BETWEEN PUBLIC AND PRIVATE ADJUDICATORY INSTITUTIONS

In the previous sections adjudication as a means of dispute-settlement has been identified with two institutions—courts and administrative agencies.   These institutions are both considered to be "public" for at least two reasons—one, they are financed by tax revenue, by public funds; and, two, individuals who are vested with the adjudicatory power are not selected by the parties to the dispute but rather by the electorate or its representatives.

However, for many years private adjudicatory institutions have coexisted with public courts and agencies.   Arbitration, the most important of private adjudicatory institutions, has secured a pre-eminent role in dispute-processing in many important areas of national life—among them labor-management relations and commercial dealings.   Arbitration is distinguished by the fact that the parties finance it, the parties select the decisionmakers, and the parties consent to the coercive power of the arbitrator.   The courts have been very hospitable to arbitration over the past two decades, especially in the area of labor relations.   There, they have by and large urged the parties to create a private jurisprudence.   Nevertheless, as in all areas where private adjudication takes place, there is even in labor relations the necessity to demarcate a boundary between the sphere in which private arrangements are proper and the realm of public concern so that public institutions may not be ousted from their authority to determine cases.   The Supreme Court recently confronted such an issue of boundary delineation in Alexander v. Gardner-Denver, 415 U.S. 36 (1974).   The labor context of the case is important, for it suggests that the Court was probably inclined to enhance the role of the private adjudicatory institution.   But another aspect of *Gardner-*

137. Compare NLRB v. Guy F. Atkinson Co., 195 F.2d 141 (9th Cir. 1952), with NLRB v. Pease Oil Co., 279 F.2d 135 (2d Cir. 1960), and NLRB v. Kobritz, 193 F.2d 8, 12–13 (1st Cir. 1951).

138. NLRB v. International Bhd. of Teamsters, 225 F.2d 343, 348 (8th Cir. 1955). The court stressed the limited

impact of its decision on the Board's ability to deal with past unlawful conduct.   .   .   .

139. NLRB v. A. P. W. Product Co., 316 F.2d 899 (2d Cir. 1963); NLRB v. Don Juan, Inc., 185 F.2d 393 (2d Cir. 1950).

Denver—the fact that it involved a claim of racial discrimination—pushed in the opposite direction. In the racial area, the Court is often impelled by the idea of public obligation to right the wrongs of discrimination.

The *Gardner-Denver* case started when a black was discharged. He filed a grievance under a collective bargaining agreement that required "just cause" for discharges and that also provided that "there shall be no discrimination against any employee on account of race." The grievance proceeded to arbitration and, as is usually the case in labor arbitration, the union prosecuted the grievance. The arbitrator ruled that the grievant had been in fact discharged for "just cause." The grievant later brought suit in federal court to adjudicate this very same dispute, only in this instance by way of enforcing his rights under Title VII of the Civil Rights Act of 1964, which similarly prohibits racial discrimination in employment. The question then arose as to what effect the arbitrator's decision should have in this court proceeding. The Supreme Court held that the arbitral decision should not be binding on the court, and thus implicitly contemplated an arrangement where public and private adjudicatory institutions formally both coexist and overlap.

In the essay that follows, Professor Meltzer explains the dynamics that might bring about what otherwise might seem to be a puzzling result. He also identifies the factors that will structure the relationship between the public and private institutions on a more dynamic level. He writes in the context of a particular case, but we believe his discussion of *Gardner-Denver* might also be understood as a study of the more general problem of the setting of boundaries between public and private adjudicatory institutions.

Bernard D. Meltzer, **Labor Arbitration and Discrimination: The Parties' Process and the Public's Purposes***

. . . In Alexander v. Gardner-Denver Co., the Supreme Court . . . reaffirmed the idea that arbitration is primarily an instrument of the parties' private purposes rather than a means for achieving public purposes reflected in the law of the land. The drawing of a bright line between private and public purposes in this context may, of course, be criticized as unreal; for arbitrators are surrounded by restraints and values expressed in law and public policy. Furthermore, the Supreme Court, as it transformed arbitration from the waif of the common law into the darling of our national labor policy, stressed the important public interest in securing the fairness, order, and peace that are the goals of arbitration and no-strike clauses. Despite this intertwining of public and private purposes, reminiscent of Adam Smith's invisible hand, the dominating fact—and one recognized by *Gardner-Denver*—is that the parties generally provide and pay for their own arbitration system in order to achieve their own private purposes, as distinguished from those reflected in external law.

* *Source*:   43 U.Chi.L.Rev. 724, 724–35
(1976). Professor of Law, University
of Chicago.

Although the Court in *Gardner-Denver* responded to that fact, it also recognized and legitimated efforts of the parties by express contractual clauses to enforce particular public policies by recourse to arbitration. Specifically with respect to discrimination, the Court understandably did not pause to question agreements that commissioned arbitrators to enforce contractual provisions similar to or duplicative of Title VII and related antidiscrimination programs.

As a purely formal matter, such private endorsement of public policy is wholly consistent with the idea of consent that lies at the core of both collective bargaining and arbitral authority. Furthermore, such endorsement appears to be a welcome symbol of the parties' special sympathy for broad social concerns. Thus the fact that collective agreements increasingly incorporate the proscriptions of Title VII may seem encouraging. But a closer look raises substantial questions about this apparently benign trend.   .   .   .

[This] type of [voluntary provision] is illustrated by the so-called *Gardner-Denver* clause, proposed at the 1974 meeting of the National Academy of Arbitrators. In essence, such a clause would (1) include "the broadest possible nondiscrimination clause;" (2) authorize "the arbitrator to apply all applicable law, including Title VII, other federal, state, and local civil rights laws, and court and agency decisions and guidelines;" (3) grant the arbitrator the same authority as a federal court, including authority to rewrite the contract after permitting the parties to negotiate necessary corrections; (4) provide for a special panel of arbitrators, established preferably by the EEOC or, alternatively, with the approval of civil rights organizations; and (5) grant "special procedural protections" for the alleged discriminatee, such as the right to select his own counsel when he is not attacking a provision of the agreement or a construction asserted by the union. Given such a clause, federal and state courts and fair employment agencies in turn should, it was also proposed, adopt a policy of deferring to both the arbitration process and completed awards.   .   .   .

In addition to the hope of increased deference and the corresponding reduction of multiple litigation, several other considerations lie behind the proposals for *Gardner-Denver* clauses. First, there is the celebrated ode to labor arbitration composed by the Supreme Court in the *Steelworkers* trilogy.[16] Second, there is the notoriously heavy backlog of the EEOC and the federal court system. Third, there is the understandable desire to be "relevant" and to play a role in meeting pressing social needs. Fourth, Title VII issues are so enmeshed with ordinary grievances that it is feared that arbitral self-limitation with respect to such issues would "decimate the arbitration process."

16. United Steelworkers of America v. American Mfg. Co., 363 U.S. 564 (1960); United Steelworkers of America v. Warrior & Gulf Navigation Co., 363 U.S. 574 (1960); United Steelworkers of America v. Enterprise Wheel & Car Corp., 363 U.S. 593 (1960).   [On this "ode," see P. Hays, Labor Arbitration: A Dissenting View (1966); Getman, The Debate over the Caliber of Arbitrators: Judge Hays and his Critics, 44 Ind.L.J. 182 (1969). Ed. Note.]

These justifications seem deficient for three principal reasons. First, these expansionist proposals understate the extent to which arbitrators are already authorized under conventional contractual clauses to deal with claims cognizable under Title VII.[19] Second, the incremental jurisdiction to invalidate specific contractual clauses that the expansionist clauses would confer is, I believe, incompatible with the nature, procedures, and essential logic of the arbitration system and would place serious strains on that system. Third, the exercise of such jurisdiction would be unlikely to ease the burdens of the federal judiciary.

I turn first to the extent to which conventional contractual clauses cover issues that substantially overlap or coincide with Title VII issues. Even though an agreement lacks a no-discrimination clause, provisions such as those requiring just cause for discipline, or job-related qualifications for promotion, would be violated if race or sex had entered into an employer's decisions. The inclusion in an agreement of terms as elastic as just cause is presumably designed to permit arbitral consideration of the developing, as well as the established, norms and values of the community. Although legislation, such as Title VII, may reinforce or crystalize such values, it is not a prerequisite for considering them. For example, new attitudes regarding dress, speech, drugs, homosexuality, or premarital heterosexual relations are likely to impinge on arbitration regardless of whether those attitudes are reflected in legislation. Contractual standards such as just cause are formulated loosely, presumably in order to permit the arbitrator to consider all relevant factors, including those values embodied in statutes and the Constitution—values that help shape standards of justice not only in the plant, but also in the larger community.[21]

. . . A *Gardner-Denver* clause, by contrast, appears to be designed to bind the arbitrator completely to the body of Title VII law, or at least its substantive if not its procedural elements.

As a consequence, *Gardner-Denver* clauses would appear to require the arbitrator to invalidate specific contractual clauses found to be repugnant to Title VII and, accordingly, to contend with the validity of contractual clauses such as these:

(1) Seniority provisions or their applications, when they are challenged as contrary to one or more of the following: Title VII, a conciliation agreement or a consent decree under that title, an EEOC guideline, and affirmative action program.

19. This understatement has been stimulated by what, in my opinion, was a mistaken implication in the Supreme Court's opinion in *Gardner-Denver*. The Court recognized that the same question may arise under Title VII and a collective bargaining agreement when an agreement's provisions track those of Title VII. See 415 U.S. at 55. It is not clear, however, that the Court also recognized that such an identity of issue might arise solely from broad contractual provisions, such as "just cause." . . .

21. . . . This point is a pervasive one; it applies not only to collective agreements but to all agreements containing malleable standards, such as the good faith standard embodied in some commercial agreements.

(2) Provisions dealing with disability payments, or paid or unpaid leaves of absence, in connection with pregnancy or maternity.

(3) Provisions calling for the use of aptitude tests.

(4) Provisions calling for equal retirement contributions on behalf of men and women and resulting in lower annual benefits to women because of their greater longevity.

Arbitral invalidation of such clauses would involve special strains; for it would nullify the consensus reflected in the parties' specific arrangements. Although the *Gardner-Denver* clause purportedly bases such nullification on the parties' consent, there is a special risk that this ostensible consent will be formal rather than real. Indeed, the incremental jurisdiction conferred by such clauses would cover issues [such as preferential treatment] that go beyond not only the core values of Title VII but also beyond any clear consensus in the plant or the larger community. . . .

If the awesome issues inherent in this dilemma are to be resolved in adjudication, the appropriate tribunal appears to be, and ultimately will be, the courts and not private adjudicators. The fundamental inadequacy of arbitration as a forum for resolving these issues is the second reason for disfavoring expansionist clauses. As the Supreme Court observed in *Gardner-Denver*, those ingredients of arbitration that make it such a valuable adjunct to a system of private ordering, compromise it as an instrument of important public purposes. These ingredients are arbitration's informality, its privacy, its emphasis on finality at the trial level, the ad hoc recruitment of its personnel, and the ecumenical nature of their credentials. Arbitrators, no matter how great their individual competence, lack the institutional credentials that give moral authority to the decisions of the federal judiciary. That authority arises from a complex of tradition and process, including selection processes, the solemnity with which judges typically function, the publicity of their forum, the respectability and expectation of appellate review, and lifetime tenure. Indeed, there is an ironic twist in attempting to provide by contract that ad hoc arbitrators—the most ephemeral of adjudicators—should have the same authority as life-tenured federal judges.

Supplementing these symbolic and traditional considerations are the more tangible difficulties that would be involved in the exercise of incremental jurisdiction under *Gardner-Denver* clauses. Such jurisdiction would, as previously suggested, encompass so-called systemic discrimination resulting from facially neutral arrangements that frequently appear to be free from any specific intention to discriminate. Cases in which such discrimination is alleged tend to involve extensive discovery, intervention by various groups, long trials, and uncertainty regarding the governing law. Such disputes would place special strains on arbitral procedure, which is designed to be quick, informal, and inexpensive.

Another and more important institutional consideration is that the attempt by arbitrators to resolve the general legal questions arising under *Gardner-Denver* clauses might well compromise the achievement of the paramount purposes of arbitration and no-strike clauses—industrial peace, fairness, and order.   Labor arbitration is, of course, a substitute not merely for court action but preeminently for economic warfare.   The relative success of conventional arbitration arrangements is directly dependent on such factors as the genuineness of the consensus reflected in the parties' agreement and the finality that typically attaches to the arbitrator's award.   In contrast, awards based on the incremental jurisdiction granted by a *Gardner-Denver* clause lack the support of these key factors and may ultimately weaken confidence in and acceptance of the results of arbitration.

Quite apart from those risks, clauses granting such incremental jurisdiction to arbitrators are not likely to help relieve the overloaded dockets of the EEOC and the federal courts.   Arbitrators under conventional agreements typically have jurisdiction over many grievances as to which the specific provisions of the collective agreement and Title VII are in accord.   Such grievances include those arising from complaints that race or sex entered into individual employment decisions, such as promotions or discharges.   Furthermore, the key questions raised by such grievances are factual, and, under *Gardner-Denver*, arbitral determinations of issues of fact may be given great weight by the courts, even though they in effect reject the claim of discrimination.   If similar weight were accorded such arbitral determinations by the EEOC and other administrative agencies, multiple litigation on questions of fact would be discouraged.   The expansionist clauses are, of course, designed to expand the arbitrator's jurisdiction to include general questions of law, such as the validity under Title VII of seniority provisions or other contractual provisions.   But it is with respect to precisely these questions that arbitrators lack any special competence.   There is, accordingly, no reason why their awards should receive special deference from courts or the losing party.   In some situations, there may, of course, be strong practical pressures on a losing party to acquiesce in what seems to be an erroneous arbitral determination of a question of external law.   But such pressures and acquiescence will be less likely when a part of the parties' bargain is being invalidated.   In any event, without formal deference from the courts or de facto deference by the losing party, the prospect that expansionist clauses will help reduce the backlogs of official tribunals is remote indeed.

The parties could improve that prospect by purporting to grant an arbitrator final and binding authority to nullify or rewrite elements of their agreements in order to bring it into compliance with Title VII and related regulations;   they could also authorize him to go beyond the minimum requirements of that law.   Courts would presumably uphold such agreements and give finality to resultant awards provided that they met minimum legal requirements.   In other words, the parties could commission arbitrators to serve as their joint legal advisors or as their compliance officers, for the purpose of Title VII and related regulations.   But the grant of arbitral authority to go beyond the requirements prescribed by Title VII would be extraordinary and should not be lightly inferred.   Under *Gardner-Denver* clauses and most contractual clauses it seems likely, therefore, that arbitral resolutions of general questions of law would be denied deference whether they were attacked in court as exceeding, or as falling below, minimum statutory requirements.   In either event, the official tribunal would have to make an independent determination as to the requirements of external law.

It has also been suggested by proponents of *Gardner-Denver* clauses that judicial deference to arbitral awards might be achieved—or at least made more likely—by setting up panels of arbitrators certified as specially qualified for discrimination cases by the EEOC or by organizations such as NOW or the NAACP. Such certification by enforcement tribunals or partisan organizations, however worthy, is a strange prerequisite for those who are to serve as surrogates for federal judges. In any event, it is doubtful that even such screening would lead to the formal judicial deference denied in *Gardner-Denver*.   .   .   .

Equally dubious is another type of proposal also spawned by the *Gardner-Denver* decision: the so-called limitist proposals. These proposals would exclude from arbitration grievances that are cognizable under Title VII. One variation would unconditionally exclude any claim asserting that race or sex entered into the employer's breach of the agreement. A less absolute variation would bar arbitration of a claim if it had been filed with a governmental tribunal. Such proposals are apparently designed to protect employers against double jeopardy with respect to the same basic claim of discrimination. Although that purpose is an appealing one, there is reason to doubt the legality as well as the desirability of such limitist clauses.

With regard to the first type of limitist clause, one objection is that the total exclusion of overlapping Title VII claims from arbitration might well be discrimination invalid under that title.   .   .   . Second, a union's acquiescence in such exclusion would arguably violate the union's duty of fair representation. Each of those objections would gain some support from the Supreme Court's recognition, in *Gardner-Denver* itself, of arbitration's usefulness in resolving claims of discrimination. Third, Title VII issues, including emerging issues of "reverse discrimination," are so pervasively intertwined with ordinary contractual issues that exclusion of arbitration in situations involving a congruence of statutory and contractual claims would drastically curtail the scope of arbitration. Such exclusion, relegating aggrieved employees to the slower statutory remedies, might increase the propensity of employees to engage in self-help in violation of no-strike clauses. Employees are not wholly unaware of the link between a no-strike clause and the existence of orderly alternatives for resolving disputes. Furthermore, curtailing the scope of arbitration would endanger specific enforcement of a no-strike clause since the underlying grievance would be nonarbitrable.

A similar weakening of the psychological and legal underpinnings of the no-strike obligation would probably accompany limitist clauses of the second type, which preclude arbitration of claims filed with official agencies. This conditional form of limitation is less objectionable than the unconditional exclusion from arbitration of all Title VII grievances; for it would bar an aggrieved employee from arbitration only if he had chosen an alternative forum.   .   .   .

––––––––

1. To what extent can Professor Meltzer's view on the proper relationship between private and public adjudicatory institutions be generalized to other types of disputes? See Cover and Aleinikoff, Dialectical Federalism:

Habeas Corpus and the Court, 86 Yale L.J. 1035 (1977), excerpted here in Chapter 7.

2. The existence of a private adjudicatory alternative raises the question of whether adjudicatory institutions should *ever* be publicly financed. In a recent article, Professors Landes and Posner address that question. Landes and Posner, Adjudication as a Private Good, 8 J.Legal Stud. 235 (1979). They first distinguish between dispute-settlement and rule-production. They acknowledge that the private production of rules or precedents is difficult to visualize. This stems in part from the difficulty of establishing property rights in those rules. More importantly, a free market in precedents would produce inconsistent rules, which in turn would destroy the value of the precedents in guiding behavior. Landes and Posner conclude, however, that dispute-settlement could be produced in a private market with limited public involvement. As they put it, "[p]ublic intervention may be necessary (1) to insure compliance with the (private) judge's decision and (2) to compel submission of the dispute to adjudication in the first place." Are there other reasons why we might be reluctant to "privatize" the dispute-settlement process altogether?

3. On the general topic of arbitration in the labor context, see Getman, Labor Arbitration and Dispute Resolution, 88 Yale L.J. 916 (1979). See also Mentschikoff, Commercial Arbitration, 61 Colum.L.Rev. 846 (1961).

SECTION B.   FORMAL ROLES AND PROCEDURAL SYSTEMS

Individuals interact within a procedural system through roles as "plaintiff," "lawyer," "judge," "juror," "witness," "arbitrator," and so forth. Indeed, a procedural system might well be understood to consist essentially of an organization of roles. See Abel, A Comparative Theory of Dispute Institutions in Society, 8 Law & Soc'y Rev. 217 (1973). Our concern here is not to construct an inventory of the roles within a procedural system, nor to show how the content of particular procedural roles is shaped by substantive theories of law. (That was the burden of Mr. Simon's essay in chapter 2.) Our purpose here is more institutional, to point to the connection between system and role, and to uncover the tensions and difficulties implicit in the very idea of a person acting through roles.

1.   AMBIGUITY IN ROLE

In the essay that follows, the brothers Kadish provide a general account of "role." They define the concept, explain how conduct is used to evaluate the way one acts in a role, and identify the various ways in which a role might be structured or defined. As they see it, the central theoretical issue to avoid is the dichotomy of the twin excesses of rigidity and permissiveness— to explain how a person might be permitted to depart from the rules that supposedly restrain his role and yet still be considered to be acting within that role. The Kadishes seek to avoid the common view which insists that people must "simply step out of their roles in order to do what must be done;" and for that purpose they introduce and develop the concept of a "recourse role." This concept formalizes and acknowledges the ambiguities inherent in any definition of role. A recourse role is one in which an individual has a liberty—though not a right—to act inconsistently with the obligations imposed by his role; these liberties are built into the very definition of the role. One need not step out of such a role "to do what must be done." The Kadishes' framework is a general one, not confined to procedural systems; but they apply it to explain a striking feature of our procedural system—the nullification power of the jury.

Mortimer R. Kadish and Sanford H. Kadish, **Discretion to Disobey** *

. . . [W]e shall understand roles as established and continuing parts in a social enterprise or institution. As such, they serve an accepted social purpose, which is why one can refer to them to justify one's actions. They are "parts" because the life of the social institution or enterprise depends upon their performance. They are "established" first in the sense that, while their agents may sometimes alter them, those agents typically encounter the rules and purposes of the role substantially given; and second in the sense that agents can refer to their role to establish their authority to deal with others. Being perceived by those who enact them and by those who receive those enactments as framed for the occupancy of others who will, or may, come later, roles are conceived as intrinsically "continuing." Agents come and go—the role remains. . . .

. . . Since a person's role activity must have a social function, it must ultimately be sustained by the role activity of others. The parent who cares for his children does not do so as a parent, but merely as a matter of fact, on his own as it were, unless his activity is in some way recognized and sustained by society. The officer cannot act as an officer unless there are other people who in their roles will accept his commands. The congressman cannot function in his role without the acceptance of the entire legal system by the other members of society; and merely to influence legislation, to whatever degree, does not make one a congressman. Therefore it is a fundamental consideration guiding role conduct that others in their roles sustain one's role activity. If they do not, the activity ceases to be such activity. And others "sustain" role activity in the sense that a person acting in a role must depend on the cooperation of others acting in their roles to achieve the ends prescribed by his, and also in the sense that those others, seeing him as a participant with them in some social enterprise, impute a kind of legitimacy to his behavior, a legitimacy often expressed by the locution that it is proper for him to be doing what he is doing. . . .

Judging in a Context of Evaluation

To act in a role does not merely mean to engage in a distinctive activity that is sustained by persons acting in other roles. It also means to make choices in a context of evaluation proper to a role. A context of evaluation determines not only whether a role agent's actions will be regarded as proper

* *Source*: Discretion to Disobey (1973), excerpts from Chapters 1 and 2. Mortimer Kadish: Professor of Philosophy, Case Western Reserve University; Sanford Kadish: Dean and Professor of Law, University of California at Berkeley.

by others but how he himself will weigh his options in a given situation. What does a context of evaluation consist of?   .   .   .

Prescribed Means.   One element of a context of evaluation, and hence one kind of standard for propositions of appropriateness, consists of what we shall call contraints on reasons—more or less explicit limitations on what reasons will be considered acceptable for undertaking actions in a particular role.   Specifying acceptable reasons serves essentially as a means by which roles may be structured to achieve their ends.   Thus a person acting in a role knows that certain considerations must not be taken into account;   that other considerations may or may not be taken into account at his own discretion; and that still other considerations must always be taken into account.   In the more complex roles the constraints on reasons include weights and priorities assigned to various aspects of the role's ends.   Thus the appropriateness of a role agent's action depends in part on whether the action is in accord with that particular role's priorities.   A person who gives great weight to that which is minimal or little to that which is overriding does not judge as a person in that role.

Only rarely are constraints on reasons adequately developed for all the occasions when a person acting in a role must make a decision.   Nevertheless, if a role is to be differentiated from other roles, some set of constraints on reasons must be distinguishable.   There is a special way of rebuking anyone who strays from such contraints, even with the best of intentions and the best of reasons, except that those reasons are not reasons of the role: "Remember," such a person is enjoined, "you are a soldier, not a social worker; a priest, not a judge;   a parent, not a stranger."   Similarly, officials of the legal and political systems may be told: "Remember, you are a judge, not a legislator;   a prosecutor, not a defense attorney."   The same holds for citizens: "Remember, you are a private citizen, not a judge.   Perhaps you would have decided the case differently.   That's not a relevant reason for refusing to comply."   Such statements say in effect that reasons acceptable in one role are precluded in another.

Constraints on actions, rather than on reasons for actions, are another element in a context of evaluation.   Whatever the constraints on reasons in a particular context of evaluation may be, there are times when no reason suffices to justify a role agent's undertaking or not undertaking a certain action. Constraints on action extend to the outcomes of any reasoning within a context of evaluation, rather than to the reasoning itself.

Constraints on actions are part of any role's context of evaluation in virtue of the distinctive and socially sustained activity that characterizes the role.   Through those constraints the structure of a role seeks to guarantee that at least the essential ends of the role will be achieved, and that the achievement of other ends, perhaps those of other roles, will not be blocked. That a soldier may not leave the battlefield without the permission of his commander is a constraint on his action;   his deferring to that rule, even in the face of death, is one of the things that makes him a soldier.   Similarly, constraints on the actions of officials follow from the nature of their office, and are essential to achieving the ends for which the office was created. And the actions of citizens are of course constrained by the legal system.

A related kind of constraint on actions consists of specifications of actions that will count as actions in the role, rather than of actions that may not or must be taken. This element appears in the context of evaluation of roles that entail the exercise of delegated powers, such as the role of an official. An official must exercise his powers by certain procedures and within certain limits if his actions are to have any effect. For example, a judge who acts in excess of his jurisdiction has in effect taken no action at all: his action counts for nothing legally. Such constraints do not apply to the citizen, however, whose role need not entail any delegated powers. To say that a citizen has not acted as a citizen means only that he has not acted properly in his role. His actions count as actions nonetheless. One might say that a citizen who refuses to pay his taxes has failed to carry out his obligations as a citizen. His refusal still stands as an action, however, and one for which he may be held accountable.   .   .   .

Prescribed Ends. All roles exist to achieve some end or ends, as we have seen. And the prescribed means just discussed are those constraints on role-agent conduct that have been fashioned to serve those ends. But sometimes a role's context of evaluation will extend to the ends of the role as well, so that the role agent may (or must) consider the mesh between the prescribed means and the role's ends in judging the appropriateness of undertaking some action. The familiar case in which the end of a role becomes part of its context of evaluation, though by no means the only one, as will be subsequently shown, occurs when a role agent is required or permitted to act at his own discretion to achieve the end of his role. It is instructive to consider now the various types of ends that sometimes enter a role's context of evaluation.

The most immediate and least abstract type of end to which a role agent may have recourse in determining appropriate action is the specific task his role is designed to accomplish. For example, the mailman's role could conceivably authorize him to choose his delivery route, to decide his hours of delivery, to give preference to pieces of mail that deserved priority, and the like, so long as he acted in accordance with the end of delivering the mail. Normally, of course, the mailman's role does not allow recourse to ends, even the end of delivering the mail. But it could be structured so that the mailman would determine his actions in accordance with his conception of his task. The same could be said, in fact, for any official role—that action will be appropriate to the degree it is in the interest of accomplishing the task and inappropriate to the degree to which it is not.

Another type of end that may become part of a context of evaluation is a role's function within a larger institution, which may itself be embedded in an entire network of institutions. To the extent that a role is so structured, judging the appropriateness of undertaking action extends to the evaluation of the role's task in the light of the larger institutional ends that the task ends are designed to serve. When this happens both the role's prescribed means and its task ends become subject to modification and interpretation by the role agent as conflicts appear. The institutional organization of society then itself becomes a factor in making judgments in a role. Obviously officials and political leaders, at least those at high levels of government, must constantly reassess the relationship of their role activity to the larger institutional framework within which their roles function. But citizens also have institutional ends they may properly take into account in certain situations. Broadly speaking, those ends are part of the general end of ensuring that the society's system of rules and competences functions successfully. Contributing to that general end will then become a relevant consideration in differentiating appropriate from inappropriate action.

The third type of end that may become part of a context of evaluation derives from commitments to norms that transcend any institutionalized role. There can be no a priori objection to incorporating in the contexts of evaluation of at least some roles, including some of those in the legal and political systems, what we shall call "background ends." Whereas task ends and institutional ends may be invoked to justify actions that serve more or less established task requirements and institutions, background ends enable an individual role agent to conceive of what is proper in his role in a more liberal or open way—or, it must be conceded, in a narrower and more wrongheaded way—and so to alter the institutional pattern in which he finds himself. He may thus invoke ends that are recognized by his society but only incompletely realized by its structure, or even ends his society has completely ignored. He may even look further afield and invoke ends that perhaps no system of roles has ever achieved or could be expected to achieve in full measure: ends such as a finer justice, kindliness, respect for other people, or human creativity. In sum, background ends may serve as a basis for criticizing and humanizing institutional ends. . . .

Knowing the Role

In order for an agent to respond to a challenge to some action of his undertaken in his role, he must first determine the nature of his role. Does the role's context of evaluation grant the role agent recourse to certain ends in justifying his actions? What tasks does it require him to perform? Such questions are not always easily answered. To determine the characteristics of a role one could reasonably consult the people who act in the role and study their behavior, but one still would not necessarily know what their reports and one's own observations signified, particularly if the two sources differed. Simply describing role behavior does not necessarily uncover the essential characteristics of the role itself. To complicate matters further, all roles need not be determinate in every respect. Roles change; roles grow; roles divide and collapse. But difficult as the task may be, it cannot be escaped by one challenged to defend undertaking some action in his role. How then are roles known?

The Ecology of Roles. The repeated observation that social roles must sustain each other suggests one direction in which an answer may be found. In order to discover what behavior is appropriate in a role and how to interpret the justification offered by role agents for their actions, one considers not only what the role agent says and does but also how persons in complementary roles respond. When do they object, and in what way? Will they refuse to cooperate, or extend cooperation only partially or provisionally? What sanctions will they administer? A role is shaped substantially by the demands of the complementary roles surrounding it; hence we may determine some of the characteristics of a role by studying its function in a complex of interdependent roles, or what we shall call the "ecology of roles." We speak of an ecology precisely because changes in specific roles tend to follow changes anywhere in the institutional environment and may radiate consequences for roles apparently far removed. By studying the ecology of roles we can see the consequences for other roles if the role in question should have one characteristic rather than another. Since there are such consequences, that a role has a given characteristic need no longer be left to simple observation; it can be confirmed against the requirements of the roles that it sustains and the roles that sustain it.

The Historical Reference. People also know the characteristics of their role, the obligations and privileges for which it provides, through the role's origins and history. In effect, roles are known through an explanation of how they got to be that way, and that is especially true of the more complex legal and political roles. But to comprehend the full meaning of a role's history, one must also trace the history of the role's developing ecology. A role's past development cannot be understood without reference to its past ecology any more than a role's present nature can be understood without reference to its present ecology. Tracing that large history also gives sense to precedents. This is so because roles are historical entities, by and large. They are established for those who come in time to fill them, and those who come in time to fill them are expected to value the way they were filled in the past. In fact, historical analysis is one means by which people often reach agreement on propositions of appropriateness.

The Systematic Reference. We said that roles are historical entities "by and large" because plainly a constitution may be written or an enterprise begun that creates a role full-grown. Such a role has no precedents. To assess its characteristics one must first turn to the constitution, statute, or agreement that produced it. If that step fails to produce a definitive result, it seems natural, as the history of constitutional law illustrates, to refer to the ecology of roles in which the constituted role was intended to operate. Nevertheless, in the case of a deliberately contrived social role one must always appeal first to the systematic reference—to the act that created the role.

Normative Judgments. A final means of determining the nature of a role deserves particular attention. It is the appeal, in some phases of some arguments about roles, to judgments of what a role should be in order to establish propositions about what it is.

Sometimes, despite ecological considerations, precedents and systematic references, disagreement over the nature of a role persists. At that point the parties to the controversy may find themselves making implicit appeals to differing normative judgments, and then continuing the argument over the role's nature by disputing one another's judgments of what the role ought to be like. For example, they might argue about whether a prosecuting attorney's role requires him to prosecute all known and provable cases that violate some portion of the penal code. A decision on the nature of his role may then depend partly on the case that can be made for the social values of having him do so.

Within the limits of ecology, history, and system, then, roles can be said to have the properties that they ought to have. Sometimes, no doubt, the constraints on the role prior to the appeal to normative judgments are so strong and definite that the normative judgment carries no weight. But at other times, particularly when events make roles as traditionally construed inadequate, it is natural to seek the nature of the role in what would be better for the role, the institution it serves, or society at large. . . .

Individuals and Roles

. . . In his role a person may be a doctor, a judge, a senator, a mail carrier, but he is also a person with his own aspirations and ethics. Thus not one but two sets of considerations, broadly speaking, guide his conduct. The first consists of what we call "role reasons"—reasons based on the constraints of his role tempered by whatever discretion recourse to role ends may afford him. The second consists of reasons that he may recognize as an individual but that in his role he cannot take into account, or what we call "excluded reasons." Frequently a person committed to a role finds himself in situations where the role reasons for undertaking an action and the excluded reasons conflict. In such a case he does not simply weigh the role reasons equally against the excluded reasons, and then act according to whichever set of reasons is greater. Instead he acknowledges his obligation to his role by imposing an extra burden, or surcharge, so to speak, on the excluded reasons, so that they must have significantly greater weight than the role reasons, rather than merely greater weight, in order to sway him. This is a familiar way of dealing with one's role commitments. Nearly everyone has had the experience of acknowledging that he would take a certain course of action if only he were not in a certain position. Usually this means that though the acknowledged merits of the case carry, in one's objective judgment, in favor of the action required, they are insufficient to overcome the demands of one's role. Very rarely, perhaps, it may mean that the excluded reasons never could carry against the role reasons, no matter what their weight.

In effect, in dealing with obligations of role, the surcharge imposed on excluded reasons is either finite, as in the first case, or infinite, as in the second. Imposing a finite surcharge is the practical result of being a person who at once accepts his obligation to a role and continues to think of himself as an individual with other commitments as well; imposing an infinite surcharge is the practical result of being a person who puts his obligation to a role unqualifiedly first. It is difficult to see how an absolutely unqualified commitment to any role can be defended. But a qualified commitment to a role, based on a finite surcharge, might be defended by seeking agreement on the whole institutional program in which that role exists, along with the implications of role deviation of the given sort for a large variety of wider interests. So the student who interrupts a class defends himself by condemning the university's structure and involvement with the military-industrial complex. He counters the accusation that he has taken his role obligations as a student too lightly by urging the overwhelming value of an alternative institutional program.   In sum, in defending his judgment of the appropriate surcharge against his action, he engages in social philosophy.   .   .   .

How Rule Departures in Roles Become Possible

Roles, including those of citizen and official, may be structured to take account of the fact that individuals acting in roles nevertheless place for the most part only a finite surcharge on excluded reasons before departing from some role requirement.   That fact is taken into account for some roles by incorporating into their contexts of evaluation a principle for acting in the role that, in effect, guides the agent in applying and sometimes extending the context itself.   Though such a role may still require a role agent to act in a certain way, it may also permit him to conclude that complying with the role's prescribed means would obstruct the role activity or defeat the role's task or institutional ends.   Or it may permit him even to conclude that the required action would defeat certain background ends, which by their nature could never be clearly delineated in the role's context of evaluation.   In effect, the role agent is permitted to incorporate into his decision what would ordinarily be excluded reasons, or to put the matter differently, to convert excluded reasons for an action into role reasons.   He is at liberty to act on his own judgment in certain circumstances, and he can expect his decision to be supported by others in related roles.   This is the finesse that introduces flexibility into role behavior and reduces the instances in which people simply step out of their roles in order to do what must be done.   .   .   .

Two requirements must be met if such rule departures are to be justified. First, extra weight must be given to achieving the role's ends through its prescribed means, including any discretion that the role may provide for; by the same token, an extra burden must be imposed on any reasons there may be for departing from the role's requirements.   In effect, the procedure used when conscientious individuals depart from roles that do not provide for justifiable rule departures must be incorporated as a feature of roles that do provide for justifiable departures.

The second requirement is that there be a constraint on the reasons for undertaking the action.   A person's reason for departing from a role's prescribed means or for failing to achieve its prescribed end must meet some standard of relevance;   otherwise the valuable distinction would be lost between the flexibility afforded by roles providing for justifiable rule departures and the exploitation and misuse of such roles.   That standard of relevance is provided by the same set of ends normally taken to guide discretionary action within the role: the task ends, institutional ends, and background ends.   Those ends establish the terms on which the role agent considering a departure from a rule, or what is a species of the same thing, an unauthorized extension of his discretion, may hope to reach agreement with those who depend on him and those on whom he depends in the ecology of roles.   If he can show that he departed from a rule in order to achieve such an end, he will have begun to make a case.   Clearly, as the range of ends a role agent may invoke to justify departing from a rule widens (to institutional ends or, at the extreme, to background ends), the possibility of justifying rule departures in a role widens also.   And the wider the possibility for justifying rule departures, the greater the opportunity for role agents both to exercise their intelligence and to commit egregious and uncontrollable violations.

Rule departures in role are made possible, then, by incorporating into the role a liberty, often of a sort that the role agent takes advantage of at his peril, to undertake actions outside the role's prescribed means to achieve the role's ends. The actions are of a sort that were the liberty not granted, they could not be justified by the role agent through any appeal to his authorized discretion, leaving him in the position of one who broke with his role. The discovery of such rule departures is not new. "An important feature of a large proportion of social roles," a group of sociologists has observed, "is that the actions which make them are not minutely prescribed, and that a certain range of variability is regarded as legitimate. Sanctions are not invoked against deviance within certain limits." [2] Our point is merely that the nature of rule departures in role has not always been squarely faced. "Deviance," which, if it means anything, means a departure from some rule or expectation, has often been hidden under the more common notion of indeterminacy, as though to deviate from a rule or requirement were the same as to assume responsibility for acting in ways "not minutely prescribed." . . .

Ambiguities in the Jury's Role

Power and Right. . . . [T]he criminal jury has evolved to a point where it exercises what might be called a sovereign power to acquit in criminal cases. The power to return a general verdict cannot be taken from it. It returns its verdict without stated reasons or justifications of any kind. If it finds the defendant not guilty, the acquittal must be given final and binding legal effect, no matter what may be thought or known about the jury's failure to follow the law. And the jury itself is fully insulated from any accountability for its action. . . .

Courts and Jury. The force of these propositions is enhanced by the way the courts have dealt with specific legal issues concerning the criminal jury. If a judge hears a criminal case without a jury and finds the defendant guilty of one charge and not guilty of another in circumstances where such a finding is illogical and inconsistent, the judgment of guilt is reversible on the ground that there can be no confidence in its correctness. But if a jury returns similar verdicts that are no less illogical and inconsistent, the verdict of guilt is regarded as irreversible. . . .

In civil cases tried before a jury the use of special interrogatories formulated by the court to assist the jury in arriving at their general verdict logically and according to the judge's instructions is a generally authorized practice. So is the special verdict, in which the jury is instructed to return only a special written finding on each issue of fact, leaving it for the court to enter judgment in accordance with the law as applied to the jury-found facts. Both devices serve as controls on the jury, functioning to ensure judgments in accordance with the law.

2. T. Parsons and E. A. Shils, eds.,
   Towards a General Theory of Action
   (New York, 1962), p. 24.

At the common law there is authority for the use of such devices in criminal cases as well, though the jury can always insist on returning a general verdict. Such devices have been even more rarely used in this country than in England, however, and current authority finds them in violation of the right to trial by jury. An instructive case is United States v. Spock, [416 F.2d 165 (1st Cir. 1969),] in which the court reversed a conviction of conspiracy to counsel evasion of the draft. The trial court had put to the jury, in addition to the general issue of guilty or not guilty, ten special questions calling for a yes or no answer. The use of this procedure was enough to require reversal of the conviction, even assuming the correctness of the questions proposed. The right to jury trial, the appellate court reasoned, would be meaningless if the jury were not free from judicial pressure. Of course, the directed verdict of guilty is the most direct of such pressures, and it is accordingly prohibited. But lesser and more indirect pressures, such as the requirement of a special verdict or the use of special interrogatories, are impermissible for the same reason.   .   .   .

Jury Tradition. The jury's obligations and freedoms are determined by tradition as well as by law. The landmark cases, particularly those involving criminal libel and sedition, in which the jury invoked its power to nullify what were widely regarded as unjust laws, are regarded not as regrettable departures from the rule of law but as historic and seminal assertions, like the Magna Carta and the Bill of Rights, of man's right to be free of unjust laws. Arguments in support of the jury's fundamental value almost always rest on the nullifying function of criminal juries.   .   .   .

Jury Behavior. Jury nullification of unjust laws is a continuing tradition. The classic historical instances include the jury's refusal to convict in a number of famous criminal libel cases until the law was changed to give juries the authority to acquit through general verdicts. Early English juries employed various strategies to avoid capital punishment, such as finding against the evidence that only 39 shillings had been stolen when to find 40 shillings or more would mean a mandatory death sentence. Later, in this country, we have witnessed the American jury's systematic nullification of the Prohibition laws during the 1920's—"the most intense example of jury revolt in recent history." [The authors then report the findings of Kalven and Zeisel's Work, The American Jury (1966), on the jury's "revolt from the law," excerpted in this volume in chapter 5.]   .   .   .

Interpreting the Jury's Role

If, now, the juror is obliged to do as he is instructed by the judge and if he may, nevertheless, do as he thinks best; if, in fact, he is afforded every protection that will make it possible for him to do as he thinks best and his function as a juror is extolled because jurors sometimes do, how is the conscientious juror to understand his role? What is he to do in his jural role if it seems to him that to follow the judge's instruction would lead to a verdict he is convinced ought to go otherwise?   .   .   .

The Conventional Interpretations. The first interpretation (Interpretation I) holds that the jury's role is to follow the judge's instructions. According to this way of understanding the situation, official formulations fully state the jury's proper role, which is strictly that of a fact-finding agency. A jury reaches its general verdict by deciding the facts of the case and applying the law as given by the judge. Of no consequence are its own sentiments concerning the law's justness, either generally or as applied to a specific case; its own conception of the law's meaning; or its own estimate of the force of any mitigating circumstances not comprehended in the law. The vaunted "sovereignty" of the jury, therefore, is a matter of power, not of right. The jury can reach a perverse verdict of acquittal and get away with it, but that does not imply the right to reach such a verdict. When juries reach verdicts that run counter to the judge's instructions, they usurp a discretion not theirs to exercise. That jury nullification has sometimes produced good results does not show that nullification is within the jury's legal role.

Such is one way of construing the jury's role. The technique is to acknowledge an inconsistency between jury power and jury duty in cases of acquittal, assume that the inconsistency cannot be, and then explain away the class of evidence that points to a jury liberty. But in fact the decision to choose jury duty over the competing value of jury liberty is arbitrary. One might equally well follow Alexander Hamilton and discover in the scrupulous protection of jury power the institution of a sovereign right. Even in ordinary matters, when people are systematically protected not only against incursions into their power to act as they think best but also against any attempt to hold them accountable for their use of the power, they assume they have the right to act as they think best.

The second interpretation (Interpretation II) holds that the jury's role is to do as it thinks best. Pound's famous distinction between the law in action and the law in books makes plausible a single, consistent interpretation of the jury's role that is precisely the reverse of Interpretation I. Instead of arguing that the jury's role demands following the judge's instructions, one may argue that the judge's instructions constitute only the formal law, whereas the real law, the law in action, leaves it to the jury to follow the judge's instructions only when so inclined. To be sure, there is the difficult question of what Pound and others who have adopted the distinction mean by the law in action. Sometimes they seem to mean that the law in action is, flatly, what people in authority do, independent of any rule. In that sense, of course, the law in action makes no requirement on juries at all: whatever they succeed in getting away with is the law in action. At other times the law in actions means the actual norms of the political-legal community as opposed to the norms announced in the books. It is in this sense that the realist distinction shores up a rule of competence for the jury: "Do as you think best. Take or leave the judge's instructions." Any jury that thought itself bound to the judge's instructions would then have misunderstood its own role. The inconsistency between duty and liberty has been overcome: the duty is merely formal; the liberty is real in the law.

But even if Interpretation II should rest on the law in action in this latter sense—that is, on the basis of a determination of what the real, rather than the apparent norms of the law may be—the question of how to determine the real norm remains. We propose that there is no direct inference from the law in action to the real norm of jury sovereignty postulated in Interpretation II without the addition of an independent preference for that condition. In the face of the history of jury acquittal, Interpretation II, like Interpretation I, needs a normative principle to select one part of the evidence rather than the other as determinative.

Such a principle is necessary because for the law in action to be law, it must define some behavior as a transgression, even if the transgressor is an official. What actual behavior cannot violate constitutes no rule. How, then, in view of the all but unpredictable course of human actions, are we to argue to the real, binding rule? Which class of behavior represents compliance with the actual norm, and which a misguided attempt to follow merely fictitious ones: the behavior of deferring to the judge's instructions or the behavior of defying them? When, in effect, does the jury deviate from the law in action, and when does it not? To ascribe to the jury a determinate role at all implies that the jury *might* deviate from the law in action. Why should the statistically far more numerous instances of compliance with court instructions carry so much less weight in determining the law in action than the far fewer instances of departure? Why should the fact of jury impunity be granted all possible weight? Such questions seem readily answerable only if one asserts a preference for one sort of jury behavior over another as a basis for determining what the law in action actually is. Then behavior that fulfills presumably valuable functions will satisfy the law in action, while behavior that fulfills no such functions but is grounded only on formal obligations becomes a misguided attempt to satisfy the law in books.

But even if the jury's role is to carry out the law in action, and even if that law can be determined by a value judgment, much that the practitioners of the legal profession consider law remains to be accounted for. Jurors are still obliged to take an oath to decide the case according to the law and the evidence. The judge does instruct the jurors in the applicable law and direct them to arrive at their verdict in accordance with it. The lawyer for the defendant typically is not permitted to argue to the jury that the law is otherwise than as stated by the judge or that it should be disregarded in any event. In these respects the jury cannot be said to have the right to act according to its own judgment in the sense that an official has the right to act according to his own judgment when the law grants him explicit discretionary authority to do so.

In short, the logical source of the notion that the jury's duty is either to follow the judge's instructions or to do as it thinks best is the commitment to the rule-of-law model for official roles. Both interpretations of the jury's role are single and consistent: in the first case, a juror must do what he is told; and in the second, he must do as he thinks best. Neither leaves room for the notion of departure from a rule.

The Jury's Role as Recourse Role. Whatever the rule-of-law model may require, logic does not prohibit an interpretation of the jury's role under the law as both requiring conformity to the judge's instructions and extending the liberty to return a general verdict of acquittal counter to those instructions. That liberty may be seen as merely reflecting the fact that the system of law extends recourse to the juror where a conflict exists within the jury's context of evaluation. A liberty does not necessarily contradict an obligation, so long as a significant surcharge is placed on the denial of the obligation; not all obligations need be unremitting. . . . Of course, an obligation ceases to be an obligation if a person can be said to have a right not to comply with it. If a jury had a right to ignore the judge's instructions for whatever reason, as Interpretation II claims, there could be no question of its being under an obligation to accept the judge's instructions. But we claim only that the jury is at liberty to depart from the judge's instructions, not that it has a right to do so at will.

In brief, the confusions in Interpretations I and II arise because the role of juror is a recourse role, while it is customary to think of official roles exclusively as either clerklike or discretionary. Under this customary assumption the role of the jury must be either to do as the court instructs or to exert a right to do as it thinks best. To be sure, this assumption of a single, consistent directive has a prima facie plausibility. To deny it seems to demand that we imagine a judge saying simultaneously, "Follow my instructions; it is your duty!" and "Use your own judgment!" One could fairly conclude that such a judge did not know what he wanted and had provided no guidance whatsoever. And such would be the case if one conceived the judge to be simultaneously placing an obligation on the jury and granting it the right not to comply with the obligation. But in fact, as we have suggested, while it can be said that the judge places an obligation on the jury, it cannot be said that he grants it the right not to comply. For one thing, the liberty to depart from the judge's instructions comes from other sources than the instructions themselves; for another, it is a liberty to depart from the instructions that those other sources extend and not a right to do so at will.

Thus the juror is the focus of a variety of claims and dispensations. He is told what he must do, but he is not forced to do it and neither he personally nor his verdict may be called to account. He is told what the law is, authoritatively; he is sworn to uphold it; and then he is left alone to reach his decision. He must judge not merely the defendant's guilt or innocence but the merit of the judge's instructions for the particular case. He has become the final judge of whether or not to fulfill his legally defined obligation as a juror. He is, in effect, the agent of a recourse role. Let us review the principal reasons why we think this is so, and then consider some likely objections.

The first reason depends on the assumption that all official roles are created to carry out certain activities according to certain prescribed procedures and constraints to achieve certain ends. So the jury has been set up to reach judgments of guilt or innocence according to certain procedures and constraints, among which are the judge's instructions, in order to achieve the ends of criminal justice. From this assumption arises both the critical problem of acting in a role and the possibility of a solution. . . . [T]hough the prescribed means for securing a role's ends are binding on the role agent, those means may from time to time prevent the role agent from achieving the role's prescribed ends. But the problem is solved if the role is structured, as the jury role is, to allow the role agent to evaluate the consequences of adhering to the role's prescribed means in terms of the role's prescribed ends—that is, if the role is structured as a recourse role. Thus the jury considers whether literal adherence to the judge's instructions will advance or impede the goals of criminal justice as well as the institutional and background ends of the society more generally. In contrast to roles that extend no liberty, the recourse role allows the agent recourse to a system of role ends that enables him to judge the applicability of his obligations and to act on that judgment. If the conflict occurs among different ends of the role itself rather than simply between some prescribed means and ends, the solution is similar. The agent may consider the role's entire structure of means and ends before making a judgment on which end or ends shall prevail and which yield.

Second, judgment by a role agent of any of his obligations is made possible, and the transition from a role that extends no liberty to a recourse role is achieved, because the reality of an obligation is not necessarily denied when the obligation is held as something less than absolute. It is on this ground that we say that the judge's instructions are binding on the jury and at the same time that the criminal jury in considering an acquittal may judge its obligation in relation to the particular case. Because the jury system requires the conscientious juror to distinguish between departing from an instruction at will and departing from an instruction because he has "damn good reason" for doing so as determined by the role ends he is committed to serve, the jury role retains the obligatory status of the judge's instructions while permitting departures from them. For in general, we regard a constraint as obligatory when we require not merely reason to deny it but overriding reason—which, of course, is the meaning of placing an extra surcharge on reasons for departing from a rule.

It may be objected that we can rid ourselves of the notion of a recourse role and preserve a single, consistent directive to act in a certain way simply by recognizing the actual definition of the role to be conditional: "If you don't have overriding reason—damn good reason—to do otherwise, then do as the judge tells you." According to this argument the current formulation of the judge's instructions to the jury is misleading. The proposed conditional formulation properly expresses the relationship between jury liberty and jury duty, without the need to introduce the concept of rule departure at all.

But this argument falls short for several reasons. The conditional formulation is spurious if its intent is really to restate the conditions met by the idea of a recourse role as a single, consistent directive that in itself generates no conflict. Liberties can always be stated to qualify obligations, but to do so does not diminish either the liberty or the obligation. Any juror hearing the above conditional would know immediately that his legal obligation weighed no less heavily simply because it was not universally compelling; the weight of his obligation, he would understand, was precisely the point of the demand for overriding reason not to carry it out. Regardless of whether the juror translated the conditional message into the language of liberty and obligation, he would face the same consequences as before: that the choice whether to obey the judge's instructions had been thrown back on him; that he would, finally, not escape making a judgment on what obligations would bind him in the instant case and what would not; that he would need to find reasons of overriding weight if he decided not to meet his obligations.

Further, the "overriding reason" condition in the above conditional requires the jury to invoke some ultimate moral or legal norm, and is only poorly understood when assimilated with simpler, more concrete conditions. "Do as the judge tells you unless the consequence is serious injustice" differs in important respects from "Assign applicants to windows according to their last names unless the line exceeds ten persons." First, there exists no routine for determining what "serious injustice" means, as there does for determining the number of people in a line. The rules of law have presumably been formulated to achieve justice. The jury liberty is extended because in some unknown and hence unstatable circumstances they may not, and the determination of those circumstances is left at large to the jury. Second, there can be no question of conflict in determining the number of people in a line, as there can be in deciding to apply some higher legal or moral norm in reaching a just verdict rather than to obey the judge. So it simply will not do to treat the introduction of an ultimate end into the deliberations as though one had merely introduced another condition in a conditional directive for attaining some end, thereby producing a consistent directive requiring the juror to decide only whether to comply or not. To mask the conflict by a conditional statement does not resolve it.

We have been arguing that one cannot rid oneself of the concept of the jury's role as a recourse role simply by recognizing the actual definition of the rule binding the jury to be conditional. We did not deny that the net effect of the constraints and powers through which the jury defines itself is to obligate the jury to follow the instructions of the judge except in the truly exceptional case where the jury finds that to follow those instructions would work a substantial disservice to the fundamental values of justice and fairness. We denied merely that the conditional formulation eliminated the recourse role as a logical possibility and assimilated the jury role into an ordinary discretionary role. Now, as a third point, we wish to observe that an explicit articulation of the jury's privilege to nullify the law where they think that to do so would serve the interests of justice constitutes one special way of engineering the legal system—a way that leads away from the preservation of the jury's role as a recourse role—while the way of engineering the jury system that has been described as the case in these pages constitutes another way. Not only are these two separate legal strategies, but there are consequences of import in the choice of which one to employ.

The different consequences underlie the debate, recently revived in prosecutions of Vietnam War resisters and protesters, over whether the judge should inform the jury of their liberty to disregard the judge's legal instructions if they find that to follow the instructions would produce an unjust conviction of the defendant.[65] The advantages of this instruction are plain enough. First, it would ensure that all juries would understand their role in the same way, and consequently that the benefit of their liberty to acquit despite the judge's instructions would be available equally to defendants in every case. Second, it would provide for fuller participation by the defendant in the processes of adjudication by allowing him to present evidence and

---

65. See the opinion of Judge Leventhal in United States v. Dougherty, 473 F. 2d 1113, 1130–37 (D.C.Cir. 1972). . . .

argue his case to the jury more fully in terms of the grounds on which the jury might properly choose to decide it.

But there would be disadvantages to such an instruction as well, disadvantages that have motivated some courts in recent years to reject the proposal. The very technique of explicitly instructing the jury, without qualification, that they are obliged to apply the law given by the judge helps ensure that they will impose the required extra surcharge on any decision to depart from the rule. One of the interesting conclusions reached by Kalven and Zeisel in their study of the behavior of the criminal jury was that while the jury does in fact make use of its power to follow its own conscience, it does not deviate from the judge's instructions very often; the jury is not, as they say, "a wildcat operation." This is so, they observe, not only because there is presently no great gap between official and popular values in criminal cases but also because the jury "has been invested with a public task, brought under the influence of a judge, and put to work in solemn surroundings." And, they conclude, "Perhaps one reason why the jury exercises its very real power so sparingly is because it is officially told that it has none."

To the extent this is so, an explicit statement that the jury may invoke their own values, even if put in terms of the highly exceptional case, would reduce the impact of the judge's instructions on the law and invite jury nullification on a greater scale. Whether this result is desirable or not is another matter. The choice turns on the value placed on jury nullification in particular stages of a legal system's development as opposed to the increased danger of arbitrary verdicts and of removing the criminal law still further from the control of court and legislature. Our task here is not to argue the issue but simply to show that there is one.

In sum, the case for characterizing the jury's role as a recourse role turns on the following propositions. First, logic does not prohibit such a role, nor does an easy reformulation make such a role dispensable. Second, recourse roles like that of the jury are functional; they serve distinct purposes in the administration of justice. Third, this characterization of the jury's role accommodates the apparently divergent themes presented by the evidence. It does not require, as alternative interpretations do, that portions of the evidence be oversimplified or explained away.

We can now answer the question posed at the beginning of this section: how is the conscientious juror to understand his role? The duty of the jury is indeed to find the facts on the basis of the evidence presented and to return a general verdict by applying those facts to the law as given by the judge. This is the rule, and it imposes an obligation to comply. But the obligation is not absolute. Sometimes considerations of common sense, or considerations of fairness to the defendant, or the jury's appraisal of the law in contrast to the judge's statement of it may weigh so heavily that the jury may justifiably depart from the rule requiring it to defer to the judge's instructions. . . .

Conditions for Legitimated Interposition

What characteristics of the legal system tend to support the interpretation of a particular official role as a recourse role—that is, as a role that provides for legitimated interposition? . . .

We have spoken in terms of classes of rule departures. But what of any particular rule departure within a class? Because the jury's role is a recourse role extending a liberty to depart from the judge's instructions, does it follow that every jury verdict contrary to those instructions is necessarily legitimated? Certainly in at least one case it does not follow. This is the case where the decision to depart is grounded on considerations that do not even purport to be part of the accepted ends of the role. A bribed juror, or one who responds to a familial relationship with the defendant or to personal fear, cannot be regarded as acting legitimately in his role. Such a juror abuses his authority in order to serve a personal interest. Yet what should we say of a jury that seeks to serve the ends of its role but grossly misinterprets them? For example, consider a Southern jury that acquits a white segregationist of killing a civil rights worker, on the grounds that in the public interest carpetbag troublemakers must be discouraged from venturing into their community, and that in any event the defendant's act was a political act that should not be punished as a common crime. Is this an instance of legitimated rule departure? The answer, we think, has to be yes. One is entitled to say that this jury is egregiously wrong in its interpretation of the ends of its role, both institutional and background; that its ventured justification rests on premises that contravene the basic ethos of the Constitution and the legal system founded on it; even that it has violated the law insofar as one may regard policies and ends of this kind as part of the law, as we do. But if our argument is correct, one cannot say that this jury has acted lawlessly, in the sense of usurping an authority it did not have, any more than one could say of a judge that he acted lawlessly when in good conscience he grossly misread the law. The liberty to make a judgment on role ends is precisely what is entailed in recourse roles; so long as the agent's judgment is conscientiously made on his view of those ends, his rule departure is legitimated. Of course, there is always the grave danger in recourse roles that the agent will act in crass and damaging ignorance, with no possibility of check or control. Any liberty may be misused. But if our interpretation is right, the law has chosen to take that chance in the case of the jury. . . .

The Possibility of a Lawful Rule Departure

. . . The usual way in which legal systems are thought to [accommodate change] is through the exercise of delegated authority within established channels. The system expands and contracts through processes that are part of its formal structure, such as the passage or repeal of statutes. But most people will acknowledge that there are also nonformal processes of change at work; our point is that retroactive ways of explaining the law obscure them. As the jury's role in acquittals illustrates, systems also change when different lines of development in a complex institution, each representing different values, come into conflict under the pressure of circumstances. In such a case the decision of which line of development shall be given precedence, and which value served, is remitted to individuals who by the nature of the situation receive only incomplete systematic guidance. The concept of legitimated interposition offers a partial explanation of how, short of revolution but beyond the system's formal structure, the legal system accommodates change. . . .

1. Is there any role in a procedural system that could not be conceptualized as a "recourse role"? For example, might the roles of advocate or judge be recourse roles, where each has liberty to avoid the duties otherwise imposed by his or her role?

2. Does the concept of a recourse role, particularly if generalized throughout the procedural system, undermine the very utility of a concept of role in either evaluating performance or making normative choices? Put another way, does a formal acknowledgment of the ambiguity inherent in all roles undermine the utility of the concept altogether in understanding a procedural system?

3. Are the Kadishes correct in assuming that legitimated interposition—through a recourse role—brings about change over time? What would be the projected pattern of change, and how large a role would interposition play in producing that change?

2. PERSON AND OFFICE

The concept of role introduces an element of impersonality into a procedural system. A distinction is made between the person and the office he occupies; his duties and rights are defined by the role, not by his personal attributes and beliefs. As the Kadishes put it, "Agents come and go— the role remains." The situation is more complex than that, however. Roles can only be occupied by persons, and the personal characteristics of the particular "officeholder" at any one time shape that role for the moment and over time. Role emphasizes the impersonal, but, in truth, the relationship between person and office is a more dynamic one. The essays that follow uncover and explore the dialectic between office and person. The first is a case study from the civil domain—*Palsgraf*. The other is Jerome Frank's well known prolegomena of Legal Realism. (On the problem of personification in the injunctive process, see the essay by Fiss in chapter 7; for a case study on the tension between office and person in the criminal process, the *Rosenberg* case, see Antonovsky, Like Everyone Else, Only More So: Identity, Anxiety, and the Jew, in M. Stein, A. Vidich, D. White (eds.), Identity and Anxiety 428 (1960).)

John T. Noonan, Jr., **The Passengers of Palsgraf***

The most famous tort case of modern times—"the most discussed and debated," as Dean Prosser put it—is Palsgraf v. Long Island Railroad Company, [248 N.Y. 339,] decided in 1928 by the most excellent state court in the United States with an opinion by the most justly celebrated of American common-law judges, Benjamin N. Cardozo. The facts of the case as stated by Cardozo were these:

> Plaintiff was standing on a platform of defendant's railroad after buying a ticket to go to Rockaway Beach. A train stopped at the station bound for another place. Two men ran forward to

* *Source*: Persons and Masks of the
Law (1976), ch. 4. Professor of Law,
University of California at Berkeley.

catch it. One of the men reached the platform of the car without mishap, though the train was already moving. The other man, carrying a package, jumped aboard the car, but seemed unsteady as if about to fall. A guard on the car, who had held the door open, reached forward to help him in, and another guard on the platform pushed from behind. In this act, the package was dislodged, and fell upon the rails. It was a package of small size, about fifteen inches long, and was covered by a newspaper. In fact it contained fireworks, but there was nothing in its appearance to give notice of its contents. The fireworks when they fell exploded. The shock of the explosion threw down some scales at the other end of the platform many feet away. The scales struck the plaintiff, causing injuries for which she sues.

Cardozo held that the plaintiff could not recover. No negligence to her by the railroad had been shown. "The risk reasonably to be perceived," Cardozo wrote, "defines the risk to be avoided, and risk imports relation; it is risk to another or others within the range of apprehension." When the guard pushed the passenger with a package, he could not have apprehended that the plaintiff was endangered by his action. In his action he did not relate to her. As to her he could not have been negligent.

William S. Andrews, who wrote an opinion in the case no less eloquent than Cardozo's, saw negligence as a breach of duty of a man to observe care toward "his fellows," not toward specific persons he should have seen as endangered by what he did. If he breached the general duty, every consequence which followed had been caused by his negligence—"we cannot trace the effect of an act to the end, if end there is." Still, "practical politics" refused to hold the negligent person liable for every consequence, and so courts drew an "uncertain and wavering line," cutting off liability at a certain degree of distance in time and space—a degree of distance which could not be set with greater specificity. Here the injury to the plaintiff was close in time and space to the original act of negligence. The defendant (the railroad) was liable, and the plaintiff could recover compensation.

Disagreement between the judges did not depend on a different reading of the facts. As Andrews put it in dissent:

> Assisting a passenger to board a train, the defendant's servant negligently knocked a package from his arms. It fell between the platform and the cars. Of its contents the servant knew and could know nothing. A violent explosion followed. The concussion broke some scales standing a considerable distance away. In falling, they injured the plaintiff, an intending passenger.

Both summaries of fact were wonderfully laconic. Andrews' was the superior in impersonality, eliminating even the sex of "plaintiff." Compelled by grammatical necessity to use a personal pronoun, Cardozo did disclose that the plaintiff was female. Otherwise, neither judge said anything about her age, marital status, maternal responsibilities, employment, or income. What injuries she had suffered, whether she had been almost decapitated or whether she had been mildly bruised, could not be learned from either opinion.

What compensation she had sought or what compensation she had been awarded—a jury had decided in her favor—was unmentioned.

No greater information was given about the defendant, except that it was a railroad or, as Cardozo chose to express it in his summary, possessed a railroad. The income and expenses, assets and liabilities, owners and directors of the defendant were unstated. Its officers and its guards or "servants" were anonymous. Defendant was as impersonally designated as plaintiff. *P* and *D* or *A* and *B* could as well have been written for their names.

The accident described by the judges had a timeless quality. It would have to have happened after 1830, since a railroad was involved. Otherwise it could have happened any time and, save for the mention of Rockaway Beach and the name of the railroad line, anywhere. Nothing was said of the hour, the day of the week, the month, the year. No notice was taken of when the plaintiff had begun her case, and of how many months or years it had taken her to reach the highest court of New York.

Cardozo and Andrews made no reference of any kind to the lawyers who had conducted the litigation. . . . The judges made no comment upon their training, their competence, their presentation of the evidence, their relationship to their clients. . . . Nothing was said as to negotiations they might have conducted with each other. Their remuneration and the bearing of the decision upon it were not touched upon.

A fortiori, the judges said nothing of themselves—their own income and investments, their marital and parental status, their professional experience, their personal experience of New York commuter trains, their own study or debate over the case. The authors of the opinion and the dissent were, if possible, less visible than the plaintiff, the defendant, and the three lawyers. Who they were was not a fact of the case. Ignoring the lawyers and themselves, stripping the litigants to their status of plaintiff and defendant, Cardozo and Andrews had performed the standard operations of opinion writers announcing the rules of law which governed their conclusions.

The Commentators' History

. . . Among all the persons who had shaped the rule [of law in *Palsgraf*] and were ignored by the analysts, there was one exception. From the beginning *Palsgraf* was linked with Cardozo. In 1928 he had sat on the Court of Appeals for fourteen years, for four years he had been Chief Judge. He had delivered in 1921 the remarkable Storrs lectures at Yale which became The Nature of the Judicial Process. He had made other decisions commemorated as turning points. Law students knew his name better than they knew the name of any other judge of a state court. The student notes in the law reviews pointed out that *Palsgraf* was a Cardozo opinion. The professorial commentators referred constantly to Cardozo as its author. The excitement of *Palsgraf* was not merely that it was a brilliant examination question; it was an examination question answered by Cardozo. . . .

[In 1939 the Columbia Law Review, Harvard Law Review, and Yale Law Journal published a joint issue commemorating the death of Cardozo. In this] memorial issue of the law reviews, Judge Learned Hand paid tribute to Cardozo's wisdom, a wisdom which depended on more than detachment from self-advancement. "I am thinking," wrote Hand, "of something far more subtly interfused. Our convictions, our outlook, the whole make-up of our thinking, which we cannot help bringing to the decision of every question, is the creature of our past; and into our past have been woven all sorts of frustrated ambitions with their envies, and of hopes of preferment with their corruptions, which, long since forgotten, still determine our conclusions. A wise man is one exempt from such a handicap .   .   .   .   Cardozo was such a man .   .   .   .   I believe it was this purity that chiefly made him the judge we so much revere." .   .   .   The portrait of Cardozo .   .   . left little place for distinguishing between the rule and the man. The person of Cardozo was recognized only to identify the man so firmly with the mask that the judge appeared merely to announce the truth.

No law review, commentator, or casebook mentioned the lawyers. Their names appearing in the printed opinion were excised when the opinion was reproduced in casebooks. The jury and the lower-court judges, even the composition of the divided sides in the Court of Appeal, received little more attention. .   .   .

The Participants

Counsel. .   .   .   The railroad was represented by Joseph F. Keany and William McNamara, who gave their addresses as "Pennsylvania Station." Keany, the senior man, had the title of General Solicitor of the Long Island Railroad and was listed as an officer of the company. .   .   .

The actual trial was conducted by Keany's junior, McNamara. He was a recent graduate of New York Law School, a proprietary institution not to be confused with New York University Law School. McNamara introduced no witnesses, cross-examined the plaintiff and her witnesses with moderate spirit but not exhaustively, and sought to bring out that a lot of people on the platform were carrying bundles. His summation to the jury, unreported, could not have taken more than fifteen minutes. He asked the judge to charge the jury that no inferences should be drawn from the defendant's failure to present witnesses, and the judge so charged. He asked the judge to charge that there was no negligence unless the defendant should have known that the package contained fireworks, and the judge declined. He asked the judge to charge that the act of assisting the passenger onto the train thereby knocking over the package was not "the proximate cause" of the plaintiff's injuries, and the judge declined. He asked the judge to set aside the verdict, and the judge refused. McNamara's performance was that of a workmanlike lawyer earning his salary with an economy of motion. He spent part of an afternoon and a morning trying the case and had given, perhaps, half a day to preparing it. If his salary, which would not have been above $6,000 a year, is prorated to this time, the railroad had spent no more than $16 in defending itself.

Opposing him was Matthew W. Wood, a solo practitioner who had an office in the tallest building then in New York, the Woolworth Building on lower Broadway. He was from Middleburgh, a small town in upstate New York. A bachelor of science from the University of Pennsylvania, he had studied law at New York Law School but had graduated from Yale Law School. He had been admitted to the bar when he was twenty-eight, and he had been in practice twenty-one years when he took Mrs. Palsgraf as a client. His biography gives the outline of a boy from the country, making with diligence a modest legal career. Only his longevity and endurance are remarkable: until his death in 1972 at the age of ninety-seven, he was listed in the standard lawyers' directory as in practice at the Woolworth Building.

Operating by himself, he was in the least prosperous category of urban practitioners and had to resort to stratagems to dig up business.   .   .   . How he and Mrs. Palsgraf had come to each other's attention and why she thought he would be a good torts lawyer are not evident. He became her lawyer two months after the accident.

Wood's preparation of the case was not elaborate. He presented the plaintiff; her two daughters, Elizabeth and Lilian; her local doctor, Karl Parshall; an engraver and his wife, the Gerhardts, who had been on the platform too; and a neurologist, Graeme M. Hammond, for thirty years professor of nervous and mental diseases and chief of clinic at the Post Graduate, with a war service record of examining 68,000 soldiers, close to eighty years old at the time of the trial.   .   .   .   On the critical question of the plaintiff's injuries, Dr. Parshall, the local physician, thought they were permanent, but McNamara brought out on cross-examination that he had never treated a similar case; the jury could have taken his name as a significant pun. The testimony of the specialist, Dr. Hammond, that his patient was suffering from "traumatic hysteria" was vital. Hammond's services were obtained the day before the trial. Wood's case, like Keany's, was an economical one, sparely presented and sparely financed.   .   .   .

Filing costs and the clerk's fee in the lower court came to $142. Dr. Hammond charged $125. Mrs. Palsgraf made $416 a year. At the time of trial, she had not yet paid Dr. Parshall's bill of $70, now three years due. It is improbable to the point of implausibility that she would have had the cash on hand to pay the court and Dr. Hammond a total of $267. It is unequally implausible that she would have had the cash to pay Wood. It is not inconceivable that her relatives could have funded the case, but it seems more probable that Wood had a fee contingent on his success and that he financed the litigation. It would not have been unusual if his contingent interest was one half the recovery after a trial—one third if a settlement was made before trial.   .   .   .

Wood asked for $50,000 in his complaint on her behalf. The discrepancy between this amount and any injuries he was able to show suggest strongly that he planned to bargain. As he did not get any expert medical opinion until the day before the trial, it may be inferred that Keany and McNamara were not interested in negotiating seriously short of what professional jargon denominates as "the courthouse steps." As McNamara's time was cheap, they may have offered only out-of-pocket expenses. Their offer was too low or Wood's expectations too high to produce a settlement at the last minute. Other negotiations, no doubt, must have gone on before the appellate division heard the appeal. The railroad would not have risked a written opinion holding it liable if it could have settled for a moderate amount.

Wood made a serious misjudgment in not compromising after the jury verdict. His mistake was the necessary condition of Cardozo stating the rule.

Clients. "Plaintiff," "Palsgraf," "Mrs. Palsgraf" bore the Christian name of Helen. She was forty-three and the mother of three children, of whom the younger two, then fifteen and twelve, were with her at the time of the accident. She was married, but neither side judged it desirable to ask who her husband was or where he was. It may be inferred that they had separated. She testified that she paid the rent, that she had always worked, and that she was "all alone."

At the time of the accident Helen Palsgraf lived in a basement flat at 238 Irving Avenue in Ridgewood, performing janitorial work in the apartment building, for which she was allowed ten dollars a month on her rent. She did day work outside the apartment, earning two dollars a day or about eight dollars a week. She spoke English intelligibly but not with complete grammatical correctness.

The day of the accident was a hot Sunday in August. She was taking Elizabeth and Lilian to the beach. It was ten o'clock. She carried a valise. She bought their tickets and walked onto the station platform, which was crowded. Lilian went for the Sunday paper. As a train started to pull out, there was the noise of an explosion. Then, "Flying glass—a ball of fire came, and we were choked in smoke, and I says 'Elizabeth turn your back,' and with that the scale blew and hit me on the side."

Fire engines and ambulances arrived. She was trembling. A policeman led her into the waiting room. A doctor from an ambulance gave her something to drink. She took a taxi home. On Monday a doctor from the Long Island Railroad Company visited her and asked her about what had happened. Tuesday she called her own doctor, Karl Parshall. He visited her several times at the house over the next two weeks, and she came about twenty times to his office in the next two months.

Helen Palsgraf had been hit by the scales on the arm, hip, and thigh. The chief perceptible effect of the accident, according to the doctors, was a stammer. Dr. Parshall said that she began to stutter and stammer about a week after the event. Dr. Hammond declared that "it was with difficulty that she could talk at all." Oral incapacitation was not reflected in the transcript of the trial, but the stenographer may have decided not to try to reproduce the stammer. The neurologist took the position that the stammer was symptomatic of a deeper trauma, associated with the litigation itself. . . .
On cross-examination, McNamara asked him "[M]ight this condition have been corrected before this time by medical treatment?" and he answered, "Not while litigation is pending. It has been my experience that it never is benefitted or relieved or cured until the source of worry disappears by the conclusion of the trial." Dr. Hammond's answers were capable of a cynical interpretation. As a clinical description of a trauma and its possible resolution by reparation for the injury, his responses attributed no malingering motive to his patient. The jury did not understand him cynically. The only way it could have estimated how much Helen Palsgraf should receive was by translating Dr. Hammond's statements about her hysteria, which had

lasted three years and which he thought would last three years after the verdict, into a cash equivalent.

The two most important facts of the case from Helen Palsgraf's perspective must have been the time it took to be heard and the size of the verdict she won. The accident took place August 24, 1924. The summons beginning her suit was served on October 2, 1924. The trial took place on May 25 and 26, 1927. For anyone who has been injured and is awaiting compensation, two years and nine months is a very long time to wait. The testimony of Dr. Hammond that this wait contributed to the continuation of Helen Palsgraf's hysteria was undisputed. When the trial was finally held, she won a verdict fourteen times her annual income. Even if she could keep only half for herself, she had a fortune in prospect. She was able to enjoy the thought of disposing of it for a whole year before the Court of Appeals took it from her, and she could nurse a faint hope for another five months until, on October 9, 1928, the Court of Appeals denied Wood's motion for reargument.

The defendant operated 366 miles of track in New York State, including the Rockaway Beach Division, running from Glendale Junction to Rockaway Park, and carried annually over 80 million passengers. Since 1900 it had been a subsidiary of the Pennsylvania Railroad, which owned 99.2 percent of its stock. . . .

In 1924 the Long Island's total assets were valued at $114 million of which $98 million was the valuation set on track and equipment. Net income from railroad operations was just over $4 million, reflecting a return just over the 4 percent that was usual for railroads of the period to show. Over 60 percent of the operating income was from passenger traffic. . . .

In 1924 the railroads of the United States killed 6,617 persons and injured 143,739 persons. A substantial number of those killed and injured were the railroads' own employees and another large fraction were classified as "trespassers," those who had no business on railroad property. Helen Palsgraf fell in the classification neither of employees nor of trespassers but of passengers, of whom 204 were killed and 6,822 were injured in 1924. . . . .

[P]robably Helen Palsgraf's accident fell within the classification of a "train service" accident, that is, it was one "arising in connection with the operation or movement of trains," for the man would not have been pushed aboard if the train had been stationary. The railroads in "train service" accidents in 1924 had killed 108 passengers and injured 3,229, and the Long Island in particular had killed 4 and injured 88. The number of "train service" injuries to passengers, even more than the number of "non-train" accidents to passengers, suggested that these injuries were necessarily incident to the operation of a railroad.

Jury and Judges. Burt Jay Humphrey presided. A country boy like Matthew Wood, from near Berkshire in Tioga County, he had read law in a judge's office and then gone west to Seattle for six years before returning to Jamaica, Long Island, to practice. He had been nominated in 1902 as county judge—a joke by the Democratic organization, which intended his

Republican opponent to win; but he had campaigned so hard that he won the office in which he remained twenty-two years. He had eventually been elected to the Supreme Court for Kings County with its higher salary of $6,-000 per year. For most of his judicial career his income from the state was no larger, but he left an estate of $200,000. When he conducted the *Palsgraf* trial, he was sixty-four; he had been on the bench twenty-five years and a judge of the New York Supreme Court for three.

Judge Humphrey's charge to the jury was balanced. He emphasized that the defendant had no duty to examine the packages of passengers. If every package was inspected, "none of us would be able to get anywhere. The purpose of railroad travel is that we can get some place." He said that if "the trainmen of the defendant" omitted to do the things which prudent and careful trainmen do for the safety of those who are boarding their trains, as well as for the safety of those who are "standing upon the platform waiting for other trains," and "the failure resulted in the plaintiff's injury," then the defendant would be liable. He described the harm done to Mrs. Palsgraf as "a nervousness which still persists and which, according to her claim, will persist for some time in the future."

The jury was drawn from Brooklyn, where Mrs. Palsgraf lived, where the accident had occurred, and where the trial took place. It would be too much to say that they were Mrs. Palsgraf's neighbors, but it may be guessed from the result that they were persons used to traveling on the Long Island and not overly sympathetic to railroads. They retired at 11:55 a. m. and returned with their verdict at 2:30 p. m.—time enough to eat lunch at the expense of the state of New York and to discuss liability and damages for at least an hour, and perhaps longer.

The case went from Judge Humphrey's court to the appellate division in Brooklyn [which sustained the award]. [A discussion of the Appellate Division judges and opinions is here omitted.] . . .

The Court of Appeals to which Keany and McNamara then took the railroad's case had been composed with that attention to religious affiliation (Protestant, Jewish, Catholic) and regional origin (upstate, metropolis) which often has exhausted political wisdom in New York. Its members were exclusively white, male, and over fifty. It consisted of Benjamin N. Cardozo of New York City, Chief Judge; William S. Andrews of Syracuse; Cuthbert W. Pound of Lockport; Frederick E. Crane of Brooklyn; Henry T. Kellogg of Plattsburgh; John F. O'Brien of New York City; and Irving Lehman of New York City. In age they ranged from Andrews, seventy, to Crane and O'Brien, fifty-four; Cardozo, Lehman, and Kellogg were in the later fifties, Pound in his middle sixties. Two had not gone to a regular day law school—O'Brien had gone nights to New York Law School, while holding a job in the office of the Corporation Counsel of New York City; Pound had read law with his father in Lockport. Cardozo was technically a dropout, having studied only two years at Columbia Law School at a time when three years had just become the requirement. Andrews, Crane, and Lehman were all actual law graduates of Columbia, as was Kellogg of Harvard.

The court was an elected body, to which no one radically outside the orbit of the Democratic-Republican norm could aspire, but an institution where electoral competition was often blunted by governors designating able men for vacancies and by the two parties agreeing, as in Cardozo's run for Chief Judge, on the same candidate. Crane, Lehman, and O'Brien had been identified as Democrats; Andrews, Pound, and Kellogg were Republicans. Cardozo had begun as an independent Democrat on a Fusion ticket and had been advanced by both a Democratic and a Republican governor.

All were members of the upper middle class, the sons of prosperous fathers, although Cardozo's father after his resignation had had to struggle; three were the sons of judges—O'Brien's father had been for eighteen years a judge of the Court of Appeals himself; Kellogg's and Cardozo's fathers had been judges of the New York Supreme Court. All, save O'Brien, had been in private practice. All, save O'Brien, had been first elected to the Supreme Court before promotion to the higher level. All now received a salary of $22,000 ($500 more for the Chief Judge) and $3,000 in lieu of expenses. The richest was Lehman, the son of Mayer Lehman, founding partner of the investment bankers, Lehman Brothers. . . .

Cardozo was a trustee of Columbia, Pound of Cornell. Neither university had in their portfolio of investments any stock in the Pennsylvania Railroad. All of the judges must, on at least a few occasions, have ridden the Long Island Railroad, but only one person on the Court of Appeals was intimate with the locale of the case—Crane, who had grown up in Brooklyn, been an assistant district attorney in Kings County, and then lived in Garden City. To him the courts of Kings and the trains of the Long Island must have been as familiar as the law reports.

An observer detached from the system might have dared to predict the outcome on the basis of class interest, but the court was so closely split that such a prediction would have been temerarious. As for the Holmesian view that law is prediction, how would one have ventured to state the law at all—so mixed were the precedents, so divided was the mind of the court? The judge who wrote the opinion had to win and keep the votes of at least three other vigorous and experienced men—to do so required a skill distinct from judging yet indispensable. . . . In the final result, in *Palsgraf*, although every vote counted, what swayed Cardozo was decisive. He was joined by Pound, Kellogg, and Lehman.

The Ingredients of the Opinion

"[T]o determine to be loyal to precedents," Cardozo had written in The Nature of the Judicial Process (1921), "and to the principles back of precedents, does not carry us far upon the road. Principles are complex bundles. It is well enough to say that we shall be consistent, but consistent with what? Shall it be consistency with the origin of the rule, the course and tendency of development? Shall it be consistency with logic or philosophy or the fundamental conceptions of justice? All these loyalties are possible." When, he continued, "the social needs demand one settlement rather than another, there are times when we must bend symmetry, ignore history, and sacrifice custom in the pursuit of other and larger ends. . . . The final cause of law is the welfare of society."

The first, though not the final, loyalty was to precedents. Cardozo marshaled two dozen opinions . . . pointing toward the result he reached. American and English treatises on torts . . . he wove into the same coherent pattern. Leading law-review articles . . . he brought into the same seamless web.

No negligence, he declared, in *Palsgraf*, existed "in the air"—the defendant must have caused a risk to a person he should have known to exist within the range of his act. . . .

Satisfied as he was that he was being loyal to precedent and "the course and tendency of development," did Cardozo consider other factors? "Affront to the personality," he wrote, "is still the keynote of the wrong." But by "personality" he meant "body." Not even mentioning Mrs. Palsgraf's physical injuries, he said nothing of the effect on her spirit of being kept suspended by the process for almost four years. What she had suffered was affront to the personality—traumatized, she had a sense of unrequited injury; but Cardozo used the phrase in a sense which put this problem out of his sight.

What place did "fundamental conceptions of justice" have? In Aristotle's classic analysis, commutative justice is equality of exchange between two parts, distributive justice is proportionate distribution from whole to part; a judge deciding between two litigants appears to be determining what is commutatively just, what is an equal exchange. When the transaction between the two parties has been involuntary, however, as it is in the case of an accident, it is not self-evident that commutative justice requires the party causing the loss to restore equality by making the victim whole—who would agree that if by chance he stepped on a firecracker igniting a blaze which destroyed the neighborhood, he should be liable for all the loss? To determine what is fair requires more than establishing who caused the injury. This intuition is clearly dominant with Cardozo. To make *A* pay *B* for causing a freak accident when *A* could have foreseen neither the accident nor its effect on *B* seems actually unfair—an inappropriate spreading to *A* of what is simply *B*'s misfortune.

If one is in a business which unavoidably produces certain types of injury, however, it seems more consistent with the Aristotelian canon to conclude that compensation for them should be a cost of the business. Who ultimately bears the cost—the stockholders, the customers, or the taxpayer—is an economic question subordinate to the larger question of fairness, of making one who voluntarily engages in an activity for his profit make restitution for injuries which are his activity's inevitable by-product. This line of argument was not considered by Cardozo. . . .

But the final cause of law, Cardozo had said, is "the welfare of society." What was socially desirable—that railroads not have the added burden of compensating passengers for all train-service accidents, or at least not have the burden where the accident was improbable, or that the loss of an innocent victim of the line be relieved? Did the economics of railroads in the 1920's show that such a burden would be absorbed as an extra cost diminishing the stockholders' return, or passed on to all the passengers, or be so substantial as to drive the railroads to bankruptcy and public ownership? However this question was resolved, was it socially preferable to have loss incurred by the user of a necessary public service confined to that user, or passed on to a going enterprise with the capacity to distribute the loss to a larger number? Was it good to stimulate the railroads to higher standards of safety by the extension of liability or better not to discourage their zeal by the imposition of rules which did not discriminate between the probable and the improbable? Was a form of transportation which was known to kill several thousand persons a year and to injure many thousands more to be treated as responsible for the injuries it generated only when its employees could reasonably have foreseen the particular persons they might injure? .   .   .

The social interests to be weighed were affected by the process by which they were presented to a court. A rule of absolute liability for injury to passengers might encourage claims against railroads by hungry tort lawyers. It might discourage delay and appeals by the railroad protracting the victim's trauma and intensifying it. If one looked at the lawyers actually before the court, circumstantial evidence, visible in the record, suggested that Matthew Wood had violated the penal code of the state [forbidding the financing of litigation as an inducement], that he should not be permitted to practice as a lawyer. Should he be rewarded with a handsome fee, perhaps half of what Mrs. Palsgraf would receive, as much as half the salary of a judge of the state supreme court? Was there not a social interest in rebuking such a stirrer-up of litigation, such a harasser of corporate enterprise? On the other hand, it might also be suspected from the record that in this close case, where the railroad had caused an injury to a passenger, the railroad's lawyers had offered no reasonable settlement. Was it socially desirable that, to establish her claim to compensation, a woman earning $416 a year had to hire a lawyer on a contingency basis and wait four years, while the defendant, with assets of over $100 million, if taken by itself, or assets of over $1 billion, if more realistically regarded as a subdivision of its parent, prolonged the contest, using more experienced counsel employed at a lower cost? .   .   .

None of these social needs or interests, none of these components of the social welfare was discussed by Cardozo. None of these questions was asked. Neither the economics of railroading nor the course of the judicial process as it affected the values at stake was mentioned. To have done any one of these things would have required looking at the litigants and their lawyers.

At the climax of his opinion, where he enunciated the central conclusion, "The risk reasonably to be perceived defines the duty to be obeyed," Cardozo cited the latest article of Warren Seavey in the [1927] Harvard Law Review, "Negligence—Subjective or Objective?" [, 41 Harv.L.Rev. 1,] a masterful analysis of the mixed (subjective and objective) components of the Prudent Man, who was the standard by whom liability for tort was measured. Seavey's presentation was, in a Holmesian vein, so avowedly neutral that he concluded that it would do no violence to his analysis to return to the medieval rule of absolute liability and, with a certain unpleasantness, indicated that was likely to be the preference of a modern society with "a mechanistic philosophy of human motives and a socialistic philosophy of the state." If Cardozo had sought a reading of modern aspirations, he had it there. He did not use Seavey for this grudging insight but for what Seavey's article really focused on—the most general and therefore the most abstract considerations of fairness in framing a rule on negligence. Seavey's "personification of a standard person" was an individual, identified with no industry, capable of existing in any environment, variously described as "*A*" or "the actor." By what was fair to this anonymous fiction Cardozo discovered the welfare of society.

The Eyes of the Oracle

. . . What Seavey later was to declare refuted by "the entire record" of Cardozo's decisions was acknowledged by Cardozo himself as sometimes determinative in difficult cases—a "compelling sense of justice" which could not be further explicated, "a semi-intuitive . . . apprehension of the spirit of our law." Cardozo personified the sentiment or intuition—they were outside the judge. Like history, custom, or social utility, they came as objective inspirations. Learned Hand in his memorial to Cardozo observed of a judge, "He must pose as a kind of oracle, voicing the dictates of a vague divinity." In The Nature of the Judicial Process Cardozo dropped the oracular pose and spoke of what came from within him as a human being:

> More subtle are the forces so far beneath the surface that they cannot reasonably be classified as other than subconscious. It is often through these subconscious forces that judges are kept consistent with themselves, and inconsistent with one another. We are reminded by William James in a telling page of his lectures on Pragmatism that every one of us has in truth an underlying philosophy of life, even those of us to whom the names and the notions of philosophy are unknown or anathema. There is in each of us a stream of tendency, whether you choose to call it philosophy or not, which gives coherence and direction to thought and action. Judges cannot escape that current any more than other mortals. All their lives, forces which they do not recognize and cannot name, have been tugging at them—inherited instincts, traditional beliefs, acquired convictions; and the resultant is an outlook on life, a conception of social needs, a sense in James' phrase of "the total push and pressure of the cosmos," which, when reasons are nicely balanced, must determine where choice shall fall. In this mental background every problem finds its setting. We may try to see things as objectively as we please. None the less, we can never see them with any eyes except our own. To that test they are all brought—a form of pleading or an act of parliament, the wrongs of paupers or the rights of princes, a village ordinance or a nation's charter.

Who decided? The person who was the judge. The detachment, the self-effacement, the freedom from one's past that Hand celebrated in his praise of Cardozo was repudiated by him in advance. The insistence of Seavey that the judge knew only precedents and weighed only interests in producing rules was denied in anticipation. If the judge were a computer, he could have conformed to Seavey's idealization. Cardozo, writing autobiography, spoke differently. The more conscious a judge was, the more creative a judge's labor, the more was he personally involved. The judge's eyes might be on God or on the rule, but it was the judge who saw things: "we can never see them with any eyes except our own." The decision depended on his vision and his perspective. If Cardozo was taken as a guide, the creation of a rule could not be fully understood apart from its creator.

. . . Facts which cannot be shown to be crucial to the disposition of a case are important in grasping how person affected person; Mrs. Palsgraf's children, Cardozo's preeminence, and others I have stated are among them. Even details which are purely extrinsic to any participant in the process have an effect on the understanding of the case. The day of the accident was "hot"—a detail of consummate irrelevance in terms of any legal principles but suggestive of the circumstances in which urban users of public transportation need to travel, a reminder of the innocence of Helen Palsgraf's seaside excursion. How such a fact should affect the outcome is nondemonstrable, yet it will play a part in the process by which judgment is reached. What is true of each additional fact is equally true of a philosophical perspective different from that enjoyed by Cardozo: it cannot be demonstrated that a shift to a less rule-focused jurisprudence would require a different judgment—it cannot be demonstrated, but having had the experience of making such a shift, I can say that my conclusion would not be Cardozo's.

The easiest way of misinterpreting such a shift is to frame a rule that persons injured on hot days should always win or that very poor persons should always win. Speculating in terms of such rules, a law professor would ask, "Suppose the day had been mild and overcast, suppose the passenger had been Mrs. Cornelius Vanderbilt, would the judgment be the same?" Such questioning is intended to force us back to the blank faces of *P* and *D*. To resort to the hypothetical, escaping the actual facts, is the mark of the mind oriented to rules. But when, in writing the history of *Palsgraf*, I call attention to the facts known to the judge and not considered relevant by him, my purpose is not to offer a new rule but to increase our understanding of the legal process. My concern is what a legal historian should record, what a legal philosopher should explain, what a law professor should teach. Only indirectly do these matters suggest how a judge should judge.

As evidence that consideration of actual persons makes a difference, I mention my modest experiment in the rewriting of *Palsgraf*. If a judge could look at all these facts available either in the record of the trial (as far as Mrs. Palsgraf is concerned) or in standard reference works (as far as the railroad is concerned) and still hold that the railroad had no liability, one could not show that he was wrong by pointing to the atmosphere of the day or the income of Mrs. Palsgraf. If, however, a judge, as he pondered these facts, was uncomfortable with reaching a result of no liability, then the enlargement of his focus would mean, perhaps, that he would select a different rule. At no point could the judge act without using a rule. Exercising his option to select a rule, the option commonly present in contested litigation, he would act less blindly the more conscious he was that he was acting as a person, using his "own eyes," and affecting other persons.

Cardozo as a person was involved in deciding Palsgraf v. Long Island Railroad.   .   .   .   Three public facts stand out. First, Cardozo never married and never had any children. He lacked the experience of conjugality and the experience of fatherhood. These lacks are not disqualifications for shaping social conduct. The judgment of the unmarried has sometimes been the finer for freedom from domestic involvement—that of St. Paul, for example, on charity, or of Tomás Sanchez on marriage. Childless, Holmes, Brandeis, and Frankfurter prescribed for generations of Americans yet to come. Personal experience is scarcely necessary to judge the quality of an act or relationship. Empathy suffices. The way accidents are perceived, the way sharing of risks is visualized, the way responsibility for a mess is understood, will be affected by the experience of marriage and fatherhood. The childless and a fortiori the unmarried will have an approach to a chain of calamities like *Palsgraf* different in outlook and emotional context from that of the reflective spouse and parent.

Second, Cardozo was the son of a Supreme Court judge, Albert Cardozo, who was a sachem of Tammany Hall when Tammany was ruled by Boss Tweed, and who as a judge was believed to have done the bidding of Jay Gould in the fight with Vanderbilt for the control of the Erie Railroad; he resigned from office after a committee of the legislature had recommended his impeachment for corruption. No further distance could exist between father and son in the universe of justice than that which seemed to exist between this father and son. No further distance could be put between himself and his father than for Benjamin Cardozo to take no interest in the identity of the contestants before him. In his court was to be only *A* or *B*.
.   .   .

Severe impartiality led in *Palsgraf* to the aspect of the decision which seemed least humane: the imposition by Cardozo of "costs in all courts" upon Helen Palsgraf. Under the New York rules of practice, costs were, in general, discretionary with the court. An old rule, laid down in 1828, was that when the question was "a doubtful one and fairly raised, no costs will be allowed." In practice, the Court of Appeals tended to award costs mechanically to the party successful on the appeal. Costs here amounted to $142.45 in the trial court and $100.28 in the appellate division. When the bill of the Court of Appeals was added, it is probable that costs in all courts amounted to $350, not quite a year's income for Helen Palsgraf. She had had a case which a majority of the judges who heard it—Humphrey, Seeger, Andrews, Crane, and O'Brien—thought to constitute a cause of action. By a margin of one, her case had been pronounced unreasonable.   .   .   .   The effect of the judgment was to leave the plaintiff, four years after her case had begun, the debtor of her doctor, who was still unpaid; her lawyer, who must have advanced her the trial court fees at least; and her adversary, who was now owed reimbursement for expenditures in the courts on appeal. Under the New York statute the Long Island could make execution of the judgment by seizing her personalty. Only a judge who did not see who was before him could have decreed such a result.

Third,   .   .   .   Cardozo had ambitions, although they were of the most exalted character. He wanted to be a reader, as he put it, of "signs and symbols given from without," a judge who would objectify not only his own "aspirations and convictions and philosophies, but the aspirations and convictions and philosophies of the men and women of my age." In this spirit, he had been in 1922 one of four reporters of a committee formed for the "Establishment of a Permanent Organization for the Improvement of the Law" and in 1923 became a member of the council, a member of the executive committee, and vice-president of the American Law Institute, which became the "Permanent Organization." The intention of the Institute, according to the organizing committee, was to remedy the principal defects in American law, and in that perspective "the most important task that the bar can undertake is to reduce the amount of the uncertainty and complexity of the law." To that task the A.L.I. and Cardozo were devoted. . . .

. . . When Cardozo acknowledged his own yearning "for consistency, for certainty, for uniformity of plan and structure," when he spoke of "the constant striving of the mind for a larger and more inclusive unity, in which differences will be reconciled, and abnormalities will vanish," when he sought this unity in the universe of law, he spoke for himself, he expressed desires which were personal and religious, but he was fortified by Holmes's example of satisfaction. Like the master, in "the remoter and more general aspects of the law," he sought "an echo of the infinite, a glimpse of its unfathomable process." That Holmes could inhabit the legal universe as its "overlord" was a sign and promise to Cardozo that pursuit of rules would produce such a resonance, that the comprehensive generality would yield such a vision. . . .

The problem of determining the cause of a rule is not unlike determining the proximate cause of an injury. Was the nomination of Burt Jay Humphrey in 1902 as a joke the cause of the *Palsgraf* case, because but for it a different judge would have sat in the Supreme Court in Kings County? Was Matthew Wood's determination or self-interest, or Keany and McNamara's stinginess in their settlement offer, the real reason why the rule was formulated? Was Helen Palsgraf's poverty and inability to present an overwhelming case, or the court's identification of the Long Island with the needs of a mobile society the decisive factor? Were Cardozo's celibacy, paternity, and idealism important to the result? No cause acts alone, and the chain of causation is endless. There is no reason, however, to limit the causes of a rule so narrowly that one looks only at the books the opinion writer cites.

Out of a sequence of events as improbable as a Rube Goldberg cartoon, reconstructed by lawyers seeking partisan advantage, on a factual basis that was probably inaccurate, above the pain of Helen Palsgraf and the plodding of Matthew Wood and the calculation of the Long Island, Cardozo fashioned a statement of clarity, symmetry, simplicity. Presented with that pervasive problem of sociology, government, and law, the "unintended consequences" of a social action, he imposed order and aesthetic design and generality. . . .

---

1. Was it only Cardozo who wore a mask? What about the lawyers, the jurors, or even the parties?

2.   Is Professor Noonan correct in asserting that a decision predicated on considerations of social welfare "would require looking at the litigants and their lawyers" in a way that Cardozo was unprepared to do?

3.   Does the cult of impersonality, so troubling to Professor Noonan, have its roots in the concept of role, or rather in the ideals of the legal system (such as formal justice—e. g., treating equals equally)? Might not these larger ideals drive towards general rules, with those rules in turn requiring that we impersonalize all the procedural rules? See, in this regard, Hoeflich and Deutsch, Judicial Legitimacy and the Disinterested Judge, 6 Hofstra L.Rev. 749 (1978). The reader may also wish to review Simon's essay in chapter 2 at this point.

———

Jerome N. Frank, **The Judging Process and the Judge's Personality***

. . . The process of judging, so the psychologists tell us, seldom begins with a premise from which a conclusion is subsequently worked out. Judging begins rather the other way around—with a conclusion more or less vaguely formed; a man ordinarily starts with such a conclusion and afterwards tries to find premises which will substantiate it. If he cannot, to his satisfaction, find proper arguments to link up his conclusion with premises which he finds acceptable, he will, unless he is arbitrary or mad, reject the conclusion and seek another.

In the case of the lawyer who is to present a case to a court, the dominance in his thinking of the conclusion over the premises is moderately obvious. He is a partisan working on behalf of his client. The conclusion is, therefore, not a matter of choice except within narrow limits. He must, that is if he is to be successful, begin with a conclusion which will insure his client's winning the lawsuit. He then assembles the facts in such a fashion that he can work back from this result he desires to some major premise which he thinks the court will be willing to accept. The precedents, rules, principles and standards to which he will call the court's attention constitute this premise.

While "the dominance of the conclusion" in the case of the lawyer is clear, it is less so in the case of the judge. For the respectable and traditional descriptions of the judicial judging process admit no such backward-working explanation. In theory, the judge begins with some rule or principle of law as his premise, applies this premise to the facts, and thus arrives at his decision.

Now, since the judge is a human being and since no human being in his normal thinking processes arrives at decisions (except in dealing with a limited number of simple situations) by the route of any such syllogistic reasoning, it is fair to assume that the judge, merely by putting on the judicial ermine, will not acquire so artificial a method of reasoning. Judicial judgments, like other judgments, doubtless, in most cases, are worked out backward from conclusions tentatively formulated. . . .

* *Source*: Law and the Modern Mind (1930), Part I, Chapter 12. Frank (1889–1957): Lecturer in Law, Yale University, and Judge, United States Court of Appeals for the Second Circuit.

But the conception that judges work back from conclusions to principles is so heretical that it seldom finds expression. Daily, judges, in connection with their decisions, deliver so-called opinions in which they purport to set forth the bases of their conclusions. Yet you will study these opinions in vain to discover anything remotely resembling a statement of the actual judging process. They are written in conformity with the time-honored theory. They picture the judge applying rules and principles to the facts, that is, taking some rule or principle (usually derived from opinions in earlier cases) as his major premise, employing the facts of the case as the minor premise, and then coming to his judgment by processes of pure reasoning.

Now and again some judge, more clear-witted and outspoken than his fellows, describes (when off the bench) his methods in more homely terms. [Judge Joseph C. Hutcheson, Jr.] essayed such an honest report of the judicial process.[a] He tells us that after canvassing all the available material at his command and duly cogitating on it, he gives his imagination play,

> and brooding over the cause, waits for the feeling, the hunch—that intuitive flash of understanding that makes the jump-spark connection between question and decision and at the point where the path is darkest for the judicial feet, sets its light along the way. . . . In feeling or 'hunching' out his decisions, the judge acts not differently from but precisely as the lawyers do in working on their cases, with only this exception, that the lawyer, in having a predetermined destination in view,—to win the law-suit for his client—looks for and regards only those hunches which keep him in the path that he has chosen, while the judge, being merely on his way with a roving commission to find the just solution, will follow his hunch wherever it leads him. . . .

And Judge Hutcheson adds:

> I must premise that I speak now of the judgment or decision, the solution itself, as opposed to the apologia for that decision; the decree, as opposed to the logomachy, the effusion of the judge by which that decree is explained or excused. . . . The judge really decides by feeling and not by judgment, by hunching and not by ratiocination, such ratiocination appearing only in the opinion. The vital motivating impulse for the decision is an intuitive sense of what is right or wrong in the particular case; and the astute judge, having so decided, enlists his every faculty and belabors his laggard mind, not only to justify that intuition to himself, but to make it pass muster with his critics.

Accordingly, he passes in review all of the rules, principles, legal categories, and concepts "which he may find useful, directly or by an analogy, so as to select from them those which in his opinion will justify his desired result."

We may accept this as an approximately correct description of how all judges do their thinking. But see the consequences. If the law consists of the decisions of the judges and if those decisions are based on the judge's

a. Hutcheson, The Judgment Intuitive: The Function of the "Hunch" in Judicial Decision, 14 Cornell L.Q. 274 (1929). Ed. note.

hunches, then the way in which the judge gets his hunches is the key to the judicial process. Whatever produces the judge's hunches makes the law.

What, then, are the hunch-producers? What are the stimuli which make a judge feel that he should try to justify one conclusion rather than another?

The rules and principles of law are one class of such stimuli. But there are many others, concealed or unrevealed, not frequently considered in discussions of the character or nature of law. To the infrequent extent that these other stimuli have been considered at all, they have been usually referred to as "the political, economic and moral prejudices" of the judge. A moment's reflection would, indeed, induce any open-minded person to admit that factors of such character must be operating in the mind of the judge.

But are not those categories—political, economic and moral biases—too gross, too crude, too wide? Since judges are not a distinct race and since their judging processes must be substantially of like kind with those of other men, an analysis of the way in which judges reach their conclusions will be aided by answering the question, What are the hidden factors in the inferences and opinions of ordinary men? The answer surely is that those factors are multitudinous and complicated, depending often on peculiarly individual traits of the persons whose inferences and opinions are to be explained. These uniquely individual factors often are more important causes of judgments than anything which could be described as political, economic, or moral biases.

In the first place, all other biases express themselves in connection with, and as modified by, these idiosyncratic biases. A man's political or economic prejudices are frequently cut across by his affection for or animosity to some particular individual or group, due to some unique experience he has had; or a racial antagonism which he entertains may be deflected in a particular case by a desire to be admired by some one who is devoid of such antagonism.

Second (and in the case of the judge more important), is the consideration that in learning the facts with reference to which one forms an opinion, and often long before the time when a hunch arises with reference to the situation as a whole, these more minute and distinctly personal biases are operating constantly. So the judge's sympathies and antipathies are likely to be active with respect to the persons of the witness, the attorneys and the parties to the suit. His own past may have created plus or minus reactions to women, or blonde women, or men with beards, or Southerners, or Italians, or Englishmen, or plumbers, or ministers, or college graduates, or Democrats. A certain twang or cough or gesture may start up memories painful or pleasant in the main. Those memories of the judge, while he is listening to a witness with such a twang or cough or gesture, may affect the judge's initial hearing of, or subsequent recollection of, what the witness said, or the weight or credibility which the judge will attach to the witness's testimony.

. . . . It is, then, a legal commonplace that a witness cannot mechanically reproduce the facts, but is reporting his judgment of the facts and may err in the making of this judgment.

Strangely enough, it has been little observed that, while the witness is in this sense a judge, *the judge, in a like sense, is a witness.* He is a witness of what is occurring in his courtroom. He must determine what are the facts of the case from what he sees and hears; that is, from the words and gestures and other conduct of the witnesses. And like those who are testifying before him, the judge's determination of the facts is no mechanical act. If the witnesses are subject to lapses of memory or imaginative reconstruction of events, in the same manner the judge is subject to defects in his apprehension of the testimony; so that long before he has come to the point in the case where he must decide what is right or wrong, just or unjust, with reference to the facts of the case as a whole, the trial judge has been engaged in making numerous judgments or inferences as the testimony dribbles in. His beliefs as to what was said by the witnesses and with what truthfulness the witnesses said it, will determine what he believes to be the "facts of the case." If his final decision is based upon a hunch and that hunch is a function of the "facts," then of course what, as a fallible witness of what went on in his courtroom, he believes to be the "facts," will often be of controlling importance. So that the judge's innumerable unique traits, dispositions and habits often get in their work in shaping his decisions not only in his determination of what he thinks fair or just with reference to a given set of facts, but in the very processes by which he becomes convinced what those facts are.

The peculiar traits, disposition, biases and habits of the particular judge will, then, often determine what he decides to be the law. In this respect judges do not differ from other mortals: "In every case of actual thinking," says F. C. S. Schiller, "the whole of a man's personality enters into and colors it in every part." To know the judge's hunch-producers which make the law we must know thoroughly that complicated congeries we loosely call the judge's personality . . . .

No one can know in advance what a judge will believe to be the "facts" of a case. It follows that a lawyer's opinion as to the law relating to a given set of facts is a guess as to (1) what a judge thereafter will guess were the facts and (2) what that judge will consider to be the proper decision on the basis of that judge's guess as to the facts. Even that is too artificial a statement. The judge, in arriving at his hunch, does not nicely separate his belief as to the "facts" from his conclusion as to the "law"; his general hunch is more integral and composite, and affects his report—both to himself and to the public—concerning the facts. Only a superficial thinker will assume that the facts as they occurred and as they later appear to the judge (and as he reports them) will invariably—or indeed often—correspond. The judge's decision is determined by a hunch arrived at long after the event on the basis of his reaction to fallible testimony. It is, in every sense of the word, ex post facto. It is fantastic, then, to say that usually men can warrantably act in reliance upon "established law." Their inability to do so may be deplorable. But mature persons must face the truth, however unpleasant.

Why such resistance to the truth? Why has there been little investigation of the actualities of the judging process? If we are right in assuming that the very subject-matter of the law activates childish emotional attitudes, we can perhaps find an answer to these questions.

It is a marked characteristic of the young child, writes [Jean] Piaget, that he does very little thinking about his thinking. He encounters extreme difficulty if asked to give an account of the "how" of his mental processes. He cannot reflect on his own reasoning. If you ask him to state how he reached a conclusion, he is unable to recover his own reasoning processes, but instead invents an artificial account which will somehow seem to lead to the result. He cannot correctly explain what he did to find this result. "Instead of giving a retrospect he starts from the result he has obtained as though he had known it in advance and then gives a more or less elaborate method for finding it again. . . . He starts from his conclusion and argues towards the premises as though he had known from the first whither those premises would lead him."

Once more these difficulties find their explanation in the child's relative unawareness of his self, of his incapacity for dealing with his own thoughts as subjective. For this obtuseness produces in the child an overconfidence in his own ideas, a lack of skepticism as to the subjectivity of his own beliefs. As a consequence, the child is singularly non-introspective. He has, according to Piaget, no curiosity about the motives that guide his thinking. His whole attitude towards his own thinking is the antithesis of any introspective habit of watching himself think, of alertness in detecting the motives which push him in the direction of any given conclusion. The child, that is, does not take his own motives into account. They are ignored and never considered as a constituent of thinking.

It would not be surprising, then, to find that, in dealing with a subject-matter which stimulates childish emotional attitudes, the inclination towards a critical analysis of the motives which lie behind thinking is not very vigorous. If we view the law as such a subject-matter, we have a key to our puzzle. Lawyers are constantly looking into the motives and biases of clients and witnesses, but are peculiarly reluctant to look into the motives and biases of judges. Yet such inquisitiveness, deliberately cultivated, is the very core of intelligent dealing with the law. That it is virtually non-existent is perhaps due to the survival of childish resistance to introspection with reference to thinking about law. The suggestion that judicial thinking can be motivated thinking is usually met with derision or amusement, as if the notion that judges had hidden motives were absurd. One recalls a dictum of Piaget in talking of the child:

"The less a mind is given to introspection the more it is the victim of the illusion that it knows itself thoroughly."

---

1.   Has Frank given a plausible account of Cardozo's performance in *Palsgraf*? As it turned out Cardozo was very much in the mind of Frank, and in a subsequent article, published under the name of Anon Y. Mous, Frank spoke of Cardozo in these terms: "All of us have some 'guiding fictions,' some images of a self or selves which we try to live up to. The word 'person' derives from the Greek theatrical word for an actor's mask through which the actor talked. There is buried truth in that word-history: every person is, in a sense, a mask, and we all have a set of masks . . . . Car-

dozo tells us that, as a young lawyer, he had a 'blind faith' that the courts would follow precedents 'inexorably to the limit of its logic.' He confesses that, as he grew older, he learned the vast amount of legal uncertainty as an unavoidable fact. He indulged in what he called 'laments' that the law is not an exact science. He acknowledged its inescapable lack of mathematical exactness but looked upon that inexactness as an 'evil against which the intellect rebels.' He wrote of 'the curse of this fluidity,' of 'an ever shifting approximation' as a curse 'that the law must bear.' Reluctantly he was 'content with many a make-shift compromise, with many a truth that is approximate and relative;' but, he conceded, he was 'yearning for the absolute.' That struggle between a yearning for the absolute in law and a recognition that it was unattainable, was doubtless an important cause of his fondness for inverted expressions, negative constructions, sinuous turns of phrases, elaborated metaphors. They signify reluctant doubt." The Speech of Judges: A Dissenting Opinion, 29 Va.L.Rev. 625, 631, 637 (1943). Earlier Frank had written to Cardozo himself and in that letter dealt with the substance of Cardozo's views and the search for certainty in the law. Letter from Frank to Cardozo, September 9, 1932, contained in the Jerome Frank Papers at Yale University Library.

2.   As a conceptual matter, one can wonder whether Judge Frank assigns far too exaggerated a role to "facts" as the "hunch producers." How does Frank understand the concept of "facts"? What is the general argument on behalf of this idea in his conceptual scheme?

3.   In the years following Frank's plea, many scholars have turned to the task of uncovering the factors that determine judicial behavior. See, generally, M. Levin, Urban Politics and the Criminal Courts (1977); Grossman, Social Backgrounds and Judicial Decision-Making, 79 Harv.L.Rev. 1551 (1966); Nagel, Political Party Affiliation and Judges' Decisions, 55 Am. Pol.Sci.Rev. 843 (1961); G. Schubert, Judicial Decision-Making (1963).

Part II

THE ELEMENTS OF ADJUDICATION

Chapter 4

ADVERSARIES

Adjudication occurs in the structured interactions among antagonists and decisionmakers. Any situation of structured antagonism creates the proper conditions for strategic behavior, that is, behavior designed to optimize an antagonist's expected outcome in a situation in which the outcome is itself partially dependent upon what the *other* antagonists do. "The term [strategy] is intended to focus on the interdependence of the adversaries' decisions and on their expectations about each other's behavior." (T. Schelling, The Strategy of Conflict 3 (1960).) Behavior of adversaries in adjudication is necessarily partly strategic—even (or especially) where "cooperation," "settlement," or informal resolution is achieved.

A theory of strategic behavior presupposes rational calculation with respect to formulated objectives. It may well be that the assumption of rational behavior does not always hold, as is seen in Professor Leff's discussion of spite. Even more important, the objectives with respect to which the rational calculation is made may not coincide with the formalized "outcome" of a single adjudication. Thus, we confront strategic behavior *within* adjudication designed to achieve the most favorable outcome of the formal event, and strategic behavior *using* adjudication in which the "game" is not defined by the outcome of the litigation but rather in terms of objectives which may include a large number of legal and non-legal events. Professor Galanter's article discusses strategic behavior of this latter sort.

Structured conflict not only introduces the concept of strategic behavior, it also underscores one important element of that structure: the ecology of roles, i. e., the patterned behavior and expectations of participants. Too often proceduralists have taken the concept of a "party" for granted, as if it were a natural, rather than a legal, concept. But, as Professor Galanter points out, there are important strategic implications in the legal construction of party status. In the articles by Professor Stone and Professor Kenneth Scott on standing, some further implications of purposeful manipulation of party status are pursued. Professor Scott pursues the question of whether some pre-existing person or organization should be "let in" to the litigation forum. Professor Stone focuses more precisely upon the issue of whether a construct should be adopted for legal personification in order to create or offset strategic advantages. Professors Landes and Posner remind us that one very common event, public agency enforcement of law, entails deliberate use of "party" status to create what are often exclusive powers to engage in litigation as a strategy to optimize the level of compliance with law. As these authors point out, the legal system, in different circumstances, uses a variable mix of private and public enforcement behavior to secure compliance with law. The Landes and Posner article suggests strategic use of the structure of antagonistic party status in pursuit of the objective of optimal levels of enforcement.

190

We next turn in this chapter to a contemporary focus for thought concerning the manipulation of party status: the aggregation of individuals into groups for purposes of litigation. In a classic article now almost forty years old, Kalven and Rosenfield considered the functions which aggregation could serve in a procedural system. The article remains as good a statement of the functional justifications for group litigation as there is. Wright's essay cast the issues in concepts of welfare economics. Professor Yeazell's article shows that the purported historical antecedents of contemporary group litigation involved a very different phenomenon. His research reveals the important discontinuities entailed in the innovations introduced over the last decade and suggests troublesome questions about a litigation device in which party constructs are so completely creatures of the legal order itself and are divorced from life in the world outside the courtroom.

Finally, our excerpt from Professor Bell's article reveals the important potential for intra-group conflict in the purposeful creation of artificial classes, as legal constructs. Professor Bell reminds us both of the critical role lawyers, with their agenda, play in the construction of the antagonistic structure of adjudication and of the lack of a perfect fit between those agenda and the life objectives of the natural persons who for litigation purposes become "all others similarly situated."

SECTION A. THE DYNAMICS OF THE CONFLICT RELATIONSHIPS: STRATEGIC BEHAVIOR

In the essay that follows, Professor Leff analyzes the strategic behavior between debtor and creditor and the part that adjudication plays within it. He employs the vocabulary of game theory. In this vocabulary "zero-sum game" is one in which whatever any player gains must come entirely out of the losses of other players. The overall sum of the gains and losses of all players must be zero. A "negative-sum game" is one in which the amount of the total losses is larger than the sum of the gains. It is a diminishing pie. A "positive-sum game" is one in which the pie expands and the sum of the antagonists' final pay-offs is greater than zero. As you read, consider how important it is to Professor Leff's analysis that collection be understood as "a minus- or negative-sum game." Why does Leff say "the source, shape, magnitude and impact of transaction costs are vitally important to understanding the transactions themselves"? What elements of debtor-creditor procedural transactions are better understood after considering the impact of "transaction costs"?

Arthur A. Leff, **Injury, Ignorance and Spite—The Dynamics of Coercive Collection***

* * *

1. Collection in Eden: Transaction Costs in the Cooperative Mode

Consider the following situation. At a particular point in time (P_0), one party (call him "C" for creditor, which he soon will be) has total wealth

Source: 80 Yale L.J. 1, 2–18 (1970).
Professor of Law, Yale University.

amounting to v, while another party (call him "D" for debtor) has zero wealth. At a later point (P_1), C transfers v to D, who promises to reconvey v or its equivalent to C at a still later point in time (P_2). The wealth positions of C and D at the relevant points in time, assuming that the value of v remains constant, may be represented as follows.[2]

	C	D
P_0	v	0
P_1	0	v
P_2	v	0

[C122]

The simplicity of this result depends on at least one important assumption, that the transactions at times P_1 and P_2 are cost-free. But in fact no transaction is cost-free. Everything one does is attended by some transaction cost,[3] even if that cost is only (and it never is only) an opportunity cost.[4] Thus if the results of the above transactions are to be presented more accurately, the chart ought to read as follows (with "t_{c1}" standing for the creditor's transactions costs at point P_1 and so on, and "t_{d1}" standing for the debtor's):

	C	D
P_0	v	0
P_1	$0 - t_{c1}$	$v - t_{d1}$
P_2	$v - (t_{c1} + t_{c2})$	$0 - (t_{d1} + t_{d2})$

[C125]

All this means, however, is that if one stipulates a system within which something of the value v is to be moved to and fro, at the end of the to, and even more at the end of the fro, there will be a progressive shrinkage of the amount of v left in the system; something will be expended in the moving which redounds to the benefit of neither party.

2. I am here excluding at least three factors which would have to be reflected in any more realistic model. First, I am leaving out any reference to what would be expected in the real commercial world, a charge for the use of v. Second, I am not reflecting the fact that at the time P_1, C would possess a claim, an account receivable, of v (or some discounted portion of that face value), and that D would have a corresponding account payable. Third, in using the concept v I will much of the time ignore the fact that the value of v, insofar as v stands for real goods, would tend to fluctuate over time because of market-price movements, normal functional depreciation, or in response to the increased or decreased likelihood of its recovery. When those possible fluctuations are of particular importance to the analysis I shall discuss them, but most of the time I shall stipulate v as a constant standing for a transfer and its agreed-upon reciprocation.

3. At this stage in this essay the term "transaction cost" refers to those costs and losses borne by a party in connection with effecting any exchange, including payments and repayments. Depending on how one looks at things, it can expand or contract meaning within very wide parameters. . . .

4. For the time being it is assumed that each party bears his own transaction costs and cannot transfer them onto the other, or externalize them onto a third party. . . .

For the economist this undeniable fact presents few theoretical difficulties. Transaction costs are to economics what friction is to classical mechanics, that which transforms pure science into engineering. For most purposes, a transaction cost is like any other cost and requires no extraordinary fuss. When an economist is speaking qua physicist rather than as an engineer he will, after noting the practical importance of transaction costs, exclude them from his theoretical model. Thus the "economics of transacting" has rarely been subjected to extended consideration by economists. Similarly, to the businessman transaction costs merit no special consideration. The costs of lending and collecting money, for instance, are part of the administrative cost of any credit business and are reflected as are any business costs in the price charged.[8] This understandable lack of theoretical interest should not, however, cause anyone to overlook the fact that the source, shape, magnitude and impact of transaction costs are vitally important to understanding the transactions themselves. To the extent that transaction costs are understood by the participants, they may significantly affect their choice of collection strategies and the overall efficiency of the collection process.

. . .

II. Collection in America: Transaction Costs in a Judicial-Coercion Game

A. Introduction: The Creditor's Dilemma

Under the American law of contracts, after the other party has fully performed his obligations it is absolutely irrational for you fully to perform yours. If you, D, refuse voluntarily to repay v in full, C would always be better off accepting from you some lesser performance, $v - x$, so long as $(v - x) > (v - t_c)$. Thus if v were 1000, and if D could force C in recovering v to expend a t_c of 100 while suffering no t_d himself, it would be rational for both C and D not to allow the coercive collection process to go to completion, but instead to settle on a repayment of anything between 901 and 999, that is, at any point on L-L_1 on the following graph:

Graph I

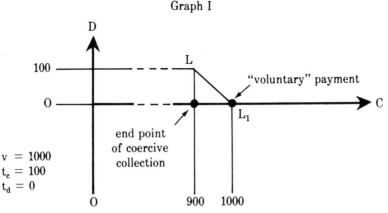

[C115]

---

8. Of course there are constraints upon the extent to which costs can be absorbed in a price, involving the competitive situation, the elasticity of demand and many other things.

For what L-L$_1$ represents is the locus of all points the sum value of which is 1000, that is, all points which, while no worse than the end point of a completed coercive collection for either party, totally conserve the v for division between C and D. No wealth is "wasted" on t. If one views coercive collection as a two-person game, and one takes account of the costs of playing it, it is not a two-person zero-sum game, but a two-person minus-sum game, and the parties can both gain by avoiding the play altogether, agreeing instead on an L-L$_1$ settlement.[15]

When D has no t$_d$, he is comparatively indifferent as to whether the game is played or not; playing cannot make him worse off than not playing can. But what if D were forced to suffer, as part of the same coercive transaction which generated the t$_c$ of 100, a t$_d$, perhaps one in excess of 100? That, pictorialized, might look like this:

Graph II

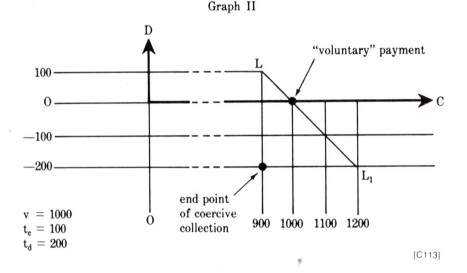

v = 1000
t$_c$ = 100
t$_d$ = 200

[C113]

15. Whether it is more economical to reach agreement than to play depends, of course, on the cost of reaching agreement compared to the sum of t$_c$ and t$_d$. . . .

Even if the parties "agree" to avoid the end-point, there is no single point on L-L$_1$ which is *the* rational solution. There are aesthetic solutions. The midpoint of L-L$_1$ (950/50), for instance, apportions equally the amount gained through cooperation. Point 999/1 bribes D with one unit above what he would end up with if he remained recalcitrant. 901/99 makes C "pay" all but one unit of his t$_c$, but still makes it one unit cheaper for him to settle than to play. These are all reasonable and attractive points to pick, but despite their natural appeal, they are no "better" than any others. . . .

The point at which C and D would finally settle depends on "bargaining power." But to make any meaningful assessment of this matter one would have to know a great deal about C and D individually, e. g., their level of effective nastiness, their intelligence, knowledge and pertinacity, and their relative marginal utilities for money. From another perspective "superior bargaining power" is what you award to someone as an accolade when you find out he got a better deal than you expected. It is an entry on his personal books that fills the same function as "good will" does on the books of a company with a lousy product and a superior earning record.

Again, playing the coercion game to completion would be minus-sum, and again both C and D would be well advised to find some point on L-L₁ at which to settle. But in this case D would not longer be indifferent as to whether the game were played or not, for a completed game, while hurting C, would hurt D more. Thus, the ultimate settlement point on L-L₁ would tend to move further southeast, that is, more to the taste of C. And if t_d could be made great enough relative to t_c, D might well decide to pay all of v in order to avoid the threatened playing of the game. Thus the actual posture of the parties will depend largely on the relative quantities of t_c and t_d which, in any particular context, coercive collection will predictably generate.

B.   The Content of t_c

.   .   .   One must to some extent be Hobbesian about it. If paid for and played from beginning to end, this expensive game does result in the acquisition of an immense bundle of power; behind every final judgment procured in any court in this country stands, ultimately, the United States Army, but even the intermediate mercenaries one buys—sheriffs, marshalls, judges—are usually sufficient unto the day. If someone has something that "belongs to" you and "the law" finally says so, so far as power can get it to you, that power will suffice. But the price one is supposed to pay for harnessing the Leviathan to one's cause is, essentially, the cost of moving it according to its own rather arcane principles, that is, the cost of due process.

The cost of due process is high for at least four reasons. First, due process demands that at the outset the court and its officers be wholly ignorant of what happened and it is expensive to educate them, at least using the pleading-and-playlet format of the common law. Second, the process of education cannot proceed on a generalized (mass-produced) basis; each case is theoretically hand-crafted. Third, save in a court of small claims it is usually specialists (e. g., lawyers) who do the crafting. Fourth, because the courts do not allocate docket space by competitive bidding between plaintiffs, the creditor with the largest claim at stake must take his place in a "queue" behind plaintiffs with smaller claims.

.   .   .   But there is another factor involved in using "the law" with respect to half-executed contracts which tends to increase the transaction costs of the party who has performed: the risk of wrongly losing, and of losing all. Assume again that C has done all that he promised D while D has done none. If nothing else were to happen at that point, C would be out v and D would be ahead v, for something "belonging to" C is at that point in D's hands. Now, assume further that D refuses to pay, and that C must go to law. Even if the law functions properly (that is, in accord with the assumed facts) the maximum that C can recover is $v - t_c$. But if the law miscarries and a "wrong" decision is made, C's post-litigation status could be as bad as $0 - t_c$. This, of course, is C's maximum exposure. Though the law does tend to formulate as many transactions as possible in yes-no terms, it is not always that rigid. While C might not get v, he might still get an amount greater than zero. But there are nonetheless innumerable accidents in legal proceedings which lead to status quo results, and for C any result which retains the status quo is more than a total loss.

What makes this risk-of-status-quo factor particularly interesting is that it is proportional to the magnitude of v. It is ordinarily less irrational to spend any given quantity of t_c as the amount of v to be recovered (which would be abandoned by abjuring the expenditure) increases. But the risk component of t_c increases as the amount of v being put in jeopardy by the litigative system increases. So long as v is not thrown into the judicial-coercive system with its power to transform C's property finally into D's, there is always hope. As soon as the final writ is executed, however, no further bargaining about v is possible; whoever it objectively belonged to, it now belongs to whoever won. Thus the greater the value of v, the more C may be irrevocably out-of-pocket, and the more dangerous it is for him to risk the irrevocable loss .   .   .   .[21]

C. The Content of t_d

The judicial-coercive process is so designed that C may have to go through a number of steps, none cost free, even though D remains totally passive. Unless one counts the cost of tearing up and throwing away an occasional summons, the process can be free for D all the way from institution of the action to execution of the judgment. C's mercenaries will have little difficult or dangerous work to do if D chooses this course of inaction, and the resultant t_c will be low, but the choice is D's. In order to increase C's costs over the bare minimum for commencing a lawsuit and taking it through to judgment, D can expend some money and effort. But the critical point is that in most cases of breach, C will be forced to spend some t_c before D need even decide whether he will spend any t_d.

Were this where the story ended, the irrationality of paying one's debts would not be merely apparent. But we all know that not fully carrying out one's obligations can bring with it a retribution that is hardly limited to social disapprobation, a guilty conscience, or an unpleasant afterlife. Translated into our formal terms, there are components of t_d in addition to those

---

21. Of course, if C does nothing and D does not pay he will lose all of v anyway. The difference between other collection methods and the judicial coercive mode is that a mistake under the latter is final. As the recalcitrance of D becomes more firm and longlasting, however, the differential risk of going to law decreases. Another way to put this is to say that if one views v as an account receivable, its actual value will decrease from face value as more and more discouraging information about this D appears, and a "final" judicial loss will be the loss of less. But the depreciation in the value of v is not a simple function of the passage of time, or even of the immovability of D in the face of other than judicial collection approaches. If one successfully sues a stubborn but solvent D, one may still eventually get all of v, less only the cost of getting the decree and execution. But until one knows that litigation is the only way, it is risky to try, and chance losing forever.

This risk-t_c factor is much more significant in situations where walking away would cost C not only v, but an adverse judicial decree could cost him much more than v, e. g., any test case situation where only one or a few litigants are likely to challenge C's right, but if one of them wins many other potential litigants, theretofore stymied by that "right," will also have an easy remedy. In such a case, it may be intelligent for C to avoid the risk altogether by buying off the active litigants with abandoned v's. This may be merely a specific application of the general rule that unknown future states are more threatening to those who have a greater stake in the status quo.

which our analysis has heretofore taken into account. . . . Not only do the courts regularly enforce contractual clauses providing that the creditor who sues successfully also recover the expenses of collection, even in the absence of any specific provision certain costs of collection are allocated to the defaulting buyer. This particular transfer payment simultaneously decreases t_c and increases t_d. A complete transfer of t_c to D will not be possible because C still must bear the risk component of his t_c, that is, the same miscarriage that would bereave C of v rightfully his will deny him that portion of t_c he would have been awarded had his suit been successful. But this is only to say that these cost-shifting devices may not by themselves be sufficient to force D into a position where it would be wholly irrational to breach, where, that is, $t_c = 0$ and $t_d > 0$.

Beyond these procedures for shifting the cost of coercive collection to D, there are for C even more powerful and threatening devices which involve no transfer payment at all. They function not as payments to C, but as mere destruction of D's wealth. But that too acts to coerce D. In a sense, of course, all t_d is like that; it hurts D without directly helping C. But some kinds of t_d, the costs of defense, for example, can be avoided by raising none. The components of t_d to be considered next cannot be avoided merely by remaining passive. Indeed such a response is likely to increase the injury.

When D has defaulted in the performance he owes to C, there are two courses open to C under modern sales law. He may attempt via self-help to get back what he gave D,[26] or he may at law attempt to get what D promised to give him. In some situations he may reclaim goods delivered under a contract (so far as that is physically feasible) and then, to the extent that that does not get him to where he would have been had the transaction gone through as planned, he may attempt to get additional things of value from D to make up the deficiency.

The attractiveness of the self-help process is obvious: it sometimes permits C to recover some large portion of v without incurring the usual expenses of going to law. It is, in effect, an opportunity to use state-of-nature power to get out of the C position without having either to buy off, or buy in, the Leviathan. It is not, of course, cost free; night work with tow trucks (or even with duplicate keys) entails expense, but seldom as much as a litigated lawsuit and subsequent execution. Moreover, it is possible in this way for C to recover all. This depends on the value to C of the goods seized and the amount of the debt outstanding at the time of the repossession, but given a high enough down payment and a low enough rate of depreciation for the goods, C may be made whole solely by retaking the goods.

But there are significant additional injuries inherent in self-help or judicially-ordered repossession which do not directly inure to C's benefit but which may so increase t_d as to inhibit D's breach. First is the loss which comes solely from being deprived of a good's use . . . . This harm can be visited on D even if C does not get use and/or resale rights in the

---

26. There are some limitations upon the manner and means of self-help repossession. At the very least, a good old medieval affray is most likely out, see Uniform Commercial Code § 9–503 (1962), though stealth and cunning seem not only lawful, but the order of the night . . . .

item, as the garageman's and lawyer's liens amply illustrate. Once deprivation is coupled with a power of resale, however, D's loss increases and becomes more permanent. There are numerous things in the world that are
worth much more to one person than they are to any other person . . . .

When there are added to this "normal" depreciation factor all the other
factors which may lower the price fetched by used goods in an aftermarket,
for example, restricted buyer pools approaching mini-monopsonies, insufficient sale advertising, unenthusiastic and incompetent selling, title uncertainties, and the lack of price-maximizing incentives, the potential loss in value
to an ex-possessor becomes substantial.[32] With consumer goods, yet another
factor enters further to drive this value-destruction vector: non-functional
depreciation, the loss in value consumer goods suffer when they move from
the category "new" to the category "used." . . .

Mere value destruction, of course, cannot do C any direct good. If his
claim is properly for more than the repossession-resale will realize, it may
do him actual harm, assuming he cannot get the deficiency from D at all,
or at least without suffering unreasonable additional costs. But the threat
of this value destruction is a threat of serious injury, available at a cost relatively low in comparison to the magnitude of the injury inflicted. It is an
increase in the applicable t_d.

The potentiality of repossession and resale to increase strikingly the ratio
of t_d to t_c by destroying value in D's hands is manifest, often to a greater degree, in the operation of the other common execution technique, garnishment. But the attractiveness of garnishment from a creditor's point of view
does not lie solely in its excitingly abusive possibilities. In theory, and often
in practice, garnishment would be a lovely remedy to have even if it threatened no excess injury to the debtor. The way it is supposed to work is that
the faucet whence liquid cash flows periodically to your debtor is directed
to divert at least a little rivulet to you, at the faucet's cost and risk, until your
cup runneth over. No need to grab possession of things, store them, manipulate them, push and shove them about until they turn into usable derefied
value. No need to follow-up, time after time, the vicissitudes of sheriffs
and auctioneers. Just wait, and to you all things will be given, slowly perhaps, but with interest. Indeed, from a creditor's point of view, garnishment is one of the most effective techniques for the non-cooperative collection
of debts ever devised . . . .

It is important to note again that as with repossession value-shrinkage,
the injury to the debtor is not simultaneously an equal direct gain to the creditor.[50] In both cases, the loss amounts initially to mere destruction of value
in the hands of the debtor. In fact, in both cases, the side effects of actually using the collection procedure decrease the likelihood that the creditor will
eventually get all of his v out of the debtor. In both cases the source of the
creditor's surcease, the things of value "owned" by the debtor, are diminished

---

32. In addition, once the debtor's default is known, his credit-replacement
cost rises because of the effects on
reputation of non-payment . . . .

50. Though in both cases the creditor
will get something, either the goods
upon repossession or the allowable portion of at least the first paycheck in
garnishment.

by the act of seizure. Of course distribution of the net loss between the parties differs; in these cases it ordinarily falls much harder on the debtor-employee than on his creditor. And that is what makes the procedure such a potent threat. But when the threats to repossess or to garnish are actually carried out, either through ignorance or to establish credibility it may fairly be said that the system is behaving "spitefully," that is, in a manner harmful to both the central participants . . . .

The most obvious and most frequent uses of game theory in the legal literature have been in connection with the settlement and the plea bargaining processes. See, e. g., H. Laurence Ross, Settled Out of Court 136–75 (1970); Nagel and Neef, Plea Bargaining, Decision Theory, and Equilibrium Models: Part I, 51 Ind.L.J. 987–1024 (1976), and Part II, 52 Ind.L.J. 1–61 (1976). See, also, Posner's discussion of settlement in his article excerpted here in chapter 1. The interested reader might examine two important general works: R. D. Luce and H. Raiffa, Games and Decisions (1957); and J. G. Cross, The Economics of Bargaining (1969).

Marc Galanter, Why the "Haves" Come out Ahead: Speculations on the Limits of Legal Change*

. . .

A Typology of Parties

. . . Because of differences in their size, differences in the state of the law, and differences in their resources, some of the actors in the society have many occasions to utilize the courts (in the broad sense) to make (or defend) claims; others do so only rarely. We might divide our actors into those claimants who have only occasional recourse to the courts (one-shotters or OS) and repeat players (RP) who are engaged in many similar litigations over time. The spouse in a divorce case, the auto-injury claimant, the criminal accused are OSs; the insurance company, the prosecutor, the finance company are RPs. Obviously this is an oversimplification; there are intermediate cases such as the professional criminal.[4] So we ought to think of OS–RP as a continuum rather than as a dichotomous pair. Typically, the RP is a larger unit and the stakes in any given case are smaller (relative to total worth). OSs are usually smaller units and the stakes represented by the tangible outcome of the case may be high relative to total worth, as in the case of injury victim or the criminal accused. Or, the OS may suffer from the opposite problem: his claims may be so small and unmanageable (the shortweighted

* Source: 9 L. & Soc'y Rev. 95, 95–151 (1974). Professor of Law, University of Wisconsin.

4. Even the taxpayer and the welfare client are not pure OSs, since there is next year's tax bill and next month's welfare check. Our concept of OS conceals the difference between pure OSs—persons such as the accident victim who get in the situation only once—and those who are in a continuing series of transactions (welfare clients or taxpayers) but whose resources permit at most a single crack at litigation.

consumer or the holder of performing rights) that the cost of enforcing them outruns any promise of benefit . . . .

Let us refine our notion of the RP into an "ideal type" if you will—a unit which has had and anticipates repeated litigation, which has low stakes in the outcome of any one case, and which has the resources to pursue its long-run interests. (This does not include every real-world repeat player; that most common repeat player, the alcoholic derelict, enjoys few of the advantages that may accrue to the RP. His resources are too few to bargain in the short run or take heed of the long run.) An OS, on the other hand, is a unit whose claims are too large (relative to his size) or too small (relative to the cost of remedies) to be managed routinely and rationally.

We would expect an RP to play the litigation game differently from an OS. Let us consider some of his advantages:

(1) RPs, having done it before, have advance intelligence; they are able to structure the next transaction and build a record. It is the RP who writes the form contract, requires the security deposit, and the like.

(2) RPs develop expertise and have ready access to specialists.[7] They enjoy economies of scale and have low start-up costs for any case.

(3) RPs have opportunities to develop facilitative informal relations with institutional incumbents.

(4) The RP must establish and maintain credibility as a combatant. His interest in his "bargaining reputation" serves as a resource to establish "commitment" to his bargaining positions. With no bargaining reputation to maintain, the OS has more difficulty in convincingly committing himself in bargaining.[10]

(5) RPs can play the odds. The larger the matter at issue looms for OS, the more likely he is to adopt a minimax strategy (minimize the probability of maximum loss). Assuming that the stakes are relatively smaller for RPs, they can adopt strategies calculated to maximize gain over a long series of cases, even where this involves the risk of maximum loss in some cases.

(6) RPs can play for rules as well as immediate gains. First, it pays an RP to expend resources in influencing the making of the rele-

---

7. Ironically, RPs may enjoy access to competent paraprofessional help that is unavailable to OSs. Thus the insurance company can, by employing adjusters, obtain competent and experienced help in routine negotiations without having to resort to expensive professionally qualified personnel . . . .

10. . . . An offsetting advantage enjoyed by some OSs deserves mention. Since he does not anticipate continued dealings with his opponent, an OS can do his damnedest without fear of reprisal next time around or on other issues. (The advantages of those who enjoy the luxury of singlemindedness are evidenced by some notorious examples in the legislative arena, for instance, the success of prohibitionists and of the gun lobby.) Thus there may be a bargaining advantage to the OS who (a) has resources to damage his opponent; (b) is convincingly able to threaten to use them. An OS can burn up his capital, but he has to convince the other side he is really likely to do so. Thus an image of irrationality may be a bargaining advantage. . . . An OS may be able to sustain such an image in a way that an RP cannot. . . .

vant rules by such methods as lobbying. (And his accumulated expertise enables him to do this persuasively.)

(7) RPs can also play for rules in litigation itself, whereas an OS is unlikely to. That is, there is a difference in what they regard as a favorable outcome . . . . The larger the stake for any player and the lower the probability of repeat play, the less likely that he will be concerned with the rules which govern future cases of the same kind. . . . On the other hand, the player with small stakes in the present case and the prospect of a series of similar cases . . . may be more interested in the state of the law.

. . . [If we were to assume] that the institutional facilities for litigation were overloaded and settlements were prevalent, [w]e would then expect RPs to "settle" cases where they expected unfavorable rule outcomes. Since they expect to litigate again, RPs can select to adjudicate (or appeal) those cases which they regard as most likely to produce favorable rules. On the other hand, OSs should be willing to trade off the possibility of making "good law" for tangible gain. Thus, we would expect the body of "precedent" cases—that is, cases capable of influencing the outcome of future cases—to be relatively skewed toward those favorable to RP. . . . In [stipulating] that RPs can play for rules, I do not mean to imply that RPs pursue rule-gain as such. If we recall that not all rules penetrate (i. e., become effectively applied at the field level), we come to some additional advantages of RPs.

(8) RPs, by virtue of experience and expertise, are more likely to be able to discern which rules are likely to "penetrate" and which are likely to remain merely symbolic commitments. RPs may be able to concentrate their resources on rule-changes that are likely to make a tangible difference. They can trade off symbolic defeats for tangible gains.

(9) Since penetration depends in part on the resources of the parties (knowledge, attentiveness, expert services, money), RPs are more likely to be able to invest the matching resources necessary to secure the penetration of rules favorable to them.

. . . What this analysis does is to define a position of advantage in the configuration of contending parties and indicate how those with other advantages tend to occupy this position of advantage and to have their other advantages reinforced and augmented thereby. This position of advantage is one of the ways in which a legal system formally neutral as between "haves" and "have-nots" may perpetuate and augment the advantages of the former . . . . .

We may think of litigation as typically involving various combinations of OSs and RPs. We can then construct a matrix such as Figure 1 and fill in the boxes with some well-known if only approximate American examples.

(We ignore for the moment that the terms OS and RP represent ends of a continuum, rather than a dichotomous pair.)

FIGURE 1

A TAXONOMY OF LITIGATION BY STRATEGIC
CONFIGURATION OF PARTIES

Initiator, Claimant

	One-Shotter	Repeat Player
One-Shotter	Parent v. Parent (Custody) Spouse v. Spouse (Divorce) Family v. Family Member (Insanity Commitment) Family v. Family (Inheritance) Neighbor v. Neighbor Partner v. Partner <center>OS vs OS</center> <center>I</center>	Prosecutor v. Accused Finance Co. v. Debtor Landlord v. Tenant I.R.S. v. Taxpayer Condemnor v. Property Owner <center>RP vs OS</center> <center>II</center>
Repeat Player	Welfare Client v. Agency Auto Dealer v. Manufacturer Injury Victim v. Insurance Company Tenant v. Landlord Bankrupt Consumer v. Creditors Defamed v. Publisher <center>OS vs RP</center> <center>III</center>	Union v. Company Movie Distributor v. Censorship Board Developer v. Suburban Municipality Purchaser v. Supplier Regulatory Agency v. Firms of Regulated Industry <center>RP vs RP</center> <center>IV</center>

Defendant (left axis label)

[C126]

On the basis of our incomplete and unsystematic examples, let us conjecture a bit about the content of these boxes:

Box I: OS vs. OS

The most numerous occupants of this box are divorces and insanity hearings. Most (over 90 per cent of divorces, for example) are uncontested. A large portion of these are really pseudo-litigation, that is, a settlement is worked out between the parties and ratified in the guise of adjudication. When we get real litigation in Box I, it is often between parties who have some intimate tie with one another, fighting over some unsharable good, often with overtones of "spite" and "irrationality." Courts are resorted to where an ongoing relationship is ruptured; they have little to do with the routine patterning of activity. The law is invoked ad hoc and instrumentally by the parties. There may be a strong interest in vindication, but neither party is likely to have much interest in the long-term state of the law (of, for instance, custody or nuisance). There are few appeals, few test cases, little expenditure of resources on rule-development. Legal doctrine is likely to remain remote from everyday practice and from popular attitudes.

Box II: RP vs. OS

The great bulk of litigation is found in this box—indeed every really numerous kind except personal injury cases, insanity hearings, and divorces. The law is used for routine processing of claims by parties for whom the making of such claims is a regular business activity. Often the cases here take the form of stereotyped mass processing with little of the individuated attention of full-dress adjudication. Even greater numbers of cases are settled "informally" with settlement keyed to possible litigation outcome (discounted by risk, cost, delay).

The state of the law is of interest to the RP, though not to the OS defendants. Insofar as the law is favorable to the RP it is "followed" closely in practice (subject to discount for RP's transaction costs). Transactions are built to fit the rules by creditors, police, draft boards and other RPs. Rules favoring OSs may be less readily applicable, since OSs do not ordinarily plan the underlying transaction, or less meticulously observed in practice, since OSs are unlikely to be as ready or able as RPs to invest in insuring their penetration to the field level.

Box III: OS vs. RP

All of these are rather infrequent types except for personal injury cases which are distinctive in that free entry to the arena is provided by the contingent fee.[34] In auto injury claims, litigation is routinized and settlement is closely geared to possible litigation outcome. Outside the personal injury area, litigation in Box III is not routine. It usually represents the attempt of some OS to invoke outside help to create leverage on an organization with which he has been having dealings but is now at the point of divorce (for example, the discharged employee or the cancelled franchisee). The OS claimant generally has little interest in the state of the law; the RP defendant, however, is greatly interested.

Box IV: RP vs. RP

Let us consider the general case first and then several special cases. We might expect that there would be little litigation in Box IV, because to the extent that two RPs play with each other repeatedly, the expectation of continued mutually beneficial interaction would give rise to informal bilateral controls. This seems borne out by studies of dealings among businessmen and in labor relations. Official agencies are invoked by unions trying to get established and by management trying to prevent them from getting established, more rarely in dealings between bargaining partners. Units with mutually beneficial relations do not adjust their differences in courts. Where they rely on third parties in dispute-resolution, it is likely to take a form (such as arbitration or a domestic tribunal) detached from official sanctions and applying domestic rather than official rules.

However, there are several special cases. First, there are those RPs who seek not furtherance of tangible interests, but vindication of funda-

---

34. Perhaps high volume litigation in Box III is particularly susceptible to transformation into relatively unproblematic administrative processing when RPs discover that it is to their advantage and can secure a shift with some gains (or at least no losses) to OSs. Cf. the shift from tort to workman's compensation in the industrial accident area . . . and the contemporary shift to no-fault plans in the automobile injury area.

mental cultural commitments. An example would be the organizations which sponsor much church-state litigation. Where RPs are contending about value differences (who is right) rather than interest conflicts (who gets what) there is less tendency to settle and less basis for developing a private system of dispute-settlement.

Second, government is a special kind of RP. Informal controls depend upon the ultimate sanction of withdrawal and refusal to continue beneficial relations. To the extent that withdrawal of future association is not possible in dealing with government, the scope of informal controls is correspondingly limited. The development of informal relations between regulatory agencies and regulated firms is well known. And the regulated may have sanctions other than withdrawal which they can apply; for instance, they may threaten political opposition. But the more inclusive the unit of government, the less effective the withdrawal sanction and the greater the likelihood that a party will attempt to invoke outsides allies by litigation even while sustaining the ongoing relationship. This applies also to monopolies, units which share the government's relative immunity to withdrawal sanctions. RPs in monopolistic relationships will occasionally invoke formal controls to show prowess, to give credibility to threat, and to provide satisfactions for other audiences. Thus we would expect litigation by and against government to be more frequent than in other RP vs. RP situations. There is a second reason for expecting more litigation when government is a party. That is, that the notion of "gain" (policy as well as monetary) is often more contingent and problematic for governmental units than for other parties, such as businesses or organized interest groups. In some cases courts may, by profferring authoritative interpretations of public policy, redefine an agency's notion of gain. Hence government parties may be more willing to externalize decisions to the courts. And opponents may have more incentive to litigate against government in the hope of securing a shift in its goals.

A somewhat different kind of special case is present where plaintiff and defendant are both RPs but do not deal with each other repeatedly (two insurance companies, for example). In the government/monopoly case, the parties were so inextricably bound together that the force of informal controls was limited; here they are not sufficiently bound to each other to give informal controls their bite; there is nothing to withdraw from! The large one-time deal that falls through, the marginal enterprise—these are staple sources of litigation.

Where there is litigation in the RP vs. RP situation, we might expect that there would be heavy expenditure on rule-development, many appeals, and rapid and elaborate development of the doctrinal law. Since the parties can invest to secure implementation of favorable rules, we would expect practice to be closely articulated to the resulting rules . . . .

Lawyers

What happens when we introduce lawyers? Parties who have lawyers do better. Lawyers are themselves RPs. Does their presence equalize the parties, dispelling the advantage of the RP client? Or does the existence of lawyers amplify the advantage of the RP client? We might assume that RPs (tending to be larger units) who can buy legal services more steadily, in larger quantities, in bulk (by retainer) and at higher rates, would get services of better quality. They would have better information (especially where restrictions on information about legal services are present). Not only would the RP get more talent to begin with, but he would on the whole get greater continuity, better record-keeping, more anticipatory or preventive work, more experience and specialized skill in pertinent areas, and more control over counsel.

One might expect that just how much the legal services factor would accentuate the RP advantage would be related to the way in which the profession was organized. The more members of the profession were identified with their clients (i. e., the less they were held aloof from clients by their loyalty to courts or an autonomous guild) the more the imbalance would be accentuated. The more close and enduring the lawyer-client relationship, the more the primary loyalty of lawyers is to clients rather than to courts or guild, the more telling the advantages of accumulated expertise and guidance in overall strategy.

What about the specialization of the bar? Might we not expect the existence of specialization to offset RP advantages by providing OS with a specialist who in pursuit of his own career goals would be interested in outcomes that would be advantageous to a whole class of OSs? Does the specialist become the functional equivalent of the RP? We may divide specialists into (1) those specialized by field of law (patent, divorce, etc.), (2) those specialized by the kind of party represented (for example, house counsel), and (3) those specialized by both field of law and "side" or party (personal injury plaintiff, criminal defense, labor). Divorce lawyers do not specialize in husbands or wives, nor real-estate lawyers in buyers or sellers. But labor lawyers and tax lawyers and stockholders-derivative-suit lawyers do specialize not only in the field of law but in representing one side. Such specialists may represent RPs or OSs. Figure 2 provides some well-known examples of different kinds of specialists:

FIGURE 2

A TYPOLOGY OF LEGAL SPECIALISTS
Lawyer

	Specialized by Party	Specialized by Field and Party	Specialized by Field
RP (Client)	"House Counsel" or General Counsel for Bank, Insurance Co., etc. Corporation Counsel for Government Unit	Prosecutor Personal Injury Defendant Staff Counsel for NAACP Tax Labor/Management Collections	Patent
OS	"Poverty Lawyers" Legal Aid	Criminal Defense Personal Injury Plaintiff	Bankruptcy Divorce

Most specializations cater to the needs of particular kinds of RPs. Those specialists who service OSs have some distinctive features:

First, they tend to make up the "lower echelons" of the legal profession. . . . (Of course the correlation is far from perfect; some lawyers who represent OSs do not have these characteristics and some representing RPs do . . . .)

Second, specialists who service OSs tend to have problems of mobilizing a clientele (because of the low state of information among OSs) and encounter "ethical" barriers imposed by the profession which forbids solicitation, advertising, referral fees, advances to clients, and so forth.

Third, the episodic and isolated nature of the relationship with particular OS clients tends to elicit a stereotyped and uncreative brand of legal services . . . .

Fourth, while they are themselves RPs, these specialists have problems in developing optimizing strategies. What might be good strategy for an insurance company lawyer or prosecutor—trading off some cases for gains on others—is branded as unethical when done by a criminal defense or personal injury plaintiff lawyer. It is not permissible for him to play his series of OSs as if they constituted a single RP.

Conversely, the demands of routine and orderly handling of a whole series of OSs may constrain the lawyer from maximizing advantage for any individual OS . . . .

The existence of a specialized bar on the OS side should overcome the gap in expertise, allow some economies of scale, provide for bargaining commitment and personal familiarity. But this is short of overcoming the fundamental strategic advantage of RPs—their capacity to structure the transaction, play the odds, and influence rule-development and enforcement policy.

Specialized lawyers may, by virtue of their identification with parties, become lobbyists, moral entrepreneurs, proponents of reforms on the parties' behalf. But lawyers have a cross-cutting interest in preserving complexity and mystique so that client contact with this area of law is rendered problematic. Lawyers should not be expected to be proponents of reforms which are optimum from the point of view of the clients taken alone. Rather, we would expect them to seek to optimize the clients' position without diminishing that of lawyers. . . .

Institutional Facilities

We see then that the strategic advantages of the RP may be augmented by advantages in the distribution of legal services. Both are related to the advantages conferred by the basic features of the institutional facilities for the handling of claims: passivity and overload.

These institutions are passive, first, in the sense that [they are] "reactive"—they must be mobilized by the claimant—giving advantage to the claimant with information, ability to surmount cost barriers, and skill to navigate restrictive procedural requirements. . . . The presiding official acts as umpire, while the development of the case, collection of evidence and presentation of proof are left to the initiative and resources of the parties.   Parties are treated as if they were equally endowed with economic resources, investigative opportunities and legal skills.   Where, as is usually the case, they are not, the broader the delegation to the parties, the greater the advantage conferred on the wealthier, more experienced and better organized party.

.   .   .   In several ways overload creates pressures on claimants to settle rather than to adjudicate:

(a) by causing delay (thereby discounting the value of recovery);

(b) by raising costs (of keeping the case alive);

(c) by inducing institutional incumbents to place a high value on clearing dockets, discouraging full-dress adjudication in favor of bargaining, stereotyping and routine processing;

(d) by inducing the forum to adopt restrictive rules to discourage litigation.

Thus, overload increases the cost and risk of adjudicating and shields existing rules from challenge, diminishing opportunities for rule-change.   This tends to favor the beneficiaries of existing rules.

Second, by increasing the difficulty of challenging going practice, overload also benefits those who reap advantage from the neglect (or systematic violation) of rules which favor their adversaries.

Third, overload tends to protect the possessor—the party who has the money or goods—against the claimant.   For the most part, this amounts to favoring RPs over OSs, since RPs typically can structure transactions to put themselves in the possessor position.

Finally, the overload situation means that there are more commitments in the formal system than there are resources to honor them—more rights and rules "on the books" than can be vindicated or enforced.   There are, then, questions of priorities in the allocation of resources.   We would expect judges, police, administrators and other managers of limited institutional facilities to be responsive to the more organized, attentive and influential of their constituents.   Again, these tend to be RPs.

Thus, overloaded and passive institutional facilities provide the setting in which the RP advantages in strategic position and legal services can have full play.

Rules

We assume here that rules tend to favor older, culturally dominant interests.   This is not meant to imply that the rules are explicitly designed to favor these interests, but rather that those groups which have become dominant have successfully articulated their operations to pre-existing rules.   To the extent that rules are evenhanded or favor the "have-nots," the limited resources for their implementation will be allocated, I have argued, so as to give greater effect to those rules which protect and promote the tangible interests of organized and influential groups.   Furthermore, the requirements of due process, with their barriers or protections against precipitate action, naturally tend to protect the possessor or holder against the claimant.   Finally, the rules are sufficiently complex and problematic (or capable of being problematic if sufficient resources are expended to make them so) that differences in the quantity and quality of legal services will affect capacity to derive advantages from the rules.

Thus, we arrive at Figure 3 which summarizes why the "haves" tend to come out ahead. It points to layers of advantages enjoyed by different (but largely overlapping) classes of "haves"—advantages which interlock, reinforcing and shielding one another. .   .   .

FIGURE 3
WHY THE "HAVES" TEND TO COME OUT AHEAD

Element	Advantages	Enjoyed by
PARTIES	— ability to structure transaction — specialized expertise, economies of scale — long-term strategy — ability to play for rules — bargaining credibility — ability to invest in penetration	— repeat players, large, professional *
LEGAL SERVICES	— skill, specialization, continuity	— organized, professional,* wealthy
INSTITU-TIONAL FACILITIES	— passivity — cost and delay barriers — favorable priorities	— wealthy, experienced, organized — holders, possessors — beneficiaries of existing rules — organized, attentive
RULES	— favorable rules — due process barriers	— older, culturally dominant — holders, possessors

[C 124]

* In the sense of "doing it for a living."

Strategies for Reform

Our categorization of four layers of advantage (Figure 3) suggests a typology of strategies for "reform" (taken here to mean equalization—conferring relative advantage on those who did not enjoy it before). We then come to four types of equalizing reform:

(1) rule-change,

(2) improvement in institutional facilities,

(3) improvement of legal services in quantity and quality,

(4) improvement of strategic position of have-not parties.

. . . [Here Professor Galanter sketches some of the possible ramifications of change on each of these four levels. We have included only the discussion relating to the improvement of the strategic position of the "have-not parties."]

The reform envisaged here is the organization of "have-not" parties (whose position approximates OS) into coherent groups that have the ability to act in a coordinated fashion, play long-run strategies, benefit from high-grade legal services, and so forth.

One can imagine various ways in which OSs might be aggregated into RPs. They include (1) the membership association-bargaining agent (trade unions, tenant unions); (2) the assignee-manager of fragmentary rights (performing rights associations like ASCAP); (3) the interest group-sponsor (NAACP, ACLU, environmental action groups). All of these forms involve upgrading capacities for managing claims by gathering and utilizing information, achieving continuity and persistence, employing expertise, exercising bargaining skill and so forth. These advantages are combined with enhancement of the OS party's strategic position either by aggregating claims that are too small relative to the cost of remedies (consumers, breathers of polluted air, owners of performing rights); or by reducing claims to manageable size by collective action to dispel or share unacceptable risks (tenants, migrant workers). A weaker form of organization would be (4) a clearing-house which established a communication network among OSs. This would lower the costs of information and give RPs a stake in the effect OSs could have on their reputation. A minimal instance of this is represented by the "media ombudsman"—the "action line" type of newspaper column. Finally, there is governmentalization—utilizing the criminal law or the administrative process to make it the responsibility of a public officer to press claims that would be unmanageable in the hands of private grievants.

An organized group is not only better able to secure favorable rule changes, in courts and elsewhere, but is better able to see that good rules are implemented. It can expend resources on surveillance, monitoring, threats, or litigation that would be uneconomic for an OS. Such new units would in effect be RPs. Their encounters with opposing RPs would move into Box IV of Figure 1. Neither would enjoy the strategic advantages of RPs over OSs. One possible result, as we have noted in our discussion of the RP v. RP situation, is delegalization, that is, a movement away from the official system to a private system of dispute-settlement; another would be more intense use of the official system.

Many aspects of "public interest law" can be seen as approximations of this reform. (1) The class action is a device to raise the stakes for an RP, reducing his strategic position to that of an OS by making the stakes more than he can afford to play the odds on, while moving the claimants into a position in which they enjoy the RP advantages without having to undergo the outlay for organizing. (2) Similarly, the "community organizing" aspect of public interest law can be seen as an effort to create a unit (tenants, consumers) which can play the RP game. (3) Such a change in strategic position creates the possibility of a test-case strategy for getting rule-change. Thus "public interest law" can be thought of as a combination of community organizing, class action and test-case strategies, along with increase in legal services . . . .

Implications for Reform: The Role of Lawyers

We have discussed the way in which the architecture of the legal system tends to confer interlocking advantages on overlapping groups whom we have called the "haves." To what extent might reforms of the legal system dispel these advantages? . . .

Our analysis suggests that change at the level of substantive rules is not likely in itself to be determinative of redistributive outcomes. Rule change is in itself likely to have little effect because the system is so constructed that changes in the rules can be filtered out unless accompanied by changes at other levels. In a setting of overloaded institutional facilities, inadequate costly legal services, and unorganized parties, beneficiaries may lack the resources to secure implementation; or an RP may restructure the transaction to escape the thrust of the new rule. Favorable rules are not necessarily (and possibly not typically) in short supply to "have-nots;" certainly less so than any of the other resources needed to play the litigation game. Programs of equalizing reform which focus on rule-change can be readily absorbed without any change in power relations. The system has the capacity to change a great deal at the level of rules without corresponding changes in everyday patterns of practice or distribution of tangible advantages. Indeed rule-change may become a symbolic substitute for redistribution of advantages.

The low potency of substantive rule-change is especially the case with rule-changes procured from courts. That courts can sometimes be induced to propound rule-changes that legislatures would not make points to the limitations as well as the possibilities of court-produced change. With their relative insulation from retaliation by antagonistic interests, courts may more easily propound new rules which depart from prevailing power relations. But such rules require even greater inputs of other resources to secure effective implementation. And courts have less capacity than other rule-makers to create institutional facilities and re-allocate resources to secure implementation of new rules. Litigation then is unlikely to shape decisively the distribution of power in society. It may serve to secure or solidify symbolic commitments. It is vital tactically in securing temporary advantage or protection, providing leverage for organization and articulation of interests and conferring (or withholding) the mantle of legitimacy. The more divided the other holders of power, the greater the redistributive potential of this symbolic/tactical role.

Our analysis suggests that breaking the interlocked advantages of the "haves" requires attention not only to the level of rules, but also to institutional facilities, legal services and organization of parties. It suggests that litigating and lobbying have to be complemented by interest organizing, provisions of services and invention of new forms of institutional facilities.

The thrust of our analysis is that changes at the level of parties are most likely to generate changes at other levels. If rules are the most abundant resource for reformers, parties capable of pursuing long-range strategies are the rarest. The presence of such parties can generate effective demand for high grade legal services—continuous, expert, and oriented to the long run—and pressure for institutional reforms and favorable rules. This suggests that we can roughly surmise the relative strategic priority of various rule-changes. Rule-changes which relate directly to the strategic position of the parties by facilitating organization, increasing the supply of legal services (where these in turn provide a focus for articulating and organizing common interests) and increasing the costs of opponents—for instance authorization of class action suits, award of attorneys' fees and costs, award of provisional remedies—these are the most powerful fulcrum for change. The intensity of the opposition to class action legislation and autonomous reform-oriented legal services such as California Rural Legal Assistance indicates the "haves" own estimation of the relative strategic impact of the several levels.

The contribution of the lawyer to redistributive social change, then, depends upon the organization and culture of the legal profession. We have surmised that court-produced substantive rule-change is unlikely in itself to be a determinative element in producing tangible redistribution of benefits. The leverage provided by litigation depends on its strategic combination with inputs at other levels. The question then is whether the organization of the profession permits lawyers to develop and employ skills at these other levels. The more that lawyers view themselves exclusively as courtroom advocates, the less their willingness to undertake new tasks and form enduring alliances with clients and operate in forums other than courts, the less likely they are to serve as agents of redistributive change. Paradoxically, those legal professions most open to accentuating the advantages of the "haves" (by allowing themselves to be "captured" by recurrent clients) may be most able to become (or have room for, more likely) agents of change, precisely because they provide more license for identification with clients and their "causes" and have a less strict definition of what are properly professional activities.

Do the characteristic advantages of RPs flow from their position in a structure for litigation, or from their position in a predominantly extra-adjudicatory distributive order? Are very well-to-do OSs in a very much different position from a typical RP? Or are poor RPs in a different position from the typical OS? If not, is there any significance whatsoever in the OS/RP distinction? Perhaps organizing RP units out of have-not OSs works, when it does work, not by virtue of changing the group's strategic position with respect to litigation, but rather by changing its relative power in the largely extra-adjudicatory political and economic orders.

SECTION B. THE PARTY AS A FUNCTIONAL CONSTRUCT: THE JUSTIFICATIONS FOR THE CREATION AND LIMITATION OF PARTY STATUS

In the preceding section Professor Galanter proposed the organization of groups as the key to the reform of a system in which the "haves" come out ahead. In the next two sections of this chapter we consider some of the conceptual devices through which the legal system "recognizes," "favors," or "facilitates" or "limits" an organization's or aggregation's uses of adjudication. In this first essay, Professor Stone proposes an artful, highly self-conscious manipulation of legal personification to satisfy certain strategic and substantive preferences. Such a proposal inevitably leads us to reflect whether the existing array of legal persons does not reflect a similar set of strategic and substantive preferences though they may have emerged in some instances from a less self-conscious process of deliberation. See J. Vining, Legal Identity: The Coming of Age of Public Law (1978).

Christopher D. Stone, **Should Trees Have Standing?—Toward Legal Rights for Natural Objects***

.   .   .   [It is not] only matter in human form that has come to be recognized as the possessor of rights. The world of the lawyer is peopled with inanimate right-holders: trusts, corporations, joint ventures, municipalities, Subchapter R partnerships, and nation-states, to mention just a few. Ships, still referred to by courts in the feminine gender, have long had an independent jural life, often with striking consequences. We have become so accustomed to the idea of a corporation having "its" own rights, and being a "person" and "citizen" for so many statutory and constitutional purposes, that we forget how jarring the notion was to early jurists. "That invisible, intangible and artificial being, that mere legal entity," Chief Justice Marshall wrote of the corporation in Bank of the United States v. Deveaux—could a suit be brought in *its* name? Ten years later, in the *Dartmouth College* case, he was still refusing to let pass unnoticed the wonder of an entity "existing only in contemplation of law." Yet, long before Marshall worried over the personifying of the modern corporation, the best medieval legal scholars had spent hundreds of years struggling with the notion of the legal nature of those great public "corporate bodies," the Church and the State. How could they exist in law, as entities transcending the living Pope and King? It was clear how a king could bind *himself*—on his honor—by a treaty. But when the king died, what was it that was burdened with the obligations of, and claimed the rights under, the treaty *his* tangible hand had signed? The medieval mind saw (what we have lost our capacity to see) how *unthinkable* it was, and worked out the most elaborate conceits and fallacies to serve as anthropomorphic flesh for the Universal Church and the Universal Empire . . . .

The fact is, that each time there is a movement to confer rights onto some new "entity," the proposal is bound to sound odd or frightening or

* *Source*: 45 S.Cal.L.Rev. 450, 452-81, 501 (1972). Professor of Law, University of Southern California.

laughable. This is partly because until the rightless thing receives its rights, we cannot see it as anything but a thing for the use of "us"—those who are holding rights at the time . . . . There is something of a seamless web involved: there will be resistance to giving the thing "rights" until it can be seen and valued for itself; yet, it is hard to see it and value it for itself until we can bring ourselves to give it "rights"—which is almost inevitably going to sound inconceivable to a large group of people.

The reason for this little discourse on the unthinkable, the reader must know by now, if only from the title of the paper. I am quite seriously proposing that we give legal rights to forests, oceans, rivers and other so-called "natural objects" in the environment—indeed, to the natural environment as a whole.[26]

As strange as such a notion may sound, it is neither fanciful nor devoid of operational content. In fact, I do not think it would be a misdescription of recent developments in the law to say that we are already on the verge of assigning some such rights, although we have not faced up to what we are doing in those particular terms. We should do so now, and begin to explore the implications such a notion would hold.

Now, to say that the natural environment should have rights is not to say anything as silly as that no one should be allowed to cut down a tree. We say human beings have rights, but—at least as of the time of this writing —they can be executed. Corporations have rights, but they cannot plead the fifth amendment; In re Gault gave 15-year-olds certain rights in juvenile proceedings, but it did not give them the right to vote. Thus, to say that the environment should have rights is not to say that it should have every right we can imagine, or even the same body of rights as human beings have. Nor is it to say that everything in the environment should have the same rights as every other thing in the environment. . . .

What it Means to be a Holder of Legal Rights

There is, so far as I know, no generally accepted standard for how one ought to use the term "legal rights." Let me indicate how I shall be using it in this piece.

---

26. In this article I essentially limit myself to a discussion of non-animal but natural objects. I trust that the reader will be able to discern where the analysis is appropriate to advancing our understanding of what would be involved in giving "rights" to other objects not presently endowed with rights—for example, not only animals (some of which already have rights in some senses) but also humanoids, computers, and so forth. . . .

As the reader will discover, there are large problems involved in defining the boundaries of the "natural object." For example, from time to time one will wish to speak of that portion of a river that runs through a recognized jurisdiction; at other times, one may be concerned with the entire river, or the hydrologic cycle—or the whole of nature. One's ontological choices will have a strong influence on the shape of the legal system, and the choices involved are not easy. . . .

On the other hand, the problems of selecting an appropriate ontology are problems of all language—not merely of the language of legal concepts, but of ordinary language as well. Consider, for example, the concept of a "person" in legal *or* in everyday speech. Is each *person* a fixed bundle of relationships, persisting unaltered through time? Do our molecules and cells not change at every moment? Our hypostatizations always have a pragmatic quality to them. . . .

First, and most obviously, if the term is to have any content at all, an entity cannot be said to hold a legal right unless and until *some public authoritative body* is prepared to give *some amount of review* to actions that are colorably inconsistent with that "right." For example, if a student can be expelled from a university and cannot get any public official, even a judge or administrative agent at the lowest level, either (i) to require the university to justify its actions (if only to the extent of filling out an affidavit alleging that the expulsion "was not wholly arbitrary and capricious") or (ii) to compel the university to accord the student some procedural safeguards (a hearing, right to counsel, right to have notice of charges), then the minimum requirements for saying that the student has a legal right to his education do not exist.

But for a thing to be *a holder of legal rights*, something more is needed than that some authoritative body will review the actions and processes of those who threaten it. As I shall use the term, "holder of legal rights," each of three additional criteria must be satisfied. All three, one will observe, go towards making a thing *count* jurally—to have a legally recognized worth and dignity in its own right, and not merely to serve as a means to benefit "us" (whoever the contemporary group of rights-holders may be). They are, first, that the thing can institute legal actions *at its behest*; second, that in determining the granting of legal relief, the court must take *injury to it* into account; and, third, that relief must run to the *benefit of it*.

To illustrate, even as between two societies that condone slavery there is a fundamental difference between S_1, in which a master can (if he chooses), go to court and collect reduced chattel value damages from someone who has beaten his slave, and S_2, in which the slave can institute the proceedings *himself*, for *his* own recovery, damages being measured by, say, *his* pain and suffering. Notice that neither society is so structured as to leave wholly unprotected the slave's interests in not being beaten. But in S_2 as opposed to S_1 there are three operationally significant advantages that the slave has, and these make the slave in S_2, albeit a slave, a holder of rights. Or, again, compare two societies, S_1, in which pre-natal injury to a live-born child gives a right of action against the tortfeasor at the mother's instance, for the mother's benefit, on the basis of the mother's mental anguish, and S_2, which gives the child a suit in its own name (though a guardian ad litem) for its own recovery, for damages to it.

When I say, then, that at common law "natural objects" are not holders of legal rights, I am not simply remarking what we would all accept as obvious. I mean to emphasize three specific legal-operational advantages that the environment lacks, leaving it in the position of the slave and the foetus in S_1, rather than the slave and foetus of S_2.

The Rightlessness of Natural Objects at Common Law

Consider, for example, the common law's posture toward the pollution of a stream. True, courts have always been able, in some circumstances, to issue orders that will stop the pollution—just as the legal system in S_1 is so structured as incidentally to discourage beating slaves and being reckless around pregnant women. But the stream itself is fundamentally rightless, with implications that deserve careful reconsideration.

The first sense in which the stream is not a rights-holder has to do with standing. The stream itself has none. So far as the common law is concerned, there is in general no way to challenge the polluter's actions save at the behest of a lower riparian—another human being—able to show an invasion of *his* rights. This conception of the riparian as the holder of the right to bring suit has more than theoretical interest. The lower riparians may simply not care about the pollution. They themselves may be polluting, and not wish to stir up legal waters. They may be economically dependent on their polluting neighbor. And, of course, when they discount the value of winning by the costs of bringing suit and the chances of success, the action may not seem worth undertaking. Consider, for example, that while the polluter might be injuring 100 downstream riparians $10,000 a year *in the aggregate*, each riparian separately might be suffering injury only to the extent of $100—possibly not enough for any one of them to want to press suit by himself, or even to go to the trouble and cost of securing co-plaintiffs to make it worth everyone's while. This hesitance will be especially likely when the potential plaintiffs consider the burdens the law puts in their way: proving, e. g., specific damages, the "unreasonableness" of defendant's use of the water, the fact that practicable means of abatement exist, and overcoming difficulties raised by issues such as joint causality, right to pollute by prescription, and so forth. Even in states which, like California, sought to overcome these difficulties by empowering the attorney-general to sue for abatement of pollution in limited instances, the power has been sparingly invoked and, when invoked, narrowly construed by the courts.

The second sense in which the common law denies "rights" to natural objects has to do with the way in which the merits are decided in those cases in which someone is competent and willing to establish standing. At its more primitive levels, the system protected the "rights" of the property owning human with minimal weighing of any values: *"Cujus est solum, ejus est usque ad coelum et ad infernos."* [34] Today we have come more and more to make balances—but only such as will adjust the economic best interests of identifiable humans. For example, continuing with the case of streams, there are commentators who speak of a "general rule" that "a riparian owner is legally entitled to have the stream flow by his land with its quality unimpaired" and observe that "an upper owner has, prima facie, no right to pollute the water." Such a doctrine, if strictly invoked, would protect the stream absolutely whenever a suit was brought; but obviously, to look around us, the law does not work that way. Almost everywhere there are doctrinal qualifications on riparian "rights" to an unpolluted stream.[36] Although these rules vary from jurisdiction to jurisdiction, and upon whether one is suing for an equitable injunction or for damages, what they all have in common is some sort of balancing. Whether under language of "reasonable use," "reasonable methods of use," "balance of convenience" or "the public interest doctrine," what the courts are balancing, with varying degrees of directness, are the economic hardships on the upper riparian (or dependent community) of abating the pollution vis-à-vis the economic hardships

---

34. To whomsoever the soil belongs, he owns also to the sky and to the depths . . . .

36. For example, courts have upheld a right to pollute by prescription . . . and by easement. . . .

of continued pollution on the lower riparians. What does not weigh in the balance is the damage to the stream, its fish and turtles and "lower" life. So long as the natural environment itself is rightless, these are not matters for judicial cognizance. Thus, we find the highest court of Pennsylvania refusing to stop a coal company from discharging polluted mine water into a tributary of the Lackawana River because a plaintiff's "grievance is for a mere personal inconvenience; and . . . mere private personal inconveniences . . . must yield to the necessities of a great public industry, which although in the hands of a private corporation, subserves a great public interest." [38] The stream itself is lost sight of in "a quantitative compromise between *two* conflicting interests." [39]

The third way in which the common law makes natural objects rightless has to do with who is regarded as the beneficiary of a favorable judgment. Here, too, it makes a considerable difference that it is not the natural object that counts in its own right. To illustrate this point, let me begin by observing that it makes perfectly good sense to speak of, and ascertain, the legal damage to a natural object, if only in the sense of "making it whole" with respect to the most obvious factors. The costs of making a forest whole, for example, would include the costs of reseeding, repairing watersheds, restocking wildlife—the sorts of costs the Forest Service undergoes after a fire. Making a polluted stream whole would include the costs of restocking with fish, water-fowl, and other animal and vegetable life, dredging, washing out impurities, establishing natural and/or artificial aerating agents, and so forth. Now, what is important to note is that, under our present system, even if a plaintiff riparian wins a water pollution suit for damages, no money goes to the benefit of the stream itself to repair *its* damages.[41] This omission has the further effect that, at most, the law confronts a polluter with what it takes to make the plaintiff riparians whole; this may be far less than the damages to the stream, but not so much as to force the polluter to desist. For example, it is easy to imagine a polluter whose activities damage a stream to the extent of $10,000 annually, although the aggregate damage to all the riparian plaintiffs who come into the suit is only $3000. If $3000 is less than the cost to the polluter of shutting down, or making the requisite technological changes, he might prefer to pay off the damages (i. e., the legally cognizable damages) and continue to pollute the stream. Similarly, even if the jurisdiction issues an injunction at the plaintiffs' behest (rather than to order payment of damages), there is nothing to stop the plaintiffs from "selling out" the stream, i. e., agreeing to dissolve or not enforce the injunction at some price (in the example above, somewhere between plaintiffs' damages

---

38. Pennsylvania Coal Co. v. Sanderson, 113 Pa. 126, 149, 6 A. 453, 459 (1886).

39. Hand, J., in Smith v. Staso Milling Co., 18 F.2d 736, 738 (2d Cir. 1927) (emphasis added) . . . .

41. Here . . . an analogy to corporation law might be profitable. Suppose that in the instance of negligent corporate management by the directors, there were no institution of the stockholder derivative suit to force the directors to make *the corporation* whole, and the only actions provided for were direct actions by stockholders to collect for damages to themselves qua stockholders. Theoretically and practically, the damages might come out differently in the two cases, and not merely because the creditors' losses are not aggregated in the stockholders' direct actions.

—$3000—and defendant's next best economic alternative). Indeed, I take it this is exactly what Learned Hand had in mind in an opinion in which, after issuing an anti-pollution injunction, he suggests that the defendant "make its peace with the plaintiff as best it can." [43] What is meant is a peace between *them*, and not amongst them and the river .   .   .   .

Toward Having Standing in its Own Right

It is not inevitable, nor is it wise, that natural objects should have no rights to seek redress in their own behalf. It is no answer to say that streams and forests cannot have standing because streams and forests cannot speak. Corporations cannot speak either; nor can states, estates, infants, incompetents, municipalities or universities. Lawyers speak for them, as they customarily do for the ordinary citizen with legal problems. One ought, I think, to handle the legal problems of natural objects as one does the problems of legal incompetents—human beings who have become vegetable. If a human being shows signs of becoming senile and has affairs that he is de jure incompetent to manage, those concerned with his well being make such a showing to the court, and someone is designated by the court with the authority to manage the incompetent's affairs. The guardian (or "conservator" or "committtee"—the terminology varies) then represents the incompetent in his legal affairs. Courts make similar appointments when a corporation has become "incompetent"—they appoint a trustee in bankruptcy or reorganization to oversee its affairs and speak for it in court when that becomes necessary.

On a parity of reasoning, we should have a system in which, when a friend of a natural object perceives it to be endangered, he can apply to a court for the creation of a guardianship .   .   .   .   [S]pecial environmental legislation could be enacted along traditional guardianship lines .   .   .   .

The potential "friends" that such a statutory scheme would require will hardly be lacking. The Sierra Club, Environmental Defense Fund, Friends of the Earth, Natural Resources Defense Counsel, and the Izaak Walton League are just some of the many groups which have manifested unflagging dedication to the environment and which are becoming increasingly capable of marshalling the requisite technical experts and lawyers .   .   .   .

In point of fact, there is a movement in the law toward giving the environment the benefits of standing, although not in a manner as satisfactory as the guardianship approach. What I am referring to is the marked liberalization of traditional standing requirements in recent cases in which environmental action groups have challenged federal government action .   .   .   .

Unlike the liberalized standing approach, the guardianship approach would secure an effective voice for the environment even where federal administrative action and public lands and waters were not involved. It would also allay one of the fears courts .   .   .   have about the extended standing concept: if any ad hoc group can spring up overnight, invoke some

43. Smith v. Staso Milling Co., 18 F.2d
736, 738 (2d Cir. 1927).

"right" as universally claimable as the esthetic and recreational interests of its members and thereby get into court, how can a flood of litigation be prevented? If an ad hoc committee loses a suit brought sub nom. Committee to Preserve our Trees, what happens when its very same members reorganize two years later and sue sub nom. the Massapequa Sylvan Protection League? Is the new group bound by res judicata? Class action law may be capable of ameliorating some of the more obvious problems. But even so, court economy might be better served by simply designating the guardian de jure representative of the natural object, with rights of discretionary intervention by others, but with the understanding that the natural object is "bound" by an adverse judgment. The guardian concept, too, would provide the endangered natural object with what the trustee in bankruptcy provides the endangered corporation: a continuous supervision over a period of time, with a consequent deeper understanding of a broad range of the ward's problems, not just the problems present in one particular piece of litigation. It would thus assure the courts that the plaintiff has the expertise and genuine adversity in pressing a claim which are the prerequisites of a true "case or controversy."

The guardianship approach, however, is apt to raise two objections, neither of which seems to me to have much force. The first is that a committee or guardian could not judge the needs of the river or forest in its charge; indeed, the very concept of "needs," it might be said, could be used here only in the most metaphorical way. The second objection is that such a system would not be much different from what we now have: is not the Department of Interior already such a guardian for public lands, and do not most states have legislation empowering their attorneys general to seek relief—in a sort of parens patriae way—for such injuries as a guardian might concern himself with?

As for the first objection, natural objects *can* communicate their wants (needs) to us, and in ways that are not terribly ambiguous. I am sure I can judge with more certainty and meaningfulness whether and when my lawn wants (needs) water, than the Attorney General can judge whether and when the United States wants (needs) to take an appeal from an adverse judgment by a lower court. The lawn tells me that it wants water by a certain dryness of the blades and soil—immediately obvious to the touch—the appearance of bald spots, yellowing, and a lack of springiness after being walked on; how does "the United States" communicate to the Attorney General? For similar reasons, the guardian-attorney for a smog-endangered stand of pines could venture with more confidence that his client wants the smog stopped, than the directors of a corporation can assert that "the corporation" wants dividends declared. We make decisions on behalf of, and in the purported interests of, others every day; these "others" are often creatures whose wants are far less verifiable, and even far more metaphysical in conception, than the wants of rivers, trees, and land.

As for the second objection, one can indeed find evidence that the Department of Interior was conceived as a sort of guardian of the public lands. But there are two points to keep in mind. First, insofar as the Department already is an adequate guardian it is only with respect to the federal public lands as per Article IV, section 3 of the Constitution.[75]   Its guardianship includes neither local public lands nor private lands.   Second, to judge from the environmentalist literature and from the cases environmental action groups have been bringing, the Department is itself one of the bogeys of the environmental movement.   (One thinks of the uneasy peace between the Indians and the Bureau of Indian Affairs.)   Whether the various charges be right or wrong, one cannot help but observe that the Department has been charged with several institutional goals (never an easy burden), and is currently looked to for action by quite a variety of interest groups, only one of which is the environmentalists.   In this context, a guardian outside the institution becomes especially valuable.   Besides, what a person wants, fully to secure his rights, is the ability to retain independent counsel even when, and perhaps especially when, the government is acting "for him" in a beneficent way

.   .   .   .

Toward Recognition of its Own Injuries

As far as adjudicating the merits of a controversy is concerned, there is also a good case to be made for taking into account harm to the environment—in its own right.   As indicated above, the traditional way of deciding whether to issue injunctions in law suits affecting the environment, at least where communal property is involved, has been to strike some sort of balance regarding the economic hardships *on human beings*.   Even recently, Mr. Justice Douglas, our jurist most closely associated with conservation sympathies in his private life, was deciding the propriety of a new dam on the basis of, among other things, anticipated lost profits from fish catches, some $12,000,-000 annually.   Although he decided to delay the project pending further findings, the reasoning seems unnecessarily incomplete and compromising. Why should the environment be of importance only indirectly, as lost profits to someone else?   Why not throw into the balance the cost *to the environment?*

The argument for "personifying" the environment, from the point of damage calculations, can best be demonstrated from the welfare economics position.   Every well-working legal-economic system should be so structured as to confront each of us with the full costs that our activities are imposing on society.   Ideally, a paper-mill, in deciding what to produce—and where, and by what methods—ought to be forced to take into account not only the lumber, acid and labor that its production "takes" from other uses in the society, but also what costs alternative production plans will impose on society through pollution.   The legal system, through the law of contracts and the criminal law, for example, makes the mill confront the costs of the first group of demands.   When, for example, the company's purchasing agent orders 1000 drums of acid from the Z Company, the Z Company can bind the mill to pay for them, and thereby reimburse the society for what the mill is removing from alternative uses.

Unfortunately, so far as the pollution costs are concerned, the allocative ideal begins to break down, because the traditional legal institutions have

75.   Clause 2 gives Congress the power "to dispose of and make all needful Rules and Regulations respecting the Territory or other Property belonging to the United States."

a more difficult time "catching" and confronting us with the full social costs of our activities.   In the lakeside mill example, major riparian interests might bring an action, forcing a court to weigh *their* aggregate losses against the costs to the mill of installing the anti-pollution device.   But many other interests—and I am speaking for the moment of recognized homocentric interests—are too fragmented and perhaps "too remote" causally to warrant securing representation and pressing for recovery: the people who own summer homes and motels, the man who sells fishing tackle and bait, the man who rents rowboats.   There is no reason not to allow the lake to prove damages to them as the prima facie measure of damages to it.   *By doing so, we in effect make the natural object, through its guardian, a jural entity competent to gather up these fragmented and otherwise unrepresented damage claims, and press them before the court even where, for legal or practical reasons, they are not going to be pressed by traditional class action plaintiffs.*   Indeed, one way—the homocentric way—to view what I am proposing so far, is to view the guardian of the natural object as the guardian of unborn generations, as well as of the otherwise unrepresented, but distantly injured, contemporary humans.   By making the lake itself the focus of these damages, and "incorporating" it so to speak, the legal system can effectively take proof upon, and confront the mill with, a larger and more representative measure of the damages its pollution causes.

So far, I do not suppose that my economist friends (unremittent human chauvanists, every one of them!) will have any large quarrel in principle with the concept.   Many will view it as a trompe l'oeil that comes down, at best, to effectuate the goals of the paragon class action, or the paragon water pollution control district.   Where we are apt to part company is here— I propose going beyond gathering up the loose ends of what most people would presently recognize as economically valid damages.   The guardian would urge before the court injuries not presently cognizable—the death of eagles and inedible crabs, the suffering of sea lions, the loss from the face of the earth of species of commercially valueless birds, the disappearance of a wilderness area.   One might, of course, speak of the damages involved as "damages" to us humans, and indeed, the widespread growth of environmental groups shows that human beings do feel these losses.   But they are not, at present, economically measurable losses: how can they have a monetary value for the guardian to prove in court?

The answer for me is simple.   Wherever it carves out "property" rights, the legal system is engaged in the process of *creating* monetary worth.   One's literary works would have minimal monetary value if anyone could copy them at will.   Their economic value to the author is a product of the law of copyright; the person who copies a copyrighted book has to bear a cost to the copyright-holder because the law says he must.   Similarly, it is through the law of torts that we have made a "right" of—and guaranteed an economically meaningful value to—privacy.   (The value we place on gold—a yellow inanimate dirt—is not simply a function of supply and demand—wilderness areas are scarce and pretty too—, but results from the actions of the legal systems of the world, which have institutionalized that value; they have even done a remarkable job of stabilizing the price.)   I am proposing we do the same with eagles and wilderness areas as we do with copyrighted works, patented inventions, and privacy: *make* the violation of rights in them to be a cost by declaring the "pirating" of them to be the invasion of a property interest. If we do so, the net social costs the polluter would be confronted with would include not only the extended homocentric costs of his pollution (explained above) but also costs to the environment per se. . . .

Toward Being a Beneficiary in its Own Right

As suggested above, one reason for making the environment itself the beneficiary of a judgment is to prevent it from being "sold out" in a negotiation among private litigants who agree not to enforce rights that have been established among themselves. Protection from this will be advanced by making the natural object a party to an injunctive settlement. Even more importantly, we should make it a beneficiary of money awards . . . . The natural object's portion could be put into a trust fund to be administered by the object's guardian. . . . Guardians fees, including legal fees, would then come out of this fund. More importantly, the fund would be available to preserve the natural object as close as possible to its condition at the time the environment was made a rights-holder.

The idea of assessing damages as best we can and placing them in a trust fund is far more realistic than a hope that a total "freeze" can be put on the environmental status quo. Nature is a continuous theatre in which things and species (eventually man) are destined to enter and exit. In the meantime, co-existence of man and his environment means that *each* is going to have to compromise for the better of both. Some pollution of streams, for example, will probably be inevitable for some time. Instead of setting an unrealizable goal of enjoining absolutely the discharge of all such pollutants, the trust fund concept would (a) help assure that pollution would occur only in those instances where the social need for the pollutant's product (via his present method of production) was so high as to enable the polluter to cover *all* homocentric costs, plus some estimated costs to the environment per se, and (b) would be a corpus for preserving monies, if necessary, while the technology developed to a point where repairing the damaged portion of the environment was feasible. Such a fund might even finance the requisite research and development . . . .

How far we are from such a state of affairs, where the law treats "environmental objects" as holders of legal rights, I cannot say. But there is certainly intriguing language in one of Justice Black's last dissents, regarding the Texas Highway Department's plan to run a six-lane expressway through a San Antonio Park.[136] Complaining of the Court's refusal to stay the plan, Black observed that "after today's decision, the people of San Antonio and the birds and animals that make their home in the park will share their quiet retreat with an ugly, smelling stream of traffic. . . . Trees, shrubs, and flowers will be mown down." Elsewhere he speaks of the "burial of public parks," of segments of a highway which "devour parkland," and of the park's heartland. Was he, at the end of his great career, on the verge of saying—just saying—that "nature has 'rights' on its own account"? Would it be so hard to do?

---

136. San Antonio Conservation Soc'y v.   U.S. 968 (1970) (Black, J. dissenting
Texas Highway Dep't, cert. denied 400   to denial of certiorari).

1.   To what extent does Professor Stone's proposal simply shift the hard question to the struggle over appointment of the guardian and/or attorney to *speak for* the tree, river, or valley?   Should the court appoint someone who lives in and alongside a natural entity to be its guardians?   Or is it preferable to appoint someone who does not live with, or in, the natural entity?   People-*users* may be seen as exploiters, but people-*lookers* may be seen as outsiders.   We may need a conception of the teleology of the natural object before we can decide which is the appropriate guardian.   For a fascinating glance at the complexities of constructing or discovering such a teleology, see J. McPhee, Coming Into the Country (1977), Part III; J. McPhee, Encounters with the Archdruid (1971).

2.   Stone points to other instances of legal personification.   But these other constructs characteristically break down when *people* struggle over their uses.   The "personhood" of a corporation is hardly helpful in analysis of situations of conflicts over who has the authority to do what with corporate resources, or in conflicts over what ought to count for corporate activity at all.   Nor would the personification of the "ship" be permitted to obscure the essential fact that a judgment against "her" ultimately operates to the detriment of persons or groups.   Cf. The Western Maid, 257 U.S. 419 (1922).   Of such "things" as parties it has been well said, "Disputes arise between human beings, not inanimate things."   Burns Bros. v. Central R. R. of N. J., 202 F.2d 910, 912–13 (2d Cir. 1953) (Hand, J.).   The fiction or construct should not serve to obscure the human conflict structure.   Does Stone's suggestion fall to such a realist's critique as well?   Why or why not?

3.   Shortly after this article was written, its theory was adopted by Mr. Justice Douglas in his dissent in Sierra Club v. Morton, 405 U.S. 727, at 741 (1972).

Kenneth E. Scott, **Standing in the Supreme Court—A Functional Analysis** *

.   .   .   The essential attribute of the standing determination has always been that it was a decision whether to decide—a determination of whether the validity of the challenged government action should be passed on for this plaintiff.   A denial of standing did not mean that the legality of the defendant's action was upheld; that question was not reached.   A grant of standing did not mean that plaintiff would prevail on the merits, even if he sustained his factual burden; when the merits were considered, the defendant's legal position might be sustained.

Why, then, should courts decline to adjudicate?   What considerations should impel a court, even assuming that the defendant government official is in error and acting contrary to statute or constitution, to go no further in the matter?   And which of these considerations should be handled by the law of standing, as opposed to other doctrines of judicial avoidance like justiciability and ripeness?   .   .   .

* *Source:*   86 Harv.L.Rev. 645, 669–92 (1973).   Professor of Law, Stanford University.

Access Standing and the Rationing of
Judicial Resources

. . . Our concern is supposed to be with the plaintiff and whether he is a "proper party" and has a "sufficient personal interest" in the litigation, not with the legal issues he raises or their suitability for judicial determination. This view of standing, however, has not always been followed by the courts and disregards another function that the doctrine has served. In order to distinguish this conception of standing from that which will be presented further on, the term "access standing" will be used. Access standing, then, means a judicial determination of whether the nature and extent of the alleged harm to a plaintiff are such as to warrant deciding his case. The purpose of this section is to inquire into the function performed by access standing in order to aid judicial thinking as to the proper scope and application of the doctrine.

1. The Economics of Judicial Services.—The usual method in our society of establishing the amount of some good or service to be produced, and the distribution of its consumption, is through the price system and market mechanism. The differing values people attach to a commodity will be reflected in the demand schedule, and (assuming no externalities) the costs of producing it will be reflected in the supply schedule, and the two will be brought into equilibrium through a market price. The services of the judiciary, however, are provided through government, substantially at the expense of taxpayers in general rather than individual litigants. Once we depart from a market solution and the principle that the users of a service shall bear the full costs of rendering it, there is no longer a way to determine precisely what is the appropriate size and capacity of our federal judicial system. It is necessary to rely on the legislature to form a judgment as to the right amount to invest in the judicial system and to appropriate annually, presumably on the basis that the social benefits created by the last dollar spent are worth at least a dollar.

The subsidization of judicial services creates a problem in determining not only the proper amount to provide, but also its distribution. Borrowing a simple diagram from economics may help to put the matter more clearly. In Figure 1 the *DD* curve represents the amount of judicial capacity that would be demanded by persons in the society at different price levels for court and trial time, and the *SS* curve represents the social costs per court hour (or other "unit" of judicial services) of supplying a court system of different sizes. On a fully costed basis the public would use and pay for a court system of size Q_1, at a price to litigants of P_1 per court hour. When society socializes most of the costs of the judicial system, leaving to litigants only some filing fees, witness fees, transcript charges and the like, the price of use of the courts drops from P_1 to P_2, with a resulting increase in demand for court services from Q_1 to Q_2. The price decrease will bring into the court system a set of additional cases.

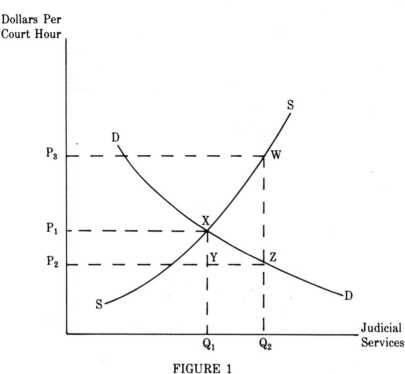

FIGURE 1

[C112]

It would be possible for the legislature, seeing this, to increase the size of the judicial system to Q_2, but this would greatly increase the cost of the judicial system for it would represent a subsidy not of P_1XYP_2 but of P_3WZP_2. The fact that the problems of court congestion and delay are chronic suggests, not surprisingly, that legislatures are habitually unwilling to supply the amount of judicial services that is in fact demanded at the artificially low prices charged to litigants by the courts. This legislative response seems quite understandable, unless the purposes of subsidizing court costs are equally applicable to all categories of litigation and all types of litigants.

If the legislature does nothing and leaves the judicial system at Q_1, there will be excess demand. One way of handling excess demand is by queues, and this characterizes in part the current practice in our judicial system. People line up and wait for their turn on the court calendar. In effect, the price of court decision is driven above P_2 by delay costs, back toward P_1, at which point the lines would no longer lengthen. Such an outcome is hardly to be desired. It increases the cost of adjudication for those whom society wished to assist and amounts to a transfer of the subsidy, in diminished amount, to those whose waiting costs are relatively low. It adds to the costs of other litigants who join the line. Furthermore, it contributes to a frequent overestimation of the effect on congestion of adding several judges to a court; as they cut into the backlog, delay costs are reduced, which in turn brings additional cases into the system.

    2. Access Screening.—Another possible response, and one that lies within the ability of the judiciary to institute by itself, is to screen cases—to weed out those actions, some of the ones brought into the court system because the price was lowered from P_1 to P_2, which society does not intend to subsidize and which are therefore, in a quite literal sense, not worth deciding.   This is a function which, in the context of judicial review of government action, a doctrine like standing can serve and, in an imperfect and not wholly conscious way, has served, in that aspect of the doctrine that is primarily concerned with the plaintiff and the injury or adverse effect that has been visited upon him . . . .

The reduction in pressure on the judicial system resulting from a standing test arises not so much from the elimination of the individual case in which plaintiff is held to lack standing as from the likelihood of the exclusion of that type of case from the demand function and from future queues.   That likelihood depends on the clarity of the exclusionary rules; and perhaps in recognition of this dependence, when the Court has denied standing to a particular party, there frequently has been a tendency to codify the denial into a rule of thumb which was thereafter applied without regard to the precise elements involved in the original case.   It became generally accepted dogma, for example, that (all) federal taxpayers lacked standing to question (all) federal expenditures.

Performing a screening function necessitates a number of judgments that are by no means easy to arrive at . . . . [I]t is worth observing that the minimum Article III inquiry is hardly sufficient to do the job.   What is more, it is highly questionable that standing doctrine has anything in turn to contribute to the implementation of the "case or controversy" requirement. We are now in a position to explore these propositions, and the exploration will form a useful prelude to an analysis of just what standards *can* be used for access screening.

3.   *Private Costs and Article III.*—Court costs are not the only or even the major component of social litigation costs; attorneys' fees and disbursements, and the time costs of preparing for and participating in litigation to the person or organization conducting it, are far more substantial.   Litigation in general is decidely expensive, and if anything, litigation with the government is yet more expensive.   The government does not lack for resources to prepare and defend the action, and plaintiffs will get no judgments by default.   The initial litigation over the FPC's approval of Consolidated Edison's Storm King reservoir cost the plaintiff conservationist organization over $250,000.   While hardly typical, it dramatizes the fact that despite the subsidization of court costs, the remaining private costs of litigation are quite sufficient to serve as an initial screening barrier of considerable height. When the "floodgates" of litigation are opened to some new class of controversy by a decision, it is notable how rarely one can discern the flood that the dissenters feared.   The plaintiff (or the organization actually funding and conducting the litigation, if legal rules force the use of nominal plaintiffs) must feel strongly enough about the issue in question to pay the bills, and that both cuts down the flood and gives us at least a partial measure of his "stake" in the outcome.

The implication of these considerations is that most of the concern over plaintiff's standing in terms of the minimal requirements of Article III, or "pure" standing, is empty.   Standing is sometimes used as a receptacle into which other "case or controversy" ingredients are dumped, such as the quite distinct problem of collusive suits. But apart from collusive suits, insofar as standing focuses on the plaintiff and whether he has a sufficient "personal stake in the outcome of the controversy," it is an idle and unnecessary Article III exercise. If plaintiff did not have the minimal personal involvement and adverseness which Article III requires, he would not be engaging in the costly pursuit of litigation.

These comments may also defuse the objections to "public actions." The suit by a "taxpayer" or "citizen" turns out on closer examination to have been brought by a rival businessman or by a person or group intensely concerned with conservation, or with church-state separation, or with some other issue. The idle and whimsical plaintiff, a dilettante who litigates for a lark is a specter which haunts the legal literature, not the courtroom.

4. Establishing a Higher Access Threshold.—Since, therefore, the law of standing and that of case or controversy should be kept entirely distinct, what process of analysis will be useful in performing access screening? A first inquiry might be whether the harm to the individual plaintiff is too slight for him to have been willing to bear the full costs of court decision— in other words, whether his is one of the actions that entered the docket only because costs were lowered from P_1 to P_2. If it is not, then we might immediately say that he has a "sufficient personal stake" in the matter for standing—i. e., to warrant deciding the case.

If the harm to the plaintiff is not great enough that he would have been willing to pay the full costs for his use of judicial services, the court must then decide if he is one whom society should subsidize. Entering into this decision will be the fact that even if the harm to the individual plaintiff, or the benefit he would derive from winning the suit, does not by itself seem adequate to pass the threshold examination, there is an externality to be weighed—the benefits which others will derive from plaintiff's victory, if he achieves it. (There is also an external cost imposed by the fact that plaintiff will generally not have to defray defendant's litigation costs even if he loses, but that is attributable to a different, though questionable, judicial doctrine.)

Such external effects characterize much litigation, to the extent that the outcome in one case establishes a precedent applicable to others, but they are especially marked in litigation with the government. When the plaintiff sues to restrain or set aside some government action or program, there are often many besides the plaintiff who will be directly and immediately affected by such an alteration in government operations. Many of the suits we are analyzing partake of the nature of class actions, whether they are brought in that form or not; the plaintiff may be viewed as representing others as well, and there may be prohibitively high costs to any substantial or direct participation by the whole class. In evaluating the plaintiff's case for threshold adequacy, it is arguable that the court should in effect add to his stake that of the affected class.

Unfortunately, as we shall see, judges have little information or legislative guidance to aid them in determining whether plaintiff's interest alone, or the interest of some class he may fairly be said to represent, is adequate to clear an appropriate access standing barrier.

(a) Plaintiff's Own Stake.—The courts face problems both in measuring the extent of plaintiff's stake and in setting the appropriate threshold level of interest. The former problem is least serious in the case of economic injury, which can be expressed in monetary terms, and the courts have responded somewhat more favorably when there is an allegation of some variety of "palpable" economic harm in the case. But what of plaintiffs complaining of injury to other values—political, or ecological, or religious? One response is to deny the reality of such injury, or to deny it any role in determining standing, which is much the same thing. That seems wholly unjustifiable, for we all know that outside the courtroom such values are taken very seriously indeed by certain individuals. The Court has already rejected this answer . . .; the proposition now seems firmly established that standing may stem from injury to noneconomic interests, such as aesthetic, conservational, recreational, or spiritual values. However, once recognized, it is difficult to measure such forms of injury for the purpose of assessing whether the case is worth deciding. We have but one objective measure: at a minimum, in his own judgment plaintiff's harm must be equivalent to the amount of the litigation costs he is incurring to reverse or forestall the government action.

If more than that is to be required, how much more? Indeed, this question applies even to cases of *monetary* damage. Although monetary damages are of course more easily measured for application of certain kinds of threshold standards, the problem of setting the level of the threshold and of identifying the relevant variables for its definition remains. Judges are simply given no clear way to decide which plaintiffs deserve subsidy, whatever the tangibility of the damage alleged.

In the area of statutory review the courts seem to have abandoned the effort—in effect coming more and more to leave the threshold to be set by the level of private litigation costs. The legislature has weighed the social costs and benefits of judicial intervention in a general way and decided in its favor, and perhaps that can be used as a ground for imposing no further limitation through restrictive interpretation of "person aggrieved." The result is to make statutory review of agency action one of the categories of litigation intentionally subsidized. Where Congress has provided for statutory review, it can be seen as a determination by our mechanism for reflecting collective social values that the subsidy is warranted in order to obtain a needed restraint on the holders of power and a procedure for correcting official deviations from legislative purposes.

In the area of nonstatutory review, there is no such explicit legislative judgment to rely on. The decision is left to the courts' unfettered discretion, at least up to the point where a denial of judicial review would transgress the due process clause of the Constitution. Where, then, and in what terms, should the line be drawn?

Again one answer is not to draw it at all—to leave the screening to private litigation costs, as in statutory review. The advantage of such an approach is that at least it provides an automatic measure of sufficient interest: the willingness of plaintiff to undertake the costs of litigation. This seems to be what Professor Davis urges, in advocating "adversely affected in fact" as the test of all standing.[128] As we have noted, persons who are not in their own view adversely affected by some governmental act do not sue to overturn it, so there should be no difficulty about satisfying the test—unless perhaps there is a catch lurking in the little phrase "in fact", whereby certain unspecified kinds of adverse effects are excluded as not factual. However, as a means of allocating subsidized judicial services, private litigation costs are not ideal, for they involve reliance on queues and delay instead of any rational principles of subsidy.

Another answer is for each judge to conduct an appraisal, by rather amorphous standards, of the injuries at stake for plaintiff and others in the suit before him. This seems a reasonably apt description of the process we have been witnessing, provided it is noted that the judge has not been thrown back entirely on his own set of values without any external guides. . . .

(b) Going Beyond the Plaintiff's Stake.— . . . [I]n a weighing of the social stake, it might be thought appropriate for the judge to go beyond the parties before him and to consider the others affected by the government action and the outcome of the case. However, as in evaluating the plaintiff's personal stake, the judge would find himself with little guidance for making this calculation. . . .

Passing beyond the special question of the degree of interference during appeal with government programs, it is also difficult for courts to take into account in general the aggregate harm to the entire group of persons affected by the government action. Such a consideration might arise in two different contexts. First, there is the situation where the plaintiff is a member of the larger group. There the injury to the plaintiff is but part of the larger injury, and it is therefore to the latter that the higher threshold standard might be applied. While this seems appropriate, it does not help to solve the problem of where to set the threshold or in what terms; it merely shifts the focus from the individual harm to that of the class.

Second, there is the situation of a plaintiff who is not affected "directly"—that is, the government action being challenged brings its coercive or incentive effects to bear in the first instance on some class of which plaintiff is not a member or chosen representative. This circumstance raises doubts as to the extent of total injury at stake: why are those who bear the direct impact of the government action not suing themselves? Sometimes this has been thought to be in itself a reason to deny plaintiff standing, but even brief reflection shows that indirectness alone should not determine the outcome. One can think of any action as setting in motion spreading circles of repercussions. Usually the magnitude of the consequences is diminished as one moves further and further away from the point of initial impact, so that second-order effects are less than first-order effects, and so on. But sometimes the government action takes a form that is much more concentrated in

128. K. Davis, Administrative Law Text
§ 22.08, at 438–39 (1972) . . . .

its second-order effects than in the first-order ones. For example, if millions of government employees are told not to join organization X, or buy from business Y, or subscribe to magazine Z, the particular restraint on the employee is on the whole a minor one, narrowing his range of choices by only a small amount, while the cumulative impact on X, Y, or Z may be concentrated and heavy. The one "directly" affected may have insufficient reason to sue, but that should not by itself constitute a reason to deny standing to the second-order plaintiff. While such a plaintiff may be seen as also representing the interests of those directly affected, it is unnecessary to place reliance on that factor. The second-order plaintiff's standing in such a case can be judged in terms of his own injury, and the fact that the nature of the government action is such that its effects are concentrated beyond the point of direct impact should serve to overcome skepticism about the extent of injury that might otherwise arise from the lack of suit by those directly affected.

A final factor which a court might consider in deciding the standing of a plaintiff where the injury extends to a larger group is whether the plaintiff is an appropriate representative of the interests of that group. This inquiry would focus not only on whether the plaintiff is able and likely to present a technically adequate case, but also on whether his interest is sufficiently representative of that of other persons affected by the government's actions that the relief sought by him will adequately protect them as well. . . .

The whole problem of representativeness may be exaggerated, however. A major practical safeguard lies in the ability of other members of the larger group to judge for themselves how adequately the plaintiff speaks for them, and to intervene or bring their own suits if he is found wanting. And while the problem of representativeness may be more substantial in that category of cases where the effect of adjudication will be to foreclose further action by other interested persons even though they are not bound by the result in a legal sense, it is doubtful that standing doctrine affords a satisfactory means of dealing with it. To evaluate which persons or organizations are most representative of the interests of all those affected by the challenged government action is a task for which courts have no suitable tools. Moreover, the point at which the issue of representativeness becomes most acute is not at the outset of the case, but rather when the remedy or settlement is being formulated. At that time particularly, the interests of those persons who are affected by the challenged government action but who are not before the court could be better protected by adopting, where feasible, some of the class action techniques, such as affording notice and opportunity to intervene to other organizations that are probably interested.

We conclude, then, that the factor of the plaintiff's representativeness, like those of the effect on the government program and the indirectness of the plaintiff's injury, should not be afforded much weight in the determination of standing. Thus, with respect to interests beyond the plaintiff's own immediate stake, as with respect to that stake itself, judges are without real guidance on how high to set the access screening threshold or what terms to use in defining it.

   5. Conclusion.—To this point we have been considering some of the difficulties presented in trying to impose on plaintiffs seeking judicial review

of government action a higher threshold requirement as to the kind or serious-
ness or extent of their grievance than is constituted by the private costs of
litigation.   The essence of the problem is that access screening imposes on
the courts a job for which they are ill-suited.   A judge has no ready way of
estimating either the extent of a plaintiff's grievance, if it falls outside the
reach of monetary damage, or the appropriate level at which to set a higher
threshold; and therefore he has at present no adequate basis for determining
if a plaintiff is one to whom subsidized access should be awarded.   Nor is he
instructed as to the very raison d'être of that subsidy—whether it is concerned
with income distribution and the lot of the poor, or with the external benefits and transaction costs associated with bringing representative actions, or
with some combination of both.

   The preferable solution lies in the hands of the legislature.   The legislature can reduce the extent of the distributional problem by generally charging for judicial services at their marginal cost and using any excess revenues
to increase judicial capacity.   It can then specify what categories of litigants
or litigation are believed to warrant subsidy in the form of providing court
services at reduced or nominal cost, and meet the ensuing level of demand
on the courts.   If the social concern is with "justice for all" and the difficulties of the poor in obtaining it, for example, it does not make much sense
to award the subsidy equally to contract disputes between large enterprises.
If it is only litigation by the poor in defense of their "essential" needs and
interests that society wishes to subsidize, the legislature is the proper body to
make that judgment and to define those needs.

   But, assuming that the legislature takes no action, the courts are faced
with a choice of unpalatable alternatives: reliance on plaintiff selection by the
judiciary or automatic selection by delay costs on top of private litigation
costs, or some blend of both.   Perhaps the process of plaintiff screening would
at least become less unsatisfactory, and less costly in terms of its own consumption of judicial resources, if it were seen, and openly discussed, in terms
of the administration of a subsidy.   .   .   .

Decision Standing and the Allocation of
Policymaking Responsibility

   In determining whether to decide plaintiff's case, the courts at times
have to consider many factors besides whether the harm being done the
plaintiff and those in a similar position warrants the expenditure of judicial
resources.   These factors are given a multitude of labels which overlap and
are never clearly defined.   Along with standing one finds ripeness, exhaustion, waiver, implied preclusion, reviewability, justiciability, political question, advisory opinion, mootness, case or controversy, and so on—the whole
arsenal of considerations and techniques for avoiding decision of the merits
of plaintiff's claim.   These devices, and a wide discretion in their use, have
been celebrated by [some] and regarded with considerable distaste, because
of their potential for unprincipled employment, by [others].   At the heart
of the matter is one of the most crucial issues of our polity: how responsibility for establishing social policy is to be shared among the different branches
of our government; and in particular how the role of the Supreme Court,

as a nonrepresentative institution in what is a largely representative government, is to be defined and limited. It is beyond the scope of this article to explore in any exhaustive way the sorts of considerations that are relevant to a court's determination of the proper extent of its policymaking role and to its application of the appropriate avoidance technique in a given case. Our task is more limited: to examine the role of standing doctrine in the process of allocating policymaking responsibility.

In theory, standing is for the most part distinguishable from these other doctrines. Standing focuses on the sufficiency of the plaintiff's interest in the case, and that means among other things that a decision adverse to him does not preclude others from litigating the same issue. Insofar as standing does involve a consideration of the legal issues raised, the concern is supposed to be with protective intent, not with the suitability of the issues for judicial determination. Thus, while the denial of standing has the effect of removing a case from the reach of judicial determination, its function is to ration scarce judicial resources, not to determine the proper scope of judicial policymaking responsibility. In short, standing narrowly and properly refers to access standing; and where the above distinctions can be applied in practice, there is considerable merit in [the] suggestion that courts should talk about standing only when their decisions are based on standing considerations. Where the grounds for their refusal to hear a case are otherwise, they should discuss justiciability, reviewability, or whatever is the appropriate term to describe those grounds.

However, courts sometimes blend together discussions of standing with these other doctrines, and the reason for the blending is not always intellectual carelessness. A particular case may raise issues of both access standing and justiciability. The application of both these doctrines is difficult, for in the area of justiciability as well as standing courts lack clear rules for making a decision. But since both doctrines relate to the same ultimate question of whether the merits of the case should be decided, it may be proper for the court, after formulating its views on each of the two issues separately, to take both into consideration in attempting to resolve that question. The resulting decision, even when referred to as a standing decision, clearly involves a different use of that doctrine than the one considered above under the heading of access standing. Here the extent and kind of injury suffered by the plaintiff is but one variable in a multivariable equation which leads to a conclusion to render decision or not. The court may in effect set a still higher access threshold, in terms of the severity or kind of plaintiff's injury or magnitude of his stake, when the case presents troublesome questions about the suitability of the issues tendered for decision by the judiciary. Or, putting it another way, concern over the decision role the court would have to assume may lead it to reject standing for a plaintiff whose injury and stake would, in a different context, pass muster. To distinguish this use of standing from access standing simpliciter, we shall refer to it hereafter as "decision standing." . . .

A . . . recent and complex application of decision standing may be seen in Flast v. Cohen.[a] The problem of access standing there was acute,

a. 392 U.S. 83 (1968). Ed. note.

for the government program being challenged [financing for parochial schools under the Elementary and Secondary Education Act of 1965] could easily be said to affect Mrs. Flast "in some indefinite way in common with people generally." . . . However, a denial of standing would have had the effect of foreclosing any widely available avenue of challenge, based on the establishment clause, to the government programs in question in a period when the federal government was embarking for the first time in its history on a course of massive aid to education including church-controlled schools. So the court may be said to have judged Mrs. Flast's case worth subsidizing or to have added the stakes of others to her own in boosting her over the access screening barrier. To this point the analysis, however controversial, was purely one of standing.

The difficulty was that by granting standing the Court was injecting itself in a major way into the field of federal expenditure and subsidy policies. To be sure, it can hardly be contended that the first amendment was designed to leave Congress an unrestricted hand in resolving these difficult questions on the basis of compromises struck among contending political forces. But federal expenditure and subsidy policies may not be deduced from some more general statutory or constitutional provision, and represent an area in which there is good cause for the judicial branch to be particularly cautious. The opinion developed in this context a standing test which . . . would permit a plaintiff to invoke only "specific" constitutional limitations in claiming entitlement to judicial decision. The Court thus both restricted the scope of the judicial intrusion and eased the search for "judicially discoverable and manageable standards." [159] Specificity is no doubt relative, but in accepting the establishment clause the Court was not thereby accepting also the due process and equal protection clauses and a potentially far larger policy role in allocating government revenues. In other words, the access standing decision to subsidize plaintiff's case or to aggregate interests was shaped by considerations more aptly described as going to justiciability, reviewability, or whatever, and yet the entire analysis was conducted under the heading of standing.

Although a court may wish to consider both the plaintiff's stake in the controversy and the scope of judicial policymaking involved in determining whether to decide a particular case, it should formulate and articulate each of the two issues separately before feeding them together into the decision whether to reach the merits. It is true that some factors may be relevant to the consideration of both. For example, where Congress has authorized judicial review of a particular set of government actions or decisions, there is less difficulty as to either the access question or that of policymaking role. As noted above, courts have tended to be more liberal in granting access standing in cases of statutory review, for there the organ of government in charge of raising and disbursing public funds has declared that the expenditure of judicial resources to review the government actions in question is warranted as a general matter. In addition, congressional authorization for review of a particular type of government decision may indicate less likelihood that the

159. Baker v. Carr, 369 U.S. 186, 217 (1962).

judicial policy role will be felt or attacked as improper. Despite such over-laps, however, access standing and the doctrines of justiciability, reviewability, and the like serve different functions and necessarily involve some different considerations. The failure to keep their initial analyses separate needlessly confuses the courts' reasoning. . . .

Moreover, it is important not only that the evaluation of the access and decision factors be kept initially separate in a case involving both, but also that the final ruling, whether in a case involving both types of standing problems or only one, make clear which aspect or aspects of standing doctrine it rests on, and how heavily. Otherwise, a ruling grounded largely on one branch of the doctrine may be mistaken for a ruling based on the other, causing the error that a recognition of the sufficiency of new forms of interest in the outcome of lawsuits will be seen as significantly enlarging the role of the judiciary in establishing public policy, or that a refusal to decide a particular case and issue will be seen as denying the plaintiff any judicial remedy for quite different legal issues which affect him in the same way.

. . . .

Conclusion

The principal concepts of the functional analysis that we have under-taken can best be summarized by applying them to an evaluation of the Court's most recent decision in the field of standing, Sierra Club v. Morton.[b] In the first place, the discussion in *Sierra Club* suffered from a confusion of the issues of court access and the judicial decision role. The underlying dispute between the opposing sides was over the balance to be struck between the preservation of wilderness and areas of particular scenic beauty, and their readier use by greater numbers of the public as recreation areas. If that had been the policy decision before the Court, there would have been most sub-stantial reasons for it to draw back; the judiciary lacks the standards and the tools for resolving such a conflict. And the Solicitor General made his standing argument in precisely such terms, attacking "government by the Judiciary." However, the questions actually presented by the plaintiff were much narrower and more amenable to judicial resolution: their decision would not require the courts to assume a policymaking role of significant magnitude; the standards to be applied were not especially vague or far-reaching; and the issues were fully developed factually. In short, the prob-lem before the Court was one of access standing, and decision standing was not involved.

On the question of access standing, the Court in *Sierra Club* . . . spoke of the need for allegations of "individualized injury" and asserted reluctance to permit judicial review "at the behest of organizations or in-dividuals who seek to do no more than vindicate their own value preferences through the judicial process." That of course was exactly how the Govern-ment had characterized Mrs. Flast. Sooner or later the Court will have to come to grips with the fact that once the reality of nonmonetary injuries is accepted, it follows than an individual who attaches more weight to some personal value than do most does suffer a differential injury from its trans-

b. 405 U.S. 727 (1972). Ed. note.

gression. He proves his "special interest" by being the one to bring suit and bear its costs, and there is no a priori reason whatever to believe that he would not do so even if he had to bear the full social costs of adjudication.
. . .

Perhaps what troubled the court in *Sierra Club* is the difficulty of measuring injury to noneconomic values, but the Court provided little in the way of a solution to that difficulty by drawing what is essentially an arbitrary line between the sometime past users or potential future users of the park and those who appreciate it pictorially or symbolically. The underlying question is and would remain whether plaintiffs would have brought the suit in a fully costed system, and if not, whether the case is one deserving of social subsidy. If the Court remains unwilling to go· the whole way and to allow private litigation costs to serve as the sole screening mechanism for access to the courts—and such unwillingness may be justified—then it should recognize the problem as one of defining and administering a subsidy, and should provide a standard and a rationale suited to that function. In the alternative, if the access screening function of standing doctrine is to be abandoned, it should be clearly distinguished from the inquiry into the policymaking role of the judiciary, so that the latter inquiry will not by error be abandoned with it.

---

1.   Do the two functions ascribed to standing—allocation of judicial resources and allocation of policymaking responsibility—correspond to two often co-existing functions of adjudication—dispute-processing and law-making? Cf. K. Scott, Two Models of the Civil Process, 27 Stan.L.Rev. 937 (1975).

2.   Must there not always be, at one and the same time, both of these dimensions in any decision to hear or not to hear a case? Does not the decision simultaneously impose an ordering of the competing claims to the judicial forum (allocation of judicial resources among claims) and an ordering of the competing authorities' claims to determine the issue (allocation of issues among competing political agencies)?

In the next selection, Professors Landes and Posner pursue a mode of analysis somewhat similar to that of Scott and turn from standing—a doctrine to limit private "party" status—to the criminal law and to the enforcement activity of public agencies. They seek to determine the proper mix of public and private enforcement of the criminal law, and they begin with a definition of the optimal level of enforcement activity: that point at which the resources devoted to enforcement (apprehension and conviction of offenders) are equal to the social loss suffered from criminal activity.

The authors establish that in a private enforcement industry the amount of resources devoted to enforcement activity will be greater than the optimal level—this is the "overenforcement theorem." The authors offer the following summary of the reasons behind the theorem:

> The intuitive explanation for the overenforcement theorem is straightforward. If the probability of apprehension and conviction

were unity, the optimum fine would be set equal to the social costs of illegal activity—i. e., to the value of crime prevention. If the value of crime prevention rose because the harm from crime was increasing, the optimum fine would rise by the same amount. This would be perceived by enforcers as an upward shift in the demand curve facing them, and would have the effect of increasing the resources devoted to crime prevention, as in the case of an ordinary product the demand for which increases. The difficulty arises because in the design of an optimum system of penalties where the probability of apprehension and conviction is less than unity, the fine is set higher than the social costs of the illegal activity not as a signal that additional resources should be devoted to the activity because its value has increased relative to other activities but rather as a device for attempting to minimize those resources. A fine so set communicates the wrong signal, from a social standpoint, to the private enforcer. In the case of public enforcement, the high fine need not be taken as a signal to invest greater resources in crime prevention, since the public enforcer is not constrained to act as a private profit maximizer.

After further theoretical elaborations of their model, the authors turn to its positive implications.

William M. Landes and Richard A. Posner, **The Private Enforcement of Law***

. . .

The Choice Between Public and Private Enforcement: Criminal Compared to Contract and Tort Cases

. . . With few exceptions, there is a public monopoly—more precisely a series of public monopolies—of criminal-law enforcement: a private individual may not prosecute for murder, or theft, or the possession of marijuana, or statutory rape.[64] Often, to be sure, the same act is both a crime and a tort (the crime of theft, for example, is the tort of conversion), and then private enforcement is possible in principle. But if the offender is judgment-proof, as is so often the case with criminal offenders, the tort remedy is ineffectual and the public enforcer has a de facto monopoly. In contrast, in areas of the law such as contracts and torts (excluding those torts that are also crimes) the main burden of enforcement falls on the private sector. Breaches of contract, and torts, are not investigated or prosecuted by the state. The state's role is limited to furnishing the court system.[65]

* *Source*: 4 J. Legal Stud. 1, 30–44 (1975). Landes: Professor of Economics, University of Chicago; Posner: Professor of Law, University of Chicago.

64. This is not universally true. In England and Western Europe, the victim of a crime is frequently permitted to prosecute if the public prosecutor declines to do so. . . .

65. Sometimes the parties to contracts opt out of the public court system by agreeing to arbitrate any issue arising under the contract. Even then, the state is in the background: the party to an arbitration proceeding can obtain a court order compelling compliance with the award of the arbitrator.

. . . [T]he essential difference between crimes, on the one hand, and torts and breaches of contract, on the other, is that with very small resources devoted to apprehension, the probability of apprehension tends to be much less than one in the former case, and to approach one in the second. The victim of a breach of contract knows who breached it; the victim of an automobile accident usually knows the identity of the other driver; [66] but the victim of a burglary does not know the burglar's identity. Where the probability of apprehension and conviction is unity, it can easily be shown that the penalty that minimizes the social loss from unlawful activity is equal to the sum of the costs of the harm inflicted by the activity and of the costs of enforcement. Thus, assuming that p [a] is approximately unity in the average tort or contract case, the problem of overenforcement . . . cannot arise. [Such a problem would arise where,] in a case where substantial resources are necessary to generate a substantial probability of apprehension, those resources can be saved by setting a very high f, [b] but the high f induces private enforcers to expend resources on apprehension—the resources that the high f was intended to conserve. If p is already unity, private enforcers will not expend any resources on trying to increase p any further.

A problem would remain if property rights were assigned to enforcers on a first-come first-served basis rather than to the victim of the tort or breach of contract. For example, if the marginal harm inflicted by the offender's conduct were $9 and the marginal costs of apprehension and conviction were $1, and hence f = $10, the enforcer who was the first to stake his claim would receive a rent of $9. The opportunity to obtain such rents might lead enforcers to stake claims simultaneously, to duplicate enforcement costs, or to engage in other methods of spending (e. g., bribing the official in charge of recording claims) that consumed resources.[68] Thus, enforcement on a first-come first-served basis would induce expenditures on enforcement in excess of $1. Victim rights eliminate this source of waste.

Thus [economics] predicts—and we in fact observe—greater reliance on private enforcement in areas such as tort, contract, property, and commercial law, where p approaches unity and victim property rights are practicable (i. e., the cost of enforcing an individual claim is low relative to the value of the claim). The criminal area presents the opposite extreme, especially in "victimless" crimes such as tax evasion and prostitution or "inchoate" crimes (various types of attempt). Most criminal acts are concealable, which means that unless substantial resources were devoted to enforcement p would be

---

66. Partly, to be sure, as a result of criminal and other regulatory statutes involving licensing of drivers, registration of vehicles, and punishment for leaving the scene of an accident.

a. p has earlier been defined as the probability of apprehension and conviction. Ed. note.

b. f has earlier been defined as the penalty payable by an offender to the enforcer. The earlier analysis begins with the assumption that all penalties are monetary. This assumption is later relaxed to allow for the use of other punishments against offenders. The coherence of the model is retained by a system of bounties adequate to offer incentive to private enforcement. Ed. note.

68. Although a bribe per se is a transfer payment rather than a cost, the opportunity to obtain bribes will attract resources into efforts to obtain the opportunity until, at the margin, cost and gain are equated.

much smaller than unity; and the cost of enforcement to the victim—if there is a victim—is high because the average criminal offender is judgment-proof. Private enforcement of the criminal law would require the institution of a comprehensive public bounty system, and any divergence between the bounty and the cost of punishment would create problems.[69]   .   .   .

The Assignment of Property Rights in Legal Claims

A system of law enforcement is implicitly a market in legal claims, and like other markets cannot function efficiently unless there are exclusive rights to the goods in the market, the claims.   Although the legal system does not characterize the matter in these terms, there are in fact exclusive rights in claims.   The victim of an alleged violation of law has the exclusive right to bring suit to redress the violation (we are abstracting now from public enforcement).   He sells that right to the defendant when the case is settled out of court.   If the case is litigated, and the defendant wins, the plaintiff's legal claim is extinguished under the doctrine of res judicata; if the plaintiff wins, the doctrine is invoked to prevent relitigation of the same issue between the same parties—i. e., to prevent the (coerced) purchase of the plaintiff's claim by the defendant from being undone.

In some cases the cost of enforcement is so high relative to the value of the claim that the legal-claims "market" would not work if the principle that the victim had the exclusive right to the claim were adhered to strictly.   A good example is a price-fixing conspiracy that imposes a small cost on each member of a large class of buyers.   The total social costs of the violation may be high, so that enforcement would be socially efficient, but none of the victims has a sufficiently large stake to be willing to bear the expenses of suit. The consumer class action is a device, although an oblique and imperfect one, for overcoming this problem.   In effect the property rights normally possessed by the victims of an alleged violation are reassigned to the lawyer for the class.   Subject to certain controls (probably rather weak) by the court, the lawyer can transfer the victims' property rights—without their consent in any meaningful sense—to the defendant.   The proceeds of the transfer are divided between the lawyer and the state with little or nothing being paid to the nominal sellers of the claim, the members of the class.

While it makes sense to assign rights on a first-come first-served basis in cases where the costs of enforcement are very high relative to the individual victim's stake, in other cases exclusive victim rights would appear to be a more efficient assignment of property rights; and this, roughly, is the pattern we observe in the real world.   A first-come first-served system would involve at least two problems [in addition to] that of external technical diseconomies. .   .   .   The first is the problem of appropriability.   Enforcer A begins an investigation of violator X, collects extensive information, and is prepared to file suit when enforcer B, having heard about A's investigation, files suit against X first.   A and B are bilateral monopolists, and while A will get something from B for the information he has collected, his gains from the investigation will be smaller than if he had had a secure property right.   The

---

69. Bribery of enforcers, if the bounty is set below the cost of punishment to prevent overenforcement; collusion between enforcers and offenders if it is set above cost.

problem of appropriability here is very similar to that in the market for inventions, and for the same reason: in both cases the commodity being produced is information.

A could have solved his problem by filing suit before beginning to investigate. This, however, suggests another problem of a first-come first-served system: excessive rewards. It would be inefficient to confer exclusive enforcement rights, potentially of great value, on people who have merely conceived the possibility of suing somebody for something. People would spend their time drafting and filing barebones complaints charging large corporations with violations of various laws, and then sit back and wait for the people with investigative skills and resources to purchase their claims. The investment of resources in drafting and filing would be socially excessive.

There are techniques for getting around these problems, embodied for example in the patent laws.[74] These laws could be adapted for use in the market for legal claims, but the result might not be very satisfactory. The patent analogy might prove useful, however, in sorting out claims among enforcers in class-action situations, where the principle of victim rights is and must be largely disregarded.

Another reason for preferring the existing system of victim rights is that efficiency sometimes requires that the victim of an unlawful act be compensated therefor. For example, under a negligence system in which the right to seek damages is owned by the victim of a negligently inflicted injury, the traveler at a railroad crossing will take only those precautions that are cost-justified, where the expected accident cost is calculated on the assumption that the railroad is complying with its duties under the negligence standard. The potential victim will not take precautions against accidents that would occur only if the railroad violated its duties—behaved negligently—because the victim of such an accident, being fully compensated for any injury resulting from it, is indifferent to whether it occurs and will incur no cost to prevent it. Suppose, however, that the victim has no right to be compensated if he is injured in a negligently inflicted accident—anyone has the right to sue in respect of that accident and to collect and retain damages from the railroad. The railroad may now have an incentive to increase the number of accidents at railroad crossings far above the optimal level. Its aim will be to make crossing a railroad track an extremely hazardous activity. At first there will be many accidents and the railroad will have to pay private enforcers—not victims—substantial judgments. Potential victims, however, not being compensated when injured no matter how negligent the railroad's conduct, will soon begin to take measures to protect themselves from crossing accidents. They may cease to use railroad crossings altogether; they may induce the municipal authorities to build an underpass. The number of accidents will fall and the result will be a reduction in the railroad's costs of accident

---

74. The requirements of novelty, utility, and nonobviousness, administered by the Patent Office, and by the courts in patent-infringement actions, are the means by which the patent laws deal with the second problem discussed above. The first is dealt with by, for example, the rule that disclosure of an invention is protected if the inventor files for a patent within a year following disclosure. . . .

liability that may exceed (even after discounting to present value) the costs of answering to private enforcers in damages for the many injuries negligently inflicted during the initial period of reckless behavior. The elimination of accidents will have been achieved by a method that is socially suboptimal.

There is another way to avoid this problem besides compensating victims, and that is to divorce liability from the infliction of injury. In our example, this would mean imposing speed limits and other forms of direct regulation on the railroad. But that implies additional public enforcement. . . .

We note in closing that the existing system of victim rights has several drawbacks. For example, legal claims are not freely transferable. A person injured in an accident cannot sell his legal claim against the injurer to a lawyer or other enforcer. This means that he cannot shift the risk created by the uncertainty of litigation (although he can share it with his lawyer by means of a contingent fee agreement) and assuming that risk aversion is prevalent the result may be underenforcement of legal claims. And current law forbids lawyers to use the corporate form to obtain capital in the capital markets, so even if they were permitted to buy claims they might find it difficult to finance their purchases.

The Public Enforcer's Budget Constraint

Another positive implication of our analysis of private enforcement relates to the fact that the budgets of public enforcement agencies tend to be small in relation to the potential gains from enforcement as they would be appraised by a private, profit-maximizing enforcer. For example, the Internal Revenue Service has repeatedly (but unsuccessfully) argued to its appropriations subcommittee that the Service is operating at a budgetary level where the marginal cost of enforcement is far below the marginal return, measured (as a private enforcer would measure it) by the additional tax revenue that additional expenditures on enforcement would generate. There is some evidence that its argument is correct. The assumption of a budget constraint would be unrealistic as applied to a private enforcer, for assuming reasonably well functioning capital markets he would be able to finance any enforcement activities where the expected monetary return exceeded the expected costs.

The agency budget constraint is at first glance puzzling. Why isn't the legislature interested in maximizing the expected value of enforcement? Why doesn't it, therefore, appropriate additional funds to any agency, such as the IRS, that could use the funds to increase the net yield of enforcement? The puzzle disappears when we reflect that a method of appropriation whereby the level of enforcement of the tax laws was allowed to rise to the level that would be reached under a system of private enforcement could . . . result in overenforcement. The effect of the budget constraint, in forcing the public enforcer to operate where marginal cost is less than marginal revenue and hence where the probability of apprehension and conviction is less than if profits were maximized, is similar to that of a tax on private enforcement designed to reduce the level of private enforcement to the socially optimal level.

There is, to be sure, an element of private enforcement in the enforcement of the federal tax laws: the government pays informers a reward of up to 10 per cent of any additional taxes collected as a result of the informer's tip. But were it not for the problem of overenforcement, it would be difficult to understand why the maximum reward has been set at such a low percentage of the revenues produced. If the objective were to carry enforcement of the tax laws to the point where marginal revenue and marginal cost were equated, a reward greatly in excess of 100 percent of the additional revenues collected might well be appropriate, since each apprehension resulting from an informer's activity would have some effect in deterring other taxpayers from underpaying their tax.[80] Alternatively, the informer, rather than being given a reward in excess of the amount of tax collected, might be given a reward equal to the additional tax plus any penalties imposed (including the monetary equivalent of the costs to the taxpayer of being imprisoned, where that was the penalty imposed). The effect of the 10 per cent ceiling is to reduce drastically the scale that the tax informer industry would attain under a system of pure private enforcement. .   .   .

Blackmail and Bribery

Blackmail may be defined as the sale of information to an individual who would be incriminated by its publication, and at first glance appears to be an efficient method of private enforcement of the law (the moral as well as the positive law). The value of the information to the blackmailed individual is equal to the cost of the punishment that the individual will incur if the information is communicated to the authorities and he is punished as a result, and so he will be willing to pay up to that amount to the blackmailer for the information. The individual is thereby punished, and the punishment is the same as if he had been apprehended and convicted for the crime that the blackmailer has discovered, but the fine is paid to the blackmailer rather than to the state.

Why then is blackmail a crime? A superficial answer is that it results in underdeterrence of crimes punished by nonpecuniary sanctions because the criminals lack the resources to pay an optimal fine. The blackmailer will sell his information to the criminal for a price lower than the cost of punishment if the criminal cannot pay a higher price. This problem, however, could be solved by a system of public bounties equal to the cost of punishment (or lower, to induce the enforcement industry to contract to optimal size). Then the blackmailer could always claim a bounty from the state if the criminal was unable to pay a price equal to the optimal fine.

A more persuasive explanation of why blackmail is a crime is that the decision to discourage blackmail follows directly from the decision to rely on a public monopoly of law enforcement in some areas of enforcement, notably criminal law. Were blackmail, a form of private enforcement, lawful, the public monopoly of enforcement would be undermined. Overenforcement of the law would result if the blackmailer were able to extract the full fine from the offenders. .   .   . Alternatively, the blackmailer might sell

---

80. This would, however, give enforcers an incentive to bribe taxpayers to violate the law. .   .   .

his incriminating information to the offender for a price lower than the statutory cost of punishment to the criminal, which would reduce the effective cost of punishment to the criminal below the level set by the legislature.

Consistently with this analysis, we observe that practices indistinguishable from blackmail, though not called by that name, are permitted in areas where the law is enforced privately rather than publicly because the overenforcement problem is not serious. No one seems to object to a person's collecting information about his or her spouse's adulterous activities, and threatening to disclose that information in a divorce proceeding or other forum, in order to extract maximum compensation for the offending spouse's breach of the marital obligations. A third party is not permitted to "blackmail" the offending spouse (unless the third party is the victimized spouse's agent) because permitting him to enforce the marital contract would undermine the assignment of the exclusive right to enforce such contracts to the victim of the breach. It is also consistent with our analysis that blackmail is forbidden in areas where there are no legal prohibitions at all—where the information would humiliate, but not incriminate, the blackmailer's victim. The social decision not to regulate a particular activity is a judgment that the expenditure of resources on trying to discover and punish it would be socially wasted. That judgment is undermined if blackmailers are encouraged to expend substantial resources on attempting to apprehend and punish people engaged in the activity.

Blackmail and bribery appear to be virtually identical practices from the standpoint of the analysis of private enforcement. The blackmailer and the bribed official both receive payment in exchange for not enforcing the law. We therefore predict that in areas where there is a public monopoly of enforcement, bribery, like blackmail, will be prohibited, while in areas where there is no public monopoly it will be permitted. And so we observe. The settlement out of court of a tort or contract or private antitrust case is a form of perfectly lawful bribery, although the term is not used in these situations (except by economists) because of its pejorative connotation.

An interesting example of "bribery" occurs in connection with the class action. As mentioned earlier, concern is frequently expressed that the lawyer for the class will be tempted to "sell out" the class by negotiating with the defendant's lawyer a settlement that will involve a combination of nominal relief in favor of the class with a large legal fee for its lawyer; the individual class member's stake in the outcome of the action is too small to warrant his exercising effective control over the lawyer for the class. This problem would not arise if the lawyer for the class were permitted to retain the entire proceeds of the class action; then his interest would be identical with that of the class. Such a solution . . . is simply a specific application of the principle of pure private enforcement, where the entire penalty imposed on the offender is received by the enforcer as compensation. Under existing law, the lawyer for the class is not entitled to receive the entire damages awarded to the class. He is entitled only to a reasonable attorney's fee, which is fixed by the court, ordinarily as a small fraction of the total damages. The difference between the total damages awarded and the attorney's fee is the equivalent of [an] enforcement tax [used] as a device for reducing the scale of private enforcement. Like the tax it drives a wedge between what the offender pays and what the enforcer receives, and thereby creates opportunities for a form of bribery, very difficult to prevent, that consists of the offender's agreeing to a settlement that involves a higher attorney's fee for the enforcer, but a lower damages bill, than the court would award. In this fashion both parties to the class action can be made better off—viewing the lawyer for the class as the real party in interest on the plaintiff's side of the action.

———

This article by Professors Landes and Posner is, in part, a response to earlier work on private enforcement that did not include the "overenforcement theorem." See, especially, Becker and Stigler, Law Enforcement, Malfeasance, and Compensation of Enforcers, 3 J.Legal Stud. 1 (1974). It should be noted, however, that Landes and Posner, much like Becker and Stigler, do not have a sanguine view of the actual performance of public enforcement. The authors qualify their statement that private enforcement is less efficient than optimum public enforcement by observing that a choice between the two strategies depends upon *actual* public enforcement, which is difficult to predict without "a theory of the behavior of public enterprises." For suggestive approaches to such a theory, compare W. Niskanen, Bureaucracy and Representative Government (1971), with Posner, The Behavior of Administrative Agencies, 1 J.Legal Stud. 305 (1972).

SECTION C. GROUP LITIGATION: FUNCTIONAL AND NATURAL BASES FOR PARTY STATUS

We have explored throughout this chapter the uneasy interpenetration of the world of adjudication and the "real" world outside. We have seen that strategic choices made with respect to broader objectives may have systematic effects upon adjudication and we have observed that the very structure of antagonism in lawsuits may be manipulated as part of the struggle over values and resources in the world outside the courtroom. In this final section of chapter 4 we consider still another set of such interactions.

1. THE FUNCTIONS OF A CLASS ACTION

Substantive law has long recognized the impact of standardized transactions upon its norms. The use of insurance concepts in torts, the acknowledgment of somewhat different rules for contracts of adhesion in contract law, and the widespread resort to public regulation of the standardized transaction itself in insurance and securities law are only a few of the many instances that could be listed. The class action and other group litigation devices have been procedure's primary response to this process. The manipulation of the conditions for group litigation cannot fail to have major strategic implications in a variety of areas. It alters the balance of advantages between the organized, centralized actors (normally defendants) and the diffuse,

small, unorganized individuals. It alters the balance between the public enforcement agencies of prosecutors or administrative agencies and the private
enforcement "industry," normally the plaintiffs' bar. It alters the balance
between court and legislative lawmaking. We have now accustomed ourselves both to the class action and to the regulatory state. It is instructive to
consider Kalven and Rosenfield's seminal article written in 1941 when the
federal class action was but three years old and the New Deal was still fairly "New." Compare this early analysis to Gerald Wright's application of
welfare-economics terminology to the same problem. Is there any advantage
to the "New" terms?

Harry Kalven, Jr., and Maurice Rosenfield, **The Contemporary Function of the Class Suit***

"The wide diffusion of securities has created a situation where the single
and isolated security holder usually is helpless in protecting his own interests
or pleading his own cause," reported the Securities and Exchange Commission
in 1937.[1] "The plight of the individual investor," the commission added,
"is accentuated where he is uninformed and unskilled in the intricacies of
finance. It is likewise accentuated where his investment is so small that it
becomes either impossible or improvident for him to expend the funds necessary to prosecute his claims or defend his position."

Although the commission's comment was made with immediate reference only to the individual investor in corporate reorganization cases, it applies equally well to many other situations. . . . The employee who is
entitled to time and a half for overtime, the stockholder who has been misled
by a false statement in a prospectus, the rate-payer who has been charged an
excessive rate, the depositor in a closed bank, the taxpayer who resists an illegal assessment, or the small business man who has been the victim of a
monopoly in restraint of trade, like the investor in the reorganization, finds
himself inadvertently holding a small stake in a large controversy. The type
of injury which tends to affect simultaneously the interest of many people is
also apt to involve immensely complex facts and intricate law, and redress for
it is likely to involve expense totally disproportionate to any of the individual claims.

Consider, for example, the plight of those who bought into the $60,-
000,000 debenture issue of Insull Utilities Investments the top holding company in the Insull hierarchy. When the system collapsed and the individual
holder discovered he was not to be paid, he was faced with the almost insuperable problem of ascertaining whether he had any basis for redress. He was
required somehow to appraise the possibilities that some of the vast number
of financial transactions involved mismanagement by the directors, or that
there were abuses in the incredible complexity of the intercompany structure,
or that perhaps the celebrated and esoteric "negative pledge" clause had been
violated. To have had any sort of knowledge or opinion on these points

* *Source*: 8 U.Chi.L.Rev. 684, 684–95,
715–21 (1941). Kalven (1914–1974):
Professor of Law, University of Chicago; Rosenfield: member of Illinois
bar.

1. Report on the Study and Investigation of the Work, Activities, Personnel
and Functions of Protective and Reorganization Committees, Part II, at 1
(1937). . . .

would have required literally months of intensive investigation and sophisticated research. To put it bluntly, the picture had become so complex that the individual could not know whether he had been "robbed" or not.

Moreover, almost no single investor's stake would warrant the enormous expense of his seeking legal redress. The investor who held, say, $10,000 in debentures, was confronted with expenses measured by a $60,000,000 lawsuit, not a $10,000 one. Clearly, if any redress was to be sought, it was imperative that it be sought on behalf of and be paid for by the debenture holders as a group. . . . The Insull case is, of course, extreme, and some of its evils have already been corrected by substantive law reforms. Nevertheless it serves to highlight the twin factors of ignorance and expense which are present in virtually all cases of large-scale group injuries.

Modern society seems increasingly to expose men to such group injuries for which individually they are in a poor position to seek legal redress, either because they do not know enough or because such redress is disproportionately expensive. If each is left to assert his rights alone if and when he can, there will at best be a random and fragmentary enforcement, if there is any at all. This result is not only unfortunate in the particular case, but it will operate seriously to impair the deterrent effect of the sanctions which underlie much contemporary law. The problem of fashioning an effective and inclusive group remedy is thus a major one.

One important answer is afforded by the development of administrative law. President Roosevelt . . . described the plight of the individual who has a small share in a large controversy and commended strongly the use of administrative bodies as the remedy: "Individual shippers could not cope in the courts with great railroad corporations over excessive charges that were small in single cases but important in the aggregate. So the Interstate Commerce Commission was created. Power consumers could not deal with electric rates, nor could individual security holders pit their strength against the concentrated power of brokerage interests, nor could individual laborers bargain on equality with the concentrated power of employers. The very heart of modern reform administration is the administrative tribunal. A 'truth in securities' act without an administrative tribunal to enforce it or a labor-relations act without an administrative tribunal to administer it, or rate regulation without a commission to supervise rates would be sterile and useless." [7]

Administrative law removes the obstacles of insufficient funds and insufficient knowledge by shifting the responsibility for protecting the interests of the individuals comprising the group to a public body which has ample funds and adequate powers of investigation. Primarily, it is a method of preventing injuries by the injunction, the stop order, and the cease and desist order; by pre-licensing and revocation; by establishing a rate for the future; or by outlining a very detailed pattern for future conduct. But it is important to note that an administrative body does not normally act to remedy wrongs which have occurred . . . .

. . . As a consequence, whether it is desirable or not, private litigation must still police large areas of modern law and provide the exclusive

7. 86 Cong.Rec. 21501 (1940).

remedy for many large-scale group injuries. It is the primary concern of this article to explore the possibilities of revitalizing private litigation to fashion an effective means of group redress.

Off-hand it might seem that a satisfactory solution to the problem is afforded by the simple expedient of multiple joinder under modern rules of procedure. Undeniably, excellent reforms have been made in recent years, and joinder statutes are almost everywhere exceedingly liberal . . . . The cardinal difficulty with joinder, however, is that it presupposes the prospective plaintiffs' advancing en masse on the courts. In most situations such spontaneity cannot arise because the various parties who have the common interest are isolated, scattered, and utter strangers to each other. Thus while the necessity for group action through joinder clearly exists, the conditions for it do not. It may not be enough for society simply to set up courts and wait for litigants to bring their complaints—they may never come.

What is needed, then, is something over and above the possibility of joinder. There must be some affirmative technique for bringing everyone into the case and for making recovery available to all. It is not so much a matter of permitting joinder as of ensuring it. There are basically two methods for doing this. The first is to organize the various claimants prior to suit and make them all parties plaintiff to the litigation; this is the committee technique. The second is to ignore the various claimants until a decree has been obtained and then to hold open the decree and to permit them upon solicitation under court auspices to participate in the benefits of the decree. The suit in form will be brought initially by any member of the group who, unchosen and unasked and without soliciting consents from the others or organizing them prior to trial, volunteers to assert the rights of all. This is the technique of the class suit.

Preliminary to an exploration of the utility of the class suit as an instrument for effective and inclusive group redress, it will be useful to take up briefly the institution of the committee as the alternative device.

It is undoubtedly true that if everyone injured were made a party plaintiff before trial an effective and inclusive group remedy would then be available. Expenses and knowledge would be shared, and the total claim of all would warrant vigorous investigation and prosecution. Finally, if the case were won all would be entitled to share in the recovery. As has already been suggested, however, the group will not voluntarily and spontaneously join in the action because of their dispersion and anonymity. If there is to be large-scale participation before trial, it is necessary that there be an aggressive, determined organization-drive, necessitating the use of something akin to the reorganization committee.

The utility of this device is subject to some serious reservations. In the first place . . . the tremendous volume of experience with reorganization committees during the depression years was disillusioning. Even those who believe that the committee could serve a useful function have advocated stringent controls over it. More serious is the fact that recent reforms in the reorganization field have tended in the direction of drastically subordinating the committee or eliminating it altogether, by delegating its functions to the bankruptcy trustee, to the indenture trustee, and to the SEC. In brief, in the one type of case in which the committee has been used extensively it has been tried and found wanting . . . .

The method of the class suit is to permit any member of the group individually, unchosen and unasked and without any organization of the class or prior consent from others, to step forward and sue on behalf of all, in the sense that if he is successful all may participate in his result. The chief difference between this method and the committee method is simply that instead of mobilizing the plaintiffs prior to trial, their participation in the case is deferred [according to the rules then in effect] until a decision is reached. In lieu of any aggressive solicitation of powers of attorney before trial, there is substituted a simple notice after the decision that relief is available. It is evident that the class suit method preserves and strengthens all the possible advantages of the committee technique. A practical opportunity for recovery is made available to all; expenses and knowledge are shared by all; and the size of the total claim of the class warrants vigorous prosecution of the rights of the class. And these advantages are obtained without the disadvantages of the committee technique. First, there is no occasion for individual fee contracts or powers of attorney—all fees are awarded by the court on a quantum meruit basis. Second, there is no unfair unleashing of adverse publicity, because prior to solicitation the case has been decided on its merits, and any solicitation is under court auspices. Finally, the method is likely to be almost completely successful inasmuch as the various members are simply notified that a completed recovery is available for them; they are not asked to put up money or to give authorizations, but are simply asked to "come and get it."

The contrast between the committee approach and the class suit approach may be seen most sharply from an examination of the familiar shareholder's derivative suit. Although serious doubts have been expressed as to its complete efficacy, there is general agreement that it furnishes the major sanction behind the fiduciary rules of corporation law. Here the theory of recovery has been completely worked out. Any shareholder may initiate the litigation, and by virtue of the fact that he is treated as derivatively asserting the corporate cause of action, his claim is the total claim of all the shareholders. If he is successful, recovery automatically inures pro rata to the benefit of each member of the class, and counsel fees and expenses are distributed over the entire class. The suit, then, is the perfect method of group redress, accomplished without any of the cumbersome paraphernalia of the committee. The really significant thing is that a single shareholder, without being asked or without procuring the authorization of other shareholders, simply volunteers to present their case as well as his own to the court. It is the best example of effective and inclusive redress through vicarious litigation.

The shareholder's suit has one advantage, it must be admitted, which is not completely available in cases where the cause of action cannot be said to belong to the entity. The corporation, by acting as a receptacle for the cause of action, makes unnecessary any solicitation and affirmative action by the beneficiaries of the plaintiff-shareholder's litigation. In cases where there is no entity, solicitation and notice after the decree provide the mechanical substitute for the entity as the device for making participation in the recovery available to all. With this one adjustment, the class suit becomes as effective a procedural form for group redress for the employee, the investor, the ratepayer, the taxpayer, et al., as the derivative suit is for the shareholder with respect to the misconduct of corporate fiduciaries.

The exact procedure envisaged for participation after the decree might be stated in somewhat greater detail, although the point is not a troublesome one. Bankruptcy, probate, equity practice in receivership, and fraudulent conveyance cases afford obvious analogies. The ordinary case will simply involve the common sense question of how best to bring everyone in and afford each one relief; clearly no exact rules of procedure are necessary or desirable, and there should be free play for the court's discretion.

In general the class suit will require the following additional steps: (1) The court should enter an interlocutory order in favor of the parties plaintiff of record and all those similarly situated who come in seasonably and establish their rights. (2) A reference should then be made to a master to administer the details of participation by the absentees. The defendant should be compelled by order to make available to the master all his information as to the names and addresses of the absentees. (3) The plaintiff's attorney or the master should prepare and submit to the court forms for proof of claims and accompanying explanatory material which the master should then mail to all absentees. (4) The absentees should file their claims within a prescribed time, and the defendant should be permitted to file objections, but only as to issues not common to the original plaintiff's case.[33] (5) The master's hearings should then be had as to the objections and, if relevant, as to damages of each claimant, and the master should file a report with the court in the customary manner. (6) The court, after disposing of all objections to the master's report, should enter a final decree ordering the defendant to pay all who have proved their claims and make provisions for expenses and fees. If the court finds that there may be a problem of collecting the judgment, it might enter the entire judgment in the name of the plaintiffs of record as trustees to collect and distribute to all who have proved claims; in such cases the court should reserve jurisdiction until the matter has been completely disposed of.

While this procedure seems quite simple, it probably represents the maximum complexity. Frequently, the process will be short circuited because the defendant may pay or be required to pay on the basis of his own records. Again, the proving of claims may become almost nominal, as in the case of investors who need only show ownership of a security. Finally, there may be a proceeding, such as bankruptcy or receivership, pending concurrently, which will provide a ready vehicle for participation and distribution and need only be adopted.   . . .

33. Where the suit is predicated upon the existence of a common question of law or fact, it is often contended with considerable rhetorical force that there are so many individual questions involved that the suit cannot be maintained. This argument sometimes involves the implicit assumption that the class suit cannot be maintained if there are any individual questions. But normally it is the common question involved which presents the real issue in the case and the minor variations among the members are trivial or irrelevant. . . .

. . . It remains by way of conclusion to make the comparison already suggested between the class suit by private litigants and action by an administrative commission as competing methods of affording group redress. It must be noted, of course, that the two methods of group redress are not as a practical matter in competition with each other . . . . Nevertheless, such a comparison may serve a double purpose. First, the contrast between private and public methods of redress for past injuries highlights certain strengths and weaknesses of the private litigation technique, and second, such a comparison may suggest possible areas for the further development of administrative law.

The choice seems then to be between the public official whose job and responsibility it is to function as an expert representative for the injured group and the amateur volunteer representative who brings the class suit. Stated in these terms, the choice is not a difficult one. But the more basic choice is between lawyers on public pay-roll and lawyers in private practice, and this choice is by no means so simple. That the representative in the administrative law method of redressing civil wrongs is the public lawyer requires no elaboration, but the exact role of the private lawyer in class suit litigation invites further comment.

It is the lawyer and only the lawyer who can properly be rewarded for the semi-public activity in a class suit. The impact of fees on the class suit is thus of prime importance. By performing services at the request of some of the group, the lawyer can, if he is successful, entitle himself to a fee based on the total claims of all. The striking thing is that although the fees may be large and attractive, they are awarded only on a quantum meruit basis. Although the result of transforming a small case into a big one is extraordinary from the lawyer's standpoint, there is no mystery as to the principle upon which the big fee is awarded. Once it has been decided that the class suit can be brought and that all can have the benefits, it follows necessarily that the successful lawyer has performed services equally valuable to all members of the class. He is awarded a large fee because he has performed a large service, and were his compensation to be measured by and paid out of the claims of his original plaintiff-client alone, there would clearly be unjust enrichment of the remainder of the class. This principle has perhaps been most definitively stated in a . . . decision of the United States Supreme Court in a case which, curiously enough, did not involve a class suit.[93] The plaintiff's original suit established a result which, solely on the doctrine of stare decisis, became immediately available to several others who were similarly situated. In allowing the plaintiff's application for an award of fees from the group, Mr. Justice Frankfurter said:

> . . . In her main suit the petitioner neither avowed herself to be the representative of a class nor did she automatically establish a fund in which others could participate. But in view of the consequences of stare decisis, the petitioner by establishing her claim necessarily established the claims of fourteen other trusts pertaining to the same bonds.

93. Sprague v. Ticonic Nat. Bank, 307 U.S. 161 (1939).

That the party in a situation like the present neither purported to sue for a class nor formally established by litigation a fund available to the class, does not seem to be a differentiating factor. . . . Whether one professes to sue representatively or formally makes a fund available for others may, of course, be a relevant circumstance in making the fund liable for his costs in producing it. But when such a fund is for all practical purposes created for the benefit of others, the formalities of the litigation— the absence of an avowed class suit or the creation of a fund, as it were, through stare decisis rather than through a decree—hardly touch the power of equity in doing justice as between a party and the beneficiaries of his litigation. . . .

It is, of course, obvious that the same result follows a fortiori in a class suit case.

It is thus seen that the class suit is a vehicle for paying lawyers handsomely to be champions of semi-public rights. It is this quality of the class suit which gives vitality to the volunteer method of representation and obviates the apathy and general disinclination of the ordinary layman to assert anyone's rights but his own. Because of the lawyer's incentive, the suit which might be brought for the original plaintiff alone is legitimately turned into a class suit for all. And more important, the suit which might not be brought at all because the demands on legal skill and time would be disproportionate to the original client's stake can, when turned into a class suit, be brought and handled in a manner commensurate with its magnitude. Thus, the class suit as a way of redressing group wrongs is a semi-public remedy administered by the lawyer in private practice—and the opposition between public and private methods of group redress is, as has been said, an opposition between the public and private lawyer.

The first objection to the private system that comes to mind is that the moving of the private system of redress into action is highly accidental and haphazard. The protection of the semi-public interest depends upon placing the case in the hands of the lawyer by the individual client. No matter how competent, informed, and eager the lawyer may be, he cannot act until at least one layman approaches him with the case.[98] By way of contrast, those administering the public system may act of their own volition and further-

---

98. Undoubtedly, the bar is not overscrupulous in observing this requirement. From one point of view the requirement of the initial client does seem anachronistic; the class is the real client and the situation does not readily adjust to orthodox notions of the lawyer-client relationship. For one thing the lawyer's stake in the litigation will frequently far exceed that of his initial client. Since the client in these cases functions primarily to put into motion the machinery of the semi-public remedy, the question naturally arises: why not permit the lawyer alone to bring a class suit without an initial client? Of course, such a re-

sult represents so drastic a deviation from contemporary professional thought, that even if it were permitted, it would probably be shunned by a very large majority of the bar. Further, the question may prove too much. It may well prove that the lawyer if he were to act without a client would be so unequivocally a public representative that there would be no point in not putting him directly on the public pay-roll. Query, whether the same might not be said of the lawyer who is permitted to sue when he has only some members of the class as his clients?

more may discover violations in the first instance through the exercise of investigatory powers and the use of official reports. But the contrast is not so complete as it may at first seem. It must be remembered that public bodies by and large do not act unless some sort of private complaint has been made. The layman asking the commission to assert his rights does not differ much from the client complaining to his lawyer.

The "personnel" which administers the private system is chosen in a haphazard fashion. The client selects not only his own lawyer but the lawyer for the others in the group. Thus, there is virtually no restriction on the selection of the representative; any lawyer may on occasion bring a class suit. The administrative personnel, on the other hand, is selected by standards which are certainly more stringent than those for general admission to the bar. The legal staffs of certain federal bodies, such as the SEC, are genuinely excellent and perhaps excel those of any law firms in the country, for it is a familiar story that in recent years the young [lawyers] have been going to Washington. Further, these staffs, by virtue of specialization, become expert in certain limited fields, and it is not at all clear but that the complexity of the situations which give rise to large scale group injuries demands the specialist's knowledge and touch. Undeniably, there have been striking instances in recent years of a distrust of the competency of private litigation to determine adequately questions of public importance. . . .

Further, due to its expert position the administrative body can view a law as a whole and have regard for a consistent, coherent, politic application of it. In the case of much new social legislation, the tempering of the enforcement of law by such discretion is of real importance. For example, the Wage and Hour Division, particularly in the first years of the law, found it wise to create good will for the law by settling close cases on the basis of the employer's affidavit to comply in the future. Where a law depends to so high a degree on the voluntary compliance of those subject to it, such judicious application of the law is an important matter of "public relations." No such restraint can be expected if the law is administered through private litigation; rather, the method will result in an insistence upon the harshest results and the most technical interpretations.

Perhaps the most serious objection to the private litigation system for redressing group wrongs is one which concerns not the competence or discretion of the private lawyer but rather what might euphemistically be called his sense of loyalty. The reorganization bar, like the reorganization committee, was not altogether satisfactory in discharging the semi-public responsibility thrust upon it by the reorganization process. But the same opportunities for abuse are not present in the ordinary class suit case. Only where there is question of compromising the suit is there any occasion for a problem. And here the controls which currently exist under the federal rule, namely, notice and court approval, are sufficient to regulate suits which reach the courts. The only remaining problem is that of the lawyer who settles before his case reaches the courts. Frequently he and his client may be handsomely paid, although most of their recovery is a reward for not bringing the class suit. While in strictly legal terms it is true that the rest of the class retains its right to sue, as a practical matter this type of settlement may seriously impair the opportunities of the rest of the class to acquire knowledge of the wrong and to assert their rights effectively.[104] The public system is not subject to being diverted in this fashion unless there is resort to out and out bribery. Not only would it be difficult to devise any controls for such settlements in the private case, but it is not at all clear that the lawyer's conduct violates any existing canons of legal ethics.

The case for the administrative agencies, however, is not without its difficulties. Some of these, of course, have been the subject of debate since the days of Adam Smith. It is, however, pertinent to observe that to impose upon public agencies the task of asserting civil sanctions on behalf of injured groups will require a substantial increase in size, personnel and expenditures . . . . Nor is the personnel picture for the public agency all sweetness and light. For many years the public lawyers who have staffed district attorney and corporation counsel offices and state commissions have frequently been primarily political appointees. Despite the great improvements in federal agencies in recent years, it is still true that there is no tradition of public service and little development of a true civil servant attitude in America. It is disquieting that so many of the young lawyers presently serving in the federal commissions regard their jobs as sort of super-apprenticeships for private practice.

Perhaps a serious difficulty with greatly expanding the scope of administrative action by adding the responsibility of civil litigation is the effect such an increase in function will have on the impartiality and balance an administrative body is supposed to assume. If the administrative body is to sue civilly, it must take sides and become an advocate. Too much can be made of this point; taking sides is not always an evil, and in fact, in exercising their injunctive powers, administrative bodies at present are in something of the advocate's position . . . .

For the sake of clarity this comparison has been in terms of exclusive alternatives. The best solution, however, is to draw upon both systems of enforcement, permitting both to develop side by side to check and complement each other. That such an arrangement is workable and valuable has already been shown by the experience with co-enforcement of the provisions of the wage and hour law by the Wage and Hour Division and by the private class suit. Certainly proposals to extend administrative law in this direction, particularly with respect to the SEC, merit serious consideration. On the other hand the power of law administration through the private lawyer should not be underestimated. The efficiency of the private lawyer when the blue chips are down—and they are down in a class suit case—can make the class suit an effective instrument in contemporary administration of justice. And in any event, not all the young [lawyers] go to Washington.

---

104. Such settlements should at least operate as affirmative concealment for the purpose of suspending the statute of limitations.

Gerald A. Wright, **The Cost-Internalization Case for Class Actions***

As the number and variety of human activities in society expand, the economy becomes increasingly sensitive to the effects that one enterprise can have on another. If such effects carry no price tag, with the result that their cost or benefit to society is not a factor in the private decisions leading to their existence, then they are known as externalities [or "external effects," "neighborhood effects," "side effects," "spillovers"]. Such externalities as sonic booms and air pollution impose large social costs that are not private costs for the airline or polluter. Since the inequality of social costs and the decisionmakers' private costs suggests that resources might be improperly allocated, economists have proposed a number of remedial measures for correcting the apparent market defect.

Proposed remedies, ranging from direct regulation to the redefinition of private legal rights, have been criticized on the basis that there is really no allocative problem at all—that the free market is capable of adjusting for externalities so as to provide efficiency [i. e., no resources are wasted or put to less than their best use] despite the apparent lack of pricing for, e. g., booms and pollution. Nevertheless, remedial measures continue to be suggested. For example, the necessity of providing a means for introducing the external sonic-boom "cost" of supersonic air transport into the balance sheet of SST operations has recently been examined . . . with the suggestion that administrative settlement of damage claims should be adopted because private lawsuits will not suffice.

This [essay] demonstrates that the supposed free-market solution to the external-cost problem is deficient . . . when consumers are involved and that remedies may indeed be necessary in that situation. Although the administrative mode may ultimately prevail for all dispute resolution, this [essay] explores the possibility of using an existing procedural device to cope with externalities in the present judicatory structure. That device is the class action.

. . . [T]here are a limited number of external costs that are particularly relevant to this discussion of the value of the class action as an internalization device. The paradigm case . . . is air pollution caused by a single polluter. The potential class is that group of people who suffer the costs—in declining property values, moving expenses, ill health—of the pollution. In general, for the class action to be appropriate there must be: (1) a class—a group of people who can make out a cause of action for similar harm from the same source; (2) a manageable cause of action, in that proof of causation is possible and damages calculable; and (3) an economically motivated and rational defendant, such as a profit-making firm or other enterprise that is concerned with minimizing its costs. . . . In the following analysis, "polluter" is to be read as standing for the potential defendant . . . .

* *Source*: 21 Stan.L.Rev. 383, 383–98, 403–04 (1969). Acting Professor of Law, University of California at Los Angeles.

The Economic Problem

Air pollution imposes on outsiders an uncompensated "cost" that is not subjected to any pricing mechanism. Many of those who are presently using the atmosphere for waste disposal are not required to pay for the privilege; conversely, there is no effective means whereby other air users may offer payment to stop the pollution. This defect in the market pricing system may prevent the various factors of production from being efficiently allocated.[10] For example, if a silent jackhammer could be manufactured and operated at only a very slight increase in cost over the present models, the aural public would presumably benefit to a greater extent than jackhammer users would be harmed.

Since economists are men of science and not philosophers, a test must be applied to determine whether silence really benefits listeners sufficiently to justify the extra cost to the builder, wrecker, or whomever. The principle of compensation serves, for if the listeners themselves *pay* the new costs of silence, the aggregate benefit is increased. The builder is no worse off, and the listeners must be better off or they would not have paid. When all the rsources of production are being utilized so that no shift of resources can benefit one person without harming another, then an efficient solution [known as Pareto optimal] has been achieved.

.   .   .   Pigou [introduced] the concept that external social costs and benefits must also be considered in any discussion of efficiency.

.   .   .   [E]fficiency could be attained only if external costs were somehow imposed on firms that seemed to produce them. Proposals to thus "internalize" the externalities have taken several forms, principally: (1) tax-subsidy schemes whereby firms are taxed to the extent of their uncompensated net social costs or subsidized for their net social benefits; (2) expansion of the firm so that all social costs and benefits accrue within the firm and are included in its profit-maximizing calculation; (3) varying degrees of government appropriation or regulation of the firm; (4) redefinition of legal rights.

The efficacy of these measures to promote efficiency has recently been subject to challenge, particularly since a 1960 article by R. H. Coase.[15] Chiefly in response to the taxation-subsidy proposals, Coase developed several propositions. First, he demonstrated that, given costless bargaining, efficient resource allocation will be achieved regardless of which party is required to bear the cost of the externality; second, he suggested that, given the subtantial bargaining costs that do exist, measures to internalize costs do not necessarily lead to an optimum solution.   .   .   .

---

10. "Allocational" questions, which concern the mix by which scarce resources are utilized, are usually considered separately from "distributional" questions, which concern how the benefits of that utilization accrue to individuals. Price theorists relegate the latter set of questions to the realms of "ethics and politics."   .   .   . Distributional decisions may, however, have important allocational effects   .   .   .   .

15. Coase, The Problem of Social Cost, 3 J.L. & Econ. 1 (1960).

Class Actions

The role of the class action as an internalization device is twofold: It reduces bargaining costs between the polluter and the pollutees, and also among the pollutees themselves. Assume that there is a single polluter, P, and a class, C, of irritated residents. The effect of these two functions is to minimize the transaction costs that prevent "costless" bargaining between P and C.

In many of the instances in which externalities become significant, the transaction costs of bargaining are of two kinds: (1) the conference costs that occur whenever a large group of people must come to common agreement, (2) the collective-good costs that result when each class member realizes that an expenditure of effort or funds on his part may not be necessary in order to gain benefits that will accrue to all class members anyway. The second cost arises in those situations where C does not have the right to prevent action by P and must offer payment to P in order to secure the benefits it desires. When C must pay, the class members will probably be unable to unite their interests effectively due to the collective-good phenomenon. Moreover, not only will there be no effective bargaining in such a situation, but claims will never be litigated: C has no enforceable right except the right to offer payment to P; P can presumably "enforce" his right to pollute without resorting to the courts. Since internalization of costs is the suggested raison d'être for antipollution litigation, and since internalization cannot occur when the single party has the enforceable right (it is unlikely that a representative of a defendant class could "bargain" with a polluter plaintiff on behalf of the class), it appears that the only effective means of structuring the subtantive law to allow internalization is to give enforceable rights to large groups rather than their single adversary. To some extent, the interpretation of class-action rules has substantive as well as procedural consequences. Substantive determinations result whenever the denial of a class action forecloses the possibility of any relief for those with small claims. To the extent that class actions succeed in establishing enforceable group rights, internalization is aided because agreement on class demands is more easily secured than agreement on a class payment offer.

Conference costs can also be reduced by the class-suit procedure. Assuming that a single pollutant source and its effects may be identified, and that there is a clearly defined right either to pollute or to be free from pollution, the mere threat of class litigation will still not induce P to reach a bargained solution with C. Even if C is given an enforceable right, there is, without a class action, no mechanism whereby a binding out-of-court agreement can be reached. It is only after a class suit is instituted and offers the prospect of judgment, including dismissal pursuant to a judicially approved settlement, that there is any way to bind all of the class members. Therefore, the class action serves not only as a means of setting group claims but as a means for awarding legal authority to the class representatives. In other words, the self-, but duly, appointed representative has the power to assert all of the class interests and thereby construct a bilateral, and manageable, "bargaining" situation from a multilateral, unmanageable situation.

The class action, then, serves two internalizing functions: (1) It provides an administratively workable means of combining group bargaining strength at minimum cost, and (2) by presenting the courts with an aggregated claim, it encourages courts to define substantive rights to the benefit of the large group, thereby creating a more effective bargaining force than exists when payments must be made from *C* to *P* . . . .

For recent developments on the class action, see, generally, Developments in the Law—Class Actions, 89 Harv.L.Rev. 1318 (1976), and the references contained therein. See pp. 80–95, supra.

2. THE NATURAL BASIS FOR GROUP LITIGATION: LIMITS UPON A LEGAL CONSTRUCT

Both the Kalven and Rosenfield essay and that by Wright presume that *intra*-group politics are relatively unproblematic. In a sense, this presumption is a natural consequence of perceiving the class action as a device for aggregating diffuse and unorganized individuals whose only commonality is formal. They claim to have "suffered" a legal injury which is identically defined by the norm. Such an aggregation is not a "group" and has no politics, though occasionally it may come to have such politics through a truly common experience of struggle against the perpetrator.

What, however, of groups that really are *groups* before the law creates them as legal entities? In the next article, Professor Yeazell considers the early history of group litigation and the differences between the 17th- and 18th-century English cases and the contemporary class action. Professor Bell in the article which concludes this chapter considers the intra-group or intra-class politics of school integration cases. His essay challenges us to consider whether the continued use of a formal construct may have an ultimately dehumanizing effect if it is imbued with a life on its own, apart from the natural persons for whom it was once a tool.

Stephen C. Yeazell, **Group Litigation and Social Context: Toward a History of the Class Action***

. . .

I.　The Conventional Wisdom and the Origins of the Class Action

[Zechariah] Chafee's . . . essay on the history and problems of the class action [published in 1950 in Some Problems of Equity] summarizes the widely accepted view of the origins of group litigation:

> Class suits began as an offshoot of bills of peace with multiple parties. A common-law action soon came to be a two-sided

* *Source*: 77 Colum.L.Rev. 866, 868–96 (1977). Acting Professor of Law, University of California at Los Angeles.

affair, usually with only one plaintiff and one defendant. .   .   .
[A] dispute of one person against many persons usually had to
come before the law courts, if at all, in the form of many separate
actions.   Hence it was far cheaper and more convenient to have a
single suit in chancery, which was accustomed to handle polygonal
controversies.   For example, bills of peace would be brought when
a lord of the manor sought to appropriate some of the village common lands for his own purposes to the loss of the manorial tenants,
as in How v. Tenants of Bromsgrove, before Lord Nottingham, or
when a vicar quarrelled with his parishioners about tithes.   In such
situations, each member of the multitude had the same interests
at stake as every other member, so that it was an obvious waste of
time to try the common question of law and fact over and over in
separate actions .   .   .   .   It was much more economical to get
everybody into a single chancery suit and settle the common questions once and for all.   In a sense, the multitude were interested in
one piece of property, the tithe, the village common or whatever
it might be.

    From such a bill of peace it was a natural step to the repre-
sentative suit.   .   .   .

Implicit in this passage are several assertions about the nature of early
group litigation and the forces shaping its development. First, there is the
assumption that efficiency was the guiding force behind Chancery's acceptance of this sort of case, the desire, as Chafee elsewhere put it, to make "one
lawsuit grow where two grew before" by aggregating multiparty common law
litigation. Second—and this is perhaps a more buried implication—we are
to read these cases, about tenants and lord, vicar and parishioners, as we would
modern ones, analogizing the rights in question to those in jointly owned
"property" and conceiving of the multitude's bond as an "interest."   Finally,
it is suggested that the sorts of cases listed are exemplary rather than exclusive. Examining these implications will be easier after a fuller description of the cases to which Chafee alludes.

    How v. Tenants of Bromsgrove [12] is typical of a line of cases in which
early group litigation doctrine took shape. How, the lord of the manor of
Bromsgrove, sued his tenants, claiming a grant of free warren [13] in certain
lands; the tenants on their part not only disputed the existence of such a
grant but also contended that even if it could be proved, its exercise would
leave them insufficient common—with the clear implication that such a finding would disenable the plaintiff from exercising his right. The somewhat
peculiar nature of this defense should signal us that a description of the dispute as one about a "piece of property" may be deceptive: the tenants argued
that the lord's grant—his claim to a piece of property—was outweighed when
measured against some other standard—the sufficiency of the commons remaining. The report is silent as to the standards by which such sufficiency

12. 23 Eng.Rep. 277 (Ch. 1681).

13. "*Free-warren* is a [royal] franchise
    .   .   .   giving the grantee a sole and
exclusive power of killing [hares, con-
eys, pheasant, and partridges] so far
as his warren extended.   .   .   ."
2 W. Blackstone, Commentaries * 38–9.

might be measured, but it assumes that such a measurement would be relevant and potentially dispositive of the case. Without further belaboring what is a brief report, we can question whether the lord was in fact trying to "appropriate some of the village common lands for his own purposes." For the heart of the villagers' defense seems to lie less in the contention that the disputed area "belonged" to them instead of to the lord, than in the assertion that even if How held title to the lands, he had—by virtue of what principle we are not told—to allow the tenants use of them because otherwise the portion left would be insufficient for their purposes. If "property" is the right category for this case, we must recognize that what is at issue is the blurred edge of property, as it shades into doctrines like waste and nuisance, rather than the sharper lines associated with title. If nothing else, then, this account of How and his tenants should suggest that analogies between seventeenth- and twentieth-century group litigation are precarious.

The second sort of case mentioned by Chafee, quarrels between vicar and parishioners about tithes, speaks of a world equally foreign to that of the modern class action. Brown v. Vermuden,[16] which he cites, involved a parish of lead miners and their parson, who asserted customary rights to purchase a tenth of the ore mined at a set price (apparently below market) per unit. The Reverend Brown was in fact attempting to enforce a right that had been decreed as a result of a former suit brought by one Carrier, his predecessor as vicar. In that action Carrier had claimed the right in question by virtue of immemorial custom; it was necessary to ground the suit on such a theory of prescription because tithes of mines, unlike tithes of agricultural produce, were not due at common law.

In order to compel payment, Carrier had apparently sued the entire parish, or at least all of the miners in it; they responded by naming four of their members to defend the suit for them. A student of the modern class action is struck by the explicitness of the "representation": in the place of talk about similarity of interest and adequacy of representation, we see representatives actually chosen by the group sued. As a result of these proceedings, "a *Decree* passed . . . that the Defendants and all the Miners would pay." At the same time, however, the court entered an order which seems strangely at odds with the apparently clear issue posed for decision, for "the Court who [*sic*] made the *Decree* held the 1d. per [unit] too little and ordered a Commission to settle some more reasonable Recompence to the Miners. . . ." One's first reaction is bewilderment: the plaintiff claims entitlement to a tenth of the ore at 1d. per unit; the court purports to uphold that claim, but in the same breath decides that one penny per unit is too little and postpones to some later date the decision of the crucial question.[20] From a practical standpoint the substance of the vicar's right is his ability to command the ore at a set price below market; to recognize the right to buy it and at the same time to throw open the question of how much he need pay is to take away with one hand what is given with the other.

16. 22 Eng.Rep. 802 (Ch. 1676).

20. The postponement in the event turned out to be indefinite; the commission that was to have issued for the adjustment of the miners' recompense was never executed . . . .

One regularly encounters such apparent anomalies in the earliest group litigation for which we have published reports, these equity suits from the seventeenth century. A number of facts strike the modern observer as peculiar. First, instances of group litigation involving defendant (as opposed to plaintiff) "classes" occur regularly. Second, the cases all involve substantive law that is largely a product of local custom rather than general common law. Third, none (including, in spite of what has already been said, Brown v. Vermuden) involve actions for money damages by or against a group. Finally, all involve disputes arising out of manor or parish communities . . . . .

II. Social Structure and Litigative Power

In the past four centuries, both peasant villagers and antibiotic purchasers have been treated by courts as entities for the purpose of litigation. Because of the different natures of these groups, their treatment as litigative units has performed different functions and has cast different political and economic reflections. Paradoxically, much of our difficulty in perceiving the significance of the old cases stems from the obviousness of the differences between villagers and pill-buyers; looking back at litigative groups of tenant farmers in the sixteenth and seventeenth centuries, we see contrasts so many and so great as to render these cases merely quaint, and this archaic cuteness blinds us to more significant structural distinctions. Seeing numerous superficial differences, we leap over a series of intermediate characteristics to assume that, *mutatis mutandis*, at the level of real importance the old and new cases deal with essentially similar problems. Yet it is precisely at the intermediate level that the most important differences appear.

For our purposes, the most significant of these facts about the old litigative groups is that the two instances cited by Chafee are not exemplary but, rather, typologically exclusive: not only *How* and *Brown* but *every* sixteenth- and seventeenth-century case of group litigation I have found involves the members of rural agricultural communities—manorial tenants, villagers, and parishioners. . . .   There is a sense in which it is even inaccurate to speak of "group litigation" as a category, but only of village, manor, and parish disputes. It follows that any understanding of these proceedings requires an examination of their social context.

A. Manor and Parish: The Status of Villagers in the Seventeenth Century

The manorial cases typically involved the successors of medieval villein tenants who owed to the manorial proprietor, by virtue of local manorial custom attaching to persons of their status, various obligations of labor and produce and who enjoyed, by virtue of the same status, certain rights in the communally cultivated glebe and commons. Originally unfree, these tenants in the course of the fourteenth and fifteenth centuries took advantage of vagaries in the labor supply and the increasing availability of employment in the cities to wring concessions from their lords; the most important of these was that of recording on the memorial rolls—and thereby freezing— the duties by which they held their tenements. Theretofore beyond the protection of royal justice, this class of farmers also succeeded in winning protection from the king's courts in the latter fifteenth century; after that time the chancellor regularly recognized and enforced manorial custom. Villein thus became copyholder and freeman; the tenement frequently became inheritable upon payment of a fine to the proprietor, and labor services were increasingly commuted to rent. The basis for the rights enjoyed and many of the duties owed still was local custom, however—some of which was unrecorded, as the "copy" often did not deal with such aspects of the tenancy as the amount of death duties.

It is the content of such customs that was at stake in much of the manorial group litigation. Thus, despite its transmutations, the original status relationship still served as the source of "law" in cases like How v. Tenants of Bromsgrove. The basis of the tenants' claim in that case, for example, was that they were entitled—by virtue of their status as copyholders—to sufficient commons land for ordinary purposes, without regard to the lord's grant. Claims of this sort were based neither on common law nor on a specific agreement, but, rather, on gradually accreted understandings between these agricultural groups and their superiors.

Such custom had emerged from the simmering tension between lord and tenants that was a constant feature of manorial life, and had the precarious durability of communal understandings that emerge from immemorial conflict. In the seventeenth-century disputes, however, one also sees a new factor. Manorial strife became more severe as lords bent on rationalizing agriculture, increasing their incomes, and (more frivolously but not insignificantly) hunting with the newly invented shotgun began to insist with full rigor on once-customary rights that had abated or fallen into desuetude. As one scholar has recently described it,

> [c]hanges affecting tenure, the exchange and consolidation of holdings, and disputes over lingering manorial obligations are commonplace throughout the seventeenth century. They were a part of the struggle by which both landlords and tenants sought to keep or gain security. . . . The litigation which often accompanied these efforts called frequently for a restatement of manorial customs (now sometimes being written down for the first time). . . . [51]

On the verge of the agricultural revolution, a social organization based on status and predicated upon a subsistence economy was being forced to confront the problems of distribution posed by a new order.

When the villagers turned from manor house to church, they confronted another network of customary duties. As residents of a parish, they were obliged to support the church. The obligation to tithe, like manorial duties, thus flowed from one's status. And like manorial duties, tithes were vigorously resisted in consequence of social change in the Restoration. Never popular, tithing for support of the established church took on a particularly distasteful quality as religious dissent spread in the late seventeenth century;

51. M. Keeler, Bibliography of British History, Stuart Period 274 (2d ed. 1970).

any tax was unpleasant, but it became odious if it went to support a religion one regarded as false. A fertile source of conflict was the tithe claimed by virtue of special prescriptive rights .   .   .   .   Such claims of custom could be challenged, however, and they were. Cases from this period in particular bespeak protracted resistance to the tithing of ore. As in Brown v. Vermuden, clergymen asserting claims to tithes were forced to sue and sue again. Those who opened new mines after the entry of a decree would assert that the prescriptive rights in question had not ripened as to them. More than "mere" custom, custom thought of as a local quirk or anomalous practice, is here at stake; it is a custom arising from a status relationship, a custom of an ancient, durable, and cohesive group, a custom shaped by the shifting balance of power between the group and its political and economic superiors.

B.   Village Organization

In both of their major social roles—as manorial tenants and as parishioners—the people involved in group litigation shared important characteristics. Most significantly, manor and parish were social and political units. On many manors the tenants lived in close proximity on a single village street.[57] Similarly, parishioners were within walking distance of the parish church. The enclosure movement that had begun before the Tudors and continued into the industrial revolution had begun to change the face of rural England, but it was still "a world of neighbors"—linked to each other by bonds of status.

More important for our purposes than the romantic notions that such a prospect may conjure up is that political organization matched this residential contiguity. For the rural village was not simply a convenient residence for tenant farmers, but an economic and political organization, with regularly chosen officers [59] and legislation governing local problems.[60] The village regulated its sowing, plowing, harvesting, marking of communally cultivated fields, maintenance of fences and roads, and pasturage of animals. Paralleling this secular organization was the parish, with its church wardens and overseers of the poor. Seventeenth-century group litigation thus grows out of two overlapping social institutions developed by rural communities to govern themselves interstitially and to deal with the secular and religious authorities that shaped their lives.

57. The nuclear village was probably the most common, though not the only, rural residential configuration.   .   .   .

59. The most common, and most important, of these locally chosen village officers was the reeve, who on most manors acted as a director and overseer of tenant efforts on the lord's land—and bore unwelcome responsibilities for the tenants' failure to perform the disliked customary duties. Officers seem to have been chosen at the required village attendance at the manorial court. In addition to choosing one of their members to serve as spokesman in relation to the lord, the villagers also chose men (often the same ones) to enforce the by-laws governing relationships among themselves.

.   .   .

60. The village by-laws characteristically set forth in minute (and to the modern observer frequently incomprehensible) detail rules to govern the use of communally-cultivated fields and the commons. Framed to deal with the intricately reciprocal behavior required for communal life in a subsistence economy, they often attain the pregnant opacity best known today to readers of the Internal Revenue Code.   .   .   .

C.   Group Litigation in a World of Status

To understand the social and political context of these cases is to question easy analogies between early group litigation and the modern class action. The differences flow from two of the features of sixteenth- and seventeenth-century social organization already sketched. First, the groups involved existed as social entities independent of the lawsuit. Second, the issues at stake involved incidents of status rather than individual claims of right. Individuals claimed or resisted their superior's claim only by virtue of their membership in the group, and all the rights and obligations involved were by definition identical since they flowed from the same relationship. Together these two circumstances quite profoundly alter what the modern observer assumes to be the causes and effects of litigation.

1.   *Transaction Costs at the Village Pond*

The first result of the social setting was that early group litigation did not perform the task which it does in modern class litigation—the overcoming of transaction costs, costs which in the typical modern representative suit are insuperable. In many modern classes, the class members are not a social group but simply those members of society who share some hypothesized interest. Because the class is not a group, class certification increases its strength. What was previously a mass of individuals becomes a litigative entity with representation and often enormous power. This newfound strength enables the group's representative both to give powerful voice to a common grievance whose dispersal over a large group made its effective communication theretofore difficult and to negotiate with its adversary from a position of aggregated strength.

No such effects attended Chancery's handling of early group litigation. First, the suit in equity did not give voice to the unvoiced grievance. Because tenants and parishioners had both social cohesion and political organization, the effort required to discover a common dissatisfaction and to communicate it to manorial and parochial superiors was very low; members of the two groups saw each other regularly, had spokesmen among whose duties it was to deal with the lord or parson in question, and possessed an official forum (assuming one was felt to be necessary) for the communication of the grievance—the manorial court or parish meeting. The same, of course, was true for the lord or parson; each was able to communicate easily with the group in question, and alleged derelictions of duty could be brought forcefully to the attention of the reeve and tithingman. Nor did the chancellor's recognition of tenants or parishioners as a group represent the sort of quantum leap in negotiating power that contemporary class certification does. Again, the pre-existing cohesion and organization of the group meant that the villagers reaped the advantages of concerted action and could insist upon treatment *as* a group without the necessity of court certification. Group cohesion and easy communication of the disputants thus meant that these early cases did not perform the functions we tend to associate with modern class litigation.

Chancery procedure reflected these social circumstances and provided that group litigation would not reach beyond this rural, communal world.

The requirements for bringing suit in such cases assumed that the group in question had chosen leaders and specifically authorized suit before seeking the court's recognition—that it had, in effect, pre-paid its transaction costs. In . . . passages from the notebooks of Lord Nottingham—passages available to earlier students of the class action only in manuscript and apparently unnoticed by subsequent scholars—the father of modern equity set forth a rule that is at odds with what we conceive to be the function of the modern class action:

> A bill to settle the customs of a manor wherein a multitude of tenants are concerned may be exhibited by any three in the name of the rest, so as they produce before the Register sufficient authority to enable them to sue in the name of the rest, and so as they be responsible for costs.[a]

To the modern observer (at least to one well-disposed toward class actions) such a requirement of individual consent in advance of the suit is at odds with the central purpose of the device—the overcoming of the costs of organizing an unconnected mass of individuals into a litigative entity. Because of the costs of communicating and negotiating with potential class members, proponents of the modern class action might quite accurately object that Lord Nottingham's procedure would vitiate its usefulness. The requirement of advance consent becomes explicable and natural, however, when one realizes that such authorization could be easily obtained in the relatively small and cohesive groups characteristic of seventeenth-century litigation.

2. *Contiguity and Collusion*

Another result of the social structure of the groups involved and their relationship to their adversaries was that at least some of the group litigation in this period was collusive. Because they could easily bargain, the parties sometimes reached settlements; after themselves resolving a dispute about custom, lord and tenants would then arrange for a collusive action in which one side would allege and the other confess the agreed-upon customs. Such a collusive suit created a permanent record in an extra-manorial forum, one which had, at least theoretically, enforcement powers and a national status that lent greater authority to the negotiated agreement. The existence of these amicable suits is important because it makes explicable the chancellor's attitude to other actions that were not friendly: with such suits frequently arranged, he showed some reluctance to impose rigid decrees in suits that were not, an attitude that makes less bizarre some of the vagueness in a decree like that entered in Carrier's suit, the predecessor case in Brown v. Vermuden.

Amicability has its limits, however, when the economic stakes are real. Then, as now, litigation implies a dispute. Thus not all suits were collusive, and decrees, whether negotiated or not, were frequently disobeyed.

---

a. Lord Nottingham's "Manual of Chancery Practice," and "Prolegomena of Chancery and Equity" 95 (D.E.C. Yale, ed. 1965). Ed. note.

3. *Social Structure and the Defendant Class*

Both in collusive and in contested suits one encounters another sign of the social universe in which villagers and parishioners dwelt—the defendant group. Today a rarity, it occurred in the sixteenth and seventeenth centuries as frequently as did the plaintiff group. The reasons lie in the characteristics of the groups in question and the limited redistributional effects of Chancery recognition. Since group litigation promised no additional power to these groups, their decisions to sue were made on the same bases as in single-party litigation: the cost of the lawsuit, the probabilities of victory, and the significance of victory.

Chancery suits were already notoriously expensive and prolonged in the seventeenth century. While a victorious party might, in the discretion of the chancellor, be awarded the costs (including attorney fees), there are some indications that chancellors in the latter seventeenth century viewed the mere bringing of such an action by tenants as a species of harassment mitigated only slightly by their having sought to litigate as a group. Under such circumstances tenants might well have felt the chances of the chancellor's discretion smiling upon them to be slight. Should they lose, on the other hand, they could be visited with their adversary's costs as well as their own. The attractions of group litigation for plaintiff groups—though not insignificant—were therefore less than overwhelming. When named as defendants, however, the group members might find litigative aggregation more useful. At that point the desirability of financing a lawsuit was no longer in question; the problem was rather how best to deal with one already thrust upon them. In such a situation it is scarcely surprising that if they decided to mount a defense at all, they should have chosen representatives to do battle as their champions.

More fundamental than any economic asymmetry, however, were the facts of social structure. Economically, socially, and politically subordinate in the relationship from which these disputes grew, copyhold tenants and parishioners seem less likely than their lords and parsons to have thought of the courts as a way of resolving a dispute. They would have had but scant familiarity with legal procedures or personnel and, it is fair to speculate, would have felt the countryman's distrust of both. They could quite accurately have sensed that the courts were populated by persons far more likely to see things through their lord's eyes than theirs and, if they thought about it at all, that the subtantive law had not been designed with their interests at heart. Under such circumstances it is less than surprising that we find villagers appearing as defendants as often as plaintiffs in such litigation; once again the apparently peculiar aspects of early group litigation flow from its contemporary role and the special characteristics of the groups involved.

4. *Status, Permanence, and the Mediatory Decree*

The permanence of the social and economic bonds involved in these cases is another characteristic that must alter our usual assumptions about the relationship between dispute and litigation. Lord and tenant, parson and parishioner were bound to each other, if not until death—for manors did occasionally change hands and parsons parishes—at least for the foreseeable future. Each could, within the bounds of his mutual rights and obligations, significantly affect the other's lot in life, and would have the power to do so for some time to come. This power had a dual significance. On one hand, it meant that the parties could apply various sorts of pressure before litigation. On the other, the permanence of the relationship meant that the parties risked less by resorting to litigation.

Unhappy tenants could bring in crops and fulfill other obligations with a reluctance verging on immobility, and a similarly disposed lord might insist on a punctilious attention to rights that made life difficult; parsons and their flocks could likewise be intransigent with each other. The sociology of contemporary litigation suggests that under such conditions the parties will resort to the courts only in cases of desperation, where the relationship has broken down completely; a corollary is that litigation will certainly bury the relationship irrevocably. Assuming that all this is true about modern litigation, we nonetheless have reasons to doubt its applicability to seventeenth-century group litigation. First, parson and parishioner, lord and tenant were tied to each other to a far greater extent than the relationships we perceive today as "permanent," e. g., marriage, long-term producer-supplier dealings. Real permanence means that the partners need not fear severance of the relationship as a result of litigation. Consequently, what a modern observer could assume to have been a relatively desperate, final gesture— the bringing of a suit—may in fact have been a far less momentous occurrence.

Such speculation finds support in a second characteristic of these cases: the nature of the decrees entered in them. One reason we tend to assume that litigation will end a long-term relationship today is that contemporary judgments tend to have a sharp, all-or-nothing quality to them: plaintiff or defendant wins; the sum claimed is or is not due; the contract has or has not been breached. Our look at *Brown* and *How* suggested that the chancellor in these cases was entering a very different sort of decree, one far less likely to have the disruptive effects on the relationship that we associate with modern judicial declarations.[86] . . .

III. Litigation as Legislation: The Decreeing of Custom

However tentative his decrees or hesitant their enforcement, the chancellor's exercise of his jurisdiction in these cases ultimately cannibalized itself; the very operation of early group litigation tended to destroy the social conditions from which it grew and thus to eliminate the basis for the jurisdiction. By depriving a body of customary law of the last element of free

86. This less disruptive effect of Chancery decrees was due to several factors. First, the effectuation of the chancellor's order often entailed a commissioner's report, and as in *Brown*, such orders were frequently not carried out. Second, because the chancellor obviously preferred that the parties settle the matter themselves, he apparently sometimes simply decreed that they should do so, as when Magdalen College was "compelled to an agreement." Prebends & Scholars of Magdalen College v. Hide, 21 Eng. Rep. 138 (Ch. 1612). Such an order gave the parties considerable negotiating room. Finally, even when the chancellor had entered a relatively certain decree, there seemed to be little reluctance to reconsider or alter it. . . .

play in its joints, Chancery hastened its demise, and with it the demise of the rural communities which created that law. With the extinction of these communities, the social context and rationale for early group litigation were gone. One result of this disappearance is the difficulty the modern observer has in understanding the significance of early group litigation. The operation of a now-vanished customary law meant that litigation had strange and to modern eyes paradoxical effects.

A. The Nature of Custom

By common understanding the issue in these cases was what the long-standing practice of a particular manor or parish had been. Because the custom at issue was supposed to be local and particular, it could, unlike the law of assault, vary from place to place without offending anyone's sense of propriety; the fines of the tenants of Wem could differ from those of Bromsgrove, and thus the actual custom in any given case was essentially a question of fact. To characterize an issue as "factual" is, of course, to release it from the legal order's myth of uniformity, to permit it to vary with the balance of power struck in any given locality.

In both practice and theory, however, this particularity was tempered, for common law and equity alike recognized boundaries to the variety of customs that they would enforce, boundaries characterized as those of "reasonableness." The injection of the doctrine of reasonableness into these cases meant that Chancery would allow great variety in the distribution of wealth among lords and tenants, parsons and parishioners, but would interfere at the edges of oppression on the ground that, as one case put it, "the Will of the Lord ought to be limited." Such boundaries of course brought a species of uniformity to practice; at the same time, they began the transformation of fact into law. As they did so, they worked important changes in the relationships of power between the parties to the custom in question. Such changes were, however, obscured and denied by the terms in which the discourse concerning them took place.

The very words of the parties' allegations concerning the custom—that it had been so done time out of mind—insisted that whatever the custom was, it was constant. In fact, we can be fairly certain that the custom was anything but static. In recent decades anthropoligical field work in societies with unwritten customary law has demonstrated that, however constant in theory, customs in practice change in response to realignments of power. Because the customs themselves reside only in memory, these changes need not be overtly acknowledged; changes in rules become submerged in disputes about who is accurately recalling past practice. . . .

B. The Decreeing of Custom

In the seventeenth century the increasing rigidity of custom had brought copyhold tenant and lord to a critical stage in their relationship. Manorial duties, once entirely a function of customary law, had long been recorded and thereby fixed. For the tenant in a time of rising prices this freezing of duties meant an increase in real income and the promise of even greater security in the future; for the lord it threatened the loss of income and social position. Rents and other obligations bore a decreasing relationship to the value of the copyhold tenement. Yet renegotiation of its terms was impossible, for the relationship did not purport to be contractual and rarely expired of its own accord; it therefore gave the tenant virtually no incentive to accede to alterations in it.

In such a situation, particularly in a period of rapid economic change like that which occurred in the sixteenth and seventeenth centuries, any remnants of customary law—still unrecorded and therefore variable—will come under considerable pressure as each side tries to use them to hold or win advantage. One avenue of escape for proprietors was an increase in the fines exacted for succession to copyhold lands; frequently unrecorded, they could be raised as other incidents, fixed by roll entry, could not. . . .

A Chancery decree, declaring the customs of the manor, fixed the duties owed and assimilated this relationship into the modern world of rational economic enterprise. The proprietor, now able to calculate with certainty the income from his holdings, could begin to enter the world of agricultural entrepreneurship that was emerging in the late seventeenth century. . . . .

Paradoxically, however, the injection of such elements of modernity into an all-but-ossified body of customary law did not enable it to survive in the brave new world of agricultural capitalism; instead it helped to kill the copyhold. A Chancery decree as to fines tended to eliminate the last area of flexibility, the last lever for negotiating adjustments in the relationship. By taking at face value the legitimating assertion of customary law —that it was unchanging—and by translating that assertion into practice, Chancery destroyed the flexibility upon which customary law in a status relationship depends. After such a declaration, the proprietor could realize the value of his land only by ignoring the decree or by abolishing the copyhold itself. The evidence suggests that in the eighteenth century the parties to such disputes at first tried to bargain over the remaining expense of enforcing the decree. Finally, however, this maneuvering room proved too small to satisfy a politically ascendant squirarchy, and copyhold was largely eradicated by Parliamentary acts in a movement characterized by Trevelyan as "radicalism of the rich, often at the expense of the poor." [b] . . .

C. An Anachronistic View of Remedies

One of the obstacles to an accurate perception of this complex relationship between custom, law, and the market has been a misunderstanding of the relief sought and granted in these early instances of group litigation. The old cases speak occasionally in terms of preventing multiplicity of suits at common law, and modern commentators have taken these statements to mean that Chancery was aggregating common law damage actions and was awarding damages for the past transgression of previously known legal standards. In fact, no such thing occurred; I have found no instance of early group litigation that involved such an aggregated claim for money damages.

Rather, the seventeenth-century cases involving groups render declarations of prospective legal obligation. In many respects the closest modern analogy to these cases is the action for a declaratory judgment; indeed the

b. G. Trevelyan, English Social History 376 (1942). Ed. note.

early cases and treatises speak in just such terms: "This Court will reduce the general Customs of a Mannor [sic] to a certainty. . . ."[115] It is in such a light that one must understand the frequently cited statements of the early cases that Chancery assumed jurisdiction to prevent multiplicity of suits. Obviously, a Chancery decree could have such an effect—not, however, because it aggregated common law damage actions as the modern class action often does, but because it established the law prospectively binding sizable groups. A modern declaratory judgment can reduce litigation by determining the legal consequences of certain courses of action before the parties have committed themselves irrevocably; similarly, a decree in Chancery, authoritatively setting forth—in advance of particular disputes—the customs of the manor or parish, could prevent the multiple lawsuits that might otherwise be brought. Indeed, in the manor or parish context, the prophylactic effect of the declaratory judgment is magnified, for it applies to numerous legally identical relationships. But it is in such ascertainment of law before the fact, rather than in the aggregation of claims afterwards, that the preventive qualities of early group litigation lie . . . .

Several of the seventeenth-century cases do in fact involve a prayer that the defendant pay damages, but not as part of group litigation in the first instance. The typical case of this sort involved two separate proceedings: first, group litigation leading to a decree embodying the relevant customs; then—and only then—a second proceeding against those who *thereafter* refused to abide by the decree. In such a procedure . . . no damages are awarded for past failure to comply with the rules reflected in the initial decree; they come only as a consequence of future departure from its regime. From a modern perspective the distinction is crucial: it marks the difference between prospective and retrospective legal action, between legislation and adjudication. Brown v. Booth,[125] a miner's case, provides a good example. There the report indicates that the plaintiff vicar was seeking an award of damages—not, however, as the immediate aftermath of a decree, but rather pursuant to a declaration of custom entered some sixty years previously. To describe such a suit as group litigation involving money damages significantly distorts its nature. Enforced payment of money could indeed follow a decree—but not until the group in question had been given notice of the terms of Chancery's resolution of the dispute.

D. The Decree as Legislation

It is not difficult to understand why the chancellor in these cases did not award damages in the first instance. . . . [H]e was engaged in a process that to a modern observer looks more like legislation than adjudication. A rule, generally applicable to a group of persons in particular social circumstances, was promulgated for the first time—a rule that, unlike a common law judgment, did not purport to result from simply applying a preexisting legal standard to particular facts. The particularity of the custom, Chancery's power to alter it in accordance with a vaguely defined standard of "reasonableness," and the chancellor's willingness to range far from the

---

115. Anon., The Practick Part of Law   125. 23 Eng.Rep. 720 (Ch. 1690).
367 (1676).

original issues posed by the parties in seeking a resolution of the dispute distinguished these cases from run-of-the-mill common law adjudication. Moreover, the decree governed future behavior of the parties, not merely in the sense that they could (as with any decided case) guide themselves by reference to its ratio decidendi, but because in its own terms it established the mode of their future conduct to one another; its command was explicit rather than implicit. One need not resort to modern conceptions of due process to understand why a seventeenth-century chancellor would hesitate to impose retroactive liability under such conditions. Chancery was self-consciously altering—and then fixing in an altered state—the balance of manorial power; with such self-awareness, the normal justification for retrospective judgments fell away.

Understanding the relief sought and given in the early cases clarifies the apparent abandon with which courts bound absent group members. Chafee [at 203] noted this tendency and wondered at "[t]he incongruity which startles us today . . . the disregard of the requirement that a man ought to have his day in court. . . . Oddly enough, this matter of binding the omitted parties did not seem to bother the older judges. . . ." Because Chafee assumed that early group litigation cases had retrospectively awarded money damages, he quite properly saw them as at odds with a concern for what we would now call due process. Once one realizes that the relief sought was a declaration of custom, the problem seems far less urgent. Having one's day in court loses some of its significance if what the court does at the end of that day is simply to declare what shall be the law tomorrow, without retrospectively applying that law to a specific dispute.

An appreciation of the differing impacts of money awards and declarations of custom does more than explain the binding of absentees; it also enables us to understand why Chancery's intervention did not destroy the copyhold long before the late eighteenth century. Decrees required enforcement in individual cases, and Chancery enforcement procedings were, by the latter seventeenth century, already notoriously uncertain and expensive. A declaration of custom thus rigidified but did not entirely freeze the parochial or manorial relationship. It lent to the prevailing side considerable strength, robbed custom of its unacknowledged slack, and made negotiation depend on willingness to ignore a specific court order—but it left some room for maneuver. Thus Chancery, apparently less by policy than through delay and cost, created at the margin of its decrees a new bargaining possibility, one much more characteristic of a modern economy than the adjustment of customary law which it had replaced. Purporting to establish relations on a prospective basis, the decrees in practice left their subjects room for difference about the realization of the new order thus decreed.

E.   "Adjudication" and Political Accommodation

Recognizing the form of relief administered in the manorial and parochial cases enables one to understand why the decrees in such cases did not eliminate copyhold at a fell swoop. It also solves Chafee's puzzlement over Chancery's willingness to bind by the decree persons who had not been parties to the suit. But it raises a new question of why, if the relief involved was invariably prospective, Chancery felt it necessary to assure itself that all the tenants had authorized suit in the first place. If Chafee's problem stemmed from the fact that in some respects Chancery failed to act as a modern court adjudicating a damage claim, the problem from our present perspective is rather why Chancery felt it necessary to behave like a modern court in *any* respect. It was, after all, engaged in a process very much like legislation or administrative rule-making, and we do not feel it necessary to obtain the consent of each potentially affected person for the introduction of a bill in the legislature or the initiation of a rule-making procedure.

Our perplexity flows from an anachronistically narrow view of the chancellor's function. Having constructed a government and numerous governmental institutions on the proposition that rule-making and adjudication are to be kept separate, we find anomalous the existence of one function within the institutional structure and procedure of the other. But there is little evidence that the chancellor saw the contrast between them that we perceive. Indeed, the whole history of Chancery jurisdiction over copyhold matters suggests that no one in the seventeenth century would have been very concerned about such a combination of functions. From the first, equity had entered this field as an instrument of royal political and social policy rather than as a strictly "adjudicative" tribunal.

Henry II's great expansion of royal jurisdiction had stopped short of the villeins, predecessors to later copyholders; to have extended the reach of the king's writs further would have seriously interfered with the jurisdiction of the manorial courts and with a baronage already upset about royal trespasses on the fees they had theretofore exacted for seignorial justice. But by the end of the Wars of the Roses in the latter fifteenth century the resurgent monarchy could safely ignore protests from an aristocracy whose members tended to be either dead or eight years old. More importantly, the Crown now had something to gain both politically and economically from an extension of royal protection to a group of farmers of much greater consequence than they had been two centuries before. Accordingly, Chancery, the branch of the judiciary most easily amenable to royal policy, began to extend at least limited protection to copyholders in the fifteenth century— at first hesitantly, but by the Tudor accession as a matter of course. Indeed, by the mid-sixteenth century the jurisdiction had become sufficiently well-established, and royal and aristocratic concern about the vagrant poor (widely believed to be former manorial tenants dispossessed by greedily enclosing lords) so intense, that even the common law was recognizing the claims of individual copyholders.

In spite of the institutionalization and acceptance of Chancery jurisdiction over the copyholder, however, we should not lose sight of the essentially political nature of the original extension of jurisdiction. Chancery was, after all, still as much an administrative arm of the Crown as a court in the modern sense of the word, and its chief executive officer exercised a correspondingly broad discretionary power. The chancellor in these manorial cases exercised this discretion to mediate between two important groups in the most significant sector of the economy. To perform this task he needed considerable flexibility, which he achieved by tempering his ability to alter a custom by reference to its unreasonableness with the prospective nature of

the relief granted.   Altering the balance of manorial power, he sweetened
the pill by giving the affected parties time to adjust to the new regime.   Seen
in this context, the requirement that all the tenants have authorized the suit
becomes less a means of justifying res judicata effects, as Chafee saw it, than
a method of assuring the court that it could rely on the point of view espoused
by the group's chosen spokesman, a means of checking the lobbyist's credentials rather than of assuring due process in an adjudication.

IV.   Procedure and Society

From the vantage point we have gained, it may be useful to look back
at our starting place.   How v. Tenants of Bromsgrove and Brown v. Vermuden take on different shapes and significance viewed from the perspective
of village organization and customary law.   *How*, for instance, seems to be
less a case about property than a dispute about the residual force of customary law, a law that the chancellor would, in his very proclaiming of it,
effectively put out of existence.   At a more basic level, however, the Chancery proceedings were not a "case" at all, as we presently conceive of the
meaning of that word; the chancellor, in declaring whether and to what
extent How enjoyed a right of free warren, was mediating and legislating—
arbitrating a dispute and declaring a rule that would prospectively govern
the parties' relations.   The chancellor *had to* announce such a rule, because
the parties' relationship was permanent and guidance for the future was
needed; he *could* do so for the whole group, because its members, possessed
of a means of communication and a political organization, had agreed to participate.   Both substance and procedure thus grow from the same manorial
soil.

Brown v. Vermuden reveals a different stage in a similar pattern.   The
stage of declaration, with which *How* is concerned, had taken place some
time before the suit; the new question was its effect on persons not party
to that action.   The defendant miner in effect argued that the previous proceedings should have been viewed as a lawsuit and that, because he was not
a party to that suit, he was not bound by its result.   The court, of course,
rejected such reasoning—and the concept of Chancery's role in group litigation that it implied—for reasons that speak more of a social and economic
vision than of a doctrine of former adjudication: "If the Defendant should
not be bound, Suits of this Nature, as in case of Inclosures, Suit against the
Inhabitants for Suit to a Mill, and the like, would be infinite, and impossible
to be ended."   The chancellor was right: suits about the content of custom
between parties in continuous relationship *would* be impossible to be ended,
because custom is elusive and accommodating.   His answer was to abolish
custom and make it into law, which, operating prospectively, would bind all
persons who came within its terms.   The miner, Vermuden, thus lost his
case, because he argued it as if it *were* a case; under the circumstances, it
was the only argument open to him, but it could not prevail if equity were
to complete the modernization of law and the destruction of custom that it
had undertaken in the previous century.

That the modernization took place under the cover of a legal fiction
must not deceive us as it did Vermuden.   By taking at face value the claim

of custom to be eternal and unchanging.   Chancery did away with it, and in the process misled the hapless miner into arguing as if the former decree had merely found a fact.   By taking at face value Chancery's claim to be merely declaring custom, we shall similarly distort beyond understanding the significance of these cases.   Such distortion may be a useful tool of legal change—indeed in the following century it proved essential [146]—but with the moment of procedural change and its concomitant need for such a passionately instrumental view of legal history in temporary abeyance, we may have more to gain from a different perspective.

By understanding what happens when something calling itself a lawsuit involves the entire universe of persons covered by the applicable law, we can more easily comprehend some of the problems in public litigation .   .   .   . By understanding the relatively insignificant effect that recognition by a court has on a group in which the costs of communication have been overcome, we can see why modern class litigation (which in effect pays such costs from the public fisc) has excited controversy, as its ancestor did not. More fundamentally, the interaction between group and law in these earliest reported instances of group litigation reminds us that the law's position as a social artifact, and the courts' function as agencies of social and economic control, preclude easy assumptions that formally similar procedural devices play similar roles in different social circumstances.   .   .   .

Derrick A. Bell, Jr., Serving Two Masters: Integration Ideals and Client Interests in School Desegregation Litigation*

.   .   .   The great crusade to desegregate the public schools has faltered. There is increasing opposition to desegregation at both local and national levels (not all of which can now be simply condemned as "racist"), while the once vigorous support of federal courts is on the decline.   New barriers have arisen—inflation makes the attainment of racial balance more expensive, the growth of black populations in urban areas renders it more difficult, an increasing number of social science studies question the validity of its educational assumptions.

Civil rights lawyers dismiss these new obstacles as legally irrelevant. Having achieved so much by courageous persistence, they have not waivered in their determination to implement *Brown* using racial balance measures developed in the hard-fought legal battles of the last two decades.   This stance involves great risk for clients whose educational interests may no longer accord with the integration ideals of their attorneys.   .   .   .

Lawyer-Client Conflicts: Sources and Rationale

A.   Civil Rights Rigidity Surveyed

Having convinced themselves that *Brown* stands for desegregation and not education, the established civil rights organizations steadfastly refuse

146.   It proved essential as Chancery adapted the old forms of group litigation to new purposes, for it handled such suits *as* adjudication.   .   .   .

* *Source*: 85 Yale L.J. 470, 470–72, 482–93, 502–16 (1976). Professor of Law, Harvard University.

to recognize reverses in the school desegregation campaign—reverses which, to some extent, have been precipitated by their rigidity. They seem to be reluctant to evaluate objectively the high risks inherent in a continuation of current policies.

1. The Boston Case

The Boston school litigation [36] provides an instructive example of what, I fear, is a widespread situation. Early in 1975, I was invited by representatives of Boston's black community groups to meet with them and NAACP lawyers over plans for Phase II of Boston's desegregation effort. Implementation of the 1974 plan had met with violent resistance that received nationwide attention. Even in the lulls between the violent incidents, it is unlikely that much in the way of effective instruction was occurring at many of the schools. NAACP lawyers had retained experts whose proposals for the 1975–1976 school year would have required even more busing between black and lower class white communities. The black representatives were ambivalent about the busing plans. They did not wish to back away after years of effort to desegregate Boston's schools, but they wished to place greater emphasis on upgrading the schools' educational quality, to maintain existing assignments at schools which were already integrated, and to minimize busing to the poorest and most violent white districts. In response to a proposal filed by the Boston School Committee, they sent a lengthy statement of their position directly to District Judge W. Arthur Garrity.

At the meeting I attended, black representatives hoped to convince the lawyers to incorporate their educational priorities into the plaintiffs' Phase II desegregation plan. The lawyers assigned to the Boston case by the NAACP listened respectfully to the views of the black community group, but made clear that a long line of court decisions would limit the degree to which those educational priorities could be incorporated into the desegregation plan the lawyers were preparing to file. That plan contained far more busing to balance the racial populations of the schools than was eventually approved by the federal court. Acting on the recommendations of appointed masters, Judge Garrity adopted several provisions designed to improve the quality of the notoriously poor Boston schools. But as in the Detroit and Atlanta cases discussed below, these provisions were more the product of judicial initiative than of civil rights advocacy.

2. The Detroit Case

The determination of NAACP officials to achieve racial balance was also tested in the Detroit school case. Having failed in efforts to obtain an interdistrict metropolitan remedy in Detroit,[42] the NAACP set out to achieve a unitary system, in a school district that was over 70 percent black. The district court rejected an NAACP plan designed to require every school to reflect (within a range of 15 percent in either direction) the ratio of whites

36. Morgan v. Hennigan, 379 F.Supp. 410 (D.Mass.), aff'd sub nom. Morgan v. Kerrigan, 509 F.2d 580 (1st Cir. 1974), cert. denied 421 U.S. 963 (1975).
. . .

42. See Milliken v. Bradley, 418 U.S. 717 (1974).

to blacks in the school district as a whole, and approved a desegregation plan that emphasized educational reform rather than racial balance.[43] The NAACP General Counsel, Nathaniel R. Jones, reportedly called the decision "an abomination" and "a rape of the constitutional rights of black children," and indicated his intention to appeal immediately.

3. The Atlanta Case

Prior to Detroit, the most open confrontation between NAACP views of school integration and those of local blacks who favored plans oriented toward improving educational quality occurred in Atlanta. There, a group of plaintiffs became discouraged by the difficulty of achieving meaningful desegregation in a district which had gone from 32 percent black in 1952 to 82 percent black in 1974. Lawyers for the local NAACP branch, who had gained control of the litigation, worked out a compromise plan with the Atlanta School Board that called for full faculty and employee desegregation but for only limited pupil desegregation. In exchange, the school board promised to hire a number of blacks in top administrative positions, including a black superintendent of schools.

The federal court approved the plan.[45] The court's approval was apparently influenced by petitions favoring the plan's adoption signed by several thousand members of the plaintiffs' class. Nevertheless the national NAACP office and LDF[a] lawyers were horrified by the compromise. The NAACP ousted the Atlanta branch president who had supported the compromise. Then, acting on behalf of some local blacks who shared their views, LDF lawyers filed an appeal in the Atlanta case. The appeal also raised a number of procedural issues concerning the lack of notice and the refusal of the district court to grant hearings on the Compromise Plan. These issues gave the Fifth Circuit an opportunity to remand the case to the district court without reaching the merits of the settlement agreement.[48] Undaunted, LDF lawyers again attacked the plan for failing to require busing of whites into the predominantly black schools in which a majority of the students in the system were enrolled. But the district court's finding that the system had achieved unitary status was upheld by the same Fifth Circuit panel.[49]

As in Detroit, NAACP opposition to the Atlanta Compromise Plan was not deterred by the fact that local leaders, including black school board members, supported the settlement. Defending the Compromise Plan, Dr. Benjamin E. Mays, one of the most respected black educators in the country, stated:

> We have never argued that the Atlanta Compromise Plan is
> the best plan, nor have we encouraged any other school system

43. Bradley v. Milliken, 402 F.Supp. 1096 (E.D.Mich.1975), . . . [subsequently aff'd, 433 U.S. 267 (1977)].

45. Calhoun v. Cook, 362 F.Supp. 1249 (N.D.Ga.1973). . . .

a. The NAACP Legal Defense Fund. Ed. note.

48. Calhoun v. Cook, 487 F.2d 680 (5th Cir. 1973). . . .

49. Calhoun v. Cook, 522 F.2d 717 (5th Cir. 1975). . . .

to adopt it. This plan is the most viable plan for Atlanta—a city school system that is 82 percent black and 18 percent white and is continuing to lose whites each year to five counties that are more than 90 percent white.

. . .

More importantly, black people must not resign themselves to the pessimistic view that a non-integrated school cannot provide black children with an excellent educational setting. Instead, black people, while working to implement *Brown*, should recognize that integration alone does not provide a quality education, and that much of the substance of quality education can be provided to black children in the interim.[50]

B.   Alternatives to the Rigidity of Racial Balance

Dr. Mays's thoughtful statement belies the claim that *Brown* can be implemented only by the immediate racial balancing of school populations. But civil rights groups refuse to recognize what courts in Boston, Detroit, and Atlanta have now made obvious: where racial balance is not feasible because of population concentrations, political boundaries, or even educational considerations, there is adequate legal precedent for court-ordered remedies that emphasize educational improvement rather than racial balance.

The plans adopted in these cases were formulated without the support and often over the objection of the NAACP and other civil rights groups. They are intended to upgrade educational quality, and like racial balance, they may have that effect. But neither the NAACP nor the court-fashioned remedies are sufficiently directed at the real evil of pre-*Brown* public schools: the state-supported subordination of blacks in every aspect of the educational process. Racial separation is only the most obvious manifestation of this subordination. Providing unequal and inadequate school resources and excluding black parents from meaningful participation in school policymaking are at least as damaging to black children as enforced separation.   .   .   .

C.   The Organization and Its Ideals

Civil rights lawyers have long experience, unquestioned commitment, and the ability to organize programs that have helped bring about profound changes in the last two decades. Why, one might ask, have they been so unwilling to recognize the increasing futility of "total desegregation," and, more important, the increasing number of defections within the black community? A few major factors that underlie this unwillingness can be identified.

1.   Racial Balance as a Symbol

For many civil rights workers, success in obtaining racially balanced schools seems to have become a symbol of the nation's commitment to equal opportunity.   .   .   .

---

50. Mays, Comment: Atlanta — Living with *Brown* Twenty Years Later, 3   Black L.J. 184, 190, 191–192 (1974).
.   .   .

2. *Clients and Contributors*

The hard-line position of established civil rights groups on school desegregation is explained in part by pragmatic considerations. These organizations are supported by middle class blacks and whites who believe fervently in integration. At their socioeconomic level, integration has worked well, and they are certain that once whites and blacks at lower economic levels are successfully mixed in the schools, integration also will work well at those levels. Many of these supporters either reject or fail to understand suggestions that alternatives to integrated schools should be considered, particularly in majority-black districts. They will be understandably reluctant to provide financial support for policies which they think unsound, possibly illegal, and certainly disquieting. . . .

Jack Greenberg, LDF Director-Counsel, acknowledges that fund-raising concerns may play a small role in the selection of cases.[57] Even though civil rights lawyers often obtain the clients, Greenberg reports, "there may be financial contributors to reckon with who may ask that certain cases be brought and others not." He hastens to add that within broad limits lawyers "seem to be free to pursue their own ideas of right, . . . affected little or not at all by contributors." The reassurance is double-edged. The lawyers' freedom to pursue their own ideas of right may pose no problems as long as both clients and contributors share a common social outlook. But when the views of some or all of the clients change, a delayed recognition and response by the lawyers is predictable.

School expert Ron Edmonds contends that civil rights attorneys often do not represent their clients' best interests in desegregation litigation because "they answer to a miniscule constituency while serving a massive clientele." [60] Edmonds distinguishes the clients of civil rights attorneys (the persons on whose behalf suit is filed) from their "constituents" (those to whom the attorney must answer for his actions). He suggests that in class action school desegregation cases the mass of lower class black parents and children are merely clients. To define constituents, Edmonds asks, "[To] what class of Americans does the civil rights attorney feel he must answer for his professional conduct?" The answer can be determined by identifying those with whom the civil rights attorney confers as he defines the goals of the litigation. He concludes that those who currently have access to the civil rights attorney are whites and middle class blacks who advocate integration and categorically oppose majority black schools.

Edmonds suggests that, more than other professionals, the civil rights attorney labors in a closed setting isolated from most of his clients. No matter how numerous, the attorney's clients cannot become constituents unless they have access to him before or during the legal process. The result is the pursuit of metropolitan desegregation without sufficient regard for the probable instructional consequences for black children. In sum, he charges,

57. Greenberg, Litigation for Social Change: Methods, Limits and Role in Democracy, 29 Record of N.Y.C.B.A. 320 (1974).

60. Edmonds, Advocating Inequity: A Critique of the Civil Rights Attorney in Class Action Desegregation Suits, 3 Black L.J. 176 (1974). . . .

"A class action suit serving only those who pay the attorney fee has the effect of permitting the fee paying minority to impose its will on the majority of the class on whose behalf suit is presumably brought."

It goes without saying that civil rights lawyers take the strongest exception to Edmonds' position. NAACP General Counsel Nathaniel Jones denies that school suits are brought only at the behest of middle class blacks, and points out what he considers to be the absurdity of attempting to poll the views of every black before a school desegregation suit is filed. But at the same time he states that his responsibility is to square NAACP litigation with his interpretation of what Supreme Court decisions require.[64]

3. *Client-Counsel Merger*

The position of the established civil rights groups obviates any need to determine whether a continued policy of maximum racial balance conforms with the wishes of even a minority of the class. This position represents an extraordinary view of the lawyer's role. Not only does it assume a perpetual retainer authorizing a lifelong effort to obtain racially balanced schools. It also fails to reflect any significant change in representational policy from a decade ago, when virtually all blacks assumed that integration was the best means of achieving a quality education for black children, to the present time, when many black parents are disenchanted with the educational results of integration. Again, Mr. Jones would differ sharply with my evaluation of black parents' educational priorities, but his statement indicates that it would make no difference if I were correct. The Supreme Court has spoken in response to issues raised in litigation begun and diligently pursued by his agency. The interpretation of the Court's response by him and other officials has then determined NAACP litigation policies.

This malady may afflict many idealistic lawyers who seek, through the class action device, to bring about judicial intervention affecting large segments of the community. The class action provides the vehicle for bringing

---

64. Letter from Nathaniel R. Jones to author, July 31, 1975:

It would be absurd to expect that each and every black person should be polled before a lawsuit is filed, or a plan of desegregation is proposed. Certainly, school boards, who resist these suits, do not poll their patrons on their views before shaping a position.

The responsibility I, as chief litigation officer of the NAACP, have, is to insure that each plan the NAACP submits to a court, or any plan upon which a court is expected to act, and the overall legal theory relied upon must square with the legal standards pronounced by the Supreme Court as necessary to effectively vindicate constitutional rights, and bring into being a unitary system.

It seems to us that the Edmonds thesis could have the effect of trading off constitutional rights in favor of expedient, short term objectives that would result in perpetuating the evil proscribed by law. This constitutes a form of plea bargaining by school systems caught with their hands in the constitutional cookie jar of black children.

Racism, which we have demonstrated in the school cases, from Little Rock to Boston, to be the basic cause of segregation of pupils, is systematic in nature. It poisons the well, so to speak, thus affecting housing, jobs and other areas in which blacks must function. The only effective way of uprooting it is to pull it out systematically and fundamentally. This is not easy nor is it painless. But we have never found the fight against racism to be so. . . .

about a major advance toward an idealistic goal.   At the same time, prosecuting and winning the big case provides strong reinforcement of the attorney's sense of his or her abilities and professionalism.   Dr. Andrew Watson
has suggested that "[c]lass actions . . . have the capacity to provide large
sources of narcissistic gratification and this may be one of the reasons why
they are such a popular form of litigation in legal aid and poverty law
clinics." [66]   The psychological motivations which influence the lawyer in taking on "a fiercer dragon" through the class action may also underlie the
tendency to direct the suit toward the goals of the lawyer rather than the
client.

Civil Rights Litigation and the Regulation
of Professional Ethics

. . . [Professor Bell first reviews NAACP v. Button, 371 U.S. 415
(1963), which held unconstitutional Virginia's attempt to prohibit the
NAACP's litigation campaign.]

Button's recognition of First Amendment rights in the conduct of litigation led to subsequent decisions broadening the rights of other lay groups
to obtain legal representation for their members.   In so doing, these decisions posed new problems for the organized bar.   The American Bar Association, faced with the reality of group practice which it had long resisted,
has attempted to adopt guidelines for practitioners; but the applicable provisions of its new Code of Professional Responsibility provide only broad
and uncertain guidance on the issues of control of litigation and conflict of
interest as they affect civil rights lawyers.

The Code of Professional Responsibility again and again admonishes
the lawyer "to disregard the desires of others that might impair his free judgment." [106]   But the suggestions assume the classical commercial conflict or
a third-party intermediary clearly hostile to the client.   Even when the Code
seems to recognize more subtle "economic, political or social pressures," the
protection needed by civil rights clients is not provided, and the suggested
remedy, withdrawal from representation of the client, is hardly desirable if the
client has no available alternatives.[107]

---

66.   Council on Legal Education for Professional Responsibility, Inc.;   Lawyers, Clients & Ethics 101 (M. Bloom
ed. 1974).

106.   EC 5–21.   Canon 5 provides: "A
Lawyer Should Exercise Independent
Professional Judgment on Behalf of a
Client."   And EC 5–1 reminds the
lawyer of his or her duty to remain
"free of compromising influences and
loyalties."

107.   EC 5–21 provides:
      The obligation of a lawyer to ex-
ercise professional judgment solely
on behalf of his client requires that
he disregard the desires of others

that might impair his free judgment.   The desires of a third person will seldom adversely affect a
lawyer unless that person is in a
position to exert strong economic,
political, or social pressures upon
the lawyer.   These influences are
often subtle, and a lawyer must be
alert to their existence.   A lawyer
subjected to outside pressures should
make full disclosure of them to his
client;   and if he or his client believes that the effectiveness of his
representation has been or will be
impaired thereby, the lawyer should
take proper steps to withdraw from
representation of his client.

The market system mentality of the drafters of the Code surfaces in another provision suggesting that problems of control are less likely to exist where the lawyer "is compensated directly by his client." [108] But solving the problem of control by relying on the elimination of compensation from a source other than the client was rejected in *Button*. All that remains is the warning that a person or group furnishing lawyers "may be far more concerned with establishment or extension of legal principles than in the immediate protection of the rights of the lawyer's individual client." [109]

The Code approach, urging the lawyer to "constantly guard against erosion of his professional freedom" and requiring that he "decline to accept direction of his professional judgment from any layman," [111] is simply the wrong answer to the right question in civil rights offices where basic organizational policies such as the goals of school desegregation are often designed by lawyers and then adopted by the board or other leadership group. The NAACP's reliance on litigation requires that lawyers play a major role in basic policy decisions. Admonitions that the lawyer make no important decisions without consulting the client [112] and that the client be fully informed of all relevant considerations [113] are, of course, appropriate. But they are difficult to enforce in the context of complex, long term school desegregation litigation where the original plaintiffs may have left the system and the members of the class whose interests are at stake are numerous, generally, uninformed, and, if aware of the issues, divided in their views.

Current ABA standards thus appear to conform with *Button* and its progeny in permitting the representation typically provided by civil rights groups. They are a serious attempt to come to grips with and provide specific guidance on the issues of outside influence and client primacy. . . . But they provide little help where, as in school desegregation litigation, the influence of attorney and organization are mutually supportive, and both are so committed to what they perceive as the long range good of their clients that they do not sense the growing conflict between those goals and the client's current interests. Given the cries of protest and the charges of racially motivated persecution that would probably greet any ABA effort to address this problem more specifically, it is not surprising that the conflict— which in any event will neither embarrass the profession ethically nor threaten it economically—has not received a high priority for further attention.

Idealism, though perhaps rarer than greed, is harder to control. . . .

The Class Action Barrier to Expression of Dissent

Even if civil rights lawyers were highly responsive to the wishes of the named plaintiffs in school desegregation suits, a major source of lawyer-client

---

108. EC 5–22 provides:
  Economic, political, or social pressures by third persons are less likely to impinge upon the independent judgment of a lawyer in a matter in which he is compensated directly by his client and his professional work is exclusively with his client. On the other hand, if a lawyer is compensated from a source other than his client, he may feel a sense of responsibility to someone other than his client.

109. EC 5–23.

111. EC 5–24.

112. EC 7–7.

113. EC 7–8.

conflict would remain. In most such suits, the plaintiffs bring a class action on behalf of all similarly situated black students and parents; the final judgment will be binding on all members of the class. As black disenchantment with racial balance remedies grows, the strongest opposition to civil rights litigation strategy may come from unnamed class members. . . .

At one time, expressions of disinterest and even disapproval of civil rights litigation by portions of the class may have been motivated by fear and by threats of physical and economic intimidation. But events in Atlanta, Detroit, and Boston provide the basis for judicial notice that many black parents oppose total reliance on racial balance remedies to cure the effects of school segregation. . . . Black parents who prefer alternative remedies are poorly served by the routine approval of plaintiffs' requests for class status in school desegregation litigation.

Basic principles of equity require courts to develop greater sensitivity to the growing disagreement in black communities over the nature of school relief. Existing class action rules provide ample authority for broadening representation in school cases to reflect the fact that views in the black community are no longer monolithic. One aspect of class action status requiring closer scrutiny is whether the representation provided by plaintiffs will "fairly and adequately protect the interests of the class." [122] Because every person is entitled to be adequately represented when his rights and duties are being adjudicated, it is incumbent upon the courts to ensure the fairness of proceedings that will bind absent class members. The failure to exercise such care may violate due process rights guaranteed by the Fifth and Fourteenth Amendments.

These problems can be avoided if, instead of routinely assuming that school desegregation plaintiffs adequately represent the class, courts will apply carefully the standard tests for determining the validity of class action allegations and the standard procedures for protecting the interests of unnamed class members.[124] Where objecting members of the class seek to intervene,

---

122. Fed.R.Civ.P. 23(a)(4). The issue of adequacy of representation is of critical importance in school desegregation cases where all members of the class are bound by the decrees entered. . . .

124. Several steps might be taken to protect class interests:

(1) *Determination of class action.* Courts should take seriously their independent obligation under Rule 23(c)(1) to decide Rule 23 issues "as soon as practicable after the commencement of an action brought as a class action," even if neither of the parties moves for a ruling. . . .

(2) *Notice to class.* Individual notice to known members of the class is required by Rule 23(c)(2) in Rule 23(b)(3) actions. Eisen v. Carlisle & Jacquelin, 417 U.S. 156 (1974). Individual notice might prove unnecessarily burdensome to plaintiffs in Rule 23(b)(2) civil rights suits and is not required. . . . But some effective means of advising the class of the existence of the suit, the type of relief to be sought, and the binding nature of the judgment should be considered by the court. See Fed.R.Civ.P. 23(d) (2). Local newspapers usually report the filing of school suits, but provide little information about the significance of the class action nature of the litigation. Notice prepared by plaintiffs might, at the court's direction, be distributed to each minority child in the school system. Precedent exists for providing each parent with a letter and questionnaire advising the parent of the pending action and inquiring whether the parent wished to be represented by the plaintiffs and their

their conflicting interests can be recognized under the provisions of Rule 23(d)(2).[125] In this regard, the class action intervention provisions are in harmony with those contained in Rule 24.

Even with the exercise of great care, the adequacy of representation may be difficult to determine, particularly at the outset of the litigation. For this reason, Professor Owen Fiss has suggested that the standard for adequacy of representation for certifying a class action should differ from that used in allowing intervention.[127] If the standards are the same, he reasons, the logical result will be that no member of the class will be allowed to intervene in a class action suit as a matter of right once it is determined that the representation is adequate as to the class. In some instances, although the representation by the named party is adequate as to a class, unnamed class members will have interests deserving of independent representation but not sufficiently important or conflicting to require that the class action be dismissed, the class representative replaced, or the class redefined to exclude the intervenors. The denial of intervention as of right whenever representation is adequate as to the class is particularly unacceptable to Fiss because the class representative is self-selected. . . .[128]

counsel. Knight v. Board of Educ., 48 F.R.D. 108 (E.D.N.Y.1969). An individual notice procedure would provide several advantages. It would:

(a) Enable a fairly accurate determination to be made as to class support for the suit and for the form of relief sought by plaintiffs;

(b) Provide the court with indications regarding the possible need for special steps that might be taken to protect the interests of the class;

(c) Provide class members with an opportunity to provide information through the questionnaire as to individual instances of discrimination they have experienced;

(d) Provide class members with an opportunity to challenge class certification; and

(e) Provide objecting class members an opportunity to intervene. (Specific provision for intervention in class is provided in subdivision (d)(2).)

(3) *Preliminary hearing on class action issue.* In those instances where members of the class raise objections to the adequacy of plaintiffs' representation or the character of relief sought, courts may hold a hearing before deciding under subdivision (c)(1) whether to allow

a class action. Challenges will seldom be made at the outset of school desegregation litigation. Subdivision (c)(1) orders are, of course, not irreversible and may be altered or amended at a later date. . . .

(4) *Partial class actions and subclasses.* Rule 23(c)(4) enables the court to authorize the class action as to only particular issues and to divide a class into appropriate subclasses. In school litigation, members of plaintiffs' class may differ substantially, but could rather easily be encompassed within the motion and hearing process normal to school litigation. . . .

125. Fed.R.Civ.P. 23(d)(2) provides:

In the conduct of actions to which this rule applies, the court may make appropriate orders . . . (2) requiring, for the protection of the members of the class or otherwise for the fair conduct of the action, that notice be given . . . to some or all of the members of any step in the action . . . to intervene and present claims or defenses, or otherwise to come into the action. . . .

127. O. Fiss, Injunctions 560–61 (1972).

128. Professor Fiss notes that in an injunction suit where damages are not sought, the defendant is unlikely to challenge the class allegations—particularly if the plaintiff's case is

Courts have been more sensitive to the differing interests of persons of varied racial, ethnic, and national backgrounds. While efforts of white parents to intervene as defendants in order to make arguments similar to those being made by school boards generally have not been successful, courts have allowed intervention in recognition of the distinct interests of Mexican- and Chinese-Americans. The disagreements among blacks as to whether racial balance remedies are the most appropriate relief for segregated schools, particularly in large urban districts, reflect interests as divergent as those which courts have recognized at the request of other ethnic minorities.

The failure to carefully monitor class status in accordance with the class action rules can frustrate the purposes of those rules and intensify the danger of attorney-client conflict inherent in class action litigation. To a measurable degree, the conflict can be traced to the civil rights lawyer's idealism and commitment to school integration. Such motivations do not become "unprofessional" because subjected to psychological scrutiny. They help explain the drive that enables the civil rights lawyer to survive discouragement and defeat and renew the challenge for change. But when challenges are made on behalf of large classes unable to speak effectively for themselves, courts should not refrain from making those inquiries under the Federal Rules that cannot fail, when properly undertaken, to strengthen the position of the class, the representative, and the counsel who serve them both.

The Resolution of Lawyer-Client Conflicts

. . . [C]ommitment to an integrated society should not be allowed to interfere with the ability to represent effectively parents who favor education-oriented remedies. Those civil rights lawyers, regardless of race, whose commitment to integration is buoyed by doubts about the effectiveness of predominantly black schools should reconsider seriously the propriety of representing blacks, at least in those school cases involving heavily minority districts. . . .

In school desegregation blacks have a just cause, but that cause can be undermined as well as furthered by litigation. A test case can be an important means of calling attention to perceived injustice; more important, school litigation presents opportunities for improving the weak economic and political position which renders the black community vulnerable to the specific injustices the litigation is intended to correct. Litigation can and should serve lawyer and client as a community-organizing tool, an educational forum, a means of obtaining data, a method of exercising political leverage, and a rallying point for public support.

But even when directed by the most resourceful attorneys, civil rights litigation remains an unpredictable vehicle for gaining benefits, such as quality schooling, which a great many whites do not enjoy. The risks involved in such efforts increase dramatically when civil rights attorneys, for idealistic

viewed as weak and his counsel incompetent. Challengers to the self-appointed class representative are not likely to be organized or to have counsel. Because the motion to intervene may be filed months and even years after the suit is initiated (although still only a short period after the conflict in interests and goals becomes apparent), courts are generally reluctant to grant intervention petitions.

or other reasons, fail to consider continually the limits imposed by the social and political circumstances under which clients must function even if the case is won. In the closest of lawyer-client relationships this continual reexamination can be difficult; it becomes much harder where much of the representation takes place hundreds of miles from the site of the litigation. . . .

In the last analysis blacks must provide an enforcement mechanism that will give educational content to the constitutional right recognized in *Brown*. Simply placing black children in "white" schools will seldom suffice. Lawyers in school cases who fail to obtain judicial relief that reasonably promises to improve the education of black children serve poorly both their clients and their cause. . . .

Political, economic, and social conditions have contributed to the loss of school desegregation momentum; but to the extent that civil rights lawyers have not recognized the shift of black parental priorities, they have sacrificed opportunities to negotiate with school boards and petition courts for the judicially enforceable educational improvements which all parents seek. The time has come for civil rights lawyers to end their single-minded commitment to racial balance, a goal which, standing alone, is increasingly inaccessible and all too often educationally impotent.

------

1. For a response to Professor Bell's charges against civil rights litigators, and an elaboration of the views set forth in footnote 64, supra p. 276, see the letter of Nathaniel Jones at 86 Yale L.J. 378 (1976).

2. Since publication of Professor Bell's article the Supreme Court has decided In re Primus, 436 U.S. 412 (1978), and Ohralik v. Ohio State Bar Ass'n, 436 U.S. 447 (1978). These cases elaborated and refined *Button's* protection in important ways and must enter into any current consideration of the power of the state to regulate the professional activities discussed by Professor Bell.

3. Will the steps outlined by Bell in footnote 124 suffice to protect the interests he has presented? For an interesting presentation of litigation as a town meeting, see Yeazell, Intervention and the Idea of Litigation: A Commentary on the Los Angeles School Case, 25 U.C.L.A.L.Rev. 244 (1977).

Chapter 5

DECISION CENTERS

An adjudicatory system vests in some person or group of persons the power to resolve disputes or to establish the norms. Adjudication is a very special type of structured conflict, involving both antagonistic participants and persons charged with the duty of deciding the conflict. Sometimes these persons are called "judges," sometimes "arbitrators," sometimes "administrative law judges," and so on. Our purpose is not to establish a typology of decision centers, nor is it to list the advantages and disadvantages of each, but rather is to locate and explore the general issues raised by the very fact that adjudication—viewed as a form of structured conflict—vests the power to decide in someone. We are concerned with the basic phenomenon of vested power and with issues that are common to all types of decision centers.

From this perspective, three topics appear central. The first concerns what we regard to be the paramount ideal of a decisionmaker in the adjudicatory context, the ideal of impartiality, or to state it in slightly more problematic terms, the ideal of independence or nonaccountability. The meaning of this ideal and its implications are explored in Martin Shapiro's essay on conflict resolution. He assumes that there is only one decision center—the court—and tries to structure the relation of that institution to the parties and to other social institutions through the concept of a "triad."

In the second section of this chapter, we alter the basic assumption of there being only a single decisionmaker. We focus on a social situation—no doubt the more typical one—in which there is not *one* court, not *one* decision center, but rather a multitude. The problem then becomes one of organizing or establishing relationships among the different decision centers. Professor Damaska identifies two alternative organizational patterns, the hierarchical and the coordinate. His essay is a comparative one, drawing on both continental and Anglo-American experience. But, for the most part, he assumes a unitary legal system and thus ignores the very special problems of organizing decision centers within a federal legal system. Damaska's coordinate model aptly fits the federal system—the elements of coordination are *accentuated* by federalism. Yet a federal system of the American variety creates its own special organizational problems, those of relating the courts of one state to those of another and of relating the state courts to the federal courts. These issues are explored in the essays by Professors von Mehren and Trautman (state-to-state relation) and by Neuborne (state-to-federal relation). Neither of these essays is an exhaustive treatment of the many professional issues concerning state and federal jurisdiction. Those issues are amply considered in an enormous and familiar literature. These articles do, however, represent important first steps in the placing of familiar professional issues within a more general theoretical framework which inquires how decision centers might be internally organized.

The third section of the chapter concerns the cognitive capacities of the decisionmaker, that is, what knowledge do we assume it has prior to making the decision? This brings the jury to the fore. Today there is great interest in the jury, in part because the Supreme Court has been redefining, in both the civil and criminal domains, the contours of the right to trial by jury and has been modifying the incidents of that right—the standards for representativeness, the unanimity rule, and the proper number of jurors. See, e. g., Ballew v. Georgia, 435 U.S. 223 (1978); Colgrove v. Battin, 413 U.S. 149 (1973); Johnson v. Louisiana, 406 U.S. 356 (1972); Apodaca v. Oregon, 406 U.S. 404 (1972); Williams v. Florida, 399 U.S. 78 (1970). We believe that the current debate within the bar presupposes some more basic issues, ones that seek to explain the differing contributions each type of decisionmaker—the lay and the professional—brings to the adjudicatory process. In chapter 3, the Kadishes discussed the nullification role of the jury as a way of underscoring the ambiguity of procedural roles. Here we focus more specifically on what the lay juror—as opposed to the judge as a decisionmaker—is supposed to bring to the decisional process. We also consider the place of the "expert" in the adjudicatory process.

In discussing the knowledge and experience of the decisionmaker, we do not intend to overlook the evidentiary components of the hearing or trial, that is, the process of assembling and presenting information to the decision maker. Such a presentation might well compensate for deficiencies in the preexisting knowledge and experience of decisional personnel. Our intent here is to isolate the question of the knowledge and the experience of the decisionmaker first. We want to understand what he or she initially brings to the adjudicatory process as a distinct theoretical issue. Then, in the next chapter, we will explore the processes by which the decisionmaker is informed in the course of the hearing.

SECTION A. THE IDEAL OF INDEPENDENCE

Martin Shapiro, **The Logic of the Triad** *

. . . The root concept employed here is a simple one of conflict and its structuring into triads. Cutting quite across cultural lines, it appears that where two persons come into a conflict that they cannot resolve themselves, one solution appealing to common sense is to call upon a third for assistance in achieving a resolution. So universal across both time and space is this simple social invention of triads that we can discover almost no society that fails to employ it. And from its overwhelming appeal to common sense stems the basic political legitimacy of courts everywhere. In short, the triad for purposes of conflict resolution is the basic social logic of courts, a logic so compelling that courts become a universal political phenomenon.

The triad, however, involves a basic instability, paradox, or dialectic that accounts for a larger proportion of the scholarly quarrels over the nature of courts and the political difficulties that courts encounter in the real world. At the moment the two conflictors find their third, the social logic of the

* *Source*: Chapter 5 ("Courts") in 5 Greenstein and Polsby, Handbook of Political Science 321–47 (1975). Professor of Law, University of California at Berkeley.

court device is preeminent. A moment later, when the third decides in favor of one of the two conflictors, a shift occurs from the triad to a structure that is perceived by the loser as two against one. To the loser there is no social logic in two against one. There is only the brute fact of being outnumbered. A substantial portion of the total behavior of courts in all societies can be analyzed in terms of attempts to prevent the triad from breaking down into two against one .   .   .   .

Consent

The most fundamental device for maintaining the triad is consent. Early Roman-law procedures provide a convenient example. The two parties at issue first met to decide under what norm their dispute would be settled. Unless they could agree on a norm, the dispute could not go forward in juridical channels. Having agreed on the norm, they next had to agree on a judge, a third person who would find the facts and apply the preagreed norm in order to decide their dispute. The eventual loser was placed in the position of having, himself, chosen both the law and the judge and thus having consented to the judgment rather than having had it imposed on him. .   .   .

Nearly every triadic conflict resolver adds another device to consent in order to avoid the breakdown into two against one. This device is the avoidance of the dichotomous, imposed solution. In examining triadic conflict resolution as a universal phenomenon, we discover that the judge of European or Anglo-American courts, determining that the legal right lies with one and against the other of the parties, is not an appropriate central type against which deviance can be conveniently measured. Instead he lies at one end of a continuum. The continuum runs: go-between, mediator, arbitrator, judge. And placement on the continuum is determined by the intersection of the devices of consent and nondichotomous, or mediate, solution. .   .   .

The Substitution of Law and Office for Consent

.   .   .   As societies become more complex they tend to substitute law for the particular consent of the parties to a particular norm for their particular dispute and office for their free choice of a particular third man to aid in the resolution of their dispute. .   .   .

The key factor in the shift from consent to law is specificity. Ethnographic and sociological materials make clear that in only a very limited number of special situations do litigants literally make their own rule of decision free of all preexisting norms. At the very minimum there is a social sense of appropriateness or natural justice, of how we always do things or what we never do.   .   .   .   Whether we express this consensus in terms of custom or fundamental principles of ordered liberty or .   .   .   as a psychic harmony of men and nature, it no doubt creates the constraints under which prospective litigants shape a norm for themselves. Indeed much of judicial ritual, particularly in the holding of public trials, consists of reminding the litigants that as good men they must consent to the overarching norms of their society. Yet the more nebulous these norms, the greater the element of immediate and real consent in achieving a precise working rule for a particular case. At one extreme we find two disputing villagers working with an elder to settle the ownership of a pig according to the ways of the ancestors. If any rule of decision is actually formulated it is likely to arise out of the adeptness of the elder in eliciting the face-to-face consent of the parties. At the other extreme we find litigants in a modern industrial state who discover at trial that their earlier behavior was governed by a detailed preexisting rule, even the existence of which was unknown to them at the time and which they consent to only in the generalized, abstract sense that all citizens agree to live under the laws of the state. The judge, then, unlike the mediator, imposes "his" rule on the parties rather than eliciting a consensual one.

Moreover, the parties may not specifically consent even to who shall impose his rule or decide under it. The most purely consensual situation is one in which the conflictors choose who shall assist them in formulating a rule and who shall decide the case under it, as the Romans initially did. In most societies, however, there seem to be instances in which it pays to choose a big man to do these tasks, whether a government official like the urban praetor or, as among the Papuans, the owner of many pigs. The disputants may turn to the big man because he knows more of the law and custom, because he has the economic, political or social power to enforce his judgment, or because his success or high position is taken as a symptom of his skill and intelligence at resolving disputes. Beyond and perhaps out of this tendency to consent to judging by big men, many societies develop the office of judge so that the parties do not choose their judge. If they choose to go to court at all, they must accept the official judge. The ultimate step, of course, is in those instances in which a legal system not only imposes the law and the officer of the law but also compels one or both parties to resort to legal processes, as in a criminal trial or civil suit. The judge, then, unlike the mediator, imposes himself on the parties rather than being chosen by them. . . .

The substitution of law and office for consent entails very major destabilizing pressures on the triadic structure. For it was essentially his consent at every preliminary stage that enabled the losing disputant to continue seeing the triad as a triad rather than as two against one. Where the loser does not specifically consent in advance to the norm, he must be convinced that the legal rule imposed on him did not favor his opponent. Thus the yearning for neutral principles of law found among contemporary lawyers. And if he did not consent to the judge, he must be convinced that judicial office itself ensures that the judge is not an ally of his opponent. Thus the yearning for a professional and independent judiciary. . . .

Social Control

. . . It is of course in the substitution of office and law for consent that the social-control aspects of courts become most evident and most clearly create tensions with conflict resolution. Where the two parties must go to a third who is an officer, it is as evident to them as to the observer that they are no longer going to a disinterested third. Instead they are introducing a third interest: that of the government, the church, the landowner, or whoever else appoints the official. To be sure, even the Papuans who mutually choose a "big man" to settle their disputes do not expect him to be neutral in the sense of having no interests of his own. Indeed the bigger he is, the broader is likely to be the web of his interlocking social and economic interests among the various genetic, economic, and social units to which the disputants belong. But the requirement of mutual consent allows the Papuans, like modern corporations in search of an arbitrator, to settle on a third who will not see his interests, whatever they may be, as parallel to those of one but not the other of the parties. . . .

When we reach the criminal law itself, and the other bodies of law that openly purport to impose the interests of the regime on individuals and groups, the vision of the triad becomes even more difficult to maintain, particularly where judicial office exists. Where the judge is himself an officer of the crown, and the dispute is in the form of the Crown v. Doe, in what sense do we have a triad as opposed to a simple inquisition? We have noted that judging is a concomitant of sovereignty or at least political authority. Where the whole tribe, or its representative jury, or the village elders meet to judge a transgression against the people or the community, in what sense do we have a folkmoot or a village "court"? Yet over the whole range of our experience we observe acts that are defined as offenses against the collectivity judged by the collectivity itself or by "judges" who are supposed to be the representatives of the collectivity.

Thus even if we could preserve the notion of the completely independent third in the realm of "pure" conflict resolution, assuming such a realm existed, we could not do so in the realm of social control because of the very nature of judicial office and proceedings in that realm. Moreover, in that realm the legal rules applied to a litigation that in form is a dispute between one party—the community—and a second party—the alleged transgressor—are rules that consciously and openly were created by and for one of the parties. Thus . . . the very facts that the proceedings are adversary and apply preexisting legal norms ensure that we will *not* have an independent judge. For even in those few societies that seek to insulate the judge from the rest of government, he is expected to administer the criminal law, that is, to impose the will of the regime on a party being prosecuted by the regime. With extremely great care to the various rituals of independence and impartiality, some criminal courts may succeed in maintaining the appearance of thirdness. However, few of the defendants in contemporary Western criminal courts are likely to perceive their judges as anything other than officers of the regime seeking to control them. So to put the matter somewhat differently, where the government or the people are one of the parties to a dispute, the triadic structure is necessarily weakened when the judge is either an officer of the government or is the people themselves.

While this weakening of the triad is clearest in criminal law, it is also fairly evident in all bodies of "public" law, that is, law setting out the relations between governor and governed. Those societies that engage in the greatest separation of powers or specialization of judicial function approach nearest to a perception of judicial independence. At least the private party engaged in a dispute with one segment of government is judged by an officer of another segment. But, as we have already seen, it is a far more typical governing arrangement to subsume judicial under administrative tasks than to create a judicial specialization. Moreover, it is typical of continental legal systems and their offspring to handle a substantial proportion of public law litigation in "administrative courts," which are less clearly differentiated from the administrative agencies than are the regular courts of the same systems. Even in the United States and Commonwealth countries, where constitutional separation of powers is most complete, a curious paradox arises because of the very inclination to separate. We encounter a common pattern in which the courts of the central government are relatively independent of the rest of that government, a federal system exists, and the highest court of the central government referees constitutional disputes between the central government and the federal units. In this situation the central court is frequently and often rightly perceived not as an independent third but as an arm of the central government imposing central control on the federal units. Particularly where the central court is imposing the will of a national majority over that of a local majority, as in many of the United States Supreme Court's race and religion decisions, the local majority sees the court not as an independent adjudicator but rather as the imposer of national uniformity over local diversity.

We have now argued that the substitution of office and law for consent gravely impairs the basic triadic logic of courts in the sphere of conflict resolution and even more particularly when courts are primarily engaged in social control. Another way of putting this is that precisely because we vest social control as well as conflict resolution in courts, their triadic position is impaired. For in most legal systems the litigants are aware that the judge is concerned not only with refereeing their two sets of interests but with imposing a third set of interests on them both. Whether the triad is maintained will then depend in large part on whether either or both parties perceive the law as neutral in relation to them or alternatively as clearly favoring the interests of the other. Indeed one of the many factors contributing to the court avoidance phenomenon found in most societies is that either one or both disputants perceive the law as inimical or irrelevant to their interests, so that a court of law is an inappropriate instrument for the particular conflict resolution task. Aid in resolution is sought elsewhere.

Courts as Lawmakers

When we move from the conflict-resolution and social-control tasks of courts to their lawmaking tasks, the triad may be even further weakened. Nearly all contemporary students of courts agree that courts do engage in at least supplementary and interstitial lawmaking, filling in the details of the statutory or customary law. In several major legal systems courts go far beyond interstitial lawmaking. The common law of the Anglo-American legal system is largely judge made. . . .

Much of the thrust of the judicial behavior literature has been toward showing that there has been a high correlation between judges' political attitudes and their decisions for and against certain categories of litigants. This literature further suggests that these judicial attitudes fall into the same relatively coherent ideological patterns found in the national political culture.

While considerably less success has been encountered in linking these patterns of political attitudes to the personal backgrounds of the judges, their modes of appointment, or the social and political structures in which they operate, the brute fact of judicial discretion, even within systems of highly articulated statutory and constitutional law, has been more than sufficiently demonstrated. In short, while the development of a political psychology of judging may be still at an early stage, the behavioral literature has fairly convincingly demonstrated that many judges are not entirely "neutral" thirds but instead bring to the triad distinct public policy preferences, which they seek to implement through their decisions.

Aside from actual empirical discovery of widespread judicial lawmaking, it is clear that such lawmaking is logically required wherever law is substituted for consent in the triadic resolution of conflict. For if the third man must resolve conflict, and if he must do so by preexisting law, then he must "discover" the preexisting law. Because no human society has ever sought to set down an absolutely complete and particularized body of preexisting law designed to exactly meet every potential conflict, judicial "discovery" must often of necessity be judicial lawmaking.

In addition to the simple fact and logical necessity of judicial lawmaking, it is clear that many societies, including even those that seek to separate judicial from administrative and legislative office, quite deliberately vest major lawmaking functions in courts. In common-law countries numerous instances may be found in which legislatures have given courts new jurisdictions without giving them new substantive statutory law for those jurisdictions. Alternatively they may have written statutes whose key operative words are common-law terms of art that incorporate past and invite future judicial lawmaking. In the United States the statutory creation of a federal labor contract jurisdiction without the provision of any substantive federal law of contracts and the Sherman Anti-Trust Act's condemnation of "conspiracies in restraint of trade" are obvious examples.   .   .   .

In a great many nations judicial independence is conceived not in terms of a tripartite constitution with checks and balances but simply in terms of a professional judiciary sufficiently insulated from other governmental influences to operate within its own sphere under the rule of law. The courts of Great Britain and Czarist Russia would show the range of this sort of independence, which may be found all the way from liberal constitutional systems emphasizing responsible but centralized political authority to pure autocracies. Obviously some political systems that seek to concentrate political authority will find that the triad is an extremely useful tool of conflict resolution. Such systems will then encounter the dynamics of the triad that we have already encountered. But they may be willing to pay the costs to centralization of creating a relatively independent judicial authority in order to reap the benefits of increased capacity for conflict resolution.

Precisely because they want such triads for routine conflict resolution among private citizens while seeking to keep political power away from the judges, such regimes necessarily encounter difficulties with their judiciaries. For we have already seen that in the course of doing conflict resolution, either under preexisting legal rules or otherwise, courts will make law, or, to express the same thing differently, exercise political power. When this inevitable phenomenon is encountered, both autocratic and constitutional regimes of centralized political authority can respond in one of four ways. First, they can yield and in the process become less centralized. Secondly, they can systematically withdraw from the legally defined competence of the judiciary all matters of political interest to themselves. Thirdly, they may intervene at will to pull particular cases out of the courts and into their own hands. Fourthly, they can create systems of judicial recruitment, training, organization, and promotion that ensure that the judge will be relatively neutral as between two purely private parties but will be the absolutely faithful servant of the regime on all legal matters touching its interests. . . .

Read in one way, the prevalence of these four tactics is testimony to the real independence of judiciaries. In many nations at many times judges have been sufficiently their own masters to require even highly centralized regimes to adopt special tactics to avoid sharing power with them. Even in highly centralized regimes, judicial lawmaking is a reality that must be dealt with, just as it is in regimes that deliberately assign substantial lawmaking authority to the judiciary.

If judges then are inevitably lawmakers, what happens to . . . independence, preexisting legal rules, adversary proceedings, and dichotomous solutions, and more particularly, what happens to the substitution of legislation for legal rules consented to by the parties? In the first place, lawmaking and judicial independence are fundamentally incompatible. No regime is likely to allow significant political power to be wielded by an isolated judicial corps free of political restraints. To the extent that courts make law, judges will be incorporated into the governing coalition, the ruling elite, the responsible representatives of the people, or however else the political regime may be expressed. In most societies this presents no problem at all because judging is only one of the many tasks of the governing cadre. In societies that seek to create independent judiciaries, however, this reintegration will nonetheless occur, even at substantial costs to the proclaimed goal of judicial independence. Thus in the United States there has been a long debate over elected versus appointed judiciaries, with the key question being the extent to which judges ought to be subordinated to the democratic political regime. This debate is ultimately unresolvable because it involves two conflicting goals: one, that triadic conflict resolvers be independent; two, that lawmakers be responsible to the people. Indeed it is because judging inevitably involves lawmaking and social control as well as conflict resolution that the tendency of judging to be closely associated with sovereignty or ultimate political authority . . . is to be found in all societies. . . .

---

1. On the mediating continuum and the role of consent in the adjudicatory process, you may also wish to look at the Golding and Eisenberg essays in chapter 3.

2. The triadic structure derives largely from the role of consent as the basis for legitimating courts (the third). A question naturally arises

as to whether there are any alternative bases for legitimacy, and, if so, whether these alternative bases would alter the conception of impartiality or independence. For example, suppose courts derive their legitimacy not from the "consent" of the parties, but rather from certain social purposes, such as "safeguarding constitutional rights." Would the structure of conflict then be triadic? Would it then be proper to identify the basic task of maintaining legitimacy as one of preventing "the triad from breaking down into two against one"? Shapiro might be correct in asserting "that the substitution of office and law for consent gravely impairs the basic triadic logic of courts" and that the triad is further impaired when courts "make law," but he still would have to explain why that impairment would amount to a special problem of legitimacy.

3. Is Professor Shapiro correct in asserting that "lawmaking and judicial independence are fundamentally incompatible"? Might *judicial* lawmaking be of a very special activity, so that courts would be able to make law and yet maintain—indeed enhance—their independence? See Wellington, Common Law Rules and Constitutional Double Standards: Some Notes on Adjudication, 83 Yale L.J. 221 (1973); R. Dworkin, Taking Rights Seriously (1977).

4. Does Professor Shapiro's thesis concerning the place of the third party in the triad provide any insight into the meaning of independence for the jury? What account might be given of the independence of the jury? The Kadishes address this issue in chapter 3, and introduce the concept of a "recourse role" as a way of formalizing the nullification power of the jury—one way of maintaining its independence. The excerpts in this chapter from Kalven and Zeisel's work, The American Jury (1966), also deal with this issue. In a more recent work, Guido Calabresi and Philip Bobbitt point to a unique dimension of jury independence, encapsulated in their characterization of the jury as an aresponsible agency: "The aresponsible agency generally has three features: It is representative, decentralized, and it gives no reasons for its decisions." G. Calabresi and P. Bobbitt, Tragic Choices 57 (1978). For them, the special appeal of the jury lies in the combination of these elements: "Juries apply societal standards without ever telling us what these standards are, or even that they exist." Id. Aresponsibility is seen by Calabresi and Bobbitt as being particularly appealing for an institution charged with making tragic choices, such as deciding who gets a scarce resource needed to sustain life (e. g., a kidney machine), or in adjudicating certain cases, such as one involving a charge of euthanasia. In such situations, great costs are incurred by the very statement of reasons. Calabresi and Bobbitt point to the value of avoiding such a statement of reasons, but one could wonder whether *that* degree of independence is desirable or consistent with the dictates of formal justice.

SECTION B.   INTERNAL ORGANIZATION OF DECISION CENTERS

1.   PATTERNS OF AUTHORITY

Mirjan Damaška, **Structures of Authority and Comparative Criminal Procedure***

.   .   .   The conventional contrast between the two systems [of criminal procedure] is one that emphasizes the adversarial (or accusatorial) aspects of the Anglo-American process, and the nonadversarial (or inquisitorial) character of the continental mode of proceeding.   This dichotomy, no matter how refined, fails to account for many important variations between the two systems, especially if one's focus moves away from the trial stage, and if one discards a preoccupation with legal mythology to consider law as it is actually applied.

In this article I shall argue that previously inexplicable differences between the continental and Anglo-American systems can be understood once the conventional trial-centered models are displaced by another set of organizing concepts.   These concepts are intended to suggest that divergences in procedural arrangements are, to a considerable extent, related to larger divergences in the conception of the proper organization of authority characteristic of the Continent and the English-speaking world.

To this end I shall offer two models of authority, the hierarchical and the coordinate, to illuminate respectively the continental and the Anglo-American systems.   For heuristic purposes, each model is premised on a very different view of the nature of justice, without any intention to imply that specific conceptions of justice historically precede or causally determine particular patterns of organizing authority.   .   .   .

I.   The Hierarchical Model

A.   General Characteristics

1.   The Object of Hierarchy

The system of values underlying the hierarchical model is characterized by the high premium placed on certainty of decisionmaking.   This preference directly affects the tradeoffs with other recognized goals of the criminal justice system, especially the desire to achieve justice in the special circumstances of each individual case.   Whenever the consideration of individualized circumstances prevents the conversion of the bases of the particular decision into a general, certain formula, such consideration must be forgone.   If one were to seek a deeper motivation for this great emphasis on certainty, the attitudinal keynote of the hierarchical model would probably be located in the rationalist desire to impose a relatively simple order on the rich complexities of life.

* *Source*:   84 Yale L.J. 480, 481–526 (1975).   Professor of Law, Yale University.

2. The Hierarchical Organization

Certainty in decisionmaking requires that uniform policies be developed. This is indubitably a centripetal striving, leading quite naturally to the centralization of authority. Thus, incumbents of authority positions have no autonomous powers: authority is only delegated to them and its exercise must be closely watched.

. . . Any structure of authority organized along its lines, except the very small ones, is inexorably driven toward rigorous hierarchical ordering. Three attributes of such ordering are important for my purposes. The first is a precise delineation of the province of each official: he must be pinned down to an exact spot determined in relation to the dominant center. Positions of super- and sub-ordination must be sharply defined and unmistakable, almost in a reenactment of the medieval adage *"nul homme sans seigneur."*
. . . The second attribute of strict ordering is that authority is allocated along a gradient of importance; the higher one climbs the "scalar" of hierarchy, the more comprehensive and important the authority one acquires. Put differently, there is a pronounced inequality among officials on various hierarchical echelons, especially in terms of the kinds of questions delegated to each for decision. The third attribute concerns the interrelationship of officials at the same level, and leads to the separation of office and incumbent: Where an individual official is delegated authority to make a decision, the decision can be changed only by hierarchical superiors. Thus it is binding on all coequal officials, and becomes a decision of an administrative unit. On the other hand, where a decision is collective, it must express the will of the group as a readily identifiable object of superior review. The group is transmogrified into an institution which assumes a life of its own, distinct and apart from the individuals comprising it. . . .

What are the most important qualifications for a position in the official hierarchy? An office holder must be a technical expert capable of efficiently applying normative standards, irrespective of what interests are thereby served. A good official is also one who has mastered the bureaucratic skills that permit the smooth functioning of the hierarchical authority structure. Generating bureaucratic minutiae is not regarded as an irksome chore, preventing an office holder from performing more important tasks. Rather, the deft handling of files and similar bureaucratic techniques are accepted as essential skills of proficient officials.

Role expectations are reinforced by a variety of mechanisms within the hierarchical model. Prominent among these mechanims are the training for official positions, recruitment techniques, and the system of promotions. Entry into a strictly ordered officialdom begins at the lowest rung of the hierarchical ladder. Established people will seldom be willing to begin at the bottom, and thus an entrant will typically be a technically skilled young man who has undergone both systematic instruction in the normative system and practical training in bureaucratic techniques. His aptitude may be tested by entrance examinations. Because there is practically no lateral entry to higher positions, important officials will be those who have ascended the ladder of hierarchy through periodic promotions which depend, at least to some extent, on performance evaluations by one's superiors . . . .

B. The Hierarchical Model and Continental Reality

1. *Centripetal Decisionmaking*

.   .   .   The comprehensive system of appellate review has a long record on the Continent.   Those wishing to trace its history must venture deep into the hidden origins of the modern state, when continental rulers began to build bureaucracies to establish their control over previously independent provincial and local authorities.   As befits a system in which decisions of subordinates are supervised by those closer to the center of power, appellate review was from its inception conceived as a comprehensive device that permitted, at least at the first level of review, a complete reconsideration of the case.   Thus criminal appeal in all modern continental systems implies a review not only of alleged legal error, but also of factual findings and even the punishment imposed.   Nor is it surprising, in light of centuries of tradition, that appellate review gradually became associated with fairness in the administration of justice.   Indeed, in modern continental countries, the "right of appeal" is usually elevated to the constitutional level. The appellate process is made very inexpensive, and is not risky for the parties.[13]   In large classes of criminal cases even supreme courts can be reached as a matter of right through the mechanism of appeals.   Of course, one consequence of this is that supreme courts lose control over their dockets and must handle a large volume of business.   Relatively large numbers of judges must be appointed to the top of the judicial hierarchy and divided into panels, some of which specialize in the adjudication of criminal cases.[14]   But the uncertainty produced while waiting for the Supreme Court to consent to decide a controversial question is almost totally absent from the continental scene, and the continental appellate mechanism is able to achieve considerable uniformity of decisionmaking on most of the important issues arising in the administration of criminal justice. . . .

A pure hierarchical model regards with great misgivings any participation of lay people in the administration of justice.   The reasons for this

---

13.   The elimination of risk is connected with the generally accepted principle prohibiting *reformatio in peius*, i. e., preventing the appellate court from using the defendant's appeal as an opportunity to modify the judgment of the court below to the detriment of the appellant.   In most continental jurisdictions, the ban applies to proceedings on retrial as well; but the limits of the prohibition in this situation differ from country to country and are uncertain and controversial.

14.   For instance the criminal law division (*La Chambre criminelle*) of the French Supreme Court (*Cour de cassation*) consists of one president, seventeen judges, and, of late, four judicial assistants (*conseillers référen-*

daires).   Inconsistencies among supreme court panels can and do arise. But various mandatory devices have been developed in all jurisdictions to assure the unity of decisionmaking. For instance, a panel is not authorized simply to deviate from a prior decision of another panel, and must submit the issue to a larger body within the supreme court for resolution.   Although the continental legal folklore maintains that judges are not formally bound by prior decisions—in the interest of uniformity of decisionmaking —this supposed rule does not apply to judges at the supreme court level. Paradoxically, they seem to have less potential freedom of action than lower judges.

attitude are not difficult to see: Laymen are usually unable and often unwilling to look at criminal cases through the prism of general rules. To laymen each case is a crisis, a unique human drama, rather than a representative of a general class. Thus, no matter what form it takes, lay participation always injects an element of unpredictability into the criminal justice system.

There are, however, important differences in the degree to which lay participation in adjudication conflicts with the hierarchical model. At one pole, and fundamentally antagonistic to the model, is the Anglo-American jury trial. Decentralized administration is inevitable where lay people are expected to apply local standards in determining guilt, and are even permitted to set aside the centrally imposed criminal law embodied in the judge's instructions. Furthermore, the largely inscrutable and often unchallengeable general verdict represents a crowning example of autonomous rather than delegated adjudicative powers.

At the other extreme, from the later Middle Ages to the French Revolution, the administration of justice on the Continent was dominated by professional adjudicators. Revolutionary times inaugurated a change. It was a period permeated by a somewhat naive intoxication with the exotic but never fully understood charm of English political institutions. It was also an epoch of great distrust of the politically reactionary judicial bureaucracy. The two circumstances in combination explain the curious phenomenon that, in the wake of the victorious French Revolution, the jury trial was transferred to the Continent, although the English ways of organizing society were quite alien to French revolutionary ideology. It is important to note, however, that the broad jury discretion was not imported; from the very beginning, professional officials retained more control over the jury than was the case in England. More importantly the transplanted jury, even in this adulterated form, never really became acculturated on the Continent. Without recounting here the exquisite misadventures of the continental jury, suffice it to note that the jury soon suffered a decline in all European countries. Nevertheless, though somewhat distorted in the transforming screen of all ideological migrations, the idea of lay participation in the adjudication of criminal cases remained a potent political force. Because the judicial bureaucracy was never powerful enough to secure a complete reversion to professional adjudication in criminal matters, the natural result, a sort of compromise, was the adoption of a milder form of lay participation. The prevailing form came to be a mixed bench on which professional and lay judges sat and decided jointly, and this is still the representative continental adjudicative body in criminal matters.

It would be an exaggeration to claim that the actual significance of lay assessors reduces everywhere to a mere nonfunctional political embellishment of the decisional body. But few would deny that the professional judge on the mixed bench is such a towering figure that the lay influence is rather negligible, and nowhere does this influence seriously impede uniformity and predictability of decisionmaking. Moreover, an appeal lies from the mixed bench to higher courts which review the entire record, and these courts are typically composed solely of professional judges . . . .

Although technically not binding, [the] normative standards [expressed by superior courts for the decisionmaking of courts below] are of extreme importance in the actual operation of criminal justice. Because the striving for uniformity and consistent decisionmaking is such an overriding tendency in all continental systems, a number of mechanisms have been designed to make lower courts accept legal propositions developed by superior courts.

Such mechanisms may operate outside actual litigation. In many countries, for example, supreme courts will formally enunciate advisory legal opinions; although usually not binding, these opinions in actual fact will be followed. Less visible, never published, but perhaps more important are various internal recommendations and circulars on legal issues flowing from higher to lower courts on diverse occasions, such as following the inspection of lower courts or perusal of their files.

Closer to the enunciation of normative propositions in actual litigation, and appearing quite bizarre to outsiders, are the "audit" procedures by which supreme courts review final decisions "in the interest of the law." Frequently their effect is solely to declare that in a decision "law was misinterpreted," but without changing the adjudication. The *effet platonique* of such supreme court decisions remains entirely incomprehensible unless their purpose is revealed as one of assuring uniformity of decisionmaking in lower courts. Finally, the pervasive appellate mechanism renders legal opinions of higher courts quite important. If the lower court judge fails to follow the legal views of his superiors, his decision inevitably will either be reversed or amended. All continental systems, mirroring the hierarchical model, have developed effective pressures against the display of obstinacy and independent assertion of views by the lower judiciary. Briefly, when the continental judge knows of a legal view expressed by his superiors and has reason to believe they still adhere to it, he will usually follow it even without any doctrinal obligation to do so. Whether this view happens to be expressed within or without the context of a particular case will be largely irrelevant to him. Instances in which trial judges actually use the freedom to develop legal standards accorded them by the system's folklore constitute quite rare deviations from the mode.

. . . To a continental judge a prior decision is not a "case," a solution to a real life problem in all the richness of its raw facts. What he is looking for in a decision is essentially a specification of a more general legal proposition that will cover the case before him. The facts of the decided case will seldom interest him; indeed, they may often constitute a regrettable distraction from his proper business of finding a precisely articulated standard. Most of the time, an abstract legal proposition, totally denuded of the enveloping factual context, will suffice for his purposes. Gone is the flexibility springing from the "distinguishing" of cases on their facts or emanating from broader and narrower formulation of holdings. Gone also is the freedom resulting from the various degrees of weight that can be attributed to precedents. The rule found in the decision either applies or it does not. This difference is of great importance, because following prior decisions in the continental fashion leads to much more rigidity than is the case under the stare decisis doctrine. While the latter does not prevent the growth of law, the former easily can . . . .

2. *Rigid Ordering of Authority*

. . . . The first characteristic [of rigid ordering] is the precise delineation of responsibilities, both internally and in relation to other branches of government. . . . [T]he continental judiciary clearly satisfies [that criterion.] . . .

Descending to details, a few examples of precise delineation of authority must be offered. A provision allocating the same matter either to a single judge or a panel, or authorizing both the trial and the appellate judge to render or alter the same decision, would be viewed in the continental systems as a serious ambiguity to be quickly remedied. Similarly, it would be unacceptable for a judge to be able to change his decision after he has announced it, even if such power extended only for a limited time period; once the decision is announced the court loses all power over it, and only the hierarchical superior can alter it. Relatively little difficulty is ever encountered in determining the proper adjudicator and relationships of super- and sub-ordination.

A second characteristic of rigorous hierarchies is the pronounced differentiation among judges at various levels, and in this the continental judiciary corresponds quite closely to the model. Let me begin with the courts of original jurisdiction. A single judge will be authorized to decide only minor offenses. More serious cases are allocated to a panel. If, however, serious felonies or sensitive matters such as political issues are involved, the criminal case will usually fall within the province of a higher trial court. More significantly for my purposes, many sensitive decisions that in other systems are made at the level of original adjudication are either taken away from the trial courts altogether and vested in appellate courts or removed from the judiciary entirely. For example, the idea that a trial judge could be entitled to determine whether a high government official is properly exercising his testimonial privilege, or what is and what is not in the interests of national security, appears almost preposterous from the continental perspective. From such a perspective, if these problems are to be entrusted to the judiciary at all, it would seem natural to vest authority to resolve them in a judicial echelon corresponding to the rank of the government official whose acts are in question. Any other solution would be regarded as a serious disruption of elementary symmetry in the allocation of authority. Consider also the power to review the constitutionality of legislation. It is probably still fair to say that continentals regard the ordinary judiciary to be an inappropriate authority to strike down statutes as unconstitutional. If judicial review is allowed, it is entrusted to a special high tribunal which deviates in many ways from "normal" courts. It would be truly alien to this system to decentralize judicial review by authorizing ordinary trial judges to declare legislation unconstitutional. Such an arrangement would introduce a serious hierarchical disharmony.

Let us move up the hierarchy to appellate courts. Here, one quite frequently encounters significant hierarchical differentiation. Judges normally decide cases in small panels; some important matters, however, come within the province of super-panels whose legal views are binding on ordinary panels.   In this manner internal or infra-court echelons of authority are created.   As shown before, this is especially important at the supreme court level.   Nor is it unusual that a rudimentary hierarchy may appear even in a single panel, in the sense that rules evolve which accord certain powers to the president and other powers to the full panel.   This should come as no surprise.   To a considerable extent, this ranking accompanies the elaborate and extensive reviewability of decisions .   .   .   .

The last demand of a rigid ordering of authority is that courts be treated as units, distinct and separate from their judges .   .   .   .

Consider first the situation in which a matter falls within the province of a single judge.   Even after a particular judge has been assigned to decide the matter, all motions and briefs must be directed to the court on which the judge sits, rather than to him personally.   And when he has rendered his decision, he has spoken for the whole court.   Thus, the same matter cannot be considered again by another member of the same bench thereby creating complexities and duplications.   For example, a party denied bail cannot turn to another judge in the hope of obtaining it.   Most of the time, however, criminal matters will be in the province of a panel whose behavior is rooted in the long continental tradition of collective decisionmaking.   Not surprisingly, the panel is elevated into an abstract, faceless legal creature, a sort of corporate personality.   It is thus not unusual to find continental systems in which opinions are not even signed by the individual judges who wrote them.   Judicial dissents are neither orally announced nor published.   While many reasons are advanced in support of this arrangement, there is only one which in my view goes beyond the surface of the continental system: Where a hierarchical organization created for the sake of assuring unity and certainty is not forced to be unisonous, especially at the top of the pyramid, the animating presuppositions of the whole structure are strained, and the criteria for decisionmaking become either completely elusive or affected with a germ of dissolution.

3.   *Preference for Determinative Rules*

.   .   .   Obviously, then, because it values appellate review so highly, the continental judiciary necessarily favors standards as lucidly defined as possible.   In the absence of the jury as the autonomous decisionmaker par excellence, this is not overly difficult.

Most comparatists would probably agree that continental criminal legislation, both substantive and procedural, purports to cover all problems that can be anticipated, including the very exceptional situation.   Permissive as opposed to mandatory language is quite rare.   This, of course, furnishes to decisionmakers only the broad framework of normative standards.   But broad legislative standards are made more concrete by the judicial hierarchy, both within and without actual litigation, and the normative output of higher courts is quite rigid.   Consistency, mutual compatibility of rules, perhaps even an order of analysis within the resulting normative universe are maintained by "legal science."

But norm-saturation is not the only relevant consideration;   attitudes towards norms are also important.   It would be a serious mistake to think that this attitude is independent of the authority structure. Comparatively speaking, the attitude of the continental judiciary toward normative standards can easily be classified as rigid and unbending. Norms are not regarded, even in procedure and practice outside the trial context, as instructions from which there are legitimate departures. The great deference of the continental judiciary toward legislation is one of the loci communes of comparative law, and this is only partially mirrored in the uneasiness of the ordinary judiciary concerning the constitutional review of statutes. Equally important is the meticulous observance of norms emanating from higher courts. In sum, rules regulating the behavior of the continental judiciary are not only relatively precise and prolific, they are also comparatively inflexible. .   .   .

4.   *Importance of Official Documents and Reports*

Implicit in the ubiquitous hierarchical control of the continental machinery of criminal justice is the importance of documentation. Traces of all official activity must be preserved for possible review by superiors. Thus files must be maintained on all official matters, and these files can be closed only in accordance with precise rules. All official activity must be recorded and even minor decisions and their justifications reduced to written form. The part played by paperwork, ministerial matters, and bureaucratic minutiae in the total effort of officialdom is quite considerable.

Documents and reports drafted by officials are highly formalized. Specific matter must be included in specific parts of documents. Exposition must be succinct and summaries made whenever possible. Even the style of writing is standardized: It frequently becomes arid, impersonal, and cliché-ridden. Personal expression, even in a jeweled and coruscated style, is anathema. Usually, tendencies toward individualism are rooted out during one's novitiate in the bureaucracy. As a consequence, anything but an impersonal stylus curiae would constitute a display of bad taste and lack of professionalism .   .   .   .

II.   The Coordinate Model

A.   General Characteristics

1.   *The Object of Coordination*

Animating the coordinate model is the aim of reaching the decision most appropriate to the circumstances of each case. Certainty of decisionmaking is recognized as an important value, but is less weighty than in the hierarchical model; what appears to be the best solution in a particular case will not be readily sacrificed to certainty and uniformity of decisionmaking. Consequently, the distinction between saying that a particular decision is just and that it is in accordance with the law cannot as easily be made as in the hierarchical model. The cast of mind underlying these value preferences attaches great importance to the rich variety of experience and is skeptical of attempts to impress general structures on the complexities of life.

2. *The Coordinate Organization*

The desire for particularized justice requires that officials be close to the concrete situations of life involved in the processing of cases, and, of course, that they be free from outside constraints in considering equities. If achieving particularized justice were indeed the sole concern in the coordinate model, the ideal system would be a single layer of authority; but the need for a degree of uniformity is recognized, and the necessary unification of policies cannot always be achieved through the voluntary cooperation of autonomous officials. Accordingly, more complex structures of authority must be composed.

When hierarchical structures of authority must be established, the basic value orientations of the coordinate model mandate that the ordering of authority be as mild as possible. Three attributes of such a mild hierarchy are important for my purposes. Because of the aversion to defining the relation of each official to the center of authority, positions of sub- and superordination are not clearly delineated. The resulting ambiguities and occasional overlappings are willingly accepted as a necessary price for the fundamental commitment to autonomous official powers. In keeping with the importance of the first layer of authority, the inequality among officials on various rungs of the hierarchical pyramid is not very pronounced; essentially, they are all homologues with similar authority inherent in their positions. And lastly, when officials must be organized into a unit, they do not thereby totally surrender their independence. Office and incumbent are not fully separated. The unit does not become an institution divorced from the real people comprising it.

Because officials must tailor their decisions to the special, sometimes unique circumstances of individual situations, the desire to predetermine the outcome of cases by precise and unbending rules is repugnant to the coordinate model. This is not to say, of course, that there are no preexisting standards for decisionmaking at all. Standards do exist, but they tend to be less precise and more flexible than in the hierarchical model. The general theme of "official discretion" runs like an obbligato through all aspects of official activity. Moreover, it is consistent with the model to entrust crucial decisions to independent bodies of laymen. In such a setting there is no need for officials to make a record of all their activities, or to write down and justify even minor rulings. And where written decisions and reports appear warranted, standardization and regimentation of style appear as unnecessary and irksome formalisms, perhaps not fully compatible with the dignity of official positions. Generally speaking, bureaucracy in the coordinate model is rudimentary.

The structure of authority emerging from the foregoing brief sketch generates quite different behavior expectations than those encountered in the hierarchical model. Obviously, the ideal official is not a technical expert applying normative directives, irrespective of what appears to him to be the best solution in the light of the circumstances of individual cases. Decisionmaking is not a technical or administrative problem with policy issues settled in advance, but rather involves the more exalted and responsible activity of finding the best solution to a social problem in light of the political and ethical values of the decisionmaker.

This different role expectation in the coordinate model is reflected in the requirements for official positions. The importance of both professional training and a period of apprenticeship is minimized or totally eliminated. A candidate for office is preferably an established person who has made his mark in society, a problem-solver attuned to community values. Since socialization to a bureaucratic world is not necessary, even the highest positions may be entered laterally, that is, by outsiders without previous experience in the machinery of criminal justice.

B. The Coordinate Model and Anglo-American Reality

1. *Centrifugal Decisionmaking*

. . . The common law jury is a classic example of an autonomous decisionmaking body in the administration of justice. No doubt, it is also a centrifugal force. Consider only the issue of jury nullification. In the face of uncontroverted evidence, and in the teeth of clear judicial instructions, the jury may bring in a verdict of acquittal and thereby refuse to apply substantive law, whether centrally imposed by the legislature or developed through judicial lawmaking. The frequent justification for this power is that jurors must bring to bear local conceptions of justice upon decisionmaking and adjust the crude substantive criminal law to the circumstances of individual cases. But even if the jury verdict is one of conviction and may therefore be set aside, decisions as to fact, law and substantive justice are so deeply entangled in the general verdict that continental review can hardly be imagined .   .   .   .

.   .   . [M]any striking features of judicial decentralization survive in the modern adjudication of criminal cases.   .   .   . [Even aside from the jury, decisionmaking is centrifugal. This results, in part, from the fact that appeals are of limited scope.]

.   .   . The lasting vitality of the notion of trial adjudication as final also accounts for the relatively limited scope of appeal. Leaving aside the fact that acquittals cannot be appealed on any ground, consider the comparatively severe limitations on the grounds for the defendant's appeal. Both the factual findings and the sentence imposed can hardly be challenged. Even when error can be appealed, *direct* reconsideration of the adjudication, as in the continental system, is not involved. Following the pattern quite understandable in the setting of the jury trial with its inscrutable general verdict, what is actually reviewed is the propriety of the material submitted to the decisionmaker for decision, rather than his "correct" use of the material. In light of the foregoing it is not at all surprising that the right to appeal is not nearly so important in Anglo-American as it is in continental systems, and that it is generally not accorded constitutional stature.

The continued importance of original jurisdiction, with the accompanying lesser importance of the appellate process, invests the Anglo-American judicial system with strong centrifugal tendencies. Judges retain important autonomous powers typical of a decentralized judiciary: Like the jury, they can nullify substantive criminal law; the unreviewability of acquittals gives them significant leeway in deciding evidentiary issues; and the scope of their sentencing power is astonishing by continental standards. As a result, centralization of policies cannot be achieved nearly so easily as it is in the hierarchical systems.

2. *Mild Ordering of Authority*

.   .   .   Characteristically, a penumbra of uncertainty exists in circumscription of judicial authority in the United States. It springs mainly from the fact that American courts, including those in the federal system, are not "creatures of legislation" in the continental sense. Judges retain certain "inherent powers," independent of the legislative delegation of authority. Nor is there much anticipatory legislation concerning the division of authority, if only because even the lower courts possess some "rulemaking" power.[93] Indeed, legislation on what could be termed judicial competence is so meager that, with its blank areas, it appears to continental lawyers to resemble early maps of Africa. Overlappings frequently occur in the jurisdiction of courts at different levels. For instance, the trial judge, for a time, following the announcement of his decision, shares with higher courts the power to alter the judgment; moreover, a stay of execution may be sought from either the court of original jurisdiction or from the appellate court. As a final illustration of ambiguous relationships, anathema to the hierarchical model, consider the power of federal *district* court judges in habeas corpus proceedings to review state *supreme* court decisions, both in deciding whether to use the existing record and in invalidating convictions of state courts rather than merely disturbing the custody of prisoners based on such convictions.

In accord with another distinguishing feature of the mild ordering of authority, trial judges are allocated many powers which a rigid hierarchy would either vest in judges at a higher level, or deny to the judiciary altogether. An obvious example is the power to strike down legislation as unconstitutional. But even more remarkable is the cause célèbre of a federal trial judge determining—albeit in the first instance only—the proper limits of the President's executive privilege. Within the hierarchical model issues of such magnitude would never be entrusted to the lowest judicial echelon.

In yet another respect the Anglo-American judiciary is accurately represented by the coordinate model: Individual judges, even when on a panel, preserve their independence and identity. Thus, for instance, the common law system has never accepted the idea, so typical of hierarchical structures, that the court as a unit has spoken when a judge belonging to its bench has rendered his decision.[97] And, when a panel issues a decision, it need not

---

93. Such rulemaking power, even if specifically delegated solely to the supreme courts, is almost beyond the comprehension of most continental lawyers. Courts with which they are familiar are mainly limited to issuing insignificant rules of order. Greater flexibility and, consequently, uncertainty also stem from the freedom of some American courts to refuse to consider a case falling within their jurisdiction. On the continent such a practice would be a clear instance of *"denegatio justiciae."*

97. For example, the denial of bail or of a stay of execution by one judge does not prevent his colleague on the court from granting it. .   .   .

speak with one voice; indeed, a requirement that individual opinions be forgone would run counter to basic ideas of the autonomy and dignity of judicial office. Consequently judges are entitled to deliver individual opinions, even if this implies, as in the Japanese fable of Rashomon, that the same story is recounted from various standpoints and there is no discernible opinion of the panel as such.

3. *Preference for Flexible Rules*

.   .   .   The Anglo-American adjudicator of criminal cases may be characterized by his freedom from settled and precise substantive law, and his flexible attitude toward rules, be they substantive or procedural.

In discussing the substantive criminal law, experts commonly assert that problems belonging to what continental lawyers would call the "general part" (such as principles of criminal liability, the unit of criminal conduct, and the definition and sufficiency of charges) are in a fluid and comparatively unrefined state. That this should be so will not surprise anyone familiar with the spirit of what I have called the coordinate model. Problems of criminal law are not authoritatively structured in advance, for it is feared that such attempts to capture reality in the mesh of rules may hamper the attainment of particularized justice. It is thought that the task of refining the law is done best in the context of individual cases, by people both familiar with the concrete details and attuned to community values. Unusual cases that contribute so much to the complexities of the law are infrequent, and prosecutors often decline to prosecute when such cases occur. Those cases that are brought within the criminal justice system are usually left to the adjudicator's general verdict, from which concrete standards simply cannot be distilled. In sum, what to continental eyes appears as a sorry state of affairs, resembling the charmingly confusing Chagallian universe of freely floating objects, represents in the setting of the coordinate model a perfectly natural and desirable arrangement.

Much more important than the relatively large areas of substantive law that are not in fact governed by rules is the Anglo-American adjudicator's disposition toward those rules that do exist. In contrast to his continental counterpart, he finds little that is sacrosanct about them and regards certain departures as perfectly legitimate. Let me present a few examples. Of course, a judge in the Anglo-American system can question the constitutionality of rules, and such rules are therefore not inviolate; and it is obvious that where a judge can decide these constitutional challenges, basic policy issues will often surface. But even in those cases where constitutional objections to rules are not raised, precedential or legislative standards will be discarded or modified whenever they indicate a result contrary to the adjudicator's strong beliefs as to the best disposition of the case. Where departures from established rules lead to the acquittal of the defendant, the adjudicator's decision usually cannot be challenged. And even where his decisions are reviewable, his attitude toward rules will be far from deferential, and departures from them may be regarded as justifiable.

Generally, then, one can observe that rules in the Anglo-American system are not much more than guidelines for average cases, guidelines susceptible of improvement and reconsideration in light of current experience and the particular circumstances of each case. The premise of this attitude resides in the desire to achieve particularized justice.

But it is important for comparative purposes to note that, in this concept of adjudication, decisionmaking becomes inevitably enmeshed in concrete situations and even minor details. Legal questions cannot be debated grosso modo, and efforts can hardly be made to develop law as a system of interrelated legal standards. . . .

4. *The Informal Style*

The autonomous manner of exercising authority that is so characteristic of the Anglo-American machinery of criminal justice must inevitably decrease the importance of official documentation and bureaucratic techniques. There is in the Anglo-American criminal process no real counterpart of the continental dossier; in fact, even writing judicial opinions is regarded by many judges as an opportunity for the expression of self, so that, by continental standards, many judicial opinions appear more like products of littérateurs than official documents . . . .

In this scheme, it would not make sense to suggest that decisionmaking should place great reliance on official documentation. Indeed, much of the law of evidence is designed to prevent such an occurrence. Summaries of testimony or of visits to the scene of crime, for example, assume the character of lifeless bureaucratic residues of reality, always defective, often spurious, and therefore such evidence is normally inadmissible at trial. The best substitute for the *viva vox* as a basis for decisionmaking at the trial is the full transcript, for this comes closest to reproducing the full complexity of reality that is so crucial to adjudication in the coordinate model . . . .

III.　The Structure of Authority and the Conventional Typology of Criminal Proceedings

. . . When the positions of the continental and Anglo-American judge are viewed from the different perspectives afforded by authority and process models, a curious puzzle emerges. The Anglo-American judge has great autonomous powers, but his ideal stance is that of a relatively passive umpire of the adversary process. His continental counterpart is less autonomous, but assumes an active role. It seems strange that the strong is expected to be passive, while the weak is supposed to be active; indeed, many would be inclined to view this combination as an analytical mismatch. . . .

Let me begin by first taking the Anglo-American side of the comparison. The passive posture of the judge is historically novel and far from being a general description of the judicial office. Instead, it applies only to a limited number of procedural contexts and to a restricted class of issues. Judicial passivity is the rule only during the guilt-determining phase of the trial, and there serves as the norm only with regard to the framing of the subject matter of the proceedings, the collection of evidence, and the presentation of proof.[112] Even in this limited segment of their activity, Anglo-American judges are not rigidly restricted: If a judge believes that abiding by his ideal role will adversely affect the proceedings or poorly serve the public interest, he will usually abandon his detached stance and vigorously intervene in the conduct of the trial.[113] And even though much of this intervention is technically limited to suggestions to the parties, these "suggestions" will typically be heeded, for both parties will be reluctant to risk unfavorable and often unchallengeable judicial decisions on other matters. Judicial passivity, however, is recognized as an ideal posture only in limited situations. In many phases of the criminal process, such as pretrial hearings, in camera examinations, and the sentencing stage, passivity and aloofness come to an end. Indeed, at these junctures in the proceedings Anglo-American judges occasionally assume outright inquisitorial postures that are without counterparts in modern continental systems.[114]

And no one would be more surprised at such powers than the continental judge at trial. It is true that he is the source of most procedural activity: He is responsible for determining the subject matter of the proceedings,[115] and for securing all evidence needed for the ascertainment of the truth. During the proceedings, he not only presides over the taking of proof, but also originates the bulk of questions. The continental trial judge, however,

112. By passivity in framing the subject matter of proceedings I refer to the arrangement whereby the parties themselves determine which claims and defenses to press or to waive. In recent times some Anglo-American jurisdictions have permitted the judge to raise certain defensive issues. . . . Where this has happened, a departure from the adversary model must be acknowledged.

By judicial passivity in collecting evidence I mean the absence of requests by the judge that the parties furnish an evidentiary source, e. g., that a witness be called. Most theoretical writers would agree that if the judge goes beyond merely suggesting to the parties that particular evidence be produced, he is deviating from the adversary style. . . . That judges should be passive in the presentation of proof is correctly viewed as less central to the ideal of adversary proceedings; asking questions of witnesses is compatible with the adversary style. . . . But if the intensity of such judicial activism exceeds a certain point, the judge clearly deviates from his proper role. Finally, it is frequently forgotten that the stance of passivity applies a fortiori to the jury.

113. Some of these deviations from the passive role can be explained by a desire to correct the malfunctioning of the adversary system. Adversary proceedings require an approximate equality between the parties in order to function properly, and if the balance of advantage is seriously affected, the judge may intervene. If his redress of the balance helps the defendant and results in acquittal, his conduct is unreviewable. If he supports the prosecution and conviction follows, the propriety of such assistance is of course subject to review . . . .

114. . . . Ever since the 19th century reforms, continental judges, whether trial or investigative, have had neither the authority to exceed prosecutorial charges nor such weapons as "provisional sentencing" to put pressure on defendants to cooperate. More generally, observe the broad equity powers of the Anglo-American judge in civil cases. It is the denial to the continental judge of comparable, flexible powers (especially of supervision) which explains more than anything else the absence of the device of the trust in the continental legal system.

115. He is, of course, confined to the prosecutor's charge, but within its limits the judge must raise all relevant issues; and thus there are, for example, no "affirmative" defenses in continental law.

must expect superior review of all his rulings as a matter of course, and is rigidly restricted by a network of rules and customary practices. He has much less independence from normative contraints than his common law counterpart, and also much less power over the parties and other participants at the trial.

It follows from the foregoing that the conventional characterizations of judicial activism in the two systems are of limited explanatory value. An analysis based on differences in the *type* of authority can provide a greater insight into a broader range of judicial activity than can the traditional dichotomy between active and passive roles. Indeed, this is the case even in those areas to which the traditional view is applicable since it must admit numerous deviations from the type of judicial behavior one would expect on the basis of the traditional dichotomy . . . .

2. CHOICE AMONG DECISION CENTERS: STRUCTURES OF COORDINATION

The coordinate model is, as Professor Damaška suggests, characterized by "overlappings." Several agencies adjudicate the same claim, and the question naturally arises as to how to structure the relationship among these agencies. Shall the choice be given to the litigant, or to some other institution, one more public and more disinterested? If it is given to the litigant, should the power be given to the plaintiff or to the defendant? What are the bounds of that choice, and what are the consequences of violating those bounds?

In the first essay here Professors von Mehran and Trautman address these questions in the context of choosing which state—taken as a separate locus of a decision center—shall have the power to adjudicate a particular claim controversy. Their concern is primarily with the American federal legal system, and the central concepts—due process and full faith and credit—are derived from a particular constitutional text. Yet the mode of analysis and the range of considerations that enter into and shape that analysis transcend that context and illuminate the more general problem of trying to structure the relationship among coordinate decision centers.

Professor Neuborne addresses the issue of coordination in the context of allocating responsibility between state and federal courts, rather than choosing between two states (the von Mehren and Trautman context). Neuborne's perspective is that of a litigator; he reveals the kinds of consideration that would lead a litigator to prefer one type of decision center to another. But our concern is with the very structure that permits the choice and with the dynamics that produce the divergent appeal of the different types of decision centers.

Arthur T. von Mehren and Donald T. Trautman, **Jurisdiction to Adjudicate: A Suggested Analysis***

. . .

I.   Preliminary Problems of Analysis

Jurisdiction to adjudicate and recognition of foreign judgments are not merely different ways of formulating a single problem; they are separate, though interrelated, questions. In the United States the two issues have tended to coalesce because the full faith and credit clause [9] of the federal constitution is taken to require jurisdiction in the rendering state court as a prerequisite to compulsory recognition in other states   .   .   .   .

But in an international context—and even within the United States in some respects—the problems of adjudicatory jurisdiction and recognition are not identical. At least in the international sphere a state may rationally wish to assert jurisdiction when it would not recognize another state's assertion of jurisdiction in a comparable situation. And a judgment can, as a practical matter, often be made fully, or at least partially, effective without relying upon its recognition elsewhere. Nonetheless, in establishing bases for jurisdiction in the international sense, a legal system cannot confine its analysis solely to its own ideas of what is just, appropriate, and convenient. To a degree it must take into account the views of other communities concerned. Conduct that is overly self-regarding with respect to the taking and exercise of jurisdiction can disturb the international order and produce political, legal, and economic reprisals.

Moreover, adjudicatory action of one jurisdiction, if it is to be fully effective, will often require the cooperation of other jurisdictions. The need for cooperation is plainest when a judgment rendered in one jurisdiction must be enforced, or a status created must be recognized, in another. More subtle forms of cooperation—or at least tolerance—are also important. For example, in any situation in which more than one jurisdiction has a significant hold upon the persons or property involved in litigation, a second jurisdiction could interfere with the first jurisdiction's handling of the matter. At the extreme, the second jurisdiction might take property from the plaintiff in the foreign action in order to compensate the defendant for a judgment he was compelled to pay. Or the second jurisdiction could enjoin a party from proceeding further in the original action. Thus jurisdictional rules ordinarily presuppose, and are designed to ensure, not only that other concerned jurisdictions will not take serious offense at the assertion of jurisdiction in the original proceeding, but that they will not act affirmatively to frustrate the results reached in the original proceeding.

---

* *Source:* 79 Harv.L.Rev. 1121, 1124–79 (1966). Professors of Law, Harvard University.

9. Article IV provides in part that: "Full Faith and Credit shall be given in each State to the public Acts, Records, and judicial Proceedings of every other State. And the Congress may by general Laws prescribe the Manner in which such Acts, Records and Proceedings shall be proved, and the Effect thereof."

The second pervasive problem of analysis is whether, as a matter of general principle, jurisdictional thinking should embody a bias in favor of the defendant or in favor of the plaintiff. For example, should the domicile of *either* party be a basis of jurisdiction, or only the defendant's domicile or residence? For purely domestic situations a general and almost universally accepted maxim favors the attacked over the complainant at least when the parties enjoy relatively equal economic strength and social standing. The status quo as between the parties is not to be lightly changed, and the burden is thus on the plaintiff. A specific application of the general domestic-law bias in favor of defendants is seen in the venue provisions developed for domestic litigation. These normally favor the defendant by allowing suit at his domicile or residence, but not at the plaintiff's domicile or residence.

The significance of jurisdictional rules favoring the defendant in litigation involving multistate elements is inevitably different from the effects of such rules in purely domestic litigation. For example, venue rules favoring defendants in litigation involving no out-of-state element ordinarily place much less of a burden on the plaintiff. The local plaintiff is not as likely to incur significant expense in transporting himself and his witnesses to the court of the local defendant's domicile or residence. Moreover, purely domestic applications of rules favoring defendants strike a balance between parties each of whom stands in the same relationship to the forum's community. In multistate litigation one of the nonlocal elements is frequently the fact that one party is a member of another community. Perhaps this difference should not be significant in a civilized international society, but its existence should be noted in any attempt to reason, with respect to problems of jurisdiction in the international sense, from domestic-law analogues. In considering the newly emerging bases of jurisdiction based on activity, we shall recur to this theme of movement away from the bias favoring the defendant toward permitting the plaintiff to insist that the defendant come to him.

The third and most perplexing problem of analysis is whether and how choice-of-law practices should be taken into account in the formulation of rules governing the assumption of adjudicatory jurisdiction. Certain other aspects of litigation are basic to all thinking about jurisdiction to adjudicate: the relation of the parties litigant to the forum and litigational and enforcement considerations (for example, convenience of witnesses and feasibility of local enforcement). But ideally, the choice-of-law question—the relationship between the underlying controversy and the forum—should be of little significance for the jurisdictional problem. The general assumption of Anglo-American practice has indeed been that choice of law operates fully and effectively, so that the relationship between the underlying controversy and the putative forum ordinarily need not be taken into account in deciding whether to exercise jurisdiction.

However, no legal order completely ignores choice of law in its thinking about adjudicatory jurisdiction. Rules respecting the assumption of jurisdiction must take the choice-of-law problem into account when *choice* is impossible either inherently or as a matter of practice—when the forum, if it adjudicates, will automatically regulate the controversy under its own domestic-law rule . . . . Thus, the propriety of allowing divorce proceedings at the moving party's domicile involves not only questions of litigational convenience and fairness but also the question whether the forum's concern for the marriage relation, as revealed by these affiliating circumstances, calls for the application of domestic-law rules. From the point of view of litigational convenience alone, the community in which the events asserted to justify divorce occurred might well seem an appropriate forum if the petitioner desires to proceed there. Jurisdiction is in practice refused, however, because these connections are not viewed as justifying the application of the forum's divorce law. Conversely, even though the forum's concerns for the parties and other litigational and enforcement considerations, standing alone, would not support an assumption of jurisdiction, the forum may take jurisdiction to adjudicate if it has a substantial interest in regulating the underlying controversy under its own law and if an otherwise more appropriate forum would apply another law. The accepted basis in American practice for divorce jurisdiction—the domicile of the moving party—again illustrates the proposition. Conventional thinking respecting jurisdiction to adjudicate would probably conclude that considerations of litigational convenience and fairness do not justify requiring the respondent to defend in the jurisdiction chosen by the moving party. However, as the Supreme Court recognized in the first *Williams* case,[17] the community in which the moving party lives has a legitimate claim to regulate his marital status under its domestic-law conceptions . . . .

     . . . To the extent that the common law approached jurisdiction to adjudicate in terms of personal service on the defendant within the territory of the judicial system, notice did not emerge as a separate problem. The asserted basis of jurisdiction served a double function, both establishing the propriety of exercising jurisdiction and notifying the defendant of the proceedings. When other bases of jurisdiction are asserted that do not of themselves notify the defendant, notice becomes a separate matter, and appropriate notice will be necessary to satisfy due process requirements . . . .

II. A Survey of Accepted Bases in American Law for Adjudicatory Jurisdiction

New developments have served to emphasize that some of the terminology conventionally employed in Anglo-American discussions of jurisdiction to adjudicate is not very helpful. A distinction has traditionally been drawn between jurisdiction over "persons" and jurisdiction over "things," but for several reasons this distinction does not seem apt or particularly useful. Adjudication always involves the determination of rights and duties of persons, natural or artificial. Things have no rights or duties but are the subjects or objects of rights and duties. An exercise of jurisdiction to adjudicate ultimately affects the rights and duties of persons; the peculiar characteristic of a true "in rem" action is simply its ability to determine the rights of all persons in the thing . . . . We shall speak, therefore, simply of jurisdiction to adjudicate, with the understanding that jurisdiction always in-

17. Williams v. North Carolina, 317 U.S. 287 (1942).

volves an exercise of power—in the sense of defining rights and duties—
with respect to one or more persons.

A further difficulty with current terminology is its failure to distinguish between the kinds of controversies appropriately adjudicated on the
basis of a particular ground of jurisdiction. In American thinking, affiliations between the forum and the underlying controversy normally support
only the power to adjudicate with respect to issues deriving from, or connected with, the very controversy that establishes jurisdiction to adjudicate.
This we call specific jurisdiction. On the other hand, American practice for
the most part is to exercise power to adjudicate any kind of controversy when
jurisdiction is based on relationships, direct or indirect, between the forum
and the person or persons whose legal rights are to be affected. This we call
general jurisdiction.

A. General Jurisdiction To Adjudicate

Two categories of general jurisdiction are found in American law: unlimited general jurisdiction, the ensuing judgment speaking without restriction to any of the judgment debtor's assets; and limited general jurisdiction,
the judgment affecting only a specified fund or assets. For example, only
limited general jurisdiction is taken when the basis for assuming jurisdiction
is the presence within the jurisdiction of assets belonging to the defendant.
When the relationship grounding jurisdiction is between the person himself
and the forum, we shall speak of directly affiliating circumstances. When
the relationship grounding jurisdiction is between a person's assets or other
interests and the forum, we shall speak of indirectly affiliating circumstances.
Each is relevant both to general jurisdiction and to specific jurisdiction.

1. Directly Affiliating Circumstances Between the Forum
and the Persons Whose Rights and Duties
are to be Affected

General jurisdiction to adjudicate has in American practice never been
based on the plaintiff's relationship to the forum. There is nothing in
American law comparable to article 126 of the Code of Civil Procedure of
The Netherlands (1827) which authorizes the assumption of jurisdiction
based on the Dutch domicile of the plaintiff, or to article 14 of the Civil
Code of France (1804) under which the French nationality of the plaintiff
is a sufficient ground for jurisdiction. American practice bases general jurisdiction to adjudicate on three types of relationship between the defendant
and the forum: his domicile or habitual residence; his presence; and his
consent, at least when it is given after the controversy has arisen or after
the action is brought.

The first of these affiliating circumstances is clearly a proper basis for
general jurisdiction; justice requires a certain and predictable place where
a person can be reached by those having claims against him. The defendant's mere presence, on the other hand, is a problematical basis for assuming
general jurisdiction. Its central role in Anglo-American law is to be explained on historical grounds. Typically, however, the defendant's presence
will be joined with one or more of the following relationships, each of which
supports in some measure the taking of jurisdiction: the forum is the plain-

tiff's domicile or residence; evidence or important witnesses are in the forum state; or the underlying controversy is closely connected with the forum state. Very few cases can arise in which a plaintiff who has no connection with the putative forum other than a desire to utilize its courts for litigation seeks to have jurisdiction to adjudicate exercised over a controversy as to which the forum has no concern and over a defendant whose only connection with the forum is his physical presence in the forum state. On one view, therefore, the presence test can be explained—and largely justified—as simply a convenient identifying element that almost invariably signals a congeries of other significant affiliations with the forum that would, upon proper analysis, ground jurisdiction. Looked at this way, it is a simple test obviating detailed inquiry in each case and a consequent increase in litigation.

The ultimate explanation of consent as a basis of jurisdiction is probably the same as has been suggested for presence: consent is an easily administered and relatively precise test which in the overwhelming majority of situations is associated in practice with other relationships supporting the taking of jurisdiction to adjudicate. Moreover, at least when consent is given after the action is brought the defendant can hardly claim that he is unfairly disadvantaged by the choice of forum. Consent obtained *before* the action is brought —indeed, before any dispute has arisen—differs in several ways from consent given after an action has been initiated: in the first place, prior consent to jurisdiction—typically embodied in a contractual stipulation—is far more important for planning. It thus finds a larger measure of support in general policies respecting the consensual ordering of human affairs and, to this extent, need not be justified solely by more strictly jurisdictional considerations. However, from the strictly jurisdictional point of view, consent given before an action is brought is more likely to produce arbitrary jurisdictional results than is consent directed to an actual litigation.[36] Further, the danger of coerced consent, for example, through the exercise of greatly superior bargaining power is great in the case of prior consent but is less likely when consent occurs in the context of an existing controversy. Of course, this difference would disappear if the courts examined all prior consents to determine whether an agreement was a fair one. But to the extent that courts decline to undertake such investigations, the difference persists and makes it easier to accept consent given after an action is instituted as a basis for jurisdiction to adjudicate.

2. *Indirectly Affiliating Circumstances Between the Forum and the Person Whose Legal Rights and Duties are to be Affected*

. . . In American practice . . . the "location" of the defendant's property within the jurisdiction remains a basis for *limited* general jurisdiction, that is, jurisdiction to adjudicate any kind of controversy

---

36. In National Equip. Rental, Ltd. v. Szukhent, 375 U.S. 311 (1964) (5-to-4 decision), the Supreme Court gave effect to a contractual stipulation that had the net result of permitting the leasing company to concentrate in its home jurisdiction all lease litigation in which the company would be plaintiff.

but limited in effectiveness to the property involved.[38]   A survey of contemporary practice in the United States can begin with land and tangible chattels.   The presence in a jurisdiction of such assets belonging to the defendant provides a basis for adjudicating any kind of claim against the defendant— regardless of whether it bears a particular relation to the asset in question— to the extent that the claim can be satisfied out of the property grounding jurisdiction.[39]   This is the most common form of the so-called "quasi in rem" jurisdiction.   .   .   .

The location within the jurisdiction of a document that embodies the rights to intangible assets—for example, a negotiable instrument—has jurisdictional consequences similar to those assigned to the presence of tangible chattels.   .   .   .   Intangible assets—in particular, monetary claims—can .   .   .   furnish a basis for limited general jurisdiction even though the claims are not embodied in an instrument.   In this form of "quasi in rem" jurisdiction, limited general jurisdiction over the defendant is acquired by garnishing a debt owed him by another; jurisdiction to garnish is typically based on either the presence or the domicile of the garnishee (the true defendant's debtor).   The classic statement of this proposition for American law is the Supreme Court decision in Harris v. Balk.[43]   The question remains whether all relationships that would ground jurisdiction in an action brought by the true defendant against his debtor are acceptable in a garnishment proceeding.   .   .   .

The propriety of this particular form of limited general jurisdiction has not gone unchallenged.   Indeed, the whole American approach basing limited general jurisdiction—as distinguished from specific jurisdiction—upon the presence of assets in a jurisdiction is of doubtful propriety.[47]   Although the American view at least avoids the absurd excesses of section 23 of the German Code of Civil Procedure, which grounds *unlimited* general jurisdiction on the presence of assets, the approach apparently adopted by France seems clearly preferable: jurisdiction—apart from exercises of *specific* jurisdiction—is as-

---

38.   In many states the limitation to specific assets does not apply if the defendant appears and contests on the merits.   .   .   .   This result is supported by the superficially plausible argument that "the defendant cannot complain of inconvenience since he has already indicated a willingness to defend the merits."   .   .   .   Even for one prepared to accept limited general jurisdiction in principle, the refusal to permit limited appearance can only constitute a pro tanto acceptance of coercion as a basis for unlimited general jurisdiction, the degree of coercion being precisely measured by the value of the defendant's property within the jurisdiction.   .   .   .   For those who agree with us that limited general jurisdiction cannot survive analysis, the refusal to permit limited appearance represents a bootstrap operation raised to the second power.   .   .   .

39.   See Pennoyer v. Neff, 95 U.S. 714 (1878) (land or immovables)   .   .   .   .

43.   198 U.S. 215 (1905).   In this case the basis of jurisdiction over the true defendant's debtor was presence. .   .   .

47.   With the emergence of specific jurisdiction, limited general jurisdiction has become increasingly less palatable; its legitimate functions are more appropriately performed by some form of specific jurisdiction.   .   .   .   [A decade after this article was written, the Supreme Court reached similar conclusions in Shaffer v. Heitner, 433 U.S. 186 (1977), which severely limited the use of quasi in rem jurisdiction. Ed. Note.]

sumed on this basis only in order to secure assets against dissipation and concealment.

3.   A Special Problem: General Adjudicatory Jurisdication Over Legal Persons With Regard to Activities Unconnected With the Forum Community

From the beginning in American practice, general adjudicatory jurisdiction over corporations and other legal persons could be exercised by the community with which the legal person had its closest and most continuing legal and factual connections.   The community that chartered the corporation and in which it has its head office occupies a position somewhat analogous to that of the community of a natural person's domicile and habitual residence. If a corporation's managerial and administrative center is in a state other than its state of incorporation, presumably general jurisdiction should exist in either community.   Indeed, if top-level managerial and administrative functions are centered rather equally in two or more communities, each such community has a legitimate claim to be treated as the corporation's head office for jurisdictional purposes.   The legal person that prefers thus to disperse its management has no legitimate ground on which to object to litigation in any of these several forums.[51]

The further question remains: should other affiliating circumstances ground truly general jurisdiction with respect to legal persons—in particular, corporations—or jurisdiction only with respect to activities connected with the forum community? .   .   .

.   .   .   In International Shoe [Co. v. Washington, 326 U.S. 310 (1945)], Mr. Chief Justice Stone summarized his understanding of the prior law as follows:

> While it has been held, in cases on which appellant relies, that continuous activity of some sorts within a state is not enough to support the demand that the corporation be amenable to suits unrelated to that activity .   .   .   there have been instances in which the continuous corporate operations within a state were thought so substantial and of such a nature as to justify suit against it on causes of action arising from dealings entirely distinct from those activities. See Missouri, K. & T. R. Co. v. Reynolds, 255 U.S. 565; Tauza v. Susquehanna Coal Co., 220 N.Y. 259, 115 N.E. 915
>
> .   .   .   .

It may be asked whether the status of this issue was affected by the new and more functional approach to the jurisdictional problem in terms of "the quality and nature of the [corporate] activity in relation to the fair and orderly administration of the laws" launched by Mr. Chief Justice Stone in *International Shoe.*   The Court emphasized that "the obligation which is here sued upon arose out of [the] .   .   .   very activities" relied upon to "establish

---

51. A degree of dispersal may be reached, however, at which the purpose of the rule—to assure a forum for all claims and to limit general jurisdiction to that forum—would better be served by abandoning the attempt to locate a "head office."   In that event, the place of incorporation would be the only appropriate forum for general jurisdiction.

sufficient contacts or ties with the state of the forum to make it reasonable and just, according to our traditional conception of fair play and substantial justice, to permit the state to enforce the obligations which appellant has incurred there." This approach suggests that, absent the kind of total, close, and continuing relations to a community implied in incorporation or in the location of a head office within a state, jurisdiction over legal persons—aside perhaps from the possibility of *limited* general jurisdiction based on the location of assets—should take the form of specific jurisdiction.   .   .   .

B. Specific Jurisdiction To Adjudicate

In the case of specific jurisdiction, the assertion of power to adjudicate is limited to matters arising out of—or intimately related to—the affiliating circumstances on which the jurisdictional claim is based.[64] It is in this area that the most significant—and most controversial—developments have occurred in contemporary American thinking and practice.

1. *Directly Affiliating Circumstances Between the Forum and the Persons Whose Rights and Duties are to be Affected*

Assertions of specific jurisdiction on the basis of circumstances directly affiliating the forum and one of the parties are few in American practice. .   .   . The more significant assertions of this variety of specific jurisdiction rely on the affiliating circumstance of the plaintiff's domicile in the forum community. For example, the principle is firmly established—and of great importance—that the plaintiff's domicile bases specific jurisdiction with respect to certain aspects of the marriage relation. Haddock v. Haddock, relying on "the inherent power which all governments must possess over the marriage relation, its formulation and dissolution," concluded that "no questions can arise on this record concerning the right of the State of Connecticut within its borders to give effect to the decree of divorce rendered in favor of the husband by the courts of Connecticut, he being at the time when the decree was rendered domiciled in that State."[66] However, under the constitutional restraint of due process, the plaintiff's domicile does not give a basis for specific jurisdiction to adjudicate all questions that arise in terminating a marriage. In particular, jurisdiction has been held not to exist to determine the absent spouse's right to financial support, for, as the Court remarked in the *Vanderbilt* case, "a court cannot adjudicate a personal claim or obligation unless it has jurisdiction over the person of the defendant."[67]   .   .   .

---

64. It is generally agreed that the defendant's appearance to defend on the merits does not ground general jurisdiction as to him   .   .   .   .

66. 201 U.S. 562, 569, 572 (1906). Since Williams v. North Carolina, 317 U.S. 287 (1942), sister states are under a full-faith-and-credit compulsion to recognize such divorces unless it can be established that the moving party was not domiciled in the rendering state.

67. Vanderbilt v. Vanderbilt, 354 U.S. 416, 418 (1957)   .   .   .   .

2. *Indirectly Affiliating Circumstances: Specific Jurisdiction Deriving from the Underlying Controversy's Relationship with the Forum*

The highly significant development in recent years of this form of specific jurisdiction reflects the growing mobility and complexity of modern life and an increasingly functional approach to jurisdictional issues. In addition, these bases have been asserted in certain contexts either because the choice-of-law process functions poorly, if at all, or because genuine conflicts in policy are involved and the forum seeks adjudicatory jurisdiction in order to vindicate its viewpoint. Finally, with commercial and economic life increasingly dominated by corporations, the emergence of jurisdiction based on indirectly affiliating circumstances removes the bias favoring defendants that is ordinarily associated with unlimited general jurisdiction, a bias that is doubtless fully appropriate as between parties of relatively equal economic power and legal sophistication but that is harder to justify when an ordinary plaintiff is thereby compelled to seek out a corporate defendant. In discussing these forms of specific jurisdiction, we find it helpful to distinguish between two-party situations and those more complex situations involving multiple or indeterminate parties.

(a) Two-Party Situations.—(1) Continuous Relationship of Defendant to the Forum.—Two kinds of continuous relationships may be the bases for asserting specific jurisdiction: doing business or carrying on a continuous course of activity within a forum, and having an interest in property located within the forum. A relatively early—and significant—case involving the first of these two bases for specific jurisdiction was Henry L. Doherty & Co. v. Goodman.[71] In that case the Supreme Court of the United States upheld jurisdiction in an action under the Iowa "blue-sky" law against an unregistered, nonresident securities dealer who had established an office in Iowa. The controversy related to stock sold to the plaintiff by the defendant's Iowa office. The Supreme Court, noting that "Iowa treats the business of dealing in corporate securities as exceptional and subjects it to special regulation," concluded that since "Doherty voluntarily established an office in Iowa and there carried on business" he was properly subject to jurisdiction. The *International Shoe* decision later generalized this trend, adopting a new analytical approach which permits the assumption of jurisdiction over any matter that bears a reasonable and substantial connection to the forum community. . . .

(2) Isolated Events or Transactions.—Without doubt some of the most significant developments in modern thinking and practice respecting jurisdiction to adjudicate relate to the increasing acceptance of specific jurisdiction based on isolated events or transactions. These developments have conduced to a rethinking of the field's methodology; they have considerably undermined the traditional jurisdictional premise that the plaintiff should seek out the defendant; and they have both increased the temptations toward parochial choice-of-law thinking and made it more imperative that these temptations be resisted.

---

71. 294 U.S. 623 (1935).

The seminal case in this area was Hess v. Pawloski.[79] The decision upheld against constitutional objections a Massachusetts nonresident motorist statute under which specific jurisdiction was asserted as to "any action or proceeding   .   .   .   growing out of any accident or collision" in which the nonresident operator was involved while operating the vehicle on a public way within Massachusetts.   Mr. Justice Butler, in his opinion for the Court, emphasized that "motor vehicles are dangerous machines" and that Massachusetts could "exclude a non-resident" until he had submitted, with respect to possible future accidents, to the jurisdiction of Massachusetts.

A more recent Supreme Court decision, basing jurisdiction on an isolated transaction in the insurance field, is McGee v. International Life Ins. Co.[82] A resident of California had purchased a life insurance policy from an Arizona corporation in 1944.   In 1948 the defendant corporation assumed the original insurer's obligation, notifying the insured by mailing him a reinsurance certificate which he accepted.   Thereafter premiums were paid by mail to the defendant's Texas office.   The insured died in 1950, and the company refused to pay the beneficiary on the ground that the insured had committed suicide.   Neither the original insurer nor the defendant ever had an office or agent in California.   "And so far as the record   .   .   .   shows, respondent has never solicited or done any insurance business in California apart from the policy involved here."   California "based its jurisdiction on a state statute which subjects foreign corporations to suit in California on insurance contracts with residents of that State   .   .   .   ."   Writing for a unanimous Court, Mr. Justice Black concluded:

> It is sufficient for purposes of due process that the suit was based on a contract which had substantial connection with   .   .   .   [California].   Cf. Hess v. Pawloski, 274 U.S. 352; Henry L. Doherty & Co. v. Goodman, 294 U.S. 623; Pennoyer, v. Neff, 95 U.S. 714, 735.   The contract was delivered in California, the premiums were mailed from there and the insured was a resident of that State when he died.   It cannot be denied that California has a manifest interest in providing effective means of redress for its residents when their insurers refuse to pay claims.   .   .   .   When claims were small or moderate individual claimants frequently could not afford the cost of bringing an action in a foreign forum—thus in effect making the company judgment proof.   Often the crucial witnesses—as here on the company's defense of suicide—will be found in the insured's locality.

The *McGee* case raises several questions.   Would the same result have been reached if the only circumstance affiliating the litigation with California had been the insured's residence?   More generally, what relations are significant for the assumption of specific jurisdiction to adjudicate in this kind of case?   In an analysis of this basis for assuming jurisdiction, is it relevant that the defendant does a significant volume of interstate business, that its insureds are typically persons of relatively modest means and that litiga-

---

79.   274 U.S. 352 (1927).   82.   355 U.S. 220 (1957).

tion expenses are presumably a relatively predictable cost of doing business and will be reflected in premium charges? . . .

(b) Multiple or Indeterminate Parties.—This is perhaps the most difficult and unsettled topic in the entire subject of adjudicatory jurisdiction. Difficulties arise even in the fully domestic context in the handling of litigation involving multiple or indeterminate parties. In litigation with multistate elements, problems of adjudicatory jurisdiction in the international sense often produce additional complications. In some instances it may be possible to obtain general jurisdiction over all relevant parties, and there has been little difficulty in handling such situations under the techniques available for comparable fully domestic litigation. For the most part, however, it is necessary to claim specific jurisdiction over one or more of the parties. The ultimate justification for the exercise of such jurisdiction rests on the practical necessity that some forum be able to speak with respect to the situation as a whole . . . .

(1) "Location" of Assets Within the Jurisdiction

(i) Land and Chattels.—Tyler v. Judges of the Court of Registration [104] upheld against federal and state constitutional objections a statute providing that a decree of registration obtained after proceedings designed to give as extensive notice as was feasible and after appropriate findings had been made, "shall bind the land and quiet the title thereto." In this opinion for the Massachusetts court, Chief Justice Holmes found no difficulty in this assertion of adjudicatory jurisdiction against the whole world: "Jurisdiction is secured by the power of the court over the *res*." However, Holmes was clear that "all proceedings, like all rights, are really against persons. Whether they are proceedings or rights *in rem* depends on the number of persons affected." In Holmes's view the ultimate basis for this assertion of adjudicatory jurisdiction was practical necessity:

> If it [this proceeding] does not satisfy the Constitution, a judicial proceeding to clear titles against all the world hardly is possible, for the very meaning of such a proceeding is to get rid of unknown as well as known claims,—indeed certainty against the unknown may be said to be its chief end,—and unknown claims cannot be dealt with by personal service upon the claimaint . . . .

(ii) Intangible Assets.—To the extent that intangible assets are taken to be embodied in a document, the document's location apparently grounds specific jurisdiction as to claims respecting the underlying assets. However, it is unclear whether specific jurisdiction over rights respecting assets that are not reified can, by analogy to Harris v. Balk, be exercised by a forum having jurisdiction over the debtor . . . .

(2) Establishment of the Legal Entity in the Jurisdiction

For certain types of problems specific jurisdiction has been recognized in the jurisdiction where the legal entity is established. Thus, in litigation

---

104. 175 Mass. 71, 55 N.E. 812, appeal dismissed 179 U.S. 405 (1900) ("the plaintiff in error has not the requiste interest to draw in question" the constitutionality of the statute).

respecting trusts, frequently the beneficiaries will be in several jurisdictions and difficulties are encountered when it is essential to bind the rights of all. For ordinary trusts the rule is emerging that "a state has judicial jurisdiction over the trustees and the beneficiaries of an express trust to determine questions relating to the validity, construction and administration of the trust if it is the state where the administration of the trust is located." The need to ensure that one forum can speak authoritatively with respect to the interests of all and the technical difficulties that had to be overcome to reach this result are especially clear in the case of common trust funds—the joint, commingled administration of many small trusts in order to gain flexibility in investment policy and administrative economies. Mullane v. Central Hanover Bank & Trust Co. made it clear that the state of establishment could exercise specific jurisdiction in these situations: [121]

> [T]he interest of each state in providing means to close trusts that exist by the grace of its laws and are administered under the supervision of its courts is so insistent and rooted in custom as to establish beyond doubt the right of its courts to determine the interests of all claimants, resident or nonresident, provided its procedure accords full opportunity to appear and be heard . . . .

(3) Totality of Contacts with the Forum

Another approach to specific jurisdiction in more complex situations is seen in Mr. Justice Traynor's decision in Atkinson v. Superior Court.[130] Separate class actions were brought in California by two groups of musicians attacking the validity of collective bargaining contracts and certain related trust agreements between their employers and the American Federation of Musicians. It was argued that the Federation had violated its duty as the musicians' collective bargaining agent and acted in fraud of their rights in agreeing with the employers that certain royalty payments and payments for reuse of motion pictures on television should be paid to a trustee for specified trust purposes instead of to the employees. General jurisdiction could have been exercised over the Federation and the employers; but the trustees were in New York and no basis existed for asserting general jurisdiction as to them. Consequently, unless a basis existed for taking specific jurisdiction, an adjudication would not bind the trustees. The trial court—taking the view that such jurisdiction did not exist—refused to proceed with aspects of the litigation involving the trustees. The jurisdictional issue came ultimately before the Supreme Court of California, which held that, under the circumstances of the case, California could exercise adjudicatory jurisdiction over the trustees.

The opinion of the court first rejected any approach seeking to "localize" the intangible rights at issue:

> In the absence of a settled rule governing the situation before us, and in light of the fact that an intangible may be subjected to the

---

121. 339 U.S. 306, 313 (1950). The requirements of notice and of the opportunity to defend are, as the decision makes clear, not absolute but a question of what is reasonable under all the circumstances.

130. 49 Cal.2d 338, 316 P.2d 960 (1957), cert. denied 357 U.S. 569 (1958).

jurisdiction of the court without personal jurisdiction over all of the
parties involved for some purposes but not for others, we conclude
that the solution must be sought in the general principles governing
jurisdiction over persons and property rather than in an attempt to
assign a fictional situs to intangibles.

The court concluded that, under all the circumstances, jurisdiction existed
over the trustees.

> The obligation plaintiffs seek to enforce grows out of their em-
> ployment by defendants here.   The payments involved are alleged
> to be consideration for work performed in this state.   The Federa-
> tion defendant is before the court.   Under these circumstances,
> fairness to plaintiffs demands that they be able to reach the fruits
> of their labors before they are removed from the state.   Moreover,
> fairness to the defendants who are personally before the court also
> demands that the conflicting claims of the trustee be subject to
> final adjudication.

(4) *The Most Appropriate Forum for Matters Needing*
a Unified Administration

Although the courts do not often place central reliance on the idea, the
suggestion at times emerges in litigation involving multiple or indeterminate
parties that specific jurisdiction to adjudicate lies with the forum providing
the most appropriate focus for matters calling for a unified administration.
This principle would suggest the taking of jurisdiction in some situations in
which it is not now taken, as well as the limiting of jurisdiction to a single
forum in situations where several forums now assume it.   An approach in
these terms may emerge more clearly as thinking respecting adjudicatory jurisdiction sheds old conceptual categories and deals in policy terms with the
various problems that press for solution.

One area in which an approach along these lines may be emerging is
that of the administration of decedent's estates.   The basic argument for such
a jurisdiction is that convenience demands an efficient, unified administration,
which cannot be provided if the estate is handled in several courts.   The movement in this area toward a single governing law may also reinforce the arguments in favor of entrusting adjudicatory jurisdiction over the entire estate to
a single forum.   The forum with the strongest claim to the exercise of this
jurisdiction would clearly seem to be in the state of the decedent's domicile
.   .   .   .

III.   Lines of Future Development

.   .   .   Will specific jurisdiction prosper and mature, or has it achieved
its full growth as the occasional and exceptional device for dealing with particular situations involving the nonresident automobile driver, securities dealer, or insurance seller? We believe that the approach in terms of reason and
fairness brought to bear on jurisdiction over corporations and other legal persons by the *International Shoe* case, whose implications already have begun
to be felt in the area of specific jurisdiction over nonresident individuals,
will continue to be extended and refined.

What policies should inform these developments and give content to "reason" and "fairness"? We submit that specific jurisdiction—with its characteristic feature of permitting the plaintiff to require the defendant to come, as it were, to him—is appropriate in two distinct classes of cases: (1) when the traditional jurisdictional bias in favor of the defendant is not justified; (2) when very strong considerations of convenience, relating not only to the plaintiff but also to the taking of evidence and other litigational considerations, point to a particular community. This second class of situations is most clearly illustrated in cases involving multiple or indeterminate parties, when jurisdiction is assumed on the basis of the location of land or other assets in the community or on that of the establishment in the community of a legal entity. And the jurisdiction asserted in Hess v. Pawloski is perhaps justified in part on this ground; considerations of litigational convenience, particularly with respect to the taking of evidence, tend in accident cases to point insistently to the community in which the accident occurred. These considerations may be determinative in the case of simple torts, but for other torts and for contracts, for example, Hess v. Pawloski would support the more general proposition that under certain circumstances the respective situations of the parties are such that the jurisdictional rule should favor the plaintiff rather than the defendant.

Why should the jurisdictional rule in Hess v. Pawloski favor the plaintiff? We suggest that the explanation lies in the multistate character of the defendant's activity giving rise to the underlying controversy, as compared with the localized nature of the plaintiff's. In addition, the defendant's activity foreseeably involved the risk of serious harm to individuals in communities other than his own. These two elements, taken together, and quite apart from considerations of litigational convenience, justify requiring the defendant to come to the plaintiff. The result is rendered still easier by the fact that the nonresident motorist—after the development of automobile insurance—usually does not handle his own case as a private person but is defended by representatives of his insurance company, whose activities are multistate and whose rates ultimately reflect the economic cost to defendants of requiring them to come to plaintiffs.

These observations suggest a point about specific jurisdiction that we consider basic to its future development: in any class of cases in which the controversy arises out of conduct that is essentially multistate on the part of the defendant, and essentially local on the part of the plaintiff, an argument exists for reversing the jurisdictional preference traditionally accorded defendants. This argument becomes very strong when the defendants as a class [140] are regularly engaged in extensive multistate activity that will produce litigation from time to time, while the plaintiffs as a class are localized in their activities. The insurance cases illustrate this proposition splendidly: insurance companies are engaged in extensive multistate activity, and their economic and legal existence is not localized; on the other hand, plaintiffs who bring actions against an insurance company typically lead a localized economic and legal existence. Under these circumstances it is appropriate to reverse the

---

140. We include the phenomenon of an insurance company conducting the defense in a case such as Hess v. Pawloski . . . .

traditional jurisdictional preference accorded the defendant, a preference that emerged, of course, in the context of litigation involving only parties who typically led localized legal and economic existences.

If our analysis is correct, the further development of specific jurisdiction should take this distinction into account.   Rather far-reaching bases for specific jurisdiction would then appear supportable with respect to certain classes of defendants, for example corporations whose economic activities and legal involvements were pervasively multistate, while the situations in which specific jurisdiction could appropriately be exercised would be far fewer when the defendant was a natural or legal person whose economic activities and legal involvements were essentially local.   With respect to this latter class of defendants, additional litigational considerations of the kind present in Hess v. Pawloski should be required before specific jurisdiction is asserted.   This analysis further suggests that specific jurisdiction is less supportable when the plaintiff's involvements are also multistate.   Thus, if the plaintiff were a nonresident, or if his own affairs were not settled in a particular locality but were spread out over several jurisdictions including the defendant's home, less reason would exist for the exercise of specific jurisdiction.   Such a plaintiff should not be able to invoke specific jurisdiction merely because the defendant's activity causing the intrusion on the plaintiff's affairs occurred in the jurisdiction whose courts are asked to entertain the litigation.   Litigational considerations, however, including the convenience of witnesses and the ease of ascertaining the governing law, may justify the exercise of specific jurisdiction. (It should be noted that the strength of such litigational considerations tends to diminish as the activity of the defendant causing the intrusion on plaintiff's affairs is less concentrated in the forum considering whether to exercise jurisdiction.)   In any event, in such situations the traditional bias in favor of the defendant should not be reversed unless the litigational considerations present are most compelling   .   .   .   .

One significant consequence of our approach   .   .   .   perhaps deserves elaboration because it marks a radical departure from traditional approaches. When the plaintiff's activities are highly localized in New York, and when litigational convenience so requires, we believe the plaintiff should be able to call the defendant to New York even though defendant has engaged in no activity in New York and has not anticipated that his multistate activity might produce consequences in New York.   It is enough, in assessing the relative fairness to plaintiff and defendant, that the plaintiff, whose affairs are essentially local, has been injured by the activity of a defendant who has involved himself in multistate activity.   Traditional approaches tend to focus on the defendant alone and to regard it as unfair, if there has been no ac-
consequences in the state were not foreseeable, to require the defendant to come to New York.   By opening up to inquiry both the question of the relative fairness to plaintiff and defendant and the question of litigational convenience, we find it difficult to escape the conclusion that cases will arise—   .   .   .   *McGee* is perhaps [an example]—in which defendant's activity in the forum is minimal or nonexistent but in which the traditional bias in favor of the defendant should be overturned.   On the other hand, foreseeability cannot of course be completely dismissed; defendant's involvement in multistate activity may not justify the imposition of a

litigational burden substantially exceeding that inherent in defendant's normal multistate activities .   .   .   .

Having discussed the policies underlying those forms of specific jurisdiction in which a bias in favor of the plaintiff should replace the traditional bias in favor of the defendant, we now consider briefly a second form of specific jurisdiction, in which strong considerations of convenience, relating not only to the plaintiff but also to the taking of evidence and other litigational considerations, point to a particular community. As has already been suggested, jurisdiction based on these considerations has been exercised sporadically in litigation involving multiple or indeterminate parties. The traditional bases for such exercises of jurisdiction have been the location of land or other assets in the community; and more recently, the establishment in the forum state of a legal entity, such as the trust in the *Mullane* case, has been recognized as an appropriate basis for the exercise of what might be called jurisdiction by necessity .   .   .   .

If specific jurisdiction enjoys the growth and undergoes the refinement just described, other changes should occur in the coming decades in the accepted bases for assuming jurisdiction to adjudicate. For reasons that have already been suggested, ultimately only general jurisdiction and specific jurisdiction should be recognized, and the only relationship basing *general* jurisdiction should come to be habitual residence except in those rare situations in which the defendant has no substantial connection with any community. *Limited* general jurisdiction should disappear entirely as various forms of specific jurisdiction emerge to permit a community to adjudicate in those situations that, in the past, have furnished the only legitimate justification for the spectrum of limited general jurisdiction cases that today runs from Pennoyer v. Neff through Harris v. Balk and perhaps even beyond.

Historically, the phenomenon of limited general jurisdiction is understandable. Specific jurisdiction was largely or completely unknown and enforcement of a foreign judgment was often difficult if not impossible. As a result the litigational convenience of proceeding where assets could be found was great, and the methodology through which jurisdictional problems were approached gave an apparent justification for such practices, concealing the true difficulties. Often, too, the presence of defendant's assets was symptomatic of other activities, or of relationships of the defendant to the forum, that functionally justified requiring the defendant to come to the plaintiff. But today all this is changing. Ultimately, all that should remain of Pennoyer v. Neff, Harris v. Balk, and their progeny is specific jurisdiction to secure assets against dissipation and concealment while a controversy is being litigated in an appropriate forum. The functions heretofore performed, often unfairly, by limited general jurisdiction can more rationally be performed by specific jurisdiction, which offers protection against the unfairness of requiring a defendant to litigate any and every question wherever his assets can be found, and also offers the plaintiff an opportunity to call the defendant to him in appropriate circumstances.

For much the same reasons, general jurisdiction based on presence, which often produces unfair results quite comparable to those reached under limited general jurisdiction, should disappear. It is, of course, appropriate to preserve some place where the defendant can be sued on any cause of action. But we submit that only the common arena of the defendant's activities should be such a place.   For an individual, the sole community where it is fair to require him to litigate any cause of action is his habitual residence; for a corporation, it is the corporate headquarters—presumably both the place of incorporation and the principal place of business, where these differ.   If specific jurisdiction matures to its full potential and is subjected to the tests based on fairness elaborated above, jurisdiction should be abandoned for many situations in which it is now asserted.

---

1.   For a similar perspective on the problems of state-court jurisdiction, see Erhenzweig, The Transient Role of Personal Jurisdiction: The "Power" Myth and Forum Conveniens, 65 Yale L.J. 289 (1956); Hazard, A General Theory of State-Court Jurisdiction, 1965 Sup.Ct.Rev. 241 (1965).

2.   The primary concern of Professors von Mehren and Trautman is with the jurisdiction of state courts within a federal political system.   Only to a lesser extent do they take up the comparable issues for federal courts. Von Mehren and Trautman see the situation of federal courts as more "ambiguous."   On one view the federal courts operate as a "unitary system," and to the extent they do, "the problem of adjudicatory jurisdiction disappears internally."   Then, von Mehren and Trautman argue, the "determination of the place of trial might well be handled administratively;" the issue would be entirely one of convenience.   On the other hand, von Mehren and Trautman recognize that this unitary assumption is not entirely correct and that to some large extent the federal courts also "are fragmented and function as organs of the distinct legal orders of the several states."   They write (in footnote 6):

> .   .   .   Perhaps because of a traditional reluctance to prescribe federal standards in the case of diversity litigation as well as an instinct for symmetry, federal law does not today directly prescribe general and comprehensive jurisdictional regulations for the federal courts in either type of litigation.   Rule 4(e) of the Federal Rules of Civil Procedure (see also rules 4(d), 4(f) and 4(i)) applies without distinction to federal-question and diversity litigation.   The rule provides for the use of federal jurisdictional standards to the extent these are furnished by "a statute of the United States."   The rule further adopts jurisdictional provisions contained in "statute[s] or rule[s] of court of the state in which the district court is held.   .   .   ."
>
> This approach incorporating state jurisdictional provisions is fully understandable for diversity cases.   .   .   .   In the absence of a complete jurisdictional scheme provided by a federal statute, the approach also seems clearly necessary and proper for federal-question cases.   .   .   .   (It can be noted that for most federal-question cases, what is in effect a restrictive jurisdictional standard is imposed by the "venue" provision of 28 U.S.C. § 1391(b), re-

quiring such suits to be brought "only in the judicial district where all defendants reside. . . .")

Rule 4(e)'s incorporative approach can, however, produce perplexities when federal claims are to be litigated. The difficulties derive from the fact that any given state necessarily views the jurisdictional problem from the perspective of its community, but, insofar as federal-law questions are concerned, the appropriate community may become the nation as a whole. Jurisdiction to adjudicate may well be properly assumed from the latter perspective though refused from the former. . . .

In connection with these observations, and their more general critique of rules unthinkingly cast in favor of the "attacked" (the defendant) rather than the "attacker" (the plaintiff), see Colby v. Driver, 577 F.2d 147 (1st Cir. 1978), cert. granted, 47 U.S.L.W. 3472 (U.S. Jan. 15, 1979) (No. 78–303) (concerning the statutory basis for and the constitutionality of nationwide service of process on federal officials who are sued in their individual capacities for acts allegedly performed under color of law).

Burt Neuborne, **The Myth of Parity***

In Stone v. Powell,[1] Justice Powell responded to the assertion that federal habeas corpus review of state exclusionary rule determinations was essential to the vigorous enforcement of the fourth amendment by rejecting any notion that federal judges are institutionally more receptive to federal constitutional norms than are their state counterparts. Rather, Justice Powell appeared to assume that state and federal courts are functionally interchangeable forums likely to provide equivalent protection for federal constitutional rights. If it existed, this assumed parity between state and federal courts, which characterizes much of the current Court's approach to problems of federal jurisdiction, would render the process of allocating judicial business between state and federal forums an outcome-neutral exercise unrelated to the merits.

Unfortunately, I fear that the parity which Justice Powell celebrated in *Stone* exists only in his understandable wish that it were so. I suggest that the assumption of parity is, at best, a dangerous myth, fostering forum allocation decisions which channel constitutional adjudication under the illusion that state courts will vindicate federally secured constitutional rights as forcefully as would the lower federal courts. At worst, it provides a pretext for funneling federal constitutional decisionmaking into state courts precisely because they are less likely to be receptive to vigorous enforcement of federal constitutional doctrine. As a result, I view forum allocation decisions like *Stone* not as outcome-neutral allocations of judicial business but as indirect decisions on the merits, which weaken disfavored federal constitutional rights by remitting their enforcement to less receptive state forums. . . .

Source: 90 Harv.L.Rev. 1105, 1105–30 (1977). Professor of Law, New York University.

1. 428 U.S. 465 (1976).

As a civil liberties lawyer for the past ten years, I have pursued a litigation strategy premised on two assumptions. First, persons advancing federal constitutional claims against local officials will fare better, as a rule, in a federal, rather than a state, trial court. Second, to a somewhat lesser degree, federal district courts are institutionally preferable to state appellate courts as forums in which to raise federal constitutional claims.[45] I know of no empirical studies that prove (or undermine) those assumptions. Yet, they frequently shape the forum selection strategy in constitutional cases today as they have in the past   .   .   .   .

A.   An Institutional Comparison: Some Preliminary Observations

The first step in assessing the relative institutional capacity of state and federal courts to enforce constitutional doctrine requires agreement on which state forum should be compared with the federal district courts to determine whether a comparative advantage exists. Generally, when the parity issue is discussed, it is in the context of a comparison that tends to measure the federal district courts against state appellate courts. While such a comparison makes sense in the context of habeas corpus, where the petitioner first will have pursued his federal claims unsuccessfully through the state court system, it is inappropriate in most constitutional cases. Even if one concedes parity between state appellate and federal district courts, corrective state appellate work does not adequately substitute for vigorous constitutional protection at the trial level. The expense, delay, and uncertainty which inhere in any appellate process render ultimate success after appeal far less valuable than speedy, accurate resolution below. Especially in the context of first amendment rights, by their nature fragile, the possibility of a lengthy, problematic appeal in order to reverse an adverse criminal or civil judgment may deter many individuals from effectively exercising their rights. Moreover, in many constitutional cases, the factfinding process plays a critical role in resolution of the contro-

---

45.   .   .   .   When comparing federal district and state appellate courts, the comparative advantage which exists at the trial level is substantially diminished. If a competence gap exists at all, it is very slight and may, indeed, favor state appellate judges. Moreover, the sense of elan and mission characterizing federal judges is also present among many state appellate courts.

Two factors exist, however, that continue to incline me toward a federal trial forum. First, appellate court ability to review findings of fact and issues of credibility is limited. The Supreme Court's increasing emphasis on intent and motive in constitutional adjudication   .   .   .   renders the integrity of the factfinding process all the more critical. Second, because of the selection processes, most state ap-

pellate courts are exposed to majoritarian pressures to nearly the same extent as are state trial courts. The same three methods used to select state trial judges   .   .   .   predominate in the selection of appellate judges.   .   .   .   Only Rhode Island, New Hampshire, Massachusetts, and New Jersey grant life tenure to supreme court justices, the latter's being conditioned on reappointment after one seven-year term. All other states require reelection at intervals from 2 to 15 years   .   .   .   .

While the evidence is far from conclusive, it is from among those appellate courts which closely approximate the independence enjoyed by the federal courts that one finds the state courts which have been most vigorous in protecting individual rights   .   .   .   .

versy. These two factors combine to render the trial forum often the most critical stage, and thus the appropriate institutional comparison should be between federal district courts and their state trial counterparts.[54]

A second preparatory step is to dispel the notion that acknowledging a comparative advantage to federal courts need imply that state trial judges violate their oaths by consciously refusing to enforce federal rights. We are not faced today with widespread state judicial refusal to enforce clear federal rights.[55] When the mandates of the Federal Constitution are clear, most state judges respect the supremacy clause and enforce them. Constitutional litigation is, however, rarely about clear law. The disputes which propel parties raising constitutional questions into court frequently pit strong legal and moral claims against each other and resolution of those competing "legitimate" claims is the real stuff of constitutional litigation. Thus, one need not intimate that state trial judges act in bad faith. Our comparison need only suggest that given the institutional differences between the two benches, state trial judges are less likely to resolve arguable issues in favor of protecting federal constitutional rights than are their federal brethren.

As a final preparatory step, another notion—that federal district judges, when called upon to enforce the fourteenth amendment against local officials, resemble an alien, occupying army dispatched from Washington to rule over a conquered province—must be dispelled. Federal judges are chosen from the geographical area they serve. Generally, they are appointed with the consent and often at the behest of a senator representing the state in which they will sit, frequently after local officials and citizen groups have had the opportunity to make their views on the nominee known. To characterize federal judges as carpetbaggers, unaware of, and insensitive to, local concerns is thus inaccurate and serves to deflect attention from the relative efficacy of state and federal forums in enforcing constitutional norms . . . .

B. Technical Competence

. . . Because it is relatively small, the federal trial bench maintains a level of competence in its pool of potential appointees which dwarfs the competence of the vastly larger pool from which state trial judges are selected. There are about twice as many trial judges in California as in the entire federal system. As in any bureaucracy, it is far easier to maintain a high level of quality when appointing a relatively small number of officials than when staffing a huge department. Additionally, there is a substantial disparity be-

---

54. Failure to perceive the trial court's importance in constitutional litigation stems in part from the prevalence of an "upper court myth" which pictures the final appellate level as the most important aspect of the American judicial process. While the appellate opinion is the more glamorous aspect of constitutional adjudication, it takes a trial court to translate the abstract norms of an appellate decision into reality. . . .

55. The widespread breakdown of Southern justice which motivated enactment of the Civil Rights Act of 1871 . . . and similar breakdowns during the height of the civil rights movement which provoked calls for significant expansions of federal jurisdiction . . . do not exist today.

tween state and federal judicial compensation which allows the federal bench to attract a higher level of legal talent than state trial courts can hope to obtain.

The selection processes utilized to staff the respective judicial posts also incline toward a federal bench of higher professional distinction. While the federal selection process is not without flaws, it does focus substantially on the professional competence of the nominee. The selection processes for state trial courts are generally less concerned with gradations of professional competence once a minimum level has been attained. Neither elections nor an appointment process based largely on political patronage is calculated to make refined judgments on technical competence.

The competence gap does not stem solely from the differences in the native ability of the judges. While it is often overlooked, the caliber of judicial clerks exerts a substantial impact on the quality of judicial output. Federal clerks at both the trial and appellate levels are chosen from among the most promising recent law school graduates for one- to two-year terms. State trial clerks, on the other hand, when available at all, tend to be either career bureaucrats or patronage employees and may lack both the ability and dedication of their federal counterparts. Moreover, while the caseload burden of the federal courts is substantial, it pales when compared to the caseload of most state trial courts of general jurisdiction. Thus, even if state and federal judges were of equal native ability, the advantages enjoyed by federal judges would probably result in a higher level of performance. When those institutional advantages are combined with the differential in native ability, the competence gap becomes pronounced.

It is fair to ask why a civil liberties lawyer is particularly concerned about the relative competence of the possible forums. Even if a competence differential exists, would not an allegedly less competent state judge be as likely to err in favor of the lawyer's position as against it? Apart from esthetics, the answer is twofold. First, since constitutional decisions serve to guide third persons seeking to conform to constitutional norms, the clarity and persuasiveness of judicial opinions in constitutional cases assume great importance. A randomly correct decision by an inarticulate court, while welcome, is of far less value to the general protection of constitutional rights than the same decision by a court which can produce an eloquent and technically precise opinion to guide similarly situated persons.[68]

Second, a technically less competent judge is not as likely to err on the side of the constitutional claimant as against him. Constitutional litigation generally involves an assault on an existing state of law or facts which enjoys the imprimatur of democratic decisionmaking, with the party asserting a constitutional claim bearing a substantial burden of explaining why the status quo

68. Assume, for example, that union organizers, seeking to inform migrant workers of their rights, are charged by a local farmer with criminal trespass for conduct which they claim is protected by the first amendment . . . . An acquittal in a justice of the peace court would be of little value to the organizers at the next migrant stop and of no help to similarly situated organizers. An articulate opinion by a technically competent trial court, while not necessarily binding at the next stop, would be of substantial assistance.

should be changed.[69] Since judicial failure to comprehend his claim renders it impossible to satisfy that heavy burden, the constitutional claimant will be generally disadvantaged in a forum of limited technical capacity.

More specifically, for the past two decades constitutional litigators have sought to implement principles inherent in a series of expansive constitutional interpretations by the Warren Court. Much of that effort has involved explaining to skeptical lower court judges why those decisions have altered much of the law they remember from law school. Our success has depended not only on our skill as advocates, but also on the technical proficiency of the trial court.

Clearly, if the Supreme Court retrenches from those expansive decisions, superior technical competence at the trial level may be as troublesome to future civil liberties lawyers seeking to enforce eroded precedents as it is currently attractive to those seeking to enforce viable ones   .   .   .   .

C. Psychological Set

Even if state and federal forums were of equal technical competence, a series of psychological and attitudinal characteristics renders federal district judges more likely to enforce constitutional rights vigorously. First, although intangible, an elite tradition animates the federal judiciary, instilling elan and a sense of mission in federal judges and exerting   .   .   .   a palpable influence on the quality of the judicial product. As heirs of a tradition of constitutional enforcement, federal judges feel subtle, yet nonetheless real pressures to uphold that tradition. State trial judges, on the other hand, generally seem to lack a comparable sense of tradition or institutional mission.

Second, federal judges often display an enhanced sense of bureaucratic receptivity to the pronouncements of the Supreme Court. State judges, of course, almost always recognize that they too are bound not to disregard the Supreme Court's interpretation of the Federal Constitution. Their bureaucratic relationship with the Supreme Court is, however, more attenuated than that of a district court judge. Although the effects of this difference are difficult to isolate with certainty, in my experience federal judges appear to recognize an affirmative obligation to carry out and even anticipate the direction of the Supreme Court. Many state judges, on the other hand, appear to acknowledge only an obligation not to disobey clearly established law. While this distinction is subtle, in the doubtful case it can exert a discernible impact on the trial level outcome. Since civil liberties lawyers frequently are engaged in urging judges to recognize Supreme Court precedent, which, while not clearly dispositive, implies judgment for the constitutional plaintiff, the forum's recognition of an institutional duty to anticipate the as yet unexpressed views of the Supreme Court is critical.

---

69. Because of the countermajoritarian character of his claim, a constitutional plaintiff will face a greater inertial burden than a plaintiff in a nonconstitutional case. At the trial level, this burden—the presumption of constitutionality generally afforded government action—becomes stronger as trial judges, mindful of their position in the judicial hierarchy, often feel constrained to leave the overturning of governmental decisions to the appellate courts.

Third, in seeking a federal forum, civil liberties lawyers hope to benefit from what can be described as an "ivory tower syndrome." The scope of federal jurisdiction, even taking account of that over federal crimes and habeas corpus, is such that federal judges are insulated from the more cynicism-breeding dimensions of constitutional law. State trial judges, conversely, especially at the criminal, family, and lower civil court levels, are steadily confronted by distasteful and troubling fact patterns which can sorely test abstract constitutional doctrine and foster a jaded attitude toward constitutional rights. The fourth amendment's exclusionary rule, for example, will command greater allegiance from a judge who has not been repeatedly exposed to the reality of the social harms inflicted by some felons whom the rule requires to be freed. Similarly, the right to hold a political demonstration or a union organizing rally will seem more obvious to a judge who need not face the disorderly conduct arrests which may arise from them. Distance from the pressures and emotions generated by the application of constitutional doctrine is conducive to a generous reading and vigorous enforcement of constitutional rights. For state trial courts, which ordinarily must be responsible both for law enforcement and the day-to-day implementation of constitutional rights, no such distance is possible. Federal trial judges, on the other hand, because of the limited nature of their jurisdiction, enjoy a degree of distance enhancing the likelihood that they will liberally and assiduously perform their function of enunciating constitutional norms.

Finally, the differences in the backgrounds of the state and federal trial judges make it more likely that a federal judge will possess certain class-based predilections favorable to constitutional enforcement than will his state court counterpart. The federal bench is an elite, prestigious body, drawn primarily from a successful, homogeneous socioeducational class—a class strongly imbued with the philosophical values of Locke and Mill (which the Bill of Rights in large measure tracks). As such, when a plaintiff asserts a constitutional claim against a state official whose socioeducational background does not include obeisance to that libertarian tradition, a federal judge generally will protect the threatened constitutional value . . . .

Most of the constitutional rights which civil liberties lawyers seek to protect fit snugly within nineteenth-century liberal thought. And since a class disparity between federal trial judges and the individual targets of constitutional enforcement is more likely than one between state trial judges and constitutional defendants, this class phenomenon will assist the constitutional plaintiff more often in the federal courts.

D.   Insulation from Majoritarian Pressures

. . . Federal district judges, appointed for life and removable only by impeachment, are as insulated from majoritarian pressures as is functionally possible, precisely to insure their ability to enforce the Constitution without fear of reprisal. State trial judges, on the other hand, generally are elected for a fixed term,[81] rendering them vulnerable to majoritarian pressure when

---

81. Three general methods for selecting state trial judges are currently in use: appointment; election, either partisan or nonpartisan; and initial appointment followed by retention election. . . .

deciding constitutional cases. Thus, when arguable grounds supporting the majoritarian position exist, state trial judges are far more likely to embrace them than are federal judges. This insulation factor, I suggest, explains the historical preference for federal enforcement of controversial constitutional norms. While the level of hostility towards any given constitutional decision varies from locality to locality, from issue to issue, and over time, constitutional adjudication still frequently involves issues which raise strong political passions. Insulation from political pressures may not be necessary in all constitutional cases; yet, where such pressures are strong, insulated judicial forums are necessary if constitutional rights are to remain viable.

E.   Some Costs of the Federal Forum Preference

Opting for a federal forum in constitutional cases admittedly entails some costs. First, an insulated federal judge may be less sensitive to the social milieu into which his decisions must fit and thus less successful in shaping decisions and remedies to the reality of that milieu. That danger, however, is minimized by the fact that "insulated" federal judges are typically drawn from, and well acquainted with, the locality in which they sit. Even so, the decisions of a politically insulated federal judge may encounter greater public resistance than the same decisions rendered by a politically accountable state judge. Clearly, to the extent that constitutional norms are enforced by a forum sensitive to the majority will, the chances of public acceptance are enhanced. Conversely, by entrusting constitutional adjudication to federal trial forums perceived as free from majoritarian influence, a measure of public acceptance is lost. That loss, however, seems necessary to insure the existence of a forum capable of protecting individual rights in the face of local political dissatisfaction.

Second, by urging a broad option to invoke federal jurisdiction in constitutional cases, civil rights lawyers exacerbate an already difficult caseload burden in the federal courts. One factor rendering federal courts desirable is their superior technical competence. Yet a failure to remedy the overburdening of the federal trial courts threatens precisely that capacity for excellence. While the caseload problem cannot be dismissed, several responses do exist. Although its small size is important in maintaining both a high level of professional ability and an elite sense of institutional mission, the current federal bench could be substantially enlarged without compromising either attribute. More fundamentally, the major justification for a system of lower federal courts is the protection of federal rights. Before that basic function is curtailed, substantial savings of federal judicial time could and should be effected by eliminating archaic heads of federal jurisdiction which lack contemporary social purpose. Moreover, barring a given case from the federal courts does not mean its disappearance. Rather, it likely will reappear on an already overcrowded state court docket. Limiting access to the federal courts, therefore, does not really solve the problem of overburdened judges. The burden is merely shifted to institutions which are often even less able to cope with the caseload.

Third, by assuming state court inferiority and by seeking to funnel important constitutional cases into federal trial courts, civil liberties lawyers may be engaged in self-fulfilling prophecy which helps perpetuate the second-class status and performance of state trial courts. Clearly, if significant constitutional cases were forced into state courts more frequently, state judges would acquire greater expertise and sensitivity in the area and would probably develop an enhanced sense of institutional responsibility for the enforcement of constitutional rights. Moreover, over time the competence gap might diminish, since such a regime would likely engender pressure from the bar and the public for upgrading the quality and the prestige of state trial benches. That, of course, would be all to the good. Channeling more cases into the state courts, however, would have no impact on their vulnerability to majoritarian pressures. Indeed, it would be likely to increase (and certainly cannot decrease) the extent to which state trial judges are exposed to such pressures. And even if state courts could be upgraded by a force feeding of constitutional cases, such an avenue of judicial reform may well require the sacrifice of several waves of litigants in the hope of achieving subsequent improvements. Where constitutional rights are at stake, that is, to my mind, too great a risk to run in order to improve the state courts.[88]   .   .   .

---

1.   Do you agree with Neuborne's assertion that "[m]ost of the constitutional rights which civil liberties lawyers seek to protect fit snugly within nineteenth-century liberal thought"? Is the phrase "civil liberties lawyer" meant to exclude "civil rights lawyers" and the cases they bring—such as school desegregation or school financing suits?

2.   Must one subscribe to Neuborne's assertions in toto in order to justify the legislative structures? See Cover and Aleinikoff, Dialectical Federalism: Habeas Corpus and the Court, 86 Yale L.J. 1035 (1977) (excerpted in chapter 7); Fiss, *Dombrowski,* 86 Yale L.J. 1103 (1977); Field, Abstention in Constitutional Cases: The Scope of the *Pullman* Abstention Doctrine, 122 U.Pa.L.Rev. 1071 (1974); Amsterdam, Criminal Prosecutions Affecting Federally Guaranteed Civil Rights: Federal Removal and Habeas Corpus Jurisdiction to Abort State Criminal Trial, 113 U.Pa.L.Rev. 793 (1965).

3.   If civil liberties litigation is often about the enunciation of constitutional rights where they are not clearly defined, and if the biases Neuborne

---

88.   If the force feeding technique for state court improvement is to be tried, it would be safer, and probably more effective, to attempt it first by abolishing diversity jurisdiction rather than by closing the federal courts to constitutional cases. Presently, much of the complex personal injury and commercial litigation arising under state law is routed into the federal courts by the corporate bar desirous of obtaining the technical advantages which federal trial courts are perceived to enjoy over their state counterparts. This continues, despite the fact that most commentators believe that the major justification for diversity jurisdiction—the need to safeguard out-of-state litigants against local bias—no longer is a significant concern.   .   .   .   Since improvement of state judicial systems will require not only pressure on the state judges themselves, but also on state political branches to increase the level of compensation and resources available for state judiciaries and to change judicial selection processes, it is important that those pressures come from politically powerful groups. While the civil rights bar is not without some clout, its political strength in any given state pales beside that which the beneficiaries of diversity jurisdiction—the corporate bar and its generally well-heeled clients—could muster for reform if given the incentive to do so.

ascribes respectively to state and federal courts are accurately stated, is it correct to conclude that federal courts are better at protecting constitutional rights? Would it not be a better and more neutral formulation to say that federal courts tend to an enlarged description of such rights while state courts read them more narrowly?

4. As Professor Neuborne suggests, considerations similar to the ones he identifies may be included (or have their counterpart) in the justification for maintaining the diversity jurisdiction of federal courts—a species of jurisdiction that presents its own problems of coordination. On this issue, see H. Friendly, Federal Jurisdiction: A General View (1973) (where Judge Friendly also deals with the problem of federal-claim jurisdiction). This book might profitably be consulted because, in contrast to Neuborne, Judge Friendly views the issues from the legislative perspective rather than that of the litigators and evinces a less ardent attachment to the underlying substantive claims.

5. The issue of coordination also arises when one decision center is private and the other public, and as such is discussed in the essay of Professor Meltzer excerpted here in chapter 3.

SECTION C. KNOWLEDGE AND EXPERIENCE OF DECISIONAL PERSONNEL

What are our expectations concerning the knowledge and experience of the people in whom we vest the power to adjudicate? In addressing this question we make a threefold distinction among these people: the professional, the layperson, and the expert.

By the "professional" we mean the professional decider, one who has special *training* that is supposed to equip him with *skills* necessary for the performance of the job of adjudication and who, over time, acquires *experience* in discharging that task. The paradigm of the professional decider is the judge. His opposite is the juror—the layperson—who has no special training whatsoever and who participates in the adjudicatory process on a "one-shot basis." To some extent, the professional adjudicator may be considered an expert, for he has special knowledge about the rules and how they might be applied or interpreted—he has a special reservoir of knowledge and experience in adjudicatory matters. But there is a different meaning for the term "expert." The "expert" we refer to has a special knowledge and experience that goes beyond the adjudicatory process; our expert typically has certain "technical" or "scientific" information about people, behavior, or institutions. In this section we first consider the allocation of authority between "lay" and "professional" decisionmakers; and next, that between general professional decisionmakers and technical experts.

1. PROFESSIONAL v. LAY

The use of lay personnel as adjudicators has long fascinated scholars. See, generally, J. Dawson, A History of Lay Judges (1960). But perhaps the most important study of that phenomenon took place at the University of Chicago Law School in the mid-1950s at the prodding of the Ford Foundation—a persistent source of change in the legal academy—and ultimately resulted in Kalven and Zeisel's book, The American Jury (1966).

Kalven and Zeisel, trying to locate the special contribution of lay personnel to the adjudicatory process, focused on the incidence of judge-jury disagreement. The study was conducted by mail questionnaire. Five hundred fifty-five trial judges completed questionnaires for 3576 trials, reporting, for criminal cases tried before them, how the jury decided each case and how they as judges would have decided it in the absence of a jury. To guard against distortion, each judge was requested to write down his projected verdict before the jury returned its verdict. The judges also gave evaluative and descriptive material about the case, the parties, and counsel. The focus was on the judge's explanation of any disagreement with the jury's actual decision. The study located five generic sources of judge-jury disagreement: (1) evidence factors, (2) facts only the judge knew, (3) disparity of counsel, (4) jury sentiments about the individual defendant, and (5) jury sentiments about the law. We start with an explanation of these categories.

Harry Kalven, Jr., and Hans Zeisel, **Reasons for Judge-Jury Disagreement***

.   .   .

Evidence factors.   Although the traditional view of the jury is that it is largely concerned with issues of fact, it turns out to be surprisingly difficult to give a thumbnail sketch of evidence as a category of judge-jury disagreement. At times the jury may evaluate specific items of evidence differently; at other times the jury might simply require a higher degree of proof. Frequently evidentiary disagreement, in our usage, refers simply to the closeness of the case, which liberated the jury to respond to non-evidentiary factors. Under these special circumstances, issues of evidence, as we were able to handle them, are properly speaking not so much a cause for disagreement as a condition for it.

Facts only the judge knew.   Here the concern is with the occasional circumstance that, during or prior to the trial, an important fact will become available to the judge but not to the jury, such as whether the defendant had a prior specific criminal record or not. Whenever the judge notes such special knowledge on his part in a disagreement case, it has been taken as a reason for his disagreement. The rationale is that judge and jury were, in fact, trying different cases, and had the jury known what the judge knew, it would have agreed with him.

Disparity of counsel.   It was possible to collect data systematically on how evenly counsel for prosecution and for defense were matched. This category covers the instances on which the superiority of either defense or prosecution counsel was given as one of the reasons for the jury's disagreement with the judge.

Jury sentiments about the individual defendant.   The type of defendant involved in a criminal case can vary across the entire spectrum of human per-

* *Source:*   Kalven and Zeisel, The American Jury (1966), excerpts from Chapters 8, 14, and 39. Kalven (1914–1974), Professor of Law, University of Chicago; Zeisel is Professor Emeritus of Law and Sociology, University of Chicago.

sonality and background, from the crippled war veteran who evokes intense sympathy to the loud mouth who alienates the jury. In this category are included all reasons for judge-jury disagreement attributable to the personal characteristics of the defendant.

Jury sentiments about the law. This category includes particular instances of "jury equity," reasons for disagreement that imply criticism of either the law or the legal result. For example, the jury may regard a particular set of facts inappropriately classified as rape, because it perceives what might be called contributory negligence on the part of the victim. A similar notion may operate in fraud cases in which the victim first hoped for an improper gain. Thus, a broader concept, contributory fault of the victim, evolves as a defense to a crime. This general category of jury sentiments about the law includes roughly a dozen sub-categories of such jury sentiments.[7]

      .   .   .   To say that the reason code fell into these five major categories is to make more than a point about coding technique. It is to state a theory. In its most general and also its least exciting form, the theory is that all disagreement between judge and jury arises because of disparity of counsel, facts that only the judge knew, jury sentiments about the defendant, jury sentiments about the law, and evidentiary factors, operating alone or in combination with each other; and as a corollary, that the judge is less likely to be influenced by these factors than is the jury. There is some gain in emphasis if we invert the statement: unless at least one of these factors is present in a case, the jury and the judge will not disagree.

      We are now ready to quantify the explanations for judge-jury disagreement. .   .   .

TABLE 23

Judge-Jury Disagreements in the 3576 Trials

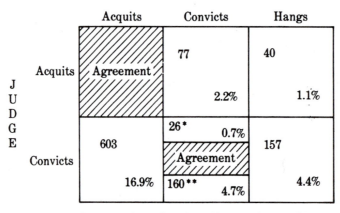

* Jury convicts of <u>major</u> offense; judge of lesser.
** Jury convicts of <u>lesser</u> offense; judge of major.

[C127]

---

7. It may be of interest at this point to preview the elements of the Senti-   ments on the Law category. The four major sentiments are: The Boundaries

The universe of disagreement can now be defined with precision. It comprises the disagreements on guilt, disagreements on charge, and the cases in which the jury hangs.[10] Reading off the relevant figures from Table 23, it can be seen that this total universe of disagreement consists of 1063 instances [out of the total of 3576 trials]. . . . Cases of disagreement where *the jury is more lenient* than the judge will be called *normal* disagreements; cases where, in the less frequent situation, *the judge is more lenient* will be called *cross-over* disagreements.

TABLE 24

Type and Direction of Disagreement

	Per Cent	*Number*
Normal disagreements on —		
Guilt	57	*603*
Charge	15	*160*
Hung Jury	15	*157*
Cross-over disagreements on —		
Guilt	7	*77*
Charge	2	*26*
Hung Jury	4	*40*
Total disagreements	100%	*1063*

The precise quest of this study then is to explain what caused the disagreements in these 1063 instances, constituting 30 per cent of all trials.

We must adjust now for the circumstance that it was not possible to find an explanation for every case of disagreement. Table 25 presents the basic tabulation of success and failure in obtaining explanations.

TABLE 25

Percentage of Unexplained Disagreements

Normal disagreements on			*Cross-overs on*			*Total*
Guilt	*Charge*	*Hung*	*Guilt*	*Charge*	*Hung*	*Disagreements*
7%	11%	19%	3%	4%	15%	10%

No explanation was forthcoming in 101 out of 1063 cases, or about 10 per cent of all disagreements. The percentage is smallest for the disagreements on guilt and largest, as might be expected, for hung juries. The percentage of failures is, on the average, smaller for the cross-over cases than it is for the normal disagreements, suggesting that the reversal of the jury's normal response is so exceptional that explanations for it are easier to see. Subtracting 101 from 1063 leaves 962 instances, or 90 per cent of all disagreement for which we have an explanation.

An exhaustive comparison of the 101 unexplained cases with the 962 explained cases revealed no marked differences between the two groups such

of Self-Defense, Contributory Fault of the Victim, De Minimis, and Unpopular Laws, followed by seven lesser sentiments: Defendant Has Been Punished Enough, Punishment Threatened Is Too Severe, Preferential Treat-ment, Improper Police Methods, Inadvertent Conduct, Insanity and Intoxication, and Crime in a Subculture.

10. . . . [W]e are excluding disagreements on penalty.

as would suggest any peculiarities in the unexplained cases. We will therefore disregard these cases in future discussion, on the assumption that even if
we knew the answers, they would not represent new sources of disagreement
but would have satisfied some one of the established categories of explanation
without changing their relative frequency.

In the future discussion, then, the relevant universe will be the 962 disagreements for which it proved possible to find an explanation. Table 26
reports the basic data for these cases in terms of the five basic reason categories.

TABLE 26

Summary Explanation of Disagreement

	Normal disagreements on			Cross-overs on			Total disagree- ments
	Guilt	Charge	Hung	Guilt	Charge	Hung	
	%	%	%	%	%	%	%
Sentiments on the law	53	59	32	49	72	26	50
Sentiments on the defendant	23	27	17	28	20	3	22
Evidence factors	78	62	84	93	100	100	79
Facts only the judge knew	7	3	3	4	4	—	5
Disparity of counsel	9	6	9	5	4	—	8
Average number of reasons per case *	1.7	1.6	1.5	1.8	2.0	1.3	1.6
Number of cases	559	142	127	75	25	34	962

* Percentages add to more than 100 because, as indicated in the Average line, some cases have more
than one reason, e. g., column one adds to 170 per cent or 1.7 reasons per case.

[C118]

The last column of Table 26 yields the first over-all measure of the relative roles of the five major reason categories in explaining the judge-jury disagreement. As might more or less be expected, in 79 per cent of all cases, or
in four out of every five cases, the disagreement in whole or in part derives
from evidence problems. At the other extreme, the over-all roles of disparity
of counsel and of differential knowledge to which the judge is privy are low
(8 per cent and 5 per cent), a result which in the case of disparity of counsel
may cause surprise. A second result that may be unexpected is that in 50 per
cent of the cases there is found a jury sentiment at odds with the law.

By way of gaining a preliminary perspective on the broader sources of
disagreement, we see that, apart from evidence difficulties, the primary sources
of disagreement are the jury sentiments about the law and about the defendant. Thus, the data in Table 26 give focus to a general theory of judge-jury
disagreement.

The data permit another basic observation. The rank order of reasons
which we obtained for the Total column, representing all cases of disagreement, remains the same for all six types of disagreements, whether it concerns

guilt, charge, or the hung jury, and whether it is in the direction of greater or of lesser jury leniency.   But although the rank order remains the same, there is a difference in emphasis: sentiments on the law are most important in respect to disagreements on charge and least important to hung juries; hung juries show a higher level of evidence issues than do the other disagreements on guilt and charge.

Thus far we have counted each reason as one.   It is helpful, however, to adjust for multiple reasons and reach a more precise estimate of the roles of the five categories.   This is the function of Tables 27, 28, and 29.

Table 27 shows that for roughly half the disagreements there is more than one reason, but in no case were all five reason categories required, and in only 1 per cent of the cases were there four reasons.

TABLE 27

Frequency of Multiple Reasons

Number of reasons * per case	Per Cent	Number of cases
1	47	456
2	41	395
3	11	105
4	1	6
5	—	—
Total disagreements	100%	962

* The term "reason" refers here only to the five major categories.   The multiplicity of reasons *within* one of these categories is ignored.   One reason is treated as sufficient to bring the category into play.   For example, the defendant may be a mother in one case, and a mother, a widow, and poor in a second case.   Yet in each case *Sentiments on the Defendant* would be counted only once as a reason for disagreement.

[C120]

Next we explore whether the five basic reason categories differ from each other in the degree to which they combine with other reasons as sources of explanation.   Table 28 shows how dependent each of the five basic categories is.

TABLE 28

Frequency with which Major Reasons Appear Alone
or with Other Reasons

	Sentiment on Law	Sentiment on Defendant	Issues of Evidence	Facts Only Judge Knew	Disparity of Counsel
	%	%	%	%	%
Appears— alone	22	8	43	2	8
with other reasons	78	92	57	98	92
Total	100%	100%	100%	100%	100%
Number of cases *	484	213	758	52	78

* The number of cases adds to 1585 although there are actually 962 cases because the same case may appear again in two or more of the five columns.

[C117]

Each of the reason categories appears more frequently in combination with other reasons than it does alone. Interestingly enough, it is the evidence category that appears alone most frequently, a point on which more will be said later.

The sharing of reasons is particularly interesting with respect to disparity of counsel and jury sentiments about the defendant, both of which combine with other reasons over 90 per cent of the time they operate. This fact has broad implications. Disparity of counsel, for the most part will not make a difference by itself but will require materials which superior counsel can exploit; the implication is that the cases do not present such material evenly. Again, sentiments about the individual defendant are seldom powerful enough to cause disagreement by themselves; rather, they gain their effectiveness only in partnership with some other factor in the case. The implication again is that for the defendant to be poor and crippled or beautiful and blonde is by itself rarely a sufficient stimulus for the jury to disagree with the judge.

Putting together the sheer frequency with which the reason categories appear in Table 26 and the perspective on multiple reasons gained in Tables 27 and 28, it is possible to show the *power* of each reason category in explaining disagreement. We have adverted earlier to the process by which multiple reasons would be weighed; they are valued inversely to their frequency in the particular case. Making these weighting computations, one obtains the profile presented in Table 29.[15]

TABLE 29

Summary of Weighted Reasons

	Per Cent
Sentiments on the law	29
Sentiments on the defendant	11
Issues of evidence	54
Facts only the judge knew	2
Disparity of counsel	4
Total	100%
Number of cases	*962*

[C121]

15. An example of the weighting process may prove helpful. It will be recalled from Table 28 that the over-all frequency of Counsel as a reason is 8 per cent, but that in 92 per cent of the cases Counsel appears with one or more other reasons. The breakdown is as follows.

(a) alone	8
(b) plus one other reason	49
(c) plus two other reasons	37
(d) plus three other reasons	6
	100%

The weighting process assigns to Counsel all of (a), half of (b), one third of (c) and one fourth of (d), totaling about 46 per cent of its over-all frequency. Since the over-all frequency is 8 per cent (Table 26), 46 per cent of it is roughly 4 per cent.

Table 29 permits a major conclusion for a theory of judge-jury disagreement.[16]   By giving weights to each of the major reason categories, it states in the large, but with precision, the answer to the question: what causes jury and judge to disagree?   Slightly over half the job of explanation falls to the evidence category.   Apart from evidence factors, the explanation for disagreements resides principally in jury sentiments on the law or jury sentiments about the defendant.   Perhaps the most interesting aspect of Table 29 is the salient role played by jury sentiments on the law in causing disagreements; jury equity looms as a significant factor.

The reason data can be arranged into one further profile.   Reducing the categories to two, as in Table 30, by simply placing the evidence category on one side and the other four categories on the other, one gets a crucial image of the jury's performance in terms of *facts* on one hand and *values* on the other.

TABLE 30

Values and Facts as Causes of Disagreement

Disagree on —	Per Cent	
Facts alone	34	
Values and Facts	45	Total facts, 79%
Values alone	21	Total values, 66%
Total	100%	
Number of cases	962	

[C119]

The conventional and official role of the jury, although it is not clear that anyone believes this, is that it is the trier of the facts and nothing else. Table 30 tells us that in only one third of the cases is the jury's fact-finding the sole source of judge-jury disagreement; in the remaining two thirds of the cases the sources of disagreement are to be seen fully only by looking beyond the official role of the jury.   On the other hand, only 21 per cent of the disagreements arise from a source having nothing to do with the facts, but purely with values or sentiments.   Thus, Table 30 serves to spotlight the peculiar difficulty that attends any effort to isolate the causes of judge-jury disagreement.   The difficulty arises because to a considerable extent, or in exactly 45 per cent of the cases, the jury in disagreeing with the judge is neither simply deciding a question of fact nor simply yielding to a sentiment or a value; it is doing both.   It is giving expression to values and senti-

16. Table 29 gives the distribution for the five reason categories in terms of total disagreement.   The breakdown as to direction is as follows.

	Normal (%)	Cross-over (%)
Sentiments on the Law	30	24
Sentiments on the Defendant	11	9
Issues of Evidence	53	64
Facts Only the Judge Knew	2	1
Disparity of Counsel	4	2
Total	100%	100%
Number of cases	828	134

[C123]

ments under the guise of answering questions of fact.   If the factual leeway is not present, the sentiments or values will as a rule have to be particularly strong to move the jury to disagree.   Conversely, if only ambiguity in the facts is present, and the directionality of the sentiment is absent, the jury will be less likely to disagree with the judge .   .   .   .

Behind this middle figure in Table [30] lies a central proposition about jury decision-making, what we shall call the liberation hypothesis.   This category of cases presents two good reasons for disagreement: there is an evidentiary difficulty to which the jury may be responding and there is also a sentiment or value to which it may be responding.   Would the jury have responded to one stimulus without the impact of the other?   The hypothesis is that in these cases both factors are needed to cause the disagreement.   The sentiment gives direction to the resolution of the evidentiary doubt;   the evidentiary doubt provides a favorable condition for a response to the sentiment.   The closeness of the evidence makes it possible for the jury to respond to sentiment *by liberating* it from the discipline of the evidence.   For this explanation, the specific sources from which the evidential doubt arises are irrelevant.   What matters is simply that, for some reason, there was doubt.

The point here is fundamental to the understanding of jury psychology and jury process.   We know, from other parts of our jury study, that the jury does not often consciously and explicitly yield to sentiment in the teeth of the law.   Rather it yields to sentiment in the apparent process of resolving doubts as to evidence.   The jury, therefore, is able to conduct its revolt from the law within the etiquette of resolving issues of fact.

At times the judge himself comes close to making this point.   In a case where the judge notes that the jury sentiments were opposed to the law in question and where he had talked with the jury after the verdict, he stresses:

> There was deliberate effort on part of some jurors to hunt for doubt.

In a second case, a drunken driving case, in which the defendant had been badly injured in the accident and there was conflicting evidence of intoxication, the judge explains:

> There was no proof that he operated his car in an unlawful manner.   .   .   .   I think the jury felt that the defendant had suffered enough; that they looked for an excuse and felt that the blood test may have been inadequate.

However intriguing the notion that a major role of the evidence is simply to liberate the jury to follow a sentiment, it cannot explain everything. We are left, as shown in Table [30], with the one third of all disagreements —those falling in the facts alone category—for which by definition some other explanation is needed.

Two lines of explanation are suggested by the familiar legal concepts of the weight and credibility of the evidence.   Obviously, if jury and judge come to different conclusions about pure issues of fact, it must in part be due to their making different responses to the credibility of the proof offered them.   For some reason the jury may tend to believe certain evidence more than does the judge, or conversely to disbelieve it.   This idea of differential credibility judgments reflects a commonplace expectation as to the role of evidence as a source of disagreement.

The law, however, adds a second and more subtle line of explanation. Some disagreements may result not because judge and jury evaluate credibility differently, but because they interpret differently the legal norm of "proof beyond a reasonable doubt." The jury may find the evidence as credible as does the judge and may weigh it the same as the judge, and yet may disagree and find the evidence wanting because in its view it falls below the required threshold.

It may be useful to summarize more formally now the three ideas we have advanced: In general, these then are the only routes by which the evidence can cause jury and judge to disagree.

(i) The liberation hypothesis. Disagreement arises because doubts about the evidence free the jury to follow sentiment.

(ii) The credibility hypothesis. Disagreement arises because one decider accepts and the other rejects a given item of proof.

(iii) The reasonable doubt hypothesis. Disagreement arises because the jury will tolerate less doubt in convicting than will the judge . . . .

[The authors then turn to a more particularized examination of the reasonable doubt hypothesis.]

. . . [I]n disagreement cases the judge often comments on reasonable doubt:

In most acquittals by juries the defense stresses "reasonable doubt" and the court must instruct the jury that if there is such doubt the jury must acquit the defendant.

Jury probably over cautious on reasonable doubt.

Reasonable doubt of guilt.

Insufficient evidence.

Didn't feel state met burden of proof.

Burden of proof not carried. I felt proof was beyond reasonable doubt. Jury did not and their conclusion was justified.

Honest difference of opinion.

It was a borderline case reasonable men could have decided either way.

At times the comment ties in with other issues as well:

Reasonable doubt and the fact that it was a circumstantial evidence case.

It was one which could go either way altho' I would have found defendant guilty. Jury may have felt defendant punished sufficiently in having killed uncle who was very close.

Child was only eight and a poor witness—could be led to say anything—Jury was intelligent and mechanically applied reasonable doubt instruction to acquit. I was nonetheless certain, down in my heart I was sure that defendant did it.

Defendants were found with a deer about 30 minutes after legal hunting began. State attempted to show by circumstantial evidence that the deer had been killed by them the night before. Reasonable men could easily differ in their interpretation of the evidence.

. . . As we probe the ambiguities in the judge's comments, we are led to refine the basic idea of reasonable doubt as an explanation for disagreement. The difficulty is to locate an independent role for it. If all evidence disagreements could be explained by the influence of a sentiment, or by differential responses to particular items of credibility, or by randomness in the resolution of very close cases, there would be no need for a reasonable doubt hypothesis. Indeed, in that event it would be difficult to assign to it any meaning. We move, therefore, to a narrower concept. If judge and jury, when unaffected by a sentiment, make the same credibility responses and yet disagree as to final outcome, and if they do this repeatedly and in the same direction, this disagreement pattern can only be explained by their having different norms as to how little doubt should be tolerated before convicting. On this view reasonable doubt is a residual but indispensable category for the complete explanation of evidence disagreements.
. . .

. . . Assume that the jury and the judge can independently rank all of the cases coming before them according to the strength of the evidence, so that they can be arranged in a continuous order from the weakest prosecution case to the strongest. The cases can then be envisioned as a series of bars of varying height. If then, pursuant to the hypothesis, we assume that the jury requires proof at a certain height before it will convict, but that the height required by the judge is measurably lower, we can plot the point at which the jury's threshold for conviction cuts the cases and can do the same for the judge's threshold. There will be some cases in which the prosecution's proof is so good that it will satisfy the jury's threshold and thus necessarily also satisfy the judge's threshold. Hence, in these cases, despite the difference in their thresholds, judge and jury will agree to convict. Similarly at the other end of the graph there will be cases in which the prosecution's proof is so weak that not even the judge's threshold will be satisfied, and once again, despite the difference in threshold, judge and jury will agree—this time to acquit. But between these two groups of cases, there will be an area in which the proof is strong enough to satisfy the judge's lower threshold but not strong enough to reach that of the jury. In these cases there will be disagreement; the judge will convict and the jury will acquit.

The model we have been describing is shown in graphic form in Table 58.

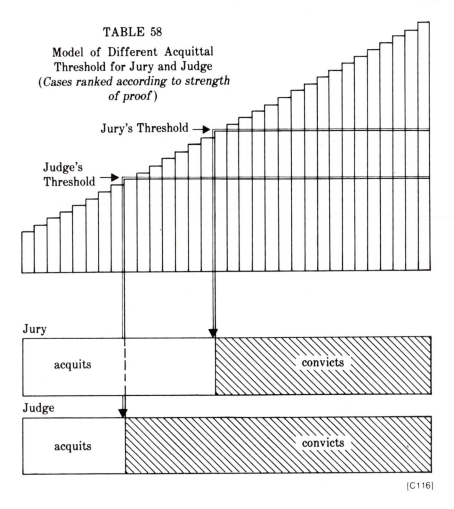

TABLE 58

Model of Different Acquittal
Threshold for Jury and Judge
(*Cases ranked according to strength
of proof*)

Jury's Threshold →

Judge's
Threshold →

Jury

acquits | convicts

Judge

acquits | convicts

[C116]

This then is a precise statement of the reasonable doubt hypothesis.   Is there any empirical way to verify its operation in evidence disagreements?

.   .   .   We have said reasonable doubt is an indispensable, residual explanation.   If it is operative there should be some cases of disagreement which cannot be explained in any other terms.   To locate these cases, then, we must first abstract from the evidence disagreements those explainable on previously established grounds.

In this process of "purification" we first eliminate all disagreements attributable to the interplay of evidence problems with sentiment; here what has been called the liberation hypothesis will be considered a sufficient explanation.   This explanation covers 46 per cent of the normal disagreements on evidence.[17]

17.   The figure of 46 per cent is derived by applying the 42 per cent disagreements on Values and Facts from Table 53 to the basis of 753 cases which on the one hand excludes all Values Alone cases from Table 53 but adds the cross-over disagreements that have evidence issues.

[For purposes of brevity we have used Table 30, tabulating the causes of all disagreements, rather than Table 53,

From the remaining group we must remove the cases resolved by the differential credibility accorded by jury and judge to defendants without criminal records. This group comprises another 21 per cent of the evidence disagreements.

The remainder requires one further purifying step in order to locate the true home of the hypothesis. One must expect that some disagreement between jury and judge in close cases is simply a random phenomenon. The cases are so close that reasonable men will decide them one way this time and another way the next time.

If we assume that the 6 per cent cross-overs which remain at this point are such random deviations, then their equivalent on the normal-disagreement side would be 6 per cent of the cases.[18]

After this third step we are left with a residual 11 per cent of the disagreements spectacularly unamenable to specific explanation. We would argue that this very difficulty provides in itself a kind of proof that the reasonable doubt hypothesis is operative. The hypothesis predicts that there will be disagreements for which there is no explanation other than that the jury takes more generously than the judge the law's admonition not to convict unless guilt is proved beyond a reasonable doubt.

The various steps we have been tracing are summarized in Table 59.

As a methodological convenience we have assigned an extremely narrow and residual role to the reasonable doubt hypothesis in order to discover whether it is at all operative as an explanatory category. Now that this has been established, there is no need to continue to view its sphere so narrowly. It may well operate as well in other evidence areas, that allocated to liberation and that allocated to credibility. We have no means of detecting how these factors may combine in producing disagreement, and for the purpose of this study it does not matter what the precise relationship might be. It is sufficient to have shown that the jury's more stringent view of proof beyond a reasonable doubt is one explanation for disagreements between the two deciders in criminal cases.

giving the causes of *normal* disagreements. The percentages differ slightly—in Table 53 the percentage disagreeing on facts alone was 34%; disagreeing on values and facts, 42%; and disagreeing on values alone, 24%. We have also renumbered the remaining footnotes in this excerpt. Ed. note.]

18. It should be understood that *random deviations* is merely a convenient term for events that cannot readily be traced to a particular cause, because they stem from a variety of causes so minute that they cannot be located individually. If, for instance, a coin is flipped, a great many small causes will determine whether one particular flip will end in heads or tails, and the individual outcome will be unpredictable. But the very fact that the result is determined by a multitude of minute causes makes it possible to predict, not the individual event, but the outcome of an aggregate of several throws; it will move around the 50–50 line. Similarly, judge and jury will in some cases produce random disagreements with each other. As to the frequency of these close-close cases, we are assuming that the residual of unexplained close cases in the cell with the smallest number of cases, the cross-over disagreement cell, determines this magnitude. As we saw, it is 6 per cent of all disagreements. This assumption will reduce the so far unexplained balance of normal disagreements to its utmost minimum.

TABLE 59

Explanation for Disagreements on the Evidence

	Normal Disagreements (Per Cent)	Crossovers (Per Cent)
Liberation hypothesis (evidence *plus* sentiments)	46%	10%
Differential credibility of defendants without record who take stand	21%	—
Random disagreements in close cases	6%	6%
Jury's greater tolerance for reasonable doubt	11%	—
Total disagreements in which evidence was a factor	84%	16%
	100%	
Number of Cases	753	

[C128]

It is well to remember a major point about the legal requirement that for conviction there be proof beyond a reasonable doubt: it is the normative or value judgment expressed in this requirement. It is a way of saying that we live in a society that prefers to let ten guilty men go free rather than risk convicting one innocent man. This is, to be sure, an almost heroic commitment to decency. In the end the point is that the jury, as an expression of the community's conscience, interprets this norm more generously and more intensely than does the judge.[19] . . .

[The authors, some chapters later, return to these themes in their concluding remarks.]

. . . Although a substantial part of the jury's work is the finding of facts, this, as has long been suspected, is not its total function in the real world. As a fact-finder it is not in any interesting way different from the judge, although it will not always reach the same conclusion. When only pure fact-finding is involved the jury tends to give more weight than the judge to the norm that there should be no conviction without proof beyond a reasonable doubt. And there is every indication that the jury follows the evidence and understands the case.

The more interesting and controversial aspects of the jury's performance emerge in cases in which it does more than find facts; where, depending on how one looks at it, the jury can be said to do equity, to legislate interstitially, to implement its own norms, or to exhibit bias.

All this is fairly familiar. The distinctive bite of this study resides in the following supplementary propositions about the jury as legislator.

First, we can estimate with some precision how frequently the jury engages in more than fact-finding. It will be recalled that about three quarters of the time it agrees with the judge; and that most, but not all of the time it agrees with him, it is not importing values of its own into the case. But roughly two thirds of the disagreements with the judge are marked by some jury response to values.

Second, the jury imports its values into the law not so much by open revolt in the teeth of the law and the facts, although in a minority of cases it does do this, as by what we termed the liberation hypothesis. The jury, in the guise of resolving doubts about the issues of fact, gives reign to its sense of values. It will not often be doing this consciously; as the equities of the case press, the jury may, as one judge put it, "hunt for doubts." Its

19. We might for a moment add a speculation as to why the jury might have a different threshold of reasonable doubt over and beyond the likelihood that it reflects a distinctive value held by laymen. It may simply turn on the fact that the jury decides as a group and by unanimous verdict. Given the ambiguity of the reasonable doubt formula, it is likely that it is not understood in exactly the same fashion by all jurors; hence, one could, theoretically, rank a population of jurors in terms of their thresholds of reasonable doubt. One could even assume that the variation among individual jurors is no different from that among judges and that the average for both groups would be at the same point. If then the group of 12 jurors decides close cases with a higher cut-off point than does a single judge, the explanation may reside simply in the unanimity requirement. The jury, to avoid disagreement, would tend in the direction of its most stringent member. One might, of course, object that the judge is not always an "average" judge nor do any 12 jurors always represent the full range of thresholds. It can, however, be mathematically proved that whenever the distribution of thresholds among jurors is by and large the same as among judges—the unanimity requirement will in the long run produce this threshold phenomenon, that is, given a sufficient number of juries and judges drawn at random to confront each other.

war with the law is thus both modest and subtle. The upshot is that when the jury reaches a different conclusion from the judge on the same evidence, it does so not because it is a sloppy or inaccurate finder of facts, but because it gives recognition to values which fall outside the official rules.

Third, we suspect there is little or no intrinsic directionality in the jury's response. It is not fundamentally defendant-prone, rather it is non-rule minded; it will move where the equities are. And where the equities are at any given time will depend on both the state of the law and the climate of public opinion.

Fourth, the extent to which the jury will disagree with the judge will depend on the selection of cases that come before the jury. Since, under current waiver rules and practice, the defendant in effect has the final say on whether there is to be a jury trial or a bench trial, the cases coming before the jury will be skewed and include a disproportionate number in which there are factors that appeal to the jury. The selection will be affected also by pleas of guilty and, to a lesser degree, by decisions of the prosecutor not to prosecute, and even in some instances by decisions of the police not to arrest. Thus the commonplace impression that the criminal jury is defendant-prone may be largely an artifact of the dynamics by which the cases are sorted out for jury trial.

Fifth, we have said the jury's reaction will in part depend on the lay of public sentiment on any given point. The extensive agreement between judge and jury indicates that there is in our society at this time widespread consensus on the values embodied in the law. As a result, a jury drawn at random from the public does not often have representatives of a dissenting view.

On some points there is sufficient dissent so that the random drawing will at times place on the jury representatives of a view contrary to the existing law. Indeed on some matters the public will even be ambivalent, with factions that deviate from the law in opposite directions.

Thus, it makes a good deal of difference in this decision-making who the personnel are. The consequence of the fact that no two juries are alike is that statements about trends in jury decision-making are probabilistic at best. We cannot assert that all juries will always feel that a man who has suffered personal disasters since committing the crime has been punished enough. We can only say that this idea is prevalent enough so that it has some chance of moving the jury away from the judge in any given instance in which it is present.

Sixth, the explanation of how a disagreement is generated requires one more fundamental point. The thesis is that to a substantial degree the jury verdict is determined by the posture of the vote at the start of the deliberation process and not by the impact of this process as rational persuasion. The jury tends to decide in the end whichever way the initial majority lies. The result is that a sentiment need be spread only so widely among the public as to produce enough representatives on the jury to yield the initial majority. On this view the study can be thought of as a study of the sentiments that will lead to initial majorities.

Seventh, and as a corollary, the deliberation process although rich in human interest and color appears not to be at the heart of jury decision-making. Rather, deliberation is the route by which small group pressures produce consensus out of the initial majority . . . .

As we attempt to step back and gain some distance from the detail of the study, it may be useful to put two quite general and interrelated questions: Why do judge and jury ever disagree, and why do they not disagree more often?

Judge and jury have experienced the same case and received the same rules of law to apply to it; why do these two deciders ever disagree? We seek for the moment an explanation more general than that offered through-out [this study] in terms of specific factors of evidence, sentiment, and defendant. Why do they not react the same way to the stimuli? Why does the judge not move over to the jury view, or the jury stay with the judge?

The answer must turn on the intrinsic differences between the two institutions. The judge very often perceives the stimulus that moves the jury, but does not yield to it. Indeed, it is interesting how often the judge describes with sensitivity a factor which he then excludes from his own considerations. Somehow the combination of official role, tradition, discipline, and repeated experience with the task make of the judge one kind of decider. The perennial amateur, layman jury cannot be so quickly domesticated to official role and tradition; it remains accessible to stimuli which the judge will exclude.

The better question is the second. Since the jury does at times recognize and use its de facto freedom, why does it not deviate from the judge more often? Why is it not more of a wildcat operation? In many ways our single most basic finding is that the jury, despite its autonomy, spins so close to the legal baseline.

The study does not answer directly, but it does lay the ground for three plausible suggestions. As just noted, the official law has done pretty well in adjusting to the equities, and there is therefore no great gap between the official values and the popular. Again, the group nature of the jury decision will moderate and brake eccentric views. Lastly, the jury is not simply a corner gang picked from the street; it has been invested with a public task, brought under the influence of a judge, and put to work in solemn surroundings. Perhaps one reason why the jury exercises its very real power so sparingly is because it is officially told it has none. . . . .

---

1. The reasons for disagreement were taken to be the reasons the judges stated in the completion of the questionnaires. No attempt was made to determine whether these were the *actual* reasons in each case behind the disagreement. Are there other methodologies for isolating the reasons for disagreement? Would these alternatives be superior to the methodology of Kalven and Zeisel? For one such critique, see Posner, The Economic Approach to Law, 53 Texas L.Rev. 757, 766 (1975). See also Walsh, The American Jury: A Reassessment, 79 Yale L.J. 142 (1969).

2.   To what extent is the Kalven and Zeisel study distorted by the presence of 101 unexplained cases?   What might account for the failure to explain in these cases, and how might these cases possibly array themselves among the five categories?

3.   In trying to quantify the role of the reasonable doubt hypothesis, the authors assume the truth of the liberation and credibility hypotheses. They then exclude any cases that might be explained by those hypotheses, leaving only the cases explainable by the reasonable doubt hypothesis.   The authors acknowledge this assumption and its arbitrary quality and at one point state that they are prepared to relax the assumption.   Is that promise ever fulfilled?   In their concluding chapter, the reasonable doubt hypothesis is downplayed—perhaps because of the quantitative role previously assigned to it (on the basis of the questionable assumptions)—and the liberation hypothesis is emphasized.   As a result of this concluding placement of emphasis, many have read the book as establishing that that principal function of the jury is to give expressions to contrary sentiments about the law.   Is this a valid interpretation?

4.   In speculating why juries might have a different threshold of reasonable doubt, Kalven and Zeisel point to the groupness or unanimity rule of the jury rather than to its lay status.   They write: "One could even assume that the variation [on the reasonable doubt standard] among individual jurors is no different from that among judges and that the average for both groups would be at the same point."   Is there any basis for such an assumption?   Given a contrary assumption, would their speculations as to the importance of the groupness or unanimity rule be persuasive?

————————

In the essay that follows, Professor Lempert pursues the "lay versus professional" issue, once again in the jury context.   He begins by setting forth a general theory of the likely contribution of each. He then applies his posited theory to two issues of current interest to the bar: jury size and the peremptory challenge.   The essay originated as testimony (prepared jointly with Dr. Jay Schulman) before a Senate subcommittee considering a bill (S. 2074, 95th Congress, 1st Session) to reduce the number of peremptory challenges in civil cases from three to two and also to *require* all federal district courts to switch from twelve-member to six-member juries.   (Now most district courts use six-member juries under local rule with the blessing of the Supreme Court.)   The bill was rejected by the subcommittee, yet the issues and larger concerns persist.

Richard O. Lempert, **Jury Size and the Peremptory Challenge***

The ideal jury (a) is representative of the people living within the jurisdiction of the court, (b) is unbiased, (c) decides a case on the basis of the evidence presented, (d) evaluates the evidence in the light of the judge's instructions on the law, and (e) in appropriate cases mitigates the rigidity of

* *Source:* Vol. 22, No. 2, Law Quad-   Professor of Law, University of Michi-
rangle Notes (U.Mich.) 8–13 (1978).   gan.

the law by reflecting in its verdict fundamental principles of justice and morality. . . .

Representatives drawn randomly from a community share the biases and prejudices that characterize members of that community. The prejudices may be irrelevant to the matter being litigated, they may be benign, or they may run counter to values that are deeply engrained in our legal system. Common prejudices include the belief that a police officer's word is better than the average citizen's as well as the belief that no police officer can be trusted. They range from the feeling that no tort judgment is excessive because . . . insurance companies exist to pay claims to the feeling that only a chiseler would seek to collect for pain and suffering. Prejudices color the way in which jurors evaluate evidence, yet often even unprejudiced jurors are likely to be incapable of appreciating the true value of evidence presented. Finally, it is clear that jurors sometimes have difficulty in understanding judicial instructions and applying them to the facts of a case.

Others have noted the tension between the demand that juries be competent, unbiased factfinders and the requirement that juries be representative of the larger community. This observation is typically the empirical linchpin in arguments made by those who, at least in civil cases, would abolish the jury and transfer its factfinding functions to the judge. But those who argue this way make a fundamental mistake. They attribute the jury's deficiencies to the fact that individuals chosen arbitrarily from the community are sometimes uneducated, sometimes uncaring, and typically legally naive. In fact, most of the drawbacks attributed to the democratic nature of the jury have little to do with the representativeness requirement. Instead they are attributable to a simpler, inescapable source: the human condition. People collect biases as they go through life. While they may differ in their ability to disregard them, there is probably no one whose observations will not at some time be affected by his biases. Even if such an individual existed, his evaluation of evidence would still be far from perfect. A substantial body of research now exists demonstrating ways in which people consistently misestimate the implications of information given them.

Judges, alas, are also human. They can no more escape the dangers of biased perception and fallible information processing than the jurors over whom they preside. If judges have an advantage over jurors in their presumed understanding of the law, they are disadvantaged in that their public position subjects them to pressures that may systematically reinforce or create biases. Indeed, judges are at times elected or appointed in part because of the appeal of biases that are ideally irrelevant in the factfinding process. Furthermore, judges typically play an administrative as well as a judicial role. As administrators they are necessarily concerned with the efficient functioning of a judicial bureaucracy. Too often behavior which promotes bureaucratic efficiency is antithetical to our system's ideal of individualized justice. In such matters as criminal sentencing, judicial behavior may be influenced by the legally irrelevant consideration of whether the court's time has been "wasted" by a jury trial. In civil trials some judges reportedly engage in considerable "arm twisting" to promote out-of-court settlements. We note these factors not to condemn judges; they would not be human if they were not at some times influenced by the bureaucratic and other pressures brought to bear on them.   But these pressures do mean that there is inherent value in an institution, such as jury trial, that guarantees the insertion of a non-bureaucratic element at a key point in the trial process.

What then is the attitude that the Congress should take toward jury reform?   It is not a romantic idealization of the jury; there is no reason to think that the jury today is a perfect factfinder or that it ever will be.   But by the same token the jury should not be regarded as an imperfect substitute for a judge, an institution that will necessarily improve as it comes more closely to resemble or be influenced by one exalted individual learned in the law. .   .   .   The continued vitality of the Sixth and Seventh Amendments should be accepted as a starting point.   This means that jury trial will necessarily be with us in the foreseeable future.   The issue is how may the institution be made more effective in promoting the valued goal of fair and accurate factfinding.   The starting point for inquiry is with the apparent weaknesses of factfinding by average individuals.

Jury Size

We specified three possible deficiencies in lay factfinding: the biases may influence perceptions, the probative weight of evidence may be distorted, and instructions on the law may be misunderstood.   These are all problems that are ameliorated by group decision making.   In groups, expressions of bias may be inhibited or properly dismissed as individuals with conflicting points of view call each other to account.   Totally apart from bias, group factual judgments tend to be more accurate than those made by individuals. An individual is at all times left to his own devices while a group may receive contributions from many individuals.   Where, for example, memory is important as in recalling the testimony of various witnesses, one individual may recall certain facts while another recalls others.   Where a problem is inescapably ambiguous, error variance is reduced when individual judgments are averaged together.   Where understanding is difficult, as with a judge's instructions, a lone decision maker is lost if he does not understand.   A person in a group may benefit from the understanding of others.   Groups, in short, are in many ways as strong as their strongest link.

These advantages of group decision making are more pronounced as group size increases, until the point where the contributions of new members are offset by increasing problems of coordination and morale.   However, even before the point of negative returns each additional new member is likely to add somewhat less to the quality of group decision making than the person before him.   The question   .   .   .   is whether differences in the quality of decisions rendered by six and twelve member groups are likely to be so great that the quality of jury justice will be decreased by mandating the smaller number.   Our feeling is that this is the case.   In clear cases, six and twelve member juries should decide similarly, although the occasional decision against the weight of the evidence will be more common with the smaller group.   In close cases, decisions of larger juries should, on the average, be better with respect to such core legal values as unbiased factfinding, thorough consideration of the evidence, and consistency across similar cases.

It can be shown statistically that minority viewpoints are substantially more likely to be represented in (more or less) randomly chosen groups of twelve than in similarly chosen groups of six. The greater heterogeneity of the larger group makes it a setting in which individual prejudices are more likely to cancel out and in which individuals with valuable specialized knowledge or particularly astute insights are more likely to be available. A further advantage enjoyed by larger juries is that they are more likely to render similar decisions in similar cases. Where individual judgments are averaged, as is often the case in civil litigation despite the official disrepute of quotient verdicts, averages taken across twelve individuals are likely to diverge less than averages taken across six. Even where judgments are not averaged, groups of twelve are more likely to resemble each other than groups of six, in that larger groups more accurately reflect the population from which they are drawn.

In short, both statistical modeling and the existing research on small groups make it clear that proponents of six member juries cannot substantiate the claim that such juries are likely to be better decision makers than juries of twelve. Indeed, even the weaker burden of showing that the switch to smaller juries will not positively harm the quality of jury justice cannot be met. While proponents of larger juries cannot specify precisely the degree to which the decisions of twelve are likely to be better than those of six, a fair reading of the evidence indicates that the advantage generally lies with twelve, perhaps by a considerable margin. . . .

Peremptory Challenges

A second proposed "reform" is reducing the number of allowed peremptory challenges in civil and criminal cases. Some who argue for fewer peremptory challenges view them as a device by which adroit attorneys can pack juries with those biased in their favor, while others believe that peremptory challenges distort juries by making them less representative of the population from which their members are drawn. While we recognize that attorneys do on occasion eliminate people because of their leadership potential or education rather than because of perceived bias, we nonetheless believe that the first view is largely mistaken. Given the limited number of peremptory challenges, their availability to both sides, and the fact that challenged jurors are replaced at random, the most an attorney can usually do is eliminate those jurors likely to be prejudiced against his or her client. Only in special circumstances, where community views disproportionately favor one party or a case appears hopeless to begin with, can an attorney afford the luxury of eliminating the unbiased.

There is more substance to the claim that the use of peremptory challenges lead to a less representative jury, but this by no means makes the case for reducing the number of peremptory challenges. Although maximizing the degree to which the jury represents the community may have value in itself, few would think this value more important than maximizing the likelihood of fair factfinding. Some viewpoints found in the community should not be represented on juries. An obvious case is the viewpoint of one so closely related to a party that his decision is likely to be colored by that relationship. Another obvious example is the viewpoint of one so convinced before trial that a certain outcome is appropriate that he will resist the influence of the evidence.

The right to challenge jurors is essential because where values clash it is more important to have jurors who can be fair in their judgments than it is to have a jury that mimics the demographic or attitudinal composition of the community. Challenges are devices for eliminating from juries individuals whose prejudices are likely to interfere with their ability to be impartial triers of fact. The group of jurors who survive the challenge process may be less representative of the community from which they are drawn than the original group of unchallenged jurors, but they are more likely to render a judgment fairly responsive to the evidence in the case. The trade-off between representativeness and fairness strengthens rather than weakens the quality of jury justice.

Many individuals accept the above argument in the case of the challenge for cause, but do not believe it applies to the peremptory challenge. Those who make this distinction do not realize how the system of challenging for cause is often administered. While there are circumstances, such as a close family relationship to one of the parties, where a challenge for cause must be allowed, the system is generally one of great judicial discretion. Many judges are reluctant to exclude jurors for cause despite an obvious source of bias if the juror states that his decision will be unaffected by the apparent cause for concern. Appellate courts typically support such lower court decisions. For example, plaintiff's attorney in a suit brought against an insurance company might wish to challenge for cause a juror whose parents were agents for some other insurance company. If the juror states that these family ties will not influence his decision, a challenge for cause will be unavailable in many courts. The decision not to exclude for cause in these circumstances may be justifiable, but it is not justifiable on the ground that the juror can be trusted to disregard the obvious source of bias. A promise to put aside one's biases is inherently suspect because people are often unaware of how their biases affect their judgments. The promise is even more suspect when it is made in a setting where one might be embarrassed to admit that he could not be fair. If the promise is suspect, the quality of jury justice is likely to be enhanced by disregarding disclaimers of prejudice where any likely source of bias is revealed on voir dire.

This alternative, however, has its disquieting aspects. People rarely ask to serve on juries and they surely do not ask to be publicly questioned in ways that cast doubt on their integrity. To dismiss for cause a juror who has asserted his capacity for separating judgment from prejudices may be perceived by the one dismissed and by others as degrading or insulting. We should be reluctant to add this kind of burden to the other burdens of jury service. Furthermore, the likelihood that a person will be influenced by apparent sources of prejudice will not always be as clear as in the example of the preceding paragraph. Judicial intuitions about when an asserted capacity for unbiased judgment should override suspicions of bias almost surely will vary from judge to judge and individual judges might well be inconsistent over time. One situation poses almost insoluble difficulties for a system

which relies on the challenge for cause to eliminate individuals whose prejudices would interfere with fair jury factfinding. This is where a suspicion
of bias is engendered not by some particular feature of the juror's biography
or by some specific prejudice, but rather by a set of diffuse attitudes that
characterize the juror's outlook on life. An individual low in tolerance of
ambiguity and high in deference toward authority might be likely to approach a criminal defendant with a presumption of guilt rather than innocence. Yet we can hardly expect a judge to attend to all the character traits
that might predict to biased judgments. We have even less reason to expect
an appellate court to declare that they do predict as a matter of law.

If we relied on judges to exclude for cause all individuals likely to be
incapable of fair judgment and if current practice is a guide, the error of
failing to strike biased jurors would be more common than the error of striking the unbiased, but both should occur. The latter error should never be
grounds for appeal since the struck juror would, in theory, be replaced by
one equally unbiased. The former error, being defined by psychological
rather than legal theory, would be very difficult for appellate courts to handle.
Hence, trial judges would be likely to be given considerable discretion which,
in practice, would be largely unreviewable. Thus, attempts to eliminate juror
bias by an expanded conception of what constitutes grounds for challenge
might lead to a system which was in practice only slightly more effective than
the current one.

The availability of peremptory challenges minimizes tensions inherent
in our system of challenges for cause. The primary virtue of the peremptory challenge is as a device for eliminating from the jury individuals whose
capacity for impartial judgment is suspect, but not so much so as to require
their exclusion as a matter of law. The peremptory challenge has the further virtue of saving face for jurors who have asserted a doubtful capacity
to decide in an unbiased fashion since these assertions are never rejected by
the court in the way that they would be if a challenge for cause was sustained. Mistakes, no doubt, continue to be made, but they are the mistakes
of the parties who suffer from them and not the mistakes of the court. Finally, the availability of peremptory challenges allow the courts to take what is,
psychologically speaking, an unduly restrictive view of when potential jurors
are likely to be impermissibly biased without endangering the quality of jury
justice as substantially as [it] would be if prejudiced jurors not challengeable
for cause could not be removed peremptorily. By limiting the situations in
which challenges for cause must be granted, appellate courts minimize the
chance of reversible error during the jury selection process.

There is no ideal number of peremptory challenges. Their availability
would vary with incidence of potentially biasing attitudes in the jury population. Generally speaking, people's biases are more likely to be activated in
criminal than in civil matters and these biases are more likely to favor the
prosecution than the defense. This justifies the decision to grant more peremptory challenges in criminal cases than in civil actions and it would also
justify a decision to grant criminal defendants more peremptory challenges
than prosecutors. While the number of available peremptory challenges
may be made to turn on whether an action is criminal or civil, it is impossible

to specify in advance appropriate numbers of peremptory challenges for different types of civil litigation.

Assuming some number is fixed for civil litigation, flexibility may be achieved by judicial administration of the challenge for cause or by judicial discretion to increase the number of peremptory challenges available to one or both parties. Where an action is likely to evoke popular prejudices, the judge should be more willing to allow challenges for cause despite disclaimers of bias than when an action appears less emotionally charged. If popular prejudice is directed largely against one side, that side should have the easier time in excluding jurors for cause or should be allowed extra peremptory challenges. If one party is to be awarded extra peremptory challenges, that party should bear a substantial burden of showing that prejudicial public opinion is widespread and deeply held. Whatever the judge's discretion with respect to challenges, the number of peremptory challenges should be sufficient to allow for the judge who is unduly rigid in his attitude toward for-cause challenges. It should allow room to challenge individuals whose attitudes suggest bias even though their biographies or acknowledged prejudices do not, and it should take into account the fact that individuals often have general biases regarding the kinds of people and organizations who are parties to typical civil actions. At the same time, it should not be so large as to allow an attorney too many opportunities to eliminate those who are likely to be unfavorable by reason of their abilities to rationally evaluate evidence rather than because of bias .   .   .   .

———————

1. A fuller and more detailed statement of Professor Lempert's views on the jury may be found in Lempert, Uncovering "Nondiscernible" Differences: Empirical Research and the Jury-Size Cases, 73 Mich.L.Rev. 643 (1975). For another approach to the issues of size and representativeness, see Klevorick, Jury Size and Composition: An Economic Approach, in M. Feldstein and R. P. Inman, Economics of Public Services (1977).

2. In pointing to the deficiencies of judges, Lempert says that "judges are at times elected or appointed in part because of the appeal of biases that are ideally irrelevant in the factfinding process." What are those biases? Lempert also suggests that judges are especially sensitive to considerations of "bureaucratic efficiency" and that such considerations are antithetical to our ideal of "individualized justice." What kinds of considerations regarding "bureaucratic efficiency" is a judge likely to introduce into the adjudicatory process? Are such considerations, in fact, antithetical to our conception of justice?

3. Against Professor Lempert's claim that "group factual judgments tend to be more accurate than those made by individuals," consider I. Janis, Victims of Groupthink (1972). Professor Janis examines foreign policy decisions, and writes: "The more amiability and esprit de corps among the members of an in-group of policy-makers, the greater is the danger that independent critical thinking will be replaced by groupthink, which is likely to result in irrational and dehumanizing actions directed at outgroups." At 198. Professor Lempert made his claim in the context of objecting to re-

ductions in size. A reduction in size might increase the likelihood of "amiabil-ity" and "esprit de corps," and thus Janis' analysis might be understood as supporting Lempert's position (though it is hard to believe that the change, say, from twelve jurors to six, will have much impact on that). On the other hand, Janis throws into question Lempert's major premise, assuming, as we do, that parallels can be found between the jury and the foreign policy decisionmaking group. Thus Janis' study, if it is correct, might influence the agenda of more ambitious reformers. The views of Professor Lempert on the value of groupness have recently been embraced by the Supreme Court. See Ballew v. Georgia, 435 U.S. 223, 233 (1978) (Blackmun, J.) (holding the line at six—a five-person jury for a state criminal trial is un-constitutional). For a recent attempt to model the deliberative process of the jury and to critically examine the majority-persuasion hypothesis of Kal-ven and Zeisel, see Klevorick and Rothschild, A Model of the Jury Decision Process, 8 J.Legal Stud. 141 (1979).

4. The ideal of jury representativeness is ambiguous. It could either mean that no cognizable social group is systematically and arbitrarily excluded from the jury, or, alternatively, that the jury (or, more plausibly, the group or pool from which it is chosen) represents a true cross section of the com-munity. Taken in the cross-sectional sense, the representativeness ideal may well conflict with another ideal of the jury, that of its impartiality. Pro-fessor Lempert acknowledges this conflict or tension. He then, however, presents the case for peremptory challenges by assigning a priority to the *impartiality* ideal. What are the assumptions behind such a preference or priority? See Spears, Voir Dire: Establishing Minimum Standards to Fa-cilitate the Exercise of Peremptory Challenges, 27 Stan.L.Rev. 1493 (1975); Phillips, Limiting the Peremptory Challenge: Representation of Groups on Petit Juries, 86 Yale L.J. 1715 (1977); Zeisel and Diamond, The Jury Se-lection in the Mitchell-Stans Conspiracy Trial, 1976 A.B.F.Res.J. 151 (1976); Zeisel and Diamond, The Effect of Peremptory Challenges on Jury and Verdict: An Experiment in a Federal District Court, 30 Stan.L.Rev. 491 (1978).

5. The jury is a distinctively Anglo-American procedural institution. Thus it is natural that most of the scholarship on lay participation in the adjudicatory process has focused on the jury. But the basic issue transcends the jury itself, and scholars have more recently turned to the examination of the participation of lay personnel within the continental adjudicatory sys-tems. See Casper and Zeisel, Lay Judges in the German Criminal Courts, 1 J.Legal Stud. 135 (1972); G. Casper and H. Zeisel, The Lay Judge in the Criminal Trial (1979) (written in German). See also J. Berman, The Cuban Popular Tribunals, 69 Colum.L.Rev. 1317 (1969).

2. EXPERTS

In this section we employ a threefold strategy. We first present, through the Donald Horowitz essay, one standard critique of the adjudicatory process: the lack of expertise in the decisional personnel. The second essay, by Joel B. Harris, starts with the same underlying premise positing the importance of expertise, but then shows how expert decisional personnel might be incorporated into the adjudicatory process—without even having to create specialized courts, such as the Commerce Court initiated by Taft to review the workings of the I.C.C. or the tax, customs, and patent courts of today. (See Frankfurter, A Study in the Federal Judicial System, 39 Harv.L.Rev. 587, 594–615 (1926); also F. Frankfurter and J. Landis, The Business of the Supreme Court 153–74 (1928).)   Harris makes his point indirectly, through a case study of litigation and the use of administrators in cases involving Title VII of the Civil Rights Act of 1964 (prohibiting racial discrimination in employment).   Finally, we conclude the subsection and chapter with an essay by Stephen Wexler which takes the discussion to a more basic level— it questions the very insistence upon expertise in decisional personnel.

Wexler is joined in this last theme by an ever-increasing number of scholars who have begun to disassemble the claim made by the Progressives and the New Deal reformers on behalf of the so-called "experts."   See, for example, J. Freedman, Crisis and Legitimacy: The Administrative Process and American Government (1978); Getman and Goldberg, The Myth of Labor Board Expertise, 39 U.Chi.L.Rev. 681 (1972); P. Hays, Labor Arbitration: A Dissenting Viewpoint (1966); Morse, Crazy Behavior, Morals and Science: An Analysis of Mental Health Law, 50 So.Cal.L.Rev. 527 (1978); Pugh, The Insanity Defense in Operation: A Practicing Psychiatrist Views *Durham* and *Brawner*, 1973 Wash.U.L.Q. 87 (1973).   In the more general literature, see I. Illich, Toward a History of Needs (1977); J. Habermas, Toward a Rational Society: Student Protest, Science, and Politics (1970) (especially Chapter 6, "Technology and Science as 'Ideology' ").

Donald L. Horowitz, **The Personnel of the Adjudicative Process** *

In a complex, highly differentiated society, the generalist role is not to be deprecated.   The interpreter, the person who stands at the synapses and makes connections between subsystems and subcultures, is a vital part of any policymaking process.   Nevertheless, the relative weight accorded to specialist and generalist opinion, and the kind of input made by each, can impart a distinctive cast to the resulting decision.   One consequence of generalist dominance in a decision process   . . .   is that, in the interstices where expertise is lacking, the generalist tends to fill in the gaps with his own "generalized normative axioms."   It is not clear that the generalized normative axioms of the lawyers, which have so far cemented the cracks of judicial decisions, are well adapted to policymaking in all of the areas to which they have been applied.

The generalist character of judges commends them as community representatives for many of the duties they must perform, but it unfits them for processing specialized information.   In fact, this is one of the jobs that many judges do with the least skill and the greatest impatience.

It has always proved difficult to integrate specialists into the adjudicative process.   Specialized information is usually provided to judges through the medium of expert witnesses and consultants or through popularized writ-

Source: D. Horowitz, The Courts and Social Policy (1977), chapter 2 ("Attributes of Adjudication"). Senior Fellow, Research Institute on Immigration and Ethnic Studies, Smithsonian Institution.

ten versions of the information . . . . The expert witnesses are paid by the respective parties, and they are almost invariably partisan. The popularizations share the usual defects of the genre. They simplify, and sometimes they mislead.

Even purely legal specialists are often not allowed to speak for themselves in court. In a complex securities case, a large law firm will send someone from the litigation department to represent the client in court. The litigator will be advised by the securities specialist who has probably handled the client's business, short of litigation, for years, but the specialist may be confined to whispering, even in non-jury cases and even during conferences in the judge's chambers. The litigator, unfamiliar though he may be with the law of securities and the problems of the client, will act as spokesman for the client and interpreter of specialized information for the benefit of the judge.

This division of responsibility is carefully geared to the character of the central actor: the judge. By virtue of the processes of recruitment and socialization and the apportionment of work, the judge of a trial or appellate court of general jurisdiction is a generalist par excellence. Those who appear before him must organize themselves and their information accordingly.

. . . We know, for example, that presidents consider the choice of Supreme Court nominees to be their prerogative, that senators have the same proprietary view of district court appointments in their states, and that court of appeals nominees fall somewhere in between. We know, too, that the American Bar Association has argued for the importance of "professional" as against "political" qualifications, and that, while there is about an even chance that a lower-court nominee will come from the ranks of public or party officeholders, the ratio of private practitioners appointed to the bench has slowly increased.

This pulling and tugging suggests that it makes a difference whether the American Bar Association or an individual senator is more influential in judicial selection. For some purposes (especially degree of party activism) it does, but there is another way to look at the recruitment process. It makes sense to view it as a mutual veto system, a system likely to throw up candidates who are not unacceptable to the main actors. The policy views of a prospective nominee have generally not played a prominent part in the selection of lower federal judges, but administrations have usually eschewed the nomination of those they regard as holding extreme views. The selection process can thus be viewed as one of narrowing down and pushing toward the least common denominator candidate. In terms of expertise, it makes little difference whether a political officeholder or a favorite private practitioner of the American Bar Association is selected. A practitioner able to obtain a high ABA rating is likely to have had some litigation experience or general corporate practice and to be exactly the kind of generalist who appears before judges.

If this suggests judicial self-perpetuation, that begins to approach the mark. About 40 percent of the Department of Justice files of the judicial appointees of the Eisenhower and Kennedy administrations contained letters from sitting judges recommending the then-prospective candidate. In both administrations, moreover, more than half the appointees to the court of appeals had themselves had prior judicial experience.   Judges beget judges.

This is what is known about the recruitment process.   What is not really known is just how this process affects the composition of the federal judiciary.   There are, as I have said, grounds for suspicion that the multiple players active in the selection process are likely to screen out specialists and approve of nominees with broad general experience.   In this connection, it is interesting that an attempt to correlate judges' basic background characteristics like political party, religion, and prior judicial experience with their judicial decisions led to inconclusive results.[12]   A very limited range of variance was explained by these social background variables.   The reason, presumably, is that there is a great deal of homogeneity on the federal bench—much more than there is diversity—and the process of recruitment may help to explain why this should be so.

Whatever the impact of the recruitment process, the socialization of judges and the apportionment of responsibilities among them impede the development of pools of expertise that might be useful in the handling of social policy matters.   These two factors are closely related, because the process of socialization is heavily directed to the manifest responsibilities of the job.

The key to the on-the-job socialization of a federal judge is the breadth of his docket.   Judges are rotated from problem to problem.   There are few things they see enough of to make them real specialists.   (The few that come to mind are criminal prosecutions, negligence cases, and prisoners' petitions.)   The basic problem for the new judge is to develop the breadth he will need.   A study of thirty new federal district judges is instructive in this regard.[13]   Almost half of this small sample consisted of "lawyer-generalists" before appointment, seven had been state-court judges, four had been United States Attorneys, and only six had been in specialist private practice.   Despite the preponderance of generalists, the overwhelming majority "pointed to many areas of federal law that they were expected to be familiar with as a judge but for which their pre-judicial careers had not prepared them."

Here the contrast with congressmen is pronounced.   Congressmen often specialize, and more senior and influential congressmen tend to specialize more.   The House of Representatives has been a notoriously decentralized body.   Much decisionmaking authority has resided in committees.   This decentralization has fostered specialization.   The growth of seniority and the related increase in safe seats over the last several decades have also permitted increased specialization.   Senior congressmen tend to be "primarily concerned with [their] committee work, and rarely develop legislation which is before another committee."   There is an informal rule in the House against serving on more than one major committee.   "This rule enforces specialization and encourages technical expertise in a small range of issues and reliance on shortcuts in most other areas."

12. Joel B. Grossman, "Social Backgrounds and Judicial Decision-Making," 79 Harv.L.Rev. 551–64 (1966).

13. Robert Carp and Russell Wheeler, "Sink or Swim: The Socialization of a Federal District Judge," 21 J. Public L. 359–93 (1972).

Not only is there specialization in practice; there is also a congressional norm of specialization. In a sampling of members of the House of Representatives, 80 percent agreed that a congressman should be a specialist, and 95 percent agreed that the important work of the House was done in committee.[18] The need for specialization was attributed to the heavy and varied workload of the House.

The same situation, therefore—heavy and varied workload—gives rise to opposite adaptations on the part of judges and congressmen. Where a congressman finds rewards in carving out a special niche for himself and acquiring credentials that differentiate him from his many colleagues, a judge finds rewards in becoming omnicompetent and more like his colleagues.

Much of the difference can be attributed to the parceling out of tasks. If judge-shopping by litigants is to be avoided and the goal of equality before the law fostered, then cases must be assigned to judges on a random or near-random basis. Furthermore, judicial decisionmaking at the district-court level is generally solitary decisionmaking: district court cases are ordinarily heard by a single judge. Both of these factors put the accent on omnicompetence, since a judge must be prepared for virtually any kind of case and cannot rely on the expertise of his colleagues. In the court of appeals, cases are also assigned on a random or near-random basis, and although that court sits in panels of three judges, the continuous reshuffling of panel members leaves little room for a division of labor or the development of spheres of expertise.

In Congress, on the other hand, the size of the body and the collegial character of all decisions permit and encourage such a division of labor. No congressman need fear that an issue outside his sphere of competence will be thrust upon him. He need decide nothing alone. Each can confidently rely on expert colleagues to counsel him in fields with which he is not familiar, secure in the knowledge that they will reciprocally consult him in areas of his special competence.

Of course, some congressmen never specialize, and some judges are indeed known as experts on particular legal subjects. But the thrust of the two institutions is quite different. Whereas both congressmen and judges start out as generalists, they tend to move in opposite directions, narrowing down in the one case, broadening out in the other. There is no judicial counterpart to the congressman who has made problems of education or health care his own special preserve. Even if there were, the chances would be slim that a suit raising such issues would find its way to him. On most of the important social policy issues that come to them, judges are bound to be novices.

The contrast with administrators is different once again. Career administrators, especially at the bureau level and below, tend to be highly specialized. Political appointees who serve in the departments and agencies tend, however, to be quite inexperienced in the programs they are expected to manage, and furthermore they often do not stay long enough to master

18. Herbert B. Asher, "The Learning of Legislative Norms," 67 Am.Pol.Sci.Rev. 499–513 (1973).

them. Where the judge, with long tenure but short case assignments, is rotated from problem to problem, the political executive, with concentrated assignments but short tenure, is rotated from job to job.

The difference is that the political executive, generalist though he is, has informational resources close at hand that are denied the judge, and, moreover, he relies on them. To be sure, the political appointee may quickly be captured by the career bureaucrats on whom he depends, and they in turn may be beholden to the interests outside their agency which they are to serve or regulate. The point here is that the unusual independence and isolation of judges is attended by the difficulties they have of informing themselves.

The generalist skills of lawyers and judges, it may be argued, are their most valuable attribute in the making of social policy. If expertise were the sole criterion of capacity to make good policy, then the established bureaucracies, interest groups, and legislative committees that possess the expertise would have made it, and there would be no need to involve the courts. Yet we know that the most specialized of all government decision-makers, the operating bureaus of government departments, often suffer from a limited vision and a propensity to become committed to one and only one version of several alternative policies. The increasing resort to the courts reflects the felt need to break loose from expertise and to gain the benefits of a more distant, uncommitted perspective on policy problems.

Perhaps so, but there is a difference between a fresh perspective and an ignorant one. That judges are generalists means, above all, that they lack information and may also lack the experience and skill to interpret such information as they may receive. On many matters, after all, the expert may know nothing of the particulars before him; what he does know, however, is the general context, and he can locate the issue in its proper place on the landscape. Judges are thus likely to be doubly uninformed, on particulars and on context. This make the process by which they obtain information crucial, for social policy issues are matters far from the everyday experience of judges.

The adjudication process conspires in a dozen small and large ways to keep the judge ignorant of social context. This may, of course, be regarded as the vestigial influence of the earlier, less ambitious functions of adjudication, structured as it was to make law only as a byproduct of responding to individual conflicts. Vestigial or not, it is with us still .   .   .   .

Joel B. Harris, **The Title VII Administrator: A Case Study in Judicial Flexibility***

The Power of the Courts to Appoint Administrators

.   .   . [T]he courts have been quite willing to fully use their broad equitable powers to issue wide-ranging decrees designed to eliminate the

Source: 60 Cornell L.Rev. 53, 55–74 (1974). Assistant U.S. Attorney, Civil Division, Southern District of New York, 1970–74; Chief, Civil Rights Unit, 1973–74; currently a member of the New York bar.

lingering effects of past discrimination. Recognizing that many unforeseen situations will arise in the course of enforcing their injunctions, several courts have appointed advisory committees or administrators to supervise various aspects of their operation. The basic function of these court-appointed officials is threefold: (1) to provide information and assistance to minority workers to enable them to take advantage of the full benefits of the court order; (2) to deal with the daily problems which arise under the decree, thereby preventing major conflicts between the parties; and (3) to provide the court with neutral expertise which can be utilized in recommending changes in employment practices designed to effectuate the purposes of the decree.

Although the use of administrative officials to supervise Title VII decrees is somewhat novel, courts of equity have long relied upon the appointment of ad hoc personnel to help them reach and enforce their decisions. The Supreme Court has recognized that courts have inherent power to provide themselves with appropriate assistance in the performance of their duties, and, indeed, in certain cases that it is the better practice for a court to obtain such assistance. This power has been used to employ auditors. In addition, it has been exercised by federal courts to appoint a master in a criminal case to examine subpoenaed files and rule on whether any of the items were privileged; an investigator to examine, in a bankruptcy context, charges of wrongful disposition of property; and a master to supervise pretrial discovery in a civil case. It has also permitted a court to appoint a commissioner to hear and determine all garnishment and attachment proceedings brought against funds or property in the custody of a court-appointed receiver. And . . . in an area related to the enforcement of Title VII, the Supreme Court [has] approved the appointment of an expert to assist a district court in preparing a workable plan for the desegregation of a public school system.

Rule 53 of the Federal Rules of Civil Procedure, providing for the use of special masters, incorporates the various officials who, under old practice, assisted the court in the hearing and disposal of litigation. Although references to masters are explicitly stated to be the exception and not the rule, masters have been appointed under Rule 53 to perform such tasks as ascertaining profits and damages, determining commissions and amounts due under a contract, rendering complex accountings, supervising discovery proceedings, superintending the election of corporate directors, taking evidence, and determining questions of foreign law. But despite this broad grant of authority, Rule 53 in no way encompasses all of the assistance to which courts are entitled; the courts retain their inherent power to appoint necessary officials.

Employment of Administrators and Committees in
Title VII Cases

The earliest use of an administrator in a Title VII context occurred in United States v. Wood Lathers Local 46, a case which was originally concluded by a consent decree.[30] The settlement agreement required the defen-

---

30. 2 EPD ¶ 10,226 (S.D.N.Y.1970). The author served as counsel for the United States in this action but has restrict- ed his remarks to matters of public record.

dant union to take various steps to achieve equal employment opportunity and provided for the appointment by the court of "an impartial person to implement the provisions of this Agreement and to supervise its performance." It delineated the administrator's powers and duties as follows:

> The Administrator shall be empowered to take all actions, including the establishment of record-keeping requirements, as he deems necessary to implement the provisions of this Agreement, to ensure the performance of this Agreement and to remedy any breach thereof. The Administrator shall decide any questions or disputes or complaints arising under this Agreement, including questions of interpretation of the Agreement and claims of violations of this Agreement acting either on his own initiative or at the request of any interested person. All decisions of the Administrator shall be in writing and shall be final.

Judge Frankel, who approved the consent decree, referred to the provisions dealing with the administrator as "[t]he somewhat novel and perhaps most interesting part of the agreement." [32] He later reflected on the responsibility of the administrator to exercise detailed supervision and directive authority to achieve the decree's purposes. In his view, "[t]he Administrator was to have not mere policing functions, but the broadly creative role, in close contact with the parties and their work, of evolving 'rules and procedures' to implement the goal of 'equal employment opportunities.' " [33] In that same opinion, the court indicated that it conceived of the administrator as a quasi-administrative body by comparing the recommendations of the administrator following his study of the industry employment needs to administrative rule-making .   .   .   .

[In] United States v. Local 638, Steam Pipefitters,[43] Judge Bonsal appointed an administrator and gave him powers similar to those possessed by the administrator in *Wood Lathers.*[44]   In addition, the *Local 638* administrator was charged with the duty to work out and submit to the court an affirmative action program to meet the minimum goal of thirty percent minority journeyman union membership by July 1, 1977, as well as to supervise the testing, publicity, and other procedures established by the court. The administrator was also required to conduct an investigation of the work referral system to determine whether it effectuated equal employment opportunities and, if not, to recommend changes in the system.

32. United States v. Wood Lathers Local 46, 328 F.Supp. 429, 433 (S.D.N.Y. 1971). When one facet of the case came before it for review, the Second Circuit commented favorably on this "innovative decree." 471 F.2d at 416.

33. United States v. Wood Lathers Local 46, 341 F.Supp. 694, 695 (S.D.N.Y. 1972), aff'd 471 F.2d 408 (2d Cir. 1973), cert. denied 412 U.S. 939 (1973).

43. 360 F.Supp. 979 (S.D.N.Y.1973), aff'd and remanded [sub nom. Rios v. Enterprise Association Steamfitters,

Local 638 of U. A., 501 F.2d 622 (2d Cir. 1974), order, 400 F.Supp. 983 (S.D.N.Y.1975)]. . . . The injunctive decree is reported at 6 EPD ¶ 8716 (S.D.N.Y.1973).

44. . . . Judge Bonsal, in appointing an "Administrator to implement the provisions of [the] decree and supervise its performance" . . . outlined the powers of the administrator as follows:

In addition to the powers specified in this decree, the Administrator

The Functioning of the Administrator:
Does the Experiment Work?

The *Wood Lathers* Case

. . . In the *Wood Lathers* case, the court appointed George Moskowitz, a seasoned labor attorney and arbitrator, to serve as administrator under the consent decree. Mr. Moskowitz assumed his position immediately, and [as of the time of this writing] has served as administrator ever since. During his four and one-half years in office, Mr. Moskowitz has tackled all of the problems which have arisen. He has arbitrated, ordered, cajoled, discussed, mediated and recommended.

Although the agreement and consent decree gave the administrator wide-ranging power, Mr. Moskowitz, perhaps conscious of his unique role, proceeded very cautiously at first, and the union continued its discriminatory conduct. Thus, although the consent decree required Wood Lathers Local 46 to prepare, within six months, a set of proposed "objective rules and procedures to implement" the "[e]qual employment opportunities" provided for therein, the administrator took no action when the union, after waiting until the very last minute, produced only a "trivial and superficial" product. The government reacted to the union's efforts with a show of despair and disgust, and proceeded to file a motion for contempt of court. After a long hearing, at which the only thing the parties agreed upon was the desirability of retaining the administrator, the district court concluded that the union's conduct had frustrated all attempts by the administrator to promote equal employment opportunities and found the union to be in contempt.

After the contempt decision, the administrator hastened his pace. First, he undertook a revision of the union's hiring hall rules at the behest of Judge Frankel, whose contempt decision was largely based on the union's discriminatory referral practices. This revision imposed a detailed regimen upon the union which became effective on August 17, 1971, and which has required the administrator to be available on a regular basis to supervise its performance. To assist him in this effort, the administrator hired a computer company, built computer capability into the hiring hall rules, and now receives periodic computer print-outs (paid for by the union) enabling him to rapidly determine whether Wood Lathers Local 46 is complying with the hiring hall rules, and to check on the validity of individual complaints.

shall be empowered to take all actions, including the establishment of such additional record-keeping requirements as he deems necessary to implement the provisions and ensure the performance of this decree. The Administrator shall hear and determine all complaints concerning the operation of this decree and shall decide any questions of interpretation and claims of violations of this decree, acting either on his own initiative or at the request of any interested person or party. All decisions of the Administrator shall be in writing and shall be appealable to the Court.

The decree also provides, as in the *Wood Lathers* case, that the administrator does not have the right to amend, modify, or change the substantive terms of the decree, and further states that he shall remain in office for an initial period of three years and thereafter for such time as the court shall determine.

Following promulgation of the hiring hall rules, Mr. Moskowitz turned his attention to a study of the industry's future employment opportunities, a task he was specifically required to perform under the consent decree. The administrator wrote a detailed study, analyzing attrition rates and work opportunities, and then estimated job openings in the industry for the succeeding five years. Based upon this data, he recommended that the union open its hiring hall by issuing work permits enabling new workers to be brought into the industry. Through the use of a one-to-one ratio of minority permits to white permits, combined with a fixed yearly minimum of new permits to be issued, his recommendations were designed to achieve approximately twenty-five percent minority participation in the industry by the end of 1975. These recommendations were adopted by Judge Frankel and affirmed by the Second Circuit. Thereafter, the administrator supervised the issuance of these work permits,[70] ensuring both the union's compliance with the order and the absence of any racial confrontation.

In addition, the administrator, whose name, address, and telephone number are posted in the hiring hall, receives a nearly continuous flow of complaints. Resolution of these complaints is itself almost a full-time job, and includes everything from simply explaining the rules to conducting evidentiary hearings.

. . . Proceeding informally, for the most part over the telephone, by mail, and at meetings with one or more of the parties, the administrator has helped to formulate practical solutions to unforeseen problems not covered by the decree.[71] He has made exceptions where decretal provisions would have resulted in an unduly harsh or unjust result,[72] and has recommended significant modifications where necessary to effectuate equal employment opportunities.

Overall the administrator's techniques have worked effectively. One phone call is often enough to correct a violation or to get a complaining minority worker a job. Instead of being allowed to intensify, problems are dealt with immediately and impartially, and potential crises are quickly defused. Gradually the union members have grown accustomed to working with minority groups and the volume of complaints of discrimination seems to have tapered off. Meanwhile, the court, and often the attorneys for the litigants, have been spared many headaches, and problems have been solved much

---

70. On one almost calamitous occasion, hundreds of men slept for days on 76th Street in New York City awaiting the issuance of the permits . . . .

71. For example, the hiring hall rules require that all persons seeking work in New York City appear in person at the hiring hall for referral. When the gasoline crisis made it difficult for many to get to the hall, the administrator considered a temporary modification of the rules for workers who lived in outlying districts and sought work near their homes . . . .

72. For instance, from time to time returning veterans (white) have applied to renew their old work permits to use the Local 46 hiring hall. The administrator has allowed renewals where the applicant had a valid permit at the time he entered military service and reapplied for such permit promptly after discharge. All other requests for renewal have been denied . . . .

more swiftly and practically than if they had been required to await formal juridical proceedings.

The *Local 638* Case

In his decision in *Local 638*, Judge Bonsal appointed Vincent Mc-Donnell, Chairman of the New York State Board of Mediation, to serve as administrator. Mr. McDonnell was given a number of immediate tasks in addition to his general duties: he was required to work with the parties to develop an affirmative action program, to supervise the testing of minority applicants for journeyman membership in the union, to formulate a new apprenticeship class of 400 members, and to study the industry referral system.

Facing immediate deadlines without having been exposed to the extensive background of the case, the administrator nonetheless performed decisively and effectively. In the first six months, 864 minority workers were scheduled to take the journeyman admission test, 488 minority workers were admitted to union membership, 175 minority apprentices were indentured, and an affirmative action proposal was adopted, all without the parties finding it necessary to return to the district court for guidance. Indeed, by the end of the seventh month the union had achieved a minority membership of 888, a staggering figure in light of its past exclusionary practices.

Like Mr. Moskowitz, Mr. McDonnell has also successfully operated informally and disposed of complaints and other problems which, if left unresolved, could have developed into serious racial disputes. Although there have been occasions when Mr. McDonnell was unavailable, causing a certain amount of delay, there can be no doubt that he too has met what Judge Frankel called the "basic goal of expert and knowledgeable management . . . avoiding an intolerable regime of daily and minute supervision by the court." . . .

The Power of the Administrator and the Form of Administration

In light of these precedents, two important questions arise: (1) what authority can and should a court delegate to the Title VII administrator, and what powers of review must the court exercise; and (2) what form should the administration take?

1. *Delegated Powers and Judicial Review*

There are definite limits to the scope of authority that a court can permissibly delegate to an administrator. Without the consent of all parties, the court must reserve to itself the duty and the right to review the evidence and the administrator's findings and conclusions. And even with consent, it is doubtful that a court could wholly delegate its responsibilities to an administrator. Thus, Rule 53(e)(4) of the Federal Rules of Civil Procedure provides that the parties can stipulate that the master's findings of fact be final, but matters of law must be left for the court's determination. It is clear, therefore, that no matter how broadly defined the administrator's powers may be there will be judicial review of his decisions.

The standard of review is less clear. Rule 53(e)(2) states that "[i]n an action to be tried without a jury the court shall accept the master's findings of fact unless clearly erroneous." In a jury trial, the findings of the master are entitled to prima facie weight. Prior to the adoption of Rule 53, some courts treated a master's findings as presumptively correct. Since the Title VII administrator is appointed pursuant to the court's inherent powers, and not under Rule 53, it is unclear whether the "clearly erroneous," "prima facie," or "presumptively correct" standard of review should be applied. And the cases decided to date offer little guidance on this point.

In the *Wood Lathers* case, there have been two occasions when decisions by the administrator have been reviewed by the district court. The first was when the administrator proposed new hiring hall rules; the second was when he recommended the issuance of new work permits. In each instance the party who concurred in the administrator's decision successfully moved in district court for an order making the recommendations effective. Once, the court stated, without citing authority, that the administrator's judgments should be given prima facie weight. There was no discussion of judicial review on the second occasion.

. . . [T]he *Local 638* decree provides only that all decisions of the administrator shall be in writing "and shall be appealable to the Court." Again, no standard of review has been provided and there are no decisions under the decree to provide guidance. At present, therefore, the amount of authority which can be delegated to an administrator is not entirely clear, although it is apparent that the court must review the administrator's findings, and that those findings are entitled to great weight.

Nevertheless, so long as some form of judicial review is retained by the district court, the impressive results obtained in the *Wood Lathers* and *Local 638* cases demonstrate that a wide scope of authority should be given to the administrator to ensure that he is equipped to deal with all unforeseen contingencies which might develop under the decree. Since flexibility combined with power is the ideal, broad general language may well be sufficient to accomplish the desired ends. Another approach is to be far more specific in detailing the administrator's powers, with a catch-all clause at the end of the decree to provide for unforeseen contingencies. It would appear to be sound practice to further define the scope of the administrator's powers and duties. This would, it is submitted, increase the power which the administrator can exercise, for it would both encourage him to act and provide him with specific language to point to if challenged. And, to some extent at least, it would reduce the likelihood that he would see himself as just as an arbitrator with a panoply of vague, unusable powers; instead, his character as a quasi-administrative agency, with specific duties to perform and specific powers to perform them with, would be clearly revealed.

It is also extremely important for the court to promulgate comprehensive and specific affirmative relief, especially in the early stages when the administrator is "getting his feet wet." Indeed, short run goals are more readily met through specific decretal language, leaving the creative role of an administrator to bear fruit in the longer-range aspects of the case. Moreover, a detailed injunction provides the administrator with a focus for the exercise of his powers and enables him to move forward swiftly to the mechanics of achieving equal employment opportunities.

To some extent, of course, a specific decree limits the powers of the administrator. Although specificity can be useful in forcing a reluctant administrator to act, it can also serve to unduly hamper a vigorous one. Great care must therefore be taken in the drafting of the decree to ensure that a proper balance is established whereby the administrator can be guided and assisted by specific provisions while at the same time he can retain sufficient flexibility to handle unexpected situations as they arise.

2. Form of Administration

Experience indicates that, on balance, a single administrator is probably more effective than a committee. A large group is cumbersome and inevitably becomes bureaucratic. Decisions and recommendations depend upon votes, and lobbying efforts by the various parties can be expected to be vigorous if a close vote appears likely. There might also be difficulty in assembling a large group for a meeting or a hearing. The impressive results attained under the *Local 638* and *Wood Lathers* decrees demonstrate that a decisive individual can speedily immerse himself in the problems of the industry, develop expertise, and then make specific recommendations for the achievement of equal employment opportunities. It is clear that the troubleshooting and negotiating aspects of the administrator's job are better handled by a single person, and that one individual can certainly operate more swiftly and more informally than a group.

On the other hand, a single administrator may be temporarily inaccessible, due to other business activities, illness or even vacation, causing delays and inconveniencing the parties. He could also die, resign, or otherwise cease functioning suddenly, leaving the parties to fend for themselves. Such problems are unlikely to arise when a committee is appointed.

Of course, the single administrator can take steps to prevent such delays and inconveniences. For example, he can appoint an assistant and have a secretary or clerk who, under his supervision, could work steadily on the matter at hand. Unfortunately, employing such additional personnel is expensive; but the continuity achieved would seem to be well worth the cost. The parties might even reap a side benefit from additional personnel to the extent that when assistants can handle the routine activities, the administrator will have more time for thought and innovation. However, none of the functioning administrators has yet developed such a procedure.

In addition, with a single administrator, personality plays an important role. Different persons approach the same problem differently, and one can expect vast differences in philosophy, temperament and style. Since the court expects to defer to the administrator's judgment, the administrator becomes an extremely important part of the proceedings. A bad or even lazy administrator would certainly impede enforcement efforts, and constant resort to the court would be expensive and time-consuming. For that reason, the administrator must be selected with great care.[103] And, if the par-

---

103. In the *Wood Lathers* and *Local 638* cases, the court requested the parties to agree upon an administrator. When they could not do so, the parties were asked to agree upon a list of acceptable candidates. In each case this list was submitted to the court which then selected one of the candidates

ties are dissatisfied with the administrator's performance, they should not hesitate to ask the court for his removal   .   .   .   .

—————

The phenomenon which Harris addresses has not been confined to Title VII cases.   Administrators or special masters have been used by courts in a great variety of suits, including those involving prisons, mental hospitals, and schools.   They are here discussed in chapter 7 (Fiss) and chapter 8 (Chayes).   See also Note, Implementation Problems in Institutional Reform Litigation, 91 Harv.L.Rev. 428 (1977); Note, Masters and Magistrates in the Federal Courts, 88 Harv.L.Rev. 779 (1975); Kaplan and Zuckerman, The *Wyatt* Case: Implementation of a Judicial Decree Ordering Institutional Change, 84 Yale L.J. 1338 (1975); Note, Monitors: A New Equitable Remedy?, 70 Yale L.J. 103 (1960).

Questions have been raised about the efficiency of such administrators or special masters, and, even more importantly, about the legitimacy of their participation in the judicial process itself.   Harris would have us read Federal Rule of Civil Procedure 53 as the basic source of their authority   Yet even he recognizes that the role contemplated for the administrator or special master does not easily fit within the bounds of that Rule.   The master contemplated by Rule 53 is to act as a "sub-judge," in much the same way as a judge acts—passive and umpireal.   He is arguably confined to consideration of the information that appears on the transcribed record which has been subject to cross examination.   He is required to make findings of fact and conclusions of law.   All such findings by the "sub-judge" are then to be reviewed by the judge.   Neither Moskowitz nor McDonnell acted in such a restricted fashion; yet their free-wheeling mode of conduct typifies the conduct of other administrators and special masters.

Geoffrey F. Aronow, in The Special Master in School Desegregation Cases: The Evolution of Roles in the Reformation of Public Institutions Through Litigation 8–9, 41 (unpublished manuscript on file in Yale Law Library, 1979), sees the special master as representing a unique procedural role, as a fusion of *party* and *sub-judge*.   He shows how the institution has evolved in school desegregation cases over the last decade, and he locates its legitimacy not in positive law, in Rule 53, but rather in the responsiveness of the institution to the special needs of a specific type of litigation, one that in its liability stages focuses on the output of bureaucratic decisionmaking

proposed by the defendant union. In both cases, all candidates were attorneys. Presumably the parties recognized that the administrator must exercise legal skills which only a trained attorney could be expected to possess. Moreover, the majority of the candidates submitted to the court were expert in the labor and/or civil rights fields, and the two eventually selected were well-known labor mediators. There is no doubt that their labor expertise facilitated the ability of the respective administrators to rapid-ly grasp the situation, and to deal speedily with the matters at hand.

Where a committee is chosen, greater flexibility in choice of personnel exists and consideration should be given to utilizing non-attorneys with specialized knowledge of areas outside the usual range of lawyers. For example, it might be desirable to include as a member of an advisory committee a person with experience in vocational testing . . . .

and that in its remedial stage requires a restructuring of the bureaucracy. He writes:

> A number of factors . . . mitigate against the success of [the] traditional [adjudicatory] structure in school desegregation cases and in related litigation concerned with the operations of other institutions, including prisons, mental institutions, and hospitals. The overriding catalyst for change is the bureaucratic nature of the violation. This feature of the litigation led to three major breakdowns in the traditional structure of the lawsuit: (1) the default of the directly affected party and the entrance into that vacuum of the organizational plaintiff; (2) the recognition of the breadth of interests affected in the remedial restructuring of public institutions; and (3) the lack of standards for evaluating a successful remedy, which enabled the defendants effectively to subvert the litigation in the remedial stage.

> . . .

> . . . [I]t seems that the role of the special master is designed to mitigate those dangers, [by abandoning the traditional adjudicatory structure,] while insuring effectiveness. The special masters allow the court to avoid being co-opted by having to take a direct role in remedial formulation, while at the same time giving the court the independent voice it needs to avoid reliance on the bureaucrats, who have a stake in the status quo. The special master brings into the litigation the consideration of the many affected interests which must be considered in the remedial formulation to assure fairness, without abandoning the focus on the remedy for a specific wrong. The special masters, in other words, by fusing aspects of judge and advocate, serve two functions simultaneously: the liberation from the formal trappings of the litigation model, but also the protection of those values of detachment, independence, consideration of all interests, and dispassionate rationality which lend the courts their legitimacy as surely as technical elements of the traditional paradigm. Many people attack the special masters because they recognize only the elements of the masters' functions which fit the first characterization; they fail to perceive the legitimacy-protecting function which the special masters also serve.

For a first-hand account of the role of a special master in a recent school desegregation case, see Berger, Away from the Court House and into the Field: The Odyssey of a Special Master, 78 Colum.L.Rev. 707 (1978). Also, the reader might at this point wish to review the consideration of "adversaries" undertaken in chapter 4.

———

Stephen Wexler, **Expert and Lay Participation in Decision Making***

Each man's right to participate in the decisions that affect him has been seriously compromised by an excessive reliance on professionals and experts. Our right to participate directly in personal decisions and our right to par-

* *Source:* 16 Nomos, Participation in Politics 186 (1975). Associate Professor of Law, University of British Columbia.

ticipate through political mechanisms in group decisions are both affected. We do not understand how and when to use professionals and experts, and so we have come to rely on them when we should not and they have gained power that they should not have. Computers are giving experts greater and greater access to information. This enhances their claims to power and increases our reliance on them.

I wish to suggest that there is a kind of question that an expert can answer for us, and another kind of question that we must answer for ourselves. Experts can *help* us with questions of the latter sort, and I shall try to outline some of the ways in which they can do so. But, though an expert can help us with such questions, they call finally for a decision that only we can make.

Without some information we cannot answer even the easiest (non-analytic) questions. If we are trying to find a way of crossing a stream and someone calls out "Will this log reach across?" we would surely want to look at both the log and the stream. We would be unable to answer even easy questions if we did not have a little information, and, therefore, when we cannot answer hard questions, we tend to think it is because we do not have enough information. We believe that getting more information always puts us in a better position to answer any question.

It is true that some information is needed to answer any question. It is not true, however, that more information is always useful. Some questions are hard to answer only because we do not have enough information. Once we have enough information the question is an easy one. But some questions are altogether different: it is not a lack of information that makes them hard to answer, and therefore, more information cannot help one answer them. There is no such thing as enough information to make such questions easy.

The distinction is important and corresponds, I believe, to a distinction made along the following lines. Simplex questions are those in which all relevant factors can be measured in the same units. "Will the log reach across the stream?" is a simplex question; it turns on the length of the log and the width of the stream, both of which can be stated in the same units.

If the log is eight feet long and the stream is twenty feet wide, "Will the log reach across?" is an easy question; it is also easy if the log is twenty feet long and the stream is eight feet wide. To answer easy questions like these we need only approximate information; a glance at the log and the stream is enough. Not all simplex questions are easy ones, however; if the log is about as long as the stream is wide, "Will the log reach across?" is a difficult question. We will want more than just a glance at the log and the stream. We will want to measure and, given the proper question, we may want to measure quite precisely.

The point to notice is that what makes a simplex question difficult is precisely that we lack information. More information is exactly what is needed to answer difficult questions of this kind.

Complex questions are those in which all the factors cannot be measured in the same units. "Should we wade across or fell a tree to bridge the stream?'' is a complex question; it involves, at least, our feelings about getting wet and our feelings about work, and these cannot be stated in the same terms. Complex questions can be reduced to simplex ones by ignoring relevant factors. Thus, "Will it take longer to wade across or bridge the stream?" is a simplex question but it ignores wetness, coldness, the difficulty of different tasks, etc.

Complex questions can be easy. Thus, if the water is very cold and we have a power saw, it is easy to decide whether to wade or bridge the stream; it is also easy if the water is pleasant and we have only hatchets. For easy complex questions as for easy simplex ones, approximate information is enough. We do not need to know the exact temperature of the water or the precise difficulty of felling a tree.

But if the water is fairly cold and bridging the stream is a fairly hard job, whether to wade or bridge is a difficult question. The important point is that a lack of information is not what makes this a difficult question, and more information will not help us answer it. Once we have said the water is *fairly* cold and felling a tree will be *fairly* hard, we have all the information that is useful. More precise information may seem to be useful, but that is illusory. What good does it do to know that the water is 56°? Suppose it had been 58°? The difficulty in this question rests not on lack of information but on having no way, in close cases, of measuring getting wet and cold against working hard.

We need no help with easy questions, simplex or complex. It is with difficult questions that we need help. It is with difficult questions that we go to experts. An expert's license indicates that he has certain information or the skill to obtain it, and so, given the proper instructions, an expert is the person best suited to answer difficult simplex questions. These questions are difficult for us because we do not have or cannot obtain certain information; for an expert this difficulty does not exist.

Can an expert "answer" our difficult complex questions? It would seem not. These questions are not difficult for lack of information: they are difficult because we must compare two or more different values and we can do so only in the grossest cases.

Can an expert decide whether we would rather be fairly wet or fairly tired? Though experts are regularly asked to answer such questions and regularly answer them, it seems to me that their licenses do not really entitle them to do so. They can be very helpful in a number of ways when we decide difficult complex questions, but they cannot decide them for us, as they can answer difficult simplex questions. Let me point out some of the ways they can help us.

1. Difficult simplex questions often underlie difficult complex ones. Thus, "Should I bring suit?" is a complex question, behind which one finds simplex questions such as "Have I a cause of action?"—precisely the sort of question a lawyer is licensed to answer. But that simplex question is not equivalent to "Should I sue?" "Should I sue?" requires a personal decision in which one must compare the advisability of suing with the hassle involved, the personal feelings between the parties, one's trust in one's lawyer, etc.

A lawyer is in no special position to decide that question. In some ways, he is in a very bad position: his training leads him to ignore all the factors that make the question complex.

If both the lawyer and I know what to expect of experts, the lawyer can be useful. Complex questions often appear to be difficult only because we have not answered simplex ones. Thus, "Should I sue (if I know there will be bad publicity)?" may seem a difficult complex question until I find out that I have no chance of winning, at which point it becomes an easy question.

We all tend to treat experts in other fields as wise men. Thus, we might be tempted to ask a doctor, "Should I tell my friend that his illness is very serious?" But how can the doctor decide whether I should obey my friend's wish that I tell him or do what is medically best? As with the lawyer, I should ask, "Is it likely to be medically bad if I tell him that his illness is serious?" If the answer is no, then what looked like a difficult decision is in fact an easy one. If the answer is yes, then I, and not the doctor, must decide what to do.

The danger is that the doctor will say "You must not tell him." And professionals often say just this sort of thing. One day, at lunch, a friend of mine who is a lawyer talked about a problem he was having:

> I don't know what to do. I've a criminal trial this afternoon and I can't decide whether to put my man on the stand. He says that the policemen who arrested him are lying about what they saw him do. I don't think the lie means much because even if he did what they said, I don't think they have a case. But my man says he wants to tell the truth. More important, if he says the police are lying, the judge is likely not to believe anything he says. I just can't decide whether he should testify or not.

It seems to me that my friend has no business making this decision. He may be able, as I have said, to help his client make the decision, by clarifying questions about evidence and judicial tendencies, but nothing in a lawyer's special training or skill entitles him to decide how important it is to tell the truth.

2. There is another way in which experts can help us decide difficult complex questions. Often, the expert will have seen other people make similar decisions, or he may have access to statistics on prior decisions. Thus, a trail guide might know that, of the people he has been out with, most of those who chose to wade the stream regretted their decision, while few of those who chose to bridge it regretted theirs. An expert may have experience as well as knowledge.[3]

---

3. There are times (for instance, when it is important to make a *quick* choice) when we can reasonably rely on an expert to decide a question we could decide. Also, making a decision may consume a great deal of time, and so we might in certain circumstances reasonably delegate it to someone else. Finally, an expert may have what is sometimes called a trained intuition; he may know something in a way he cannot explain. It sometimes makes sense to trust an expert's intuition. I believe we rely on experts too much, but that is not really the point here. Whether we increase, decrease, or continue our reliance on experts, we should know why we rely on them and whether we have good grounds for doing so.

This experience can be useful if the expert has seen many cases, if they have been substantially the same, and if the results have not been the product of the expert's biases.   However, there is no reason why the expert cannot give us the details of his experience rather than summary advice.   Instead of telling me what to do, he should tell me what he knows and let me decide what to do.   The expert's experience only answers the simplex question "What percentage of the people have regretted wading?"—i. e., "How likely is it that I will regret wading?"

But "How likely is it that I will regret wading?" is not the same as "Should I wade?"   I might sensibly say, "Well, though it is likely that I will regret wading, nevertheless I will do so."

Let me illustrate: "Is Jones lying about what he did Friday night?" is a complex question (unless I know for certain what Jones did Friday night).[4] To answer this question I must weigh Jones' past record for telling the truth against his demeanor, against his reasons for lying, against the plausibility of his story, etc.   A psychologist may be able to tell me that people like Jones are, in his experience, very likely to lie in cases such as this, but he cannot answer the question "Is Jones lying?"

It seems quite clear to me that even after I have heard the psychologist, I will still want to talk to Jones: I will want to talk to Jones because I might conclude, "Though it seems likely that a man like Jones would lie in a case like this, nevertheless I believe him."

3.   An expert may help us decide complex questions by pointing out relevant factors that we have neglected.   Thus, if we are trying to decide whether to encourage small farmers to move to the cities, and we are weighing the loss of rural life styles against increased farm yield, an expert might tell us that we have forgotten to note the increased welfare costs entailed by forcing workers into a tight economy.

4.   An expert can help us to know that the complex question we face is a difficult one.   In some cases only an expert will be able to give us the approximation we need to see the problem.   Thus, we may not know that felling a tree is *fairly* hard work.   Or that putting a road through a town will cause *fairly* serious social upheavals.

We do need *some* information to know that there is a real question, and experts can often give that to us.   But more information will not help to decide it.

If we face a simplex question and an expert tells us the tree is about eight feet long and the stream is about eight feet wide, we can usefully send him back for a closer measurement.   If he returns and says, "The tree is eight feet plus a little less than one inch long and the stream is eight feet plus a little less than one inch wide" we can send him back again.   We can push him back through as many decimal places as is necessary to get an answer.   Approximations will not do.

4. If I know for certain what Jones did, then "Is Jones lying about what he did?" is a simplex question and I am an expert on the matter; I have all the information needed to decide.

But if the expert tells us the road will be *fairly* useful and the number of families up-rooted will be *about* 400, he has served his purpose. If we ask for, and he obtains, more accurate information, he has given us something useless. So it is exactly 396 families. So what?

Now I wish to raise and deal with a very important objection. If the information that experts bring us is sometimes useful and at worst useless, why not get as much of it as we can? There are at least four good reasons not to do so—four good reasons why we should remember that information, and therefore experts, can play only a very limited role in the decision of difficult complex questions.

1. If we neglect to distinguish between questions an expert can answer and questions we must decide ourselves, we may inadvertently ask the expert the wrong one and he may answer it, thereby preempting our decision. So, if we ask an economist whether we should encourage small farmers to move to the cities, he may compute the costs and the profits and say "Yes," and we will forget to count the loss of the rural life style.

2. If we forget that there are some questions we must decide for ourselves, we will come to rely on experts too much. They will become wise men for us. The Pentagon Papers reveal that Lyndon Johnson gave away the American people's ability to participate through their elected officials in deciding whether to make war in Vietnam. And he did so because he developed an improper reliance on body counts, kill-ratios, and cost-benefit analyses and the people who prepared them.

3. If we remember that precise information is not always essential in making decisions, we foreclose one of the arguments of those who would take away our right to participate. "Do you know exactly how many megatons the bomb on Amchitka will be?" "Don't tell me lots of people get killed, tell me how many get killed." "Can you be sure that putting mercury in the lake will kill the fish? Professor so-and-so is not sure." "When were you in Cambodia last?" When we are deciding difficult complex questions, an argument that rests on the other fellow's lack of precise information is spurious.

4. Most important, once we have invested time and money to get information, we will be tempted to use it. A friend of mine once decided to build a brick wall. She ordered the bricks, and by the time they came she was no longer sure she wanted the wall. But she had spent a lot of money on the bricks and so she *decided* to build the wall. If an expert tells us that the water is 57.3°, we are likely to say, "Well, it's more than 57°, so let's wade."   .   .   .

Chapter 6

INFORMATION AND KNOWLEDGE

Adjudication entails a process of (1) informing the adversaries, their representatives, and the decisionmaker of relevant matters; (2) assessing that information; and (3) arriving at relevant conclusions. Thus, the process entails communication of information, the transformation of information into knowledge, and the arrival at decisions under conditions of uncertainty.

These processes have important practical ramifications. Lawyers and their clients constantly make judgments about whether it is worth spending an additional dollar to try to discover something which may produce a more favorable outcome. They confront the costs of information and the fact that its ultimate value may be highly uncertain. Managers and designers of procedural systems also must consider the costs and avenues of information. They must decide whether some, or all, parties should be fully or partially subsidized in their quest for relevant information and whether, and to what extent, a party seeking information should be able to impose part of the costs upon others.

But such questions of tactics and of design, with the many associated ethical issues, hardly exhaust the problematic dimension of information in procedure. There are larger theoretical issues implicating communication theory, economics, epistemology, and the sociology of knowledge—though these issues have often been hidden beneath their essentially institutional guise, e.g., the composition and functions of decisionmaking bodies (especially juries), the role characteristics of deciders, and the attributes of impartiality. In this chapter we present material which addresses the underlying theoretical questions.

We present here four such theoretical questions in the design of procedural systems for communication. First, we ask whether the participants, as products of differing social experience, might not be systematically incapable of understanding one another; and, as a corollary, whether that incapacity increases with social distance. Second, we ask whether the system is satisfactory as a channel for information, assuming the participants to be capable of understanding each other's messages. Third, we ask how deciders should treat conditions of uncertainty. Finally, we ask whether the behavior of participants is systematically affected by formal characteristics of the proceeding itself. Where there has been an article which explicitly links these theoretical questions to legal issues, we have presented that article even if it illustrates but a small portion of the relevant problem area. Thus, Professor Martin Shapiro's explicit discussion of stare decisis in terms of communication theory and Professor Tribe's consideration of the possible uses of formal treatments of uncertainty in decisions both proceed at the level of integration of law and theory for which we have searched. Professor Damaška's article is a searching critique of social psychology methods and theories of addressing the behavioral questions. Unfortunately, we have not found a similar article integrating the insights of modern epistemology

376

or of the sociology of knowledge into an explicit legal discussion. In the absence of such a piece, we have chosen to present the general summary of the major issues in the sociology of knowledge contained in Robert Merton's classic survey, Social Theory and Social Structure (1965). The function of this inclusion is simply to alert the student of procedure to an area where important conceptual work might be undertaken. Consider as you read Merton's brief description of the sociology of knowledge what relevance its assertions have for our usual assumptions regarding adjudication.

SECTION A.   KNOWLEDGE AND BELIEF AS SOCIAL CONSTRUCTS

Robert K. Merton, **The Sociology of Knowledge***

The sociology of knowledge takes on pertinence under a definite complex of social and cultural conditions. With increasing social conflict, differences in the values, attitudes and modes of thought of groups develop to the point where the orientation which these groups previously had in common is overshadowed by incompatible differences. Not only do there develop distinct universes of discourse, but the existence of any one universe challenges the validity and legitimacy of the others. The co-existence of these conflicting perspectives and interpretations within the same society leads to an active and reciprocal *distrust* between groups. Within a context of distrust, one no longer inquires into the content of beliefs and assertions to determine whether they are valid or not, one no longer confronts the assertions with relevant evidence, but introduces an entirely new question: how does it happen that these views are maintained? Thought becomes functionalized; it is interpreted in terms of its psychological or economic or social or racial sources and functions. In general, this type of functionalizing occurs when statements are doubted, when they appear so palpably implausible or absurd or biased that one need no longer examine the evidence for or against the statement but only the grounds for its being asserted at all.[3] Such alien statements are "explained by" or "imputed to" special interests, unwitting motives, distorted perpectives, social position, etc. In folk thought, this involves reciprocal attacks on the integrity of opponents; in more systematic thought, it leads to reciprocal ideological analyses. On both levels, it feeds upon and nourishes collective insecurities.

Within this social context, an array of interpretations of man and culture which share certain common presuppositions finds widespread currency. Not only ideological analysis and *Wissenssoziologie* [the sociology of knowl-

* *Source:* R. Merton, Social Theory and Social Structure (revised and enlarged edition) 457–60 (1965). Professor of Sociology, Columbia University.

3. Freud had observed this tendency to seek out the "origins" rather than to test the validity of statements which seem palpably absurd to us. Thus, suppose someone maintains that the center of the earth is made of jam. "The result of our intellectual objection will be a *diversion of our inter-*ests; *instead of their being directed on to the investigation itself,* as to whether the interior of the earth is really made of jam or not, *we shall wonder what kind of man it must be who can get such an idea into his head. . . .*" Sigmund Freud, New Introductory Lectures 49 (New York: W. W. Norton, 1933). On the social level, a radical difference of outlook of various social groups leads not only to ad hominem attacks, but also to "functionalized explanations."

edge], but also psycho-analysis, Marxism, semanticism, propaganda analysis, Paretanism and, to some extent, functional analysis have, despite their other differences, a similar outlook on the role of ideas. On the one hand, there is the realm of verbalization and ideas (ideologies, rationalizations, emotive expressions, distortions, folklore, derivations), all of which are viewed as expressive or derivative or deceptive (of self and others), all of which are functionally related to some substratum. On the other hand are the previously conceived substrata (relations of production, social position, basic impulses, psychological conflict, interests and sentiments, interpersonal relations, and residues). And throughout runs the basic theme of the unwitting determination of ideas by the substrata; the emphasis on the distinction between the real and the illusory, between reality and appearance in the sphere of human thought, belief, and conduct. And whatever the intention of the analysts, their analyses tend to have an acrid quality: they tend to indict, secularize, ironicize, satirize, alienate, devalue the intrinsic content of the avowed belief or point of view. Consider only the overtones of terms chosen in these contexts to refer to beliefs, ideas and thought: vital lies, myths, illusions, derivations, folklore, rationalizations, ideologies, verbal façade, pseudo-reasons, etc.

What these schemes of analysis have in common is the practice of discounting the *face value* of statements, beliefs, and idea-systems by re-examining them within a new context which supplies the "real meaning." Statements ordinarily viewed in terms of their manifest content are debunked, whatever the intention of the analyst, by relating this content to attributes of the speaker or of the society in which he lives. The professional iconoclast, the trained debunker, the ideological analyst and their respective systems of thought thrive in a society where large groups of people have already become alienated from common values; where separate universes of discourse are linked with reciprocal distrust. Ideological analysis systematizes the lack of faith in reigning symbols which has become widespread; hence its pertinence and popularity. The ideological analyst does not so much create a following as he speaks for a following to whom his analyses "make sense," i. e., conform to their previously unanalyzed experience. . . .

The "Copernican revolution" in this area of inquiry consisted in the hypothesis that not only error or illusion or unauthenticated belief but also the discovery of truth was socially (historically) conditioned. As long as attention was focused on the social determinants of ideology, illusion, myth, and moral norms, the sociology of knowledge could not emerge. It was abundantly clear that in accounting for error or uncertified opinion, some extra-theoretic factors were involved, that some special explanation was needed, since the reality of the object could not account for error. In the case of confirmed or certified knowledge, however, it was long assumed that it could be adequately accounted for in terms of a direct object-interpreter relation. The sociology of knowledge came into being with the signal hypothesis that even truths were to be held socially accountable, were to be related to the historical society in which they emerged. . . .

1.   Merton states that the sociology of knowledge is itself the product of increasing social conflict and differences in values.   To what extent are these social conditions convergent with conditions that might be expected to lead to large-scale litigation and adjudication as a dominant dispute-settlement tool?

2.   If litigation is used as a device for processing disputes among groups, will not divergent ideologies constitute an obstacle to agreement on both the factual and the normative premises of the conflict to be settled? How could such obstacles be overcome?

3.   In McDougall, The Case for Black Juries, 79 Yale L.J. 531, 550 (1970), the author argues that "[i]t is in [a] society, with its cities torn apart by racial disorder, with lawlessness and violence plaguing the black community—that black juries are of such critical importance."   Under what circumstances would one expect the antagonistic interests of litigants to merely distort their perception and understanding of reality?   Under what circumstances would we expect antagonists to bring radically different structures of mind to the dispute-processing battlefield?   How do the propositions of the sociology of knowledge change our conception of the meaning of "neutrality," "impartiality," and "fairness" in an adjudicator?

4.   A somewhat tangential clarification: "Ideology" is a word which recently has been prominent among historians of law.   E. P. Thompson, in his book Whigs and Hunters (1975), concluded with a muted fanfare for the rule of law.   He stated that "[t]he essential precondition for the effectiveness of law, *in its function as ideology*, is that it shall display an independence from gross manipulation and shall seem just."   At 263 (emphasis added).   Thompson's perspective on law as ideology is shared by Douglas Hay, whose article entitled Property, Authority and the Criminal Law we have excerpted in chapter 7.   In this chapter, however, we are concerned with a somewhat different, though related, problem.

Thompson and Hay are interested in the way in which the idea and experience of law are used to justify and criticize existing institutions and patterns of domination.   Law is seen as an element of thought, discourse, and experience which, in important respects, is shared both by the dominator and by the dominated.   In such a view, law is the justification for each (with varying degrees of success) of his or her respective position.   The problems that we wish to raise in this chapter are not those which understand "law" as performing these ideological tasks within a culture.   Rather, we wish to emphasize that the activities of the law—more particularly, adjudication—require interaction among persons and/or groups whose very *minds* are problematic to one another by virtue of their differing social experiences.   It would be conclusory—and a very optimistic conclusion at that —to say that the law provides a successful means of mediating the ideological differences of participants since the law itself is in some measure "autonomous."   You may wish to return to consider the questions raised here after you have read the Hay excerpt in chapter 7.

SECTION B. LEGAL DISCOURSE AS A COMMUNICATION SYSTEM

Examination of the issue or problem of ideology directs itself to a prominent source of difficulty in communication and decisionmaking. The concept views the participants in communication not simply as receptors of messages, but also as participants in the process entailing the giving of meaning to those messages. We may wish, however, to focus on other aspects of the problem of communication; for, whether or not the social determinants of the human mind create different conditions of knowledge, perception, and action, in all cases such conditions depend as well upon the information received.

In the essay which follows, Martin Shapiro focuses upon some characteristics of this flow of information. He has applied several important concepts from communication theory to the pronouncements of courts—primarily appellate courts—to yield a refreshing alternative conception of stare decisis.

Martin Shapiro, **Toward a Theory of Stare Decisis***

.   .   .   Communications theory is not a unified body of thought. It has three quite distinct branches. The first, "syntactics," is concerned with the logical arrangement, transmission, and receipt of signals or signs. It is the domain of the electrical engineer; its concern is with the transmission of signals, whatever their meaning. The second is "semantics," which is concerned with the meaning of the signals to people. The third is "pragmatics," which is the study of the impact of signal transmission on human behavior . . . .

The key concepts of syntactics, for our purposes, are "information," "redundancy," and "feedback," of which the first two are best discussed together. For the telegraphic engineer, information is the content of a signal that could not have been predicted by the receiver; it is a probability concept. The more probable the transmission of a given sign, the less information its actual transmission conveys. "Redundancy" is the opposite of information. It is the introduction of repetition or pattern into the message. If the telegrapher sends each message twice, his second sending is redundant and contains less information than his first. If we establish the convention, rule, or pattern that two dashes will always be followed by a dot, then the actual transmission of the dot after the two dashes will be redundant and contain no information because the dot placement in the sequence could always be predicted without actual transmission.

The ideal transmission, then, in terms of pure "information," would contain absolutely no repetition and no pattern. The engineer finds it wise, however, to introduce redundancy at the cost of reducing the information content of a message, because otherwise any loss of information due to malfunctions in the transmission system would be undetectable and

* *Source:* 1 J.Legal Stud. 125, 125–34 (1972). Professor of Law, University of California at Berkeley.

irremediable.   It is only when we can predict, at least partially, what message we are going to receive that we can spot an erroneous omission or substitution in the message and call for its correction.   The ideal message,
then, will contain the highest proportion of information and the lowest proportion of redundancy necessary to identify and correct errors in transmission.

Thus it will be seen that redundancy and information, in syntactic
terms, are reciprocals of each other; but the situation is more complex when
we consider the semantic dimension of communication, for both information and redundancy convey meaning.   And the line is even more
blurred when we consider the pragmatics of communication.   Writing
on the "New Communication," John H. Weakland has said ". . . there
is no 'redundancy' . . .,"[3] his point being, of course, that repetition and patterns in messages do have behavioral significance to the participants in the communications process.   Such redundancies carry a freight
of meaning, knowledge and/or stimuli to the receiver and in this important
sense are not redundant.

Redundancy may be introduced into messages to facilitate the diagnosis
of information-transmission errors and the transmission back to the sender
of messages enabling him to correct his errors.   This identification and transmission back is feedback.   It is important to distinguish syntactic from cybernetic feedback.   The former involves transmission back concerning error
in the sense of incorrect transmission or receipt of information between sender and receiver within the system; the latter involves transmission concerning error in the sense of incorrect adjustment by the system to the outside
world.   Thus high levels of syntactic feedback indicate trouble in the transmission facilities of the system, rather than the sensitivity and learning that
are typically imputed where high levels of cybernetic feedback are present.
Simply to speak of feedback in general is quite misleading.

.   .   .   [M]ost attempts to apply communications theory to legal
processes have foundered on a failure to keep clear these important distinctions among the relevant concepts of communications theory.   It would
appear a worthwhile undertaking to attempt an application of such concepts
as information, redundancy, and feedback that paid due regard to their
origins in syntactics and clearly labeled all shifts from syntactic to cybernetic
or semantic or pragmatic levels of analysis.   The remainder of this article is
devoted to that endeavor, beginning with some general remarks on legal
communication.   .   .   .

At the most superficial level, it is obvious that legal discourse organized
by the rules of stare decisis emphasizes, and itself insists that its success rests
upon, high levels of redundancy and, therefore, remembering our original
theoretical formulation, low levels of information.   The strongest legal argument is that the current case, on its facts, is "on all fours" with a
previous case and that the decision in that case is deeply embedded in a long
line of decisions enunciating (repeating) a single legal principle.   In other
words, the strongest argument is that the current case, treated as an input,

3.   Communications and Behavior—An
Introduction, 10 Amer.Behav.Sci. 1, 2
(1967).

is totally redundant, and under the rules of stare decisis the duty of the judge is to transmit a message that is equally redundant. Of course the facts of a new case are never exactly on all fours with an old, and no line of precedents is ever totally clear and consistent. The point is that the rules of legal discourse seem to require each attorney to suppress as much information and transmit as much redundancy as possible.

At the semantic level, legal discourse is conducted in terms of highly redundant symbols. The string citation comes to mind in which authorities are piled up endlessly in support of a statement of the law in the opinion, brief, or text.

Legal communication is also replete with highly redundant synonym use. In what has come to be referred to as the "noisy marble" experiment,[5] subjects isolated from one another had to communicate to each other, by written message, the color of marbles. At first, plain, solid color marbles were used. Then cloudy, mottled and indistinct marbles, still quite different from one another, were supplied. Those subjects who succeeded with the more difficult (noisy) marbles did so by markedly increasing the number of synonyms they used in describing their marble rather than by seeking the single "best" descriptive word. When they finally had induced the receiver to understand which of the array of noisy marbles their synonyms were aimed at designating, they could in future communications use any single one of the synonymous words to designate that marble accurately. As the experimenters pointed out: "Once the redundant coding has been used, and the errors reduced thereby, we may assume that the receiver remembers the synonyms used for a given symbol in the redundant code, and that in future messages these synonyms or alternate codes are understood even though not physically present." [6]

In the "craftsmanlike" appellate opinion or brief, the argument is built sentence by sentence, with each sentence—often many of the phrases within each sentence—supported by a citation. A skilled lawyer, seeing the sequence of citations alone, could predict the argument, or, seeing the argument alone, could predict the citations. Thus, either the argument or the citations are —and are supposed to be—redundant. Furthermore, the optimum situation for authoritative appellate decision-making is one where each citation is to a "leading" case that is "leading" precisely because its reasoning has been repeated (and it itself cited) in many other cases. The citation of a leading case name incorporates, in effect, other synonymous cases so that, as in the noisy-marble experiment, we may assume that the receiver remembers the synonyms used for a given symbol in the redundant code, and that in future messages these synonyms or alternate codes are understood even though not physically present . . . . It is significant, too, that a well-constructed legal opinion is likely to make the same point many different ways—in canvassing the issues, in meeting the counterarguments, etc. . . . [T]he very practice of citation is the assertion that "I am not saying anything new; I am only repeating what has already been said."

. . . It remains to consider why the legal system tolerates or requires such high levels of redundancy.

5. See Josiah Macy, Jr., et al., Codins Noise in a Task-Oriented Group, 48 J. Abnor. Psychol. 401 (1953).

6. Id. at 403.

"Redundancy may be said to be due to an additional set of rules, whereby it becomes increasingly difficult to make an undetectable mistake." [7] When we speak of stare decisis, we are speaking of such a set of rules. The importance of redundancy in error correction has been overshadowed by the somewhat imprecise adoption in political science of cybernetic models, with their emphasis on feedback. As noted earlier, cybernetic feedback involves messages to the organism correcting errors in its adjustment to the environment. It thus draws attention away from the problem whether the receiver within the organism has received currently the message from the sender within the organism. Here I wish to stick to the sender-receiver problem and thus view redundancy and feedback as two sides of the coin of correcting message errors. The question why there are high levels of redundancy in the legal system thus inescapably entails the question, are there—and if so why—high levels of communication error?

It seems a reasonable hypothesis that complex organizations are necessarily involved in high levels of signaling. High levels of signaling will lead to high levels of syntactic noise (the larger the number of signals, the more likely they are to interfere with one another), and even higher levels of semantic noise will occur since the subjects of the messages of our complex organization will themselves be complex and ambiguous—noisy in the sense the mottled marbles were. High levels of noise should invite the deliberate introduction of high levels of redundancy to counteract the noise, but the high levels of redundancy, by reducing the information content of the organization's messages, will handicap the organization's ability to meet changing circumstances unless some strong countervailing mechanism is present.

This reasoning seems plausible—but does it apply to the legal system? The answer, I believe, is that it does. I have been engaged recently in studying the evolution of policy formulation in tort law *as if* the fifty state supreme courts, the United States Supreme Court and the British courts constituted a single organization marked by decentralized, non-hierarchical and yet coordinated decision-making.[9] I stress the "as if," because I am working by analogy and assuming what is to be proved—that there are sufficient interconnections between my 52 decision-makers to justify treating them as an organization. On the side of my assumption is a massive and visible flow of messages among them and a policy product sufficiently unified to suggest something more than totally independent action and sufficiently diversified to suggest more than multiple, independent but highly determined responses to a single overriding cause. Against my assumption is the suspicion that tort policy is so socially determined that 52 totally independent decision-makers would arrive at almost the same policy outputs, given the similarities between the communities in which they operate, even if there were no links between them. At the very least I think it is possible to ask how these courts managed to arrive at relatively unified *forms* of legal doctrine even if the general social environment independently, and without the aid of coordinating mechanisms, dictated the unified *substance* of policy.

---

7. Colin Cherry, On Human Communications: A Review, a Survey, and a Criticism 185 (1957).

9. See Martin Shapiro, Decentralized Decision-Making in the Law of Torts, in Political Decision Making (S. Sidney Ulmer ed., 1970).

Viewed in organizational terms a central problem quickly emerges in the tort area. How do a large number of decision-makers manage to arrive at well-coordinated policy decisions (policy decisions are the output of this organization) when the organization is bereft of all the mechanisms of hierarchical control that we associate with classical organizational structures? None of the state supreme courts is legally subordinated to any of the others, nor, in the tort field, are they collectively subordinated to the Supreme Court, which, due to the sparseness of its tort docket, is far from being even primus inter pares.

Once the problem is stated in this way, our attention is immediately drawn to communications phenomena. A logical first guess would be that the organization has developed some set of special communications techniques that allow its decision-makers to cooperate—to substitute, somehow, mutual influence for command from above. Because of the large number of decision-makers, and the very large volume of decisions necessary to keep tort policy attuned to a changing society, we would expect these communications techniques to absorb a disproportionately large share of the organization's resources.

In fact we discover that most of the participants in the organization have spent much of their educational and subsequent professional lives learning coding rules. More important, we find a vast body of communications personnel. The litigational market assures that thousands of lawyers will devote their energies to carrying messages from one court to the next, keeping each informed of what the others are doing. This flow of communications is not controlled by conscious plan or carefully structured communications networks, but rather by hundreds of thousands of individual decisions guided by the desire for personal profit. I use the term litigational market precisely because I wish to suggest an "invisible hand."

For this market, like Adam Smith's, has many rules and conventions that harness individual greed to a higher cause. Under the rules of the game, the lawyer-communicator has the highest chance of winning if he can show a court that his client must prevail if the court keeps doing exactly what it has been doing; the next highest chance if he can persuade the court that it should do exactly what some other court has been doing; the next highest chance if he can convince it to do something slightly different from what it or some other court has been doing; and the worst prospect if he must argue that the court should do something markedly different from what it and other courts have done in the past.

It will be seen that the litigation market encourages the flow of a very large number of *confirmation* messages between independent decision-makers, reassuring each that the others have been agreeing with it. From

10. To the outside observer, using a cybernetic approach, they might appear to be positive feedback, *if* he had made the quite independent determination that what the organization had been doing was an "error" vis-à-vis its environment. Then such supportive messages would have the effect of making the organization persist in its past behavior and thus make more and more errors. It is necessary to keep "error" in the syntactic sense clearly separated from error in the broader cybernetic sense of failure to adjust to the environment.

the standpoint of syntactics, these messages are redundant, and they are *not* feedback, since they are neither occasioned by, nor do they report, error.[10] When messages indicating *differences* between decision-makers are introduced, they are added in small numbers to the stream of reassurances, they emphasize the smallness of the differences, and they tend to suppress or conceal larger ones. Often they are syntactic feedback in the sense of exposing minor errors in understanding or phrasing rather than real policy differences.

In an earlier analysis of this material, basing myself on incremental theories of decision-making, I argued that this form of communication was the substitute for the rational-hierarchical control structures that play a major role in coordinating policy in other organizations. In other words, the tort organization goes to an extreme form of incremental decision-making in which there is a very strong bias against any change at all, only very small changes are ever considered, and differences between organizational units are deemphasized, suppressed, or quickly mediated by requesting each unit to make small step changes in the direction of the other. Faced with a conflict between the authoritative cases in State *A* and State *B*, the lawyer is not likely to state the conflict clearly and ask the judge in State *C* to take his choice. Instead the lawyer will seek to "harmonize" the authorities by bending each a little. If the judge in State *C* will accept the harmonization, then the new mediate position of State *C* will be used in future litigation to lever States *A* and *B* off their initial positions. The potential for conflict among 52 decision-makers is high and the style of decision-making I have described seems designed to create an atmosphere of mutual reassurance, support, and compromise and to avoid the emergence of rationally stated major policy differences, particularly differences stated as matters of principle.

But I now see that this analysis is incomplete. An important activity of the tort organization and its litigational market operating under the rules of stare decisis is to ensure extremely high levels of redundancy in the communications linking the decision-making units. A system that inevitably generates a great deal of noise, and one in which high levels of random error would jeopardize coordination, fully employs the standard techniques for the reduction of noise-caused transmission error. What appears in one light as an incremental (and thus non-rational) technique of decision-making appears in another as the most orthodox and rational solution to the noise problem.

It is well to recall at this point the argument that redundancies at the syntactic level are not redundant at the semantic level, because they transmit the knowledge that the sender is repeating or patterning his message. The rules of legal discourse create redundancy in the first sense in that they make it easier for the receiver to spot unintentional errors in transmission and, more important, to spot intentional ones—for remember that the transmission channels here are lawyers with their own interests. In the same sense, redundancy in tort discourse reduces noise-caused errors in a net with many overlapping signals, and reduces receiving errors by decreasing the workload of each receiver—the amount of information he must process—to manageable proportions.

In the broader semantic sense the redundancy of tort communication, pre-cisely because it conveys the additional knowledge that senders are repeating their messages, provides supportive reassurance to each of the communicator decision-makers that his fellows are with him. The adding of new informa-tion (requests for changes) only in very small quantities not only ensures the ability of the receiver to process the information but his willingness to ac-cept and retransmit that information. Redundancy in this sense is a major solution to the problem of coordinating output in non-hierarchical organiza-tions.

In this light we can begin to explain the survival of stare decisis, partic-ularly in "common law" areas of law, as the dominant mode of legal dis-course. Its strength lies in its dual and mutually supporting contents of syntactic and semantic redundancy. Stare decisis viewed as redundancy is a fully rational, probably indispensable, method of solving the problem of syn-tactic noise in a system with very high message loads—which any system that proceeds case by case inevitably is. At the same time, the redundancy intro-duced for this syntactic purpose automatically and simultaneously becomes, at the semantic level, a heavy stream of the kind of information necessary to operate an incremental system of decision-making—information about mutual support and agreement in the form of constant repetition of previous agreement.

Of course the danger to an organization that relies very heavily on re-dundancy is that it may process so little information that it cannot learn. It is routinely argued, in the broader cybernetic context, that such organizations, if they are to survive, must have high levels of feedback to counterbalance redundancy. Such an argument illustrates the danger of failing to differ-entiate clearly between syntactic and cybernetic feedback. Cybernetic feed-back is itself information. If the system employs high levels of syntactic redundancy, it does not have the "space" to transmit much cybernetic feed-back information to its receiving parts. To say high redundancy with high feedback is to say low information with high information.

The tort organization does have a partial solution to this paradox. The content of the litigational market's communications is highly redundant al-though some level of cybernetic feedback is maintained in the form of re-quests for small changes. Here the virtue of stare decisis lies in the peculiar nexus it provides for syntactic and cybernetic phenomena. Following the rules of stare decisis, requests for legal changes, which are actually inspired by the failure of law to adjust correctly to the environment, and are thus cybernetic feedback, are put in the form of syntactic feedbacks, statements that some judge or lawyer has not correctly received the real message that was transmitted by the previous cases (their "true principles"). In this way much cybernetic feedback information can be squeezed into a communications system that demands very high levels of redundancy, and it can be squeezed in without interfering with that sense of mutual support necessary to the coordination of non-hierarchical organizations. . . .

It would seem appropriate, therefore, to examine the opinion-writing activity of courts in the context of communication, and once we do, a striking finding emerges. The style of legal discourse that we summarize in the expression stare decisis is not a unique phenomenon peculiar to the Anglo-American legal system, not a unique method or form of reasoning or logic, but an instance of redundancy, the standard solution predicted by communications theory for any acute noise problem. And there is a further finding: the characteristic style of Anglo-American legal discourse persists because its rather standard and routine solution to the noise problem of a non-hierarchical organization like the courts yields at the very same time a pattern of redundant communication that is extremely useful, perhaps essential, to the incremental mode of decision-making that organizations of this sort typically adopt. If this suggestion has any merit, it should be possible for social scientists to treat the phenomenon of stare decisis as a problem in human communications rather than as exclusively one of logic and/or obfuscation.

———

1. Professor Shapiro applies communications theory primarily to the law-making or rule-creating function of courts. You may ask yourself how these same theoretical concepts might be applied to the dispute-resolution function as well. How might the concepts of information, redundancy, and feedback be used in the dispute-resolution context to help analyze the presentation of evidence, the relationship between judge and jury, or the relation between trial and appellate courts?

2. To what extent might our extensive system of coordinate jurisdiction be understood in terms of its providing extensive "cybernetic feedback"? For a treatment of questions closely related to this one, see Professor Shapiro's article, Decentralized Decision-Making in the Law of Torts, in Political Decision Making (S. Ulmer ed. 1970), which suggests reasons for a multiplicity of decision centers, although not for a particular pattern of coordinate and quasi-hierarchical arrangements such as ours. You might keep Shapiro's formulations in mind when reading Cover and Aleinikoff, Dialectical Federalism: Habeas Corpus and the Court, excerpted in the next chapter, and the essays in section B of chapter 5 dealing with the organization of decision centers.

3. There have been several formulations of what Shapiro labels a "cybernetic" theory of decision which use terms such as redundancy and feedback in ways that Shapiro distinguishes from their use in "syntactics." See, e. g., J. Steinbruner, The Cybernetic Theory of Decisions (1974), which in substance relies heavily on R. Cyert and J. March, A Behavioral Theory of the Firm (1963), and D. Braybrooke and C. Lindblom, A Strategy of Decision (1963). Again, Professor Shapiro has been at the forefront in applying these ideas to judicial action. See Shapiro, Stability and Change in Judicial Decision-Making: Incrementalism or Stare Decisis?, 2 L.Transition Q. 134 (1965).

SECTION C. FROM INFORMATION TO DECISION

The decisionmaking process in adjudication may be conceptualized as a decision under conditions of uncertainty in which the process of taking evidence is conceived of as the progressive acquisition of information which affects the nature and degree of uncertainty as to relevant questions. The "policy sciences" have spawned a proliferation of formal devices for analysis of decisions made under conditions of uncertainty.

In the following article, Laurence Tribe attacks the use of formal mathematical treatment of uncertainty in adjudication. This article is part of a major debate on the subject precipitated by the decision of the California Supreme Court in People v. Collins, 68 Cal.2d 319, 438 P.2d 33, 66 Cal. Rptr. 497 (1968), in which that court held improper a prosecutor's attempt to introduce formal probability-theory treatment of evidence linking the defendants to a robbery. Not long after that decision, an article appeared by M. O. Finkelstein and W. B. Fairley entitled A Bayesian Approach to Identification Evidence, 83 Harv.L.Rev. 489 (1970). The excerpted article which here follows is, in part, an answer to Finkelstein and Fairley. After the publication of Professor Tribe's article, a rebuttal and surrebuttal followed: Finkelstein and Fairley, A Comment on "Trial by Mathematics," 84 Harv.L.Rev. 1801 (1971), and Tribe, A Further Critique of Mathematical Proof, 84 Harv.L.Rev. 1810 (1971). A further interesting elaboration on the principal theme of this debate is to be found in Lempert, Modeling Relevance, 75 Mich.L.Rev. 1021 (1977).

The reader may remember that Professor Tribe is among those characterized as a "ritualist" by William Simon in the Ideology of Advocacy, excerpted here in chapter 2. One of Simon's most telling points against the "ritualists" was his criticism of their celebration of dignity and fraternal values in processes which, in reality, bestow dignity and fraternity upon the professionals—i. e., lawyers—while heaping indignity, patronization, or abuse upon lay participants—i. e., witnesses and parties. Are the values extolled by Tribe here and/or his application of them to the particular problem of inference methodology amenable to this criticism?

Laurence H. Tribe, **Trial by Mathematics** *

       . . .   In deciding a disputed proposition, a rational factfinder probably begins with some initial, a priori estimate of the likelihood of the proposition's truth, then updates his prior estimate in light of discoverable evidence bearing on that proposition, and arrives finally at a modified assessment of the proposition's likely truth in light of whatever evidence he has considered. When many items of evidence are involved, each has the effect of adjusting, in greater or lesser degree, the factfinder's evaluation of the probability that the proposition before him is true. If this incremental process of cumulating evidence could be given quantitative expression, the factfinder might then be able to combine mathematical and non-mathematical evidence in a perfectly natural way, giving each neither more nor less weight than it logically deserves.

A quantitative description of the ordinary process of weighing evidence has long been available. Before deciding whether that description can be put to the suggested use of enabling the factfinder to integrate mathemati-

* Source: Tribe, Trial by Mathematics: Precision and Ritual in the Legal Process, 84 Harv.L.Rev. 1329, 1350–77 (1971). Professor of Law, Harvard University.

cal and non-mathematical evidence, it will be necessary to develop the description briefly here.

Suppose X represents a disputed factual proposition; that is, the question for the trier is whether X is true or false. And suppose E represents some other proposition, the truth of which has just been established. Prior to learning E, the trier's subjective probability assessment of X was $P(X)$. After learning E, the trier's assessment of X will typically change. That is, the trier's subjective probability for X *given the fact that E is true*, designated $P(X|E)$,[70] will ordinarily differ from the trier's prior subjective probability for X. The problem is to determine exactly how $P(X|E)$, the probability of X given E, can be calculated in terms of $P(X)$ and such other quantities as are available—to discover, that is, how the receipt of evidence E quantitatively transforms $P(X)$ into $P(X|E)$.

The solution to that problem, commonly known as Bayes' Theorem, will be summarized verbally after its mathematical formulation has been explained. The theorem follows directly from two elementary formulas of probability theory: if A and B are any two propositions, then:

(1) $P(A \,\&\, B) = P(A|B) \cdot P(B)$

(2) $P(A) = P(A \,\&\, B) + P(A \,\&\, \text{not-B}).$[72]

These formulas can be shown to imply

(3) $P(X|E) = \left[\dfrac{P(E|X)}{P(E)} \right] \cdot P(X)$

and

(4) $P(E) = P(E|X) \cdot P(X) + P(E|\text{not-X}) \cdot P(\text{not-}X).$[73]

And, using (4) to calculate $P(E)$ in (3), we obtain

(5) $P(X|E) =$

$$\left[\frac{P(E|X)}{P(E|X) \cdot P(X) + P(E|\text{not-X}) \cdot P(\text{not-X})} \right] \cdot P(X).$$

[C171]

70. $P(X|E)$ is usually read "*P* of *X* given *E*," or "the probability of *X* given the truth of *E*."

72. To make these formulas intuitively transparent, consider exactly what they assert. The first asserts that the probability that *A* and *B* are *both* true equals the product of two other probabilities: the probability that *B* is true, multiplied by the probability that *A* would also be true *if B were true* . . . .

The second formula asserts that the probability that *A* is true equals the sum of two other probabilities: the probability that *A* is true and *B* is *true*, plus the probability that *A* is true and *B* is *false*. Of course, *B* is either true or false, mutually exclusive possibilities, so the second formula reduces to the assertion that the probability that one of two mutually exclusive events will occur equals the sum of the probabilities of each event's occurrence. For example, if a well-shuffled deck contains ten white cards, ten gray cards, and eighty black cards, the probability that a card chosen randomly from the deck will be either white or gray equals .2, the sum of the probability that it will be white (.1) and the probability that it will be gray (.1).

73. Formula (1) implies that P(E & X) = P(E|X) • P(X). But E & X is identical with X & E so P(E & X) = P(X & E) = P(X|E) • P(E). Thus P(X|E) • P(E) = P(E|X) • P(X), from which we obtain formula (3) by dividing P(E) into

Formula (5), known as Bayes' Theorem, determines $P(X|E)$ in terms of $P(X)$, $P(E|X)$, and $P(E|\text{not-}X)$.[74] In the abbreviated form of formula (3), Bayes' Theorem expresses the common sense notion that, to obtain $P(X|E)$ from $P(X)$, one multiplies the latter by a factor representing the probative force of *E*—that is, a factor equal to the ratio of $P(E|X)$ (designating the probability of *E* *if* *X* is true) to $P(E)$ (designating the probability of *E* whether or *not* *X* is true).

Perhaps the easiest way to express Bayes' Theorem for the non-mathematician, though it is not the most convenient expression for actual use of the theorem, is to say that

$$(6)\ \ P(X|E) = \frac{P(E\ \&\ X)}{P(E)} = \frac{P(E|X)\cdot P(X)}{P(E)}.$$

This simply asserts that the probability of *X* being true if *E* is known to be true, designated $P(X|E)$, may be determined by measuring how often, out of all cases in which *E* is true, will *X* *also* be true—that is, by calculating the ratio of $P(E\ \&\ X)$ to $P(E)$. That ratio, in turn, equals $P(E|X)\cdot P(X)$ divided by $P(E)$, which completes the equation in Bayes' Theorem.

To give a concrete example, let *X* represent the proposition that the defendant in a particular murder case is guilty, and let *E* represent the evidentiary fact that the defendant left town on the first available plane after the murder was committed. Suppose that, prior to learning *E*, an individual juror would have guessed, on the basis of all the information then available to him, that the defendant was approximately twice as likely to be guilty as he was to be innocent, so that the juror's prior subjective probability for the defendant's guilt was $P(X) = \frac{2}{3}$, and his prior subjective probability for the defendant's innocence was $P(\text{not-}X) = \frac{1}{3}$. What effect should learning *E* have upon his probability assessment—i. e., $P(X|E)$? The answer to that question will depend, of course, on how much more likely he thinks a guilty man would be to fly out of town immediately after the murder than an innocent man would be.

Suppose his best guess is that the probability of such flight if the defendant is guilty, designated $P(E|X)$, is twenty percent, and that the probability of such flight if the defendant is innocent, designated $P(E|\text{not-}X)$, is ten percent. Then $P(E|X) = \frac{1}{5}$ and $P(E|\text{not-}X) = \frac{1}{10}$. Recall formula (4):

$$P(E) = P(E|X)\cdot P(X) + P(E|\text{not-}X)\cdot P(\text{not-}X).$$

As applied to this case, we have

$$P(E) = (\tfrac{1}{5})(\tfrac{2}{3}) + (\tfrac{1}{10})(\tfrac{1}{3}) = \tfrac{1}{6}.$$

In other words, given his prior assessment of $P(X) = \frac{2}{3}$, the juror's best estimate of the probability of the defendant's flight, $P(E)$, would have

both sides of this equation. Formula (2) implies that $P(E) = P(E\ \&\ X) + P(E\ \&\ \text{not-}X)$. Applying formula (1), we know that $P(E\ \&\ X) = P(E|X)\cdot P(X)$ and that $P(E\ \&\ \text{not-}X) = P(E|\text{not-}X)\cdot P(\text{not-}X)$, from which we obtain formula (4) by adding these two terms.

74. The only other variable in (5), P (not-X), is equal to $1 - P(X)$.

been ⅙. But if he knew that the defendant were in fact guilty, his best estimate of the probability that the defendant would flee, $P(E|X)$, would be ⅕. Learning that he actually did flee should thus multiply the juror's prior assessment by the ratio

$$\frac{P(E|X)}{P(E)} = \frac{⅕}{⅙} = \frac{6}{5}.$$

Applying formula (3),

$$P(X|E) = \left[\frac{P(E|X)}{P(E)}\right] \cdot P(X),$$

or

$$P(X|E) = \left[\frac{6}{5}\right] \cdot \frac{2}{3} = \frac{4}{5}.$$

Therefore, his subsequent probability assessment of the defendant's guilt, after learning of his flight, should be ⅘. The evidence of flight should thus increase the juror's subjective probability estimate of the defendant's guilt from ⅔ to ⅘—assuming that he thinks there would be a ⅕ probability of flight if the defendant were guilty and a 1⁄10 probability of flight if he were not.

Given this precise a tool for cumulating evidence in a quantitative way, there might seem to be no obstacle to assimilating mathematical evidence into the trial process. Indeed, two commentators—one a lawyer, the other a statistician—have proposed doing exactly that. . . . Michael Finkelstein and William Fairley recently suggested [in A Bayesian Approach to Identification Evidence, 83 Harv.L.Rev. 489 (1970),] that mathematically expert witnesses might be employed to explain to jurors the precise probative force of mathematical evidence in terms of its quantitative impact on the jurors' prior probability assessments. As . . . this article tries to show, although their analysis is both intriguing and illuminating, neither the technique proposed by Finkelstein and Fairley, nor any other like it, can serve the intended purpose at an acceptable cost. It will be necessary first, however, to review the method they have suggested. To that end, it is useful to begin with the hypothetical case Finkelstein and Fairley posit.

A woman's body is found in a ditch in an urban area. There is evidence that the deceased quarreled violently with her boyfriend the night before and that he struck her on other occasions. A palm print similar to the defendant's is found on the knife that was used to kill the woman. Because the information in the print is limited, an expert can say only that such prints appear in no more than one case in a thousand. The question Finkelstein and Fairley ask themselves is how the jury might best be informed of the precise incriminating significance of that finding.

By itself, of course, the "one-in-a-thousand" statistic is not a very meaningful one. It does not . . . measure the probability of the defendant's innocence—although many jurors would be hard-pressed to understand why not. As Finkelstein and Fairley recognize, even if there were as few as one hundred thousand potential suspects, one would expect approximately one hundred persons to have such prints; if there were a million potential suspects, one would expect to find a thousand or so similar prints. Thus the palm print would hardly pinpoint the defendant in any unique way.

To be sure, the finding of so relatively rare a print which matches the defendant's is an event of significant probative value, an event of which the jury should almost certainly be informed. Yet the *numerical index* of the print's rarity, as measured by the frequency of its random occurrence, may be more misleading than enlightening, and the jury should be informed of that frequency—if at all—only if it is also given a careful explanation that there might well be many other individuals with similar prints. The jury should thus be made to understand that the frequency figure does not in any sense measure the probability of the defendant's innocence.

Finkelstein and Fairley are distressed that this might leave the jury with too little information about the print's full probative value. The solution they propose to meet this difficulty is the use at trial of Bayes' Theorem; it is this solution to which I particularly object. Let X represent the proposition that the defendant used the knife to kill his girlfriend, and let E represent the proposition that a palm print resembling the defendant's was found on the knife that killed her. $P(E|X)$ is the probability of finding a palm print resembling the defendant's on the murder weapon if he was in fact the one who used the knife to kill, and $P(E|\text{not-}X)$ is the probability of finding a palm print resembling the defendant's on the murder weapon if he was *not* the knife-user. $P(X)$ represents the trier's probability assessment of the truth of X *before* learning E, and $P(X|E)$ represents the trier's probability assessment of the truth of X *after* learning E. Finally, $P(\text{not-}X)$ represents the trier's probability assessment of the falsity of X before learning E, so that $P(\text{not-}X) = 1-P(X)$. Recall now Bayes' Theorem:

$$P(X|E) = \left[\frac{P(E|X)}{P(E|X) \cdot P(X) + P(E|\text{not-}X) \cdot P(\text{not-}X)} \right] \cdot P(X).$$

In applying this formula, Finkelstein and Fairley "assume for simplicity that defendant would inevitably leave such a print," so that $P(E|X) = 1$. They also state that the probability $P(E|\text{not-}X)$ equals "the frequency of the print in the suspect population." In other words, they assume that the probability of finding a print like the defendant's on the knife, if the defendant did not in fact use the knife to kill his girlfriend, is equal to the probability that a randomly chosen person would have a print like the defendant's. In a later section of this article, I will try to show that both of those assumptions are entirely unrealistic, that this error substantially distorts the results derived by Finkelstein and Fairley, and—most importantly—that the error reflects not so much carelessness in their application of mathematical methods as an inherent bias generated by the use of the methods themselves in the trial process.

For now, however, my only purpose is to see where the method, as Finkelstein and Fairley apply it, leads us. They undertake, using Bayes' Theorem, to construct a table showing the resulting value of $P(X|E)$ for a range of prior probabilities $P(X)$ varying from .01 to .75, and for a range of different values for the frequency of the print in the suspect population varying from .001 to .50. Nine typical values for P(X|E) taken from the table Finkelstein and Fairley obtain (using the two simplifying assumptions noted above) are as follows:

Posterior Probability of *X* Given *E* as a Function
of Frequency of Print and Prior Probability

	Prior Probability, P(X)		
Frequency of Print	.01	.25	.75
.50	.019	.400	.857
.10	.091	.769	.967
.001	.909	.997	.9996

The table shows, for example, that if a print like defendant's occurs with a frequency of one in a thousand, and if the trier's prior assessment of the probability that defendant used the knife to kill his girlfriend is one in four before he learns of the palm-print evidence *E*, then the palm-print evidence should increase to .997 the trier's posterior assessment of the probability that defendant used the knife to kill: $P(X|E) = .997$.

Finkelstein and Fairley would first have each juror listen to the evidence and arrive at a value for P(X) based upon his own view of the non-mathematical evidence (in this case, the prior quarrels and violent incidents). Then an expert witness would in effect show the jury the appropriate row from a table like the above, choosing the row to correspond with the testimony as to the print's frequency, so that each juror could locate the appropriate value of P(X|E) as his final estimate of the probability that the defendant was in fact the knife-user. If the print's frequency were established to be .001, for example, the jurors need only be shown the last row; if it were .10, the jurors need only be shown the second row. In this way, Finkelstein and Fairley argue, the frequency statistic would be translated for the jury into a probability statement which accurately describes its probative force. And, the authors add, most of the respondents in an informal survey conducted by them would have derived higher final probabilities by this method than they did without the assistance of Bayes' Theorem. "Probably the greatest danger to a defendant from Bayesian methods," the authors conclude, "is that jurors may be surprised at the strength of the inference of guilt flowing from the combination of their prior suspicions and the statistical evidence. But this, if the suspicions are correctly estimated, is no more than the evidence deserves."

Is it? . . .

1. The Distortion of Outcomes.—*a. The Elusive Starting Point*—
It is of course necessary, if the trier is to make any use at all of techniques like that proposed by Finkelstein and Fairley, for him first to settle on a numerical value for P(X), his assessment of the probability of X prior to the mathematical bombshell typically represented by the evidence *E*. But the lay trier will surely find it difficult at best, and sometimes impossible, to at-

tach to P(X) a number that correctly represents his real prior assessment. Few laymen have had experience with the assignment of probabilities, and it might end up being a matter of pure chance whether a particular juror converts his mental state of partial certainty to a figure like .33, .43, or somewhere in between. An estimate of .5 might signify for one juror a guess in the absence of any information and, for another, the conclusion of a search that has narrowed the inquiry to two equally probable suspects. And a juror's statement that he is "four-fifths sure"   .   .   .   is likely, in all but the simplest cases, to be spuriously exact   .   .   .   .

   b.   The Case of the Mathematical Prior.—Finkelstein and Fairley consider the application of their technique primarily to cases in which the prior probability assessment of a disputed proposition is based on non-mathematical evidence and is then modified by the application of Bayes' Theorem to some further item of evidence that links the defendant to the case in a quantifiable way or sheds some quantifiable light upon his conduct. When statistical evidence is so used to modify a prior probability assessment, it is true, as the authors claim, that

> Bayesian analysis would demonstrate that the evidentiary weight
> of an impressive figure like one in a thousand—which might other-
> wise exercise an undue influence—would depend on the other evi-
> dence in the case, and might well be relatively insignificant if the
> prior suspicion were sufficiently weak.

   What they ignore, however, is that in most cases, whether civil or criminal, it will be none other than this "impressive figure like one in a thousand" that their general approach to proof would highlight. For, in most cases, the mathematical evidence will not be such as to modify a prior probability assessment by furnishing added data about the specific case at hand. Instead, the mathematical evidence will typically bear only upon the broad category of cases of which the one being litigated will be merely an instance.   .   .   .   In such cases, *E* can *only* shed light on what initial value to assign to P(X).[100] Thus, the statistical information in these cases will, if given to the jury, create a high probability assessment of civil or criminal liability—and there is no assurance that the jury, either with or without the aid of Bayes' Theorem, will be able to make all of the adjustments in that high prior assessment that will be called for by the other evidence (or lack of it) that the rest of the trial reveals. The problem of the overpowering number, that one hard piece of information, is that it may dwarf all efforts to put it into perspective with more impressionistic sorts of evidence. This problem of acceptably combining the mathematical with the non-mathematical evidence is not touched in these cases by the Bayesian approach.

   In situations of the sort being examined here, however, when the thrust of the mathematical evidence is to shed light on the probability assessment

100. When the mathematical evidence *E* simply describes the *class* of cases of which the litigated case is one, the truth or falsity of the litigated proposition *X* in no way affects the probability of the truth of *E*; i. e., P(E|X) equals P(E). Bayes' Theorem then simply asserts that P(X|E) = P(X). *See* equation (3)   .   .   .   . Hence, in all such cases, *E* can suggest what *initial* value to assign to P(X) but cannot serve to *refine* that initial value—as can, for example, evidence of the palm-print variety   .   .   .   .

with which the trier ought rationally to begin, there is at least one way to take the evidence into account at trial without incurring the risk that the jury will give it too much weight when undertaking to combine the mathematical datum with fuzzier information.   Let the judge rather than the jury weigh the probabilistic proof in order to determine whether it might not be both equitable and conducive to an accurate outcome to shift to the other side the burden of producing some believable evidence to take the case outside the general rule seemingly established by the probabilities.[101]   If one is to avoid a distortion in results, however, any such proposal must be qualified, at least when the question is one of the defendant's identity, by the principle that a party is not entitled to a jury verdict on statistical evidence alone absent some plausible expanation for his failure to adduce proof of a more individualized character.

But the difficulty that calls forth this solution is not limited to cases in which the mathematics points to a readily quantifiable prior assessment. The problem—that of the overbearing impressiveness of numbers—pervades all cases in which the trial use of mathematics is proposed.   And, whenever such use is in fact accomplished by methods resembling those of Finkelstein and Fairley, the problem becomes acute.

   c. The Dwarfing of Soft Variables.—The syndrome is a familiar one: If you can't count it, it doesn't exist.   Equipped with a mathematically powerful intellectual machine, even the most sophisticated user is subject to an overwhelming temptation to feed his pet the food it can most comfortably digest.   Readily quantifiable factors are easier to process—and hence more likely to be recognized and then reflected in the outcome—than are factors that resist ready quantification.   The result, despite what turns out to be a spurious appearance of accuracy and completeness, is likely to be significantly warped and hence highly suspect.

The best illustration is none other than the computations performed by Finkelstein and Fairley themselves in their palm-print hypothetical. To begin with, they assume that, if the defendant had in fact used the knife to kill his girlfriend, then a palm print resembling his would certainly have been found on it, i. e., $P(E|X) = 1$.   Had they not been moved by the greater ease of applying Bayes' Theorem under that assumption, the authors would surely have noted that a man about to commit murder with a knife might well choose to wear gloves, or that one who has committed murder might wipe off such prints as he happened to leave behind.   Thus $P(E|X)$ equals not 1, but 1–g, where g represents the combined probability of these contingencies and of the further contingency, later considered by Finkelstein and Fairley, that such factors as variations within the suspected source [105] might prevent a print left by the defendant from seeming to match his palm.

101. For example, in line with the suggested approach, the judge might decide to employ the doctrine of res ipsa loquitur . . . or any of a variety of rebuttable presumptions . . . . One of the traditional functions of the use of presumptions, at least those rebuttable by any substantial contrary evidence, is "to make more likely a finding in accord with the balance of probability . . . . "

105. The same palm might leave a variety of seemingly different partial prints.

Far more significantly, Finkelstein and Fairley equate the frequency of the palm print in the suspect population with $P(E|not\text{-}X)$, the probability of finding a print like the defendant's on the knife if he did not use it to kill. That equation, however, strangely assumes that finding an innocent man's palm print on the murder weapon must represent a simple coincidence. If that were so, then the likelihood of such a coincidence, as measured by the print's frequency in the population, would of course yield the probability that a print like the defendant's would appear on the knife despite his innocence.[108] But this ignores the obvious fact that the print might have belonged to the defendant after all—without his having used the knife to kill the girl. He could simply have been framed, the real murderer having worn gloves when planting the defendant's knife at the scene of the crime. . . . Finkelstein and Fairley . . . overlook the risk of frame-up altogether—despite the nasty fact that the most inculpatory item of evidence may be the item most likely to be used to frame an innocent man.[111]

One can only surmise that it was the awkwardness of fitting the frame-up possibility into their formula that blinded even these sophisticated authors, one a legal scholar and the other a teacher of statistical theory, to a risk which they could not otherwise have failed to perceive. And if *they* were seduced by the mathematical machinery, one is entitled to doubt the efficacy of even the adversary process as a corrective to the jury's natural tendency to be similarly distracted.

As it turns out, the frame-up risk would have been awkward indeed to work into the calculation, increasing $P(E|not\text{-}X)$ from a value equal to the frequency of the palm print, hereinafter designated f, to a value equal to $f + F$, where F represents the probability of frame-up.[113] Bayes' Theorem would then have assumed the messy form

$$P(X|E) = \left[\frac{(1-g)}{(1-g)\,P(X) + (f + F)\,P(not\text{-}X)} \right] \cdot P(X).$$

This formula may be easy enough to use when one assumes, with Finkelstein and Fairley, that $g = 0$ and $F = 0$, but is rather more troublesome to handle when one has no real idea *how* large those two probabilities are.

Moreover, it makes quite a difference to the outcome just how large the probabilities, g and f, turn out to be. Consider again the case in which

108. Even this is somewhat over-simplified since it neglects to multiply the frequency by the factor $(1-g)$. . . . .

111. A quite distinct problem, more serious in cases relying on human identification than in cases where identification is based on physical evidence, is that the characteristics of the defendant relied upon in the probabilistic formula may not in fact have been shared by the actually guilty individual or individuals because of some mistake in observation or memory. Such risks of error, like the risk of frame-up, are hard to quantify and hence likely to be underemphasized in a quantitative analysis, but differ from the risk of frame-up in that they need not perversely increase as the apparent probative value of the evidence increases.

113. More precisely, $P(E|not\text{-}X)$ equals not simply $f + F$, but $(1-g)f + F$. . . . This fact makes the final computation even more complex, although it changes the outcome only slightly if g is small in relation to f or F.

the print is assumed to occur in one case in a thousand, so that $f = .001$, and in which the prior assessment is $P(X) = .25$. On those facts, Finkelstein and Fairley conclude—by treating g and F as though they were both zero—that $P(X|E) = .997$, an overwhelming probability that the defendant did the killing. If, however, we assume that $g = .1$ and $F = .1$, then the same initial values $f = .001$ and $P(X) = .25$ yield the strikingly different conclusion $P(X|E) = .75$, a very much lower probability than Finkelstein and Fairley calculated.

What, then, is one to tell the jurors? That each of them should arrive somehow at his own values for g and F, as to neither of which any evidence will be available, and should then wait while a mathematician explains what $P(X|E)$ turns out to be given those values? Surely we have by now strained the system beyond its breaking point. If the jurors are to work with mathematical proof in any capacity beyond that of passive observers, they will in the end have to be given the numbers computed by Finkelstein and Fairley and asked to draw their own conclusions, keeping in mind—unless the judge who instructs them is as blinded by the formulas as the authors were—that possibilities such as frame-up distort the figures in the table so that they overstate the truth by some indeterminate amount.

But then we have come full circle. At the outset some way of integrating the mathematical evidence with the non-mathematical was sought, so that the jury would not be confronted with an impressive number that it could not intelligently combine with the rest of the evidence, and to which it would therefore be tempted to assign disproportionate weight. At first glance, the use Finkelstein and Fairley made of Bayes' Theorem appeared to provide the needed amalgam. Yet, on closer inspection, their method too left a number—the exaggerated and much *more* impressive $P(X|E) = .997$ —which the jury must again be asked to balance against such fuzzy imponderables as the risk of frameup or of misobservation, if indeed it is not induced to ignore those imponderables altogether.

What is least clear in all of this is whether the proponents of mathematical proof have made any headway at all. Even assuming with Finkelstein and Fairley that the accuracy of trial outcomes could be somewhat enhanced if *all* crucial variables could be quantified precisely and analyzed with the aid of Bayes' Theorem, it simply does not follow that trial accuracy will be enhanced if *some* of the important variables are quantified and subjected to Bayesian analysis, leaving the softer ones—those to which meaningful numbers are hardest to attach—in an impressionistic limbo. On the contrary, the excessive weight that will thereby be given to those factors that can most easily be treated mathematically indicates that, on balance, more mistakes may well be made with partial quantification than with no quantification at all.

d. Asking the Wrong Questions.—Throughout the preceding discussion, I have referred to $P(X)$ and to $P(X|E)$, deliberately eschewing the terminology employed by Finkelstein and Fairley. Instead of X, they write G—implying the $P(X|E)$ represents the probability that the defendant is *guilty of murder* if a palm-print matching his is found on the murder weapon. But of course it represents no such thing, for murder means much more than causing death. To say that $P(X|E) = .997$ is to say that, given the palm-print evidence, there is a probability of .997 that the defendant used the knife to kill the deceased. It is to say nothing at all about his state of mind at the time, nothing about whether he intended to cause death, nothing about whether the act was premeditated.[119] To be sure, these elements can be called to each juror's attention, but his eyes are likely to return quickly to that imposing number on the board.

It is no accident that such matters as identity—matters that are objectively verifiable in the world outside the courtroom—lend themselves more readily to mathematical treatment than do such issues as intent—issues that correspond to no verifiable "fact" outside the verdict of the jury . . . .

One consequence of mathematical proof, then, may be to shift the focus away from such elements as volition, knowledge, and intent, and toward such elements as identity and occurrence—for the same reason that the hard variables tend to swamp the soft. It is by no means clear that such marginal gains, if any, as we may make by finding somewhat more precise answers would not be offset by a tendency to emphasize the wrong questions.[121]

  e. The Problem of Interdependence.—Essential to the application of Bayes' Theorem to derive $P(X|E)$ from $P(X)$ is that the trier be able somehow to make a prior estimate of $P(X)$, the probability of the disputed proposition X. If that estimate is arrived at after knowing or even suspecting E, then to use the information provided by E to refine the estimate through Bayes' Theorem to obtain $P(X|E)$ would obviously involve counting the same thing twice. Particularly when the proposition X goes to the identity of the person responsible for an alleged wrong, and when the tendency of E is to pinpoint the defendant as the responsible person, the knowledge or suspicion of E is likely to have entered into the plaintiff's choice of this particular defendant. . . . [H]aving found a latent palm print on the murder weapon, the State was less likely to file an indictment against a person whose palm print *failed* to match. And the trier would be hard put to disregard those obvious realities in attempting to derive a value for $P(X)$. The accurate application of Bayes' Theorem along the lines proposed by Finkelstein and Fairley necessarily assumes that the evidence E of quantifiable probative value can be made independent of the prior suspicion, but in most trials the two will be hopelessly enmeshed.

Indeed, even if $P(X)$ is arrived at without any reliance whatever upon E, the straightforward application of Bayes' Theorem will still entail a distorted outcome if some or all of the evidence that *did* underlie $P(X)$ was related to E, in the sense that knowing something about the truth of X and of that underlying evidence would yield information one way or the other about the likely truth of E. To take a simple example, suppose that an armed robbery taking fifteen minutes to complete was committed between

---

119. Although such matters will rarely be at issue in cases where the defense rests in part on a claim of mistaken identity, it is of course possible for both identity and intent to be disputed in the same case.

121. This difficulty would be somewhat easier to correct than any of the others identified thus far—through the use of special instructions to the jury, or perhaps through special verdicts.

3:00 a. m. and 3:30 a. m. The trier first learns E_1: that the accused was seen in a car a half-mile from the scene of the crime at 3:10 a. m. Based on this information, the trier will assess a subjective probability $P(X)$ of the accused's likely involvement in the robbery. Then the trier learns E_2: that the accused was also seen in a car a half-mile from the scene of the crime at 3:20 a. m. By itself, E_2 appears to make X, the proposition that the accused was involved, more likely than it would have seemed without any evidence as to the accused's whereabouts, so that $P(X|E_2)$ will exceed $P(X)$ if computed by applying Bayes' Theorem directly, i. e., by multiplying $P(X)$ by the ratio $P(E_2|X)/P(E_2)$. Yet this is surely wrong, for if E_1 and E_2 are *both* true, then X must be false, and $P(X|E_2)$ should equal zero. One can with some effort make the appropriate adjustment—by using Bayes' Theorem to compute [125]

$$P(X|E_1 \& E_2) = \left[\frac{P(E_2|X \& E_1)}{P(E_2|E_1)} \right] \cdot P(X|E_1).$$

This means, however, that the theorem cannot be applied sequentially, with one simple multiplication by $P(E|X)/P(E)$ as each new item of evidence, E, comes in, but must instead be applied in the terribly cumbrous form shown above, unless one knows somehow that the item of evidence to which the theorem is being applied at any given point is not linked conditionally to any evidence already reflected in one's estimate of $P(X)$. Finkelstein and Fairley ignore that requirement; taking it into account in order to avoid grossly inaccurate outcomes would make the machinery they propose so complex and so unwieldy that its operation, already hard enough for the juror to comprehend, would become completely opaque to all but the trained mathematician.

2. The End of Innocence: A Presumption of Guilt?—At least in criminal cases, and perhaps also in civil cases resting on allegations of moral fault, further difficulties lurk in the very fact that the trier is forced by the Finkelstein-Fairley technique to arrive at an explicit quantitative estimate of the likely truth at or near the trial's start, or at least before some of the most significant evidence has been put before him.[129]

To return for a moment to the palm-print case posited by Finkelstein and Fairley, a juror compelled to derive a quantitative measure $P(X)$ of the defendant's likely guilt after having heard no evidence at all, or at most only the evidence about the defendant's altercations with the victim, cannot escape the task of deciding just how much weight to give the undeniable fact that the defendant is, after all, not a person chosen at random but one strongly suspected and hence accused by officials of the state after extended investigation. If the juror undertakes to assess the probative value of that

---

125. By successive applications of equations (1) and (3).

$$P(X|E_1 \& E_2) = \frac{P(X) \cdot P(E_1 \& E_2|X)}{P(E_1 \& E_2)} = \frac{P(X \& E_1 \& E_2)}{P(E_1 \& E_2)} =$$

$$\frac{P(X \& E_1) \cdot P(E_2|X \& E_1)}{P(E_1 \& E_2)} = \frac{P(E_1) \cdot P(X|E_1) \cdot P(E_2|X \& E_1)}{P(E_1) \cdot P(E_2|E_1)} =$$

$$\frac{P(E_2|X \& E_1) \cdot P(X|E_1)}{P(E_2|E_1)}.$$

129. The crucial factor is not so much that of time sequence as that of priority in thought. Even if all of the evidence has in fact been introduced before the trier is asked to quantify the probative force of a limited part of it without taking account of the rest, the problems discussed here still obtain.

fact as realistically as he can, he will have to give weight to whatever information he supposes was known to the grand jury or to the prosecutor who filed the accusation. To the extent that this supposed information contains facts that will be duplicated by later evidence, such evidence will end up being counted twice, and will thus be given more weight than it deserves. And, to the extent that the information attributed to the prosecutor or the grand jury is *not* duplicative in this sense, it will include some facts that will not be, and some facts that cannot properly be, introduced at trial as evidence against the accused. Inviting jurors to take account of such facts is at war with the fundamental notion that the jury should make an independent judgment based only on the evidence properly before it, and would undercut the many weighty policies that render some categories of evidence legally inadmissible.

Moreover, even if no such problem were present, directing the jury to focus on the probative weight of an indictment or other charge, or even directing it simply to assess the probability of the accused's guilt at some point before he has presented his case, would entail a significant cost. It may be supposed that no juror would be permitted to announce publicly in mid-trial that the defendant was already burdened with, say, a sixty percent probability of guilt—but even without such a public statement it would be exceedingly difficult for the accused, for the prosecution, and ultimately for the community, to avoid the explicit recognition that, having been forced to focus on the question, the rational juror could hardly avoid reaching some such answer. And, once that recognition had become a general one, our society's traditional affirmation of the "presumption of innocence" could lose much of its value.

That presumption . . . "represents far more than a rule of evidence. It represents a commitment to the proposition that a man who stands accused of crime is no less entitled than his accuser to freedom and respect as an innocent member of the community." [133] In terms of tangible consequences for the accused, this commitment is significant because it can protect him from a variety of onerous restraints not needed to effectuate the interest in completing his trial; because the suspension of adverse judgment that it mandates can encourage the trier to make an independent and more accurate assessment of his guilt; and because it may help to preserve an atmosphere in which his acquittal, should that be the outcome, will be taken seriously by the community. But no less important are what seem to me the intangible aspects of that commitment: its expressive and educative nature as a refusal to acknowledge prosecutorial omniscience in the face of the defendant's protest of innocence, and as an affirmation of respect for the accused—a respect expressed by the trier's willingness to listen to all the accused has to say before reaching any judgment, even a tentative one, as to his probable guilt.

It may be that most jurors would suspect, if forced to think about it, that a substantial percentage of those tried for crime are guilty as charged. And that suspicion might find its way unconsciously into the behavior of at

133. Tribe, An Ounce of Detention: Preventive Justice in the World of John Mitchell, 56 Va.L.Rev. 371, 404 (1970).

least some jurors sitting in judgment in criminal cases.   But I very much doubt that this fact alone reduces the "presumption of innocence" to a useless fiction.   The presumption retains force not as a *factual* judgment, but as a *normative* one—as a judgment that society *ought* to *speak* of accused men as innocent, and *treat* them as innocent, until they have been properly convicted after all they have to offer in their defense has been carefully weighed.   The suspicion that many are *in fact* guilty need not undermine either this normative conclusion or its symbolic expression through trial procedure, so long as jurors are not compelled to articulate their prior suspicions of guilt in an explicit and precise way.

But if they *are* compelled to measure and acknowledge a factual presumption of guilt at or near each trial's start, then their underlying suspicion that such a presumption would often accord with reality may indeed frustrate the expressive and instructional values of affirming in the criminal process a normative presumption of innocence.   Jurors cannot at the same time estimate probable guilt and suspend judgment until they have heard all the defendant has to say.   It is here that the great virtue of mathematical rigor—its demand for precision, completeness, and candor—may become its greatest vice, for it may force jurors to articulate propositions whose truth virtually all might already suspect, but whose explicit and repeated expression may interfere with what seem to me the complex symbolic functions of trial procedure and its associated rhetoric.   .   .   .

3.   The Quantification of Sacrifice.—This concern for the expressive role of trial procedure is no less relevant to the trial's end than to its start. Limiting myself here to the ordinary criminal proceeding, I suggest that the acceptance of anything like the method Finkelstein and Fairley propose, given the precision and explicitness its use demands, could dangerously undermine yet another complex of values—the values surrounding the notion that juries should convict only when guilt is beyond real doubt.[137]

An inescapable corollary of the proposed method, and indeed of any method that aims to assimilate mathematical proof by quantifying the probative force of evidence generally, is that it leaves the trier of fact, when all is said and done, with a number that purports to represent his assessment of the probability that the defendant is guilty as charged.   Needless to say, that number will never quite equal 1.0, so the result will be to produce a quantity—take .95 for the sake of illustration—which openly signifies a measurable (and potentially reducible) margin of doubt, here a margin of .05, or $\frac{1}{20}$.

Now it may well be   .   .   .   that there is something intrinsically immoral about condemning a man as a criminal while telling oneself, "I be-

137. Although this notion is readily confused with the presumption of innocence,   .   .   .   it is in fact quite different and rests on a partially overlapping but partially distinct set of objectives. To some extent, in fact, the concept that conviction is proper only after all real doubt has been dispelled may tend to undercut the purposes served by the presumption of innocence, for that concept suggests that a defendant's acquittal signifies only the existence of some doubt as to his guilt, whereas one function of the presumption of innocence is to encourage the community to treat a defendant's acquittal as banishing all lingering suspicion that he might have been guilty .   .   .   .

lieve that there is a chance of one in twenty that this defendant is innocent, but a ½₀ risk of sacrificing him erroneously is one I am willing to run in the interest of the public's—and my own—safety." It may be that—quite apart from the particular number—there is something basically immoral in this posture, but I do not insist here on that position. All I suggest is that a useful purpose may be served by structuring a system of criminal justice so that it can avoid having to proclaim, as the Finkelstein-Fairley procedure would force us to proclaim, that it will impose its sanctions in the face of a recognized and quantitatively measured doubt in the particular case.

If the system in fact did exactly that, such compelled candor about its operation might have great value. It could generate pressure for useful procedural reform, and it should probably be considered worthwhile in itself. But to let the matter rest there would be wrong, for the system does *not* in fact authorize the imposition of criminal punishment when the trier recognizes a quantifiable doubt as to the defendant's guilt. Instead, the system dramatically—if imprecisely—insists upon as close an approximation to certainty as seems humanly attainable in the circumstances. The jury is charged that any "reasonable doubt," of whatever magnitude, must be resolved in favor of the accused. Such insistence on the greatest certainty that seems reasonably attainable can serve at the trial's end, like the presumption of innocence at the trial's start, to affirm the dignity of the accused and to display respect for his rights as a person—in this instance, by declining to put those rights in deliberate jeopardy and by refusing to sacrifice him to the interests of others.

In contrast, for the jury to announce that it is prepared to convict the defendant in the face of an acknowledged and numerically measurable doubt as to his guilt is to tell the accused that those who judge him find it preferable to accept the resulting risk of his unjust conviction than to reduce that risk by demanding any further or more convincing proof of his guilt. I am far from persuaded that this represents the sort of thought process through which jurors do, or should, arrive at verdicts of guilt. Many jurors would no doubt describe themselves as being "completely sure," or at least as being "as sure as possible," before they vote to convict. That some mistaken verdicts are inevitably returned even by jurors who regard themselves as "certain" is of course true but is irrelevant; such unavoidable errors are in no sense *intended*,[143] and the fact that they must occur if trials are to be conducted at all need not undermine the effort, through the symbols of trial procedure, to express society's fundamental commitment to the protection of the defendant's rights as a person, as an end in himself. On the other hand, formulating an "acceptable" risk of error to which the trier is willing deliberately to subject the defendant would interfere seriously with this expressive role of the demand for certitude—however unattainable real certitude may be, and however clearly all may ultimately recognize its unattainability.

143. Tolerating a system in which perhaps one innocent man in a hundred is erroneously convicted despite each jury's attempt to make *as few mistakes as possible* is in this respect vastly different from instructing a jury to *aim* at a 1% rate (or even a .1% rate) of mistaken convictions . . . .

In short, to say that society recognizes the necessity of tolerating the erroneous "conviction of some innocent suspects in order to assure the confinement of a vastly larger number of guilty criminals" is not at all to say that society does, or should, embrace a policy that juries, *conscious of the magnitude of their doubts in a particular case,* ought to convict in the face of this acknowledged and quantified uncertainty. It is to the complex difference between these two propositions that the concept of "guilt beyond a reasonable doubt" inevitably speaks. The concept signifies not any mathematical measure of the precise degree of certitude we require of juries in criminal cases, but a subtle compromise between the knowledge, on the one hand, that we cannot realistically insist on acquittal whenever guilt is less than absolutely certain, and the realization, on the other hand, that the cost of spelling that out explicitly and with calculated precision in the trial itself would be too high.

4. *The Dehumanization of Justice.*—Finally, we have been told by Finkelstein and Fairley that jurors using their method may find themselves "surprised" at the strength of the inference of guilt flowing from the combination of mathematical and non-mathematical evidence. Indeed they may, and in a far deeper sense than with other equally obscure forms of expert testimony, for such testimony typically represents no more than an input into the trial process, whereas the proposed use of Bayesian methods changes the character of the trial process itself. When that change yields a "surprisingly" strong inference of guilt in a particular case, it is by no means clear that, so long as one keeps one's numbers straight, "this . . . is no more than the evidence deserves." Methods of proof that impose moral blame or authorize official sanctions [150] on the basis of evidence that fails to penetrate or convince the untutored contemporary intuition threaten to make the legal system seem even more alien and inhuman than it already does to distressingly many. There is at stake not only the further weakening of the confidence of the parties and of their willingness to abide by the result, but also the further erosion of the public's sense that the law's fact-finding apparatus is functioning in a somewhat comprehensible way, on the basis of evidence that speaks, at least in general terms, to the larger community that the processes of adjudication must ultimately serve. The need now is to enhance community comprehension of the trial process, not to exacerbate an already serious problem by shrouding the process in mathematical obscurity.

It would be a terrible mistake to forget that a typical lawsuit, whether civil or criminal, is only in part an objective search for historical truth. It is also, and no less importantly, a ritual—a complex pattern of gestures comprising what Henry Hart and John McNaughton once called "society's last line of defense in the indispensable effort to secure the peaceful settlement of social conflicts." [151]

---

150. The argument I am here advancing applies with greatest force in the criminal context, but it also has some significance in much ordinary civil litigation.

151. Hart & McNaughton, Evidence and Inference in the Law, in Evidence and Inference 48, 52 (D. Lerner ed., 1958) . . . .

One element, at least, of that ritual of conflict-settlement is the presence and functioning of the jury—a cumbersome and imperfect institution, to be sure, but an institution well calculated, at least potentially, to mediate between "the law" in the abstract and the human needs of those affected by it. Guided and perhaps intimidated by the seeming inexorability of numbers, induced by the persuasive force of formulas and the precision of decimal points to perceive themselves as performing a largely mechanical and automatic role, few jurors—whether in criminal cases or in civil—could be relied upon to recall, let alone to perform, this humanizing function, to employ their intuition and their sense of community values to shape their ultimate conclusions.

When one remembers these things, one must acknowledge that there was a wisdom of sorts even in trial by battle—for at least that mode of ascertaining truth and resolving conflict reflected well the deeply-felt beliefs of the times and places in which it was practiced. This is something that can hardly be said of trial by mathematics today . . . .

---

1. Can the "ritual" function of the trial be severed from its search for historical truth? Could the trial continue to effectively "secure the peaceful settlement of social conflicts" in a society such as our own without also convincing us that it is an effective, albeit imperfect and costly, device in the search for historically-accurate factual premises for our ascriptions of responsibility?

2. Should Professor Tribe's argument lead to different conclusions about the use of Bayes' theorem depending upon whether the case is tried to a judge or to a jury?

3. It must be stressed that the characterization of adjudication as a search for historical truth is, at best, a drastic simplification. For the making of a decision in adjudication may entail simultaneous decisions about what in fact did occur and about the appropriateness of the categories of norms to be applied. Adjudication does not, cannot, and should not merely apply law to facts. And while it may be appropriate (though there are those "frequentists" who would disagree) to speak of the probability, given the evidence, of the defendant having stabbed the victim, it is surely impossible, as Tribe indicates, to speak coherently of the *probability* that that stabbing constitutes murder (except in the circular sense of the probability that a given court will *convict* the defendant of murder).

4. For an article which explores some of the inherently nonquantifiable characteristics of adjudication, see Ball, The Play's the Thing: An Unscientific Reflection on Courts under the Rubric of Theater, 28 Stan.L.Rev. 81 (1975).

SECTION D. MEASURING THE IMPORTANCE OF STRUCTURAL VARIABLES IN THE INFORMATIONAL PROCESSES

The use of probability theory in trials entails a normative stance towards the fact-finding process. It assumes a position on how we ought rationally to treat certain evidence in the deciding of a case. Over the past decade there has developed a body of material which pursues a different systematic inquiry, one seeking answers as to how certain variables in procedural structures actually influence decisions. The lead in these inquiries has been taken by social psychologists together with legal scholars. Most prolific among these scholars have been Professors John Thibaut and W. Laurens Walker of the University of North Carolina. Their book, Procedural Justice: A Psychological Analysis (1975), and a variety of articles published together with various associates, have produced interesting and controversial insights into such "mundane" characteristics of our process as the *order* of presentation. See, e. g., Walker, Thibaut, and Adreoli, Order of Presentation at Trial, 82 Yale L.J. 216 (1972). Other researchers have pursued avenues similar to those of Thibaut and Walker. See, e. g., Marshall, Marquis, and Oskamp, Effects of Kind of Question and Atmosphere of Interrogation on Accuracy and Completeness of Testimony, 84 Harv.L.Rev. 1620 (1971); Lind, Erickson, Friedland, and Dickenberger, Reactions to Procedural Models for Adjudicative Conflict Resolution, 22 J. Conflict Resolution 318 (1978). Rather than put forward a single, necessarily very limited, piece of research from an interrelated and extensive corpus, we have reprinted here a critical article by Professor Mirjan Damaška. He undertakes both an account of some of the social-psychology literature and a sketch of the proper and necessary limits on the claims that can be made for this literature. He draws on some of the themes developed at greater length in his essay in chapter 5.

Mirjan Damaška, **Presentation of Evidence and Factfinding Precision**[*]

For at least a century a debate has been raging about the relative advantages of the adversary and nonadversary presentations of evidence as tools in the quest for the truth . . . .   In our age, so enamoured of scientific methodology and so desirous of replacing "soft" by "hard" data, the question almost naturally arises: can at least some themes involved in the debate be translated into a form susceptible of empirical analysis? If the answer is in the affirmative, perhaps products of disinterested science can replace our prejudice, parochialism, and irrational attachments to existing arrangements, no matter how "efficient" these existing arrangements may be. In the present [essay] I propose to express my reflections on this subject, reflections that were stimulated by a piece of research presented in a series of recent, thought-provoking empirical studies.[2] . . .

[*] *Source:* 123 U.Pa.L.Rev. 1083, 1083–1106 (1975). Professor of Law, Yale University.

2. Thibaut, Walker & Lind, Adversary Presentation and Bias in Legal Decisionmaking, 86 Harv.L.Rev. 386 (1972).

I. Theoretical Propaedeutic

A. Preliminary Remarks on the Object of Proof

The problem whether the adversary or the nonadversary mode of presenting evidence is better equipped to lead to the truth cannot be analyzed in vacuo. "Truth about what?" is the question that must be answered at the very outset. It must be determined with sufficient precision what is the referent to which the characterization "truth" or "falsity" applies.

Following in the path of the studies mentioned a moment ago, I shall be concerned solely with issues involved in arriving at a judgment concerning the guilt or innocence of the criminal defendant. But this restriction is far from sufficiently precise. To begin with, consider that the issues disposed of in a judgment do not all have the same epistemological status: The meaning of the symbol "truth" changes considerably as we attach it to its different component parts.

     .   .   .   [I]magine a manslaughter charge arising out of reckless driving. The decisionmaker must determine the truth of a certain number of propositions regarding "external facts," such as the speed of the automobile, the condition of the road, the traffic signals, the driver's identity, and so on. The mental operations required to ascertain such "external facts" belong primarily to the sphere of sensory experience. The inquiry here appears to be relatively objective,[3] and the "truth" about such facts does not seem to be too elusive.

But many "internal facts" will also have to be established in the imagined case. They regard aspects of the defendant's knowledge and volition, to the extent to which these are important for the application of the relevant legal standard. The ascertainment of such facts is already a far less objective undertaking than the ascertainment of facts derived by the senses: processes of inductive inference from external facts are the most frequently traveled cognitive road. Even so, we do not hesitate to accord roughly the same cognitive status to findings regarding these internal facts as we do to findings of external facts. The characterizations "true" and "false" retain their respective meanings.

The situation changes, however, when the facts ascertained must be assessed in the light of the legal standard. Whether a driver has deviated from certain standards of care—and if so to what degree—are problems calling for a different type of mental operation than that used in dealing with external facts. It is, of course, a matter of free semantic choice whether to

---

. . . Additional pieces of research have been described in a number of subsequent articles. See Lind, Thibaut, & Walker, Discovery and Presentation of Evidence in Adversary and Nonadversary Proceedings, 71 Mich.L. Rev. 1129 (1973); Walker, Thibaut, & Andreoli, Order of Presentation at Trial, 82 Yale L.J. 216 (1972).

3. I say relatively objective, for an element of subjectivity suffuses even such psychological activities as perception. The latter has been shown to be far from a passive registration of stimuli: it depends on interests, previous habits, even on the creative act of grasping structures, thus implying a degree of inferential construction. Implications of the "creativity" of perception have been traced in various areas. See R. Arnheim, Perceptual Abstractions and Art, in Toward a Psychology of Art 27, 33 (1972); T. Kuhn, The Structure of Scientific Revolutions 126 (2d ed. 1970).

characterize the outcome of legal evaluation as "true" or "false," or to use some other pair of symbols. But if one decides to stick with the former, he must recognize that these symbols acquire a different meaning in the new context. In essence they convey the idea that the result of the activity is either correct (coherent) or incorrect (incoherent) within a given framework of legal reference. . . .

Notwithstanding marginal uncertainties and philosophical arguments on some aspects of this problem, it is generally agreed that the presentation of evidence is directed toward establishing the veracity of factual propositions, rather than the correctness of legal reasoning.[7] In what follows I shall therefore, be restricted solely to the *factual segment* of the judgment, as the only proper object of proof-taking. Within this factual segment, the problems of findings regarding external facts will bulk largest. They seem a very convenient object of empirical study, in that the processes of their determination are relatively objective.

Where empirical research is contemplated, is this restriction to the factual segment of the adjudicatory activity a workable proposition? Can this segment be extirpated from the whole in any fashion other than through logical analysis? This thought occurs quite naturally to lawyers in the Anglo-American legal culture, where the largely inscrutable jury verdict is so central. But even in continental systems, where decisionmakers are, as a rule, required to provide separate reasons for factual findings and legal determinations, skepticism can easily arise. The mandate to provide separate reasons can easily be viewed as implying rationalizations: what is in reality intertwined is presented post-festum in two neatly separated categories. It is indeed the most sophisticated modern view on the continent that, in arriving at a judgment, the mind of the decisionmaker constantly travels from facts to law and back to facts again, in a simulacrum of regenerative feedback.[8]

The constant interaction between fact and law thus cannot be denied. It poses serious problems for the empirical study of the factual segment of adjudication in isolation. If the actual criminal litigation were the object of study, these problems would be insuperable.[9] But there is another strategy of research. The presentation of evidence can be observed at simulated trials, under controlled laboratory conditions, and under this method the activity may be limited to factual issues only, even to the determination of external facts. . . .

It cannot be denied that the separation of the factual from the totality necessarily infects the results of the study with an element of artificiality and

---

7. As the reader knows, a legal proposition may sometimes be made an object of proof. But the aim of the evidentiary activity is to prove that a rule exists, and not that a certain legal solution is appropriate in the case.

8. . . . The view of sophisticated modern writers may be stated briefly as follows. You cannot decide which facts matter unless you have already selected, at least tentatively, applicable decisional standards. But most of the time you cannot properly understand these legal standards without relating them to the factual situation of the case . . . .

9. But, for independent reasons, actual systems can hardly be studied to determine the accuracy of their adjudicative outcomes. A formidable problem is how to determine the reality against which the actual disposition of cases could be matched.

distortion. The latter element is more pronounced in the Anglo-American system, where the place of the factual in the whole of the adjudication is less certain than on the continent. But this is hardly news to the scientist who deals with parts of totality all the time. It only means to him that the results must be interpreted with reserve and caution. . . .

B.   Two Contrasting Modes of Developing Evidence

Let me then try to present in some detail what is involved in the opposition of the two proof-taking styles [—adversary and nonadversary]. . . . Although my method here necessarily implies a degree of imprecision in depicting a much more complex phenomenon, for the sake of brevity I shall limit my discussion to the development of evidence through the examination of witnesses.

1.   *The Nonadversary Mode*

Under this variant, there are no separate witnesses for the prosecution and the defense. All witnesses are evidentiary sources of the bench, and it is the judge, not the parties, who has the primary duty to obtain information from them. The parties are not supposed to try to affect, let alone to prepare, the witnesses' testimony at trial. "Coaching" witnesses comes dangerously close to various criminal offenses of interfering with the administration of justice.[12]

At trial, the witness is first asked by the judge to present a narrative account of what he knows about the facts of the case. His story will be interrupted by questions from the bench only to help the witness express himself, to clarify a point, or to steer the witness back from the labyrinth of utter irrelevancy.[13] Only when this very informal communication comes to an end does the judge proceed to the interrogation. But even this interrogation process may sometimes strike an Anglo-American observer as more of an informal conversation than a rigorous succession of questions and short answers. Some of the questions go to the credibility of the witness and serve, to a moderate extent, as a functional equivalent of cross-examination. When the interrogation from the bench has been completed, the two parties are permitted to address questions to the witness, in an attempt to bring out omitted aspects favorable to them, or to add emphasis to certain points on which testimony has already been obtained. In brief, the bulk of information is obtained through judicial interrogation, and only a few informational crumbs are left to the parties.

But how can the judge effectively interrogate? It stands to reason that there can be no meaningful interrogation unless the examiner has at least some conception of the case and at least some knowledge about the role of the witness in it. Thus, under the nonadversary mode of develop-

---

12. In a number of continental countries this practice is also contrary to professional canons of ethics, no matter how fantastic this may seem to American lawyers . . . .

13. The paucity of continental rules on what is admissible evidence permits such an informal arrangement. In some continental countries the failure to permit the witness to offer a narrative account may constitute reversible error . . . .

ing evidence, the judge is typically given a file (dossier) containing summaries of what potential witnesses know about the case sub judice.

It is easy to see what lies at the core of the described manner of presenting evidence. The decisionmaker is active; he uses the informational sources himself. Information does not reach him in the form of two one-sided accounts; he strives to reconstruct the "whole story" directly.

After the proof-taking phase of the trial is over, the predominantly unilateral style of proceeding comes to an end. Then summations of facts and legal argumentation must be presented. Each side makes his own one-sided assessment of the evidence heard and advances his legal arguments. Exchange is permitted, but the defense must have the last word. Before the bench retires, the defendant is given the chance to make a final statement, which usually contains a potpourri of what can be classified as testimonial statements and exhortations to render certain decisions.

2.   *The Adversary Mode*

Under this arrangement, each party calls his own witnesses and tries to obtain from them information favorable to his case. In order to do this effectively, the party must often prepare the witness for the court appearance; what is later to be testimony is often told in the lawyer's office first. After one party has elicited information from his witness, his adversary takes over the interrogation process. Now the reliability of the other party's witness will be questioned, or an attempt will be made to obtain from him reliable information in favor of the cross-examiner's thesis. And it is through such rival use of evidentiary sources that the factfinding stage of the trial unfolds.

It is true that this adversary presentation may be moderated by the intervention of the factfinder, if he happens to be a judge.[16] He can ask questions that "cry out to be asked," or he may obtain immediate clarification of points from the perspective of his cognitive needs. But this judicial intrusion into an adversary development is necessarily limited. Too extensive an intervention may lead to reversal of the judgment. Apart from this consideration, it is exceedingly hard for a judge to ask meaningful questions, innocent as he must be of any prior knowledge of the case.

The essence of this second arrangement is obvious: The decisionmaker is passive, and the informational sources are tapped by two procedural rivals. The information about the facts of the case reaches the adjudicator in the form of two alternating one-sided accounts.

C.   The Perspective of Experimental Witness Psychology

As I am interested in the problem of which of the two described arrangements leads to more accurate factual findings, the insights offered by experimental psychology become valuable. And it is just one of many melan-

---

16. The jury is largely doomed to passivity, at least until the trial is over. This fact is important from the point of view of experimental psychology . . . .

choly facts unraveled by this relatively young discipline that all interrogation techniques exert some distorting influences . . . .

Let me first allude to a number of problems with the nonadversary mode of developing testimonial evidence. It will be recalled that the judge must have some prior knowledge of the case in order to become an effective interrogator at trial. But his necessary prior knowledge is, at the same time, a considerable shortcoming from the epistemological point of view. Being somewhat familiar with the case, the judge inevitably forms certain tentative hypotheses about the reality he is called upon to reconstruct. More or less imperceptibly, these preconceptions influence the kinds of questions he addresses to witnesses. More importantly, there is an ever-present danger that the judge will be more receptive to information conforming to his hypotheses than to that which clashes with them. Although the resulting dangers to accurate decisionmaking are somewhat decreased by the fact that judges are usually aware of this distorting psychological mechanism, the shortcomings of this arrangement cannot be entirely eliminated.

Consider now the adversary manner of developing evidence. It is designed in such a way that the art of suspended judgment can be practiced for a much longer period of time by the adjudicators. They are not driven by the duty to lead an inquiry into forming early tentative theories about the facts of the case. This is, of course, an advantage of the adversary mode. There may be yet another one, although it is much less certain in terms of experimental witness psychology. It is possible that an interrogator "hostile" to the witness may be in a better position to bring out potential conscious or unconscious distortion mechanisms inherent in his testimony (e.g., inaccurate perception, faulty memory images, mystifications, etc.).

But all this is only part of the story: there are important cognitive costs of the adversary arrangements . . . . [L]et us explore various epistemological pitfalls that lie in the tactical wake of letting two adversaries control the development of evidence at trial . . . .

It may be in the narrow interest of only one party, or in the common interest of both, that some items of information which the witness possesses do not reach the adjudicator—even though their relevancy in the quest for the truth is beyond dispute. Evidence unsupportive of one's case has no function in the adversary litigation process, nor do matters which the parties decide to leave out of the disputation. And, as the witness is limited to answering relatively narrow and precise questions, much information may effectively be kept away from the decisionmaker who presumably is responsible for finding the truth within the limits of the charge. Accordingly, the factual basis for the decision may be incomplete.[22]

22. I assume that the total number of facts to be established and the total number of evidentiary sources to be used is the same under both systems discussed.   In other words, many variables that influence the completeness of the factual and evidentiary materials submitted to the decisionmaker are held constant under the adversary and nonadversary trial processes. The remark in the text on the completeness of material only refers to the possibility that, as a result of different styles of examining witnesses, the quantum of information obtained from the *same* witness may be unequal under the two arrangements: the discrepancy between what the witness knows and what he communicates to the decisionmaker may vary

But there are much more important costs of the development of evidence through rival use of informational sources. The damage to testimony inflicted by the preparation of witnesses is very serious. Parties can hardly be expected to interview the potential witnesses in relatively detached ways that minimize the damage of interrogation to memory images. During the sessions devoted to "coaching," the future witness is likely to try to adapt himself to expectations mirrored in the interviewer's one-sided attitude. As a consequence, gaps in his memory may even unconsciously be filled out by what he thinks accords with the lawyer's expectations and are in tune with his thesis. Later, in court, these additions to memory images may appear to the witness himself as accurate reproductions of his original perceptions. Another important cost accompanies the cross-examination technique, which, with its challenge to the credibility of witnesses, is a two-edged sword . . . . Even with the best of intentions on the cross-examiner's part, reliable testimony may easily be made to look debatable, and clear information may become obfuscated.

Finally, observe the procedural position of the passive decisionmaker. It is old hat in experimental psychology that people display different cognitive needs; they try to reach knowledge and understanding along different paths. It therefore stands to reason that decisionmakers may sometimes require a different method of presentation than that of the clash of two one-sided versions, and that, at a psychologically crucial point, they would sometimes like to ask a specific question of a witness, which in their passivity they cannot do.

significantly under the two modes of developing evidence. Let me allude parenthetically, however, to three important variables of crucial importance for the larger problem whether the factual basis for the adjudication of guilt is equal under the adversary and nonadversary systems of structuring the trial.

The first variable concerns the *range of facts* that the decisionmakers have to determine. Under the adversary system of trial, the parties may agree not to submit certain facts to the decisionmaker even though these facts are within the compass of a charge. Or, one party may decide not to raise an issue relevant to the charge (e. g., a defense). Both these practices are alien to the nonadversary system, in which inter-party arrangements concerning facts are prohibited, and in which it is the court's duty to extend its inquiry to all relevant facts within the limits of the charge.

The second variable involves the different strategies of the *search for evidence*. Under the adversary system, the parties collect evidence to support their respective theses. Under the nonadversary model, the gathering of evidence is primarily the duty of a state agency. Obviously, different problems of transmitting information about detected evidence spring from this variation: the adversaries are often reluctant to exchange information about the evidence discovered, while the nonadversary agency entrusted with preparation of the case for trial will, as a rule, transmit all it has unearthed to the court.

The third variable involves different rules of admissibility. Under the adversary system much logically relevant and cognitively valuable information never reaches the factfinder, while the filtering mechanism in the nonadversary system is much cruder.

What is the cumulative effect of these and other variables? It is probably that the total volume of information under the nonadversary system is somewhat greater (assuming that the number of relevant facts is the same). But this does not preclude the possibility that the information obtained under the nonadversary process is less reliable. . . .

.   .   .   [C]an empirical tests tell us which evidentiary arrangement, if either, leads to a better approximation of the evanescent reality that we seek to reconstruct in the criminal process?   .   .   .

II.   Laboratory Experimentations with Presentation of Evidence

A.   The Experiment by Thibaut, Walker, and Lind

This group of researchers has set out to explore whether the adversary manner of presenting evidence is better suited to counteracting the decision-maker's bias than the nonadversary.   Bias was understood as "the tendency to judge too swiftly in terms of the familiar that which is not yet fully known."   It was concretely structured so as actually to mean the expectation on the part of the decisionmaker that the criminal defendant is guilty.   .   .   .

A test case was constructed by the researchers.   It involved a tavern brawl in the course of which one person, later to be indicted, reacted to an assault by using force.   The issue raised by the case was that of the limits of lawful self-defense.   Details of the test case were embodied in fifty brief factual statements, half of which were designed under a scaling technique to induce a belief that self-defense was justified, and the remaining half to suggest that the use of force was unjustified.   The decisionmakers were selected from among college students.   In half of them, the expectation was implanted that the defendant was guilty, while the other half remained "unbiased."   Panels of student judges were formed, some with biased and others with unbiased students.   They were all instructed about two alternative standards for decision: in order to repel an attack a person is not justified in using more force than he thinks necessary (a subjective criterion), or more force than a reasonable person would consider necessary in the circumstances of the case (an objective criterion).   The task of the panels was to decide whether the violent reaction of the defendant to assault was lawful or not.

Next, stylized models of adversary and nonadversary presentation were constructed.   In the simulation of the adversary mode, the facts were to be announced to the decisionmakers by two students, seated at separate tables bearing the words "prosecution" and "defense."   One student, the prosecutor, was to announce the twenty-five factual propositions damaging to the defendant, while the other, counsel for the defense, was to relate the twenty-five factual statements favorable to the defendant.   In the simulation of the nonadversary presentation, all fifty factual statements were to be announced by one person only, but the classification of the facts into two separate groups was to be maintained.   Under both simulated models the decisionmakers were expected to be passive, limited to listening to the informational input of a third person (or persons).   After completion of some preliminaries that do not concern me here, the simulated trials took place.

.   .   .   In unbiased judges, the different presentation of factual state-ments failed to produce a statistically significant difference in the determination of guilt.   But in biased judges, there was a statistically significant higher number of decisions of guilt (i. e., decisions consistent with their bias) in the simulated nonadversary presentation than in the simulated adversary presentation. This difference was most pronounced in the interim measurements taken after biased decisionmakers had been exposed, under the nonadversary mode, to presentation only of the factual statements designed to create the belief that the defendant was probably guilty. Those exposed to the adversary presentation better resisted this bias. . . .

The researchers tell us that their investigation focused on two modes of presenting evidence. But, in light of my brief initial sketch of the adjudicative process, the reader must already have had second thoughts about the accuracy of this claim. In the experiment, the decisionmakers were not presented evidence and then asked to ascertain facts. Instead, they were conveyed propositions of fact and apparently expected to assume that these were true. There is no indication in the description of the study that the decisionmakers were supposed to question the accuracy of factual propositions that were transmitted to them. What then is a better description of their activity? They were supposed to implement one of two very general decisional standards in light of the supplied factual information and were expected to arrive at a decision of guilt or innocence, at a legal determination. Under the subjective legal standard (whether the defendant *believed* that the use of force was necessary) they were also asked to establish "internal" facts (the beliefs of the defendant). But even on this point there was no outward evidentiary activity of any sort: The decisionmakers were engaged solely in inferences and evaluations. Consequently, what the researchers actually studied was the effect of unilateral as opposed to bilateral announcements to the adjudicator of the results of *already completed* evidentiary activity. This, to my mind, more nearly resembles closing arguments before the judge than the presentation of evidence to him.[30]

Was the experiment addressed to the problem of which arrangement is more likely to produce the truth? Of course not. If the main activity involved in the simulated adjudication was indeed the making of a legal decision,[31] it stands to reason that this decision cannot be characterized as "true" or "false" in the same sense in which this characterization applies to the objects of my concern—factual findings. Borrowing a phrase from Wittgenstein, one can say that different language games are involved. Nor were the decisions evaluated in terms of their "coherence" or "correctness" within the legal universe. No independent criterion was supplied against which to judge whether the defendant's reaction to the assault was indeed lawful or not. The researchers' *direct* concern was the efficacy of the two different arrangements in counteracting the adjudicator's bias, understood as an inclination to follow the expectation that the defendant is guilty. It seems, however, that those who designed the experiment may have hoped to provide indirectly some data on the question of which arrangement leads to

---

30. Of course, the difference remains that the judge is not expected to assume the accuracy of the factual underpinnings of the partisan closing arguments.

31. An argument could be made that the supplied "objective" standard for decision (i. e., what force a reasonable person would believe necessary) involves a factual determination. Although it is true that many such standards could be made the objects of surveys and similar sociological factfinding techniques, they are actually treated as normative propositions.

greater accuracy.   There is a passage in their text pointing to the widespread belief in the correlation between the adjudicator's bias (read "expectation of guilt") and an erroneous decision.   But one cannot rule out the possibility, no matter how unpleasant the thought, that those who followed their bias made the "correct" finding of unlawfulness, while those who resisted it erred.   I would not be the first beautiful assumption slain by ugly facts.[33]

.   .   .   [But let us assume, for the sake of argument,] that the researchers were indeed focusing on the presentation of evidence, and that they were in fact measuring, albeit indirectly, the truth-finding potential of the two different evidentiary arrangements.   The problem then becomes whether their two simulated models express the opposition between the adversary and nonadversary development of evidence.   My answer, clearly following from my previous discussion of this contrast, is definitely in the negative.

As I understand it, and mine is not an unorthodox conception, the quintessence of the nonadversary arrangement is that the decisionmaker be active, that he develop the evidence himself.   If this feature is absent, so are all the possible advantages of the arrangement.   And it is precisely this characteristic of proof-taking that was not included among the planned variations used in constructing the simulated models.   Under both models the decisionmakers were passive listeners, a desirable stance only within the adversary mode.   Under both models adjudicators were exposed to an informational input that neatly classified factual propositions as either favorable or damaging to the defendant.   This again is true only to the adversary style.   The only difference between the two arrangements was that the dividing line between the two kinds of information was thrown into sharper relief under what was supposed to be the simulation of the adversary model, by assigning the announcement of different categories of facts to different persons.   The contrast between adversary and nonadversary modes of presenting evidence can hardly be found in the simulated model.   Nor is the contrast devised by the researchers expressive of continental as opposed to Anglo-American styles of arguing before the court.   All modern nonadversary systems or-

---

33.   It is true that an arrangement that better counteracts the adjudicator's predisposition toward guilt is better equipped to minimize the number of false convictions.   But whether such an arrangement leads to the truth in a greater number of cases is another question.   Minimizing the *total number of inaccurate outcomes* and minimizing *false positives* are two different concerns.   As long as one remains in the sphere of procedural epistemology, the two issues must not be confused.   The question about the optimal distribution of error is based on values other than the desire to establish the truth, and thus falls outside the purview of this article.

There is another problem, however, that deserves brief mention in connection with the impact of the decisionmaker's bias in the described experiment.   It concerns the balanced nature of the test case.   The factual basis for the legal decision was in equipoise: twenty-five propositions suggested guilt and twenty-five propositions indicated innocence.   Jean Buridan would surely claim that this is exactly the situation he illustrated with his donkey between two equal haystacks: In order to have any movement, an impetus must first be provided.   See M. Clagett, The Science of Mechanics in the Middle Ages 537 (1959).   The study of bias in this unusual situation is sui generis.   Imagine that the adjudicators in this case were further instructed about the reasonable doubt standard.   It is not inconceivable that, even with biased decisionmakers, the two variations would show no statistically significant difference.

ganize arguments in a disputational form, and whatever differences remain were not picked up by the simulation.

In summarizing my comments about the experiment, I am led to conclude that the researchers promised one thing and delivered another. They supplied empirical support for the following hypothesis: In close cases a bilateral summation of established facts is better suited than a unilateral one to counteract the decisionmaker's inclination to render a judgment in accordance with his expectation that the defendant is probably guilty. They told us nothing about the relative advantages of adversary and nonadversary modes of presenting evidence in the divination of truth.   .   .   .

B.   An Alternative Test Proposal

If one wants to embark on a study of factfinding accuracy he must, of course, establish criteria of reality. This is neither too costly nor overly difficult if simulated trials are contemplated. For instance, having written certain facts into the script, one could film an event simulating a crime (for example, a manslaughter by a drunken driver), and by careful and repeated viewing of the motion picture compile an exhaustive list of all facts that a viewer of the film might possibly observe. Criteria have now been obtained for checking the accuracy of future factual findings at the simulated trial.

What we need next are witnesses. A number of persons should be invited to watch the motion picture closely.   .   .   .   A false witness could be produced and later planted at the simulated trials to measure the extent to which false testimony can distort the outcome, if this variable is of interest.

Finding suitable factfinders and defining their role may be more difficult.   .   .   .   [T]he nonadversary trial calls for factfinders who are both skilled examiners and adjudicators; such people are hard to come by in countries where the personal union of the investigator and the adjudicator is viewed askance.   .   .   .   To hold constant factors stemming from the different composition of various decisionmaking bodies, single judges seem on many counts to be preferable to panels.

Much as in the preceding experiment, some judges would then have to be implanted with an expectation that the defendant is guilty (they would have to be biased). It is true that the sole task of the judges will be to establish a factual basis for a finding of guilt, but this by no means implies that factfinding, even in the context of a simulated trial, is such a "neutral" activity as not to be influenced by bias.[37] This bias could be induced, for instance, by exposing some of the future judges to series of film clips, designed to induce specific preconceptions about what usually happens under circumstances similar to those in the filmed event.

Following the simulated trials, the task of the judges would be to submit a list of precisely described factual findings about the event. Naturally, standards of what facts are relevant would have to be deveolped and made

---

37. How bias can affect factfinding in our context is easy to show. Even if conduct is not a crime, preconceptions about what has happened influence the factfinder's inquiry (where he conducts it) and sensitize him more to certain information than to other information. Expectation also affects the mechanism of "logical completion" of memory images   .   .   .   .

uniform for all judges, no matter what the mode of trial. The expected decision would be in the nature of a special rather than a general verdict.

Nonadversary development of evidence would be designed in such a way that the factfinder would invite witnesses to present a narrative account, and then submit them to interrogation. There would be a possibility of confronting witnesses whose testimonies clashed. If thought necessary for effective questioning, a file containing brief summaries of what witnesses saw could be supplied to decisionmakers. In order to avoid undue complexity in an experiment under laboratory conditions, there would be no subsidiary questioning by counsel, and many other characteristics of the nonadversary model would not be replicated.

The adversary manner of presenting evidence would be designed to unfold through examination-in-chief and cross-examination of witnesses before a passive factfinder. For this skilled lawyers would be needed, and each would be assigned a number of "his" witnesses to prepare for testimony. The methodological problem would be, of course, how to create a contest between two counsel. . . . For instance, lawyers could be divided into two groups; one would be invited to try to prove the factual basis for a conviction on the manslaughter charge, the other to establish the facts supporting a verdict of innocence. At all times the circumstances would have to be checked to determine whether the factfinding efforts under the two modes of proof-taking are directed toward the same facts.

As a result of four variables (adversary versus nonadversary proof-taking, and biased versus unbiased factfinders) four types of differently structured simulated trials would have to be held. The decisionmakers would then be expected, following the criteria of relevancy, to hand in their factual findings. These findings would be measured and statistically analyzed, at least insofar as the findings under the adversary and nonadversary presentations overlap and concern the same facts.[38]

The results could be quite interesting. Those who believe in the superiority of the continental style would probably expect that the latter, even when used to a biased judge, would still yield a more precise factfinding result. Those who believe in the potency of cross-examination would probably expect this weapon to secure better results even before a biased judge. In any event, data obtained would, I believe, tell us much more about the two differing styles of proof-taking than the study described before.

III.   A Glance at a Larger Epistemological Problem

A much debated problem has now hopefully been presented in a form susceptible of empirical testing. Quite unrealistically, let me assume that experimentation has proven conclusively that one manner of presenting evidence leads to more precise factual findings than the other. What would be

---

38. It is possible that, notwithstanding the uniform criteria of relevancy, one or another mode comes up with a richer harvest of facts. For instance, the partisan perspective followed by the adversary system may embrace within its two narrow searchlights a smaller number of facts than the unfocused narrative of the witness in the nonadversary system. Accuracy of findings must then be measured only with regard to the factual overlap.

the significance of such an empirical datum for the question of which evidentiary arrangement is preferable?

As the criminal process is not an untrammeled exercise in cognition, it does not take much imagination to realize that from the standpoint of other important values, an epistemologically inferior technique may on the whole be preferable. Preoccupation with the rationality of one component can be irrational when judged from the point of view of the entire scheme. But the perspective of such other values does not concern me here, limited as I am to the sphere of the quest for truth in the criminal process. Observing, then, the presentation of evidence in this narrow, artificial light, would the datum mentioned above not put an end to the debate about the relative merits of the two manners of presenting evidence? To answer this question I must, before closing, return once again to the object of proof-taking.   .   .   .

.   .   .   Anglo-American decisionmakers are traditionally strongly attached to individualized justice and strive to arrive at the just result in the light of concrete circumstances of the case: justice to them can hardly be separated from details. The continental decisionmakers are relatively more concerned about uniformity and predictability: they are much more ready than the common-law adjudicator to neglect the details of the case in order to organize the world of fluid social reality into a system.

This unequal value orientation leaves an unmistakable imprint on decisional standards in the two legal cultures. Those of the Anglo-American judge are traditionally in the form of precedents. It is typical of precedents that the decisional standard contained in them can hardly be translated into an abstract rule. What is important in factual details of such professional anecdotes can be approached from different perspectives, and hardly can be stated with precision. Meanwhile, standards of the continental judge are preferably in the form of precise rules, contained in authoritative texts. The consequence of this difference in standards for factual determination, and therewith for the object of proof-taking, is not difficult to see. The Anglo-American criteria of relevancy make the factual basis of a decision closer to social reality, where fact and value are intertwined. The foundation of the continental decision is drained of much of the concreteness of real life situations. It is frozen, as it were, into a relatively artificial world of technical relevancy, untainted by social conflict. Now, the more one is removed from the fullness of life, the more limited but also the more precise is our knowledge: there is one fixed perspective. On the other hand, the closer one remains to the complexity of real life processes, the more encompassing but also less certain is one's understanding: as in cubism, our sensations come from multiple viewpoints and there is more than one side to every story. The truth appears elusive, often a matter of feeling and intuition.

If I am right, and there is indeed a subtle discrepancy in the "realities" constituting the object of proof in the two systems, then it is only natural that methods of inquiry into such different realities need not be exactly the same. The continental system would tend to embrace a paradigm closer to that of scientific investigation. The Anglo-American system, where truth is so much a matter of perspective, would tend to espouse a variation of the dialectic method for the divination of the elusive truth.

Note how differently the "scientific" and the "dialectic" paradigms conceive of the ideal position of the judge. In the continental jurisdictions, the judge who has prior knowledge of the case will not automatically be viewed with suspicion. He is, mutatis mutandis, like a scientist who, by having formed tentative theories about the object of his exploration, has not thereby surrendered his claims to impassivity. Only when he has a personal stake in the decision, or when his mind is closed on the case, may there be a ground for disqualification. In the Anglo-American system, prior knowledge of the case on the part of the judge is more readily associated with bias. The reasons for this are quite straightforward. If the judge obtains knowledge about the case independently of the dialectical process of courtroom inquiry, he can hardly decide which side emerged victorious from the disputation about the truth; he will be siding all the time with the party whose version of the facts accords with his independent knowledge.[45] Nor is this all. Quite ominously, the two parties will no longer be stimulated to invest their energies in a full adversary clash, for that method of inquiry will no longer be decisive, having formed a mésalliance with an alien epistemological approach. . . .[46]

---

1.   Thibaut and Walker conducted further research to examine some of the components which Damaška found missing in their earlier articles. In particular, they have been more aware that participation values may be critically important in some situations—perhaps even more important than truth-finding. In their book (Procedural Justice (1975), chapters 8–12) and in certain articles (see, especially, Thibaut, Walker, LaTour, and Houlden, Procedural Justice as Fairness, 26 Stan.L.Rev. 1271 (1974)) they have attempted to measure the feelings of participants concerning alternative structures which entail varying degrees of participation or imposed-decision attributes. See also Thibaut and Walker, A Theory of Procedure, 66 Cal.L. Rev. 541 (1978).

2.   Would Professor Damaška's proposed experiment meet the rigors of the scientific method and at the same time adequately illuminate reality?

---

45. Continentals are often puzzled at the requirement that jurors have no knowledge of any facts whatsoever. A good example of this was the continental reaction to the voir dire in the trial of Jack Ruby, who was seen by millions on TV to have shot Lee Harvey Oswald. What does the Anglo-American system want, a continental mind is inclined to ask? Surely it does not want that the courtroom process of truth divination come up with a finding contrary to the TV "reality." Why then should the Anglo-American system assume that those who know about the killing will be partial judges in other matters that must be determined?

46. The particular conception of bias found in the Anglo-American system surfaces in the study by Thibaut, Walker, and Lind. The orientation of their "comparative" research has a built-in common law slant. But, for the same reasons, the research paradigm suggested by me expresses a continental perspective, in that the fragmentation of the "totality" of adjudication, and the emphasis on precise determination, do less violence to the continental than they do to the Anglo-American system of administering justice.

One might begin to answer this question by wondering whether there are any differences between viewing a movie (e. g., about manslaughter by a drunken driver) and witnessing the event itself. See S. Cavell, The World Viewed (1971).

Chapter 7

ADJUDICATORY ACTION: ITS FORMS AND MEANING

In this chapter we shift the focus from inputs and consider instead the outcome of the informational process—the judgment, the decision, the decree, the order, the sentence. The material concentrates on judicial action, though there is every reason to believe that actions of other adjudicators, such as the arbitrator or the administrative agency, would raise comparable issues and problems.

We start from the overwhelming fact of contemporary litigation, namely, that the action of a judge can take a multitude of forms. This phenomenon accentuates the choice of remedy issue. It necessitates an examination of the connection between alternative, overlapping, and sometimes antithetical forms of action. We also maintain that the same judicial action could have many different meanings. Through two case studies—one involving the judgment of Solomon and the other involving judicial mollification of the Black Act of eighteenth-century England—we suggest how the latent function of judicial action might be understood. In the final section of the chapter we return to the contemporary scene to study the problems of efficacy. We focus on two striking instances of modern public adjudication, the school prayer and school desegregation cases, to identify the conditions that determine the efficacy of judicial action and to reveal how the very desire to be efficacious shapes the terms of judicial action—and perhaps even threatens its meaning.

SECTION A. THE FORMS OF ACTION: THEIR VARIETY AND INTERRELATIONSHIPS

A modern account of the forms of action must be guided by two rules. The first is that such an analysis must be truly comprehensive. The account must start with a unified conception of legal procedure, must span the gap between equity and law, and, to mention an even more difficult challenge, must span the gap between actions denominated "civil" and those denominated "criminal" and "administrative." The emergence of the legislature as a prime lawmaking agency and the willingness of the legislature to delegate more and more power to administrative agencies and to bring more and more conduct within the reach of criminal prohibitions means that, when we speak of the forms of action, we can no longer use only the common-law civil categories.

Secondly, a modern account must give a primacy to two remedies traditionally assigned a secondary or minor position—the injunction and habeas corpus. The preeminence of the injunction today can be traced to Brown v. Board of Education, 347 U.S. 483 (1954), 349 U.S. 294 (1955), and to the revolution that that case wrought in our substantive and even our procedural law. Similarly, during that same era, habeas corpus emerged as a central and quite common mode of action in the federal courts. It expressed the very special quality of the commitment of the Warren Court to "the constitutionalization of criminal procedure."

In the essays that follow, we acknowledge these two rules and try to set the foundations for a modern account of the various forms of judicial action.

Owen M. Fiss, **The Civil Rights Injunction—The Sources of Uniqueness***

.   .   .   The law has long embraced a pluralism with regard to injunctions, accepting the idea that there are categories or species of injunctions. But for the most part the pluralism has been too limited—content to distinguish interlocutory and final injunctions, or perhaps mandatory or prohibitory ones. I would like to expand the pluralism and introduce three new categories: the preventive injunction, which seeks to prohibit some discrete act or series of acts from occurring in the future; the reparative injunction, which compels the defendant to engage in a course of action that seeks to correct the effects of a past wrong; and the structural injunction, which seeks to effectuate the reorganization of an ongoing social institution   .   .   .   .

Equipped with these new categories, I think we will be in a better position to assess the alleged uniqueness of the injunction. Classic doctrine, such as the irreparable injury requirement, has been primarily addressed to the preventive injunction, and paradoxically, that injunction bears a striking resemblance to other remedies. The preventive injunction might be viewed as a mini-criminal statute, though more individuated, more decentralized, and with greater power invested in the judge. With the newer categories, those with roots in civil rights litigation, we seem to move in two different directions. The reparative injunction closely resembles the damage judgment and might be viewed as an in-kind damage award, while the structural injunction emerges, so I will maintain, as a truly unique legal instrument.

A.   The Content of the Injunction

1.   Prevention

Justice Story described the unique office of the injunction as preventive justice: the injunction is an instrument designed to prevent a wrong from occurring in the future. There are two important senses in which this proposition is false: it overstates the claim of uniqueness and takes insufficient account of reparative and structural injunctions.

In asserting the supposed uniqueness of the injunction, Story is comparing it to the damage award or criminal conviction; these remedies have an effect upon the future conduct of both the individual against whom a judgment is entered (specific deterrence) and society in general (general deterrence). Yet they are retrospective remedies, because a necessary condi-

* *Source:* The Civil Rights Injunction
7–37 (1978), chapter II. Professor of
Law, Yale University.

tion for each (putting aside the category of inchoate crimes) is that a wrong has occurred. This is not true for the classic injunction, the preventive one.

Story's claim of uniqueness, however, involves a false comparison. The preventive injunction should not be compared to the damage award or the criminal conviction, but rather to the rules of conduct underlying those judicial judgments—the liability rule or the criminal prohibition. Both the liability rule and the criminal prohibition are addressed to the future, and neither requires a past wrong in order to become operative. Each controls conduct through deterrence—the liability rule is backed by a threat to impose costs, and the criminal prohibition by a threat to punish. The preventive injunction operates in a similar fashion.

This can be seen more clearly if the injunctive process is divided into two phases: the issuance phase, in which the tribunal promulgates the rule of conduct, and the enforcement phase, in which sanctions are imposed for noncompliance with the previously promulgated rule of conduct. The enforcement phase can properly be compared to the damage action or criminal prosecution; all are retrospective in the sense that they are responsive to an antecedent wrong—a violation of a rule of conduct. The issuance phase of the injunctive process, on the other hand, should be compared with the promulgation of a rule of liability or a criminal prohibition: a past wrong is not a necessary condition for either, and the concern of each is to establish standards of future conduct.

The standard account also misleads in suggesting that prevention is the only concern of the injunction .   .   .   .   [T]here are at least two species, two important species, that are more backward-looking.

The first is the structural injunction—the injunction seeking to effectuate the reform of a social institution. The most notable example is a decree seeking to bring about the reorganization of a school system from a "dual system" to a "unitary nonracial school system." Antecedents of these decrees might be found in the railroad reorganizations at the turn of the century or, more recently, in the antitrust divestiture cases. But it was school desegregation, I maintain, that gave these types of injunctions their contemporary saliency and legitimacy; in the wake of this experience, courts have attempted the structural reorganization of other institutions, such as hospitals and prisons, not just to vindicate a claim of racial equality, but also to vindicate other claims, such as the right against cruel and unusual punishment or the right to treatment.

The other backward-looking injunction is the reparative injunction— an injunction that seeks to eliminate the effects of a past wrong, in this instance conceived as some discrete act or course of conduct. To see how it works, let us assume that a wrong has occurred (such as an act of discrimination). Then the mission of an injunction—classically conceived as a preventive instrument—could be said to be to prevent the recurrence of the wrongful conduct in the future (stop discriminating and do not discriminate again). But in United States v. Louisiana,[5] a voting discrimination case, Justice Black identified still another mission for the injunction—the elimination of the *effects* of the past wrong (the past discrimination). .   .   .

5. 380 U.S. 145 (1965).

[I]n that vein, election officials have been ordered not only to stop discriminating in future elections but also to set aside a past election and to run a new election as a means of removing the taint of discrimination that infected the first one. Similarly, public housing officials have been ordered both to cease discriminating on the basis of race in their future choices of sites and to build units in the white areas as a means of eliminating the effects of the past segregative policy (placing public housing projects only in the black areas of the city).

The mission of these backward-looking injunctions—both the structural and the reparative variety—might be described so as to reduce the tension with the classical conception of the injunction as an exclusively preventive instrument. For the structural injunction it might be said that the purpose of reorganizing an institution is to prevent a wrong from recurring. And for the reparative injunction it might be said that being subjected to the continuing effects of a past wrong is itself an independent wrong, a wrong that is to occur in the future, and that the purpose of the injunction is to prevent *that* wrong. Without wholly denying the analytic integrity of these attempted reconceptualizations, let me suggest that both strain and obscure the underlying social realities.

The attempted reconceptualization of the structural injunction assumes that the wrong exists independently of the organizational structure, and that assumption is incorrect. The constitutional wrong is the structure itself; the reorganization is designed to bring the structure within constitutional bounds—not to minimize the chance of some other, discrete wrong occurring. Moreover, at least as a practical matter, a past wrong is required for the issuance of a structural injunction; the mere threat of a wrong in the future is not likely to be deemed sufficient to trigger the reform enterprise, even though such a threat is sufficient for the classic preventive injunction. A structural injunction is unlikely to issue without a judgment that the existing institutional arrangement is illegal, is now a wrong, and will continue to be wrongful unless corrected.

The attempt to make the reparative injunction appear preventive is similarly flawed. The redefinition fails to reflect the derivative nature of the future wrong—that the wrong supposedly to be prevented by the reparative injunction is analytically derived from a past wrong. A past wrong and its effects must be identified before we can even understand the future wrong to be prevented. The reconceptualization of the reparative injunction is no more persuasive than would be the claim that the damage award is preventive because it prevents the future wrong of leaving the victim uncompensated for his injuries. Both conceptions are highly contrived. And there is so little to be gained. It would be better to abandon this analytic scrimmage and simply accept one important lesson from the civil rights experience —that the office of the injunction need no longer be exclusively preventive.

2.   Individuation

If I am correct in asserting that the preventive injunction is best compared to the liability rule or the criminal prohibition, in that all are preventive instruments, one striking difference readily comes to mind, namely, the individuated quality of the injunction. A liability rule or criminal prohibition, for example, makes it unlawful for landowners to use their property in a way that unreasonably interferes with the enjoyment of land by others. The injunction rests on or assumes these same generalized standards of conduct, but then introduces an individuated quality—it prohibits the defendant's cement factory from emitting smoke onto the plaintiff's land. The individuation of the injunction arises from the fact, first, that it is *addressed* to some clearly identified individual, not just the general citizenry; second, the *act* prohibited or required is described with a degree of specificity not found in a liability rule or criminal prohibition; and third, the *beneficiaries* of the decree are also more specifically delineated.

. . . [The] fundamental point to note is that individuation is but a *potential*. The injunction can be individuated, but it need not be; and to the extent that it is not, the resemblance increases between the injunction— particularly of the preventive variety—and other preventive instruments such as liability rules and criminal prohibitions . . . .

. . . Almost all preventive injunctions in the civil rights area contain a provision that does little more than track the prohibition of the appropriate statute or constitutional command—do not discriminate on the basis of race. The broader the command the greater the threat to due process values, and the harder it is to impose severe sanctions—adequate notice of what constitutes a violation is likely to be lacking. On the other hand, broad commands make evasion more difficult and may deter even though severe sanctions are unlikely. Costs are imposed on the defendant by the very assertion of a claim of violation and the necessity of defending an enforcement proceeding.

With the other types of civil rights injunctions, the decreed act has been more individuated. The reparative injunction—promising to give in-kind compensation—has been specific in terms of the act prohibited or required. The very purpose of the injunction is to specify the compensation. With the structural injunction the story is more complicated: over time the decreed act becomes more and more specific, for example, detailing the dates on which choice forms are to be distributed, the ratio of blacks and whites in each school, the amount to be spent on books, etc. But this specificity emerges as a last resort. The original impulse in these structural cases was just the opposite—to use almost no specificity in describing the act required.

For the first decade, 1954–64, the typical school decree, to take the most common structural injunction, had two parts—one a broad prohibition (do not discriminate on the basis of race; do not maintain a "dual school system"), and the other a requirement for the school board to submit a plan for transforming the "dual school system" into a "unitary, nonracial school system." This plan-submission technique was an attempt to have the defendants—as opposed to the plaintiffs or the court—specify their own remedial steps. It reflected doctrinal uncertainty (a lack of clarity as to what "unitary nonracial school system" meant); strategic considerations (a desire to go slowly or to be as uncoercive or unobtrusive as possible); and a desire to capitalize on the expertise of the school board. The technique of plan submission made eminent sense, and yet in time courts saw the obvious—

that these generalized decrees would not effectively change the status quo. The same dynamics that led to the violation in the first place would prevent the defendant from using its knowledge and imagination against itself, from tying its own hands too effectively or too stringently. The school boards failed to plan for themselves. During the second *Brown* decade, 1964–74, the courts began to write their own plans and thus to be increasingly specific in describing the steps for the structural reformation. The Supreme Court was anxious to emphasize, however, that these "specifics" were to be viewed as mere expedients—perhaps only of a temporary duration— necessary to cope with the absence of good faith.

The absence of individuation in the beneficiary component of civil rights injunctions is even more striking, and does not vary greatly between reparative, structural, and preventive injunctions. The beneficiary of the typical civil rights injunction is not an individual, or even a collection of identifiable individuals; rather it is a social group—the blacks. The contours of the benefitted group are determined not by the personal characteristics of the person who happens to be the named plaintiff, but rather by considerations of who should—as a matter of fairness, efficacy, and equal protection theory—receive the benefit. This is not due to the procedural vessel, the fact that the suits are formally brought as representative actions; it is due instead to the group character of the underlying substantive claim—the fact that racial discrimination impairs the status of an already disadvantaged group, blacks, and for that very reason is proscribed by the Equal Protection Clause. Form follows substance .   .   .   .

Developments in the addressee component paralleled the loss of individuation in the act and beneficiary components. Civil rights injunctions were typically addressed to the office, rather than the person. This was true even in cases where abuse of office was charged. Operationally this meant that in determining whether an injunction was needed, the misconduct of the predecessors in office would automatically be attributed to the incumbent; there was a tacking of misconduct. It also meant that after issuance the automatic substitution rule of Federal Rule of Civil Procedure 25(d) would be invoked. Rule 65(d) of the Federal Rules, which originated in the Clayton Act of 1914 as an attempt to confine the labor injunction, omits the word "successor" in the list of persons bound by a decree. Yet virtually no attention was given that omission in designing civil rights injunctions. The word "successor" was included in almost all civil rights injunctions, premised on the insight that the most important determination of official conduct is not the person but the office—defined not by the formal job description but by the traditions, culture, and surrounding political structures.

This shift from person to office as addressee occurs along a vertical axis—over time. No one pays much attention to the person who happens to occupy the office at any particular time. It should also be noted that there has been a comparable development along the horizontal axis—at any one time large numbers of persons have been bound by the decree; injunctions have been made to "run against the world."

There was a need for a broad injunction in labor disputes. These disputes often involved mass conduct—countless picketers, strikers, and labor organizers—many of whom were not known to the employer. Often the labor injunction   .   .   .   was addressed to anyone who happened to get actual notice of it. In the reaction to the labor injunction this scope was identified as an "abuse," a derogation of the principle enunciated by Lord Elden that only parties are bound. This view obtained legislative approval in the Clayton Act of 1914 and was carried over to Federal Rule 65(d). It confined federal court injunctions to the parties (and their agents). By the 1930s, however, what appeared to be at stake was not just an English dictum or a congressional command, but, in the words of Justice Brandeis, "established principles of equity jurisdiction and procedure"—a phrase that has the same resonance as a claim about the requirements of due process. Individuation was not just a practice, but rather an ideal.

The civil rights experience called this ideal into question. The substantive claim did not cause us to ignore procedural values, but rather to look at them with greater scrutiny. There was an urgent need for a legal instrument to deal, for example, with white political leaders and citizens' groups—not parties to the underlying school desegregation case—who were preventing black children from exercising rights under the decree, i. e., from attending formerly all white schools. This was manifest in one response to the Little Rock crisis—the enactment of 18 U.S.C. § 1509—making it a crime for *anyone* to interfere forcibly with the exercise of rights arising from a federal court decree. The validity of the decree was not open to relitigation, and the individual who interfered with rights emanating from that decree was subject to criminal penalties. In that sense the nonparty was bound by the decree. A second departure from the ideal also had its roots in the Little Rock crisis, and in the crises surrounding the school closing in Alabama (1963) and the registration of James Meredith at Ole Miss (1962). What emerged from these crises was an antiobstruction injunction—an injunction prohibiting interferences with the rights granted by another decree.

Initially these antiobstruction injunctions were granted against named individuals such as Governors Faubus, Barnett, and Wallace, and only after hearings, although the defendants in these antiobstruction proceedings were not allowed to question the correctness of the findings and conclusions of the underlying injunction. But starting in about 1966, in order to cope with the faceless mob, the antiobstruction decree took the form of an ex parte temporary restraining order against anyone with actual notice of the decree. Federal Rule 65(d) was brushed aside on the theory that it was only a codification of, rather than a limitation upon, the courts' common law powers. The underlying injunction (the one now being protected by the antiobstruction injunction) was described as having, "in effect, adjudicated the rights of the entire community with respect to the racial controversy surrounding the school system." [19]   .   .   .

19. United States v. Hall, 472 F.2d 261,
      267 (5th Cir. 1972) . . .

B.   The Nature of the Injunctive Process

1.   The Power of Initiation

Our legal system is characterized by two different models for formally allocating the power of initiating a judicial process: one allocates it to officers, the other to the citizenry. With the officer model, the power to initiate a lawsuit is centralized in the sense that it is vested in a limited number of governmental officials—the district attorney or Secretary of Labor. The citizen's role is a modest one. He may file a complaint with the government official, and, under the new jurisprudence disfavoring administrative discretion, he may even utilize procedures to make certain that the government official responds to the complaint in a nonarbitrary manner. But the power of initiation is in the government official. In contrast, the citizen model contemplates a wider dispersion of the power of initiation. The exercise of the power may be conditioned on certain requirements, some procedural (e. g., filing a complaint), some substantive (e. g., stating a claim for which relief can be given), and others financial (e. g., paying filing fees); and yet access is not formally blocked by some government officer who decides whether or not to proceed. The power to initiate litigation is vested in the citizen.

The injunctive process, like the damage process and unlike the criminal one, conforms to the decentralized citizen model. The power of initiation is allocated to the citizenry. This classification of injunctive proceedings needs no qualification if one focuses on the issuance phase and if the concern is with the property injunction. Qualifications must be introduced, however, if one's attention shifts to the enforcement phase and if sufficient account is taken of developments with the labor injunction, developments that are renewed by the civil rights injunction. Before turning to these qualifications, I should emphasize that even with them the predominant motif in the initiation sphere remains one of decentralization, comparable to the damage system.

Assume that a citizen initiates an injunctive suit, an injunction is issued, and the defendant does the act prohibited by the injunction. The citizen-plaintiff can commence an enforcement proceeding designed to coerce compliance with the injunction (the defendant is jailed until assurances are received that he will refrain from the prohibited act). He can also seek to obtain compensation for the harm caused by the violation. With these two varieties of contempt—the first is conditional-order civil contempt and the second is compensatory-damage civil contempt—the power of initiation is allocated to the citizen. There is a third type of contempt proceeding—criminal contempt; here the sanction is a finite jail sentence or fine, and the allocative scheme is more complicated. The power to initiate is shared by court and citizen.

As a purely formal matter the power to initiate criminal contempt is allocated to the tribunal. It is important to recognize, however, that even on a formal level there is more decentralization in this allocative scheme than in that of the criminal system, where the power of initiation is vested in a district attorney or the Attorney General. For we are talking about an allocation to many trial judges. Each judge has considerable leeway. True, initiation in the criminal sphere may be delegated to an assistant district attorney, but in contrast to the assistant district attorney, each individual judge views himself as an autonomous actor. This view in part derives from the independence of the judge's commission and from the absence of the usual hierarchical controls by superiors (the appellate judges) over the incidents of the job, e. g., pay and promotion. It is reinforced by the knowledge that a decision *not* to proceed is generally unreviewable, and by the fact that even if it is reviewable, the standard of review is the lax abuse-of-discretion one.

Moreover, as a practical matter, the citizen plays a large role in criminal contempt, perhaps even larger than the one he plays in the criminal system (as complaining witness). For the court, more than the district attorney, is conceived of as a passive institution. On occasion a judge can transcend that mind set and abandon his passive role. Yet, in order to do so, the judge has to overcome inertia, doctrines requiring him to act on the basis of general rules (often an inappropriate basis for making prosecutorial decisions), and the absence of proper staff for this function (e. g., investigators). Thus, for the most part, the tribunal depends heavily on the initiatives of the individual citizen for bringing the violation to light, and often for the presentation of the case. As a consequence, the practical allocation—though not the formal allocation—may be thought to be to the citizenry.

The relationship between the injunction and the decentralized citizen model for initiation is purely contingent much like individuation. The officer model can be introduced even in the issuance phase. . . . [There is a] question . . . whether it is necessary to have congressional authorization for the Attorney General to commence injunctive suits on behalf of the United States. . . . But there is no doubt that with congressional authorization the officer model may be used. . . . The result is an amalgamation—officer and citizen models coexist.

Sometimes this coexistence is more formal than real. I have in mind the structural injunction, in which Executive participation is often decisive. The power of the Executive derives from the special dependency of court and citizen in the structural context. In part the dependency stems from special evidentiary problems in the issuance phase—more than a few isolated incidents are needed before a point can be made about structure, before a judge is likely to be persuaded that he should undertake so ambitious a project as reconstructing an ongoing institution. The dependency also stems from the intractable problems of policing performance in the structural context. It takes resources as significant as those of the Department of Justice to conduct regular inspections and to evaluate the periodic reports that are usually required of the defendant in the structural context.

Since the power of the Executive derives from a dependency, and that dependency derives from needs endemic to the remedial enterprise, the power is not easily curtailed. Decentralization is not easily restored. The special needs of the structural context may to some extent be met by greater reliance on institutional litigators (e. g., the NAACP Legal Defense Fund). In the Republican years (1969–77)—when the courts could no longer count on the Department of Justice—these private institutions achieved a new importance.

Even more striking has been the improvisation of the trial judges who sought to create new agencies (e. g., Human Rights Councils, special masters) to meet the special needs of structural reform; these agencies are charged with policing performance and making proposals for framing and modifying the decree .   .   .   .

2.   The Power of Decision

Under the classical view, there was little point in distinguishing between the issuance and enforcement phases of the injunctive process—in both, the decisional authority was the judge.   .   .   .   [R]ecent developments, some statutory, others constitutional, have complicated the picture.   Today a complete account of the allocative scheme governing the power to decide must once again distinguish between the enforcement and issuance phases.

In the issuance phase, where the court promulgates the standard of conduct, the decisional authority is the judge.   The uniqueness of this allocation is hard to gauge.   For the reparative injunction the uniqueness is undeniable; the correct comparison is with the damage action, where the primary decisional agency has been the jury.   Structural injunctions have no ready standard of comparison, and the uniqueness might be thought to derive as much from the nature of the enterprise as the decisional agency.   With the preventive injunction, commentators have stressed the uniqueness of the decisional agency because they have used a false standard of comparison.   The comparison has been made to the jury—the primary decisional agency in damage actions or criminal prosecutions.   I have maintained, however, that the preventive injunctions should be compared not with the damage award or judgment of conviction, but rather with the liability rule or criminal prohibition.   Viewed from that perspective, the decisional authority for preventive injunctions appears less unique.

Today the promulgation of criminal prohibitions is viewed as a legislative task.   But this was not true of most of our history.   Common law crimes prevailed in most of the states well into the twentieth century and under that regime the criminal prohibitions were promulgated by judges.   The common law system for federal crimes ended at an early point in our history, and in the federal domain statutes have predominated.   But the federal domain has never occupied a pivotal conceptual position in the American criminal law system; up to now, criminal law has largely been the work of the states.   In any event many of the federal statutes gave a centrality to judges, calling upon them to define amorphous concepts (e. g., a conspiracy to defraud the United States) in order to establish the standards of conduct.   The similarity of injunctions to liability rules is .   .   .   even clearer because judges have always been the primary authority for promulgating those standards.

In recent years the legislature has not only played an increasingly important role in setting liability rules and criminal prohibitions, but has also emerged in the injunctive process.   This is true even in the civil rights domain.   .   .   .   The legislative commands have been cast in the most general terms (e. g., do not discriminate on the basis of race), and the leeway of the judiciary in fashioning the substantive rules of conduct has been considerable. Under this institutional arrangement, which is not by any means confined to civil rights, but is found throughout our legal system, the judiciary is not the exclusive decisional agency. It is a coordinate agency, exercising power delegated to it by the legislature.

Looking at the injunctive process from the enforcement perspective, the proper standard of comparison is the jury. The question whether an individual violated a criminal prohibition or a liability rule is, as a formal matter, generally allocated to the jury, and that is the type of question to be resolved in the enforcement proceeding—did the defendant violate the injunction? Historically . . . that question was allocated to the judge. Two developments have modified that allocative scheme and have introduced the jury into the enforcement phase. One has been specific legislative enactments guaranteeing the trial by jury . . . . The other has been *Bloom v. Illinois* [31] (1968). There the Supreme Court held that criminal contempt was to be included in the constitutional category of "crimes" or "criminal proceedings," thereby guaranteeing trial by jury in all criminal contempts in which the punishment was not petty—imprisonment for more than six months.

I believe, then, that even in the enforcement phase allocation of the decisional authority is not as unique as it was previously: the jury has been introduced. Differences nevertheless persist, and they should be carefully delineated. (1) For purposes of applying the *Bloom* rule in the criminal context, the severity of the punishment is determined on the basis of the maximum the judge is *authorized* to impose. In the injunctive context, the determining factor for "severity" is punishment *actually* imposed. This rule in effect gives the judge the power to settle for an imprisonment of less than six months as a means of avoiding the vagaries of a jury trial and the attendant risk of nullification. (2) In the criminal system, all fines in excess of $500 are serious. In the injunctive process the seriousness of a fine is not determined on an absolute basis, but rather must reflect the financial resources of the contemnor. *Muniz v. Hoffman* (1975)[32] introduced this principle of progressivity; it held that $10,000 for a union was not "severe." (3) The jury has remained out of the enforcement phase when the sanction is civil contempt rather than criminal contempt, regardless of whether the civil contempt takes the form of a conditional order (jail until compliance) or a compensatory-damage award.

Having deployed this analytic distinction between the issuance and the enforcement phases, we must not let it obscure the underlying reality: the centrality of the judge in the injunctive process. The judge is the primary decisional agency: this is the theme that unites both phases. The legislature may play a role in the issuance phase, but it is essentially one of delegator of authority. The jury might play a role in the enforcement phase, but the judge has the power to insulate his decision from jury review by settling for civil contempt or for a criminal contempt sanction (e. g., five months in prison) that might be legally deemed "petty" when in truth it is severe. The injunctive process should then be seen as *concentrating* or *fusing* the decisional power in the judge; it represents the antithesis of separation of powers.

31. 391 U.S. 194 (1968).   32. 422 U.S. 454 (1975)

It should also be emphasized that this concentrated or fused power is *decentralized*. The power is not allocated to the judiciary as much as it is allocated to the multitude of individual trial judges. As *Brown II* teaches, they are our chancellors. Of course, the trial judges are related to one another through a judicial hierarchy, a system of appeals, but that hierarchy is not strong enough to produce centralization. For one thing, the trial judges —at least in the federal system—tend to view themselves as independent, autonomous decisional centers. . . . Doctrines of discretion, so pervasive in injunctive litigation, contribute to the decentralization of decision-making authority; they may be the functional equivalent of the leeway allowed the jury and result in the same degree of decentralization introduced by the jury.

The decisional authority in the injunctive process is not only concentrated and decentralized; it is also peculiarly personalized. The recipient of the injunctive power is a person, in contrast to other recipients of nondemocratically controlled power, such as the jury—a group that in effect requires facelessness for membership and that exists for one discrete event of limited duration (a trial). The issuance or enforcement of an injunction becomes an expression of a person, as much as it is an expression of an office, and represents a striking instance of the personification of the law—when we speak of the decisional authority in the injunctive process we often talk not of *the law* or even of *the court*, but of Judge Johnson or Judge Garrity.

Personification stems not only from the individual character of the recipient of power but also from the fact that the power is both concentrated and decentralized. These features are inherent to the injunction, and thus personification can be expected in all types of injunctions. With the structural injunction, however, there is an additional factor that makes the personification even more pronounced—the judge maintains a continuous relationship with the institution over a significant period of time. There is no easy, one-shot method of reconstructing an institution; a series of interventions are inevitable, for the defendants' performance must be evaluated, and new directions issued, time and time again. Structural injunctions entail a process of continuous interaction, and that has the effect of further projecting the person rather than the office.

3. The Hearing Itself

Two types of injunctions—preliminary injunctions and temporary restraining orders—do violence to the norms that generally govern judicial behavior. Preliminary injunctions may be issued after a truncated presentation of the facts and law. The ordinary opportunities for discovery may be curtailed. The rules of evidence (such as the hearsay rule) may be abandoned; heavy reliance is likely to be placed on documents rather than on live testimony to establish a factual point; the ordinary opportunities for cross-examination are curtailed; and often the judge must decide without adequate opportunity to study either the law or the facts. Temporary restraining orders are procedurally one degree—one significant degree—more irregular: they may be issued even without notice to the other side.

Interlocutory injunctions thus abrogate or severely modify the conception of a hearing that permeates the rest of the judicial system. This uniqueness should be acknowledged, and yet at the same time, one must avoid the danger of generalizing: preliminary injunctions and temporary restraining orders are very special legal instruments designed to preserve the status quo pending a judicial determination of the underlying controversy (in which the plaintiff may be seeking damages rather than an injunction). By definition interlocutory injunctions are of limited duration, and the violation of the usual procedural norms occurs in the name of preserving the opportunity to have a claim adjudicated. They are preservative of the right to have a claim heard by a court. The ordinary injunction, the final or permanent injunction, does not make the same kind of demand for expedition. The issuance of those injunctions must be preceded by a hearing and one that generally conforms to the standard procedural norms. Accordingly, when the focus is on final rather than interlocutory injunctions, the nature of the hearing preceding issuance turns out not to be a source of uniqueness for injunctions.

Turning to the enforcement phase, there are two aspects of the hearing that do introduce elements of uniqueness. The first is the rule of Walker v. City of Birmingham [38] which denies the criminal contemnor the right to contest the constitutional validity of the outstanding decree. To be more precise, *Walker* held that it was not denial of due process for a state to foreclose a constitutional challenge to a restraining order in a criminal contempt proceeding where the restraining order was not patently invalid and where the contemnor had not moved to dissolve the restraining order before disobeying. Of course, courts are free to adopt a contrary rule; *Walker* only held that they were not constitutionally obliged to. More radically, the *Walker* rule could be flatly repudiated as being inconsistent with a basic precept of our legal system—prohibiting the imposition of sanction without an adequate opportunity to contest the constitutional validity of the underlying rule of conduct. (It is ex parte restraining orders, we should remember, that *Walker* galvanizes.) But until the day comes that *Walker* is repudiated or made unavailing, we must recognize that the limitation on the defenses that could be tendered in a criminal contempt hearing is a source of uniqueness. *Walker* introduces a radical incompleteness to the criminal contempt hearing.

A second, and more subtle, distortion is introduced by the nature of the issue posed in an enforcement proceeding—whether the defendant violated the outstanding decree. In the issuance proceeding (for a final injunction) the hearing is structured on the contest model, one that is prevalent throughout all American procedure: two parties vying against one another, with the judge as an impartial umpire. Once we enter the enforcement phase, however, it is likely that the triadic structure will collapse, or at least get blurred, and realignment will occur, with the judge and plaintiff now aligned against the defendant.

In criminal contempt this realignment occurs at a formal level: the judge is invested with the power of initiation: he makes the prosecutorial decision.

---

38. 388 U.S. 307 (1967).

In all contempts it is likely to arise on a practical level, given the very nature of the charge—that the defendant defied the judge's decree. In the adjudication of such a charge, it is unrealistic to expect the judge to maintain his umpireal pose in all its purity; he may be indifferent to the question of the defendant's innocence, but he has more than the usual investment in obtaining compliance with the standard of conduct. It is *his* decree. And of course, to the extent that there is not one enforcement proceeding, but an endless series of them, as is typically the case in the structural context, the problem is compounded and the realignment all the more pronounced. The defendant has been found in noncompliance several times, and thus the judge is not likely to approach the question of the defendant's innocence unpredisposed; at the same time the judge's investment in the standard of conduct has increased through the very process of issuing a series of supplemental decrees. It is not surprising to learn that judges engaged in implementing structural decrees have special difficulty in maintaining their distance from the plaintiffs and the adjunct agencies used to implement the decree (e. g., amicus, special masters, the Department of Justice). The triadic structure is all but gone.

This realignment is not without parallels in either the damage or criminal system, once liability or guilt is established and the question is one of sanction. Moreover, this triadic structure can be restored to some degree by using different judges in the issuance and enforcement phases; in fact, this has been constitutionally mandated in direct contempts (where the disobedience occurs in the presence of the court, such as the disruption of a trial). The effectiveness of this proposal, admittedly, is limited by collegial ties and institutional identification, and, in any event, it may entail a loss of specialized knowledge (viewed as a form of expertise). When the same judge is retained for both issuance and enforcement phases, he can bring his familiarity with the terms and purposes of the decree to bear on the issues of enforcement, determining whether there was a violation and what the sanction should be. Ironically, this specialized knowledge is all the more important in the context of a structural decree, and yet that is the context in which the greatest strain is placed on the judge's umpireal posture—he must direct or manage the reconstruction of an ongoing social institution.

C. The Sanctioning System

. . . Both liability rules and criminal prohibitions operate through deterrence: both acknowledge the risk of disobedience to the underlying command or rule of conduct and threaten to impose sanctions upon the violator. The critical difference lies in the level of the sanctions. With a liability rule, the sanctions are set at the level of costs to the victim, thereby causing the perpetrator to internalize the costs of his action. With a criminal prohibition, the sanctions are set at a higher level, sufficient not only to bring the costs of the damage caused the victim to bear on the perpetrator, but to stop the proscribed conduct altogether. . . .

In terms of this framework, the sanctioning system of the classic injunction, the preventive injunction, can be seen to resemble that of the criminal prohibition. In issuing a preventive injunction the court promulgates a rule of conduct and also (implicitly) threatens to impose sanctions—jail or fine—for a violation; and what is more to the point, the level of the sanctions is not tied to the level of damages caused. The sanctions *might* be set at a level sufficient to discourage the individual defendant from ever violating this injunction again (the deterrence is specific in terms of the injunction and the individual—and hence I refer to it as double-specific deterrence), or to discourage this individual from violating any other injunction issued by the court (individual-specific deterrence); to discourage any other addressee of this injunction from violating it (injunction-specific deterrence), or to discourage anyone from violating any other injunction that might be issued by the court (general deterrence). In all these cases—all instances of criminal contempt—the aim is not simply to internalize the costs to the victim but to stop the prohibited act or to enhance the power of the court to stop acts that it might prohibit. Of course, as with criminal prohibitions, on occasion the ambition of the preventive injunction may go unfulfilled. To state the obvious, an injunction can be violated. The rule of Walker v. City of Birmingham—denying a criminal contemnor the right to contest the constitutional validity of the injunction—may strengthen the threat of punishment by enhancing the certainty of infliction, but it does not guarantee that the threat will be successful in preventing the proscribed conduct.

This account accurately captures the criminal contempt sanction; it is roughly analogous to the sanctioning system of the criminal law. But we must also consider civil contempt. What is so curious about civil contempt, and thus the injunctive sanctioning system, is that civil contempt consists of two quite distinct strands, each pushing in an opposite direction. One strand, the conditional order, pushes the injunction toward the criminal regime, and the other, the compensatory-damage award, pushes it toward the tort regime.

The most common form of civil contempt is the conditional order: the injunction prohibits the defendant from doing X (e. g., dumping waste in the river); the defendant does X once (e. g., he dumps one load in the river), and, as a form of civil contempt, the defendant is jailed until he stops doing X or until the court is thoroughly satisfied through promises, etc. that he will not do X. Though called civil, this form of contempt is a variant of double-specific deterrence: its ambition is to prevent this particular individual from violating this particular injunction again, and the court applies whatever pressure is necessary to bring about the result. The uniqueness of conditional-order contempt lies in its refinement. The conditional order is a more *calibrated* form of specific deterrence than is available in the criminal prosecution (or in criminal contempt): the judge need not rely on his estimate of the probable impact of a certain quantum of punishment on an individual's future behavior. After one violation, the burden is cast on the contemnor to assure the judge of the likelihood of his compliance in the future.

The other form of civil contempt, an order requiring the contemnor to pay the victim damages as compensation, makes the injunction seem more like a liability rule than like a criminal prohibition. But such a reductionism would be incorrect. The preventive injunction is like a mini-criminal statute, though individuated, decentralized, and judge-issued. As long as the criminal contempt sanction remains available (and it does even if civil contempt is in fact utilized, either in its compensatory or conditional guise), the injunction will be viewed as having more stringent ambitions than a liability rule. In gauging deterrent effect, what is crucial is the expected sanction (multiplied by the probability of imposition), and that must include the whole range of sanctions possible, high and low.

Of course, the formal availability of a strong (criminal-like) sanction may be impeached by a declaration of the judge that disobedience will be met only with an award of compensatory damages or by practices to a like effect. But such declarations are rare indeed, and the award of compensatory damages as the sole or exclusive sanction has not been sufficiently pervasive to alter the conception of an injunction as a criminal prohibition. We often decry the "softness" of the judicially imposed contempt sanction, but that complaint has its counterpart in the evaluation of the criminal system as well.

Our analysis thus far—suggesting that the injunction should be viewed as a mini-criminal statute—holds for the preventive injunction. The reparative injunction uses the same sanctioning system, yet the analogy with the criminal statute collapses because the reparative injunction seeks to undo the effects of a past wrong and thus is more like an in-kind damage judgment. Contempt in the reparative context is analogous to using criminal sanctions to collect damage judgments (rather than the seizure and sale of assets—an enforcement mechanism that is awkward [48] since we are dealing with compensation in kind).

With the structural injunction the analogy to the deterrence system of the criminal law is even less successful. For structural injunctions the sanctioning system primarily consists of supplemental decrees, not contempt, either civil or criminal. The usual scenario in the structural context is for the judge to issue a decree (perhaps embodying a plan formulated by the defendant), to be confronted with disobedience, and then not to inflict contempt but to grant a motion for supplemental relief. Then the cycle repeats itself. In each cycle of the supplemental relief process the remedial obligation is defined with greater and greater specificity. Ultimately, after many cycles of supplemental decrees, the ordinary contempt sanctions may become realistically available, but the point to emphasize is that it is *only* then—only at the end of a series—that the threat of contempt becomes credible.

The gradualism of the structural sanctioning system might be attributable to political considerations (such as a desire to "go slow" so as to build wide popular support for the remedial enterprise). In a similar vein, it might be said that it reflects an ambivalence toward the underlying decree. I suspect, however, that the gradualism has deeper roots—uncertainties in the goal to be achieved (e. g., what is a "unitary nonracial" school system) or shortcomings in our knowledge and ability to restructure ongoing institutions —and thus is less tractable. The gradualism stems from the very nature of the remedial enterprise.

---

48. Awkward though not inconceivable: with in-kind judgments the functional equivalent of seizure and sale would be some form of receivership, where a judicial officer would be put in charge of the defendant and would dispense the benefits according to the terms of the decree. . . .

The unique sanctioning system of structural decrees coalesces with another characteristic identified earlier—the fact that structural decrees are not preventive. A structural decree—one of the most distinctive legacies of the civil rights experience—should not be viewed as an instrument seeking to prevent a future wrong through deterrence. Rather, it should be viewed as a means of initiating a relationship between a court and a social institution.[49] The issuance of the injunction is not so much a coercive act, such as issuing a command, as it is a declaration that henceforth the court will *direct* or *manage* the reconstruction of the social institution, in order to bring it into conformity with the Constitution. The first ploy of any manager is to induce collaboration; authoritative directives are reserved as a last resort.

———

1.   This essay employs a comparative perspective and, as promised, tries to span both the civil and criminal domains. But has sufficient account been taken of the type of action which is undertaken by administrative agencies? Might not the structural injunction appear less unique if the standard of comparison were administrative rather than judicial action? See O. M. Fiss, The Civil Rights Injunction (1978) at 110 n.7.

2.   Even once the injunction is properly defined and the sources of uniqueness are identified, the normative task of setting the conditions for its use still remains. This issue is addressed in the second part of The Civil Rights Injunction. Traditional doctrines—such as the irreparable injury requirement and the prior restraint doctrine—are there evaluated and found to be without any justification. It is proposed, in contrast to the traditional remedial hierarchy, that the choice of remedy be made on a context-specific basis, with due regard to the technical advantages and the system of power-allocation implied in each remedy. Would this view collapse the distinction between substance and procedure? Properly so? See chapter 2 supra. See also Calabresi and Melamed, Property Rules, Liability Rules, and Inalienability: One View of the Cathedral, 85 Harv.L.Rev. 1089 (1972).

3.   On the structural similarity between damage judgment and criminal punishment, see, generally, Becker, Crime and Punishment: An Economic Approach, 76 J. Political Econ. 169 (1968). It should be noted that in recent years the damage judgment, like the injunction, has been transformed; perhaps the counterpart of the structural injunction is fluid class recovery in omnibus class actions. See Note, Developments in the Law—Class Actions, 89 Harv.L.Rev. 1318 (1976).

---

49. From this perspective, the structural injunction might profitably be compared to the parole and probation components of the criminal process.

Robert M. Cover and T. Alexander Aleinikoff, **Dialectical Federalism:**
Habeas Corpus and the Court*

. . .

A.   The Value of Equality and the Choice of Habeas Corpus

The dominant theme of the Warren Court's innovations in constitutional law was equality.   This theme was manifest in the Court's work
in areas such as race relations and reapportionment.   In the criminal procedure area, the primacy of equality is obvious in the many cases affording
indigent defendants the right to state-provided equipage for effective litigation, whether those cases relied on the equal protection clause, the right to
counsel, or the due process clause.

The value of equality is equally powerful if less explicit in cases like
Miranda v. Arizona,[9] which adopted exclusionary rules to compensate for
the courts' presumed inability to otherwise penetrate and control low visibility
police conduct that was believed (rightly or wrongly) to typify police relations with lower class and minority group suspects.   *Miranda* suggested that
the state was obligated to take affirmative measures to equalize the ability
of defendants to assert rights;   defendants had to be informed of their rights,
particularly the right to assistance of counsel.   There is language in the case
which suggests that the cumulative effects of background circumstances
should not be permitted to produce different outcomes in a criminal process.
Chief Justice Warren stressed the impact of private interrogation on an "indigent Mexican defendant" who "was a seriously disturbed individual with
pronounced sexual fantasies," and on "an indigent Los Angeles Negro who
had dropped out of school in the sixth grade."   Across-the-board standards
of police behavior were then enunciated in order to protect the weakest actors
in the criminal process.

In implementing constitutional innovations in reapportionment and
civil rights, the Warren Court was driven to a substantial expansion of federal equity power.   Such an eruption in the chancery was not wholly unfamiliar to students of the history of the labor injunction or of equity re-
ceiverships prior to the enactment of statutory provisions for corporate reorganization.   But the application of the injunction to governmental units
and for the purposes of the Fourteenth Amendment required both imagination and structural elaborations distinct from, if no more intrinsically complex than, those of the past.   The injunctive remedy that was grafted to
Brown v. Board of Education [13] and Reynolds v. Sims [14] was direct and coercive.   It was a remedy that called for conforming behavior from the persons
directly responsible for the alleged injury.   It threatened to use the "contempt" power as a sanction for resistance.   The injunction also, and less
visibly, provided a forum for negotiation of the terms of future conduct.
Defendants were directly involved as participants in "settling" the terms of
the decree.   The equity court provided a forum for compulsory bargaining,
often with rather stringent limitations upon the terms of the settlement.
The "state plan," which became an institutional feature in desegregation and

* *Source:* 86 Yale L.J. 1035, 1037–54,
1066–67 (1977). Cover is Professor of
Law, Yale University; and Aleinikoff
is a member of the New York bar.

9.   384 U.S. 436 (1966) . . . .

13.   347 U.S. 483 (1954).

14.   377 U.S. 533 (1964).

reapportionment decrees, was the means by which compulsory bargaining took place. In this way equity became the midwife of constitutional innovation. It was assisted by the Warren Court's expansion of liability rules for constitutional torts and by its resurrection of enforcement of criminal laws protecting civil rights.

Despite substantive thematic continuities between race relations and criminal justice, no such remedial steps followed the expansion of constitutional doctrine into the domain of state administration of the criminal law. It is remarkable that decisions as far reaching as Gideon v. Wainwright,[20] In re Gault,[21] Griffin v. Illinois,[22] Brady v. Maryland,[23] Duncan v. Louisiana,[24] Robinson v. California,[25] Miranda v. Arizona, and Mapp v. Ohio [27] would be announced with no remedial instrument whatsoever acting directly, coercively or prospectively upon the persons whose behavior was purportedly controlled. No injunction ordered that counsel be afforded felony defendants or juveniles. No "state plan" was demanded to establish an adequate system of providing counsel to meet *Gideon* or *Gault* standards. No decrees were issued against prosecutors or police to structure their behavior in future disclosure, arrest or search situations. Furthermore, civil liability rules were not developed for judges and prosecutors. Indeed, immunity doctrines were reaffirmed and perhaps enlarged.[28] Finally, federal court displacement of inadequate state institutions was eschewed by very narrow construction of the civil rights removal statute.[29] The absence of a remedy acting directly upon these personnel is startling, especially if we understand state courts and state law-enforcement officials to be the targets of this program for constitutional change. . . .

What the Warren Court did produce as remedial counterpart to the constitutionalization of criminal procedure was an expanded federal writ of habeas corpus. Fay v. Noia [42] and Townsend v. Sain [43] were decided on the same day as Gideon v. Wainwright and Douglas v. California.[45] The habeas corpus that *Fay* and *Townsend* created was to be the vehicle for the reform in which *Gideon* and *Douglas* were key elements. Habeas corpus (like appellate review) is a remedy that acts not upon those persons whose behavior is the target of reform but upon institutional outcomes. Policemen are not penalized for illegal searches; judges are not fined for failures to appoint counsel, to empanel proper juries or to exclude illegal evidence. Rather, the

20. 372 U.S. 335 (1963).

21. 387 U.S. 1 (1967).

22. 351 U.S. 12 (1956).

23. 373 U.S. 83 (1963) (prosecutor must divulge exculpatory evidence to state defendant).

24. 391 U.S. 145 (1968) (holding Sixth Amendment right to jury trial applicable to states).

25. 370 U.S. 660 (1962) (criminal punishment cannot be imposed for status of narcotics addiction).

27. 367 U.S. 643 (1961).

28. Pierson v. Ray, 386 U.S. 547 (1967), upheld the common law's grant of absolute immunity to judges in the context of a § 1983 action. . . .

29. See City of Greenwood v. Peacock, 384 U.S. 808 (1966) (construing 28 U.S.C. § 1443 (1970)); Georgia v. Rachel, 384 U.S. 780 (1966) (same).

42. 372 U.S. 391 (1963).

43. 372 U.S. 293 (1963).

45. 372 U.S. 353 (1963).

defendant's release is held out as the incentive to redo the process until it is done correctly.

The Court's expansion of habeas corpus ensured the active participation of federal courts in the protection and definition of constitutional rights. Justice Brennan made clear this underlying premise of *Fay* by recognizing "the manifest federal policy that federal constitutional rights of personal liberty shall not be denied without the fullest opportunity for plenary federal judicial review." This "manifest policy," favoring independent federal adjudications free from the impact of structural deficiencies in state criminal processes, employed redundancy as a safeguard. If two overlapping or redundant processes are to serve as a check on one another, they must be independent in the sense that malfunction of one does not affect the functioning of the other. *Fay* guaranteed such broad independent review in three ways. First, it reaffirmed the doctrine of Brown v. Allen[a] that state court adjudications could not estop federal court adjudication. Second, it held that defendants could not lose their opportunity to raise federal claims in federal court unless they had "deliberately bypassed" state procedures for adjudicating such claims. This high waiver standard[50] was reinforced by a third principle: waiver depended upon "the considered choice" of the defendant; the acts of counsel would not automatically bind the client . . . .

The choice of the indirect remedy of habeas corpus, however, sacrificed some of the momentum for reform of state criminal justice. While *Fay* . . . secured the federal tribunal's independence from the state courts and superiority in the sense of the independent power to block state institutional outcomes in a particular case, [it] did not and could not secure the power to impose upon the state courts the main elements of the Warren Court's program. The relief afforded by habeas corpus is almost always extended only to a single petitioner, and the form of relief is limited to release from confinement.[54] Thus, habeas corpus was not always the most appropriate remedy for furthering the Warren Court's goal of equality. The rules of Mapp v. Ohio and *Miranda,* for example, as enforced through broad habeas, were likely to be less effective in protecting disadvantaged groups from illegal police practices than a remedy akin to the civil rights injunction.[56] As we shall see below, state courts retained the power legitimately to resist

a. 344 U.S. 443 (1953) Ed. note.

50. For purposes of this article, the phrase "high waiver standard" will refer to a requirement that the court only find a waiver after it is convinced that the defendant's failure to raise a claim was knowing and voluntary. It is a standard which makes it relatively difficult to infer a waiver.

54. Since a successful petition for a writ of habeas corpus results only in discharge of the petitioner, the potential of federal habeas corpus to impose direct structural reform of state institutions is slight. Of course, the threat of release could induce structural change, and the remedy of release could be conditioned upon the state's failure to act in some designated fashion. However, the state always retains the option of ignoring the threat and suffering the consequences of a prisoner's discharge.

56. The relative inefficacy of habeas corpus relief is due to two factors: the small number of state convictions that are successfully challenged in federal court . . . and the likelihood of a low correlation between frustration of outcomes (reversal of convictions) and altered "front-line" police behavior . . . .

lower federal court determinations of what the Constitution required of the state criminal courts. Such resistance would be purchased at the price of some released petitioners and many retrials, but a state court willing to pay such a price remained in a relatively independent position under *Fay*.

A strategy of redundancy, although limited by these factors, had correlative advantages. First, the Court avoided the Russian Winter of direct enforcement of an unpopular constitutional innovation. By 1963 the Court had faced massive resistance to Brown v. Board of Education through much of the South, and was aware how difficult the remedial process could become. Second, habeas corpus and the redundancy it afforded seemed to meet the principal needs and demands of those most directly affected by constitutional deficiencies in the criminal process: defendants and prisoners wanted reversals of convictions and release, not institutional reform. Appellate review and habeas corpus were the traditional and natural remedies.

Fay's strategy of redundancy also had a significant impact on the creation and reliability of protection of constitutional rights. Reliability of protection was, in fact, a major reason for the Warren Court's choice of habeas corpus: it increased the probability that constitutional rights would not be wrongfully denied. The impact upon the creation of rights was perhaps an unforeseen but potentially more profound development. *Fay* permitted and encouraged a dialogue between state and federal courts that helped define and evolve constitutional rights.

B. Redundancy and Constitutional Rights

1. *Reliability*

Defenders of a broad habeas corpus jurisdiction have often pointed to the special competence and zeal that federal judges possess in protection of federal constitutional rights. Their concern is nurtured by institutional factors. As Professor Abraham Sofaer argued long ago in a brilliant student note, the habeas corpus proceeding as contemplated by *Fay* encourages successful vindication of federal rights by isolating them from other elements in the criminal process and making them the special concern of a special forum.[59]

But even without the special awareness and position of federal judges, redundancy fosters greater certainty that constitutional rights will not be erroneously denied. A simple exercise will establish that the probability of two independent courts both acquiescing in upholding a conviction with a given constitutional error is the product of the respective probabilities of error of the two courts. If each court has a probability of this sort of error of .1, then the probability of such an error surviving the double scrutiny, given a unanimity decision rule, is .01—a measurable gain in certainty. This rise in certainty that a conviction will not stand where there has been an erroneous adjudication of a constitutional right, however, entails a corresponding increase in the probability that there will be an erroneous failure to convict. That is, the probability that one of two courts will make an er-

---

59. Sofaer, Federal Habeas Corpus for State Prisoners: The Isolation Prin-   ciple, 39 N.Y.U.L.Rev. 78 (1964)
      . . . .

roneous recognition of a constitutional right is greater than the probability that one court acting alone will do so.   Redundancy—as limited to reconsideration of defendants' claims of error—therefore establishes a biased decision rule against convictions with erroneous adjudications of constitutional rights.   Some would argue against such a rule.   But the mandate of *Fay* was clear: it was the deprivation of constitutional rights that was to be avoided.   .   .   .

Redundancy could also spark a reduction of constitutional errors on the part of the states.   If state courts knew that errors would be corrected by a federal court requiring a retrial, they might be more solicitous toward claims brought before them.   Moreover, as Justice Brennan has argued in cases and articles, the existence and exercise of federal habeas corpus jurisdiction may stimulate the states to develop and improve procedures for the adjudication and protection of constitutional rights.

2. *Dialectical Federalism*

The biased decision rule of *Fay* in favor of   .   .   .   constitutional rights was no doubt intended by the Court.   But the Court was probably less conscious that the choice of habeas corpus also was consistent with a special model of federalism and the establishment of a unique dynamics, a dialectic between state and federal courts.   This dialectic is an important yet unrecognized device for translating those values which the Court has identified as significant into specific constitutional rights.

a. *Rights and Remedial Strategies*

Discussions of the appropriate role of federal law in altering state institutions often proceed little beyond the staking out of initial positions. Two paradigms are developed and defended: a model of hierarchical imposition of federally determined values; and a model of fragmentation, justifying value choices by the states.   Political and prudential factors may be conceded as qualifications of either pure model, but we have no affirmative image of a middle ground.

The classic paradigm of hierarchical imposition entails: (a) federal (Supreme Court) articulation of a value; (b) federal court definition of the rights which flow from that value; and (c) direct and coercive federal court imposition of the rights on state personnel and institutions.   Under this model, states are left little or no room to influence the choice or shape of developing rights.   Alternatively, the fragmentation model posits fifty-one social laboratories, each freely pursuing its own definition of values.   States retain the major role in evolving rights subject only to some vague limits on arbitrariness and irrationality.[64]   The theory does not specify a method by which one laboratory's results are chosen over another's.

---

64. This role for the states can be fostered by at least two Supreme Court strategies.   The Court may decide that the Constitution simply does not speak on a particular issue.   For example, it can hold that the Constitution creates no protected interest in reputation, and that, therefore, the states may choose to protect the interest as they see fit.   .   .   .   Or, the Court may find a constitutional right implicated by certain state actions, but decide that the states are to be trusted to implement constitutional requirements.   .   .   .

Both paradigms create a sense that conflict and indeterminacy are dysfunctional. At the hierarchical end of the spectrum such conflict is called resistance or interposition and is a violation of Article VI. At the fragmentation end, it is called federal interference with states' rights. Under both theories one system has exclusive or preeminent voice as to the value to be chosen or imposed. Such a political model suffers from the lawyer's disease of sovereignty.

A third model of federal-state interaction is possible, premised upon conflict and indeterminacy Values become rights when lawyers fight about their implications. This model obtains whenever jurisdictional rules link state and federal tribunals and create areas of overlap in which neither system can claim total sovereignty. Conflicts will arise where values identified by the Supreme Court are interpreted differently by the two court systems. Where the Supreme Court refuses to impose a solution, an open-ended dialogue can ensue. The "dialectical federalism" that emerges becomes the driving force for the articulation of rights.

A federal-state dialogue can proceed with varying levels of attentiveness, depending on the linkage of the two systems. For example, in situations of concurrent jurisdiction, a competition for judicial business may exist. This may lead to the elaboration of legal doctrine, as courts vie for prestige or influence with an eye to the other system's developments. The dialogue becomes most intense when state and federal court systems both have input into the resolution of a single dispute. Thus, the availability of Supreme Court review of state court adjudications of federal claims has an impact on state decisions. Similarly, state adjudications affect federal decisions through the abstention doctrine.[67]

Perhaps the most dramatic example of dual input is habeas corpus. Given the unanimity rule for a valid conviction, the habeas relationship demands mutual respect and awareness. Habeas corpus has often served to dramatize conflicting values. In the pre-Civil War era, habeas corpus served as a crucible for the abolitionist-pro-slavery debate. Similarly, federal habeas corpus has functioned throughout our history as a mechanism for arguing over notions of fundamental fairness. But it is Brown v. Allen, Fay v. Noia and Townsend v. Sain that openly embrace a dialectical approach to programmatic reform of the criminal process. These cases, by ensuring broader overlap of state and federal court determinations, engage these tribunals in an exploration of constitutional principles. For such jurisdictional ties to produce a *dialogue* requires satisfaction of two preconditions: that there be no foreordained answers to the relevant questions, and that there be two distinct voices.

Thus, the dialogue occurs only where the Supreme Court has not spoken with specificity. There exists an obligation on the part of the lower court judges not only to obey a writ of the Supreme Court when it runs to them, but to defer to the words of the Court when those words apply to the case

---

67. The abstention doctrine, deriving from Railroad Comm'n v. Pullman Co., 312 U.S. 496 (1941), holds that federal courts should refuse to render a judgment on the constitutionality of a state statute if state court construction of the statute could obviate the need for a federal determination . . . .

before them.   If Cohens v. Virginia [70] decided the first point firmly and forever, the second was as firmly announced in Cooper v. Aaron.[71]   Cooper v. Aaron, which reads into every official's oath of office an obligation to obey in good faith the constitutional doctrine of the Supreme Court, means that once the Supreme Court has spoken, it has exhausted the space for constitutional colloquy.   But where the Court has not spoken, or has spoken so broadly that its statements do not answer particular questions, there is much room for federal-state dialogue.   Competing principles and policies may be presented to a host of different tribunals each of which is independently capable of reaching a solution.   Until Cooper v. Aaron comes into play, judges may act, in good faith, according to their preferred constitutional theory without risk of violating their obligations under Article VI.   And state and federal judges act on a level of constitutional equality: the constitutional decisions of inferior federal courts are not binding on state courts; Cooper v. Aaron applies only to the high Court's pronouncements.

The absence of, or lacunae between Supreme Court opinions, then, permits state and federal courts to speak from their own perspectives.   A dialogue is created when the two systems in fact represent different viewpoints.   This has generally been the case with the criminal law, where federal and state courts have tended to adopt divergent positions.   We shall call these two positions "utopian" and "pragmatic" constitutionalism, respectively . . . .

The different institutional roles that state and federal courts play make it likely that within each court system one tendency will dominate.   State courts are likely to hold up the pragmatic end of the dialogue about our system of mass criminal justice.   State courts are employed at the firing line. They have a major role in determining which cases will be processed, how many will be processed at what rate of speed, what resources will be expended on these cases, by what procedures cases will be decided, and, of course, what the decision will be.   These tasks entail coordination of independent or quasi-independent elements in the criminal justice system—prosecutors, defense counsel, prison and probation officials, police.   They also involve sizeable managerial problems with respect to the courts themselves and their own personnel.   Finally, they involve the difficulties of decisions about guilt, innocence, and disposition.   The constraints of "constitutional rights" permeate the ways in which these tasks may permissibly be carried out. Clearly, the simultaneous pursuit of so many objectives is facilitated if constraints, which hinder efficient assembly-line processes, are eliminated or read loosely.   In short, given the quite difficult and legitimate objectives of the state court systems, one would hardly expect them to have a utopian perspective on constitutional rights relevant to the criminal process.

To a large extent, the utopian perspective has characterized the efforts of lower federal courts.   Because of the definition of their jurisdiction, these courts play a significant role in the creation of a constitutional common law of criminal procedure.   Since they can overturn state convictions only on constitutional grounds, they necessarily speak the language of constitutional imperatives.   Thus the expansion of federal habeas after Fay v. Noia has meant more than giving defendants another chance to cart out their claims.

70. 19 U.S. (6 Wheat.) 264 (1821).   **71.** 358 U.S. 1 (1958).

It has enlarged the federal-state dialogue by giving rise to thousands of claims articulated in constitutional terms and assessed by state courts and the inferior federal tribunals.

There are several reasons why federal courts tend to support the utopian end of the dialogue. The federal courts are not themselves as tied to the practical realities of administration of the criminal law as are the state courts. Although the increased activity of the federal criminal law has somewhat obscured this distinction, it is still broadly true. Furthermore, the jurisdiction of the federal court is invoked by claims about the constitutionality of the state process. The practical aspects of administration are at most a backdrop; the constitutional inquiry is in bold relief. The federal court's inquiry also obscures the defendant's conduct. The guilt, innocence, or dangerousness of the defendant can rarely be the object of focused inquiry in federal court. Whether desirable or not, this fact makes it likely that the federal court will be less systematic in construing claims of deprivation of constitutional rights in light of the character of the defendant.

b. *The Habeas Corpus Dialogue*

What then are the consequences of such contrary tendencies existing simultaneously in two sets of tribunals both of which have a major part in the criminal process? The structure of habeas corpus jurisdiction determines the consequences. First, no conviction can stand unless both tribunals concur, provided that the federal forum is invoked. This unanimity rule puts the federal courts in an initially strong position. Their decisions may release the particular petitioner and threaten to release other prisoners similarly situated in the state process. The influence of a federal habeas decision may cross state boundaries as well. Since a decision to release a state prisoner is by definition a constitutional pronouncement, a utopian decision anywhere in the system—particularly by a circuit court—must be considered seriously by a state court adopting a pragmatic approach. Even if the utopian decision is not in the circuit in which the state is located, it constitutes a perilous possibility as a precedent unless the home circuit has recently rejected such a rule. The federal system need not be composed solely of utopian courts, therefore, to exert a utopian tug on state courts. It is this fact that distinguishes utopian decisions from law review articles.

The state courts, however, are not helpless before federal power. First, the unanimity rule is seriously mitigated in its practical effect by the fact that most state convictions never come before federal courts. Furthermore, the sequential nature of the proceedings means that the federal courts will be confronted with the state system's adjudication of the facts, one that federal courts are neither likely nor permitted to treat lightly. The sequential nature also permits the state to demonstrate the practical constraints under which it operates; such pragmatic briefs may elicit acquiescence from the reviewing federal court.

State courts may also openly resist federal utopian decisions. Clearly, state courts are not bound to respect the doctrinal statements of the inferior federal tribunals insofar as they understand those statements not to be compelled by the Supreme Court. As the Florida Supreme Court has recently noted: "It is axiomatic that a decision of a federal trial court, while persuasive if well-reasoned, is not by any means binding on the courts of a State." [82] This means that the last word which the federal court has as to the continued restraint of a petitioner is not the last word with respect to the future orientation of the state court system that generated the case. Such resistance may frustrate federal utopian purposes, particularly if one understands the objective of a utopian decision to be institutional reform—i. e., if the aim of the utopian court is not simply or mainly the release of a given petitioner, but a general change in the practices of a court. Since the federal court lacks administrative supervisory power over the state courts, and since the political constituencies of the two courts are largely distinct, the reformative strategy of the utopian court can be effectively blocked by the state court's non-acceptance of a new constitutional rule. While the state court pays a price in released prisoners, it can exact a price from the federal court by frustrating that court's objectives in the majority of cases which will never eventuate in a petition for federal habeas corpus. Thus, there are incentives for each court system to acknowledge and, if possible, satisfy some of the more reasonable demands of the other. With this approximate equality of power, or at least mutual ability to frustrate, we may expect some movement from original starting points. Even if there is no movement, the elaboration of the respective positions may, over time, inform the Supreme Court with textured experience as well as opposing arguments. The Supreme Court is not, however, simply choosing between competing lower court orientations. The high Court may itself be oriented to either a pragmatic or utopian perspective on the criminal law. Its orientation will constitute part of a larger dialectic between law and politics which has been a primary subject of constitutional scholarship . . . .

The dialogue itself, regardless of its effect on the development of constitutional doctrine, may be justified because it articulates a basic tension in our society's view of the criminal process. We are deeply troubled by the implications of constitutional values in the criminal law. The parallel forum in the criminal law permits society to enact, ritualize, project its own ambivalence in jurisdictional terms. The dialectical federalism of Fay v. Noia permits us both to act as if we were not committed to these uncertain constitutional values and to cherish them as indispensable. We try on both garments. And it is surprising how often both fit—how clearly each image of the process makes perfect sense so long as we suppress the other . . . . But just as both waves and particles are complementary, necessary models to adequately account for the behavior of light, so utopian and pragmatic perspectives on the criminal process may both be indispensable to a complete account of our ambivalent and contradictory social selves. If we are in such a state, it may be as foolish to give up one of our "redundant" forums as it would be for the physicist to forgo either his wave or his particle model. Thus the Warren Court's movement to habeas corpus may have been due to its inability to settle us or itself into an unambiguous commitment to equality in the criminal law . . . .

82. Bradshaw v. State, 286 So.2d 4, 6 (Fla.1973), cert. denied 417 U.S. 919 (1974) . . . .

1.   How would a desire to maintain a dialogue shape the character and quality of the judicial action? For example, is it true that "once the Supreme Court has spoken, it has exhausted the space for constitutional colloquy"? How could a dialogue proceed within a hierarchical structure when the commands are specific?

2.   To what extent could the dialectical model be generalized? Suppose the Warren Court had employed an alternative remedial strategy and had placed weight on injunctions and damages rather than habeas corpus as the primary instruments for realizing the ideal of equality in the criminal process. Could that interaction still be understood in terms of a dialectic? Could the relationships between courts and other adjudicatory agencies, such as arbitrators and administrative agencies, be understood in those terms? How about the relationship between courts and the political process? See generally, A. Bickel, The Least Dangerous Branch: The Supreme Court at the Bar of Politics (1962), portions of which appear at the end of this chapter.

SECTION B.   THE LATENT FUNCTION OF JUDICIAL ACTION

The sociology of knowledge, described in the selection from Robert Merton in Chapter 6, teaches that we should not take beliefs or knowledge at their face value, but rather should understand them as an expression of an underlying set of social forces.   In this section we pursue that insight.   We apply it not to the knowledge of the decisionmaker, nor to the information he receives, but rather to the output of the decisional process: his judgment. How might judicial action be understood, we ask, if it is not to be taken at its face value?

The essays that follow seek an answer to that question; but they do not express a single unified conception of the latent function.   To the contrary, the particular essays were chosen because they define that function in divergent ways, they express our doubt as to the desirability or usefulness of striving for a single, unified conception of the latent function.   Martha Minow's essay on the judgment of Solomon, a fresh interpretation of probably the most famous of all judicial decisions, casts the function in essentially personal terms: the judgment of Solomon—to divide the child—should be understood as a test, itself a trial, which transforms the participants.   Douglas Hay, on the other hand, sees the function in essentially social terms: the judicial decisions of eighteenth-century England, which at first seem inconsistent with the manifest severity of the Black Act and the unwillingness of Parliament to repeal these laws, can be interpreted as furthering the broader aims of the ruling class—the maintenance of their authority.

Each of these essays should be evaluated on its own merits.   It is also important, however, to locate the premises that lead the authors in divergent directions, and also to ask whether the latent meaning of judicial action might be found in still other domains.   These essays are examples of a methodology, of an approach toward understanding the actions of adjudicators.   They are not meant to exhaust that methodology, but rather to reveal its possibilities —to suggest a sociology of judicial action.

Martha L. Minow, **The Judgment of Solomon and the Experience of Justice***

And the wise king judged the two women before him. Each had a child newly born, but one child had died. Each woman claimed the living child as her own. And the king said,

"Fetch me a sword."

And they brought him a sword. And the king said,

"Divide the living child in two,
and give half to the one,
and half to the other."

Then spoke the woman whose the living child was, for her heart yearned upon her son, and she said, "Oh, my lord, give her the living child and in no wise slay it." But the other said, "It shall be neither mine nor thine; divide it." Then the king answered and said,

"Give her the living child,
and in no wise slay it;
she is the mother of the child."

And all Israel heard of the judgment which the king had judged; and they feared the king; for they saw that the wisdom of God was in him, to do justice.

—Kings 4:16–28

I

What "wisdom of God" did the people see in Solomon? Perhaps it was the insight that allowed him to identify the "true" mother from the pretender. The pretender exposed by Solomon clung to the trappings of the role without being able to mimic the response of the "true mother" to the test of the sword.

Solomon's decision seems to resemble his trick before the Queen of Sheba. The Queen teased Solomon: she had heard he was the wisest of all judges; but could he distinguish between a garland of real flowers and an artificial creation designed to appear identical to the original? Indeed, the two garlands appeared to have no differentiating features, the false one was so marvelous. Solomon ordered that a window be opened. A bee entered through the window, flew directly to one of the garlands, and settled on it. "That is the garland of real flowers," announced Solomon. And the Queen of Sheba asked that she be allowed to sit at his feet and learn his wisdom.

Introducing the bee allowed Solomon to bypass a wager on one of the garlands. Raising the sword permitted him to avoid weighing the women's identical claims to the child. The surprise in both stories then is not that Solomon made the right decision. The surprise is that he obtained evidence which had not previously been imagined, and thereby acquired a reliable picture of the truth. In both instances, the new information seemed so close-

* *Source:* Previously unpublished paper
written by a 1979 graduate of the Yale
Law School.

ly linked to the question posed, that all who witnessed the presentation of evidence would agree with the judge's decision. What a relief must the judge have felt: he unearthed information and avoided a perilous prediction; he formed a decisive judgment on a close question and still acted within the ambit of the community's own assumptions.

Yet Solomon's wisdom in raising the sword passed beyond mere fact-finding about an enduring state of affairs. Solomon's sword challenged the women to think about the issues in a new way; it challenged them to consider the ultimate welfare of the child. In this way, the test of Solomon's sword is different from the test of the bee. Although in both instances Solomon looked for a sign to reveal the true alternative, his sword provoked a new response. He did not employ a trick or signal to illuminate the constant reality; his sword test stirred one woman to change. She saw the issue differently when the sword was poised above the child's very life. She dropped her claim and withdrew from the competition to win the child because her understanding of the situation changed, not because she stayed the same. She withdrew because she realized that winning was not all.

The test of the bee disclosed an essential reality which had existed and which would always exist. It solved a contest of identities. The "true mother," however, experienced a new insight. She grew in her response to the king. Solomon was wise and fearsome because he saw this. Indeed, he was wise and fearsome because he created the opportunity for this to happen.

II

The two women argued their claims before the judge: "This is my child." "No, mine." Solomon rejected any inquiry into these claims of right. He disposed of their arguments and pleas; he demanded that they submit to his authority. He demanded that they believe in his power. In the court of law, he brought forth his sword to threaten the life of the child.

The women had no advocates to speak their case to this judge. They themselves did not know what would convince Solomon, and they had to persuade him to their own views about the custody of the child—and now to their views about the child's life.

Each woman responded to Solomon's sword with a rule from within her own experience and hopes. Each urged a rule upon the judge to guide his decision. "Above all, life," said one. The other said, "No, above all, equal treatment, even equal suffering." The first said, "Better one should win and not me, and there be life." The second said, "No, better none should win." They trembled because they themselves had not known that this was how they felt.

With no shield against the king's sword, no protection against his challenge to their thinking, the women waited for his decision. They waited to submit to his decision, which could well be to slay the child.

In fact, both women had to believe that the judge could, and would, divide the living child. The woman who changed, the one who urged life for the child, she had to believe that the king was capable of performing this horrible act. If only for an instant, she had to imagine the death of the child. At that moment, she learned for herself the order of concerns for the child: first, life. Only if life were guaranteed could she persist in her exclusive claim to the child. Until then, she must seek the child's life, apart from her own claim.

The other woman too must have believed that the king would slay the child. She thought she might use the threatened force to inflict harm on another, and thereby spread her sorrow. If she could not win, no one should win. So to express her resentment of the loss, she must have believed in the judge's will to do what he threatened to do.

The judge who had refused to weigh their initial claims to the child now heard the women. He heard the rules of law they offered, yet that was not what he weighed. He never said, "Yes, to choose life is better than to choose equal treatment." He never referred to other cases or rules. He who had rejected their facts, and who had threatened to slay the child, he looked not at law but at what the claimants revealed about themselves. He challenged them to relinquish their original claims and to become vulnerable before him.

In this personal encounter between the judge and the women, no special talisman of truth, no external authority, no predetermined boundaries guided the judge. Instead, the impress of personality, vital to an extended family and to the texture of tribal ties, marked the judge's conduct. Solomon himself introduced something new to the dispute. It was he who posed a challenge and looked to see who would take a step beyond the dispute as first presented. It was he who looked for the one who would move from a personal stake to a stake in life, and above all else, a commitment to the child.

Because he did not simply look for a sign of the true or the innocent, because he did not accept the evidence initially brought by the parties, this judge was beyond the bounds of the rules which restrained the people and the rules which the people used to judge one another. A judge who posed a new problem for the contestants could not be judged by the terms of the law as they knew it. A judge who could raise a sword in the courtroom and pose an unthinkable alternative was beyond the people and the law which governed them.

The judge answered the woman who pried herself from the child to urge the life of the baby under the other woman's care. The judge did not praise her, nor did he threaten her. He answered, he took part. He heard, he saw, and then he declared what should be done.

And as soon as he did, the people knew he was right. The women knew he was right. The test he used was not a magic test employed to catch a glint of truth from some other world. It was not a blood test, not a bee test, not a test of constancy. He did not use a trick to uncover what always was—he did not tell them to try to win the wrong way and then find who could not force herself to do that wrong. He asked the women to respond to the possible destruction of the thing they most wanted. Then all witnesses could discern who deserved the reward and the responsibility of caring for the life of the child.

Thus, when the people heard the king's judgment and were afraid, it was not because he had decided wrongly or had surprised them with the conclusion he drew from the evidence. He had not drawn out a sign of the constant truth which usually evades human comprehension. The people did not see in his judgment the preknowledge or omniscience of God. No, the people were afraid because they saw the wisdom of God to do justice—to demand more than the pleadings, more than the facts, more even than a choice of rules. They saw the judge who tested the people, who challenged them and shared the challenge with them. They saw the judge who turned the court into a stage on which the people could grow.

III

Perhaps because contemporary trial judges consider child custody determinations the most agonizing kind of decision they are required to make, the swift and sure judgment of Solomon commands persistent awe. Some legal observers explicitly express their yearning to grasp Solomon's sword. Some even yearn to "sharpen it" because Solomon's sword is not fine enough to parse the competing considerations in child custody suits brought today.

Others try to formulate verbal tests or rules which embody Solomon's incisive determination. One judge concluded that when a child's interests seem imperiled by a particular parent's demand for custody, "the parent's insistence on his right to custody despite the harm that would clearly result to his child will itself be evidence of his unfitness." A psychiatrist suggested as a rule that courts should not divide a child's loyalties by ordering the adverse parties to share custody of the child. These rules, at best, are only partial expressions of Solomon's test. They draw on Solomon's focus on the child, not on the opportunity he gave for the parents to grow.

Even if Solomon's test were more fully articulated in a rule, its very expression in rule form would not satisfy the needs of the parties in these contested suits. Once the rule is publicized, it could no longer serve to reveal truth or provoke change. Further, a rule by its very nature cannot accord the individual attention required. We lack consensus on what is good parenting, much less a shared sense about which of competing claimants deserves a child. We lack reliable information about the interests of children, must less solid evidence on what alternatives serve those interests. Precisely because we know so little in general, society owes at least individual attention in considering the contested placement of a child. The judging process should reflect the significance of the decision in the lives of the individuals, even if the decision is made with less certainty than Solomon's judgment. The bang of a gavel aimed specifically at the parties may be necessary for them to obey a decision made by an outsider. Custody disputes are bitterly contested; they are frequently indeterminate; they are sometimes destructive to the child. No wonder Solomon's stroke, with its certitude and its power to provoke change, inspires continuing awe. Solomon's test rested on a simple ploy: he threatened to destroy what was most precious to the women. This is the tactic of the terrorist, here practiced by the wisest king and judge. Because of his unique position, because of his wisdom, Solomon's use of power was not challenged. But is this an approach which should be generalized in the resolution of disputes?

Douglas Hay, **Property, Authority and the Criminal Law** *

The rulers of eighteenth-century England cherished the death sentence. The oratory we remember now is the parliamentary speech, the Roman periods of Fox or Burke, that stirred the gentry and the merchants. But outside Parliament were the labouring poor, and twice a year, in most counties in England, the scarlet-robed judge of assize put the black cap of death on top of his full-bottomed wig to expound the law of the propertied, and to execute their will. "Methinks I see him," wrote Martin Madan in 1785, "with a countenance of solemn sorrow, adjusting the cap of judgement on his head . . . . His Lordship then, deeply affected by the melancholy part of his office, which he is now about to fulfill, embraces this golden opportunity to do most exemplary good—He addresses, in the most pathetic terms, the consciences of the trembling criminals . . . shows them how just and necessary it is, that there should be laws to remove out of society those, who instead of contributing their honest industry to the public good and welfare, have exerted every art, that the blackest villainy can suggest, to destroy both . . . He then vindicates the *mercy*, as well as the *severity* of the law, in making such examples, as shall not only protect the innocent from outrage and violence, but also deter others from bringing themselves to the same fatal and ignominious end. . . . He acquaints them with the certainty of speedy death, and consequently with the necessity of speedy repentance— and on this theme he may so deliver himself, as not only to melt the wretches at the bar into contrition, but the whole auditory into the deepest concern— tears express their feelings—and many of the most thoughtless among them may, for the rest of their lives, be preserved from thinking lightly of the first steps to vice, which they now see will lead them to destruction. The dreadful sentence is now pronounced—every heart shakes with terror—the almost fainting criminals are taken from the bar—the crowd retires—each to his several home, and carries the mournful story to his friends and neighbours;—the day of execution arrives—the wretches are led forth to suffer, and exhibit a spectacle to the beholders, too aweful and solemn for description.[1]"

This was the climactic moment in a system of criminal law based on *terror* . . . . The most recent account suggests that the number of capital statutes grew from about 50 to over 200 between the years 1688 and 1820. Almost all of them concerned offences against property. . . .

Yet two great questions hang over this remarkable code. The first concerns the actual number of executions. The available evidence suggests that, compared to some earlier periods, the eighteenth-century criminal law claimed few lives. At the beginning of the seventeenth century, for example, it appears that London and Middlesex saw four times as many executions as 150 years later. Equally interesting is the fact that in spite of the growth in trade and population, the increasing number of convictions for theft, and the continual creation of new capital statutes throughout the eighteenth

* *Source:* E. P. Thompson, ed., Albion's Fatal Tree (1975), Chapter 1. Professor of History, Memorial University of Newfoundland.

1. Martin Madan, Thoughts on Executive Justice with Respect to our Criminal Laws, particularly on the Circuit, 1785, pp. 26–30.

century, the number of executions for offences against property remained relatively stable, especially after 1750. The numbers of executions did not increase to match the number of convictions because of the increasing use of the royal pardon, by which transportation could be substituted for hanging, on the recommendation of the judges. . . . [It has been argued] that Parliament intended their legislation to be strictly enforced, and that the judges increasingly vitiated that intention by extending pardons freely. But this is an unsatisfactory conclusion. A conflict of such magnitude between Parliament and the judiciary would have disrupted eighteenth-century politics, and nothing of the sort happened. . . .

This first problem is related to a second one. Most historians and many contemporaries argued that the policy of terror was not working. More of those sentenced to death were pardoned than were hanged . . . . The critics of the law argued that the gibbets and corpses paradoxically weakened the enforcement of the law: rather than terrifying criminals, the death penalty terrified prosecutors and juries, who feared committing judicial murder on the capital statutes. Sir Samuel Romilly and other reformers led a long and intelligent campaign for the repeal of some laws, arguing from statistics that convictions would become more numerous once that fear was removed. The reformers also used the arguments of Beccaria, who suggested in 1764 that gross and capricious terror should be replaced by a fixed and graduated scale of more lenient but more certain punishments. . . . Yet Parliament resisted all reform. Not one capital statute was repealed until 1808, and real progress had to wait until the 1820s and 1830s.

Why the contradiction? If property was so important, and reform of the criminal law would help to protect it, why did gentlemen not embrace reform? . . . Two immediate explanations are commonly given. The gentry undoubtedly refused to create a regular police force, a necessary part of the Beccarian plan. Moreover, the lack of secondary punishments, and the unsatisfactory nature of those in use, such as transportation, made it seem desirable to keep the death penalty for the incorrigible rogue. Neither fact, however, explains why there was such unbending opposition to the repeal of even those capital statutes that were seldom used. This determination of Parliament to retain all the capital statutes, even when obsolete, and to continue to create new ones, even when they were stillborn, suggests that the explanation for the failure of reform lies deeper in the mental and social structure of eighteenth-century England. . . . For it is difficult to believe that Parliament would have been so complacently conservative about the unreformed law unless they were convinced that it was serving their interests . . . . .

Timothey Nourse antedated Beccaria and Romilly by a good half-century, but he expressed an enduring belief of the gentry when he declared that many of the common people were "very rough and savage in their Dispositions, being of levelling Principles, and refractory to Government, insolent and tumultuous." Civility only made them saucy. . . . The instruments to deal with such "stubborn, cross-grain'd rogues" were at hand: "*Beadles, Catchpoles, Gaolers, Hangmen,* . . . such like Engines of

Humanity are the fittest Tools in the World for a Magistrate to work with in the Reformation of an obdurate Rogue, all which, I say, may be so used and managed by him as not to endanger his own Fingers, or discompose his thoughts." [2] . . . Nourse knew instinctively that the criminal law is as much concerned with authority as it is with property. For wealth does not exist outside a social context, theft is given definition only within a set of social relations, and the connections between property, power and authority are close and crucial. The criminal law was critically important in maintaining bonds of obedience and deference, in legitimizing the status quo, in constantly recreating the structure of authority which arose from property and in turn protected its interests.

But terror alone could never have accomplished those ends. It was the raw material of authority, but class interest and the structure of the law itself shaped it into a much more effective instrument of power. Almost a century after Nourse, another defender of the unreformed system described the other side of authority: "Could we view our own species from a distance, or regard mankind with the same sort of observation with which we read the natural history, or remark the *manners,* of any other animal," he wrote in 1785, "there is nothing in the human character which would more surprise us, than the almost universal subjugation of strength to weakness—than to see many millions of robust men, in the complete use and exercise of their faculties, and without any defect of courage, waiting upon the will of a child, a woman, a driveller, or a lunatic. And, although . . . we suppose perhaps an extreme case; yet in all cases, even in the most popular forms of civil government, *the physical strength lies in the governed.* In what manner opinion thus prevails over strength, or how power, which naturally belongs to superior force, is maintained in opposition to it; in other words, by what motives the many are induced to submit to the few, becomes an inquiry which lies at the root of almost every political speculation. . . . Let civil governors learn hence to respect their subjects; let them be admonished, that the physical strength resides in the governed; that this strength wants only to be felt and roused, to lay prostate the most ancient and confirmed dominion; that civil authority is founded in opinion; that general opinion therefore ought always to be treated with deference, and managed with delicacy and circumspection.[3] "

These are the words of Archdeacon Paley, and they were published a few years after the Gordon Riots. Paley is not usually quoted as an exponent of "delicacy and circumspection", but as the most eloquent defender of the old criminal law as a system of selective terror. He was cited by almost every subsequent opponent of reform, and has often been considered by later writers as little more than an ingenious apologist or uncritical conservative. But he was in fact an acute observer of the bases of power in eighteenth-century England, and although he did not make the connection explicit, the criminal law was extremely important in ensuring, in his words, that "opin-

2. Timothy Nourse, Campania Foelix (2d ed., 1706). . . .

3. William Paley, Principles of Moral and Political Philosophy, 1785, Book VI, ch. 2.

ion" prevailed over "physical strength." The opinion was that of the ruling class; the law was one of their chief ideological instruments. It combined the terror worshipped by Nourse with the discretion stressed by Paley, and used both to mould the consciousness by which the many submitted to the few. Moreover, its effectiveness in doing so depended in large part on the very weaknesses and inconsistencies condemned by reformers and liberal historians. In considering the criminal law as an ideological system, we must look at how it combined imagery and force, ideals and practice, and try to see how it manifested itself to the mass of unpropertied Englishmen. We can distinguish three aspects of the law as ideology: majesty, justice and mercy. Understanding them will help us to explain the divergence between bloody legislation and declining executions, and the resistance to reform of any kind.

Majesty

If we are to believe an undated couplet from Staffordshire, at first sight the majesty of the law did not always impress:

COUNTRYMAN: What mummery is this, 'tis fit only for guisers!

TOWNSMAN: No mummery Sir, 'tis the Stafford Assizes,

for coupled with wealth, a considered use of imagery, eloquent speech, and the power of death, the antics surrounding the twice-yearly visits of the high-court judges had considerable psychic force . . . . The assizes were a formidable spectacle in a country town, the most visible and elaborate manifestation of state power to be seen in the countryside, apart from the presence of a regiment. . . . [T]he court arrived in town with traditional, and calculated, panoply: "The judges," wrote a French observer, "upon their approach are received by the sheriff, and often by a great part of the wealthiest inhabitants of the county; the latter come in person to meet them, or send their carriages, with their richest liveries, to serve as an escort, and increase the splendour of the occasion. They enter the town with bells ringing and trumpets playing, preceded by the sheriff's men, to the number of twelve or twenty, in full dress, armed with javelins. The trumpeters and javelinmen remain in attendance on them during the time of their stay, and escort them every day to the assize-hall, and back again to their apartments.[4]" In the court room the judges' every action was governed by the importance of spectacle. Blackstone asserted that "the novelty and very parade of . . . [their] appearance have no small influence upon the multitude:"[5] scarlet robes lined with ermine and full-bottomed wigs in the seventeenth-century style, which evoked scorn from Hogarth but awe from ordinary men. The powers of light and darkness were summoned into the court with the black cap which was donned to pronounce sentence of death, and the spotless white gloves worn at the end of a "maiden assize" when no prisoners were to be left for execution.

---

4. Charles Cottu, The Administration of Criminal Justice in England, 1822, p. 43 . . . . .

5. Blackstone, Commentaries, vol. III, p. 356.

Within this elaborate ritual of the irrational, judge and counsel displayed their learning with an eloquence that often rivalled that of leading statesmen.   There was an acute consciousness that the courts were platforms for addressing "the multitude."   Two stages in the proceedings especially were tests of the rhetorical power of the bench.   The first, the charge to the grand jury, was ostensibly directed to the country gentry.   Judges gave close attention to content and to delivery.   .   .   .   The flavour of paternalism was important, for usually the charge was also directed at the wider audience in the courtroom.   It was often a secular sermon on the goodness of whichever Hanoverian chanced to be on the throne, the virtues of authority and obedience, the fitness of the social order:

"It is the king's *earnest Desire,* as well as his *truest Intent,* that all his subjects be easy and happy.   In this he places his greatest Security & Glory; and in the preservation of the Laws of the Kingdom, & of ye liberties of his People, the Chief support of his title & Government.   .   .   .   Without order [continued Hardwicke in this charge to Somerset Assizes], how miserable must be the condition of the People?   Instead of a regular observance and a due execution of the laws, every man's lust, his avarice, his revenge, or his ambition would become a law to himself, and the rule of his dealing with his neighbour."

The second rhetorical test for the judge demanded not the accents of paternalism, but the power and passion of righteous vengeance.   The death sentence, we have suggested, was the climactic emotional point of the criminal law—the moment of terror around which the system revolved.   As the cases came before judge and jury at assizes, the convicted were remanded for sentencing on the last day;   and on that day the judgements were given in ascending order of severity, reserving the most awful for the last.   Before passing sentence of death, the judge spoke about the crimes and the criminals   .   .   .   .

.   .   .   The aim was to move the court, to impress the onlookers by word and gesture, to fuse terror and argument into the amalgam of legitimate power in their minds.   For execution was a fate decreed not by men, but by God and Justice.   The judge might deepen the effect when visibly moved himself   .   .   .   .

In its ritual, its judgements and its channelling of emotion the criminal law echoed many of the most powerful psychic components of religion.   The judge might   .   .   .   emulate the priest in his role of human agent, helpless but submissive before the demands of his deity.   But the judge could play the role of deity as well, both the god of wrath and the merciful arbiter of men's fates.   For the righteous accents of the death sentence were made even more impressive by the contrast with the treatment of the accused up to the moment of conviction.   The judges' paternal concern for their prisoners was remarked upon by foreign visitors, and deepened the analogy with the Christian God of justice and mercy   .   .   .   .

Justice

"Justice" was an evocative word in the eighteenth century, and with good reason. The constitutional struggles of the seventeenth had helped to establish the principles of the rule of law: that offences should be fixed, not indeterminate; that rules of evidence should be carefully observed; that the law should be administered by a bench that was both learned and honest. These achievements were essential for the protection of the gentry from royal greed and royal tyranny, and for the regulation, in the civil side of the courts, of the details of conveyancing, entailing, contracting, devising, suing and releasing. Since the same judges administered the criminal law at its highest levels, on the same principles, even the poorest man was guaranteed justice in the high courts. Visitors remarked on the extreme solicitude of judges for the rights of the accused, a sharp distinction from the usual practice of continental benches. It was considered to be good grounds for requesting a royal pardon if the judge "did (contrary to the usual custom) lean against the prisoner." The assize judge's attention to the rights of the prisoner did much to mitigate the prohibition against legal counsel in felonies . . . .

Equally important were the strict procedural rules which were enforced in the high courts and at assizes, especially in capital cases. Moreover, most penal statutes were interpreted by the judges in an extremely narrow and formalistic fashion. In part this was based on seventeenth-century practice, but as more capital statutes were passed in the eighteenth century the bench reacted with an increasingly narrow interpretation. Many prosecutions founded on excellent evidence and conducted at considerable expense failed on minor errors of form in the indictment, the written charge. If a name or date was incorrect, or if the accused was described as a "farmer" rather than the approved term "yeoman", the prosecution could fail. The courts held that such defects were conclusive, and gentlemen attending trials as spectators sometimes stood up in court and brought errors to the attention of the judge. These formalisms in the criminal law seemed ridiculous to contemporary critics, and to many later historians. Their argument was (and is) that the criminal law, to be effective, must be known and determinate, instead of capricious and obscure. Prosecutors resented the waste of their time and money lost on a technicality; thieves were said to mock courts which allowed them to escape through so many verbal loopholes. But it seems likely that the mass of Englishmen drew other conclusions from the practice. The punctilious attention to forms, the dispassionate and legalistic exchanges between counsel and the judge, argued that those administering and using the laws submitted to its rules. The law thereby became something more than the creature of a ruling class—it became a power with its own claims, higher than those of prosecutor, lawyers, and even the great scarlet-robed assize judge himself. To them, too, of course, the law was The Law. The fact that they reified it, that they shut their eyes to its daily enactment in Parliament by men of their own class, heightened the illusion. When the ruling class acquitted men on technicalities they helped instil a belief in the disembodied justice of the law in the minds of all who watched. In short, its very inefficiency, its absurd formalism, was part of its strength as ideology . . . .

Mercy

The prerogative of mercy ran throughout the administration of the criminal law, from the lowest to the highest level. At the top sat the high court judges, and their free use of the royal pardon became a crucial argument in the arsenal of conservatives opposing reform. At the lowest jurisdiction, that of the Justice of the Peace, the same discretion allowed the magistrate to make decisions that sometimes escaped legal categories altogether. Although he frequently made obeisance to the rules when convicting, as we have seen, he could dispense with them when pardoning, and the absence of a jury made it even easier for him to do so . . . . This element of discretion impressed Weber when he examined the office of JP. He compared it to Arabic "khadi justice"—a formalistic administration of law that was nevertheless based on ethical or practical judgements rather than on a fixed, "rational" set of rules. It could combine rigid tradition with "a sphere of free discretion and grace of the ruler".[6] Thus it allowed the paternalist JP to compose quarrels, intervene with prosecutors on behalf of culprits, and in the final instance to dismiss a case entirely. The right of the pardon was not limited, however, to high court judges and Justices of the Peace. The mode of prosecution, the manner of trial and the treatment of condemned convicts gave some of the same power to all men of property. "Irrationality", in the sense used by Weber, and the "grace of the ruler" which grew from it pervaded the entire administration of the law.

Almost all prosecutions were initiated by private persons, at their discretion, and conducted in accordance with their wishes . . . . The victim of the crime could decide himself upon the severity of the prosecution, either enforcing the letter of the law, or reducing the charge. He could even pardon the offence completely by not going to court. The reformers' objections to this system are well known. Private prosecution was capricious and uncertain, and too often rogues escaped due to the distaste, compassion or fear of their victims. But reformers failed to acknowledge the great power this conferred on the prosecutor to make the law serve his own purposes. In Cottu's words, the accuser became "the arbitrator of the culprit's fate", and the law became an expression of his will. In short, it was in the hands of the gentleman who went to law to evoke gratitude as well as fear in the maintenance of deference.

In a rural parish with a relatively settled population there were many alternatives to a rigorous prosecution. The accused man could be made to post a bond not to offend again, or be given the choice of leaving the neighbourhood. The threat of prosecution could be held over his head to ensure his future good behaviour. He might also be allowed to escape the law by making compensation for his crime. . . . Other accused men simply

6. From Max Weber, ed. by H. H. Gerth and C. Wright Mills, 1970, pp. 216–21 . . . .

appealed to the merciful feelings of the man who held them in his power. The wretched thief begging on his knees for forgiveness is not a literary conceit, but a reality described in many legal depositions. Critics of the law objected, however, that many prosecutions were dropped through fear as well as compassion. Certainly it is true that feeling against some prosecutors ran so high that they went in fear of their lives from popular opinion, or felt obliged to defend their actions in the press. Yet where certainty of enforcement had to be sacrificed to public opinion, even then graciously granted mercy could produce gratifying deference. Especially where the prosecutor was a landed gentleman, acts of mercy helped create the mental structure of paternalism . . . .

The nature of the criminal trial gave enormous discretion to men of property other than the prosecutor. Because the law did not allow those accused of felony to employ an attorney to address the jury, a poor man's defence was often a halting, confused statement. If he had a clear alibi he was lucky: to establish innocence in more complicated cases might be very difficult, even when the judge was sympathetic. Character witnesses were thus extremely important, and very frequently used. It was not uncommon for a man accused of sheep-stealing, a capital offence, to bring a dozen acquaintances to court to testify to his honesty. If the jury did convict, such favourable testimony might still induce the judge to pass a lesser sentence, or recommend a pardon. Yet in character testimony too, the word of a man of property had the greatest weight. Judges respected the evidence of employers, respectable farmers and neighbouring gentlemen, not mere neighbours and friends. A labourer accused of a serious crime learned again his enormous dependence on the power of property to help him, or abandon him, as it chose . . . . If respectable character witnesses did not succeed in convincing the jury to acquit, their support was the first step in influencing the judge to consider a pardon. A free or conditional pardon from the king was the hope of almost every capital convict in the eighteenth century, and many men under lighter sentences also struggled to obtain it. For the historian it epitomizes the discretionary element of the law, and the use of mercy in justifying the social order.

Pardons were very common. Roughly half of those condemned to death during the eighteenth century did not go to the gallows, but were transported to the colonies or imprisoned. In many cases the judge made the decision before he left the assize town, but if he did not intend to recommend mercy, it was still possible to petition the king, through the Secretary of State, up to the moment of execution. The grounds for mercy were ostensibly that the offence was minor, or that the convict was of good character, or that the crime he had committed was not common enough in that county to require an exemplary hanging. The judges also used the pardon when necessary to meet the requests of local gentry or to propitiate popular feelings of justice. The bench could ultimately decide whom to recommend for mercy and whom to leave to hang, but they were not usually willing to antagonize a body of respectable feeling . . . . The judges were well aware that the gentry of the county were charged with government and criminal justice between assize times, and hence usually gave their opinions a serious hearing. The pardon could be used, however, to show mercy when the death penalty seemed too severe, and this discretion became part of the explicit justification of the law to the poor .   .   .   .

.   .   .   The pardon allowed the bench to recognize poverty, when necessary, as an excuse, even though the law itself did not.   But the manner in which a pardon was obtained made it an important element in eighteenth-century social relations in three other ways.   In the first place, the claims of class saved far more men who had been left to hang by the assize judge than did the claims of humanity.   Again and again in petitions the magic words recur: "his parents are respectable persons in Denbighshire"; his father is "a respectable farmer"; his brother is "a builder of character and eminence in London".   There are very few petitions that plead what one in 1787 called "the common excuse for larceny, poverty and distress".   It may have been the common excuse, but those requesting pardons knew it held little weight—only two of the hundreds of petitions that year bothered to mention it.   In contrast, the excuse of respectability was pleaded in extenso

.   .   .   .   .

The pardon thus served to save a good many respectable villains.   It was all very well to hang Dr. Dodd and Lord Ferrers, but to hang every errant son of the rich who tried his hand at highway robbery to pay gambling debts would have made too great a carnage in the better circles.   Pardons also favoured those with connections for another reason: mercy was part of the currency of patronage.   Petitions were most effective from great men, and the common course was for a plea to be passed up through increasingly higher levels of the social scale, between men bound together by the links of patronage and obligation.   The bald language of place-seekers recurs here too;   trading in life and death became part of the game of interest .   .   .   .

Beyond class favouritism and games of influence, the pardon had an equally important role to play in the ideology of mercy.   The poor did not see the elaborate ramifications of interest and connection.   Although the convolutions of the patronage system at the lowest level were known to every man who wished to become a tidewaiter, the law was set apart, and no gentleman wished to admit too openly that justice itself was but another part of the system.   Moreover, pardon-dealing went on at the highest levels only, well concealed from the eyes of the poor.   Therefore the royal prerogative of mercy could be presented as something altogether more mysterious, more sacred and more absolute in its determinations.   Pardons were presented as acts of grace rather than as favours to interests.   At the lowest levels, within the immediate experience of the poor, pardons were indeed part of the tissue of paternalism, expressed in the most personal terms.   The great majority of petitions for mercy were written by gentlemen on behalf of labourers.   It was an important self-justification of the ruling class that once the poor had been chastised sufficiently to protect property, it was the duty of a gentleman to protect "his" people .   .   .   .

Petitions for pardons were occasionally opposed, but usually by determined prosecutors.   Where a prosecutor had second thoughts or wished to indulge his humanity after exacting terror and recovering his property, he sometimes was the first to add his name to a plea for mercy—and thereby gave it greater weight.   Most successful petitions, however, were begun by other men of respectable position, with good connections, and their activity on behalf of the condemned could only enhance their reputations as men of compassion and magnanimity. To the poor, the intercession of a local gentleman was proof of his power to approach the throne. He took no blame if the petition failed, for an unanswered plea was attributed to the determination of the king, who was popularly believed to sign all death warrants. A successful outcome was attributed to mercy at the same exalted height. .   .   .   And all the chaplains, country gentlemen and peers who had helped to obtain a pardon shared somewhat in the reflected glory of the merciful ruler.

The pardon is important because it often put the principal instrument of legal terror—the gallows—directly in the hands of those who held power. In this it was simply the clearest example of the prevailing custom at all levels of criminal justice. Here was the peculiar genius of the law. It allowed the rulers of England to make the courts a selective instrument of class justice, yet simultaneously to proclaim the law's incorruptible impartiality, and absolute determinacy. Their political and social power was reinforced daily by bonds of obligation on one side and condescension on the other, as prosecutors, gentlemen and peers decided to invoke the law or agreed to show mercy. Discretion allowed a prosecutor to terrorize the petty thief and then command his gratitude, or at least the approval of his neighbourhood as a man of compassion. It allowed the class that passed one of the bloodiest penal codes in Europe to congratulate itself on its humanity. It encouraged loyalty to the king and the state:

> And Earthly Power doth then show likest God's
> When mercy seasons justice.

And in the countryside the power of gentlemen and peers to punish or forgive worked in the same way to maintain the fabric of obedience, gratitude and deference. The law was important as gross coercion; it was equally important as ideology. Its majesty, justice and mercy helped to create the spirit of consent and submission, the "mind-forged manacles", which Blake saw binding the English poor   .   .   .   .

Delicacy and Circumspection

.   .   .   There is a danger, which perhaps this essay has not avoided, of giving the impression that a system of authority is *something*, rather than the actions of living men. The invisible hand of Adam Smith's political economy was metaphor, shorthand for an effect rather than a cause; it was a description of recurrent patterns of useful behaviour forged out of the energy, conflicts and greed of thousands of individuals in a capitalist market. In a somewhat similar way, much of the ideological structure surrounding the criminal law was the product of countless short-term decisions. It was often a question of intuition, and of trial and error. In handling a mob it was useful to appeal to ideals of English justice: but that was a lesson that was slowly learned over many generations, and rarely raised to the level of theory. The necessity of gauging reactions to executions was an immediate problem of public order, not a plot worked out by eighteenth-century experts in public relations for a fee. The difficulty for the historian of the law is twofold.

He must make explicit convictions that were often unspoken, for if left unspoken we cannot understand the actions of the men who held them. Yet in describing how convictions and actions moulded the administration of justice, he must never forget that history is made by men, not by the Cunning of Reason or the Cunning of System. The course of history is the result of a complex of human actions—purposive, accidental, sometimes determined— and it cannot be reduced to one transcendent purpose. The cunning of a ruling class is a more substantial concept, however, for such a group of men is agreed on ultimate ends. However much they believed in justice (and they did); however sacred they held property (and they worshipped it); however merciful they were to the poor (and many were); the gentlemen of England knew that their duty was, above all, to rule. On that depended everything. They acted accordingly . . . .

The second question raised by a discussion of the law as ideology is evidential: how can we prove that it worked? Much of the evidence cited here comes from the avowed intentions and observations of the rulers, not the ruled. Perhaps much of what the gentry interpreted as the deference and gratitude of the poor was in fact conscious deception. Perhaps the ordinary Englishman played the role assigned to him, but was never convinced by the play. The eighteenth century produced much genteel cant about justice, but it also produced a large popular literature marked by cynicism and disrespect for the law. And there were many more forceful demonstrations of incredulity, including riots at executions, and rogues who mocked their judges.

Much research remains to be done before we can give confident answers to some of these questions. But two general points may be made. In the first place, most of the evidence that we have of loud popular disrespect for the law comes from London, and London differed in important ways from the rest of eighteenth-century English society. It had a highly transient population, and a large body of disorderly and parasitic poor, living on the gathered wealth of commerce, the port and the disorderly and parasitic rich. In sharp contrast to the provinces, the men hanged at Tyburn were mostly born in distant places. They had come to London from the country, and in doing so left behind the close and persisting personal relationships that still characterized much of English society. And it was in such intimate dealings of fear and gratitude that much of the ideology of justice was realized. Some historians have suggested that "urban alienation" accounts for London disorder and crime in the eighteenth century. It may be more correct to say that the instruments of control there were weaker, in part because the class relationships that fostered deference were. Resistance to the law, disrespect for its majesty, scorn for its justice were greater. Equally, judicial mercy in London was more often a bureaucratic lottery than a convincing expression of paternalism.

The provinces too erupted in disorder: food riots, militia riots, excise riots, turnpike riots, gang poaching, endemic and often violent smuggling. The hegemony of the law was never complete and unbroken, even in the most deeply rural, most traditional counties. The fabric of authority was torn and reknit constantly. The important fact remains, however, that it was reknit readily. The closer mesh of economic and social ties in rural society, the public nature of those relationships compared to the complexity and obscurity of much of metropolitan life, allowed the creation of an ideology that was much more pervasive than in London. When it was momentarily challenged in a county riot or by a defiant labourer, no serious harm resulted; the prevailing code was, in fact, usually strengthened. An ideology endures not by being wholly enforced and rigidly defined. Its effectiveness lies first in its very elasticity, the fact that men are not required to make it a credo, that it seems to them the product of their own minds and their own experience. And the law did not enforce uniform obedience, did not seek total control; indeed, it sacrificed punishment when necessary to preserve the belief in justice. The courts dealt in terror, pain and death, but also in moral ideals, control of arbitrary power, mercy for the weak. In doing so they made it possible to disguise much of the class interest of the law. The second strength of an ideology is its generality. Provided that its depths are not explored too often or by too many, it remains a reservoir of belief throughout the society and flows into the gaps made by individual acts of protest. Therefore, those using it are concerned above all with surface appearances. Undoubtedly the gentleman accepting an apology from the man in his power, the thief or the rioter, would have been gratified to know that the contrition was absolute, from the soul. But provided that the act of contrition was public and convincing, that it served to sustain general belief in the justice of the social order, it sufficed. It became part of the untested general idea, the ideology which made it possible to stigmatize dissent as acts of individuals, of rogues and criminals and madmen.

The hypothesis presented here is that the criminal law, more than any other social institution, made it possible to govern eighteenth-century England without a police force and without a large army. The ideology of the law was crucial in sustaining the hegemony of the English ruling class. . . .

There was . . . a division of interest among propertied Englishmen about the purpose of the criminal law. The reformers' campaign spoke to humanitarians of all classes, men revolted by the public agonies of the condemned at the gallows. But their argument that capital punishment should be replaced by a more certain protection of property appealed mostly to that great body of "middling men", almost half the nation, who earned from £25 to £150 a year at mid-century, and created more than half England's wealth. Although they could use the discretionary elements of the law to a limited degree, their property was the prey of thieves undeterred by terror. Their complaints did not impress a tiny but powerful ruling class, whose immense personal property in land was secure, who could afford to protect their other goods without public support, and who in any case were most concerned with the law as an instrument of authority.

It is in such terms that we must work toward a definition of the ruling class of eighteenth-century England. Far from being the property of Marxist or *marxisant* historians, the term is a leitmotiv in studies of the period. Partly this is due to the testimony of the sources: gentry and aristocracy claimed the title with complete assurance. Its historical usage, however, remains imprecise. Usually it has been defined in terms of income or status: the rents of the great landed estate, or the exact meaning contemporaries gave to the word "gentleman". Class, however, is a social relationship, not simply an aggregate of individuals. As a relationship based upon differences of power and wealth, it must be sought in the life of the institutions that men create and within which they meet. The law defined and maintained the bounds of power and wealth, and when we ask who controlled the criminal law, we see a familiar constellation: monarchy, aristocracy, gentry and, to a lesser extent, the great merchants. In numbers they were no more than 3 per cent of the population. But their discretionary use of the law maintained their rule and moulded social consciousness. An operational definition of the ruling class—asking who controlled a critical institution like the law, and how they manipulated it—is a more useful approach than drawing horizontal lines in Blackstone's list of forty status levels. For it is necessary to define in detail what it means to rule.

Many historians, confronted with the hegemony of the eighteenth-century ruling class, have described it in terms of absolute control and paternal benevolence. Max Beloff argued that after the Restoration they enjoyed an unparalleled sense of security which explained "the leniency with which isolated disturbances were on the whole treated, when compared with the ferocity shown by the same class towards their social inferiors in the times of the Tudors and early Stuarts." [7] It seems more likely that the relative insecurity of England's governors, their crucial dependence on the deference of the governed, compelled them to moderate that ferocity. More recent writing has stressed the importance of patronage; Harold Perkin has argued [in The Origin of Modern Society 32–49 (1969)] that this was the central bond of eighteenth-century society. Patronage created vertical chains of loyalty; it was, in fact, "the module of which the social structure was built". Powerful men bound less powerful ones to them through paternalism, controlling the income, even the "life-chances" of the dependent client or tenant or labourer. Such ties, repeated endlessly, formed a "mesh of vertical loyalties". Social control in the eighteenth century seems a gentle yoke from this perspective: a spontaneous, uncalculated and peaceful relationship of gratitude and gifts. The system is ultimately a self-adjusting one of shared moral values, values which are not contrived but autonomous. At one point the author concedes that insubordination was "ruthlessly suppressed". But mostly social solidarity grew quietly: "those who lived within its embrace . . . [called it] friendship." Coercion was an exceptional act, to handle exceptional deviance.

Yet it is difficult to understand how those loyalties endured when patronage was uneven, interrupted, often capricious. Many contemporaries testified to the fickleness of wealth: disappointed office-seekers, unemployed labourers or weavers, paupers dumped over parish boundaries. Riot was a commonplace; so too were hangings. Benevolence, in short, was not a simple positive act: it contained within it the ever-present threat of malice. In economic relations a landlord keeping his rents low was benevolent because he could, with impunity, raise them. A justice giving charity to a wandering beggar was benevolent because he could whip him instead. Benevolence, all patronage, was given meaning by its contingency. It was the ob-

7. Max Beloff, Public Order and Popular Disturbances 1660–1714, 1938, p. 154 . . . .

verse of coercion, terror's conspiracy of silence. When patronage failed, force could be invoked; but when coercion inflamed men's minds, at the crucial moment mercy could calm them.

A ruling class organizes its power in the state. The sanction of the state is force, but it is force that is legitimized, however imperfectly, and therefore the state deals also in ideologies. Loyalties do not grow simply in complex societies: they are twisted, invoked and often consciously created. Eighteenth-century England was not a free market of patronage relations. It was a society with a bloody penal code, an astute ruling class who manipulated it to their advantage, and a people schooled in the lessons of Justice, Terror and Mercy. The benevolence of rich men to poor, and all the ramifications of patronage, were upheld by the sanction of the gallows and the rhetoric of the death sentence.

––––––

1.   Clearly Ms. Minow's interpretation is not the only possible interpretation of Solomon's judgment, nor is Hay's the only possible interpretation of the eighteenth-century judicial action. Imagine alternative explanations and then ask yourself what criteria should be used for choosing among the competing interpretations. How does one "validate" a claim about the latent function of judicial action? Is the standard of validity one of empirical truth, one of internal coherence or consistency, or one of quasi-aesthetic appeal—let's call it resonance—the capacity of the interpretation to render a body of experience meaningful and intelligible?

Empiricism obviously has a limited claim in explanations that purport to identify latent functions—the stated reasons are by definition not the real reasons. The criterion of internal consistency is not particularly selective; many interpretations will meet that standard. And the resonance criterion is so heavily dependent on each individual's world views and prior dispositions as almost to deny the possibility of the existence of a "valid" interpretation.

2.   Two other scholars, Eugene Genovese, Roll, Jordan, Roll (1974) (Chapter 2, "The Hegemonic Function of Law"), and E. P. Thompson, Whigs and Hunters: The Origin of the Black Act (1976), have put forth accounts of law and judicial action quite similar to that of Douglas Hay. As pointed out above, all three share a similar theoretical structure (which probably can be traced to Gramsci, Prison Notebooks; see James Joll, Antonio Gramsci (1977), chapter 7) and all three apply it in a historical context. All three authors are historians. One wonders whether the relationship between the sociology of judicial action and history in such accounts is partly *contingent*, or whether distance in time—also exemplified in Ms. Minow's mythical study—is an important precondition for isolating, or even speculating about, the latent functions of judicial action. Does history give one a perspective, for example, about the constructed quality of social phenomena that otherwise appear so real, or is it that history gives us a *freedom*—a license—to speak the language of latency?

3.   See also O. Kirchheimer, Political Justice: The Use of Legal Procedure for Political Ends (1961); M. Foucault, Discipline and Punish: The

Birth of the Prison (1977) (especially Part IV, "Prison"); Hoeflich and Deutsch, Judicial Legitimacy and the Disinterested Judge, 6 Hofstra L.Rev. 749 (1978).

SECTION C. EFFICACY

All forms of adjudicatory action seem to have one trait in common: the desire to be effective, to settle a dispute, to change people's behavior. In this section we first consider the difficulty of achieving that desire, that is, how judicial action is circumscribed and limited by many conditions beyond the reach of the tribunal. We then take a more daring tack. We suggest how the very desire to be effective shapes—or twists—the nature and terms of the tribunal's action.

1. THE CONDITIONS OF EFFICACY

In recent years a number of social scientists—primarily political scientists and sociologists—have sought to study the conditions that determine the efficacy of judicial action. See, e. g., S. Goldman and T. Jahnige, The Federal Courts as a Political System (2d ed. 1976), Chapter 7; S. Wasby, The Impact of the United States Supreme Court: Some Perspectives (1970); H. Rodgers and C. Bullock, Law and Social Change: Civil Rights Laws and their Consequences (1972); K. Dolbeare and P. Hammond, The School Prayer Decisions (1971); F. Wirt, Politics of Southern Equality: Law and Social Change in a Mississippi County (1970); T. Becker and M. Feeley, The Impact of Supreme Court Decisions (2d ed. 1973). Some have aspired to a statement of a general theory. That aspiration has largely gone unfulfilled: the empirical knowledge has been incomplete, the variables too manifold, or the basic concepts too simplistic. We have, therefore, settled for two of the more important case studies appearing in the literature—that of William Muir on the school prayer decision; and that of Robert Crain on school desegregation. Both of the judicial decisions studied faced formidable obstacles—well-entrenched patterns of behavior and deeply-held beliefs; they represented testing situations. The studies do not describe the typical but are intended to provide the material out of which a general theory of efficacy might be constructed.

Muir's essay focuses explicitly on law, on *Schempp* and the conditions of its efficacy. Crain's essay is more indirect. Crain asks why school desegregation was so painful, so violent, and so precarious in New Orleans. He places no special emphasis on the fact that the desegregation was court-ordered. He fails to give any special attention to the place in New Orleans society of the trial judge, J. Skelly Wright, then a federal district judge in the Eastern District of Louisiana, now of the U. S. Court of Appeals for the District of Columbia. How is it possible, you may wonder, to analyze the conditions of efficacy of a judge's decree in terms of elite theory without understanding the place of that judge in the elite structure of his community? Not all federal district judges are part of the "civic elite," particularly in a "feudal" or "traditionalist" society such as New Orleans.

Robert L. Crain, **The Politics of School Desegregation—Why New Orleans?** *

Why did violence occur in New Orleans and not in other cities? Several different kinds of explanations could be made. First, there is the "national climate" theory—that southern school integration took many communities to the brink of violence, and that, as school integration moved into the Deep South, some school system would go over the edge—if it had not been New Orleans, it would have been somewhere else. The three major crises—Little Rock, New Orleans, and Birmingham—were neatly spaced at three-year intervals. Does this suggest that 1960 was a year for trouble, and that New Orleans happened to be unlucky?

We do not believe this to be a useful explanation. First, the early incidents of violence—Sturgis, Clinton, Mansfield, and Little Rock—each occurred because of a new and unexpected factor, each demonstrated some new principle, and each set an example for other cities. From Clinton, police learned the danger of the traveling provocateur. From Mansfield, we learned that the state could intercede to prevent voluntary integration, and from Little Rock, we learned what lay in store for the state that tried to fight the federal courts. From Virginia, we learned that southerners would not tolerate disbanding the public education system, and that private schools simply would not work. But there was nothing new about New Orleans. No rational person could look at New Orleans and believe that school integration could be avoided by the same old mobs and pickets that had been used in Little Rock. Furthermore, people in New Orleans and Atlanta knew the price that Little Rock had paid in its unsuccessful attempt to find some way around the *Brown* decision. Nor can we accept the idea that New Orleans had to be violent just because it was the first city to desegregate in the Deep South. New Orleans had a history of desegregated colleges to accustom it to desegregation. In any case, even if 1960 was a time to expect trouble, this hypothesis does not explain why New Orleans did so little to prepare for it, while Atlanta, which did not desegregate until 1961, was already taking steps to ease the process.

A second possible explanation for New Orleans is that the segregationist activity centered around mass demonstrations of great magnitude, which were beyond control from the start. This also seems implausible. If it were the case, then there are certainly many southern cities where segregationist opposition would be even greater, and the large rural areas of the South should have been consumed in a bonfire of segregationist activity.

A third possible explanation is a purely political one—that the political leadership at the state and federal level was responsible. At the state level, this at first seems quite plausible. . . . [T]he state legislature passed a long list of rather ingenious bills. But it must be remembered that nearly all this legislation was voided by Judge Wright before it could have any lasting impact. The state was unable to compel the closing of the schools, to

Source: R. Crain, The Politics of School Desegregation (1967), chapter 16.

16. Senior Social Scientist, The Rand Corporation.

enforce the boycott, or to provide funds to support private schools for the boycotters. . . .

In Louisiana the state was limited to little more than a harassing rearguard action. We do not believe that this in itself would have been sufficient to create and maintain a year-long boycott. In addition, we should recall that the relationship between New Orleans and the state was a two-way interaction. Even when it became fairly obvious that the state legislature was trying to disrupt the New Orleans schools without any hope of actually preventing desegregation, the New Orleans delegation, Mayor Morrison, and other local political leaders made only a token fight. Georgia could have harassed the Atlanta schools in the same way (and Atlanta represents a smaller portion of the Georgia population that New Orleans does in Louisiana). Again, why New Orleans and not Atlanta?

. . . [A]t various times the federal government was slow to take action to prevent school desegregation crises. We might apply this consideration in explaining the crises in other cities, but it is more difficult to apply it to New Orleans. The United States Justice Department could have entered the New Orleans case much earlier. But on the other hand, Judge Skelly Wright acted with astonishing speed in invalidating various efforts of the state to interfere. And federal marshals escorted the Negro girls to school every day and, beginning with the ninth of December, escorted the white pupils as well. The federal government did as much or more in New Orleans as it did anywhere else. Furthermore, the federal police role is by definition reactive—it could only appear after a crisis had begun.

Fourth, we can advance the hypothesis that the New Orleans crisis resulted from a chance accumulation of various factors and that there is no general explanation. . . . While this explanation makes some sense—there is a good deal of chance in any action—it does not strike us as a particularly good explanation. The list of accidents is not so very long. . . . Summing all the accidents does not give us the impression that 1960 was an unlucky year for New Orleans. And some of these accidents cannot be treated as mere chance occurrences . . . .

One way to demonstrate that there was more than chance involved in 1960 is to contrast the behavior of the actors in 1960 with that in 1961, when the second year of desegregation began. In 1961 the school board again employed the computer [to select the schools and children for desegregation]. This time, when the computer again produced the names of slum schools for desegregation, the program was changed until the school board could get some schools that it wanted—in this case, schools in the silk-stocking area where support for desegregation was greatest. In addition, in 1961 the police were under orders to disperse crowds, rather than merely to prevent violence. Finally, the civic and economic elite in the city purchased an advertisement, calling for peaceful desegregation, before school opened. . . . [T]he civic elite was out in full force in 1961 for the first time. In the course of our interviewing, we asked twenty-two respondents to designate those persons most influential in local decisions. This yielded a list of fourteen men.

. . . [T]he leaders signed the ad supporting Sutherland [a] and the ad supporting peaceful desegregation in 1961, but they did not sign the ad calling for support of the school board in 1960. The contrast between 1960 and 1961 is clear. The 1960 ad supporting the school board did not come until December, when the boycott [of the desegregated schools] was two months old and business was hard hit, yet the ad still lacked the signatures of most of the top leaders.

The changed approach of the school board, the police, the mayor, and the civic elite in 1961 seemed to pay off. The newly desegregated schools had only minor difficulties, and the Frantz enrollment soared to 100 (out of a capacity of 575). Five Negroes and fifteen whites enrolled at McDonogh No. 19. The continuing boycotts at Frantz and McDonogh No. 19 are really not surprising; these children had been in other schools with little or no tuition, and for many of them there was no real advantage to transferring back.

We think that the events of 1961 indicate that the situation in 1960 was controllable and that something more than mere accident, or a coincidence of several accidents, caused the difficulty.

What hypotheses do seem to be reasonable explanations, then? First, we must consider that some of the difficulty arose because of the behavior of the school board. They maintained a head-in-the-sand attitude for over four years, when they could have been letting the public know that desegregation was coming. It was not until the beginning of July, 1960, that the board members decided to work to keep the schools open. Yet even during the school board election, as late as the first week of November, board members were pledging their full cooperation to Governor Davis if he could keep the schools open and segregated. Though the board held little hope for Davis' efforts (Sutherland cautioned, the voters on the necessity of facing the issues "as they are, not as we would have them to be"), the board members nevertheless did not say flatly that desegregation was unavoidable. And on November 18, after the first week of desegregation, the school board once again asked the federal courts to delay desegregation. Although it is impossible to demonstrate, we think that had the school board acted earlier, the rest of the community would have had more time to make adjustments and begin to build a save-the-schools movement.

Second, the school board could have avoided the fiasco caused by their choice of schools to integrate. Even if we dismiss as mere Monday-morning quarterbacking the claims made by various respondents that they had expressed their opposition to the computerized selection, the fact remains that the school board had ample reason to know that there were more favorable alternatives. They had been invited to send Negro students to two silk-stocking schools, and they had rejected the invitation. They knew that their

---

a. School Board member Matthew Sutherland successfully campaigned for reelection in November of 1960 on the platform that he was a segregationist but that he was going to keep the schools open even if they were desegregated. The day before the election, and ad supporting Sutherland and signed by 98 important business and professional men appeared in the New Orleans Times-Picayune Ed. note.

main support groups, [Save Our Schools] and [Committee for Public Education], had been unable to organize in the ninth ward [where the schools chosen to be desegregated were located]. The school board members told us that they had refused to intervene in the selection of schools and had ordered the use of the computer because they did not want to have a part in deciding who would have to suffer integration. In other words, this was part of the syndrome: first refusing to believe that integration was coming, then refusing to draw a plan, so that Skelly Wright played school administrator in addition to his other roles in this crisis, and finally refusing to have anything to do with selecting the schools.

But the board did look for ways to build public support. First, the parents were polled to see whether they preferred "a small amount of integration" to closing the schools. The reader might object that the school board should have been telling the voters that schools would be open rather than asking their opinion, but we interpret the referendum as a shrewd maneuver to build support. On its face, it looks as if the "loaded" questions should have received a favorable response. Why did they not? The best explanation we can offer is that the questionnaire was administered too early.

The postcard questionnaires were sent out April 22, 1960. At that time there was simply no public discussion of the issue. It was not until May 16, 1960, when Judge Wright issued his decision setting the date for September, that the city became aware of the immediacy of the issue.[1] Six months later, after prolonged public discussion of the issue, Sutherland ran on a save-the-schools platform and won reelection. Of course he was an incumbent and had a well-organized campaign; even so, it seems hard to believe that an electorate deeply committed to closing the schools would have supported him. This leads us back to our initial point: the school board should have taken a public position earlier. Even if the initial reaction to their position had been hostile, an early stand would have generated earlier the kind of public discussion which eventually led to Sutherland's victory in November. Had the postcard poll been conducted after some public discussion instead of before it, [School Board President Lloyd] Rittiner's faith in the attachment of New Orleans parents to the public schools might have been borne out.

Of course, the school board received very little help from the other actors in the community. Morrison did nothing; the economic elite did nothing; even "the Girls" [the reformist women of New Orleans] were slow to organize. The save-the-schools campaign reached its peak . . . when the boycott was in its third month. The school board had made private overtures to all these people without success. This brings us to our principal hypothesis—that the New Orleans crisis arose from a general failure of community leadership, resulting in a breakdown of social control over the masses. The school board, the mayor, and the civic elite all shied away from taking action. To make a more general statement, we propose that the New Or-

---

1. .   .   .   In February of 1960 there was no space whatsoever devoted [in the Times-Picayune] to the subject; in the first half of May there were only sixty column inches. But in the fifteen days following Wright's order, there were 320 column inches, and the number increased thereafter. In Atlanta, by contrast, the story was front-page news in 1958.

leans civic elite has always been reluctant to become involved in local politics, and that this withdrawal contributed not only to the crisis, but also has tended to produce the kind of mayor, and the kind of school board that New Orleans had in 1960.

The civic elite's withdrawal from the school desegregation controversy is important primarily because these men have power and at the same time are much more insulated from public opinion than are the elected officials. Their power takes several forms: they have the money with which to influence political campaigns and to influence public opinion, they have personal influence over many leaders in the community, and they hold the positions of highest prestige, especially in a southern city. Other people have power, but most of them are also vulnerable—ministers can be fired, politicians defeated, and anyone who is an employee can lose his job.

If the civic elite had decided early enough to support peaceful desegregation, they could have taken several steps. The Times-Picayune could have supported peaceful desegregation and the save-the-schools movement. An advertising campaign could have been conducted (Dallas businessmen, for example, bought advertising space on streetcars). The elite could have persuaded ministers to make public appeals for peace. Our respondents who were close to Morrison reported that he would definitely have made a public statement if he had had support from the top leaders. The businessmen could have made it clear to Morrison that they did not want—indeed, would not tolerate—street disturbances that would damage business in the city. In turn, Morrison could have had the police disperse the demonstrators and arrest those who resisted. (In Atlanta, police permitted no crowd to gather in front of the desegregated schools. The few who refused to move on were arrested and given jail sentences. That ended the loitering.) The top businessmen could have offered jobs and job security to those white parents who wanted to send their children to school. Many would-be demonstrators would have been deterred had they seen their employers listed as leaders in the save-the-schools movement. Above all, the economic elite could have let the board know that they could support them if the school board would begin the public discourse by taking an early stand. The economic elite, most of them supporters of Governor Davis, could have put some public pressure on Davis to stop interfering in the New Orleans school situation. Again, these are all obvious steps, which in other cities have ordinarily led to a chain reaction and to a strong community consensus in favor of peaceful desegregation.

Why did the New Orleans elite fail to act? The first and most obvious hypothesis is that there is a power vacuum—that leadership is diffuse, fractionated, and invisible and therefore difficult to coordinate. This does not seem to be the case, however. We asked twenty-two respondents (including school board members, other actors in the desegregation crisis, and those they named as community influentials) to name the city's influential men. We found a surprising amount of agreement. One man was named by twenty of the twenty-two respondents, and six of these respondents immediately named him as the single most influential person. Another man was named eleven times, two were named seven times, and one was named six times.

In addition, there is a strong grapevine connecting the top elites to one another. From the interview data available to us, we believe that a full-scale study would indicate that New Orleans has a power structure similar to that . . . existing in Atlanta. To some extent our sample is biased since it includes many respondents who were involved in school desegregation. But we do not think that the list of influentials consists of an elite specializing in race relations. The leaders identified by this listing include those responsible for the present efforts to attract industry to Louisiana. Most important, as we have already stressed, these men did not specialize in race relations; they were not involved in the school desegregation struggle. Although we did not systematically attempt to study other issues, we collected enough incidental information to indicate that the men listed as influential did have influence.

We find a similar pattern in two other racial issues. In 1963, Negroes were threatening to hold public demonstrations because they were not allowed to sit on the benches in the public park. The mayor (Schiro) refused to meet with the Negroes—he had a meeting to attend, he said. But the man who was at the top of our list of influential citizens called the mayor out of the meeting and ordered him to meet with the Negroes. The mayor did. In 1962, 1963, and 1964, Negro leaders made extensive efforts to get the mayor to appoint a public biracial committee to handle racial problems. Many moderates (including some of the elite) backed this proposal. The mayor let it be known that he would favor such a committee if he could get the backing and participation of the city's top influentials. But because two of the top men on our list opposed the formation of such a committee, no such committee was formed. (Meanwhile, the governor of Louisiana, elected originally as a segregationist, saw fit to form a state biracial committee; so now New Orleans is lagging behind the state of Louisiana in at least this one principal aspect of racial relations.)

Thus, not only do the men on our list have the reputation of being influential, but when they wanted the mayor to do something, he did it. When they opposed something the rest of the community wanted and the mayor was willing to go along with, it did not get done. When these men would not endorse peaceful desegregation, the city did not have it. And when these men backed peaceful desegregation, the city had peaceful desegregation. So apparently there is a power structure. But we hypothesize that the power structure does not want to wield influence in New Orleans.

First, there is a general withdrawal of the elite from politics. This may seem strange, since Morrison was elected on the basis of a reform vote and was generally seen as a reform mayor interested in economic development. And Morrison certainly had the support of the economic elite. But in contrast to other southern cities, the economic leaders did not play a prominent role in his election. He was not a candidate chosen by the elite, nor was he a member of their group. If the economic leaders had wished to recruit a candidate to run against Mayor Maestri in 1946, it is unlikely that they would have chosen Morrison. He was from the right section of town (the uptown silk-stocking section) and he had "good breeding"—he was the scion of a 150-year-old Creole family. But a handsome thirty-four year old playboy who moves in a fast crowd is hardly the type of candidate business leaders generally seek to represent their interests in the city government. One must keep in mind, in trying to understand why Morrison was drafted for the position, that no one else wanted to run and that Maestri was considered to be a shoo-in. No one, of course, knew what "the Girls" could accomplish. And no one knew what they were getting when they elected Morrison. What they got was a non-local, a man with a burning ambition to become president some day. With his city in crisis in the late 1950's and in 1960, Morrison was pursuing the governorship of a segregationist state and taking the stance that he thought would enhance that personal goal. By contrast, the mayor of Atlanta was completely a local with little time for anything but the city's business and no ambitions beyond the mayor's office.

Oddly enough, though Maestri was Long's man, the anti-Long business leaders seemed quite content with him and even praised the wisdom of those who declined to battle him. All it took was a little conservatism on Maestri's part to wed the anti-Long economic elites of New Orleans to the machine that, throughout the thirties, had plundered the city and destroyed self-government in New Orleans. The New Orleans economic elites withdrew from the political battlefront for two decades, until after Morrison was elected by the clubwomen.

The failure of the elite to play major roles in politics is equally pronounced in the school board elections. When the Independent Women's Organization began its drive to reform the schools, they were unable to find any man who would run for the board, and had to elect Mrs. Jackie Leonhard instead. Later on they were also to recruit men, but in general these were men active in the middle-class associations, rather than in the circles of the elite.

Related to this withdrawal from politics is the fact that the elite seem to have only a mild interest in such matters as economic development. The drive to develop the Port was spearheaded by Morrison, and one respondent remarked that in that effort Morrison brought the economic leaders together in a concerted campaign for economic development for the first time. It is of course difficult to know why New Orleans has been unable to attract new industry, but whatever the reason, New Orleans does not have a strong "booster" spirit or any strong organizations committed to attracting industry.

Without this strong interest in economic development, the proponents of peaceful desegregation could gain little leverage by threatening the elite with "another Little Rock." In Atlanta, the mayor hired a management consultant firm to produce a report on the failure of new plants to move to Little Rock, and the report was a best-seller among the elite. In New Orleans, a Little Rock businessman was brought into the city, only to discover that no one wanted to hear him.

Finally we arrive at the conclusion that, whatever the reason, the New Orleans elite is simply more traditional than the elite of Atlanta or Baton Rouge. In many ways, New Orleans is dominated by its old wealth. In an effort to pursue the implications of this, we asked six members of the civic elite—including three of the four men most frequently named as influentials —how long they had lived in New Orleans and how they felt about the city.

Four of the six volunteered the information that their family had been in New Orleans for over a century. In response to the second question, two of them added that "money means little in New Orleans," and they unanimously praised New Orleans for its "way of life"—its "pleasant and gracious" set of social relations. If they were critical of New Orleans, it was only of the climate, and the one man who complained that the city was resistant to change was also the one man who was not named as one of the elite.

In some of these interviews, we brought up the subject of Atlanta and Houston—New Orleans' two rival cities. (In 1920, New Orleans was larger than Houston and Atlanta combined; if present trends continue, however, it will soon be the smallest of the three.) It was here that the comment that money was unimportant in New Orleans became relevant. The two rival cities are considered to be not truly southern; they are money-grubbing, ruled by the nouveau riche, and made repugnant by their brashness and boosterism, their lack of culture and civility. As one top influential put it, "Yes, but who'd want to live there?"

In cities like Atlanta and Houston, money and achieved status count for everything. But in New Orleans, being a native and coming from a good family count for everything. New Orleans is thus an anachronism—a traditionalist society in mid-twentieth-century America. We find attitudes in New Orleans which were prevalent in the traditionalist societies of the nineteenth-century South, the most obvious of which is a resistance to new ideas and new values. Since new values are brought in by new wealth and by outsiders, the economic elite of New Orleans is predictably not as hospitable to new industry as the elites in other southern cities. We saw a dramatic illustration of this point when we learned of some real estate speculators and contractors with ambitious plans for downtown New Orleans. They were either northerners or came from working-class origins, and thus they found New Orleans a very unfriendly city.

A second attitude inherent in the traditionalist ideology is aloofness from politics and governmental affairs. To the nineteenth-century capitalist, business was more important than government (unless he wanted to buy a city streetcar franchise). A third attitude typical of the southern traditionalist is so obvious that we might almost overlook it here—racial prejudice . . . . [W]e may find a .   .   .   concrete example of the ramifications of prejudice in the elite if we recall that the Times-Picayune (whose publisher and editor were both listed as influentials) could not decide which would be a worse disaster—integration or closing the schools. Another of the top leaders refused to support the school board because the school toilets would be unsegregated.

There were three groups of people in New Orleans who had power that could have been used to prevent the breakdown of social control, and each of these groups used too little influence too late to prevent the crisis. The school board waited until the last possible moment to begin a campaign to keep the schools open, and even then they were hesitant to commit themselves. The elected officials kept a minimum amount of law and order and used little of their influence on the state legislature. The civic elite did not act at all on the issue of race until January, although it did lend its support to the Sutherland campaign. For each group there is an explanation: the school board was insecure and conservative on racial matters, Mayor Morrison had an eye on the governor's mansion, the civic elite was traditional and aloof from civic activity and politics. Furthermore, these are not three random factors that happened to coincide. The school board was weak because it did not include the first-line elite (such as those who serve in Columbus), the second-line elite (as in Montgomery), or even the third-line elite (as in Atlanta). If Morrison was ambitious, it must be added that only one who was ambitious would have been willing to undertake a last-minute campaign against the Maestri machine.

New Orleans is politically disorganized almost to the point of having a power vacuum. The one well-organized group with money, prestige, control over communications, and technical skill is the civic elite—and it has taken little more than a casual interest in city politics. The city had been reformed, true; but the most powerful political organization behind this reform was a collection of women's clubs.

William K. Muir, Jr., Law and Attitude Change—Prayer in the Public Schools *

Can law change deep-rooted attitudes? Can legislation promote racial or religious tolerance or a democratic spirit? Can law affect the hearts of men: their feelings about themselves, their reactions toward others, their ideas about the world in which they live?

To probe these questions, I explored in some depth the attitudes of a group of educators toward schoolhouse religion—the daily recitation of the Lord's Prayer and Holy Scripture in the public schools of one American city [called "Midland"]. Assessments of their attitudes were made before and after the United States Supreme Court's decision in the *Schempp* case,[1] by which "religious exercises" in the nation's public schools were prohibited as unconstitutional. The assumption of this study was that if we are eventually to answer the grander questions posed above, we ought to start with the microscopic problem, Did *Schempp* have an effect on the attitudes of a group of educators toward schoolhouse religion? . . .

Over and over again in the interviews the officials described the personal impact of the prayer cases in physical terms. The law touched a "sore point"; it made a "wound"; it took a "slice out of our thunder"; it left a "scar." To these men and women the change in attitude which they had undergone was like a medical operation in which the morbid part of an organ is excised.

If I follow through with the surgical metaphor to which the respondents naturally gravitated, it highlights four important circumstances about the

---

* *Source:* Law and Attitude Change 1, 122–38 (1974). Professor of Political Science, University of California at Berkeley.

1. School District of Abington Township v. Schempp, 374 U.S. 208 (1963).

[The first interviews were begun in February 1963; the follow up ones, in January 1964. In March 1964, a new controversy flared up, over the school board's racial imbalance plan. Ed. note.]

process of attitude change. A successful physical operation requires a patient who is willing to undergo its discomforts; it needs surgeons and nurses whom the patient trusts; it calls for the use of sharp and functional instruments to minimize the intrusion; and there must follow a convalescent period in which new tissues can form to bind the incision. Not too dissimilarly, attitude change involves the individual's incentive to excise old attitudes, trustworthy associates who aid the individual to adapt, the intellectual tools to confine psychological repercussions to a minimum, and a social environment sufficiently compatible to permit new attitudes to develop.

The Motive to Change

Most of the twenty-eight men and women we have observed were originally equivocators. To some degree they espoused two or more incompatible attitudes on the same subject at the same time. These inconsistencies stemmed from discrete experiences. They learned in childhood that the Supreme Court was valuable and in adolescence that judges were hypocrites. Their priests told them that religion was the basis of morality; their history teachers described the religious persecutions which sent the Pilgrims to America; and their college professors said that a non-sectarian religious ceremony gave a nice tone to the classroom. In the period before the *Schempp* case the average Midland official hardly thought twice about the inconsistency which existed, for example, between his personal belief in the more religion the better and his preference for a school policy permitting only a hurried recital of a fifty-word prayer.

Until the *Schempp* case few officials had any motive to integrate their attitudes into a consistent pattern. No one rebuked them for being equivocal. In fact, harboring incompatible attitudes allowed them to adjust to incompatible groups of friends.

The law, however, motivated officials all the way down the line to get their indecision under control. They knew that at least a part of their mixed feelings was outside the law and was bound to get them into trouble with those whom the law vindicated. Furthermore, the teachers looked to the principals, the principals to the school board, and so on, for answers of how to keep out of court or what to do if they were hailed before a magistrate. Everyone in the Midland educational system seemed to know that certain organized groups were looking to this decision as an answer to things they had been hoping for.

The threat of [a] civil law suit [to enforce *Schempp*] was especially convincing to the average Midland educator because the potential complainants appeared to him so bizarre; they were "atheists", "free thinkers", the "little religions", the "ultraliberals", "a bunch of crackpots", the "inverse bigots," and "hypersensitive communicants," "individualists that like to be a little different", people who indulge in "tactics like the Fascists used", "Communists (Khruschev is an atheist)", persons to whom "something bad psychologically has happened." Schelling has pointed out the special bargaining force of men who refuse to be sensible. "If a man knocks at a door and says that he will stab himself on the porch unless given $10, he is more likely to get the $10 if his eyes are bloodshot." [2]　Like the drunk too inebriated to know better, the minority groups that looked to the prayer cases as an answer to things they had been hoping for were likely to be too obstinate or too unintelligent to realize what they were doing when they brought a lawsuit.

The threat made the official's inherited equivocal feelings an issue.　He had a choice: either he had to get his feelings into some kind of coincidence himself, or he could look upward to higher officials to give him guidelines.　Somewhere, however, "the buck has to stop" . . . . A decision had to be made to deal with the imminent threat.

To illustrate the intensity of the pressure upon officials to resolve their indecisiveness, let us look at the fate of State Commissioner Foley.　He was a popular man before the *Schempp* case.　The former president of Midland's Teachers' College, he was respected by most of the staff in the Midland public school system.

The day *Schempp* was decided, Rynne [a junior high school principal] telephoned him.　Miss Barber [an elementary school principal] wrote him.　The school board waited expectantly to see what he would do.　Other school boards explicitly asked his advice.

Foley did not want to spare time for a decision which he rightly regarded as counterproductive.　Miss O'Brien [another elementary school principal], in her remote little way, was accurate when she said, "The way I see it, he was not excited by it."　And so, to Rynne on the phone, "he wouldn't give a definite yes or no."　In reply to Miss Barber, "his letters weren't too strong."　To Chairman [of the School Board] Rizzuto waiting for some guide, "He just didn't make any sense: he said nothing at all about it; it was a lot of doubletalk and worse."

Foley did not resolve his mixed feelings when everyone demanded that he . . . "develop some arguments pro or con the decision or come up with some compromise."　Foley did not want to do his homework and to undergo the discomforts of making a commitment one way or the other.　Later, when he was confronted with an adversary like Goldman [a lawyer and School Board member] who had arranged his "intellectual, emotional and ethical feelings . . . into some kind of coincidence," his equivocation looked foolish.　Former friends . . . watched his position be refuted by the opinion of Goldman.　Former detractors . . . were more firmly convinced that he lacked leadership.

Foley suffered a personal disaster, in terms of his reputation and personal affection, as a result of his equivocation.　As a state education commissioner, he competed for the attention of teachers and citizens with local school boards, irate parents, educational critics, educators in the national and state governments, and private educational groups—even university presidents.　In one evasive moment he lost whatever competitive advantage he possessed in Midland.　Thereafter, his aspirations to accomplish important things would be far more likely to be frustrated until this disaster somehow could be redeemed.　No school board was likely to defer to a man who was a

2.　Thomas C. Schelling, The Strategy of Conflict (Cambridge, Mass.: Harvard University Press, 1960), p. 22.

"chicken," whose positions were "unspeakable," who "never says what [he] thinks," who talked "doubletalk," and who was unwilling to get embroiled in an unpopular issue. If he were to get the Board in a tough spot, he might leave it dangling and   .   .   .   "not help us out at all."

The law forces an official to be a leader or a fool. One does not equivocate in the immediate vicinity of a law suit. [As it turned out, in July the Commissioner interpreted *Schempp* to permit prayers. The Midland board took the opposite position. In November, the State Attorney General supported the board and rebuked the Commissioner.]

Every school administrator in Midland, large or small, had at some time or another undergone an experience analogous to Foley's, and the memory of such a personal debacle was a spur to resolving long-standing inconsistencies. They knew that the protection of other goals depended upon their personal reputations for decisiveness.

A Trustworthy Environment: Voluntarism

What determined the direction in which the equivocation was resolved? Of all the factors within the Midland educational organization, the most crucial was the informal group with which the individual official was affiliated   .   .   .   .

In any small group of friends there is a commitment to stay together. Each member has a stake in maintaining pleasantry and in keeping the group going. The rewards of friendship justify compromises. With trustworthy comrades working in the same profession, a Midland official had a chance to relax and to talk shop indiscreetly, knowing his confidence would be kept. He took solace from people who saw his troubles as he did, and received praise from friends who shared his triumphs.

Within each of these voluntarist groups there were forces tending to disintegration: divisive issues unexpectedly intruded, and decisions over the allotment of group time to one subject or another produced friction. To protect the group from fragmentation, its members worked centripetally, agreeing on the need to get agreement, to have unity.

Each of the informal voluntarist groups within the system in its turn worked for, enjoyed, and lauded itself for its little unities. When a divisive issue intruded, every member pitched in to define a common meeting point on which all his friends could converge to form a practical unanimity.

Within the friendship group, however, each partner was also an adversary, wanting collective agreement which was as close to his own starting point as possible. In this mixed adversary-friend situation, a potential meeting place which was qualitatively unique had an irresistible attraction. It was not that a particular unique focal point was substantively the most attractive to the majority of the members; indeed, all members of the group might be unhappy with it. But the strongest argument for accepting a unique point of compromise was the rhetorical question "If not here, then where?" The law in the *Schempp* case was just such a focal point. No doubt it was satisfactory to very few members of the Midland school system, but members of the small groups could find no other single point of coordination. Some point of agreement had to be reached before the small group fragmented or the threatened law suit materialized, and the rule of *Schempp,* almost by default, won the day in one informal group after another. After all, if the agreement was not at the separatist point designated by the Supreme Court, where else could it be? Add to the pressing need for agreement the fact that some of these groups contained an educator whose original separatist convictions had been vindicated by the prayer case and whose determination to stand up for her rights was clear to her friends in the group, and it is not overly difficult to see the possibility of widespread agreement to comply, although initially the majority of persons in the organization opposed compliance.

. . . [S]mall informal groups function within an organization to maintain a zone of indifference. In the Midland school system, such was the case. The member of the small informal group who modified his attitudes in accordance with *Schempp* was compensated by his fellows with both praise and gratitude redeemable in the future. Mrs. Hanna [a board member] noted, for example, that Rizzuto "played the game, and he decided with us." Because the school board was an on-going informal group, a compromising member like Rizzuto could count on his colleagues to reciprocate on some other issue in the future.

If an informal group had been together for a long time and had attained unity on a series of issues, the experience of solidarity increased the self-confidence of its members. Whenever one member persuaded an accommodating friend to accept his attitude, the persuading partner hardened his own convictions. . . . The willingness of members in a productive small informal group to accommodate their fellows worked a kind of self-persuasion, eliminating doubts and reducing equivocation.

Within these groups of trustworthy persons, mutually desiring to find a point of agreement on any divisive issue, the Midland official aired his deepest convictions on the matter of schoolhouse religion. He unashamedly let his equivocations rise to the surface, where they were examined by his friends. In resolving his own inconsistencies, he listened to their "guidance" without feeling diminished by his dependence on their help.

Visualize, for example, the always vocal principal Miss Mercer listening to her troubled and apolitical friends Miss Battistella and Miss FitzGerald [all three were elementary school principals and Roman Catholics]. Then, as the conversational initiative returned to her, she gently filled in for them the historical background of the Court's positions on separation of church and state. . . . She began by admitting, woman to woman, her own misgivings about the *Schempp* case (for example, she agreed with Miss Battistella that the public school prayer ban might encourage Catholic parents to place their children into parochial institutions), but as she continued she introduced the bright side. After all, the new program of character education might be successful; the firm stand of the board prevented public upheaval; and news media were generally favorable to the prayer ban; the Midland school system, in other matters, was really going places; and so forth. In this trusting, unthreatening, and pleasant association, the overcoming of the resistance to change was begun.

The Tools

What happened to the participants in these intimate conversations? The principal contribution of these informal talks was to provide officials important intellectual tools. These tools permitted the individuals to accept the Supreme Court decision and at the same time to preserve undamaged the absolute maximum of their old attitude structures. Miss O'Hara remarked on the origins of the sharp verbal distinction which had enabled her to accept the fact that the Court's separatism and the teacher's obligation to her pupils were compatible.

> Being Catholic, I could not make a distinction between guidance and prayer. I did not see how I would still be free to function as I had a guide after the board policy. . . . Dr. Bartkowitz [the superintendent] pointed out I could still. As a school person I gave a great deal of guidance to individuals, and it had a religious bent to it. . . . But Dr. Bartkowitz saw no reason why I could not still function in a moral guidance position to the individual student, because the rule was only that students as a group could not participate in a prayer ritual at the school.

This differentiation between guidance and prayer was of the utmost consequence to Miss O'Hara. Without it, she faced the dilemma of disobedience or demoralization, of being a bad citizen or a bad teacher. With the opportunity to talk matters out with her co-religionist Dr. Bartkowicz, the dilemma dissolved.

> . . . By partly redefining familiar concepts, the individual distinguished between philosophy and religion, between individual prayers and collective prayers, between manners and meditation, and between guidance to individuals and ritual. Small groups provided the social areas in which there took place this process of breaking up previously unitary concepts into their good and bad components.

Differentiation was not the only intellectual tool developed in these intimate conversations among friends. . . . The interviews provided at least one striking instance of a small group consensually arriving at a reinterpretation of a prior attitude. In the small group composed of the school board and superintendents, eight of the nine participants expressed a variation of [this] theme.

> As I say, it's purely hypothesis now, but I have a feeling that the concern that has been occasioned by the necessity to fill the vacuum in character education will have a very good effect. I think this will be very salutary.

That is, the prayer ban, in the short run, did produce bad effects (old attitude), but concern about the bad effects, in the long run and in terms of the quality of family life and of school curriculum, has been very salutary (the sweet lemon twist). In small groups whose members wished to preserve their solidarity, such Candide-like techniques were well received.

A third intellectual device disseminated within friendship groups was remedial reanalysis. The official reexplained why his old beliefs were true.

For example, the realist Miss Barrone re-searched [sic] the causal connection between schoolhouse prayers and the strengthening of underprivileged children. She came to the conclusion that the most important effect of prayer was that it tended to calm middle-class teachers, who consequently were more patient with their students. With this analysis of the causalties involved, Miss Barrone had begun to look for other ways to bolster the teacher's strength. In small groups articulate researchers such as Miss Barrone tended to dominate conversation.

Differentiation, sweet lemons, remedial research—in common these intellectual tools involved reanalysis of concepts, values, and relationships. In the decentralized privacy of friendship groups, the reanalysis was made; and when it was completed for each individual, the relief from the pressure of equivocation was very pleasant.

External Protection

A man's attitudes are not neutral, but affect others. His friends and neighbors come to rely on the stability of his inclinations.

Attitude change toward schoolhouse religion, imminent or completed, threatened the status quo, and invariably these reliant friends and neighbors took countervailing action: they retaliated, they blackmailed, they entreated, they tried to make the change so costly to the individual that he would return to the fold . . . .

. . . [Those who inwardly denied the virtue of the decision] were never able to cope with the assaults within their social circles when they tentatively tried the new separatist attitudes. The challenge of this social denunciation was too severe for [them], and they retreated. Loss of comradeship and pleasantry, then, was one effective cost the external community could inflict.

Another cost was diminution of political status. The politician Farley [an elementary school principal] and the seven other professionals . . . had a stake in the cooperative relationships they had established with their colleagues and their neighborhoods. These officials had to worry about jeopardizing this hard-won political goodwill. It was extremely vulnerable to attack.

Third, attitude change had economic implications. Irate parents and teachers had the option of removing their children to suburban public schools or to Midland parochial and private schools, thereby diminishing a sizeable part of the business of Midland's school system.

Fourth, there was physical jeopardy from the persons who took the law into their own hands. Rynne, the former athlete, told a story of one father who "came in waving his fist at me and said he was going to accompany his son to school and they would get down on their knees in the classroom and pray." . . .

In sum, when an official changed his attitude on the issue of school house prayers, he incurred certain social, political, economic, and physical dangers which he could avoid if he recanted. If law was to be effective in inducing permanent psychological change, it had to provide a benign, post-operative environment where the individual needed only to flex his muscles, not depend on them for his very life.

In Midland, the legal system was at least in part successful in providing protection. Its first assistance was largely negative. The lawyers, at least the prominent ones, did not divide on the issue. The profession looked monolithic, despite the fact that an election campaign highlighted the legal issue. The newsworthy lawyers acted in concert . . . . As a result, whenever irate citizens looked for legal and philosophical weapons to hurl at some vulnerable official, they found none, at least in the legal realm. Without a news maker sufficiently expert to define the portents of the prayer ban, social retaliation flagged.

The second device was that law had national application, and invited vindicated citizenry simultaneously and in every town to enforce it. Thus, while the prayer ban conceivably disadvantaged Midland, the school systems of Chicago and Cleveland suffered the same handicap concomitantly. The old saying about garlic eaters, "An odor common to both is offensive to none," applies as well to the law.

As a matter of fact, however, the law was not invoked uniformly. Both Midland suburbs, Northland and Milltown, resisted the prayer cases without incurring the costs of a civil suit. It was a fortuity that Midland as a locality had sufficient unrelated advantages to compensate for this legal discrimination. In an evenly matched competition, however, the disparity might have invited backlash, for the effect was to give the lawbreaker a relative advantage over the compliant.

So, too, with the Midland private parochial and non-sectarian schools. If, in fact, the public and private schools had been in closer competition, the prayer ban, with its application limited to governmental schools, might have worked invidiously. The public and private schools were not competitive, however, because the government retained the significant advantage of providing education free of charge. It enjoyed a monopoly of gratuitous schooling. While even-handed enforcement of the law is essential, it need exist only for effective competitors.

Finally, the political elite, with control over the instruments of public order, were ready to punish lawbreakers within Midland itself. Criminal retaliation against the law-abiding never became a serious threat, because punishments by the guardians of the public order were so certain and so severe. It was not even thinkable . . . .

Unanimity among legal spokesmen, even-handed enforcement of the law among competitors, certain punishment for the illegal posse—these factors ameliorated the Midland environment in which the school system was set. Without the law's protection, however, the compliant, gently nursing his new feelings, would have had to reverse his legal commitment. There was too much else at stake to be left dangling in the open . . . .

The Significance

Judge Learned Hand, late of the federal Court of Appeals, once cautioned:

> I often wonder whether we do not rest our hopes too much upon constitutions, upon laws and upon courts. These are false hopes; believe me, these are false hopes. Liberty lies in the hearts of men and women; when it dies there, no constitution, no laws, no court can save it; no constitution, no law, no court can even do much to help it. While it lies there it needs no constitution, no law, no court to save it.[3]

Because Judge Hand is so highly regarded, because his premise of legal inefficacy runs through the controversy regarding judicial activism and restraint, and because analysis of what he said brings out the importance of this study, it warrants examination.

"The spirit of liberty" Hand defines as "the spirit which is not too sure that it is right." It is tolerance, empathy, compromise, compassion, humility —in short, a certain kind of deep-rooted attitude, to use the language of the present study.

According to Judge Hand, such profound attitudes can not be shaped by legal institutions. The family, education, friends and experience will create and preserve such attitudes, but not law. We need only to reflect on the experience of the backlashers [the law accentuated the very attitudes to be changed] and the nulists [the law had no effect on the attitudes] to recognize the wisdom contained in Hand's caution.

There are, however, two fallacies in Hand's argument. First, while it is true that law is unlikely to save any important attitudes if it is solidly opposed by all other social institutions, the same holds true of any institution which breeds moral attitudes—the churches and the schools, for example—which also would be unable to preserve a spirit of liberty if it were alone in a hostile world. Where there is no monolithic trend, however, where the population is ambivalent or indecisive or divided, where the life or death of a deep-rooted attitude is still uncertain, then legal institutions can and apparently do shore up the partisans (or detractors) of that attitude. For every situation where all institutions disintegrate at once (as Hand's remarks presuppose), there are a dozen marginal situations where opposing factions are nearly equal and where a small but decisive factor (such as a legal decision) can make a difference.

Which leads to the second fallacy, the fallacy of ignoring contexts. Hand wrote, "While [the spirit of liberty] lies [in the hearts of men], it needs no constitution, no law, no court to save it." It depends.

If a tolerant man exists in circumstances where unless legal institutions can protect him he will suffer the loss of his dignity, friends, or customers if he behaves tolerantly, then Judge Hand is wrong when he observes that law is unnecessary to save the spirit of liberty. As a general proposition there

---

3. Learned Hand, The Spirit of Liberty
(New York: Vintage, 1959), p. 144.

are some circumstances (such as the tolerant man in the intolerant society) where law is both necessary and effective in shaping and preserving deep-rooted attitudes.

These two fallacies I call the Fallacies of Cataclysm and Overabstraction. The Fallacy of Cataclysm refers to ignoring the importance of small factors in a state of near equilibrium. The Fallacy of Overabstraction refers to ignoring the differences in social contexts in which persons live. Hand was too wise an observer of the human condition to have committed these fallacies unwittingly; he was urging a point by overstating it. Nonetheless, his cautionary words about placing too many hopes in the law have given some succor to those who have resisted recent legal changes begun by legislatures and, particularly, by the Supreme Court of the United States. . . .

At the same time, law is a sensitive social tool. Ineptly used, it produces backlash. Even properly used, law causes friction when it encounters a contrary community opinion, which wears away the reputation of lawmakers. This damage to the goodwill of legal institutions has to be calculated in counting the costs of employing the law to alter widely held social attitudes.

Awareness that law is a delicate tool does not, however, imply its need for overprotection. Factors exist in American society which strengthen the effectiveness of legal institutions. The first is the development of an organized law profession, with professional standards and national training, a body of lawyers which can and sometimes does act in concert to support lawmakers. Among the profession is a growing number of respected lawyers strongly identified with the law-making institutions. In the development of this identification a factor of importance is the experience young lawyers get as clerks to federal and state judges. If Goldman is typical, a youthful apprenticeship to the judiciary [he was once a judicial clerk] results in an enduring loyalty.

Second, there is the tradition of written judicial opinions and their dissemination. The judicial opinion, in conjunction with judicial review of legislation, contains a description and justification of the action of lawmakers and bureaucrats. Thus, in effect, judges are made the spokesmen for legal institutions in general, and publication of their opinions gives them as such spokesmen a communication initiative that is comparable to the advantage a president of the United States enjoys when he uses his press conferences effectively. The idiom of the judicial opinion shapes the idiom of political debate. Language, we have observed, facilitates attitude change, and in the molding of attitudes the written judicial word, widely published in a literate society, has a substantial influence.

The third advantage is that American legal institutions have been organized so that the concerned private citizen can invoke and indirectly enforce the law. The threat of law does not depend entirely, or even in large part, upon the whim of bureaucrats. Rather, as was the fact in *Schempp,* enforcement of law comes by way of a civil action, brought by persons and interest groups seeking civil, not criminal, remedies. The subtlety of the common law procedure may be that it puts the responsibility for calling the law into effect in the lap of the private citizen with a stake in the matter. To sharpen the point: perhaps one reason for the ineffectiveness of Prohibition was its dependence for enforcement upon criminal means exclusively. No private rights to invoke judicial power in its name were created.

The organization of the legal profession, the written judicial opinion, and the tradition of the civil remedy—these three distinctively legal factors, coupled with the social factors of pluralism, voluntarism, and literacy, account in large part for the potential power of the law in the United States.

.   .   .

———

In thinking about Muir's study and the essay of Alexander Bickel that follows next, you might speculate on the consequences of placing the school prayer decision on an all-deliberate-speed basis. Would that have enhanced its effectiveness?

2.   THE DESIRE FOR EFFICACY AND ITS INFLUENCE

Alexander M. Bickel, **The Supreme Court at the Bar of Politics***

.   .   .   I have suggested that the rule of principle in our society is neither precipitate nor uncompromising, that principle may be a universal guide but not a universal constraint, that leeway is provided to expediency along the path to, and alongside the path of, principle, and finally, that principle is evolved conversationally not perfected unilaterally. All this the decision in the *School Segregation Cases* illustrates. But it illustrates also .   .   .   what is commonly more obscure—another sort of colloquy that can take place after the declaration of governing principle by the Court, and another sort of reprise that is open to the political institutions and to society at large.

Everybody knows that the lifetime of applied principle is often no longer than one or two generations. Principle may endure beyond that, of course, but not necessarily as formulated in the application; if it does endure, it will often be through a process of renewal. And so what one means by the ultimate, final judgment of the Court is quite frequently a judgment ultimate and final for a generation or two. That, however, is quite long enough to worry about, and the really interesting question, therefore, is what happens within the generation or two. Here the history of the *School Segregation Cases* sheds its light.

Composing for the Anthologies

The *School Segregation Cases* were five suits by individual Negro children praying that they be admitted to previously all-white schools, from which the local authorities had excluded them on the ground that they were Negroes and must attend schools reserved solely for Negroes. Thus was the issue raised whether separate schools for the two races are permissible in principle. The Court decided that they are not and that Negro children must have full entry to a common public-school system, free of restrictions or classifications based on race; so that, there being no other valid

* *Source:* A. M. Bickel, The Least Dangerous Branch 244–53 (1962), Ch. 6.   Bickel (1924–74): Professor of Law, Yale University.

reason for excluding a Negro child from a school previously reserved for whites, race could not be erected into such a reason, and the Negro child must be admitted. That was the decision of May 17, 1954. But no decrees issued from the Court on that date. The formulation of appropriate decrees presented, the Court said, "problems of considerable complexity." Therefore, the Court called the parties to another argument at which they were to address themselves to these problems. Must it, the Court asked, order the immediate admission of Negro children to schools of their choice, within the limits of normal school districting, or may the Court "permit an effective gradual adjustment to be brought about from existing segregated systems to a system not based on color distinctions"?

Like poetry, then, as a verse by Auden tells us, the great *School Segregation* decision of May 17, 1954, made nothing happen. But only like poetry. Only as it may sometimes seem that nothing but power, purposefully applied, can affect reality, only thus could it be said that this first decision had no consequences. And this is a species of romantic illusion. In fact, announcement of the principle was in itself an action of great moment, considering the source from which it came. Immediately, in the phrase Lincoln used about slavery, segregation was placed "where the public mind shall rest in the belief that it is in course of ultimate extinction"; and very shortly, in many places, there was a palpable effect. By early 1955, although there had as yet been no decree and there was thus no command outstanding which bound anyone to act, more than five hundred school districts had abandoned policies of segregation. This did not represent a large percentage of all segregated districts, and the number of Negro pupils actually admitted to white schools was even less impressive. Still, some 250,000 Negro pupils were affected. Although by far not all were now in white schools, some were, and, in any event, the racial barrier had been removed. This degree of integration had taken place in St. Louis and elsewhere in Missouri, in Baltimore, in West Virginia, Kentucky, Oklahoma, Tennessee, Texas, New Mexico, and Arizona, and in two school districts in Arkansas, where later the crisis of Little Rock was to strike. None of these cities and states was a party to the actual Supreme Court cases. Integration had taken place also in Delaware and Kansas, which were involved in the litigated cases, and most massively in Washington, D. C., also a litigant.

In the fall of 1954, there had been some minor trouble. Segregation may be a way of life, but it subsumes racism, and that, in turn, is an idea, and it can be a fighting idea. So provoked sometimes by itinerant agitators, a few riots flared up here and there in Delaware, Maryland, and West Virginia. They were promptly and easily quelled by local officials who knew what they were doing and why. One small community in Delaware, which had integrated eleven Negroes in a school with 665 whites, gave up in the face of some rioting. But this was an isolated instance. On the whole, what followed immediately upon the Court's pronouncement of principle was encouraging and edifying. It spoke well for the effective role of the institution in the American system.

Very edifying, a demonstration of the spell the Court is capable of casting, a manifestation of its prestige, of the force of its mystique, and of the dominion of ideas. But the Court does not sit to make precatory pronouncements. It is not a synod of bishops, nor a collective poet laureate. It does not sit, Mr. Freund has remarked, "to compose for the anthologies." [5] If it did, its effectiveness would be of an entirely different order; and if it did, we would not need to worry about accommodating its function to the theory and practice of democracy. The Court is an organ of government. It is a court of law, which wields the power of government in disposing of concrete controversies. Therefore, although pronouncement of the principle of May 17, 1954, was in itself not an ineffectual act, it did not alone discharge the function of the Court. Jurisdiction having been assumed, that function required issuance of a legal decree.

All Deliberate Speed

In the vast majority of cases—barring those that are dismissed outright as not suitable for adjudication—the normal and expected judgment of the Court is a crisp and specific writing which tells one of the parties exactly what he must do, such as pay a judgment, deliver certain real estate, cease from doing something or indeed, go to jail. The equivalent in these cases would have been a decree ordering the named children, and perhaps, since these were class actions, all children in the five school districts affected who were similarly situated, to be admitted forthwith to the white schools of their choice. The question is, why should the Court not have issued such a decree? Indeed, one might have asked whether the Court could do other than issue such a decree?

If the Court, at the other extreme from merely composing for the anthologies, sat merely to render ad hoc judgments applicable solely to the precise circumstances of a controversy immediately before it, then also it would not be the powerful institution it is, and its function would need no elaborate justification. The matrix paradox of all paradoxes concerning the Court is . . . that the Court may only decide concrete cases and may not pronounce general principles at large; but it may decide a constitutional issue only on the basis of general principle. In the performance of this function—to use a fittingly lofty phrase of Chief Justice Hughes—the Court's "mental vision embraces distant scenes." [6] Hence, while the cases immediately before the Court exemplified and concretized the issue of principle, they could not be treated as if they involved only the admission of three or four dozen children to a dozen schools. Rather, these five cases did necessarily bring into view the total situation in all the states having school districts which are organized on a segregated basis.

The admission of a few dozen children to a few dozen schools would have presented no very grave difficulties calling for a study of means of gradual adjustment. Seen in its totality, however, as involving some 5,000 school districts, nearly nine million white children and nearly three million colored, the situation exhibited great variety and complexity. To begin with, a vast number of statutes and regulations, incorporating centrally or mar-

5. Freund, The Supreme Court and Civil Liberties, 4 Vand.L.Rev. 533, 552 (1951) . . . .

6. C. E. Hughes, "Mr. Justice Brandeis," in F. Frankfurter, ed., Mr. Justice Brandeis (New Haven: Yale University Press, 1932), p. 3.

ginally the rule of segregation, would require change in order to conform
to the new principle. In most places, pupils are assigned to schools in accordance with the location of their homes. Where there were two schools,
one white and one Negro, residential lines would now have to be drawn
purely on a geographical basis, rather than, as previously, in accordance with
both geography and race. But the two schools may not have been of equal
size or otherwise of equal character. Thus elimination of the racial criterion may create a new and expensive problem before solving the old one. In
general, running two segregated school systems is more expensive than running a single integrated one. But that is not to say that the process of integration might not require some immediate additional expenditures. And
the cost of money is either money or time. Further complications: New assignments and other administrative arrangements for teachers, including
Negro teachers, would have to be made. School transportation would have
to be rearranged. No doubt, since Negro schools had seldom been fully
equal to white ones, and since many Negro pupils came from economically
and culturally depressed families, differences in educational background
and aptitudes would be found between Negro and white pupils, and allow-
ance might have to be made for these in the process of integration.

These and yet additional problems varied greatly from place to place,
from cities to rural districts, and in relation, among other things, to the
ratio of Negro to white pupils in a given district. No solution could be
fabricated and made effective overnight, no matter what anyone might
wish. Moreover, the Court itself bore some responsibility for the situation it
now faced. The practice of segregation was no invention of the Court, to be
sure. But segregation had prospered and come to full flower at least partly
in reliance upon the Court's decision [in Plessy v. Ferguson], in 1896, that
it conformed to constitutional principle. No one hearing the late John W.
Davis, who argued to the Court in behalf of South Carolina, emphasize how
pervasive and how solidly founded the present order was could fail to be
sensible of the difficulties to be encountered in uprooting it. "Sometime to
every principle," Mr. Davis remarked, "comes a moment of repose when
it has been so often announced, so confidently relied upon, so long continued, that it passes the limits of judicial discretion and disturbance." Mr.
Davis was intimating that the existing order was no longer subject to judicial change, that no principle of its alteration could now be announced.
This was to deny the essence of the Court's function, and on the basis of
no more than an inadmissibly static view of society. But the suggestion that
judicial alteration of so deep-rooted an order of things raises special problems to which the Court must have due regard—that could not be ignored.

It is unusual but not unheard of for the Court—for all courts, in the
general run of business, constitutional and otherwise—to be faced with practical factors that make it impossible to achieve immediately a result called for
by the Court's decision. Thus in applying the antitrust laws the Court may
find—has in fact found—that a large corporation, the American Tobacco
Company, for example, was a near-monopoly and violated the antitrust laws,
and that it should be dissolved and split into its component parts. Or the
Court may find, as it recently did, that ownership by the DuPont Corporation of a potentially controlling block of shares in the General Motors Cor-

poration violates the antitrust laws, and that the relationship should be severed. But such things cannot be made to happen in a day.[9] Here is the elemental demonstration of the truth that very often society can only strive to attain the rule of principle through a tangle of perverse and intractable existing facts, which are themselves man-made but which are not any the less real for that. Pupil-assignment rules were willfully scrambled by men pursuing racist ends rather than ordained of God; but that does not render them any easier to unscramble overnight, once the racist principle has been extracted. There is embedded in Anglo-American law, quite aside from the peculiar function of constitutional adjudication, the recognition that, on occasion, the law proposes but, for a time at least, the facts of life dispose. The mainstream of Anglo-American legal development has been the common law, administered by judges who evolved and reasoned from principle. But there soon flowed alongside the common law another stream, the equity jurisdiction, whose headwaters were in the discretionary royal prerogative. Equity was a more flexible process, more unprincipled, initially quite ad hoc. It often worked the accommodation that made the rigorous principles of the common law fit to live with. Our courts in general now combine both functions—common law and equity—and so does the process of judicial review.

The considerations I have recited are significant and would by themselves have led the Court, in the exercise of equity discretion, to allow southern communities some time in which to comply with the principle of integration; these considerations nevertheless leave out of account the most important factor. This is the unpalatable but undeniable fact that the principle of the integration of the races ran counter to the views and the strong emotions, not merely the customary practice, of a majority of the people to whose way of life it was to be chiefly applicable; that is to say, most southern whites. Despite the prefatory work that had been in progress . . . for over a generation, despite many hopeful steps toward the integration of universities in the South, and, in any event, the absence of any concerted political offense against such integration or against other judicial measures enforcing equal treatment of the races—despite all that, resistance could be expected. This does not mean that the principle of integration was wrong or not suitable for pronouncement by the Court in discharge of the constitutional functions, nor even that the Court should have had more pause before announcing it, fearing that it was not a fundamental presupposition "to which widespread acceptance may fairly be attributed." First, even if the task of the Court were . . . to follow the election returns, surely the relevant returns would be those from the nation as a whole, not from a white majority in a given region. Fragmented returns cannot count, any more than early ones. Secondly, as we have seen, the Court's principles are required to gain assent, not necessarily to have it. Yet the fact of foreseeable opposition, like the fact of confident reliance, "so long continued," that Mr. Davis stressed, could not be ignored; it constituted an additional problem.

The problem was not simply one of enforcement. The task of the Court is to seek and to foster assent, and compliance through assent. Of

9. United States v. American Tobacco Co., 221 U.S. 106 (1911); United States v. E. I. duPont de Nemours & Co., 366 U.S. 316 (1961).

course, we normally enforce some of our law—the criminal law, for example—forthwith and without recourse. But the analogy from the *Segregation Cases* to criminal statutes and the like fails completely. The latter are generally based on almost universal acceptance and need to be enforced only against an infinitesimal minority, consisting of the irreducible number of the antisocial. When they are not so based, they are commonly ineffective. Witness the great prohibition experiment. Witness also anti-gambling statutes, most sex laws, and other laws policing morals. Indeed, we have built-in devices for ensuring the ineffectiveness of such laws—for example, the discretion of prosecutors, who are most often politically sensitive officers, and the grand and petit jury systems. When we say, as we often do, that government should not try to enforce morality by law, we mean that in our system it cannot enforce it, if it is merely an idiosyncratic morality or a falsely professed morality, not the generally accepted one. It follows that in achieving integration, the task of the law—and all the more, the task of judicial rather than legislative law—was not to punish law breakers but to diminish their number. For what was to be foreseen was the resistance, not of a fringe of misfits, but of a populace. In such circumstnces, it may not be prudent to force immediate compliance.

This brings me to a third and very closely connected reason that the Court did not order sudden execution of the principle pronounced in the *Segregation Cases*. The foreseeable opposition was localized, indeed isolated; but, by the same token, it was entrenched in a cluster of states, where it formed a majority. Thus concentrated, it could wield power disproportionate to what its numbers would give if it were distributed nationwide. Hence, just possibly, the cooperation of the political branches might be needed in fostering the necessary acceptance; and it could well be looked for, since the Solicitor General of the United States, responding to the Court's request for an expression of views as amicus curiae, had appeared and supported the cause of the Negro plaintiffs. Normally, to be sure, the Court relies on its own great and mystic prestige and on the skilled exertion of its educational faculty, and finds them quite sufficient even to overcome or otherwise direct the will of the political branches. But here exceptional circumstances were in prospect. Moreover, there might be, not only resistance to the full reach of the new principle, but even difficulty with the enforcement of specific decrees. In an enforcement crisis of any real proportions, the judiciary is wholly dependent upon the Executive. The Court commands no significant police power of its own. It is true that both in practice and in theory the Executive is obliged to come to the judiciary's support in any such crisis. Good order demands it, regardless of the merits. But there are degrees of enthusiasm in rendering executive support, and there are ways of emphasizing order above, rather than alongside of, the decision that is to be enforced. If, then, one of those rare occasions was to be foreseen when the cooperation of the political institutions might be needed both in fostering consent and quite possible in administering enforcement, the Court was entitled to consider that those institutions are uncomfortable in the presence of hard and fast principles calling for universal and sudden execution. They respond naturally to demands for compromise, and, of course, they contain within themselves representatives of the opposition that was to be foreseen.

They can most readily be expected to exert themselves when some leeway to expediency has been left open. Therefore, time and an opportunity for accommodation were required not only for the other reasons I have mentioned; they were needed also to form part of the invitation that the Court might be extending to the political institutions to join with it in what amounted to a major enterprise of social reform.

It was argued to the Court by the National Association for the Advancement of Colored People, which represented the Negro children, that the task of making the Court's principle accepted and effective would be facilitated by a sort of shock treatment, an order of immediate and sudden execution, rather than by allowing time for accommodation. The argument was that "gradualism, far from facilitating the process, may actually make it more difficult; that, in fact, the problems of transition will be a good deal less complicated than might be forecast. . . . Our submission is that this, like many wrongs, can be easiest and best undone, not by 'tapering off' but by forthright action." Conceivably this might have been so, but certainly it was not a broadly shared view. What the Court was more widely urged to do, especially by the Solicitor General, and what it did was in effect to require the local school boards to submit to the lower federal courts plans providing for a start toward integration—that is, to begin with, the admission of a few children here and there on some staged scheme. Any such plan would have to contain also the promise of eventual full compliance, meaning an eventually unified school system in which children would be assigned to schools without distinction of race, although other criteria, including residential ones, might still be effective. The Court set no deadlines. None was seriously urged, it being realized, as the Solicitor General pointed out, that conditions vary and "that maximum periods tend to become minimum periods." The test for each plan would be whether it was moving in good faith toward integration "with all deliberate speed."

.   .   .

The remedial strategy of *Brown* had two aspects: (1) the remand to the district courts to fashion the specifics of the dsegregation plans; and (2) the legitimation of gradualism in dismantling dual school systems. The first branch has not been seriously controverted. The dual school system existed at the time in some five thousand school districts throughout the United States. All agreed that the district courts—rather than the Supreme Court—were the most appropriate forums for working out the specifics of each desegregation plan, for taking into account the "variety" and "complexity" of local conditions.

The second branch, the legitimation of gradualism, was of an entirely different order. It seemed vulnerable on two grounds. The first was a question of social engineering: was it true that the compromise with principle was likely to enhance the effectiveness of the pronouncement? As Professor Bickel notes, the plaintiffs argued that it was not. They contended that gradualism revealed a weakness in the commitment to principle and would be read as an invitation to resistance—i. e., if we drag our feet long enough and hard enough, there is a chance that the Court will change its mind. There is much in the subsequent history to suggest that the plaintiffs were right in their analysis. See, e. g., Cooper v. Aaron, 358 U.S. 1 (1958); Wright v. Georgia, 373 U.S. 284 (1963); see also the Crane and Muir essays above. But Professor Bickel does not let the plaintiffs have the benefit of hindsight. He dismisses their view on two grounds—one, that, at the time, their view "was not a broadly shared view;" and two, that it was not the position urged by the Solicitor General. Is either point sufficient?

The plaintiffs would surely point to the fact that the Solicitor General was a political officer as much as he was a lawyer and officer of the court. As such, he was likely to reflect the (well-known) ambivalence of his president, Eisenhower. See R. Kluger, Simple Justice: The History of Brown v. Board of Education and Black America's Struggle for Equality (1976). The plaintiffs would also surely insist that the so-called "broadly shared view" did not exist in fact, or was at best only a mask for the hostility towards the Court's pronouncement. For our purposes, the more important question is not to decide which side was correct—either prospectively or retrospectively. Rather, our purpose is to ask how a court is supposed to make that choice?

The excruciating quality of that decision relates to the second ground for finding fault with gradualism and the compromise with principle that it implies: why should a court be saddled with the burdens, uncertainties, and anxieties inherent in the task of trying to engineer social conduct? Why shouldn't the Court find its efficacy in other domains—in establishing the principles of our public morality—and not compromise its contribution in that domain by gestures designed to generate assent to its own pronouncements? Bickel writes: "[T]he Court does not sit to make precatory pronouncements. It is not a synod of bishops, nor a collective poet laureate . . . . The Court is our organ of government. It is a court of law, which wields the power of government in disposing of concrete controversies." Are you persuaded?

Chapter 8

THE INTERRELATIONSHIP OF STRUCTURAL ELEMENTS —ALTERNATIVE CONCEPTIONS OF ADJUDICATION

We have analyzed adjudication by fragmenting it into a series of elements. We have looked at party structure and the role of representatives; at the attributes and organization of decisional personnel; at the processes of information acquisition and exchange; and, lastly, at the forms and meaning of judicial action. Now the moment has come to look at adjudication as an integrated whole, to see how these various individual elements relate to one another. For this purpose, we turn to the essay of Abram Chayes, who attempts this reconstructive process. He proceeds by positing an overview and then mapping the changes that have accrued over time. He suggests that today we are at a distinct historical phase in our conception of adjudication, a turning point in the history of procedure.

Abram Chayes, **The Role of the Judge in Public Law Litigation***

.   .   . We are witnessing the emergence of a new model of civil litigation and, I believe, our traditional conception of adjudication and the assumptions upon which it is based provide an increasingly unhelpful, indeed misleading framework for assessing either the workability or the legitimacy of the roles of judge and court within this model.

In our received tradition, the lawsuit is a vehicle for settling disputes between private parties about private rights. The defining features of this conception of civil adjudication are:

(1) The lawsuit is *bipolar*. Litigation is organized as a contest between two individuals or at least two unitary interests, diametrically opposed, to be decided on a winner-takes-all basis.

(2) Litigation is *retrospective*. The controversy is about an identified set of completed events: whether they occurred, and if so with what consequences for the legal relations of the parties.

(3) *Right and remedy are interdependent*. The scope of the relief is derived more or less logically from the substantive violation under the general theory that the plaintiff will get compensation measured by the harm caused by the defendant's breach of duty—in contract by giving plaintiff the money he would have had absent the breach; in tort by paying the value of the damage caused.

(4) The lawsuit is a *self-contained* episode. The impact of the judgment is confined to the parties. If plaintiff prevails there is a simple compensatory transfer, usually of money, but occasionally the return of a thing or the performance of a definite act. If

* *Source:* 89 Harv.L.Rev. 1281, 1282–
1305, 1308–09, 1313–16 (1976). Professor of Law, Harvard University.

defendant prevails, a loss lies where it has fallen. In either case, entry of judgment ends the court's involvement.

(5) The process is *party-initiated* and *party-controlled*. The case is organized and the issues defined by exchanges between the parties. Responsibility for fact development is theirs. The trial judge is a neutral arbiter of their interactions who decides questions of law only if they are put in issue by an appropriate move of a party .   .   .   .

Whatever its historical validity, the traditional model is clearly invalid as a description of much current civil litigation in the federal district courts.[12] Perhaps the dominating characteristic of modern federal litigation is that lawsuits do not arise out of disputes between private parties about private rights. Instead, the object of litigation is the vindication of constitutional or statutory policies. The shift in the legal basis of the lawsuit explains many, but not all, facets of what is going on "in fact" in federal trial courts. For this reason, although the label is not wholly satisfactory, I shall call the emerging model "public law litigation."

The characteristic features of the public law model are very different from those of the traditional model. The party structure is sprawling and amorphous, subject to change over the course of the litigation. The traditional adversary relationship is suffused and intermixed with negotiating and mediating processes at every point. The judge is the dominant figure in organizing and guiding the case, and he draws for support not only on the parties and their counsel, but on a wide range of outsiders—masters, experts, and oversight personnel. Most important, the trial judge has increasingly become the creator and manager of complex forms of ongoing relief, which have widespread effects on persons not before the court and require the judge's continuing involvement in administration and implementation. School desegregation, employment discrimination, and prisoners' or inmates' rights cases come readily to mind as avatars of this new form of litigation. But it would be mistaken to suppose that it is confined to these areas. Antitrust, securities fraud and other aspects of the conduct of corporate business, bankruptcy and reorganizations, union governance, consumer fraud, housing discrimination, electoral reapportionment, environmental management—cases in all these fields display in varying degrees the features of public law litigation.

The object of this article is first to describe somewhat more fully the public law model and its departures from the traditional conception, and second, to suggest some of its consequences for the place of law and courts in the American political and legal system.

12.   .   .   .   There are, I think, corresponding departures from the traditional model in the state courts. There, litigation itself has declined in importance, and the overwhelming bulk of cases is disposed of either ad- ministratively, through the mechanism of default (as in consumer credit and landlord-tenant cases), or by manipulation of consent (as in divorce and criminal matters) .   .   .   .

I. The Received Tradition

The traditional conception of adjudication reflected the late nineteenth century vision of society, which assumed that the major social and economic arrangements would result from the activities of autonomous individuals. In such a setting, the courts could be seen as an adjunct to private ordering, whose primary function was the resolution of disputes about the fair implications of individual interactions.   The basic conceptions governing legal liability were "intention" and "fault."   Intentional arrangements, not in conflict with more or less universal attitudes like opposition to force or fraud, were entitled to be respected, and other private activities to be protected unless culpable.   Government regulatory action was presumptively suspect, and was tested by what was in form a common law action against the offending official in his private person.   The predominating influence of the private law model can be seen even in constitutional litigation, which, from its first appearance in Marbury v. Madison, was understood as an outgrowth of the judicial duty to decide otherwise-existing private disputes.

Litigation also performed another important function—clarification of the law to guide future private actions.   This understanding of the legal system, together with the common law doctrine of stare decisis, focussed professional and scholarly concern on adjudication at the appellate level, for only there did the process reach beyond the immediate parties to achieve a wider import through the elaboration of generally applicable legal rules. So, in the academic debate about the judicial function, the protagonist was the appellate judge (not, interestingly enough, the appellate *court*), and the spotlight of teaching, writing, and analysis was almost exclusively on appellate decisions .   .   .   .

In contrast to the appellate court, to which the motive power in the system was allocated, the functions of the trial judge were curiously neglected in the traditional model.   Presumably, the trial judge, like the multitude of private persons who were supposed to order their affairs with reference to appellate pronouncements, would be governed by those decisions in disposing smoothly and expeditiously of the mine-run of cases.   But if only by negative implication, the traditional conception of adjudication carried with it a set of strong notions about the role of the trial judge.   In general he was passive.   He was to decide only those issues identified by the parties, in accordance with the rules established by the appellate courts, or, infrequently, the legislature.

Passivity was not limited to the law aspects of the case.   It was strikingly manifested in the limited involvement of the judge in factfinding. Indeed, the sharp distinction that Anglo-American law draws between factfinding and law declaration is itself remarkable.   In the developed common law system, these were not only regarded as analytically distinct processes, but each was assigned to a different tribunal for performance.   The jury found the facts.   The judge was a neutral umpire, charged with little or no responsibility for the factual aspects of the case or for shaping and organizing the litigation for trial.

Because the immediate impact of the judgment was confined to the parties, the traditional model was relatively relaxed about the accuracy of its factfinding. If the facts were not assumed as stated in the pleadings or on the view most favorable to one of the parties or determined on the basis of burdens or presumptions, they were remitted to a kind of black box, the jury. True, some of the law of evidence reflects an active suspicion of the jury. And if the evidence adduced would not "rationally" support a finding for one party or the other, the case could be taken from the jury. But the limits of rationality are inevitably commodious. Even law application, unless there was a special verdict (never much favored in this country), was left to the jury's relatively untrammeled discretion. Indeed, one of the virtues of the jury was thought to be its exercise of a rough-hewn equity, deviating from the dictates of the law where justice or changing community mores required.

The emphasis on systematic statement of liability rules involved a corresponding disregard of the problems of relief. There was, to be sure, a good deal of discussion of measure of damages, as a corollary to the analysis of substantive rights and duties. Similarly, the question of the availability of specific performance and other equitable remedies came in for a share of attention. But the discussion was carried forward within the accepted framework that compensatory money damages was the usual form of relief. Prospective relief was highly exceptional in the traditional model and was largely remitted to the discretion of the trial judge. . . .

Besides its inherent plausibility in the nineteenth century American setting, the traditional model of adjudication answered a number of important political and intellectual needs. The conception of litigation as a private contest between private parties with only minimal judicial intrusion confirmed the general view of government powers as stringently limited. The emphasis on the appellate function, conceived as an exercise in deduction from a few embracing principles themselves induced from the data of the cases, supplied the demand of the new legal academics for an intellectual discipline comparable to that of their faculty colleagues in the sciences, and for a body of teachable materials. For practitioners and judges, the same conception provided a professional methodology that could be self-consciously employed. Most importantly, the formulation operated to legitimate the increasingly visible political consequences of the actions of a judiciary that was not politically accountable in the usual sense.

II.   The Public Law Litigation Model

Sometime after 1875, the private law theory of civil adjudication became increasingly precarious in the face of a growing body of legislation designed explicitly to modify and regulate basic social and economic arrangements. At the same time, the scientific and deductive character of judicial lawmaking came under attack, as the political consequences of judicial review of that legislation became urgent.

These developments are well known and have become an accepted part of our political and intellectual history. I want to address in somewhat greater detail the correlative changes that have occurred in the procedural structure of the lawsuit. Most discussion of these procedural developments, while recognizing that change has been far-reaching, proceeds on the assumption that the new devices are no more than piecemeal "reforms" aimed at improving the functional characteristics or the efficiency of litigation conducted essentially in the traditional mode. I suggest, however, that these developments are interrelated as members of a recognizable, if changing, system and that taken together they display a new model of judicial action and the judicial role, both of which depart sharply from received conceptions.

A.   The Demise of the Bipolar Structure

Joinder of parties, which was strictly limited at common law, was verbally liberalized under the codes to conform with the approach of equity calling for joinder of all parties having an "interest" in the controversy. The codes, however, did not at first produce much freedom of joinder. Instead, the courts defined the concept of "interest" narrowly to exclude those without an independent legal right to the remedy to be given in the main dispute. The definition itself illustrates the continuing power of the traditional model. The limited interpretation of the joinder provisions ultimately fell before the banners of "rationality" and "efficiency." But the important point is that the narrow joinder rule could be perceived as irrational or inefficient only because of a growing sense that the effects of the litigation were not really confined to the persons at either end of the right-remedy axis.

The familiar story of the attempted liberalization of pleadings under the codes is not dissimilar. Sweeping away the convolutions of the forms of action did not lead to the hoped-for elimination of technicality and formality in pleading. The immediate response was the construction of cause-of-action rules that turned out to be almost as intricate as the forms themselves. The power of the right-remedy connection was at work here too, but so also was the late nineteenth century impulse toward systemization, which tended to focus attention on accurate statement of legal theory. The proponents of "efficiency" argued for a more informal and flexible approach, to the end that the courts should not have to rehear the same complex of events. This argument ultimately shifted the focus of the lawsuit from legal theory to factual context—the "transaction or occurrence" from which the action arose. This in turn made it easier to view the set of events in dispute as giving rise to a range of legal consequences all of which ought to be considered together.[44]

This more open-ended view of the subject matter of the litigation fed back upon party questions and especially intervention. Here, too, the sharp constraints dictated by the right-remedy nexus give way. And if the right to participate in litigation is no longer determined by one's claim to relief at the hands of another party or one's potential liability to satisfy the claim, it becomes hard to draw the line determining those who may participate so as to eliminate anyone who is or might be significantly (a weasel word) affected by the outcome—and the latest revision of the Federal Rules of Civil Procedure has more or less abandoned the attempt.

---

44. The transaction or occurrence thus became the basis for defining the unit that ought to be litigated as one "case." . . .

The question of the right to intervene is inevitably linked to the question of standing to initiate litigation in the first place. The standing issue could hardly arise at common law or under early code pleading rules, that is, under the traditional model. There the question of plaintiff's standing merged with the legal merits: On the facts pleaded, does this particular plaintiff have a right to the particular relief sought from the particular defendant from whom he is seeking it? With the erosion of the tight structural integration of the lawsuit, the pressure to expand the circle of potential plaintiffs has been inexorable. Today, the Supreme Court is struggling manfully, but with questionable success, to establish a formula for delimiting who may sue that stops shorts of "anybody who might be significantly affected by the situation he seeks to litigate."

"Anybody"—even "almost anybody"—can be a lot of people, particularly where the matters in issue are not relatively individualized private transactions or encounters. Thus, the stage is set for the class action . . Whatever the resolution of the current controversies surrounding class actions, I think it unlikely that the class action will ever be taught to behave in accordance with the precepts of the traditional model of adjudication. The class suit is a reflection of our growing awareness that a host of important public and private interactions—perhaps the most important in defining the conditions and opportunities of life for most people—are conducted on a routine or bureaucratized basis and can no longer be visualized as bilateral transactions between private individuals. From another angle, the class action responds to the proliferation of more or less well-organized groups in our society and the tendency to perceive interests as group interests, at least in very important aspects . . . . .

B.   The Triumph of Equity

One of the most striking procedural developments of this century is the increasing importance of equitable relief. It is perhaps too soon to reverse the traditional maxim to read that money damages will be awarded only when no suitable form of specific relief can be devised. But surely, the old sense of equitable remedies as "extraordinary" has faded.

I am not concerned here with specific performance—the compelled transfer of a piece of land or a unique thing. This remedy is structually little different from traditional money-damages. It is a one-time, one-way transfer requiring for its enforcement no continuing involvement of the court. Injunctive relief, however, is different in kind, even when it takes the form of a simple negative order. Such an order is a presently operative prohibition, enforceable by contempt, and it is a much greater constraint on activity than the risk of future liability implicit in the damage remedy. Moreover, the injunction is continuing. Over time, the parties may resort to the court for enforcement or modification of the original order in light of changing circumstances. Finally, by issuing the injunction, the court takes public responsibility for any consequences of its decree that may adversely affect strangers to the action.

Beyond these differences, the prospective character of the relief introduces large elements of contingency and prediction into the proceedings. Instead of a dispute retrospectively oriented toward the consequences of a closed set of events, the court has a controversy about future probabilities. Equitable doctrine, naturally enough, given the intrusiveness of the injunction and the contingent nature of the harm, calls for a balancing of the interests of the parties. And if the immediate parties' interests were to be weighed and evaluated, it was not too difficult to proceed to a consideration of other interests that might be affected by the order.

The comparative evaluation of the competing interests of plaintiff and defendant required by the remedial approach of equity often discloses alternatives to a winner-takes-all decision. An arrangement might be fashioned that could safeguard at least partially the interests of both parties, and perhaps even of others as well. And to the extent such an arrangement is possible, equity seems to require it. Negative orders directed to one of the parties—even though pregnant with affirmative implications—are often not adequate to this end. And so the historic power of equity to order affirmative action gradually freed itself from the encrustation of nineteenth century restraints. The result has often been a decree embodying an affirmative regime to govern the range of activities in litigation and having the force of law for those represented before the court . . . .

The interests of absentees, recognized to some extent by equity's balancing of the public interest in individual suits for injunction, become more pressing as social and economic activity is increasingly organized through large aggregates of people. An order nominally addressed to an individual litigant—the labor injunction is an early example—has obvious and visible impact on persons not individually before the court. Nor must the form of the action be equitable: A suit against an individual to collect a tax, if it results in a determination of the constitutional invalidity of the taxing statute, has the same result for absentees as a grant or denial of an injunction. Statutory construction, for example of welfare or housing legislation, may have a similar extended impact, again even if the relief is not equitable in form. Officials will almost inevitably act in accordance with the judicial interpretation in the countless similar situations cast up by a sprawling bureaucratic program.[65] We may call this a stare decisis effect, but it is quite different from the traditional image of autonomous adjustment of individual private transactions in response to judicial decisions. In cases of this kind, the fundamental conception of litigation as a mechanism for private dispute settlement is no longer viable. The argument is about whether or how a government policy or program shall be carried out . . . .

C.   The Changing Character of Factfinding

The traditional model of adjudication was primarily concerned with assessing the consequences for the parties of specific past instances of conduct. This retrospective orientation is often inapposite in public law litigation, where the lawsuit generally seeks to enjoin future or threatened action, or to modify a course of conduct presently in train or a condition presently existing. In the former situation, the question whether threatened action

---

65. Several courts have refusd to certify as class actions suits challenging government policy because if the plaintiff were successful, the government would certainly change its behavior in all instances . . . .

will materialize, in what circumstances, and with what consequences can, in the nature of things, be answered only by an educated guess. In the latter case, the inquiry is only secondarily concerned with how the condition came about, and even less with the subjective attitudes of the actors, since positive regulatory goals are ordinarily defined without reference to such matters. Indeed, in dealing with the actions of large political or corporate aggregates, notions of will, intention, or fault increasingly become only metaphors.

In the remedial phases of public law litigation, factfinding is even more clearly prospective. . . . [T]he contours of relief are not derived logically from the substantive wrong adjudged, as in the traditional model. The elaboration of a decree is largely a discretionary process within which the trial judge is called upon to assess and appraise the consequences of alternative programs that might correct the substantive fault. In both the liability and remedial phases, the relevant inquiry is largely the same: How can the policies of a public law best be served in a concrete case?

In public law litigation, then, factfinding is principally concerned with "legislative" rather than "adjudicative" fact. And "fact evaluation" is perhaps a more accurate term than "factfinding." The whole process begins to look like the traditional description of legislation: Attention is drawn to a "mischief," existing or threatened, and the activity of the parties and court is directed to the development of on-going measures designed to cure that mischief. Indeed, if, as is often the case, the decree sets up an affirmative regime governing the activities in controversy for the indefinite future and having binding force for persons within its ambit, then it is not very much of a stretch to see it as, pro tanto, a legislative act.

Given these consequences, the casual attitude of the traditional model toward factfinding is no longer tolerable. The extended impact of the judgment demands a more visibly reliable and credible procedure for establishing and evaluating the fact elements in the litigation, and one that more explicitly recognizes the complex and continuous interplay between fact evaluation and legal consequence. The major response to the new requirements has been to place the responsibility for factfinding increasingly on the trial judge. The shift was in large part accomplished as a function of the growth of equitable business in the federal courts, for historically the chancellor was trier of fact in suits in equity. But on the "law side" also, despite the Supreme Court's expansion of the federal right to jury trial, there has been a pronounced decline in the exercise of the right, apart, perhaps, from personal injury cases.[76]

The courts, it seems, continue to rely primarily on the litigants to produce and develop factual materials, but a number of factors make it impossible to leave the organization of the trial exclusively in their hands. With the diffusion of the party structure, fact issues are no longer sharply drawn in a confrontation between two adversaries, one asserting the affirma-

---

76. Some indication of the decline in the number of jury trials in civil cases can be derived from data of the Administrative Office of the United States Courts. In 1960, for example, 3,035 of 6,988 civil trials were jury trials. See 1960 Administrative Office of the United States Courts Ann. Rep. 103. In 1974, although the total number of civil trials had almost doubled to 10,972, jury trials remained at 3,569. 1974 id. at 318.

tive and the other the negative. The litigation is often extraordinarily complex and extended in time, with a continuous and intricate interplay between factual and legal elements. It is hardly feasible and, absent a jury, unnecessary to set aside a contiguous block of time for a "trial stage" at which all significant factual issues will be presented. The scope of the fact investigation and the sheer volume of factual material that can be exhumed by the discovery process pose enormous problems of organization and assimilation. All these factors thrust the trial judge into an active role in shaping, organizing and facilitating the litigation. We may not yet have reached the investigative judge of the continental systems, but we have left the passive arbiter of the traditional model a long way behind.

D.   The Decree

The centerpiece of the emerging public law model is the decree. It differs in almost every relevant characteristic from relief in the traditional model of adjudication, not the least in that it *is* the centerpiece. The decree seeks to adjust future behavior, not to compensate for past wrong. It is deliberately fashioned rather than logically deduced from the nature of the legal harm suffered. It provides for a complex, on-going regime of performance rather than a simple, one-shot, one-way transfer. Finally, it prolongs and deepens, rather than terminates, the court's involvement with the dispute.

The decree is also an order of the court, signed by the judge and issued under his responsibility (itself a shift from the classical money judgment).[79] But it cannot be supposed that the judge, at least in a case of any complexity, composes it out of his own head. How then is the relief formulated?

The reports provide little guidance on this question. Let me nonetheless suggest a prototype that I think finds some support in the available materials. The court will ask the parties to agree on an order or it will ask one party to prepare a draft. In the first case, a negotiation is stipulated. In the second, the dynamic leads almost inevitably in that direction. The draftsman understands that his proposed decree will be subject to comment and objection by the other side and that it must be approved by the court. He is therefore likely to submit it to his opponents in advance to see whether differences cannot be resolved. Even if the court itself should prepare the initial draft of the order, some form of negotiation will almost inevitably ensue upon submission of the draft to the parties for comment.

The negotiating process ought to minimize the need for judicial resolution of remedial issues. Each party recognizes that it must make some response to the demands of the other party, for issues left unresolved will be submitted to the court, a recourse that is always chancy and may result in a solution less acceptable than might be reached by horse-trading. Moreover, it will generally be advantageous to the demanding party to reach a solution through accommodation rather than through a judicial fiat that may be performed "in a literally compliant but substantively grudging and unsatisfactory way." Thus, the formulation of the decree in public law litigation introduces a good deal of party control over the practical outcome. Indeed,

79. The judgment in a common law action was not an order to the defendant to pay but a recital that "it is considered that plaintiff do recover so much from the defendant."   .   .   .

relief by way of order after a determination on the merits tends to converge with relief through a consent decree or voluntary settlement. And this in turn mitigates a major theoretical objection to affirmative relief—the danger of intruding on an elaborate and organic network of interparty relationships.

Nevertheless it cannot be supposed that this process will relieve the court entirely of responsibility for fashioning the remedy. The parties may fail to agree. Or the agreement reached may fail to comport with the requirements of substantive law as the judge sees them. Or the interests of absentees may be inadequately accommodated. In these situations, the judge will not, as in the traditional model, be able to derive his responses directly from the liability determination, since, as we have seen, the substantive law will point out only the general direction to be pursued and a few salient landmarks to be sought out or avoided. How then is the judge to prescribe an appropriate remedy?

If the parties are simply in disagreement, it seems plausible to suppose that the judge's choice among proposals advanced by the *quondam* negotiators will be governed by his appraisal of their good faith in seeking a way to implement the constitutional or statutory command as he has construed it. The interest in a decree that will be voluntarily obeyed can be promoted by enforcing a regime of good faith bargaining among the parties. Without detailed knowledge of the negotiations, however, any attempt to enforce such a regime can rest on little more than an uneasy base of intuition and impression. Where a proposed decree is agreed upon among the parties, but is inadequate because the interests shared by the litigants do not span the range that the court thinks must be taken into account, resubmission for further negotitaion may not cure this fundamental defect. Here too, the judge will be unable to fill the gap without a detailed understanding of the issues at stake in the bargaining among the parties.

For these reasons, the judge will often find himself a personal participant in the negotiations on relief. But this course has obvious disadvantages, not least in its inroads on the judge's time and his pretentions to disinterestedness. To avoid these problems, judges have increasingly resorted to outside help—masters, amici, experts, panels, advisory committees —for information and evaluation of proposals for relief. These outside sources commonly find themselves exercising mediating and even adjudicatory functions among the parties. They may put forward their own remedial suggestions, whether at the request of the judge or otherwise.

Once an ongoing remedial regime is established, the same procedure may be repeated in connection with the implementation and enforcement of the decree. Compliance problems may be brought to the court for resolution and, if necessary, further remediation. Again, the court will often have no alternative but to resort to its own sources of information and evaluation.

I suggested above that a judicial decree establishing an ongoing affirmative regime of conduct is pro tanto a legislative act. But in actively shaping and monitoring the decree, mediating between the parties, developing his own sources of expertise and information, the trial judge has passed beyond even the role of legislator and has become a policy planner and manager.

E.   A Morphology of Public Law Litigation

The public law litigation model portrayed in this paper reverses many of the crucial characteristics and assumptions of the traditional concept of adjudication:

(1) The scope of the lawsuit is not exogenously given but is shaped primarily by the court and parties.

(2) The party structure is not rigidly bilateral but sprawling and amorphous.

(3) The fact inquiry is not historical and adjudicative but predictive and legislative.

(4) Relief is not conceived as compensation for past wrong in a form logically derived from the substantive liability and confined in its impact to the immediate parties; instead, it is forward looking, fashioned ad hoc on flexible and broadly remedial lines, often having important consequences for many persons including absentees.

(5) The remedy is not imposed but negotiated.

(6) The decree does not terminate judicial involvement in the affair: its administration requires the continuing participation of the court.

(7) The judge is not passive, his function limited to analysis and statement of governing legal rules; he is active, with responsibility not only for credible fact evaluation but for organizing and shaping the litigation to ensure a just and viable outcome.

(8) The subject matter of the lawsuit is not a dispute between private individuals about private rights, but a grievance about the operation of public policy.

In fact, one might say that, from the perspective of the traditional model, the proceeding is recognizable as a lawsuit only because it takes place in a courtroom before an official called a judge.   But that is surely too sensational in tone.   All of the procedural mechanisms outlined above were historically familiar in equity practice.   It is not surprising that they should be adopted and strengthened as the importance of equity has grown in modern times .   .   .   .

III.   A First Appraisal

One response to the [public] law model of litigation would be to condemn it as an intolerable hodge-podge of legislative, administrative, executive, and judicial functions addressed to problems that are by their nature inappropriate for judicial resolution.   Professor Lon Fuller has argued that when such functions are given to the judiciary they are parasitic, in the sense that they can be effectively carried out only by drawing on the legitimacy and moral force that courts have developed through the performance of their inherent function, adjudication according to the traditional conception. A certain limited amount of such parasitism can be accommodated, but too much undermines the very legitimacy on which it depends, because the non-traditional activities of the judiciary are at odds with the conditions that ensure the moral force of its decisions.

From one perspective, the Burger Court may be seen to be embarked on some such program for the restoration of the traditional forms of adjudication. Its decisions on standing,[95] class actions,[96] and public interest attorneys' fees,[97] among others, achieve a certain coherence in this light. On the other hand, it is hard to believe that the Court is actuated by concern for jurisprudential orthodoxy. One suspects that at bottom its procedural stance betokens a lack of sympathy with the substantive results and with the idea of the district courts as a vehicle of social and economic reform . . . .

In any event, I think, we have invested excessive time and energy in the effort to define—on the basis of the inherent nature of adjudication, the implications of a constitutional text, or the functional characteristics of courts—what the precise scope of judicial activity ought to be. Separation of powers comes in for a good deal of veneration in our political and judicial rhetoric, but it has always been hard to classify all government activity into three, and only three, neat and mutually exclusive categories. In practice, all governmental officials, including judges, have exercised a large and messy admixture of powers, and that is as it must be. That is not to say that institutional characteristics are irrelevant in assigning governmental tasks or that judges should unreservedly be thrust directly into political battles. But such considerations should be taken as cautionary, not decisive; for despite its well rehearsed inadequacies, the judiciary may have some important institutional advantages for the tasks it is assuming:

First, and perhaps most important, is that the process is presided over by a judge. His professional tradition insulates him from narrow political pressures, but, given the operation of the federal appointive power and the demands of contemporary law practice, he is likely to have some experience of the political process and acquaintance with a fairly broad range of public policy problems. Moreover, he is governed by a professional ideal of reflective and dispassionate analysis of the problem before him and is likely to have had some experience in putting this ideal into practice.

Second, the public law model permits ad hoc applications of broad national policy in situations of limited scope. The solutions can be tailored to the needs of the particular situation and flexibly administered or modified as experience develops with the regime established in the particular case.

95. E. g., Warth v. Seldin, 422 U.S. 490 (1975).

96. E. g., Eisen v. Carlisle & Jacquelin, 417 U.S. 156 (1974); Zahn v. International Paper Co., 414 U.S. 291 (1973).

97. Alyeska Pipeline Serv. Co. v. Wilderness Society, 421 U.S. 240 (1975).

Third, the procedure permits a relatively high degree of participation by representatives of those who will be directly affected by the decision, without establishing a liberum veto.

Fourth, the court, although traditionally thought less competent than legislatures or administrative agencies in gathering and assessing information, may have unsuspected advantages in this regard. Even the diffused adversarial structure of public law litigation furnishes strong incentives for the parties to produce information. If the party structure is sufficiently representative of the interests at stake, a considerable range of relevant information will be forthcoming. And, because of the limited scope of the proceeding, the information required can be effectively focused and specified. Information produced will not only be subject to adversary review, but as we have seen, the judge can engage his own experts to assist in evaluating the evidence. Moreover, the information that is produced will not be filtered through the rigid structures and preconceptions of bureaucracies.

Fifth, the judicial process is an effective mechanism for registering and responding to grievances generated by the operation of public programs in a regulatory state. Unlike an administrative bureaucracy or a legislature, the judiciary *must* respond to the complaints of the aggrieved. It is also rather well situated to perform the task of balancing the importance of competing policy interests in a specific situation. The legislature, perhaps, could balance, but it cannot address specific situations. The bureaucracy deals with specific situations, but only from a position of commitment to particular policy interests.

Sixth, the judiciary has the advantage of being non-bureaucratic. It is effective in tapping energies and resources outside itself and outside the government in the exploration of the situation and the assessment of remedies. It does not work through a rigid, multilayered hierarchy of numerous officials, but through a smallish, representative task force, assembled ad hoc, and easily dismantled when the problem is finally resolved . . . .

There are also counter-instances and counter-arguments for each of the advantages of the public law model suggested above. Can the disinterestedness of the judge be sustained, for example, when he is more visibly a part of the political process? Will the consciously negotiated character of the relief ultimately erode the sense that what is being applied is law? Can the relatively unspecialized trial judge, even with the aid of the new authority and techniques being developed in public law litigation, respond adequately to the demands for legislative and predictive fact-finding in the new model? Against the asserted "responsiveness" of the courts, it may be argued that the insensitivity of other agencies represents a political judgment that should be left undisturbed. And although the courts may be well situated to balance competing policy interests in the particular case, if as is often true the decree calls for a substantial commitment of resources, the court has little basis for evaluating competing claims on the public purse. Each of these considerations needs exploration in much more detail—although I would hope that the discussion would proceed on the basis of what has been happening in the cases rather than a priori . . . .

IV. Some Thoughts on Legitimacy

. . . As the traditional model has been displaced in recent years, . . . questions of judicial legitimacy and accountability have reasserted themselves . . . .

. . . For it cannot be denied that public law litigation explicitly rejects many of the constraints of judicial method and procedure in which we have characteristically sought respite from the unease. Now, I do not deny that the law, like other creative and performing arts, encompasses a recognizable (and teachable) technique; and this technique plays an important part in the development of the medium and in the criticism and evaluation of its practitioners. But in the law, as elsewhere, technical virtuosity has never been a guarantee of acceptable performance.

Moreover, an amalgam of less tangible institutional factors will continue to operate to shape judicial performance in the public law system as in the past: general expectations as to the competence and conscientiousness of federal judges; professional traditions of conduct and performance; the accepted, often tacit, canons and leeways of office. These are amorphous. They mark no sharp boundaries. Their flexibility and vagueness can be abused. But other kinds of constraint are no less vulnerable; and the historical experience is that egregious violation has invariably activated a countervailing response.

More fundamentally, our transformed appreciation of the whole process of making, implementing, and modifying law in a public law system points to sources other than professional method and role for the legitimacy of the new model lawsuit. As we now begin to see it, that process is plastic and fluid. Popular participation in it is not alone through the vote or by representation in the legislature. And judicial participation is not by way of sweeping and immutable statements of *the* law, but in the form of a continuous and rather tentative dialogue with other political elements—Congress and the executive, administrative agencies, the profession and the academics, the press and wider publics. Bentham's "judge and company" has become a conglomerate. In such a setting, the ability of a judicial pronouncement to sustain itself in the dialogue and the power of judicial action to generate assent over the long haul become the ultimate touchstones of legitimacy.

In my view, judicial action only achieves such legitimacy by responding to, indeed by stirring, the deep and durable demand for justice in our society. I confess some difficulty in seeing how this is to be accomplished by erecting the barriers of the traditional conception to turn aside, for example, attacks on exclusionary zoning and police violence, two of the ugliest remaining manifestations of official racism in American life. In practice, if not in words, the American legal tradition has always acknowledged the importance of substantive results for the legitimacy and accountability of judicial action. . . .

---

1. For a parallel account of the tensions of civil adjudication, suggesting also a movement from (private) dispute settlement to (public) norm

declaration and enforcement, see Scott, Two Models of the Civil Process, 27 Stan.L.Rev. 937 (1975).

2.   Have the criminal and administrative processes also evolved along the lines suggested by Professor Chayes for civil litigation?   Or can it be said that the evolution in civil litigation represents a move toward a unified conception of legal procedure?   To the extent that civil litigation is moving closer to a public law model, it might be thought to be moving toward the criminal and administrative processes, generally considered to be paradigmatic instances of "public law" adjudication.   See, e. g., Packer, Two Models of the Criminal Process, 113 U.Pa.L.Rev. 1 (1964); Griffiths, Ideology in Criminal Procedure, or a Third "Model" of the Criminal Process, 79 Yale L.J. 359 (1970); Stewart, The Reformation of American Administrative Law, 88 Harv.L.Rev. 1669 (1975).

3.   In Chapter 1 we suggested, particularly through the essays of Professors Felstiner and Leff, that procedural systems are to a large extent limited by social structure.   Assuming this to be true, what changes in contemporary American social structure might account for the procedural changes that Professor Chayes describes?   Can it be that the basic unit of social structure has changed from the *individual* to the large-scale *organization*? How might this claim or, for that matter, even Chayes' claims about the procedural changes—the emergence of a new *model* of adjudication—be verified?

4.   In the closing passage of his essay, Professor Chayes considers the question of the legitimacy of the so-called new mode of adjudication.   He suggests that conformity to the traditional conception of role is neither a necessary nor a sufficient criterion of legitimacy.   Indeed, for Chayes, role fidelity may be inconsistent with the proper grounds of legitimacy—"the power . . . to generate assent over the long haul" or "substantive results."   But one wonders whether these latter criteria of legitimacy are in fact independent of or antithetical to the demand that individuals be faithful to their roles.   Can the justice of the "substantive result" be understood independently of performance in a role which is in large part defined by tradition?   Does the capacity "to generate assent" ultimately depend on fidelity to role?   Compare R. M. Cover, Justice Accused: Antislavery and the Judicial Process (1975), with O. M. Fiss, The Civil Rights Injunction (1978).

————

In assessing the legitimacy of the new model of adjudication, Professor Chayes took as his point of departure Professor Lon Fuller's essay, The Forms and Limits of Adjudication—it seemed to represent the tradition he was trying to surmount.   Fuller's essay was first prepared in 1957 and was widely circulated in mimeographed form (both within the Harvard Law School and beyond) for the next twenty years.   It had an important impact on a number of scholars in addition to Chayes.   (Portions of the essay were published in two articles by Fuller: Adjudication and the Rule of Law, 54 Proc.Am. Soc'y Int'l L. 1 (1960), and Collective Bargaining and the Arbitrator, 1963 Wis.L.Rev. 3 (1963).)   When Fuller died in 1978, the essay was not in finished form, yet it was of sufficient importance in the intellectual history of procedure to warrant publication by the Harvard Law Review.

Chayes' enterprise is primarily positivistic—he tries to describe the evolution of procedural forms. The normative questions—those of appraisal and the legitimacy of the emergent forms—are treated but secondarily. Fuller mirrors Chayes' emphases: he is primarily normative, and secondarily descriptive. Fuller maintains that there exists an essential core to the idea of adjudication, and he uses that as a standard for evaluation. His normative stance does not imply anything about what is or is not happening in the history of procedure, but it does strongly suggest that there are limits to what may rightly claim to be adjudication. These limits are exceeded only at some distinct moral risk.

Fuller emphasizes two ideas in formulating what is supposed to be the core of adjudication—one, a special kind of *participation*, and the other, *polycentrism*. The first concept determines the *form* that adjudication is to take—for example, how the judge is supposed to behave. The second sets the *limits* on the kinds of tasks suitable for adjudication—polycentric disputes are beyond the reach of adjudication. As it turns out, polycentric limitation is derived from the distinctive mode of participation (form)—rationalistic.

Fuller visualizes adjudication in the broadest terms: adjudication is not simply a method of dispute resolution—it is also a form of social ordering. As a form of social ordering, it is to be distinguished from other forms of social ordering, such as contract and elections, by the mode of participation by the affected party. The distinctive mode of participation for contracts is negotiation; for elections, voting; and for adjudication, presentation of proof and reasoned arguments. From this premise and the further premise that idealizes the distinctive mode of participation (as he puts it, adjudication is "institutionally committed" to acting on the basis of reasoned argument), Fuller proceeds to identify a number of attributes that are necessary and desirable for an adjudicatory process.

The first attribute, as you might imagine, is an adversary presentation by a lawyer. In the original text of this essay the discussion of this attribute was limited to a heading and a reference to a statement Professor Fuller coauthored with John D. Randall entitled Professional Responsibility: Report of the Joint Conference (appearing in 44 A.B.A.J. 1159 (1958)). Another attribute of adjudication remained only a heading in the essay—"Moot Cases and Declaratory Judgments." (Professor Fuller wrote: "There has not been time to consider seriously the problems presented by this title.") Due to these omissions, we have taken the liberty of dropping the identifying numbers that he used for his headings in the section entitled "The Forms of Adjudication." Also, we dropped the headings in the section entitled "The Limits of Adjudication."

One further point, perhaps also attributable to the unfinished nature of the essay, needs to be added by way of introduction. It concerns Fuller's very special conception of rationality—it is not just that adjudication is "institutionally committed" to reasoned argument, but more importantly that it is committed to a very special type of reasoned argument. This qualification appears most clearly when Fuller tries to defend his claim that poly-centric tasks are not suitable for adjudication. Taking the construction of a bridge as a paradigmatic polycentric task, Fuller acknowledges that "there are rational principles for building bridges." The problem is, as he sees it, that "there is no rational principle which states, for example, that the angle between girder A and girder B must always be 45 degrees. This de-pends on the bridge as a whole. One cannot construct a bridge by construct-ing successive separate arguments concerning the proper angle for every pair of intersecting girders. One must deal with the whole structure." Fuller leaves the reader to wonder why the rationalistic participatory mode that is said to mark adjudication cannot as a normative matter, as a statement of an ideal, embrace reasoned arguments about "whole structures."

In the decade immediately following the first appearance of Fuller's essay, adjudication in the guise of the federal court injunction became the principal form of "social ordering" used to reorganize a broad variety of "whole structures"—schools, prisons, mental hospitals—so as to bring them within the bounds of the Constitution. See, generally, O. M. Fiss, The Civil Rights Injunction (1978); see also pp. 361 and 421, supra. Fuller's essay cir-culated for some twenty years but it was never modified to address the chal-lenges posed—both positive and normative—by the litigative experience of the civil rights era. The essay was published in the late 1970s, but strikingly it always remained a statement of the late 1950s.

—————

Lon L. Fuller, **The Forms and Limits of Adjudication***

. . .

Adjudication and Rationality

. . . It may be said that the essence of adjudication lies not in the manner in which the affected party participates in the decision but in the office of judge. If there is a judge and a chance to appear before him, it is a matter of indifference whether the litigant chooses to present proofs or reasoned arguments. He may, if he sees fit, offer no argument at all, or pitch his appeal entirely on an emotional level, or even indicate his willing-ness that the judge decide the case by a throw of the dice. It might seem, then, that our analysis should take as its point of departure the office of judge. From this office certain requirements might be deduced, for exam-ple, that of impartiality, since a judge to be "truly" such must be impartial. Then, as the next step, if he is to be impartial he must be willing to hear both sides, etc.

The trouble with this is that there are people who are called "judges" holding official positions and expected to be impartial who nevertheless do not participate in an adjudication in any sense directly relevant to the sub-ject of this paper. Judges at an agricultural fair or an art exhibition may serve as examples. Again, a baseball umpire, though he is not called a judge, is expected to make impartial rulings. What distinguishes these functionaries

* *Source:* The Forms and Limits of Ad-judication, 92 Harv.L.Rev. 353, 365–71, 381–404 (1978). Fuller (1902–1978): Professor of Law, Harvard University.

is not that they do not hold governmental office, for the duties of a judge at a livestock fair would scarcely be changed if he were an official of the Department of Agriculture. What distinguishes them from courts, administrative tribunals, and boards of arbitration is that their decisions are not reached within an institutional framework that is intended to assure to the disputants an opportunity for the presentation of proofs and reasoned arguments. The judge of livestock may or may not permit such a presentation; it is not an integral part of his office to permit and to attend to it . . . .

It may be objected at this point that "reasoned argument" is, after all, not a monopoly of forensic proceedings. A political speech may take the form of a reasoned appeal to the electorate; to be sure, it often takes other forms, but the same thing may be said of speeches in court. This objection fails to take account of a conception that underlies the whole analysis being presented here the conception, namely, of a form of participating in a decision that is institutionally defined and assured.

When I am entering a contract with another person I may present proofs and arguments to him, but there is generally no formal assurance that I will be given this opportunity or that he will listen to my arguments if I make them . . . . During an election I may actively campaign for one side and may present what I consider to be "reasoned arguments" to the electorate. If I am an effective campaigner this participation in the decision ultimately reached may greatly outweigh in importance the casting of my own single vote. At the same time, it is only the latter form of participation that is the subject of an affirmative institutional guarantee. The protection accorded my right to present arguments to the electorate is almost entirely indirect and negative. The way will be held clear for me, but I shall have to pave it myself. Even if I am given an affirmative right (for example, under the "equal time" rule of the FCC) I am given no formal assurance that anyone will listen to my appeal. The voter who goes to sleep before his television set is surely not subject to the same condemnation as the judge who sleeps through the arguments of counsel.

Adjudication is, then, a device which gives formal and institutional expression to the influence of reasoned argument in human affairs. As such it assumes a burden of rationality not borne by any other form of social ordering. A decision which is the product of reasoned argument must be prepared itself to meet the test of reason. We demand of an adjudicative decision a kind of rationality we do not expect of the results of contract or of voting. This higher responsibility toward rationality is at once the strength *and the weakness* of adjudication as a form of social ordering.

In entering contracts, men are of course in some measure guided by rational considerations. The subsistence farmer who has a surfeit of potatoes and only a handful of onions acts reasonably when he trades potatoes for onions. But there is no test of rationality that can be applied to the result of the trade considered in abstraction from the interests of the parties. Indeed, the trade of potatoes for onions, which is a rational act by one trader, might be considered irrational if indulged in by his opposite number, who has a storehouse full of onions and only a bushel of potatoes. If we asked one party to the contract, "Can you defend that contract?" he might answer,

"Why, yes. It was good for me and it was good for him." If we then said, "But that is not what we meant. We meant, can you defend it on general grounds?" he might well reply that he did not know what we were talking about. Yet this is precisely the kind of question we normally direct toward the decision of a judge or arbitrator. The results that emerge from adjudication are subject, then, to a standard of rationality that is different from that imposed on the results of an exchange.

I believe that the same observation holds true when adjudication is compared with elections. The key to the difference lies again in the mode in which the affected party participates in a decision. If, as in adjudication, the only mode of participation consists in the opportunity to present proofs and arguments, the purpose of this participation is frustrated, and the whole proceeding becomes a farce, should the decision that emerges make no pretense whatever to rationality. The same cannot be said of the mode of participation called voting. We may assume that the preferences of voters are ultimately emotional, inarticulate, and not subject to rational defense. At the same time there is a need for social order, and it may be assumed that this need is best met when order rests on the broadest possible base of popular support. On this ground, a negative defense of democracy is possible; the will of the majority controls, not because it is right, but—well, because it *is* the will of the majority. This is surely an impoverished conception of democracy, but it expresses at least one ingredient of any philosophy of democracy, and it suggests a reason why we demand of adjudication a kind of rationality that we do not expect of elections .   .   .   .

Now if we ask ourselves what kinds of questions are commonly decided by judges and arbitrators, the answer may well be, "Claims of right." Indeed, in the older literature (including notably John Chipman Gray's The Nature and Sources of the Law (1909)) courts were often distinguished from administrative or executive agencies on the ground that it is the function of courts to "declare rights." If, then, we seek to define "the limits of adjudication," a tempting answer would be that the proper province of courts is limited to cases where rights are asserted. On reflection we might enlarge this to include cases where fault or guilt is charged (broadly, "the trial of accusations"), since in many cases it is artificial to treat the accuser (who may be the district attorney) as claiming a right. Though it is not particularly artificial to view the lawbreaker as violating "a right" of the state, to say that when the state indicts the lawbreaker it is claiming a remedial "right" against him does seem to reflect a misguided impulse toward forcing a symmetry between civil and criminal remedies. To avoid any such manipulations of natural modes of thought, let us then amend the suggested criterion to read as follows: The proper province of adjudication is to make an authoritative determination of questions raised by claims of right and accusations of guilt.

Is this a significant way of describing "the limits of adjudication"? I do not think so. In fact, what purports here to be a distinct assertion is merely an implication of the fact that adjudication is a form of decision that defines the affected party's participation as that of offering proofs and reasoned arguments. It is not so much that adjudicators decide only issues presented by claims of right or accusations. The point is rather that *whatever* they decide, or *whatever* is submitted to them for decision, tends to be converted into a claim of right or an accusation of fault or guilt. This conversion is effected by the institutional framework within which both the litigant and the adjudicator function.

Let me spell out rather painstakingly the steps of an argument that will show why this should be so. (1) Adjudication is a process of decision that grants to the affected party a form of participation that consists in the opportunity to present proofs and reasoned arguments. (2) The litigant must therefore, if his participation is to be meaningful, assert some principle or principles by which his arguments are sound and his proofs relevant. (3) A naked demand is distinguished from a claim of right by the fact that the latter is a demand supported by a principle; likewise, a mere expression of displeasure or resentment is distinguished from an accusation by the fact that the latter rests upon some principle. Hence, (4) issues tried before an adjudicator tend to become claims of right or accusations of fault.

We may see this process of conversion in the case of an employee who desires an increase in pay. If he asks his boss for a raise, he may, of course, claim "a right" to the raise. He may argue the fairness of the principle of equal treatment and call attention to the fact that Joe, who is no better than he, recently got a raise. But he does not have to rest his plea on any ground of this sort. He may merely beg for generosity, urging the needs of his family. Or he may propose an exchange, offering to take on extra duties if he gets the raise. If, however, he takes his case to an arbitrator he cannot, explicitly at least, support his case by an appeal to charity or by proposing a bargain. He will have to support his demand by a principle of some kind, and a demand supported by principle is the same thing as a claim of right. So, when he asks his boss for a raise, he may or may not make a claim of right; when he presents his demand to an arbitrator he *must* make a claim of right. . . .

If the analysis presented here is correct, three aspects of adjudication that seem to present distinct qualities are in fact all expressions of a single quality: (1) the peculiar mode by which the affected party participates in the decision; (2) the peculiarly urgent demand of rationality that the adjudicative process must be prepared to meet; and (3) the fact that adjudication finds its normal and "natural" province in judging claims of right and accusations of fault. So, when we say that a party entering a contract, or voting in an election, has no "right" to any particular outcome, we are describing the same fundamental fact that we allude to when we say that adjudication has to meet a test of rationality or of "principle" that is not applied to contracts and elections. . . .

I have suggested that it is not a significant description of the limits of adjudication to say that its proper province lies where rights are asserted or accusations of fault are made, for such a statement involves a circle of reasoning. If, however, we regard a formal definition of rights and wrongs as a nearly inevitable product of the adjudicative process, we can arrive at what is perhaps the most significant of all limitations on the proper province of adjudication. Adjudication is not a proper form of social ordering in those areas where the effectiveness of human association would be destroyed if it were organized about formally defined "rights" and "wrongs." Courts have, for example, rather regularly refused to enforce agreements between husband and wife affecting the internal organization of family life. There are other and wider areas where the intrusion of "the machinery of the law" is equally inappropriate. An adjudicative board might well undertake to allocate one thousand tons of coal among three claimants; it could hardly conduct even the simplest coal-mining enterprise by the forms of adjudication. Wherever successful human association depends upon spontaneous and informal collaboration, shifting its forms with the task at hand, there adjudication is out of place except as it may declare certain ground rules applicable to a wide variety of activities.

These are vague and perhaps trite observations. I shall attempt to bring them into sharper focus in a later part of this paper, particularly in a discussion of the relative incapacity of adjudication to solve "polycentric" problems. Meanwhile, the point I should like to stress is that the incapacity of a given area of human activity to endure a pervasive delimitation of rights and wrongs is also a measure of its incapacity to respond to a too exigent rationality, a rationality that demands an immediate and explicit reason for every step taken. Back of both of these incapacities lies the fundamental truth that certain kinds of human relations are not appropriate raw material for a process of decision that is institutionally committed to acting on the basis of reasoned argument.   .   .   .

The Forms of Adjudication

.   .   .   [The reader] should not [be] misled into thinking that this paper condemns all departures of adjudication from a state of pristine purity. Certain mixed forms are valuable and almost indispensable, though their use is often attended by certain dangers.

In determining whether a deviant or mixed form impairs the integrity of adjudication the test throughout will be that already stressed repeatedly: Does it affect adversely the meaning of the affected party's participation in the decision by proofs and reasoned arguments?   .   .   .

May the Arbiter Act on His Own Motion in Initiating the Case?

.   .   .   [I]n most of the practical manifestations of adjudication the arbiter's function has to be "promoted" by the litigant and is not initiated by itself. But is this coy quality of waiting to be asked an essential part of adjudication?

It would seem that it is not. Suppose, for example, the collision of two ships under circumstances that suggest that one or both masters were at fault. Suppose a board is given authority to initiate hearings in such a case and to make a determination of fault. Such a board might conduct its hearings after the pattern of court proceedings. Both masters might be accorded counsel and a full opportunity for cross-examination. There would be no impairment of the affected parties' full participation by proofs and reasoned argument; the integrity of adjudication seems to be preserved.

Yet I think that most of us would consider such a case exceptional and would not be deterred by it from persisting in the belief that the adjudicative process should normally not be initiated by the tribunal itself. There are, I believe, sound reasons for adhering to that belief.

Certainly it is clear that the integrity of adjudication is impaired if the arbiter not only initiates the proceedings but also, in advance of the public hearing, forms theories about what happened and conducts his own factual inquiries. In such a case the arbiter cannot bring to the public hearing an uncommitted mind; the effectiveness of participation through proofs and reasoned arguments is accordingly reduced. Now it is probably true that under most circumstances the mere initiation of proceedings carries with it a certain commitment and often a theory of what occurred. The case of the collision at sea is exceptional because there the facts themselves speak eloquently for the need of some kind of inquiry, so that the initiation of the proceedings implies nothing more than a recognition of this need. In most situations the initiation of proceedings could not have the same neutral quality, as, for example, where the occasion consists simply in the fact that a corporation had gone two years without declaring a dividend.

. . . [To take a more central example, it] seems clear that a regime of contract (more broadly, a regime of reciprocity) implies that the determination whether to assert a claim must be left to the interested party.

A contrary suggestion is advanced by Karl Llewellyn in The Cheyenne Way [written with E. A. Hoebel in 1941]. In answer to the question "Why do we leave it to the affected party whether to assert his claim for breach of contract?" he gives the startling explanation that this is because as a matter of actual experience the motive of self-interest has proved sufficient to maintain a regime of contract. He suggests that if in the future this motive were to suffer a serious decline, then the state might find itself compelled to intervene to strengthen the regime of contract. This curious conception is symptomatic of a general tendency of our times to obscure the role of reciprocity as an organizing principle and to convert everything into "social policy," which is another way of saying that all organization is by common aims (or by the aims that in the mind of the "policymaker" ought to be common).

. . . To enforce a contract for a party who is willing to leave it unenforced is just as absurd as making the contract for him in the first place. (I realize, of course, that there are contracts required by law, but this is obviously a derivative phenomenon which would lose all meaning if every human relation were imposed by the state and were called a "contract.")

The belief that it is not normal for the arbiter himself to initiate the adjudicative process has, then, a twofold basis. *First*, it is generally impossible to keep even the bare initiation of proceedings untainted by preconceptions about what happened and what its consequences should be. In this sense, initiation of the proceedings by the arbiter impairs the integrity of adjudication by reducing the effectiveness of the litigant's participation through proofs and arguments. *Second*, the great bulk of claims submitted to adjudication are founded directly or indirectly on relationships of reciprocity. In this case, unless the affected party is deceived or ignorant of his rights, the very foundations of the claim asserted dictate that the processes of adjudication must be invoked by the claimant.

Must the Decision Be Accompanied by a Statement of the Reasons for It?

We tend to think of the judge or arbitrator as one who decides and who gives reasons for his decision. Does the integrity of adjudication require that reasons be given for the decision rendered? I think the answer is, not necessarily. In some fields of labor arbitration (chiefly, I believe, where arbitration is a facility made available without charge by the state) it is the practice to render "blind" awards. The reasons for this practice probably include a belief that reasoned awards are often misinterpreted and "stir up trouble," as well as the circumstance that the arbitrator is so busy he has no time to write opinions. Under the procedures of the American Arbitration Association awards in commercial cases are rendered usually without opinion. (Written opinions are, however, usual in *labor* cases.) . . .

By and large it seems clear that the fairness and effectiveness of adjudication are promoted by reasoned opinions. Without such opinions the parties have to take it on faith that their participation in the decision has been real, that the arbiter has in fact understood and taken into account their proofs and arguments. A less obvious point is that, where a decision enters into some continuing relationship, if no reasons are given the parties will almost inevitably guess at reasons and act accordingly. Here the effectiveness of adjudication is impaired, not only because the results achieved may not be those intended by the arbiter, but also because his freedom of decision in future cases may be curtailed by the growth of practices based on a misinterpretation of decisions previously rendered.

May the Arbiter Rest His Decision on Grounds Not Argued by the Parties?

Obviously the bond of participation by the litigant is most secure when the arbiter rests his decision wholly on the proofs and argument actually presented to him by the parties. In practice, however, it is not always possible to realize this ideal. Even where all of the considerations on which the decision rests were touched on by the parties' arguments, the emphasis may be very different. An issue dealt with only in passing by one of the parties, or perhaps by both, may become the headstone of the arbiter's decision. This may mean not only that, had they foreseen this outcome, the parties would have presented different arguments, but that they might also have introduced evidence on very different factual issues.

If the ideal of a perfect congruence between the arbiter's view of the issues and that of the parties is unattainable, this is no excuse for a failure to work toward an achievement of the closest approximation of it. We need to remind ourselves that if this congruence is utterly absent—if the grounds for the decision fall completely outside the framework of the argument, making all that was discussed or proved at the hearing irrelevant—then the adjudicative process has become a sham, for the parties' participation in the decision has lost all meaning. We need to analyze what factors influence the desired congruence and what measures may be taken to promote it.

One circumstance of capital importance is the extent to which a particular process of adjudication takes place in a context of established rules. In branches of the law where the rules have become fairly settled and certain, it may be possible for lawyers to reach agreement easily in defining the crucial issues presented by a particular case. In such an area the risk is slight that the decision will fall outside the frame of reference set by the proofs and arguments. On the other hand, in areas of uncertainty, this risk is greatly increased. There are, to be sure, dangers in a premature crystallization of standards. On the other hand, one of the less obvious dangers of a too long delayed formulation of doctrine lies in the inevitable impairment of the integrity of adjudication that is entailed, for the reality of the parties' participation is reduced when it is impossible to foretell what issues will become relevant in the ultimate disposition of the case.

These are considerations often overlooked in criticisms of the conduct of administrative agencies and labor arbitrators. Ex parte posthearing conferences with the parties are often motivated by a well-intentioned desire to preserve the reality of the parties' participation in the decision. Where the standards of decision are vague and fluctuating, when the time comes for final disposition of the case it may be apparent that most of what was argued and proved at the public hearing has become irrelevant. A desire to give a litigant a meaningful "day in court" may, paradoxically, lead to giving him a lunchhour out of court. In many cases this conduct should be characterized as inept, rather than wicked.

Those inexperienced in legal procedures often do not know of devices which have been developed by courts that will eliminate much of the need for such practices. In particular, requests for a reargument and the device of the tentative decree, with something like an order to show cause why it should not be made final, could often be used with advantage by labor arbitrators and administrative tribunals. This is not to say that these expedients will solve all problems. An arbitrator paid on a per diem basis by the parties may hesitate to run up his bill by requesting a second argument. In some situations a tentative decree may arouse expectations of such an intensity that a later modification becomes very difficult. The fundamental point made here, however, is that before we demand of lay arbiters that they act like judges, we must place them in a context, and arm them with procedures, that will make it possible for them to do their job properly and still act throughout like judges. . . .

Qualifications and Disqualifications of the Arbiter

. . . I shall merely suggest that the problem of securing a properly qualified and impartial arbiter be tried by the same touchstone that has been used throughout—what will preserve the efficacy and meaning of the affected party's participation through proofs and arguments? Obviously, a strong emotional attachment by the arbiter to one of the interests involved in the dispute, is destructive of that participation. In practice, however, another kind of "partiality" is much more dangerous. I refer to the situation where the arbiter's experience of life has not embraced the area of the dispute, or, worse still, where he has always viewed that area from some single vantage point. Here a blind spot of which he is quite unconscious may prevent him from getting the point of testimony or argument. By and large, I think the decisions of our courts in commercial cases do not represent adjudication at its highest level. The reason is a lack of judicial "feel" for the problems involved.

A sailor was once brought before a three-judge German court for violation of a provision of the criminal code which made it a serious offense to threaten another with bodily harm. Uncontradicted testimony proved that the prisoner had been heard to say, "I'll stick a knife in your guts and turn it around three times." Two judges, who had spent their lives in genteel surroundings far from the waterfront, were with great difficulty persuaded by the third to acquit.

Must the Decision Be Retrospective?

In practice both the decisions of courts and the awards of arbitrators are retrospective, both as to their effect on the litigants' rights and their effect as precedents for the decisions of other cases. A paradox is sometimes squeezed from this traditional way of acting, to the effect that courts, in order to avoid the appearance of legislating, cast their legislative enactments in the harshest possible form, making them ex post facto.

The philosophy underlying the retrospective effect of the judicial decision can be stated somewhat as follows: It is not the function of courts to create new aims for society or to impose on society new basic directives. The courts for various reasons analyzed previously are unsuited for this sort of task. Perhaps the most compelling objection to an assumption of any such function lies in the limited participation in the decision by the litigants who (1) represent generally only themselves and (2) participate in the decision only by proofs and arguments addressed to the arbiter. On the other hand, with respect to the generally shared aims and the authoritative directives of a society, the courts do have an important function to perform, that of developing (or even "discovering") case by case what these aims or directives demand for their realization in particular situations of fact. In the discharge of this function, at times the result is so obvious that no one thinks of a "retroactive effect." Theoretically, a court might distinguish between such decisions and those which announce a rule or standard that seems "new," even though it may represent a reasoned conclusion from familiar premises. But if an attempt were made to apply such a distinction pervasively, so that some decisions would be retrospective, some prospective only, the resulting confusion might be much less bearable than the situation that now obtains.

Generally the same considerations apply also to arbitration awards. It is not a matter of "concealing" the legislative nature of the arbitrator's award which makes him give it a retrospective effect. It is rather a conservative philosophy about the proper functions of adjudication, a philosophy which seeks to keep meaningful the adversary presentation, the participation of litigants only through appeals to reason, etc.

How is Adjudication Affected by the Source of the Arbiter's Power?

The power to adjudicate may represent a delegated power of government, as in the case of a judge, or it may derive from the consent of the litigants, as in most forms of arbitration. Are these two basically different "forms" of adjudication? Obviously it has been a tacit assumption of this paper that they are not.

On the other hand, this does not mean that the discharge of the arbiter's function is wholly unaffected by the source of his power. In a summary way we may say that the possible advantages of adjudication supported by governmental authority are: (1) The judge is under less temptation to "compromise" than is the contractually appointed arbitrator. (2) The acceptability of the judge's decision may be enhanced by the fact that he seems to play a subservient role, as one who merely applies rules which he himself did not make.

Among the possible advantages of adjudication which derives its power from a contract of the parties are the following: (1) Being unbacked by state power (or insufficiently backed by it in the case of an ineffective legal sanction), the arbitrator must concern himself directly with the acceptability of his award. He may be at greater pains than a judge to get his facts straight, to state accurately the arguments of the parties, and generally to display in his award a full understanding of the case. (2) Being relatively free from technical rules of procedure, the wise and conscientious arbitrator can shape his procedures upon what he perceives to be the intrinsic demands of effective adjudication. Thus, the "due process" which animates his conduct of the hearing may appear to the parties as something real and not something that has to be taken on faith, as allegedly inhering in technical rules that seem quite arbitrary to the layman.

As a special quality of contractually authorized arbitration, which cannot unequivocally be called either an "advantage" or "disadvantage," we may note that the contract to arbitrate may contain explicit or implicit limits upon the adjudicative process itself. The arbitrator often comes to the hearing with a feeling that he must conduct himself in a way that conforms generally to the expectations of the parties and that this restriction is implicit in the contract of submission. Thus, if both parties desire and expect a more "literal" interpretation than the arbitrator himself would prefer, he may feel obligated to adopt an attitude of interpretation that he finds intellectually uncongenial.

The Limits of Adjudication

Attention is now directed to the question, What kinds of tasks are inherently unsuited to adjudication? The test here will be that used throughout. If a given task is assigned to adjudicative treatment, will it be possible to preserve the meaning of the affected party's participation through proofs and arguments?

[For purposes of addressing the question of limits, this] section introduces a concept—that of the "polycentric task—which has been derived from Michael Polanyi's book The Logic of Liberty [(1951)]. In approaching that concept it will be well to begin with a few examples.

Some months ago a wealthy lady by the name of Timken died in New York leaving a valuable, but somewhat miscellaneous, collection of paintings to the Metropolitan Museum and the National Gallery "in equal shares," her will indicating no particular apportionment. When the will was probated the judge remarked something to the effect that the parties seemed to be confronted with a real problem.   The attorney for one of the museums spoke up and said, "We are good friends.   We will work it out somehow or other."   What makes this problem of effecting an equal division of the paintings a polycentric task?   It lies in the fact that the disposition of any single painting has implications for the proper disposition of every other painting.   If it gets the Renoir, the Gallery may be less eager for the Cezanne but all the more eager for the Bellows, etc.   If the proper apportionment were set for argument, there would be no clear issue to which either side could direct its proofs and contentions.   Any judge assigned to hear such an argument would be tempted to assume the role of mediator or to adopt the classical solution: Let the older brother (here the Metropolitan) divide the estate into what he regards as equal shares, let the younger brother (the National Gallery) take his pick.

As a second illustration suppose in a socialist regime it were decided to have all wages and prices set by courts which would proceed after the usual forms of adjudication.   It is, I assume, obvious that here is a task that could not successfully be undertaken by the adjudicative method.   The point that comes first to mind is that courts move too slowly to keep up with a rapidly changing economic scene.   The more fundamental point is that the forms of adjudication cannot encompass and take into account the complex repercussions that may result from any change in prices or wages.   A rise in the price of aluminum may affect in varying degrees the demand for, and therefore the proper price of, thirty kinds of steel, twenty kinds of plastics, an infinitude of woods, other metals, etc.   Each of these separate effects may have its own complex repercussions in the economy.   In such a case it is simply impossible to afford each affected party a meaningful participation through proofs and arguments.   It is a matter of capital importance to note that it is not merely a question of the huge number of possibly affected parties, significant as that aspect of the thing may be.   A more fundamental point is that each of the various forms that award might take (say, a three-cent increase per pound, a four-cent increase, a five-cent increase, etc.) would have a different set of repercussions and might require in each instance a redefinition of the "parties affected."

We may visualize this kind of situation by thinking of a spider web.   A pull on one strand will distribute tensions after a complicated pattern throughout the web as a whole.   Doubling the original pull will, in all likelihood, not simply double each of the resulting tensions but will rather create a different complicated pattern of tensions.   This would certainly occur, for example, if the doubled pull caused one or more of the weaker strands to snap.   This is a "polycentric" situation because it is "many centered"—each crossing of strands is a distinct center for distributing tensions.   .   .   .

It should be carefully noted that a multiplicity of affected persons is not an invariable characteristic of polycentric problems.   This is sufficiently illustrated in the case of Mrs. Timken's will.   That case also illustrated the fact that rapid changes with time are not an invariable characteristic of such problems.   On the other hand, in practice polycentric problems of possible concern to adjudication will normally involve many affected parties and a somewhat fluid state of affairs.   Indeed, the last characteristic follows from the simple fact that the more interacting centers there are, the more the likelihood that one of them will be affected by a change in circumstances, and, if the situation is polycentric, this change will communicate itself after a complex pattern to other centers.   .   .   .

Now, if it is important to see clearly what a polycentric problem is, it is equally important to realize that the distinction involved is often a matter of degree.   There are polycentric elements in almost all problems submitted to adjudication.   A decision may act as a predecent, often an awkward one, in some situation not foreseen by the arbiter.   Again, suppose a court in a suit between one litigant and a railway holds that it is an act of negligence for the railway not to construct an underpass at a particular crossing.   There may be nothing to distinguish this crossing from other crossings on the line. As a matter of statistical probability it may be clear thát constructing underpasses along the whole line would cost more lives (through accidents in blasting, for example) than would be lost if the only safety measure were the familiar "Stop, Look & Listen" sign.   If so, then what seems to be a decision simply declaring the rights and duties of two parties is in fact an inept solution for a polycentric problem, some elements of which cannot be brought before the court in a simple suit by one injured party against a defendant railway.   In lesser measure, concealed polycentric elements are probably present in almost all problems resolved by adjudication.   It is not, then, a question of distinguishing black from white.   It is a question of knowing when the polycentric elements have become so significant and predominant that the proper limits of adjudication have been reached.   .   .   .

The final question to be addressed is this: When an attempt is made to deal by adjudicative forms with a problem that is essentially polycentric, what happens?   As I see it, three things can happen, sometimes all at once. *First,* the adjudicative solution may fail.   Unexpected repercussions make the decision unworkable; it is ignored, withdrawn, or modified, sometimes repeatedly.   *Second,* the purported arbiter ignores judicial proprieties—he "tries out" various solutions in posthearing conferences, consults parties not represented at the hearings, guesses at facts not proved and not properly matters for anything like judicial notice.   *Third,* instead of accommodating his procedures to the nature of the problem he confronts, he may reformulate the problem so as to make it amenable to solution through adjudicative procedures.

Only the last of these needs illustration.   Suppose it is agreed that an employer's control over promotions shall be subject to review through arbitration.   Now obviously an arbitrator cannot decide whether when Jones was made a Machinist Class A there was someone else more deserving in the plant, or whether, in view of Jones' age, it would have been better to put him in another job with comparable pay.   This is the kind of allocative problem for which adjudication is utterly unsuited.   There are, however, two ways of obtaining a workable control over promotions through arbitration.   One of these is through the posting of jobs; when a job is vacant, interested parties may apply for promotion into it.   At the hearing, only those who have made application are entitled to be considered, and of course only the posted job is in issue. Here the problem is simplified in advance to the point where it can be arbitrated, though not without difficulty, particularly in the form of endless arguments as to whether there was in fact a vacancy that ought to have been posted, and whether a claimant filed his application on time and in the proper form, etc. The other way of accommodating the problem to arbitration is for the arbitrator to determine not who should be promoted but who *has* been promoted. That is, the contract contains certain "job descriptions" with the appropriate rate for each; the claimant asserts that he is in fact doing the work of a Machinist A, though he is still assigned the pay and title of a Machinist B. The controversy has two parties—the company and the claimant as represented by the union—and a single factual issue, Is the claimant in fact doing the work of a Machinist A?

In practice the procedure of applying for appointment to posted jobs will normally be prescribed in the contract itself, so that the terms of the agreement keep the arbitrator's function with respect to promotions within manageable limits. The other method of making feasible a control of promotions through arbitration will normally result from the arbitrator's own perception of the limitations of his role. The contract may simply contain a schedule of job rates and job classifications and a general clause stating that "discharges, promotions, and layoffs shall be subject to the grievance procedure." If the arbitrator were to construe such a contract to give him a general supervision over promotions, he would embark himself upon managerial tasks wholly unsuited to solution by any arbitrative procedure. An instinct toward preserving the integrity of his role will move him, therefore, to construe the contract in the manner already indicated, so that he avoids any responsibility with respect to the assignment of duties and merely decides whether the duties actually assigned make appropriate the classification assigned by the company to the complaining employee. . . .

In closing this discussion of polycentricity, it will be well to caution against two possible misunderstandings. The suggestion that polycentric problems are often solved by a kind of "managerial intuition" should not be taken to imply that it is an invariable characteristic of polycentric problems that they resist rational solution. There are rational principles for building bridges of structural steel. But there is no rational principal which states, for example, that the angle between girder *A* and girder *B* must always be 45 degrees. This depends on the bridge as a whole. One cannot construct a bridge by conducting successive separate arguments concerning the proper angle for every pair of intersecting girders. One must deal with the whole structure.

Finally, the fact that an adjudicative decision affects and enters into a polycentric relationship does not of itself mean that the adjudicative tribunal is moving out of its proper sphere. On the contrary, there is no better illustration of a polycentric relationship than an economic market, and yet the laying down of rules that will make a market function properly is one for which adjudication is generally well suited. The working out of our common law of contracts case by case has proceeded through adjudication, yet the basic principle underlying the rules thus developed is that they should promote the free exchange of goods in a polycentric market. The court gets into difficulty, not when it lays down rules about contracting, but when it attempts to write contracts. .   .   .

————

Professor Melvin Eisenberg has written an article commenting upon Fuller's The Forms and Limits of Adjudication. In it he explicitly compares Fuller's twenty-year-old work to the more recent work of Chayes. He concludes that "no element of the public law model is inconsistent with Fuller's concept of participation." Eisenberg, Participation, Responsiveness, and the Consultative Process: An Essay for Lon Fuller, 92 Harv.L.Rev. 410, 427 (1978). Nevertheless, Eisenberg concedes that Chayes' descriptions of or prescriptions for the remedial process in the public law model makes the decree look "very much like a discretionary regime addressing a problem governed by .   .   . polycentric criteria." Id. at 428. And it should be noted, however, that Chayes views the decree as "[t]he centerpiece of the emerging public law model," though he, in a spirit congenial to Fuller, also sees the court—even in its remedial phase—as a midwife to the parties' labors to achieve an acceptable, consensual solution. Eisenberg concludes with a question (at 431): "Whether expansion of the public law model will undermine the moral force of adjudication, whether Fuller's view will be shown to have been too confining, or whether the publication of Forms and Limits will itself influence the lines of future development in the public law area, remains to be seen."

AFTERWORD: A MAP FOR MISREADING

Although the structure of these readings was determined by our own pedagogic and theoretical concerns, the materials may be integrated into a traditional civil procedure course and will broaden the focus of any of the widely used casebooks in the field. This afterword suggests how this might be done, by explaining the relationship between our categories and those found in the five major casebooks: Cound, Friedenthal & Miller (West, 2d ed. 1974) (CF + M); Carrington & Babcock (Little, Brown; 2d ed. 1977) (C + B); Louisell and Hazard (Foundation Press, 3d ed. 1973) (L + H); Field, Kaplan & Clermont (Foundation Press, 4th ed. 1978) (FK + C); and Rosenberg, Weinstein, Smit and Korn (Foundation Press, 3d ed. 1976) (RWS + K).

A. Valuing Process

All of the major casebooks begin with introductory material usually designed to give the student an overview of civil adjudication. (C + B is an exception and its early pages are more in harmony with the issues put forward in this reader.) The student is introduced to the idea of formulating objectives for a client, to the stages of a lawsuit, and, albeit briefly, to the uses of such stages in achieving particular objectives. But this early phase in the student's immersion in procedure ought to be used, as well, to ask what the objectives of the system of procedure are from the point of view of the society, of the system designer, and of the observer. We thus urge the introduction of material which explicitly asks what the value of process might be. Chapter 1 of these readings includes such material. The teacher may wish to introduce only the Michelman, Posner, and Mashaw pieces at first, leaving the Leff and Felstiner articles for a retrospective rethinking of basic questions towards the end of the course. Felstiner (and also Golding in chapter 2) is particularly useful for introducing the student to the range of dispute-processing devices and to the general social and cultural context within which adjudicatory values must be set.

B. The Independence of Procedure

Chapter 2 of this book invites the reader to devote serious attention to the relation between "substance" and "procedure." In one sense, the problem is a traditional one usually found in a procedure course. Every casebook considers the issue at least in the context of the *Erie* problem and of the Federal Rules. Most books flag the issue as well in distinguishing between the "substantive" sufficiency of a pleading and its "formal" adequacy. Some of the readings included in this chapter might well be introduced when the *Erie* issue is considered; they help provide a sense of how the procedure/substance distinction and interaction remains intellectually important in a variety of contexts. The Cover and Grey articles consider, in different ways, whether procedure may be understood as being "autonomous" from substance. They are useful in connection with considerations of the *Erie* problem, the promulgation of the Federal Rules, and principles of interpretation in procedural matters. If procedural due process cases are considered in a casebook, as in the first part of C + B, the Grey article is a natural companion.

The Scott article in chapter 2 demonstrates exactly how substance has changed through procedure. It might be read in connection with a consideration of the traditional subject of "parties." But it might also be introduced together with the Cover article in considering the Rules Enabling Act and the rule promulgation process. The Simon article, which begins the chapter, invites an examination of the place of procedure in a general theory of law. It is of obvious relevance to explicit considerations of the adversary system or of the legal profession.

C. The Concept of a Formal Procedural System

Many casebooks speak of alternatives to adjudication by court. They usually conceptualize the issue as one of a predefined dispute which can go through one of several dispute-resolving "black boxes." The materials in chapter 3 enlarge upon this focus. First, they do not assume that adjudication is primarily *private* dispute resolution; thus public processes, such as legislation, are included within the matters considered. More importantly, however, the essays are attentive to the complex interplay of process, structure, and outcomes in the society. Thus, the "dispute" which goes to arbitration may have to be understood as being definitionally different in that very respect from an otherwise apparently similar dispute adjudicated by a court. The essays in this chapter may be keyed to materials on arbitration, settlement, or negotiation, where such material exists in a casebook. CF + M chapter X, Section C, would be placed in a quite enlarged field of consideration by using some of this chapter. F, K + C contains some interesting parallel material in Part One, Topic C, §§ 1 and 2. Part VI of L + H is directed to many similar questions.

In section B of this chapter we also introduce the concept of the formal role. The essays here are designed to raise general questions, about "role" and its formal embodiments as problematic, albeit pervasive, dimensions of adjudication. These materials can be introduced together with traditional consideration of judge, jury, and their respective functions. The Noonan piece might even be used to provide an interesting enlargement of a traditional discussion of the small "technical" issue of assignment of costs.

D. Adversaries

The material in chapter 4 of this book easily fits into a traditional procedure course at several points. First, the material on group litigation can simply be used as a supplement to a consideration of the class action. Second, the material on the creation and limitation of party status can be introduced either as a parallel to discussions of standing or as an introduction to a general consideration of parties. The natural case-law link is to the standing issue of Sierra Club v. Morton and related cases. The material at the beginning of the chapter does not "fit" as neatly into the traditional framework, but is of great intellectual importance in the rethinking of procedure. The Leff article can be linked to the cases in a provisional remedies section. If this is done, it will turn what is often a minor topic into a discussion of a major issue: the structuring of strategic advantages. The Galanter article may be used either at the beginning of the parties issue or in discussion of the provision of legal counsel, proceedings in forma pauperis, or other equalizing tactics.

E. Decision Centers

Chapter 5 of this reader corresponds fairly neatly to traditional categories such as jurisdiction, judge, and jury. We recommend the use of Shapiro, Damaška, Neuborne, and von Mehren and Trautman when dealing with jurisdiction. We believe the Shapiro and Damaška articles, in particular, are important in that they analyze institutional arrangements at a level not readily obvious from cases and the traditional commentaries.

The Kalven and Zeisel and the Lempert materials on juries should be introduced as part of a conventional consideration of the composition and functions of the jury. The Kalven and Zeisel work is among the most familiar of materials that is reprinted in this book. But we believe it useful for the student to read such a classic, the insights of which still remain important.

The Wexler article might be used during a consideration of the expert witness either at trial or in discovery. It would be used most profitably if the course considers explicitly the expert alternatives to general court adjudication, i. e., specialized courts, administrative agencies, and/or arbitration. The Harris and Horowitz excerpts should be used in considering either masters or complex litigation, if the course has such categories.

F. Information and Knowledge

Much of the material in Chapter 6 is equally appropriate for either an evidence course or a procedure course. We have noted that most procedure courses are caught "betwixt and between" in considering the trial. On the one hand it seems too important a component of the process to simply ignore in a chronological organization of procedure. On the other hand, it is, to a large extent, the proper domain of the evidence course.

Most case books attempt to focus on the kind of event the trial ideally ought to be without necessarily considering matters such as hearsay or privilege in great detail. Unfortunately, the material used in striking this compromise usually tends to be a summary or generalization about the law of evidence or some rather general statement about the adversary process. We believe that the usual existence of a separate evidence course in the traditional curriculum provides an opportunity not simply to preview or epitomize its content, but also to introduce systematic and analytic explorations of the problems of epistemology and communications which adjudication presents. We would, therefore, recommend assignment of the Merton, Tribe, and Damaška articles as substitutes for or supplements to that material which attempts to present evidence in a nutshell. CF + M: 856–69; L + H: 1002–35, 1171–82, 1287–1300, and especially 1002–35; RNS + K: 917–35; FK + C: 229–96, 486–514. C + B uses an original organization which cuts across the "stages" in an interesting way. The material in their Chapter IV, at 389–424, provides interesting counterpoints to our Chapter 6. The Shapiro article in Chapter 6 might be assigned when considering the appellate process, or in an explicit consideration of stare decisis or lawmaking via adjudication. It could also be assigned with *Erie* material.

G. Adjudicatory Action

Our Chapter 7 corresponds in part to the traditional category of remedies. The excerpts from the Fiss book and from the Cover and Aleinikoff article may be easily integrated into a remedies section of a procedure course. The Crain, Muir, and Bickel excerpts are also readily grafted to such a course segment since they explore the limitations imposed by the social environment upon remedial efficacy. Our category of "action" is somewhat more comprehensive than "remedies," however, and includes the *latent* dimensions of action. These dimensions include therapeutic, and ideological functions. As a consequence, the Minow and Hay articles are less readily integrated into the traditional course. Both, but especially Minow, might be read with remedies materials as demonstrations of the limits of traditional categories—the missing dimensions in legal thought. Alternatively, they might be introduced as introductory materials.

H. Alternative Conceptions of Adjudication

We conclude our book in Chapter 8 with a long excerpt from Professor Chayes' article, The Role of the Judge in Public Law Litigation. This article has already found its way, in bits and snippets, into the most recent editions of some casebooks. We have, nevertheless, reprinted much of it here because it integrates so many of the ideas running through our other chapters into an alternative model of litigation. Since we believe that so much conventional procedural thought is, in fact, tied to a paradigm of atomistic, private litigation we find it useful to have alternative models put forward even if they may eventually prove wrong in some respects. We have also included Lon Fuller's classic statement of the traditional model.

The Chayes article is most naturally introduced in an explicit consideration of "complex" litigation. Some procedure courses link consideration of this subject to the multidistrict-litigation problem. We believe that the proper contours of the subject are more nearly approximated by taking the analytic path of Chayes' article than by considering 28 U.S.C. § 1407 and related case law. The multidistrict-litigation problem is one technical issue often, but not always, associated with "complex" cases. And many multidistrict cases are relatively simple or traditional in Chayes' terms. This article may also be introduced in a course segment on remedies or class actions if the teacher does not wish separate consideration of complex litigation.

Although we hope these readings will be useful as an afterthought to the traditional procedure course, our larger ambition is to have them spur innovation in the organization of the course itself. We have found in our own teaching that the categories suggested by our chapter and subchapter headings and introductions are a beginning in such a reorganization. We hope they may be helpful to others in this task and we quite candidly solicit the experience and thoughts of others for their further development.

ACKNOWLEDGMENTS

We are grateful to the recent generations of Yale Law students, who with their good humor and critical eyes, have endured the curriculum reform represented by this book. They have added spirit to the dialectic between "real procedure" and "metaprocedure" (to use the terms of their jibes); they have forced us critically to examine our ideas and categories; and they have opened new avenues of inquiry. It is they who make teaching at the Yale Law School such a special experience.

There are also a number of individuals who we wish to thank. Our colleague Burke Marshall has participated in this collaberation from the very outset, and has been an important source of ideas and encouragement. Bruce Ackerman and Geoffrey Hazard of Yale, Paul Brest of Stanford, and Richard Lempert of Michigan have commented on this work at various stages, and helped enormously by bringing new material to our attention. Cathy Kiselyak, of the Class of 1980, guided us through the early stages of assembling the readings and integrating them with the cases. Our secretaries, Diane McDougal and Lorraine Nagle, must be thanked for their commitment to the task and their patience with us. Finally something must be said about Steven Bonville, for he is special. He is a member of the Class of 1979 and has been our research assistant during the final stages. He has been the indispensable force that brought this collaboration to fruition. He organized all the technical work. He organized us. He performed both chores with such style, such thoroughness, and such tact, that we look back at the whole process and his role in it with a touch of amazement.

We wish to thank Diane Cover for the front cover design and drawing and to express our appreciation to the following authors and publishers for their permission to reprint the included works:

Frank I. Michelman, The Supreme Court and Litigation Access Fees: The Right to Protect One's Rights, 1973 Duke L.J. 1153, 1172–77 (1973). Copyright © 1974 by Duke Law Journal. Reprinted with permission. Originally published at 1973 Duke L.J. 1153.

Richard A. Posner, An Economic Approach to Legal Procedure and Judicial Administration, 2 J. Legal Stud. 399, 400–20, 441–48 (1973). Copyright © 1973 by The University of Chicago.

Jerry L. Mashaw, The Supreme Court's Due Process Calculus for Administrative Adjudication in Mathews v. Eldridge: Three Factors in Search of a Theory of Value, 44 U.Chi.L.Rev. 28, 28–30, 46–59 (1976). Copyright © 1977 by The University of Chicago.

Arthur A. Leff, Law and, 87 Yale L.J. 989, 989–1005 (1978). Reprinted by permission of The Yale Law Journal Company and Fred B. Rothman & Company from The Yale Law Journal, Vol. 87, pp. 989–1005.

William L. F. Felstiner, Influences of Social Organization on Dispute Processing, 9 L. & Soc'y Rev. 63, 63–89 (1974). Copyright © 1974 by the Law and Society Association, reprinted by permission from Law & Society Review, its official publication.

William H. Simon, The Ideology of Advocacy: Procedural Justice and Professional Ethics, 1978 Wis.L.Rev. 29, 30–64, 91–113 (1978). Copyright © 1978 by The University of Wisconsin.

Robert M. Cover, For James Wm. Moore: Some Reflections on a Reading of the Rules, 84 Yale L.J. 718, 722–40 (1975). Reprinted by permission of The Yale Law Journal Company and Fred B. Rothman & Company from The Yale Law Journal, Vol. 84, pp. 718–40.

Hal S. Scott, The Impact of Class Actions on Rule 10b–5, 38 U.Chi.L.Rev. 337, 337–71 (1971). Copyright © 1971 by The University of Chicago.

Thomas C. Grey, Procedural Fairness and Substantive Rights, in 18 Nomos, Due Process 182, 190–202 (1977). Copyright © 1977 by New York University Press.

Martin P. Golding, Dispute Settling and Justice, chapter 6 of Philosophy of Law 106–25 (1975). Copyright © 1975. Adapted by permission of Prentice-Hall, Inc., Englewood Cliffs, New Jersey.

Melvin A. Eisenberg, Private Ordering Through Negotiation: Dispute-Settlement and Rulemaking, 89 Harv.L.Rev. 637, 638–65 (1976). Copyright © 1976 by the Harvard Law Review Association.

David L. Shapiro, The Choice of Rulemaking or Adjudication in the Development of Administrative Policy, 78 Harv.L.Rev. 921, 921–57 (1965). Copyright © 1965 by the Harvard Law Review Association.

Bernard D. Meltzer, Labor Arbitration and Discrimination: The Parties' Process and the Public's Purposes, 43 U.Chi.L.Rev. 724, 724–35 (1976). Copyright © 1976 by the Bureau of National Affairs, Inc.

Mortimer R. Kadish and Sanford H. Kadish, Discretion to Disobey 15–31, 50–52, 54–68, 70 (1973). Reprinted from Discretion to Disobey: A Study of Lawful Departures from Legal Rules, by Mortimer R. Kadish and Sanford H. Kadish with the permission of the publishers, Stanford University Press. Copyright © 1973 by the Board of Trustees of the Leland Stanford Junior University.

John T. Noonan, Jr., The Passengers of *Palsgraf,* chapter 4 in Persons and Masks of the Law (1976). Copyright © 1976 by John T. Noonan, Jr.

Jerome N. Frank, The Judging Process and the Judge's Personality, in Law and the Modern Mind (Part I, chapter 12) (1930). Selections from Law and the Modern Mind by Jerome N. Frank, Copyright 1930, 1933, 1949 by Coward-McCann, Inc., copyright 1930 by Brentano's Inc., are from Anchor Books edition, 1963; copyright renewed in 1958 by Florence K. Frank. Reprinted by arrangement with estate of Barbara Frank Kristein.

Arthur A. Leff, Injury, Ignorance and Spite—The Dynamics of Coercive Collection, 80 Yale L.J. 1, 2–18 (1970). Reprinted by permission of The Yale Law Journal Company and Fred B. Rothman & Company from The Yale Law Journal, Vol. 80, pp. 1–18.

Marc Galanter, Why the "Haves" Come Out Ahead: Speculation on the Limits of Legal Change, 9 L. & Soc'y Rev. 95, 95–151 (1974). Copyright © 1974 by the Law and Society Association; reprinted from Law & Society Review, its official publication.

Christoper D. Stone, Should Trees Have Standing?—Toward Legal Rights for Natural Objects, 45 S.Cal.L.Rev. 450, 452–81, 501 (1972). Copyright © 1972 by The University of Southern California.

Kenneth E. Scott, Standing in the Supreme Court—A Functional Analysis, 86 Harv.L.Rev. 645, 669–92 (1973). Copyright © 1973 by the Harvard Law Review Association.

William M. Landes and Richard A. Posner, The Private Enforcement of Law, 4 J. Legal Stud. 1, 30–44 (1975). Copyright © 1975 by The University of Chicago.

Harry Kalven, Jr. and Maurice Rosenfield, The Contemporary Function of the Class Suit, 8 U.Chi.L.Rev. 684, 684–95, 715–21 (1941). Copyright © 1941 by The University of Chicago.

Gerald A. Wright, The Cost-Internalization Case for Class Actions, 21 Stan. L.Rev. 383, 383–98, 403–04 (1969). Copyright © 1969 by the Board of Trustees of the Leland Stanford Junior University.

Stephen C. Yeazell, Group Litigation and Social Context: Toward a History of the Class Action, 77 Colum.L.Rev. 866, 868–96 (1977). Copyright © 1977 by the Directors of The Columbia Law Review Association, Inc.

Derrick A. Bell, Jr., Serving Two Masters: Integration Ideals and Client Interests in School Desegregation Litigation, 85 Yale L.J. 470, 470–72, 482–93, 502–16 (1976). Reprinted by permission of The Yale Law Journal Company and Fred B. Rothman & Company from The Yale Law Journal, Vol. 85, pp. 470–516.

Martin Shapiro, Courts, chapter 5 in 5 Greenstein and Polsby, Handbook of Political Science 321–47. Copyright © 1975 by the Addison-Wesley Publishing Company.

Mirjan Damaška, Structures of Authority and Comparative Criminal Procedure, 84 Yale L.J. 480, 481–526 (1975). Reprinted by permission of The Yale Law Journal Company and Fred B. Rothman & Company from The Yale Law Journal, Vol. 84, pp. 480–526.

Arthur T. von Mehren and Donald T. Trautman, Jurisdiction to Adjudicate: A Suggested Analysis, 79 Harv.L.Rev. 1121, 1124–79 (1966). Copyright © 1966 by the Harvard Law Review Association.

Burt Neuborne, The Myth of Parity, 90 Harv.L.Rev. 1105, 1105–30 (1977). Copyright © 1977 by the Harvard Law Review Association.

Harry Kalven, Jr. and Hans Zeisel, excerpts from chapters 8, 14, and 39 of The American Jury (1966). Copyright © 1966 by Kalven and Zeisel.

Richard O. Lempert, Jury Size & the Peremptory Challenge, Vol. 22, No. 2, Law Quadrangle Notes (U.Mich.) 8–13 (1978).

Donald L. Horowitz, The Personnel of the Adjudicative Process, in chapter 2 of The Courts and Social Policy 25–31 (1977). Published and copyright © 1977 by The Brookings Institution.

Lon L. Fuller, The Forms and Limits of Adjudication, 92 Harv.L.Rev. 353, 365–71, 381–404 (1978). Copyright © 1978 by Lon Fuller and the Harvard Law Review Association. Reprinted by permission of Mrs. Marjorie Fuller and the Harvard Law Review.

It should be noted that in most articles or excerpts the original footnote numbers have been retained. The three exceptions are the Kalven and Zeisel, Hay, and Muir excerpts where the footnotes have been renumbered. Where we have added editorial footnotes, they are denoted by lower case letters. Parenthetical references in the Felstiner article were omitted.

SELECTED BIBLIOGRAPHY

Abel, Richard L. "A Comparative Theory of Dispute Institutions in Society," 8 Law & Society Review 217 (1973).

Albert, Lee A. "Standing to Challenge Administrative Action: An Inadequate Surrogate for Claim for Relief," 83 Yale Law Journal 425 (1974).

Alschuler, Albert W. "The Defense Attorney's Role in Plea Bargaining," 84 Yale Law Journal 1179 (1975).

Alschuler, Albert W. "The Prosecutor's Role in Plea Bargaining," 36 University of Chicago Law Review 50 (1968).

Amsterdam, Anthony G. "Criminal Prosecutions Affecting Federally Guaranteed Civil Rights: Federal Removal and Habeas Corpus Jurisdiction to Abort State Criminal Trial," 113 University of Pennsylvania Law Review 793 (1965).

Amsterdam, Anthony G. "Perspectives on the Fourth Amendment," 58 Minnesota Law Review 349 (1974).

Antonovsky, Aaron. "Like Everyone Else, Only More So: Identity, Anxiety, and the Jew," in Maurice R. Stein, Arthur J. Vidich, and David M. White, (eds.), Identity and Anxiety 428. Glencoe, Illinois: Free Press, 1960 (on the *Rosenberg* case).

Arnold, Thurman W. The Symbols of Government. New Haven: Yale University Press, 1935.

Aronow, Geoffrey F. "The Special Master in School Desegregation Cases: The Evolution of Roles in the Reformation of Public Institutions Through Litigation." Unpublished manuscript, on file at Yale Law Library, 1979.

Arrow, Kenneth J. The Limits of Organization. New York: Norton, 1974.

Aubert, Vilhelm. "Competition and Dissensus: Two Types of Conflict and of Conflict Resolution," 7 Journal of Conflict Resolution 26 (1963).

Aubert, Vilhelm, ed. Sociology of Law. Baltimore: Penguin, 1969.

Auerbach, Jerold S. Unequal Justice: Lawyers and Social Change in Modern America. New York: Oxford University Press, 1976.

Ball, Milner S. "The Play's the Thing: An Unscientific Reflection on Courts under the Rubric of Theater," 28 Stanford Law Review 81 (1975).

Becker, Gary S. "Crime and Punishment: An Economic Approach," 76 Journal of Political Economy 169 (1968).

Becker, Gary S., and William M. Landes, eds. Essays in the Economics of Crime and Punishment. New York: Columbia University Press, 1974.

Becker, Gary S., and George J. Stigler. "Law Enforcement, Malfeasance, and Compensation of Enforcers," 3 Journal of Legal Studies 1 (1974).

Becker, Theodore L., and Malcolm M. Feeley, eds. The Impact of Supreme Court Decisions (2d ed.). New York: Oxford University Press, 1973.

Bell, Derrick A., Jr. "Serving Two Masters: Integration Ideals and Client Interests in School Desegregation Litigation," 85 Yale Law Journal 470 (1976).

Berger, Curtis J. "Away from the Court House and into the Field: The Odyssey of a Special Master," 78 Columbia Law Review 707 (1978).

Berman, Jesse. "The Cuban Popular Tribunals," 69 Columbia Law Review 1317 (1969).

Bernstein, Roger. "Judicial Economy and Class Actions," 7 Journal of Legal Studies 349 (1978).

Bickel, Alexander M. The Least Dangerous Branch. Indianapolis: Bobbs-Merrill, 1962.

Blumberg, Abraham S. "The Practice of Law as a Confidence Game: Organizational Cooptation of a Profession," 1 Law & Society Review 15 (1967).

Bohannan, Paul. Justice and Judgment among the Tiv. New York: Oxford University Press, 1957.

Borosage, Robert, et al. "The New Public Interest Lawyers," 79 Yale Law Journal 1069 (1970).

Braybrooke, David, and Charles E. Lindblom. A Strategy of Decision. New York: Free Press, 1963.

Cahn, Edgar S., and Jean Camper Cahn. "Implementing the Civilian Perspective—A Proposal for a Neighborhood Law Firm," 73 Yale Law Journal 1317 (1964).

Calabresi, Guido, and Philip Bobbitt. Tragic Choices. New York: W. W. Norton, 1978.

Calabresi, Guido, and A. Douglas Melamed. "Property Rules, Liability Rules, and Inalienability: One View of the Cathedral," 85 Harvard Law Review 1089 (1972).

Cappelletti, Mauro. "Governmental and Private Advocates for the Public Interest in Civil Litigation: A Comparative Study," 73 Michigan Law Review 794 (1975).

Cappelletti, Mauro; James Gordley; and Earl Johnson, Jr. Toward Equal Justice: A Comparative Study of Legal Aid in Modern Societies. New York: Oceana Publications, 1976.

Cardozo, Benjamin N. The Nature of the Judicial Process. New Haven: Yale University Press, 1955.

Carp, Robert, and Russell Wheeler. "Sink or Swim: The Socialization of a Federal District Judge," 21 Journal of Public Law 359 (1972).

Casper, Gerhard, and Hans Zeisel. "Lay Judges in the German Criminal Courts," 1 Journal of Legal Studies 135 (1972).

Chafee, Zechariah, Jr. Some Problems of Equity. Ann Arbor: University of Michigan Law School, 1950.

Chayes, Abram. "The Role of the Judge in Public Law Litigation," 89 Harvard Law Review 1281 (1976).

Christensen, Barlow F. Lawyers for People of Moderate Means: Some Problems of Availability of Legal Services. Chicago: American Bar Foundation, 1970.

Clark, Charles E. "The Role of the Supreme Court in Federal Rule-Making," 46 Journal of the American Judicature Society 250 (1963).

Coase, R. H. "The Problem of Social Cost," 3 Journal of Law & Economics 1 (1960).

Cohen, Jerome A. "Chinese Mediation on the Eve of Modernization," 54 California Law Review 1201 (1966).

Cook, Walter Wheeler. The Logical and Legal Bases of the Conflict of Laws. Cambridge: Harvard University Press, 1942.

Coons, John. "Approaches to Court Imposed Compromise—The Uses of Doubt and Reason," 58 Northwestern University Law Review 750 (1964).

Cover, Robert M. "For James Wm. Moore: Some Reflections on a Reading of the Rules," 84 Yale Law Journal 718 (1975).

Cover, Robert M. Justice Accused: Antislavery and the Judicial Process. New Haven: Yale University Press, 1975.

Cover, Robert M., and T. Alexander Aleinikoff. "Dialectical Federalism: Habeas Corpus and the Court," 86 Yale Law Journal 1035 (1977).

Crain, Robert L. The Politics of School Desegregation. Chicago: Aldine Publishing Co., 1968.

Cross, John G. The Economics of Bargaining. New York: Basic Books, 1969.

Curtis, Charles P. "The Ethics of Advocacy," 4 Stanford Law Review 4 (1951).

Cyert, Richard M., and James G. March. A Behavioral Theory of the Firm. Englewood Cliffs, N.J.: Prentice-Hall, Inc., 1963.

Dam, Kenneth W. "Class Actions: Efficiency, Compensation, Deterrence, and Conflict of Interest," 4 Journal of Legal Studies 47 (1975).

Damaška, Mirjan. "Evidentiary Barriers to Conviction and Two Models of Criminal Procedure: A Comparative Study," 121 University of Pennsylvania Law Review 506 (1973).

Damaška, Mirjan. "Presentation of Evidence and Factfinding Precision," 123 University of Pennsylvania Law Review 1083 (1975).

Damaška, Mirjan. "Structures of Authority and Comparative Criminal Procedure," 84 Yale Law Journal 480 (1975).

Danzig, Richard, and Michael J. Lowy. "Everyday Dispute and Mediation in the United States: A Reply to Professor Felstiner," 9 Law & Society Review 675 (1975).

Davis, Kenneth Culp. Discretionary Justice. Urbana, Illinois: University of Illinois Press, 1970.

Dawson, John P. A History of Lay Judges. Cambridge: Harvard University Press, 1960.

Dawson, John P. The Oracles of Law. Ann Arbor: University of Michigan Law School, 1968.

Deutsch, Morton. The Resolution of Conflict: Constructive and Destructive Processes. New Haven: Yale University Press, 1973.

"Developments in the Law—Class Actions," 89 Harvard Law Review 1318 (1976).

Dolbeare, Kenneth M., and Phillip E. Hammond. The School Prayer Decisions. Chicago: University of Chicago Press, 1971.

Dworkin, Ronald. Taking Rights Seriously. Cambridge: Harvard University Press, 1977.

Eckhoff, Torstein. "Impartiality, Separation of Powers, and Judicial Independence," 9 Scandanavian Studies in Law 9 (1965).

Edmonds, Ron. "Advocating Inequity: A Critique of the Civil Rights Attorney in Class Action Desegregation Suits," 3 Black Law Journal 176 (1974).

Ehrenzweig, Albert A. "The Transient Rule of Personal Jurisdiction: The 'Power' Myth and Forum Conveniens," 65 Yale Law Journal 289 (1956).

Ehrlich, Isaac. "The Deterrent Effect of Capital Punishment," 65 American Economic Review 397 (1975).

Eisenberg, Melvin A. "Participation, Responsiveness, and the Consultative Process: An Essay for Lon Fuller," 92 Harvard Law Review 410 (1978).

Eisenberg, Melvin A. "Private Ordering Through Negotiation: Dispute-Settlement and Rulemaking," 89 Harvard Law Review 637 (1976).

Ely, John Hart. "The Irrepressible Myth of *Erie*," 87 Harvard Law Review 693 (1974).

Felstiner, William L. F. "Avoidance as Dispute Processing: An Elaboration," 9 Law & Society Review 695 (1975).

Felstiner, William L. F. "Influences of Social Organization on Dispute Processing," 9 Law & Society Review 63 (1974).

Field, Martha A. "Abstention in Constitutional Cases: The Scope of the *Pullman* Abstention Doctrine," 122 University of Pennsylvania Law Review 1071 (1974).

Finkelstein, Michael O., and William B. Fairley. "A Bayesian Approach to Identification Evidence," 83 Harvard Law Review 489 (1970).

Finkelstein, Michael O., and William B. Fairley. "A Comment on 'Trial by Mathematics,'" 84 Harvard Law Review 1801 (1971).

Finman, Ted. "OEO Legal Services Programs and the Pursuit of Social Change: The Relationship Between Program Ideology and Program Performance," 1971 Wisconsin Law Review 1001 (1971).

Fiss, Owen M. The Civil Rights Injunction. Bloomington: Indiana University Press, 1978.

Fiss, Owen M. "*Dombrowski*," 86 Yale Law Journal 1103 (1977).

Fiss, Owen M. "The Fate of an Idea Whose Time Has Come: Antidiscrimination Law in the Second Decade after *Brown v. Board of Education*," 41 University of Chicago Law Review 742 (1974).

Fiss, Owen M. Injunctions. Mineola, N.Y.: Foundation Press, 1972.

Fleming, Macklin. The Price of Perfect Justice. New York: Basic Books, 1974.

Foucault, Michel. Discipline and Punish: The Birth of the Prison. New York: Pantheon Books, 1977.

Frank, Jerome N. Courts on Trial: Myth and Reality in American Justice. Princeton: Princeton University Press, 1949.

Frank, Jerome N. Law and the Modern Mind. Garden City, N.Y.: Anchor Books, 1963.

Frankfurter, Felix. "A Study in the Federal Judicial System," 39 Harvard Law Review 587 (1926).

Frankfurter, Felix, and James M. Landis. The Business of the Supreme Court. New York: Macmillan, 1928.

Freedman, James O. Crisis and Legitimacy: The Administrative Process and American Government. New York: Cambridge University Press, 1978.

Fried, Charles. "The Lawyer as Friend: The Moral Foundations of the Lawyer-Client Relation," 85 Yale Law Journal 1060 (1976).

Friedman, Lawrence M., and Robert V. Percival. "A Tale of Two Courts: Litigation in Alameda and San Benito Counties," 10 Law & Society Review 267 (1976).

Friendly, Henry J. Federal Jurisdiction: A General View. New York: Columbia University Press, 1973.

Fuller, Lon L. "The Forms and Limits of Adjudication," 92 Harvard Law Review 353 (1978).

Fuller, Lon L. "Human Interaction and the Law," 14 American Journal of Jurisprudence 1 (1969).

Fuller, Lon L. "Mediation—Its Forms and Functions," 44 Southern California Law Review 305 (1971).

Fuller, Lon L. The Morality of Law (rev. ed.). New Haven: Yale University Press, 1969.

Fuller, Lon L. "Two Principles of Human Association," in 11 Nomos, Voluntary Associations 3. Cambridge, Mass.: Harvard University Press, 1969.

Galanter, Marc. "Afterword: Explaining Litigation," 9 Law & Society Review 347 (1975).

Galanter, Marc. "Why the 'Haves' Come Out Ahead: Speculations on the Limits of Legal Change," 9 Law & Society Review 95 (1974).

Gellhorn, Walter. Children and Families in the Courts of New York City. New York: Dodd, Mead; 1954.

Gellhorn, Walter. Ombudsmen and Others: Citizens' Protectors in Nine Countries. Cambridge: Harvard University Press, 1966.

Getman, Julius G. "Critique of the Report of the Shreveport Experiment," 3 Journal of Legal Studies 487 (1974).

Getman, Julius G. "The Debate over the Caliber of Arbitrators: Judge Hays and his Critics," 44 Indiana Law Journal 182 (1969).

Getman, Julius G. "Labor Arbitration and Dispute Resolution," 88 Yale Law Journal 916 (1979).

Getman, Julius G., and Stephen B. Goldberg. "The Myth of Labor Board Expertise," 39 University of Chicago Law Review 681 (1972).

Gluckman, Max. The Ideas in Barotse Jurisprudence. New Haven: Yale University Press, 1965.

Gluckman, Max. The Judicial Process among the Barotse. Manchester (Eng.): University of Manchester Press, 1967.

Goffman, Erving. Interaction Ritual: Essays on Face-to-Face Behavior. New York: Doubleday, 1967.

Golding, Martin P. Philosophy of Law. Englewood Cliffs, N.J.: Prentice-Hall, 1975.

Golding, Martin P. "Preliminaries to the Study of Procedural Justice," in Graham Hughes (ed.), Law, Reason and Justice. New York: New York University Press, 1969.

Goldman, Sheldon, and Thomas P. Jahnige. The Federal Courts as a Political System (2d ed.). New York: Harper & Row, 1971.

Goldstein, Abraham S. "Reflections on Two Models: Inquisitorial Themes in American Criminal Procedure," 26 Stanford Law Review 1009 (1974).

Goldstein, Abraham S. "The State and the Accused: Balance of Advantage in Criminal Procedure," 69 Yale Law Journal 1149 (1960).

Goldstein, Joseph. "Police Discretion Not to Invoke the Criminal Process: Low Visibility Decisions in the Administration of Justice," 69 Yale Law Journal 543 (1960).

Gould, John P. "The Economics of Legal Conflicts," 2 Journal of Legal Studies 279 (1973).

Greely, Henry T. "The Equality of Allocation by Lot," 12 Harvard Civil Rights–Civil Liberties Law Review 113 (1977).

Greenberg, Jack. "Litigation for Social Change: Methods, Limits and Role in Democracy," 29 Record of New York City Bar Association 320 (1974).

Grey, Thomas C. "Procedural Fairness and Substantive Rights," in 18 Nomos, Due Process 182. New York: New York University Press, 1977.

Griffiths, John. "Ideology in Criminal Procedure or a Third 'Model' of the Criminal Process," 79 Yale Law Journal 359 (1970).

Griffiths, John, and Richard E. Ayres. "A Postscript to the Miranda Project: Interrogation of Draft Protestors," 77 Yale Law Journal 300 (1967).

Grossman, Joel B. "Social Backgrounds and Judicial Decision-Making," 79 Harvard Law Review 1551 (1966).

Grossman, Joel B., and Jack Ladinsky. "Law and Society: A Selected Bibliography," 7 Law & Society Review 497 (1973).

Gulliver, Philip H. "Negotiation as a Mode of Dispute Settlement: Towards a General Model," 7 Law & Society Review 667 (1973).

Gulliver, Philip H. Social Control in an African Society. Boston: Boston University Press, 1963.

Hallauer, Robert. "The Shreveport Experiment in Prepaid Legal Services," 2 Journal of Legal Studies 223 (1973).

Harris, Joel B. "The Title VII Administrator: A Case Study in Judicial Flexibility," 60 Cornell Law Review 53 (1974).

Hart, H. L. A. The Concept of Law. Oxford: Clarendon Press, 1961.

Hart, Henry M., Jr., and John T. McNaughton. "Evidence and Inference in the Law," in Daniel Lerner (ed.), Evidence and Inference 48. Chicago: The Free Press of Glencoe, 1959.

Hay, Douglas. "Property, Authority and the Criminal Law," in E. P. Thompson, (ed.), Albion's Fatal Tree. New York: Pantheon Books, 1975.

Hays, Paul R. Labor Arbitration: A Dissenting Viewpoint. New Haven: Yale University Press, 1966.

Hazard, Geoffrey C., Jr. Ethics in the Practice of Law. New Haven: Yale University Press, 1978.

Hazard, Geoffrey C., Jr. "A General Theory of State-Court Jurisdiction," 1965 Supreme Court Review 241 (1965).

Hazard, Geoffrey C., Jr. "Law Reforming in the Anti-Poverty Effort," 37 University of Chicago Law Review 242 (1970).

Hazard, Geoffrey C., Jr. "Representation in Rule-making," in The American Assembly, Law and the American Future (M. L. Schwartz, ed.). Englewood Cliffs, N.J.: Prentice-Hall, 1976.

Hazard, Geoffrey C., Jr. "Social Justice Through Civil Justice," 36 University of Chicago Law Review 699 (1969).

Hazard, Geoffrey C., Jr. "Undemocratic Legislation" (book review), 87 Yale Law Journal 1284 (1978).

Hirschman, Albert O. Exit, Voice and Loyalty: Responses to Decline in Firms, Organizations and States. Cambridge: Harvard University Press, 1970.

Hoeflich, Michael H., and Jan G. Deutsch. "Judicial Legitimacy and the Disinterested Judge," 6 Hofstra Law Review 749 (1978).

Horowitz, Donald L. The Courts and Social Policy. Washington: Brookings Institution, 1977.

Horwitz, Morton J. The Transformation of American Law—1780–1860. Cambridge: Harvard University Press, 1977.

Hutcheson, Joseph C., Jr. "The Judgment Intuitive: The Function of the 'Hunch' in Judicial Decision," 14 Cornell Law Quarterly 274 (1929).

Jaffe, Louis L. "The Citizen as Litigant in Public Actions: The Non-Hohfeldian or Ideological Plaintiff," 116 University of Pennsylvania Law Review 1033 (1968).

Johnstone, Quintin, and Dan Hopson, Jr. Lawyers and Their Work: An Analysis of the Legal Profession in the United States and England. Indianapolis: Bobbs-Merrill, 1967.

Jones, Nathaniel R. Letter to the Editors, 86 Yale Law Journal 378 (1976) (responding to Professor Bell's "Serving Two Masters . . . ," listed above).

Kadish, Mortimer R., and Sanford H. Kadish. Discretion to Disobey. Stanford: Stanford University Press, 1973.

Kadish, Sanford H. "Methodology and Criteria in Due Process: A Survey and Criticism," 66 Yale Law Journal 319 (1957).

Kalven, Harry, Jr. "The Dignity of the Civil Jury," 50 Virginia Law Review 1055 (1964).

Kalven, Harry, Jr. "The Jury, the Law, and the Personal Injury Damage Award," 19 Ohio State Law Journal 158 (1958).

Kalven, Harry, Jr., and Maurice Rosenfield. "The Contemporary Function of the Class Suit," 8 University of Chicago Law Review 684 (1941).

Kalven, Harry, Jr., and Hans Zeisel. The American Jury. Boston: Little, Brown: 1966.

Kaplan, Benjamin; Arthur T. von Mehren; and Rudolf Schaeffer. "Phases of German Civil Procedure," 71 Harvard Law Review 1193, 1443 (1958).

Kaplan, Diane S., and Richard M. Zuckerman. "The *Wyatt* Case: Implementation of a Judicial Decree Ordering

Institutional Change," 84 Yale Law Journal 1338 (1975).

Kirchheimer, Otto. Political Justice: The Use of Legal Procedure for Political Ends. Princeton: Princeton University Press, 1961.

Klevorick, Alvin K. "Jury Size and Composition: An Economic Approach," in Feldstein Martin S. and Robert P. Inman, The Economics of Public Services. New York: Halsted Press, 1977.

Klevorick, Alvin K., and Michael Rothschild. "A Model of the Jury Decision Process," 8 Journal of Legal Studies 141 (1979).

Kluger, Richard. Simple Justice: The History of *Brown v. Board of Education* and Black America's Struggle for Equality. New York: Alfred A. Knopf, 1976.

Kornstein, Daniel J. "A Bayesian Model of Harmless Error," 5 Journal of Legal Studies 121 (1976).

Landau, Martin. "Redundancy, Rationality, and the Problem of Duplication and Overlap," 29 Public Administration Review 346 (1969).

Landes, William M. "The Bail System: An Economic Approach," 76 Journal of Political Economy 79 (1973).

Landes, William M. "An Economic Analysis of the Courts," 14 Journal of Law & Economics 61 (1971).

Landes, William M., and Richard A. Posner. "Adjudication as a Private Good," 8 Journal of Legal Studies 235 (1979).

Landes, William M., and Richard A. Posner. "The Independent Judiciary in an Interest-Group Perspective," 18 Journal of Law & Economics 875 (1975).

Landes, William M., and Richard A. Posner. "The Private Enforcement of Law," 4 Journal of Legal Studies 1 (1975).

Leff, Arthur A. "Economic Analysis of Law: Some Realism about Nominalism," 60 Virginia Law Review 451 (1974).

Leff, Arthur A. "Injury, Ignorance and Spite—The Dynamics of Coercive Collection," 80 Yale Law Journal 1 (1970).

Leff, Arthur A. "Law and," 87 Yale Law Journal 989 (1978).

Lempert, Richard O. "Jury Size and the Peremptory Challenge," Law Quadrangle Notes (U. Mich.), vol. 22, no. 2, p. 8 (1978).

Lempert, Richard O. "Mobilizing Private Law: An Introductory Essay," 11 Law & Society Review 173 (1976).

Lempert, Richard O. "Modeling Relevance," 75 Michigan Law Review 1021 (1977).

Lempert, Richard O. "Uncovering 'Non-discernible' Differences: Empirical Research and the Jury-Size Cases," 73 Michigan Law Review 643 (1975).

Lesnick, Howard. "The Federal Rule-Making Process: A Time for Re-examination," 61 American Bar Association Journal 579 (1975).

Lev, Daniel. "Judicial Institutions and Legal Culture in Indonesia," in Claire Holt et al. (eds.), Culture and Politics in Indonesia 246. Ithaca: Cornell University Press, 1972.

Levin, Martin A. Urban Politics and the Criminal Courts. Chicago: University of Chicago Press, 1977.

Lind, E. Allan; Bonnie E. Erickson; Nehemia Friedland; and Michael Dickenberger. "Reactions to Procedural Models for Adjudicative Conflict Resolution," 22 Journal of Conflict Resolution 318 (1978).

Lind, E. Allan; John Thibaut; and Laurens Walker. "Discovery and Presentation of Evidence in Adversary and Nonadversary Proceedings," 71 Michigan Law Review 1129 (1973).

Llewellyn, Karl N. The Common Law Tradition. Boston: Little, Brown; 1960.

Llewellyn, Karl, and E. Adamson Hoebel. The Cheyenne Way: Conflict and Case Law in Primitive Jurisprudence. Norman, Okla.: University of Oklahoma Press, 1941.

Lubman, Stanley. "Mao and Mediation: Politics and Dispute Resolution in Communist China," 55 California Law Review 1284 (1967).

Luce, Robert D., and Howard Raiffa. Games and Decisions. New York: Wiley, 1957.

Maine, Sir Henry J. S. Dissertations on Early Law and Custom. New York: H. Holt and Co., 1886.

Maitland, Frederic W. The Forms of Action at Common Law, edited by A. H. Chaytor and W. J. Whittaker. Cambridge (Eng.): The University Press, 1968.

Mannheim, Karl. Ideology and Utopia. New York: Harcourt, Brace and Company; 1955.

Marshall, Burke. "The Control of the Public Lawyer," in The American Assembly, Law and the American Future (M. L. Schwartz, ed.) 167. Englewood Cliffs, N.J.: Prentice-Hall, 1976.

Marshall, James; Kent H. Marquis; and Stuart Oskamp. "Effects of Kind of Question and Atmosphere of Interrogation on Accuracy and Completeness of Testimony," 84 Harvard Law Review 1620 (1971).

Mashaw, Jerry L. "The Supreme Court's Due Process Calculus for Administrative Adjudication in *Mathews v. Eldridge*: Three Factors in Search of a Theory of Value," 44 University of Chicago Law Review 28 (1976).

McChesney, Fred S. "On the Procedural Superiority of a Civil Law System: A Comment," 30 Kyklos 507 (1977).

McDougall, Harold A., III. "The Case for Black Juries," 79 Yale Law Journal 531 (1970).

Meltzer, Bernard D. "Labor Arbitration and Discrimination: The Parties' Process and the Public's Purposes," 43 University of Chicago Law Review 724 (1976).

Mentschikoff, Soia. "Commercial Arbitration," 61 Columbia Law Review 846 (1961).

Merton, Robert K. "Manifest and Latent Functions," in Robert K. Merton, Social Theory and Social Structure (revised and enlarged edition) 19. New York: The Free Press, 1965.

Michelman, Frank I. "Formal and Associational Aims in Procedural Due Process," in 18 Nomos, Due Process 126. New York: New York University Press, 1977.

Michelman, Frank I. "The Supreme Court and Litigation Access Fees: The Right to Protect One's Rights—Part I," 1973 Duke Law Journal 1153 (1973); "Part II," 1974 Duke Law Journal 527 (1974).

Milgram, Stanley. Obedience to Authority: An Experimental View. New York: Harper & Row, 1974.

Minow, Martha L. "The Judgment of Solomon and the Experience of Justice." Previously unpublished, on file at Yale Law Library, 1979.

Milsom, S.F.C. Historical Foundations of the Common Law. London: Butterworths, 1969.

Moore, Sally Falk. "Law and Social Change: The Semi-Autonomous Social Field as an Appropriate Subject of Study," 7 Law & Society Review 719 (1973).

Morse, Stephen J. "Crazy Behavior, Morals and Science: An Analysis of Mental Health Law," 50 Southern California Law Review 527 (1978).

Moulton, Beatrice A. "The Persecution and Intimidation of the Low-Income Litigant as Performed by the Small Claims Court in California," 21 Stanford Law Review 1657 (1969).

Muir, William K., Jr. Law and Attitude Change. Chicago: Phoenix Books, 1974.

Nader, Laura. "Styles of Court Procedures: To Make the Balance," in Laura Nader, ed., Law in Culture and Society. Chicago: Aldine, 1969.

Nagel, Stuart S. "Political Party Affiliation and Judges' Decisions," 55 American Political Science Review 843 (1961).

Nagel, Stuart S., and Marian Neef. "Plea Bargaining, Decision Theory, and Equilibrium Models, Part I," 51 Indiana Law Journal 987; "Part II," 52 Indiana Law Journal 1 (1976).

Nelson, William E. Americanization of the Common Law: The Impact of Legal Change on Massachusetts Society. Cambridge: Harvard University Press, 1975.

Neuborne, Burt. "The Myth of Parity," 90 Harvard Law Review 1105 (1977).

Newman, Donald J. Conviction: The Determination of Guilt or Innocence without Trial. Boston: Little, Brown; 1966.

Niskanen, William A., Jr. Bureaucracy and Representative Government. Chicago: Aldine Publishing Co., 1971.

Nonet, Philippe. Administrative Justice: Advocacy and Change in a Government Agency. New York: Russell Sage Foundation, 1969.

Nonet, Philippe. Law and Society in Transition: Toward Responsive Law. New York: Octagon Books, 1978.

Noonan, John T., Jr. Persons and Masks of the Law. New York: Farrar, Straus and Giroux, 1976.

Note, "Implementation Problems in Institutional Reform Litigation," 91 Harvard Law Review 428 (1977).

Note, "Masters and Magistrates in the Federal Courts," 88 Harvard Law Review 779 (1975).

Note, "Monitors: A New Equitable Remedy?," 70 Yale Law Journal 103 (1960).

Nottingham, Heneage Finch, 1st Earl of. Manual of Chancery Practice and Prolegomena of Chancery and Equity (D.E.C. Yale, ed.). Cambridge (Eng.): University Press, 1965.

Ordover, J. A., and Phillip Weitzman. "On the Efficient Organization of Trials: A Comment," 30 Kyklos 511 (1977).

Packer, Herbert L. The Limits of the Criminal Sanction. Stanford: Stanford University Press, 1968.

Phillips, Bradley S. "Limiting the Peremptory Challenge: Representation of Groups on Petit Juries," 86 Yale Law Journal 1715 (1977).

Posner, Richard A. "The Behavior of Administrative Agencies," 1 Journal of Legal Studies 305 (1972).

Posner, Richard A. An Economic Analysis of Law (2d ed.). Boston: Little, Brown; 1977.

Posner, Richard A. "The Economic Approach to Law," 53 Texas Law Review 757 (1975).

Posner, Richard A. "An Economic Approach to Legal Procedure and Judicial Administration," 2 Journal of Legal Studies 399 (1973).

Pospisil, Leopold J. Anthropology of Law: A Comparative Theory. New York: Harper & Row, 1971.

Pugh, Daniel D. "The Insanity Defense in Operation: A Practicing Psychiatrist Views *Durham* and *Brawner*," 1973 Washington University Law Quarterly 87 (1973).

Rabin, Robert L. "Job Security and Due Process: Monitoring Administrative Discretion Through a Reasons Requirement," 44 University of Chicago Law Review 60 (1976).

Rabin, Robert L. "Lawyers for Social Change: Perspectives on Public Interest Law," 28 Stanford Law Review 207 (1976).

Raiffa, Howard. Decision Analysis: Introductory Lectures on Choices Under Uncertainty. Reading, Mass.: Addison-Wesley, 1968.

Rawls, John. A Theory of Justice. Cambridge: Belknap Press of Harvard University Press, 1971.

Reich, Charles A. "The New Property," 73 Yale Law Journal 733 (1964).

Robinson, Glen O. "The Making of Administrative Policy: Another Look at Rulemaking and Adjudication and Administrative Procedure Reform," 118 University of Pennsylvania Law Review 485 (1970).

Rodgers, Harrell R., and Charles S. Bullock III. Law and Social Change: Civil Rights Laws and their Consequences. New York: McGraw-Hill, 1972.

Rosenthal, Douglas E. Lawyer and Client: Who's in Charge? New York: Russell Sage Foundation, 1974.

Ross, H. Laurence. "Insurance Claims Complaints: A Private Appeals Procedure," 9 Law & Society Review 275 (1975).

Ross, H. Laurence. Settled Out of Court: The Social Process of Insurance Claims Adjustments. Chicago: Aldine, 1970.

Sarat, Austin. "Alternatives in Dispute Processing: Litigation in a Small Claims Court," 10 Law & Society Review 339 (1976).

Sarbin, Theodore, and Vernon Allen. "Role Theory," in Gardner Lindzey and Elliot Aronson (eds.), The Handbook of Social Psychology. Reading, Mass.: Addison-Wesley, 1968.

Sax, Joseph. Defending the Environment: A Strategy for Citizen Action. New York: Knopf, 1971.

Scheingold, Stuart A. The Politics of Rights: Lawyers, Public Policy and Political Change. New Haven: Yale University Press, 1974.

Schelling, Thomas C. The Strategy of Conflict. Cambridge, Mass.: Harvard University Press, 1960.

Schubert, Glendon A., ed. Judicial Decision-Making. New York: Free Press, 1963.

Schwartz, Murray L., and Daniel J. B. Mitchell. "An Economic Analysis of the Contingent Fee in Personal-Injury Litigation," 22 Stanford Law Review 1125 (1970).

Scott, Hal S. "The Impact of Class Actions on Rule 10b–5," 38 University of Chicago Law Review 337 (1971).

Scott, Kenneth E. "Standing in the Supreme Court—A Functional Analysis," 86 Harvard Law Review 645 (1973).

Scott, Kenneth E. "Two Models of the Civil Process," 27 Stanford Law Review 937 (1975).

Sedler, Robert Allen. "Standing to Assert *Jus Tertii* in the Supreme Court," 71 Yale Law Journal 599 (1962).

Shapiro, David L. "The Choice of Rulemaking or Adjudication in the Development of Administrative Policy," 78 Harvard Law Review 921 (1965).

Shapiro, David L. "Some Thoughts on Intervention Before Courts, Agencies, and Arbitrators," 81 Harvard Law Review 721 (1968).

Shapiro, Martin. "Courts," in Fred I. Greenstein and Nelson W. Polsby (eds.), 5 Handbook of Political Science 321. Reading, Mass.: Addison-Wesley Pub. Co., 1975.

Shapiro, Martin. "Decentralized Decision-Making in the Law of Torts," in S. Sidney Ulmer (ed.), Political Decision-Making. New York: Van Nostrand, 1970.

Shapiro, Martin. "Stability and Change in Judicial Decision-Making: Incrementalism or Stare Decisis?," 2 Law in Transition Quarterly 134 (1965).

Shapiro, Martin. "Toward a Theory of Stare Decisis," 1 Journal of Legal Studies 125 (1972).

Simon, Herbert A. Administrative Behavior. New York: The Macmillan Company, 1947.

Simon, William H. "The Ideology of Advocacy: Procedural Justice and Professional Ethics," 1978 Wisconsin Law Review 29 (1978).

Skolnick, Jerome H. Justice without Trial: Law Enforcement in Democratic Society. New York: Wiley, 1966.

Smith, Reginald H. Justice and the Poor. Chicago: American Judicature Society [Bulletin VII], 1919; Chicago: National Legal Aid and Defenders Association (reprinted), 1967.

Sofaer, Abraham D. "Federal Habeas Corpus for State Prisoners: The Isolation Principle," 39 New York University Law Review 78 (1964).

Spaeth, Harold J.; David B. Meltz; Gregory Rathjen, and Michael V. Haselswerdt. "Is Justice Blind?: An Empirical Investigation of a Normative Ideal," 7 Law & Society Review 119 (1972).

Spears, Jay M. "Voir Dire: Establishing Minimum Standards to Facilitate the Exercise of Peremptory Challenges," 27 Stanford Law Review 1493 (1975).

Steinbruner, John D. The Cybernetic Theory of Decisions. Princeton: Princeton University Press, 1974.

Stewart, Richard B. "The Reformation of American Administrative Law," 88 Harvard Law Review 1669 (1975).

Stigler, George J. "The Economics of Information," in The Organization of Industry 171 (1968).

Stigler, George J. "The Optimum Enforcement of Laws," 78 Journal of Political Economy 526 (1970).

Stone, Christopher D. "Should Trees have Standing?—Toward Legal Rights for Natural Objects," 45 Southern California Law Review 450 (1972).

"Symposium on The *Paper Label* Sentences," 86 Yale Law Journal 590 (1977).

Thibaut, John W., and W. Laurens Walker. Procedural Justice: A Psychological Analysis. New York: Halsted Press, 1975.

Thibaut, John, and W. Laurens Walker. "A Theory of Procedure," 66 California Law Review 541 (1978).

Thibaut, John; W. Laurens Walker; Stephen LaTour; and Pauline Houlden. "Procedural Justice as Fairness," 26 Stanford Law Review 1271 (1974).

Thibaut, John; W. Laurens Walker; and Allan E. Lind. "Adversary Presentation and Bias in Legal Decisionmaking," 86 Harvard Law Review 386 (1972).

Thompson, E. P., (ed.) Albion's Fatal Tree. New York: Pantheon Books, 1975.

Thompson, E. P. Whigs and Hunters: The Origin of the Black Act. New York: Pantheon Books, 1976.

Tribe, Laurence H. "A Further Critique of Mathematical Proof," 84 Harvard Law Review 1810 (1971).

Tribe, Laurence H. "An Ounce of Detention: Preventive Justice in the World of John Mitchell," 56 Virginia Law Review 371 (1970).

Tribe, Laurence H. "Structural Due Process," 10 Harvard Civil Rights—Civil Liberties Law Review 269 (1975).

Tribe, Laurence H. "Trial by Mathematics: Precision and Ritual in the Legal Process," 84 Harvard Law Review 1329 (1971).

Tribe, Laurence H. "Triangulating Hearsay," 87 Harvard Law Review 957 (1974).

Tullock, Gordon. "On the Efficient Organization of Trials," 28 Kyklos 745 (1975). Also, Fred S. McChesney, "On the Procedural Superiority of a Civil Law System: A Comment," 30 Kyklos 507 (1977); J. A. Ordover and Phillip Weitzman, "On the Efficient Organization of Trials: A Comment," 30 Kyklos 511 (1977); Gordon Tullock, "Reply to McChesney, and Ordover and Weitzman," 30 Kyklos 517 (1977).

Underwood, Barbara D. "The Thumb on the Scales of Justice: Burdens of Persuasion in Criminal Cases," 86 Yale Law Journal 1299 (1977).

van Velsen, J. "Procedural Informality, Reconciliation, and False Comparisons," in Max Gluckman (ed.), Ideas and Procedures in African Customary Law. New York: Oxford University Press, 1969.

Vining, Joseph. Legal Identity: The Coming of Age of Public Law. New Haven: Yale University Press, 1978.

von Mehren, Arthur T., and Donald T. Trautman. "Jurisdiction to Adjudicate: A Suggested Analysis," 79 Harvard Law Review 1121 (1966).

Vose, Clement E. Caucasians Only. Berkeley: University of California Press, 1959.

Vose, Clement E. "Interest Groups, Judicial Review, and Local Government," 19 Western Political Quarterly 85 (1966).

Vose, Clement E. "Litigation as a Form of Pressure Group Activity," 319 Annals of the American Academy of Political and Social Science 20 (1958).

Wald, Michael S., et al. "Interrogations in New Haven: The Impact of *Miranda*," 76 Yale Law Journal 1521 (1966).

Walker, Laurens; John Thibaut; and Virginia Andreoli. "Order of Presentation at Trial," 82 Yale Law Journal 216 (1972).

Walsh, Michael H. "The American Jury: A Reassessment" (book review), 79 Yale Law Journal 142 (1969).

Wasby, Stephen L. The Impact of the United States Supreme Court: Some Perspectives. Homewood, Illinois: Dorsey Press, 1970.

Weber, Max. Law in Economy and Society (Max Rheinstein, ed.). Cambridge: Harvard University Press, 1954.

Wechsler, Herbert. "Toward Neutral Principles of Constitutional Law," in Herbert Wechsler, Principles, Politics and Fundamental Law. Cambridge: Harvard University Press, 1961.

Weisbrod, Burton A., in collaboration with Joel F. Handler and Neil K. Komesar. Public Interest Law: An Economic and Institutional Analysis. Berkeley: University of California Press, 1978.

Wellington, Harry H. "Common Law Rules and Constitutional Double Standards: Some Notes on Adjudication," 83 Yale Law Journal 221 (1973).

Wexler, Stephen. "Expert and Lay Participation in Decision Making," in 16 Nomos, Participation in Politics 186. New York: Lieber-Atherton, 1975.

Wirt, Frederick M. Politics of Southern Equality: Law and Social Change in a Mississippi County. Chicago: Aldine Publishing Co., 1970.

Wright, Gerald A. "The Cost-Internalization Case for Class Actions," 21 Stanford Law Review 383 (1969).

Yeazell, Stephen C. "Group Litigation and Social Context: Toward a History of the Class Action," 77 Columbia Law Review 866 (1977).

Yeazell, Stephen C. "Intervention and the Idea of Litigation: A Commentary on the Los Angeles School Case," 25 University of California at Los Angeles Law Review 244 (1977).

Zeisel, Hans, and Sheri Seidman Diamond. "The Effect of Peremptory Challenges on Jury and Verdict: An Experiment in a Federal District Court," 30 Stanford Law Review 491 (1978).

Zeisel, Hans, and Sheri Seidman Diamond. "The Jury Selection in the Mitchell-Stans Conspiracy Trial," 1976 American Bar Foundation Research Journal 151 (1976).

Zeisel, Hans; Harry Kalven, Jr.; and Bernard Buchholz. Delay in the Court (2d ed.). Westport, Conn.: Greenwood Press, 1978.

*

INDEX

References are to Pages

Access to Courts, 56, 223, 231, 233, 330
  Filing fees, 3, 5, 427
  Right to initiate, 427–429
Adjudication, 40, 115–133, 144, 148, 190,
  267–270, 271–280, 283, 513–521
    See also Administrative Agencies;
      Arbitration; Litigation
  Finality, 437–446, 484
  Hearing, 8, 17, 20, 22, 25, 135, 139, 432
  Mediation, 41–46
  Models of, 292–306, 427, 428, 492–512
  Notice, 135, 309
  Polycentrism, 507–508, 512, 517–521
  Principles, role of, 115–133, 508–521
  Rationality, 508–512
  Therapeutic integration, 45, 447–451
Administrative Agencies
  Adjudication, 8, 18–19, 134–135, 244,
    288
  Role in structural reform, 422, 424
  Rulemaking, 134–144
Adversary System, 292–306, 409–412, 507
  See also Class Actions
Advisory Opinions
  See Cases and Controversies
Allocation of Cases
    See also Jurisdiction; Jury
  Comity, 307–332
  Erie doctrine, 47, 75–85
  Full faith and credit, 306–307
  Substance and procedure, 2, 6, 47, 50,
    53–57
Amicus Curiae, 136–137, 489
    See also Attorney General; Parties
  Appellate review, 25, 297–298, 301
Arbitration, 144, 145–150, 203, 285, 510,
  511, 513
Attorney General, 427–428
Attorneys, 170, 204–206, 217, 248–251, 458
  Civil rights attorneys, 271–282, 327–331
  Fees, 10, 172, 178, 211, 225, 246, 503
  Organization, 41, 483
  Partisanship, 32, 183
  Professional responsibility, 45, 50, 73,
    277–278, 281–282
  Role, 31, 41, 48–74, 183, 186–187, 281–
    282, 416
  Specialization, 205–206, 250

Burden of Proof, 11, 12, 388–419
  See also Information; Presumptions

Bureaucracy, 24, 61, 292–306, 349–350
  See also Special Masters

Capacity to Sue
  See Adversary System; Parties;
    Standing to Litigate
Cases and Controversies, 225–226, 230
    See also Adversary System; Par-
      ties; Settlement; Standing to
      Litigate; Strategy
  Advisory opinions, 230, 296
  Justiciability, 222, 230, 232
  Mootness, 230
  Political question, 230
  Ripeness, 222, 230
  Test cases, 281
Choice of Law, 306, 308–309
  See also *Erie* Doctrine; Jurisdiction
Class Actions, 75–95, 209, 211, 218, 242–
  280, 497, 503
  Adequacy of representation, 280, 281
  Binding effect, 254, 318
  Cost internalization, 252–255
  Federal rules requirements, 80, 271–282
  Intervention, 280–281
  Intra-class conflicts, 272–280
  Notice, 246, 250, 273
  Relief available, 266
  Settlement, 241, 250
  Strike suits, 55
Collateral Estoppel
  See Res Judicata
Complaint
  See Pleadings
Conflict of Laws
  See Choice of Law
Contempt, 427, 432, 433, 434–435, 438
  See also Remedies
Costs
  Information, 376
  Litigation, 12–17, 45
  Process, 2, 3, 7, 195
  Transaction costs, 8, 191–199, 253–254,
    261
Courts
    See also Adjudication; Judicial
      Role; Special Masters
  Assizes, 451, 454–457
  Chancery, 256, 271, 421–436, 484–490

Courts—Cont'd
  Expertise, 15, 333–349, 361–369
  Roles, 44–45
Criminal Law, 160, 235, 287, 292–306, 429,
    451–464, 489, 506
  See also Burden of Proof
  Death penalty, 160, 451–464
  Pardon, 457–460
  Rights of accused, 4, 7, 16, 59, 60

Damages
  See Remedies
Declaratory Judgments
  See Remedies
Delay, 3, 15
Desegregation, 271–282, 422, 424–426,
    466–474, 484–491, 493
Discovery, 15, 431
  See also Information
Due Process Clause, 2, 18, 306, 309
  See also Access to Courts; Adjudica-
      tion
  Absolute duty of obedience (*Walker*
      rule), 432
  Collapse of triadic structure, 421–436

Economic Analysis
  See also Class Actions; Settlement;
      Transaction Costs
  Cost internalization, 6, 252–255
  Pareto optimality, 253
  Social costs, 8–11, 14–17
Equity
  See Injunctions
Erie Doctrine, 47, 75–85
  See also Allocation of Cases
Evidence
  See Burden of Proof; Information
Exclusionary Rule, 7, 56, 324, 329
Experts, 15, 17, 284, 293, 300, 357, 375,
    433, 493, 504
  See also Administrative Agencies; In-
      formation; Judicial role; Jury;
      Special Masters

Federal Courts, 16, 324–331
  Habeas corpus, 437–446
Federal Rules of Civil Procedure, 75, 82–
    86, 281
  Rule 4, pp. 323–324
  Rule 23, pp. 80–84, 86–87, 89, 94, 280
  Rule 24, p. 280
  Rule 25, p. 425
  Rule 53, pp. 262, 366–367, 369
  Rule 65, pp. 425–426
Federalism, 283, 288, 324–331
  Comity, 283, 302, 306
Full Faith and Credit, 306–307
  See also Allocation of Cases; Jurisdic-
      tion; Venue

Game Theory, 191–199
  See also Ritual; Strategy; Trial
  Zero-sum game, 124, 126, 191, 194

Habeas Corpus, 302, 324–325, 329, 437,
    446
  See also Federal Courts; Remedies
  Waiver, 439

Ideology, 48–75, 451–464, 473
  See also Judgment; Positivism; So-
      ciology of Knowledge; Substan-
      tive Law
Indigence
  See also Access to Courts; Costs;
      Parties
  Bar to access, 3, 56
Indispensable Parties
  See Parties
Information, 205, 376, 419, 447–450, 501
  See also Burden of Proof; Presump-
      tions; Stare Decisis
  Evidence, 17, 23, 32, 54, 284, 304, 311,
      340, 349, 388–419, 431, 456
  Judicial notice, 15
  Witnesses, 308, 311, 415
Injunctions, 307, 421–437, 438, 497, 498
  See also Contempt; Interlocutory In-
      junctions; Remedies
Interlocutory Injunctions, 421, 432
  See also Injunctions; Remedies
  Preliminary injunction, 431, 432
  Temporary restraining order, 431–432
Intervention
  See Class Actions; Parties

Judge
  See Judicial Role
Judgment
  See also Obedience to Judicial De-
      cree; Precedent; Stare Decisis
  Efficacy of, 16, 106–115, 466–491
Judicial Review, 19, 26, 140–141, 225, 297,
    302, 366–368, 495
Judicial Role, 26, 61, 179–188, 415, 447–
    450, 492–512
  See also Adversary System; Ex-
      perts; Information; Jury; Spe-
      cial Masters
  Centrality in injunctive process, 427–
      437
  Efficacy of judicial action, 17, 293,
      465–490
  Impartiality, 29, 51, 66, 283–290, 300,
      302, 329, 361, 432, 508
  Judge-jury disagreement, 332–349
  Judicial notice, 15
  Neutrality, 51, 493, 494
  Passivity, 19, 20, 304–306, 500, 502

Judicial Role—Cont'd
Personification, 212–221
Precedent, 24, 296, 300, 303
Recruitment of judges, 289, 326–327, 358, 361
Ritualism, 31–40, 455
Triadic structure, 32, 40, 125, 283, 284–290, 432, 433
Written opinion, 172, 184, 299, 300, 302–304, 483

Jurisdiction
See also Allocation of Cases; Federalism; Venue
Administrative agencies, 144
Arbitrators, 147–149
General jurisdiction, 310–314
Habeas corpus, 444–445
In personam, 309
In rem, 309, 311–312, 317
Quasi in rem, 312
Specific jurisdiction, 310, 312, 314–323
Subject matter jurisdiction, 309

Jury, 15, 159–168, 170, 175, 291, 295, 333–356
See also Roles
Factfinding functions, 161, 166, 291, 298, 339, 389–419, 494
Historical source of right, 295
Instructions, 161, 164
Judge and jury disagreement, 332–349
Jury controls, 295, 349
Jury trial, right to, 16, 284, 430
Nullification, 152, 160, 161, 165–166, 291, 301
Number of jurors, 32, 351–352, 355–356
Preemptory challenge, 352–355, 356
Representativeness of jury, 284, 349, 350, 356
Unanimous verdict, 284, 335
Verdict, 301
Voir dire, 356

Justiciability
See Cases and Controversies

Legal Realism, 55–56
Legitimacy, 20, 22, 40, 284–291, 505
Litigation, 31, 54, 137, 170, 173, 178, 199–211
See also Adjudication
Complex litigation, 13, 23, 308, 500
Public law litigation, 3, 5, 249–251, 271, 281–282, 492–505
Ritual, 31, 33, 37–38, 48–74

Masters
See Special Masters
Mediation, 40, 41–45, 285, 518
See also Adjudication; Settlement

Mootness
See Cases and Controversies; Settlement

Multidistrict Litigation
See Litigation

Negotiation, 115–133, 500–505
See also Mediation; Settlement; Strategy

Obedience to Judicial Decrees, 433–436, 466–491
See also Desegregation; Judgment
Ombudsmen, 46
Organizational Patterns of Courts, 292–332

Parties, 190–191, 199–211, 308
See also Attorney General; Class Actions; Standing to Litigate
Adversary party, 493
Intervention, 496–497
Joinder of parties, 245, 496
Participatory rights, 511, 514
Party initiative, 427–429

Pleadings, 496
Answer, 16, 31
Complaint, 16, 31, 427
Discovery, relation to, 431
Prayer for relief, 427

Political Questions
See Cases and Controversies
Positivism, 50–59, 507
Precedent, 123–125, 141, 201, 516
See also Information; Stare Decisis
Preclusion
See Res Judicata
Presumptions, 21, 399–403
See also Information
Process
Values of, 2–46

Remedies, 5, 128–129, 486–490, 495, 502
Compensation, 12, 28, 495
Damages, 16, 432, 495
Garnishment, 198, 199
Habeas corpus, 302, 324–325, 329, 437–446
Injunction, 307, 421–437, 438, 486, 497, 498, 500–502
Interlocutory injunction, 421
Repossession, 197–199
Structural injunction, 422, 423, 435–436
Temporary restraining order, 431–432
Representation, 504
See also Attorneys; Class Actions; Parties
Res Judicata, 15, 237, 270
See also Stare Decisis

Rights, 4, 6, 52, 122–123, 207, 212–234, 237, 257–258
Ripeness
  See Cases and Controversies
Ritual, 40, 285, 403–404
  Drama, 31, 33, 45, 62–68, 388–404
  Games, 34–38, 67–71
Roles, 45, 151–188
  See also Judicial Role; Parties
Rules Enabling Act, 81

Settlement, 7–18, 178, 191–199, 201–207
  See Cases and Controversies; Mediation; Negotiation
Sociology of Knowledge, 377–379, 446
  See also Information
Special Masters, 362, 370, 429, 493, 501
  See also Bureaucracy; Experts; Judicial Role
Standing to Litigate, 75–85, 212–221, 222–234, 497, 503
  See also Access to Courts; Parties
  Functional basis, 222–234
  Guardianship, 77, 79, 217–219
Stare Decisis, 248, 296, 303, 380–387, 494, 498
  See also Information; Precedent
Strategy, 12–13, 15, 54, 57, 190, 200, 206, 209–211, 376

Strategy—Cont'd
  See also Economic Analysis; Game Theory
  Avoidance, 42–44
  Forum selection, 325–326
  Strike suits, 55
  Test cases, 281
Substantive Law, 6–8, 11, 15, 54
  Relation to procedure, 2, 6, 47, 50, 53–74, 75

Temporary Restraining Order
  See Injunctions; Interlocutory Injunctions; Remedies
Transaction Costs, 7, 191–199, 253–254, 261
  See also Economic Analysis
Trial, 67
  See also Information; Jury
  Ritual, 31–33, 37–38, 67, 388–404

Utilitarianism, 6–22

Venue, 308, 323–324
  See also Jurisdiction
Verdict
  See Judgment; Jury
Voir Dire
  See Jury

University Textbook Series

May, 1993

Especially Designed for Collateral Reading

HARRY W. JONES
Directing Editor
Professor of Law, Columbia University

ADMINISTRATIVE LAW AND PROCESS, Second Edition (1992)
Richard J. Pierce, Jr., Professor of Law, Columbia University.
Sidney A. Shapiro, Professor of Law, University of Kansas.
Paul R. Verkuil, President and Professor of Law, College of William and Mary.

ADMIRALTY, Second Edition (1975)
Grant Gilmore, Professor of Law, Yale University.
Charles L. Black, Jr., Professor of Law, Yale University.

AGENCY (1975)
W. Edward Sell, Dean of the School of Law, University of Pittsburgh.

ANTITRUST LAW, PRINCIPLES OF (1993)
Stephen F. Ross, Professor of Law, University of Illinois.

BANKRUPTCY, THE ELEMENTS OF (1992)
Douglas G. Baird, Professor of Law, University of Chicago.

BUSINESS ORGANIZATION AND FINANCE, Fifth Edition (1993)
William A. Klein, Professor of Law, University of California, Los Angeles.
John C. Coffee, Jr., Professor of Law, Columbia University.

CIVIL PROCEDURE, BASIC, Second Edition (1979)
Milton D. Green, Professor of Law Emeritus, University of California, Hastings College of the Law.

COMMERCIAL TRANSACTIONS, INTRODUCTION TO (1977)
Hon. Robert Braucher, Associate Justice, Supreme Judicial Court of Massachusetts.
Robert A. Riegert, Professor of Law, Cumberland School of Law.

CONFLICT OF LAWS, COMMENTARY ON THE, Third Edition (1986) with 1991 Supplement
Russell J. Weintraub, Professor of Law, University of Texas.

CONSTITUTIONAL LAW, AMERICAN, Second Edition (A TREATISE ON) (1988)
Laurence H. Tribe, Professor of Law, Harvard University.

CONTRACT LAW, THE CAPABILITY PROBLEM IN (1978)
Richard Danzig.

CONTRACTS, CONCEPTS AND CASE ANALYSIS IN THE LAW OF, Second Edition (1993)
Marvin A. Chirelstein, Professor of Law, Columbia University.

CORPORATE TAXATION, FEDERAL, Second Edition (1990)
Howard E. Abrams, Professor of Law, Emory University.
Richard L. Doernberg, Professor of Law, Emory University.

CORPORATIONS, Second Edition (1971)
Norman D. Lattin, Professor of Law, University of California, Hastings College of the Law.

CORPORATIONS IN PERSPECTIVE (1976)
Alfred F. Conard, Professor of Law, University of Michigan.

CRIMINAL LAW, Third Edition (1982)
Rollin M. Perkins, Professor of Law, University of California, Hastings College of the Law.
Ronald N. Boyce, Professor of Law, University of Utah College of Law.

CRIMINAL PROCEDURE, Third Edition (1993)
Charles H. Whitebread, II, Professor of Law, University of Southern California.
Christopher Slobogin, Professor of Law, University of Florida.

ESTATES IN LAND & FUTURE INTERESTS, PREFACE TO, Second Edition (1984)
Thomas F. Bergin, Professor of Law, University of Virginia.
Paul G. Haskell, Professor of Law, University of North Carolina.

EVIDENCE: COMMON SENSE AND COMMON LAW (1947)
John M. Maguire, Professor of Law, Harvard University.

JURISPRUDENCE: MEN AND IDEAS OF THE LAW (1953)
The late Edwin W. Patterson, Cardozo Professor of Jurisprudence, Columbia University.

LABOR RELATIONS THE BASIC PROCESSES, LAW AND PRACTICE (1988)
Julius G. Getman, Professor of Law, University of Texas.
Bertrand E. Pogrebin, Member, New York State Bar.

LEGAL CAPITAL, Third Edition (1990)
Bayless Manning.

LEGAL RESEARCH ILLUSTRATED, Fifth Edition with 1990 Assignments Supplement
J. Myron Jacobstein, Professor of Law, Emeritus, Stanford University.
Roy M. Mersky, Professor of Law, Director of Research, University of Texas.

LEGAL RESEARCH, FUNDAMENTALS OF, Fifth Edition with 1990 Assignments Supplement
J. Myron Jacobstein, Professor of Law, Emeritus, Stanford University.
Roy M. Mersky, Professor of Law, Director of Research, University of Texas.

PROCEDURE, THE STRUCTURE OF (1979)
Robert M. Cover, Professor of Law, Yale University.
Owen M. Fiss, Professor of Law, Yale University.

PROPERTY, PRINCIPLES OF THE LAW OF, Third Edition (1989)
John E. Cribbet, Dean, Chancellor, Professor of Law Emeritus, University of Illinois.
Corwin W. Johnson, Professor of Law Emeritus, University of Texas.

TAX, FEDERAL INCOME, Second Edition (1992)
Douglas A. Kahn, Professor of Law, University of Michigan.

UNIVERSITY TEXTBOOK SERIES—Continued

TAXATION OF S CORPORATIONS, FEDERAL INCOME (1992)
John K. McNulty, Professor of Law, University of California, Berkeley.

TAXATION, FEDERAL INCOME, Sixth Edition (1991)
Marvin A. Chirelstein, Professor of Law, Columbia University.

TAXATION, PARTNERSHIP INCOME (1991)
Alan Gunn, Professor of Law, University of Notre Dame.

TORTS, Second Edition (1980)
Clarence Morris, Professor of Law, University of Pennsylvania.
C. Robert Morris, Professor of Law, University of Minnesota.

WILLS AND TRUSTS, THE PLANNING AND DRAFTING OF, Third Edition (1991)
Thomas L. Shaffer, Professor of Law, University of Notre Dame.
Carol Ann Mooney, Associate Professor of Law, University of Notre Dame.

WILLS, TRUSTS AND ADMINISTRATION, PREFACE TO (1987)
Paul G. Haskell, Professor of Law, University of North Carolina.